DIE ERSTE SEITE

11. SEPTEMBER 2001

VERLAG KARL MÜLLER

11.09.2001

Inhalt

Vorwort

Am 11. September 2001 stockte der Welt der Atem. Mit einer bis dahin unvorstellbaren Entschlossenheit rasten Terroristen mit entführten Passagierflugzeugen kurz nacheinander in die Wahrzeichen des Kapitalismus und zerstörten die Machtsymbole der USA. Das Ausmaß der Tragödie war gewaltig. Der 11. September war ein Tag, der die Welt veränderte.

Die Presse berichtete rund um den Globus über die Anschläge, oft mit minimaler zeitlicher Verschiebung. Es galt, nicht über ein ungewöhnliches Ereignis, sondern über eine entsetzliche Katastrophe, über eine unglaubliche Nachricht zu schreiben. In fliegender Eile wurden Sonderausgaben gedruckt und auch Tage später verblasste das Entsetzen in den Medien nicht. Rund um den Globus war man bemüht, das Unfassbare zu fassen. Angesichts der Tragweite des Geschehens verstummten selbst die wortgewaltigsten Blätter.

Das vorliegende Buch dokumentiert diese Reaktionen der internationalen Presse auf die Ereignisse des 11. Septembers 2001. Im Zentrum steht die Titelseite, das Gesicht einer jeden Zeitung. Die Titelseite wird zum Maßstab für den journalistischen Umgang mit den Ereignissen, zeigt im internationalen Kontext kulturelle Unterschiede auf und spiegelt die Bemühungen des seriösen und des Boulevard-Journalismus, über die schockierenden Vorfälle in angemessener Form in Bild und Text zu berichten.

Die Grundlage der Dokumentation bildet eine breite Auswahl unterschiedlichster Zeitungen aus aller Herren Länder, die in der Woche nach dem 11. September erschienen sind. Dabei spielte es keine Rolle, ob es sich um eine überregionale, regionale oder auch lokale Ausgabe handelte. Auch Wochenzeitungen und einige ausgewählte Magazine wie »Time« oder der »Spiegel« wurden berücksichtigt. Ziel war es, die globale Bedeutung der Ereignisse darzustellen und so auch jeden Kontinent durch mehrere Zeitungen zu repräsentieren. Als Orientierungshilfe für den Leser visualisiert daher ein Globus den Erscheinungsort der jeweiligen Zeitung. Darüber hinaus wurden zum besseren Verständnis die Schlagzeilen und Vorspanne der ausländischen Zeitungen ins Deutsche übersetzt. Dabei tritt mit der Kommentierung der Ereignisse auch immer ein interessantes Dokument der Weltsicht des jeweiligen Landes zu Tage.

Neben der Konzentration auf die US-amerikanische sowie die internationale Presse liegt ein Schwerpunkt auf der deutschen Berichterstattung. Hier ist – neben den großen überregionalen Zeitungen, Wochenzeitungen und Magazinen unterschiedlichster politischer Couleur – jedes Bundesland mit einer Zeitung vertreten. Eine weitere aufschlussreiche Perspektive bietet die Titelseite der Allgemeinen Jüdischen Zeitung als Deutschlands einziger überregionaler jüdischer Zeitung. Mit dem Osservatore Romano wird auch die Sicht der katholischen Kirche berücksichtigt.

+++ Zwei Flugzeuge rasen am Morgen des 11. 9. 2001 in die Zwillingstürme des World Trade Centers in New York. Die oberen Teile der Wolkenkratzer gehen nach den Explosionen in Flammen auf.

Terror, Krieg, Entsetzen – so lauteten einhellig die internationalen Schlagzeilen in den Zeitungen. Während die einen mit Bildern im Posterformat und riesigen Schlagzeilen (Libération, Kronen Zeitung, Blick, Times, Postimees, Milliyet, Washington Post), oder sogar Stoßgebeten (Bild), vor allem die Emotionen des Lesers ansprechen, setzen die anderen – auch unter der Gefahr, doch nur die längst bekannten Informationen aus Funk, Fernsehen und Internet zu wiederholen – auf Dokumentation und Artikel im Sinne des »traditionellen« Journalismus (Le Monde, New York Times, Dawn). Dennoch: Die meisten Zeitungen machten zunächst auf ihren Titelseiten Platz für das Bild und räumten ihm mehr Platz als üblich ein. Mit zunehmendem Abstand zu den Ereignissen nimmt dann die Zahl und Größe der Bilder wieder ab. Die Renmin Ribao, quasi offizielles Organ der chinesischen Berichterstattung, veröffentlichte am Tag nach den Terrorattacken als eine der wenigen Ausnahmen kein Foto zu den Ereignissen auf der Titelseite.

Wie eine Medienanalyse der Universität Leipzig ergab, wichen zum Beispiel in Deutschland viele meinungsbildende Zeitungen vom gewohnten Layout ab. Die FAZ druckte am 12. September erstmals in ihrer über 50-jährigen Geschichte zwei Fotos ohne Bildunterschrift auf ihrer Titelseite. Anders als gewohnt war auch das Erscheinungsbild der Süddeutschen Zeitung und der Frankfurter Rundschau, die über fünf bis sechs Spalten titelten. Und die Rhein-Zeitung aus Koblenz erschien am 13. 9. 2001 angesichts der Ereignisse nicht in Farbe, sondern schwarz-weiß.

Auch im internationalen Vergleich sind bemerkenswert gestaltete Titelseiten zu entdecken. Das Wirtschaftsblatt aus Österreich tritt mit einer überdimensionalen Infografik zur erschütterten Weltwirtschaft hervor. In Frankreich beispielsweise bezog die Libération die Rückseite mit in die Gestaltung ein, indem sie ein riesiges Foto über beide Seiten abdruckte, das sie nur durch das Datum des Schreckenstages kommentierte. Aus der Masse relativ ähnlich gestalteter Titelseiten sticht auch die griechische Zeitung Ta Nea heraus. In einer riesigen Todesanzeige mit weißer Schrift auf schwarzem Grund drückt sie ihr Mitgefühl mit den Opfern und Angehörigen der Anschläge aus.

Festzuhalten bleibt, dass uns die Reaktionen der Presse auf den 11. September 2001 die Bedeutung des Bildes für die Kommunikation im 21. Jahrhundert vor Augen führen. Bilder dominierten in den Zeitungen, transportierten das Thema, lösten die stärksten Emotionen aus und gestalteten die dramatischsten Titelseiten. Diese Titelseiten aus aller Welt sind mahnende, zeithistorische Dokumente wider das Vergessen.

+++ Blick auf die gewaltige Rauchsäule kurz nach dem Anschlag. Innerhalb von 18 Minuten sind zwei von terroristischen Selbstmordattentätern gesteuerte Flugzeuge in die Gebäude gestürzt.

+++ Feuerwehrleute eilen nach dem Terroranschlag zur Rettung an den Ort des Schreckens.

+++ Vor einer meterhohen Wand aus dichtem Rauch flieht ein Mann vor den Trümmern der einstürzenden Türme.

11. September

EXTRA

MILD
HIGH 60, LOW 48 – B12

The Washington Times

www.washingtontimes.com TUESDAY, SEPTEMBER 11, 2001 ★R★★ SUBSCRIBER SERVICE: (202) 636-3333 Prices may vary outside metropolitan Washington area 25 cents

8:48 a.m.: A commercial plane slams into the north tower of the World Trade Center.
9:06 p.m.: A second commercial plane ploughs into the south tower.
10:02 a.m.: The south tower collapses.
10:20 a.m.: A third commercial plane crashes into the southwestern side of the Pentagon.
10:28 a.m.: The north tower of the World Trade Center collapses.
10:30 a.m.: Evacuations under way at the White House and other federal buildings.
10:37 a.m.: United Airlines Flight 93 reportedly crashes near an airport southeast of Pittsburgh.
10:42 a.m.: Federal aviation officials shut down air traffic and divert transatlantic flights.
11:25 a.m.: Mayor Rudolph Giuliani urges evacuation of lower Manhattan.

1 HORROR

AP

4 In this image from television, a ball of fire explodes from one of the towers at the World Trade Center in New York after a plane crashed into it. The aircraft was the second to fly into the towers Tuesday morning.

2 Plane smashes into Pentagon, shuts down D.C.

By Stephen Dinan and Tom Ramstack
THE WASHINGTON TIMES

A plane crashed into the Pentagon this morning, throwing the region into panic, setting the federal government on high alert and shutting down the downtown area of the District.

Officials had not yet determined this afternoon if the plane that hit the Pentagon was an American Airlines jet that disappeared after taking off from Dulles with 64 people aboard earlier today.

The incident in Washington came about an hour after planes crashed into both towers of the World Trade Center in New York City.

There were unconfirmed reports of other attacks in the region, and people across the area reported feeling a second explosion while watching the smoke from the Pentagon.

The Associated Press reported that American Airlines Flight 77 from Dulles to Los Angeles, a Boeing 757, with 58 passengers, four flight attendants and 2 pilots, is one of two aircraft American says it "lost."

Witnesses described hearing a plane flying low over Arlington, as if one were off course on its way to Ronald Reagan Washington National Airport, at about 9:40 a.m., and then described hearing a big explosion.

Television footage showed a hole in the roof and upper wall of one of the five sides of the Pentagon, which is in Arlington, just across the Potomac River from the District.

There were no immediate details on any deaths from the explosion, but witnesses in the Pentagon area said they were sure there would be deaths.

Qawiy Sabre, a data processor at the Pentagon, was

see PLANE, *page A3*

Agence France-Presse

5 Smoke billows from the Pentagon in Washington today after an airplane crashed into it. At the same time, two passenger planes were crashed into the twin towers of the World Trade Center in New York City.

3 Terrorists attack World Trade Center, Pentagon

By Frank J. Murray
THE WASHINGTON TIMES

Terrorists flying airliners hijacked from Boston and Dulles airports today demolished both towers of the World Trade Center and part of the Pentagon in coordinated sneak attacks on the most visible symbols of U.S. military and financial power.

Thousands of the 50,000 people arriving at work in New York City's landmark twin towers were presumed dead, police said, and uncounted others are missing after both 110-story buildings collapsed.

As maimed and dead bodies were carried from the New York disaster, the rest of the country went on the defensive against an unseen enemy using Pearl Harbor-style tactics that killed at least 156 passengers on two commercial airliners.

Minutes after the second World Trade Center impact, President Bush blamed "an apparent terrorist attack on our country" and headed back to the capital from Florida.

"Terrorism against this nation will not stand," the president said, invoking the memorable line-in-the-sand phrase his father used when Saddam Hussein's forces invaded Kuwait. That attack eventually was repelled by conventional desert forces fighting a uniformed enemy.

One wire service report said the radical Islamic Jihad movement called the attacks "a consequence of United States policy in the Middle East." It was not clear if the organization was claiming full responsibility.

The airliner that hit one of the World Trade Center towers apparently was the hijacked American Airlines Flight 11 from Boston to Los Angeles, carrying 92 per-

see ATTACK, *page A2*

1 Entsetzen

2 Flugzeug stürzt ins Pentagon und isoliert D. C.

3 Terroristen greifen das World Trade Center und das Pentagon an

4 Dieses Fernsehbild zeigt den Feuerball, der aus einem der Türme des World Trade Centers in New York schlägt, nachdem ein Flugzeug hineingekracht ist. Es war das zweite Flugzeug, das Dienstagmorgen in die Türme raste

5 Rauch steigt aus dem Pentagon in Washington auf, nachdem heute ein Flugzeug hineingestürzt ist. Zur selben Zeit wurden zwei Passagierflugzeuge in die Zwillingstürme des World Trade Centers in New York City gelenkt

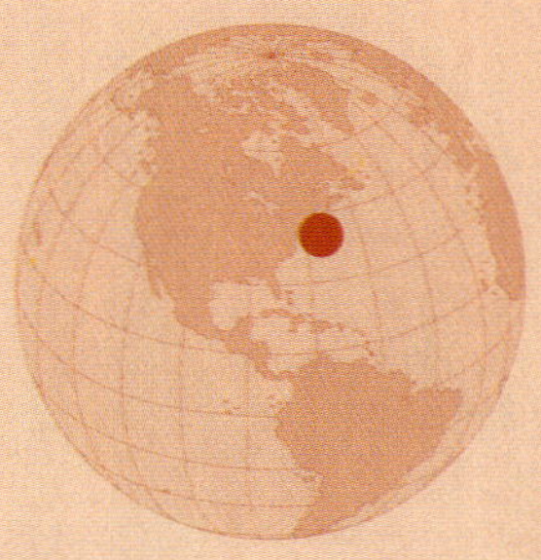

Nordwest Zeitung

EXTRA BLATT KOSTENLOS

OLDENBURGER NACHRICHTEN

Dienstag, 11. September 2001

Terrorkrieg in USA: Tausende Todesopfer

Zwei Jets rasen ins World-Trade-Center – Pentagon in Flammen – Panik auf den Straßen

Die Anschlagserie in den USA hat für einen Schock und Entsetzen weltweit gesorgt. Die amerikanischen Behörden befürchten, dass bei einer Serie schwerster Terroranschläge Tausende von Menschen ums Leben gekommen sind.

ap **New York.** Die USA sind gestern vor den Augen der ganzen Welt von einer beispiellosen Terrorwelle überrollt worden, bei der wahrscheinlich hunderte, möglicherweise tausende Menschen getötet wurden. Ziele waren die Symbole der amerikanischen Macht: die Millionenstadt New York und die Hauptstadt Washington. Es herrschte das völlige Chaos.

Zuerst stürzten sich im Kamikazestil im Abstand von 18 Minuten offenbar zwei Passagierflugzeuge in die beiden Hochhaustürme des World Trade Centers in New York, in denen etwa 50 000 Menschen arbeiten. Beide Türme stürzten ein, Manhattan war völlig in Rauch und Qualm gehüllt. Etwas später stürzte ein Flugzeug auf das Pentagon, das ebenfalls teilweise einstürzte. Vor dem Außenministerium explodierte eine Autobombe. In Manhattan explodierte offenbar noch ein weiteres Gebäude in Manhattan.

Das Verteidigungsministerium, das Weiße Haus und alle weiteren Regierungsgebäude wie das Außen- und das Finanzministerium wurden evakuiert. US-Präsident George W. Bush sprach von einem „offenkundigen Terroranschlag auf unser Land". Der Präsident, der zum Zeitpunkt der Anschläge in Florida war, wollte umgehend nach Washington zurückkehren.

Aus Geheimdienstkreisen verlautete, die Urheber seien nicht bekannt. „Das war nicht das Werk eines schlecht ausgerüsteten Feindes. Aber es ist noch zu früh, um etwas zu sagen." Wie es hieß, wurde mindestens eines der Flugzeuge in Boston entführt. Es war eine Boeing 767 der American Airlines, die auf dem Weg nach Los Angeles war. Das zweite Flugzeug wurde offenbar in Newark in New Jersey entführt. In den USA wurden danach alle Flugzeugstarts abgesagt. Alle Brücken und Tunnel nach Manhatten wurden geschlossen. Die Anschlagsserie begann kurz vor 9 Uhr Ortszeit. In New York rannten die Menschen in Panik auf die Straße. In der Nähe von Pittsburgh in Pennsylvania stürzte eine Boeing 767 ab. Dazu lagen zunächst keine näheren Einzelheiten vor. Es wurde auch hier ein Zusammenhang mit den Anschlägen vermutet.

Die Welt war Zeuge dieser beispielosen Terroranschläge. Der Sender CNN zeigte noch die Bilder des World Trade Centers, in das ein Flugzeug

hineingerast war. Und vor laufenden Kameras stürzte dann 18 Minuten nach dem ersten ein zweites Passagierflugzeug in die Mitte des zweiten Turms des 110-stöckigen Gebäudekomplexes.

Ein Bild wie im Krieg: Das World Trade Center, Wahrzeichen New Yorks und wirtschaftliches Herz der USA, steht in Rauch gehüllt. Zwei Flugzeuge treffen die Türme. Die Terrorkatastrophe erschüttert auch den US-Präsidenten Bush, der sich in Florida aufhielt.

Passanten blutüberströmt auf New Yorker Straßen

Krankenhäuser überfordert – Menschen suchen schreiend Schutz vor einstürzenden Mauern – „Unvorstellbarer Verlust von Menschenleben"

Von Gabriele Chwallek und Herbert Winkler

Washington. Die Terrorschläge gegen die Supermacht USA kamen aus heiterem Himmel. Ohne Vorwarnung rasten zwei Flugzeuge in die Zwillingstürme des World Trade Centers in New York: Feuerbälle stiegen auf, dunkler Qualm verdunkelte den blauen Himmel, beide Türme stürzten teilweise ein. Die Szenerie wirkte wie einem Katastrophenfilm entnommen. Ungläubig und entsetzt starrten die Amerikaner auf ihre Fernsehschirme. Dann herrschte an der schrecklichen Wirklichkeit kein Zweifel mehr: „America under Attack" meldeten Fernsehen und Internetseiten in riesigen roten Lettern. Mehrere Flugzeuge wurden vermisst - möglicherweise entführt und in terroristische „Waffen" verwandelt.

Ein todernster Präsident George W. Bush, der im Sonnenstaat Florida für seine Schulreform werben wollte, musste der schockierten Bevölkerung von einer „nationalen Tragödie" berichten. Die Polizei sprach von einem „unvorstellbaren Verlust an Menschenleben". Es sei „offensichtlich" ein terroristischer Angriff, sagte Bush und gab sich stark: „Wir werden Terrorismus gegen unser Land nicht zulassen." Er ordnete die Mobilisierung aller Reserven an, um die Täter zu finden. Doch es war klar: Mit den beiden Türmen des Trade Centers kippte auch das Selbstbewusstsein der USA, dem Terror Herr zu werden. Die USA wirkten wie gelähmt, als ein Schlag dem anderen folgte. Das schlug rasch in Panik und Alarm um. In New York suchten die Menschen schreiend Schutz, als riesige Trümmerstücke von den einstürzenden Türmen auf die Straßen fielen. Passanten lagen blutüberströmt auf dem Pflaster. Die Krankenhäuser waren so überfordert, dass von einer verzweifelten Lage die Rede war.

In Washington wurden die Menschen, die in der warmen Sonne spazieren gingen oder auf dem Weg zur Arbeit und noch ahnungslos waren, durch rasende Feuerwehrautos und ununterbrochenes Sirenengeheul aufgeschreckt.

Zunehmend gab es im Zentrum der Stadt mit dem Weißen Haus, dem Kapitol und dem nationalen Pressegebäude kein Durchkommen mehr. Straßen wurden abgesperrt, Polizeiwagen blockierten Bürgersteige. Der U-Bahn-Verkehr verlief zunächst noch normal, aber mit jeder Minute wuchs die Unruhe.

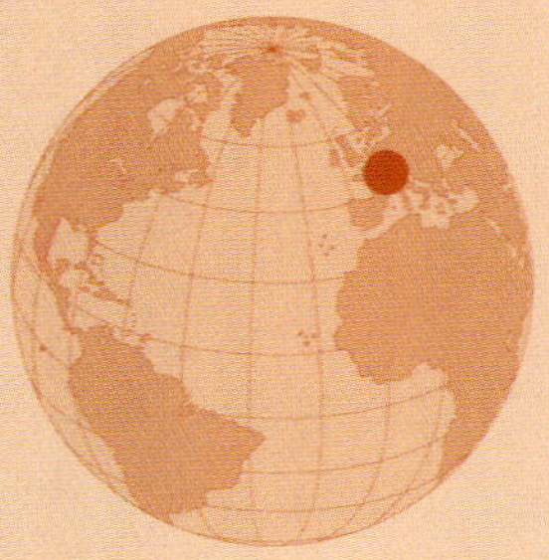

Nordwest Zeitung
www.nwz-online.de
Deutschland, Oldenburg

Express & Star

Disaster Special

Telephone 01902 31 31 31 | Tuesday, September 11, 2001 | www.westmidlands.com | 30p

❶ Doomsday

❷ Day the world caught fire

New York inferno: Shocking pictures Page 4, 5, 6, 7, 8, 9, 10 and 11

❶ Der jüngste Tag

❷ Der Tag, an dem die Welt in Brand geriet

Express & Star
www.expressandstar.com
Grossbritannien, Wolverhampton

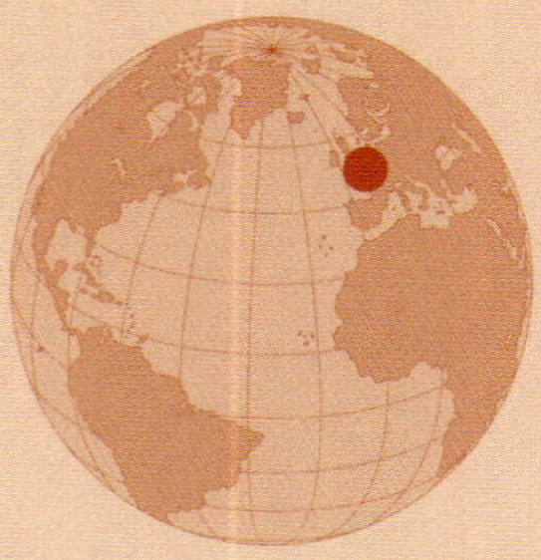

11

Express & Star WOLVERHAMPTON The Millennium City

Telephone 01902 31 31 31 Tuesday, September 11, 2001 www.westmidlands.com 30p

Terror jets blow up skyscrapers

Terrorists hijacked two jet airliners and crashed them into the World Trade Centre in New York at 300mph within minutes of each other today.

Horrified onlookers were wondering how a jet had crashed into the 110-storey skyscraper on such a clear day when they saw a second jet fly directly into the other tower.

It was then that they realised they were witnessing what could be the world's worst terrorist atrocity rather than a dreadful air accident.

Fifty thousand people work at the World Trade Centre. It is not yet known how many people were on the planes, nor how many people have been killed in the Trade Centre.

Both planes, which are twin engined jet liners remain embedded in the building.

New York inferno: Dramatic pictures Page 4

1 Terrorflugzeuge jagen Wolkenkratzer in die Luft

2 Inferno in New York: Dramatische Bilder Seite 4

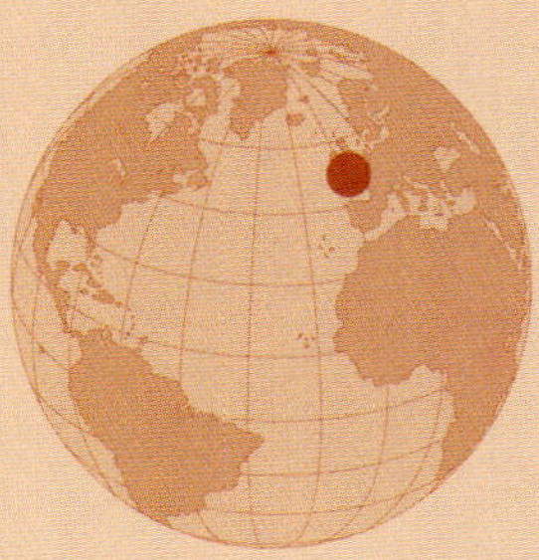

Express & Star
www.expressandstar.com
Grossbritannien, Wolverhampton

11

+++ Der Tag nach dem verheerenden Anschlag. Dort, wo einst die beiden berühmten Zwillingstürme standen, steigt nur noch Rauch auf.

+++ Bergungshelfer beginnen mit der Beseitigung der Trümmer des World Trade Centers, dessen Ruine im Hintergrund zu sehen ist.

+++ Erschüttert sitzt ein erschöpfter Feuerwehrmann auf einem Bordstein.

12. September

"All the News That's Fit to Print"

The New York Times

Late Edition
New York: **Today**, sunny, a few afternoon clouds. High 77. **Tonight**, slightly more humid. Low 65. **Tomorrow**, sun then clouds. High 81. **Yesterday**, high 81, low 63. Weather map, Page C19.

VOL. CL . . No. 51,874 — Copyright © 2001 The New York Times — NEW YORK, WEDNESDAY, SEPTEMBER 12, 2001 — $1 beyond the greater New York metropolitan area. — 75 CENTS

1

U.S. ATTACKED

2

HIJACKED JETS DESTROY TWIN TOWERS AND HIT PENTAGON IN DAY OF TERROR

3

A CREEPING HORROR

Buildings Burn and Fall as Onlookers Search for Elusive Safety

By N. R. KLEINFIELD

It kept getting worse.

The horror arrived in episodic bursts of chilling disbelief, signified first by trembling floors, sharp eruptions, cracked windows. There was the actual unfathomable realization of a gaping, flaming hole in first one of the tall towers, and then the same thing all over again in its twin. There was the merciless sight of bodies helplessly tumbling out, some of them in flames.

Finally, the mighty towers themselves were reduced to nothing. Dense plumes of smoke raced through the downtown avenues, coursing between the buildings, shaped like tornadoes on their sides.

Every sound was cause for alarm. A plane appeared overhead. Was another one coming? No, it was a fighter jet. But was it friend or enemy? People scrambled for their lives, but they didn't know where to go. Should they go north, south, east, west? Stay outside, go indoors? People hid beneath cars and each other. Some contemplated jumping into the river.

For those trying to flee the very epicenter of the collapsing World Trade Center towers, the most horrid thought of all finally dawned on them: nowhere was safe.

For several panic-stricken hours yesterday morning, people in Lower Manhattan witnessed the inexpressible, the incomprehensible, the unthinkable. "I don't know what the gates of hell look like, but it's got to be like this," said John Maloney, a security director for an Internet firm in the trade center. "I'm a combat veteran, Vietnam, and I never saw anything like this."

The first warnings were small ones. Blocks away, Jim Farmer, a film composer, was having breakfast at a small restaurant on West Broadway. He heard the sound of a jet. An odd sound — too loud, it seemed, to be

Continued on Page A7

Steve Ludlum

4

President Vows to Exact Punishment for 'Evil'

By SERGE SCHMEMANN

Hijackers rammed jetliners into each of New York's World Trade Center towers yesterday, toppling both in a hellish storm of ash, glass, smoke and leaping victims, while a third jetliner crashed into the Pentagon in Virginia. There was no official count, but President Bush said thousands had perished, and in the immediate aftermath the calamity was already being ranked the worst and most audacious terror attack in American history.

The attacks seemed carefully coordinated. The hijacked planes were all en route to California, and therefore gorged with fuel, and their departures were spaced within an hour and 40 minutes. The first, American Airlines Flight 11, a Boeing 767 out of Boston for Los Angeles, crashed into the north tower at 8:48 a.m. Eighteen minutes later, United Airlines Flight 175, also headed from Boston to Los Angeles, plowed into the south tower.

Kelly Guenther for The New York Times

SECOND PLANE United Airlines Flight 175 nearing the trade center's south tower.

Then an American Airlines Boeing 757, Flight 77, left Washington's Dulles International Airport bound for Los Angeles, but instead hit the western part of the Pentagon, the military headquarters where 24,000 people work, at 9:40 a.m. Finally, United Airlines Flight 93, a Boeing 757 flying from Newark to San Francisco, crashed near Pittsburgh, raising the possibility that its hijackers had failed in whatever their mission was.

There were indications that the hijackers on at least two of the planes were armed with knives. Attorney General John Ashcroft told reporters in the evening that the suspects on Flight 11 were armed that way. And Barbara Olson, a television commentator who was traveling on American Flight 77, managed to reach her husband, Solicitor General Theodore Olson, by cell phone and to tell him that the hijackers were armed with knives and a box cutter.

In all, 266 people perished in the four planes and several score more were known dead elsewhere. Numerous firefighters, police officers and other rescue workers who responded to the initial disaster in Lower Manhattan were killed or injured when the buildings collapsed. Hundreds were treated for cuts, broken bones, burns and smoke inhalation.

But the real carnage was concealed for now by the twisted, smoking, ash-choked carcasses of the twin towers, in which thousands of people used to work on a weekday. The collapse of the towers caused another World Trade Center building to fall 7 hours later, and several

Continued on Page A14

5

A Somber Bush Says Terrorism Cannot Prevail

By ELISABETH BUMILLER with DAVID E. SANGER

WASHINGTON, Sept. 11 — President Bush vowed tonight to retaliate against those responsible for today's attacks on New York and Washington, declaring that he would "make no distinction between the terrorists who committed these acts and those who harbor them."

"These acts of mass murder were intended to frighten our nation into chaos and retreat, but they have failed," the president said in his first speech to the nation from the Oval Office. "Our country is strong. Terrorist acts can shake the foundation of our biggest buildings, but they cannot touch the foundation of America."

His speech came after a day of trauma that seems destined to define his presidency. Seeking to at once calm the nation and declare his determination to exact retribution, he told a country numbed by repeated scenes of carnage that "these acts shattered steel, but they cannot dent the steel of American resolve."

Mr. Bush spoke only hours after returning from a zigzag course across the country, as his Secret Service and military security teams moved him from Florida, where he woke up this morning expecting to press for his education bill, to command posts in Louisiana and Nebraska before it was determined the attacks had probably ended and he could safely return to the capital.

It was a sign of the catastrophic

Continued on Page A4

Justin Lane for The New York Times

Paul Hosefros/The New York Times

AMERICAN TARGETS A ball of fire exploded outward after the second of two jetliners slammed into the World Trade Center; less than two hours later, both of the 110-story towers were gone. Hijackers crashed a third airliner into the Pentagon, setting off a huge explosion and fire.

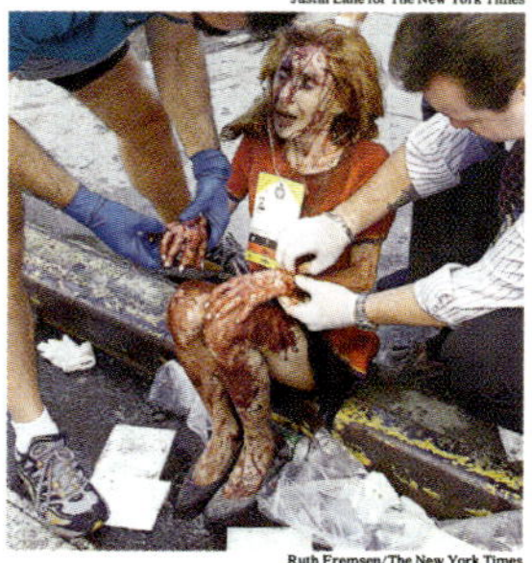

Ruth Fremsen/The New York Times

6

Awaiting the Aftershocks

Washington and Nation Plunge Into Fight With Enemy Hard to Identify and Punish

By R. W. APPLE Jr.

News Analysis

WASHINGTON, Sept. 11 — Today's devastating and astonishingly well-coordinated attacks on the World Trade Center towers in New York and on the Pentagon outside of Washington plunged the nation into a warlike struggle against an enemy that will be hard to identify with certainty and hard to punish with precision.

The whole nation — to a degree the whole world — shook as hijacked airliners plunged into buildings that symbolize the financial and military might of the United States. The sense of security and self-confidence that Americans take as their birthright suffered a grievous blow, from which recovery will be slow. The aftershocks will be nearly as bad, as hundreds and possibly thousands of people discover that friends or relatives died awful, fiery deaths.

Scenes of chaos and destruction evocative of the nightmare world of Hieronymus Bosch, with smoke and debris blotting out the sun, were carried by television into homes and workplaces across the nation. Echoing Franklin D. Roosevelt's description of the attack on Pearl Harbor as an event "which will live in infamy," Gov. George E. Pataki of New York, a Republican, spoke of "an incredible outrage" and Senator Charles E. Schumer of New York, a Democrat, spoke of "a dastardly attack."

But mere words were inadequate vessels to contain the sense of shock and horror that people felt.

As Washington struggled to regain a sense of equilibrium, with warplanes and heavily armed helicopters crossing overhead, past and present national security officials earnestly debated the possibility of a Congressional declaration of war — but against precisely whom, and in what exact circumstances? Warships were maneuvering to protect New York and Washington. The North American Air Defense Command, which had seemed to many a relic of the cold war, adopted a pos-

Continued on Page A24

MORE ON THE ATTACKS

1 USA angegriffen

2 Entführte Flugzeuge zerstören die Zwillingstürme und treffen das Pentagon an einem Tag des Terrors

3 Ein schleichendes Grauen

4 Präsident schwört, Bestrafung für das Böse einzufordern

5 Ein düsterer Bush sagt, der Terrorismus könne nicht siegen

6 Warten auf die Nachbeben

THE NEW YORK TIMES
WWW.NYTIMES.COM
USA, NEW YORK (NEW YORK)

(平成元年1月23日第三種郵便物認可) (日刊但、土曜及び日曜を除く) NO. 3314, WEDNESDAY, SEPTEMBER 12, 2001

VIA SATELLITE FROM LORAL CYBERSTAR™ www.usatoday.com

INTERNATIONAL

USA TODAY

AVAILABLE AROUND THE WORLD

By Jym Wilson, USA TODAY

Chaos: Smoke covers Pentagon after plane hits military nerve center.

Terror hits Washington, 4A

By Shannon Stapleton, Reuters

Rescue: Victim evacuated from World Trade Center.

New York panic

'Everyone was screaming' as towers collapsed. Story, 3A

Wednesday, September 12, 2001

U.S. under attack

Hundreds feared dead as passenger jets destroy New York's World Trade towers, slam into Pentagon ■ Hijackers likely piloted planes themselves, experts say ■ Bush vows to punish those responsible

Newsline

■ News ■ Money ■ Sports ■ Life

By Paul J. Richards, AFP

Bush learns of air attacks

White House chief of staff Andrew Card interrupts President Bush during an education event in Florida as news breaks of the terrorist attacks. 4A.

Bin Laden viewed as chief suspect

Terrorism experts say the exiled Saudi dissident has the capability to order coordinated attacks such as Tuesday's assault on U.S. facilities. 4A.

Terrorism coverage blankets TV

Viewers who tuned in to TV coverage of the terrorist attacks in New York and Washington found the grimmest form of reality television. 9B.

Weather: Clouds in London, Tokyo

European cities: London, partly cloudy; Paris, partly cloudy. Asian/Pacific cities: Tokyo, partly cloudy. U.S. cities: New York, sunny. 12A.

■ **Money: Wall Street reacts to attacks**

Terrorist attacks disrupt communication, travel, and force the closing of the U.S. stock market. 9A.

■ **Sports: Games cancelled**

Major league baseball games were postponed. 1B.

■ **Life: Emmy Awards postponed**

The 53rd annual Emmy awards ceremony in Los Angeles was cancelled. No new date was set.

By Douglas Stanglin

USA TODAY .com Get breaking news updated 24 hours a day, 7 days a week. Visit us on the web at www.usatoday.com

USA TODAY Snapshots®

Learning about others

When asked how frequently they attempted to learn about cultures that were neither their own nor those of their ancestors, respondents said:

Very often	24%
Often	21%
Sometimes	31%
Seldom	15%
Never	8%

Note: Numbers do not add up to 100 because of rounding.

Source: Maritz Marketing Research survey of 1,005 adults. Margin of error: ±3 percentage points.

By Lori Joseph and Marcy E. Mullins, USA TODAY

Crossword	8B
Editorial	7A
Nation	4A
State-by-state	6A
Stocks	11A
World	6A

©COPYRIGHT 2001 USA TODAY, a division of Gannett Co., Inc.

ABC News via AP

Fireball of destruction: One of two hijacked airliners plunges Tuesday morning into one of the towers at the World Trade Center in lower Manhattan. Both of the 110-floor New York landmarks later collapsed onto neighboring streets and buildings. Losses from the attacks were feared to be enormous, officials said.

U.S. premise: Attacks will be renewed

By Richard Willing and Jim Drinkard
USA TODAY

The nation went on a full wartime alert Tuesday after terrorist attacks in New York City and Washington left an unknown number of killed and wounded and shook the nation as perhaps nothing had since the Japanese attack on Pearl Harbor nearly 60 years ago.

"Freedom itself was attacked this morning by a faceless coward, and freedom itself will be defended," President Bush said early Tuesday afternoon, from a Louisiana air base to which he had been evacuated.

Death and injury tolls were not immediately available, but were expected to reach perhaps into the thousands.

"Make no mistake – the United States will hunt down and punish those responsible for these cowardly acts," Bush said.

Cover story

Bush spoke after apparently hijacked commercial airliners loaded with passengers crashed into both twin towers of the World Trade Center in New York City, causing them to collapse, and the Pentagon near Washington during rush hour Tuesday morning. The coordinated strikes came without warning.

At about 10:40 a.m., 2 hours after the first crash, a fourth apparently hijacked plane crashed near Somerset County Airport near Johnstown, Pa. Federal officials believe it was en route to Washington to participate in the attack.

The federal government moved quickly to place the nation on a full-scale security alert commensurate with an enemy attack.

Intelligence officials said that for at least the past 10 days they had anticipated a possible attack by followers of Osama bin Laden, the Saudi-born financier of Islamic terror groups. But the officials said they had expected the attacks, if any, to come against American targets abroad. American embassies and military installations overseas were on high alert Tuesday.

National security sources said they are working under the premise that the attacks will be renewed. No credible group has claimed responsibility for the attacks. But authorities believe that the coordination involved and the willingness of the attackers to die to kill others point to a radical Islamic group.

Please see COVER STORY next page ▸

For the latest breaking news 24 hours a day, 7 days a week... JUST CLICK HERE USA TODAY .com
Visit us on the Web at www.usatoday.com

HK FF UK ML

1 Angriff auf die USA

Hunderte Todesopfer befürchtet, als Passagierflugzeuge die New Yorker WTC-Türme zerstören und ins Pentagon einschlagen • Experten vermuten, dass die Luftpiraten die Flugzeuge selbst steuerten • Bush schwört, die Verantwortlichen zur Rechenschaft zu ziehen

2 Bush erfährt von den Luftangriffen

3 Die USA gehen davon aus, dass weitere Anschläge folgen

USA TODAY, INTERNATIONALE AUSGABE
WWW.USATODAY.COM
USA, MCLEAN (VIRGINIA)

www.usatoday.com THE NATION'S NEWSPAPER 50 CENTS

Wednesday, September 12, 2001

USA TODAY

NO. 1 IN THE USA

Special Report

37 pages on America's day of terror

'Tears most of the day'

Coast to coast, Americans turn to each other. 8A

Carnage in New York

Horror, disbelief and tears cascade city. 6A

Pentagon in flames

Jetliner tears into symbol of U.S. might. 7A

'Act of war'

Terrorists strike; death toll 'horrendous'

Bush to nation: U.S. 'saw evil'

Vows to avenge strikes. 3A

Crowds rush blood centers

'Touching' response. 10D

Crisis deepens economic woes

'The wrong time.' 1B

86% say attacks are acts of war

USA TODAY/CNN Poll. 2A

Drama of day in pictures

Color pullout. 10-11A

By Chao Soi Cheong, AP

Second impact: Flames and debris explode from a World Trade Center tower as a jetliner slams into the structure Tuesday. Both towers in Manhattan collapsed into a pile of rubble shortly thereafter.

Newsline	3A
Money	1B
Sports	1C
Life	1D
Crossword	11D
Editorial	18-19A
Lotteries	11C
Marketplace	10D
State-by-state	14A
Weather	20A

COPYRIGHT 2001 USA TODAY, a division of Gannett Co., Inc. Subscriptions, customer service 1-800-USA-0001 www.cs.usatoday.com

Minute by minute, fear envelops the country

As jetliners strike U.S. landmarks, America's sense of security is shattered

It may have been the bloodiest day in U.S. history, when our two biggest office towers were obliterated and the Pentagon, symbol of our military authority, was ripped open like an egg carton.

Our commercial jetliners were turned into weapons of mass murder, and we had to stop doing things we always do, from trading stocks to going to Disney World.

Cover story

By Rick Hampson
USA TODAY

People ran through the ash-covered streets of lower Manhattan like extras in a nuclear winter fantasy, chased by a mighty cloud of dust and debris from the office towers they once occupied. Others, some on fire, jumped from 30, 40, 80 stories. One couple held hands as they leapt.

Even if Sept. 11, 2001, was not our deadliest day, it was surely our worst. Americans talked of "a second Pearl Harbor" and "an act of war," but the comparisons faltered.

This time it was civilians dying in the nation's political and financial centers, not soldiers and sailors in a distant Pacific territory. This time the targets were not outdated battleships, but buildings familiar to every schoolchild.

And if this really was war – 86% of Americans in a USA TODAY/CNN/Gallup Poll Tuesday said it was – who was the enemy? What did he want? When was the next battle?

Suspicion focused on an individual, indicted Saudi terrorist Osama Bin Laden, not a nation.

As some called for a congressional declaration of war, Rep. Jim Moran of Virginia asked, "Who do you declare war on?"

History will find that something about America changed at 9 a.m. Tuesday, predicted John Morton Blum, a retired Yale historian and World War II scholar.

"Americans aren't used to being in a war zone," he said. "From here on, they are. No superpower has ever been hit like this."

Sen. John McCain, R-Ariz., struck an apocalyptic note: "I don't think our lifestyles will be the same for a long time."

The prime casualty was America's sense of safety. When Arab terrorists bombed the World Trade Center 8 years ago, six people died, and the complex came back better than ever.

But by noon Tuesday, the Trade Center looked like a smoldering dump and America looked like a nation in retreat – office workers ran up Broadway, and men and women in uniform walked from the Pentagon past Arlington National Cemetery and the Iwo Jima Marine Memorial. They glanced fearfully behind them, as though afraid of what

See COVER STORY next page ▸

"Pearl Harbor brought us together to face a problem. Maybe this can do the same."

—Former Secretary of State Lawrence Eagleburger.

1 »Kriegshandlung«

Terroristen schlagen zu, die Zahl der Todesopfer ist »grauenvoll«

2 Spezial-Report – »Tränen den ganzen Tag«

3 Blutbad in New York

Pentagon in Flammen

4 Bush an die Nation: USA »sahen das Böse« | Ansturm auf Blutspendezentren | Krise vertieft wirtschaftliche Probleme | 86 % meinen, die Angriffe seien Kriegshandlungen |Das Drama des Tages in Bildern

5 Von Minute zu Minute umklammert Angst das Land.
Als die Flugzeuge die Wahrzeichen der USA trafen, wurde Amerikas Gefühl der Sicherheit zerschmettert

USA Today
www.usatoday.com
USA, McLean (Virginia)

12

0912A01NELA0 NE Main section 0912A01NELA0 ZALLCALL 71 21:16:38 09/11/01 B

NATIONAL EDITION

Los Angeles Times

On The Internet: WWW.LATIMES.COM — WEDNESDAY, SEPTEMBER 12, 2001 — COPYRIGHT 2001 $1.00 Designated Areas Higher

TERRORISTS ATTACK NEW YORK, PENTAGON

Thousands Dead, Injured as Hijacked U.S. Airliners Ram Targets; World Trade Center Is Destroyed

AP photos / CARMEN TAYLOR via KHBS/KHOG-TV

United Flight 175, left, heads for the south tower of the World Trade Center, then explodes on impact while the north tower burns from an attack 20 minutes earlier.

Tragedy: Assault leaves Manhattan in chaos. Three of the flights were en route to L.A., one to San Francisco. President Bush puts military on highest alert, closes borders and vows to 'find those responsible.'

By GERALDINE BAUM and MAGGIE FARLEY
TIMES STAFF WRITERS

NEW YORK—Terrorists struck at the preeminent symbols of America's wealth and might Tuesday, flying hijacked airliners into the World Trade Center and the Pentagon, killing and injuring thousands of people.

As a horrified nation watched on television, the twin towers of the World Trade Center in lower Manhattan collapsed into flaming rubble after two Boeing 767s rammed their upper stories. A third airliner, a Boeing 757, flattened one of the Pentagon's famed five sides.

A fourth hijacked jetliner crashed in western Pennsylvania. Authorities said the hijackers might have been trying to crash the plane at the presidential retreat at Camp David, Md.

The assaults, which stirred fear and anxiety across the country and evoked comparisons to Pearl Harbor, were carefully planned and coordinated, occurring within 50 minutes. No one claimed responsibility, but official suspicion quickly fell on Saudi fugitive Osama bin Laden.

Addressing the nation Tuesday night, President Bush vowed to "find those responsible and bring them to justice." This country, he said, would retaliate against "those behind these evil acts" and any country that harbors them.

Altogether, the four downed planes carried 266 people.Scores of people jumped to their deaths or died in fires and the collapsing superstructure at the World Trade Center. New York Mayor Rudolph W. Giuliani said earliest reports counted 2,100 people injured, about 150 of them in critical condition.

Estimates of the death toll at the Pentagon ranged from 100 to 800.

Please see ATTACK, A10

NEWS ANALYSIS

President Shoulders Historic Weight

By RONALD BROWNSTEIN and DOYLE McMANUS
TIMES STAFF WRITERS

WASHINGTON—The greatest challenge any American president can face is war—and George W. Bush, who won the presidency at a moment of peace and prosperity, is abruptly facing a sterner test than anyone expected.

Tuesday's attacks on New York and Washington were almost certain to rank as the most damaging ever against U.S. territory, with the final death toll expected to exceed Japan's 1941 attack on Pearl Harbor.

Bush's initial response—after an awkward day, dictated by security concerns, in seclusion on military bases—was a brief statement pledging "to find those responsible and to bring them to justice."

"We will make no distinction between the terrorists who committed these acts and those who harbor them," Bush said, warning countries such as Afghanistan that they can no longer count on U.S. restraint.

But the real test of the new president's leadership will come in the weeks to come: Can he unify the nation in grief and anger? Can he choose an effective military response? And can he find ways to prevent another attack from occurring?

Please see BUSH, A6

A Struggle to Escape Fiery Chaos

Scene: For those who got out of the burning towers, it was a day of fear and heroism.

By GERALDINE BAUM and PAUL LIEBERMAN
TIMES STAFF WRITERS

NEW YORK—People likened it to a bomb, to midnight, to a hurricane and, finally, when the air was choked with soot and smoke, to hell.

In the aftermath of the explosions Tuesday morning that shook the twin towers of the World Trade Center, thousands struggled to escape. Some were lucky and fast enough to find elevators still functioning. Others walked and crawled and groped their way down hundreds of stairs.

Many, no one yet knows their number, could not escape, blocked by fire or fear. Experts said blazing jet fuel inside the building would have driven temperatures to beyond 1,400 degrees Fahrenheit, hot enough to melt steel, which it did, and hot enough to kill, which it did as well. Some people, unable to withstand the flames, jumped or were sucked out into the high empty air, their bodies tumbling like dolls all the way to the ground.

At 8:45 a.m., Robert Lipiak had just unlocked the door to Cosmos Service America on the 89th floor of the north tower, the first to be struck and the second to collapse. He still had his key in the lock when the explosion rocked the building, sending him flying across the office, crashing into a desk. Others came in and he made them lie on the floor and covered them with towels.

Then he gathered them up and herded them toward the stairwell, which was locked. Police arrived, unlocked the exit and Lipiak's people joined what would become a throng on the route down.

Four floors below, Geoffrey Heineman, managing partner of a law firm on the 85th floor of One World Trade Center, had taken an early train from his home in Garden City, N.Y., because it was "a special day," his oldest son's 11th birthday, "and I wanted to get home for the party."

The firm's offices take up more than half the 85th floor, with spectacular views of New York Harbor and the Statue of Liberty. Ohrenstein & Brown has 90 people at peak hours, but only the early wave had arrived, maybe 15 in all. Heineman was the first in and, by 8:20, had already finished his first phone conference of the day, about a case in New Jersey, when he heard the thud and felt the building sway.

"There was a big bang, an explosion. The building has always swayed in windy weather, but it was nothing like that," he said. "Then it swayed back. I came out of my office, and said, 'Let's round up the people.' "

He figured a helicopter or small plane had accidentally struck the tower because, as he explained, "we often see small planes flying by, below the top of the tower."

Please see DESCENT, A12

Associated Press

A woman watches the World Trade Center burn. Both towers collapsed within two hours of the first hit by a hijacked jet.

The Choreography of Carnage Was Precisely Timed, FBI Says

Terrorism: The hijackers penetrated susceptible security systems before authorities could react to impending disaster.

By RICHARD A. SERRANO and DAVID WILLMAN
TIMES STAFF WRITERS

WASHINGTON—The air attacks Tuesday morning in New York and Washington and a jetliner crash in Pennsylvania were the work of a conspiracy that deftly skirted a beleaguered U.S. airport security system and placed terrorists on four planes, senior FBI officials believe.

Authorities suspect that the terrorists had help from airport ground crews, that they chose cross-country flights because the planes would be heavily loaded with fuel, and that their ranks included hijackers who could fly planes.

But what investigators found most surprising was the timing. They marveled at how teams of hijackers working in at least three cities simultaneously overpowered commercial planes in the air before federal authorities could shut down all flights across the country.

In doing so, the terrorists penetrated an airport security net that many have warned previously is inadequate.

Lewis Schiliro, who as head of the FBI office in New York helped oversee investigations into the explosion aboard TWA Flight 800 and an earlier bombing at the World Trade Center, was left in utter disbelief by what he saw unfold Tuesday morning.

"I've been chilled by a lot of things," Schiliro said. "But this is something I just can't begin to comprehend. They put this together very, very neatly."

In the past, terrorist acts in the U.S. have been marked by disarray. Even the last attack on the World Trade Center in 1993, which killed six people, failed to deliver the carnage intended.

Please see PROBE, A16

Special Coverage

The buildings: Terrorists struck the World Trade Center towers at their most vulnerable spot, structural engineers say, **A2**

Washington: In the nation's crippled capital, dazed people flee federal buildings and wander the streets as the Pentagon burns, **A5**

Pittsburgh crash: A passenger aboard United jet calls 911 to report a hijacking. Moments later, the plane plunges to earth, **A8**

Planes grounded: For the first time, the FAA halted all U.S. air traffic. Stricter security measures are expected, **A15**

The suspects: Preliminary evidence indicates that Osama bin Laden is behind the attacks, U.S. officials say, **A16**

The victims: At least three people aboard the hijacked jets make cell phone calls to alert others of the danger, **A20**

1 **Terroristen greifen New York und das Pentagon an**

2 Tausende Tote und Verletzte, nachdem entführte US-Passagierflugzeuge ihre Ziele rammen; World Trade Center ist zerstört

3 Der Kampf, dem brennenden Chaos zu entkommen

4 Präsident stellt sich der historischen Bürde

5 Laut FBI war der Ablauf des Blutbads genau festgelegt

THE WALL STREET JOURNAL.

© 2001 Dow Jones & Company, Inc. All Rights Reserved.

VOL. CCXXXVIII NO. 51 EE/PR ★★★★ WEDNESDAY, SEPTEMBER 12, 2001 WSJ.com $1.00

TERRORISTS DESTROY WORLD TRADE CENTER, HIT PENTAGON IN RAID WITH HIJACKED JETS

Nation Stands In Disbelief And Horror

Streets of Manhattan Resemble War Zone Amid Clouds of Ash

What's News—

Business and Finance

World-Wide

Death Toll, Source of Devastating Attacks Remain Unclear; U.S. Vows Retaliation as Attention Focuses on bin Laden

By David S. Cloud And Neil King

Hour of Horror Forever Alters American Lives

Attacks Will Force People To Make Adjustments In Ways Large and Small

U.S. Airport Security Screening Long Seen as Dangerously Lax

New Measures Are Likely To Add Inconvenience And Costs for Passengers

The Eye of the Storm: One Journey Through Desperation and Chaos

A Nightmare of Falling Bodies, Acrid Smoke and Heroism: 'It's Coming Down! Run!'

By John Bussey

Attacks Raise Fears of a Recession

By Greg Ip and John D. McKinnon

A Day of Terror

NOTICE TO READERS

THE WALL STREET JOURNAL
WWW.WSJ.COM
USA, CHICOPEE (MASSACHUSETTS)

1 **Terroristen zerstören das World Trade Center und treffen das Pentagon durch Anschläge mit entführten Flugzeugen**

2 Nation sieht sich in Fassungslosigkeit und Entsetzen

3 Zahl der Todesopfer und Ursprung der vernichtenden Angriffe bleiben weiterhin unklar. USA schwören Vergeltung, während sich die Aufmerksamkeit auf bin Laden richtet

4 Die Stunde des Entsetzens verändert das Leben der Amerikaner für immer

5 US-Flugsicherheitskontrollen gelten schon lange als gefährlich nachlässig

6 Angriffe wecken Furcht vor einer Rezession

ONLINE UPDATES ON WWW.ADN.COM

■ **21 PAGES:** Coverage of Tuesday's attack on the nation inside. See sections A, B, C and E.

50 cents

State Final Edition

Anchorage Daily News

Wednesday, September 12, 2001 — ALASKA'S NEWSPAPER — www.adn.com

TERROR

Thousands feared dead as hijacked jets topple World Trade Center towers

■ **CATASTROPHE:** Other planes strike Pentagon, crash near Pittsburgh; government suspects Osama bin Laden.

By SERGE SCHMEMANN
The New York Times

NEW YORK — Hijackers rammed jetliners into each of New York's World Trade Center towers Tuesday morning, toppling them in a hellish storm of ash, glass, smoke and leaping victims, while a third jetliner crashed into the Pentagon in Virginia.

There was no official count, but President Bush said thousands of people perished, and in the immediate aftermath the calamity was being ranked as the worst and most audacious terror attack in American history.

The attacks seemed carefully coordinated. The hijacked planes were all en route to California and therefore gorged with fuel, and their departures were spaced within an hour and 40 minutes.

The first, American Airlines Flight 11, a Boeing 767 out of Boston bound for Los Angeles, crashed into the north tower at 4:48 a.m. ADT. Eighteen minutes later, United Airlines Flight 175, also headed from Boston to Los Angeles, plowed into the South Tower.

Then an American Airlines Boeing 757 left Washington's Dulles International Airport bound for Los Angeles but instead hit the western part of the Pentagon, the military headquarters where 24,000 people work, at 5:40 a.m. ADT.

Finally, United Airlines Flight 93, a Boeing 757 flying from Newark to San Francisco, crashed near Pittsburgh, raising the possibility that its hijackers had failed in whatever their mission was.

Within an hour of the initial attack on the World Trade Center, the fires in the building had grown so hot that first the North Tower and then the South Tower collapsed in an explosion of thick, gray dust, molten metal and hundreds of tons of shattered glass. Office supplies were sent flying three miles from the collapsing building.

In all, 266 people died in the four planes, but establishing a comprehensive death toll could take weeks. Numerous firefighters, police officers and other rescue workers who responded to the initial disaster in lower Manhattan were killed or injured when the buildings collapsed. Hundreds

See Back Page, **TERROR**

Anchorage looks for answers after East Coast devastation

■ **GRAPPLING:** City has scares after attacks on the other side of the continent.

Daily News staff

Anchorage awoke Tuesday morning to the jarring news: terrorist attacks in New York and near Washington, D.C., with horrific reports of immense casualties and smoky devastation.

Before the sun rose above the Chugach Mountains, the aftershocks from events on the other side of the continent began to rattle the lives of Alaskans on a scale not seen since the 1964 Good Friday earthquake — with evacuations, closures, traffic delays and extra police on the street.

Airports were closed statewide and flights grounded, isolating scores of communities and stranding travelers all over, from hunters in the Bush to the season's last tourists.

The Alaska Command jumped to high alert and sharply restricted access to military bases statewide, while fighter jets scrambled at least once to investigate a suspicious airliner headed toward the city.

The city activated its emergency command center and filled the streets with a double-shift of police and loaded fire stations with extra personnel. Customs officials were at heightened alert at Alaska's four highway crossings into Canada.

False alarms were inevitable. About 9:15 a.m., a school bus was evacuated and examined by police after someone

See Back Page, **HIGH ALERT**

Above, a fire ball erupts from the upper floors of the south tower of the World Trade Center after a second plane hit the complex on Tuesday.

KRISTEN BROCHMANN
The New York Times

At right, an emergency worker helps a woman after she was injured in the terrorist attack Tuesday on the World Trade Center in New York.

GULNARA SAMOILAVA
The Associated Press

Glance inside

TOWERS

■ **WHY THEY CRUMBLE[D]** World Trade Center's twi[n] ers couldn't withstand th[e] er of the attack and ensu[ing] fire. No building designe[d] could. **Pages A-2, 3**

SURVIVORS

■ **THEIR TALES:** "I heard muffled boom and I thou[ght] everything was just going [to] collapse," said Richard C[...] who was in the World Trade Center. **Page A-3**

TERRORISTS

■ **WEAKNESS EXPLOIT[E]D:** Terrorists probably [u]sed their own pilots, [ex]perts said. "No pilot, [ev]en with a gun to his [h]ead, is going to fly into [th]e world towers," said [...]ene Poteat, president [of] the Association of [Fo]rmer Intelligence Offi[ce]rs. **Page A-7**

PASSENGER

■ **FINAL PLEA:** A passenger on United Airlines Flight 93 called on his cellphone from a locked bathroom: "We are being hijacked; we are being hijacked!" **Page A-8**

WASHINGTON

■ **ATTACK HOBBLES PENTAGON:** After a plane struck the Pentagon, Washington turned into a massive sea of chaos, smoke and terror. **Page A-8**

DOOGAN

■ **WE'RE ALL SOLDIERS:** In the war against terrorism, every place is a battlefield and every person is a soldier. **Alaska, Page B-1**

OUR STUDENTS

■ **WITNESS TO HISTORY:** Textbooks were closed in East High School teacher Jackie Hoover's U.S. government class as a chapter of history unraveled before students' eyes. **Alaska, B-1**

HELP

■ **WHERE TO TURN:** Check our listing of how you can help, local church services and other information. **Alaska, B-3**

SPORTS

■ **GAMES CANCELLED:** Competitions in Alaska and throughout the country were postponed. **Sports, C-1**

BUSINESS

■ **SLOPE DRILLING CURBED:** On the North Slope, operators restricted access to the oil fields and curbed drilling activities. **Business, E-1**

OUR VIEW

■ **A GAPING HOLE:** There is today a gaping hole in the Manhattan skyline – and a gaping hole in the American heart. The nation has been stunned, and the giant is awakening again. **Opinion, B-6**

HAMILTON

■ **NO SAFE HARBOR:** The coordinated hijacking of commercial airplanes to be the weapons in this act of war brings the threat of terrorism into virtually every American's life. **Opinion, B-6**

Full coverage in Sections A, B, C and E.

INDEX

❶ Terror

❷ Tausende Tote befürchtet, als entführte Flugzeuge in die WTC-Türme krachen

❸ Katastrophe: Weitere Flugzeuge treffen das Pentagon, zerschellen nahe Pittsburgh; die Regierung verdächtigt Osama bin Laden

❹ Anchorage sucht nach der Verwüstung an der Ostküste nach Antworten

Anchorage Daily News
www.adn.com
USA, Anchorage (Alaska)

WEDNESDAY, SEPTEMBER 12, 2001

Detroit Free Press

METRO FINAL ••• ON GUARD FOR 170 YEARS 50 cents outside 6-county metropolitan area 35 cents

WWW.FREEP.COM

AMERICA'S DARKEST DAY

SHOCK WAVES
Tuesday's attack caused many Detroit area schools, workplaces, courts and shopping malls to close. Some will reopen today. **PAGES 4A-5A**

A RUSH ON GAS
Worried motorists line up for gasoline, and some stations charge up to $5. **PAGE 13A**

MITCH ALBOM
We've all been hijacked, he writes. Rochelle Riley, Desiree Cooper and Brian Dickerson also comment. **PAGE 12A**

SURVIVOR'S TALE
Michigan native was on 30th floor of World Trade Center but escaped to safety. **PAGE 8A**

THE ECONOMY
Consumers and markets are likely to recoil, Susan Tompor writes. Plus other fallout for banking, trading and for brokerages. **PAGE 7A**

FLIGHTS HALTED
Metro Airport and the nation's air traffic system are shut down until at least noon today. Airports may soon turn into armed camps. **PAGE 6A**

EDITORIAL
Free Press readers and Mike Thompson react to the tragedy. **PAGES 14A-15A**

MATTHEW McDERMOTT/Corbis Sygma

IN RUINS: With the skeleton of the World Trade Center looming behind them, firefighters search through the rubble left by the terrorist attack.

Terrorists will be hunted down, Bush tells the nation

Photo from ABC-TV

MOMENT OF IMPACT: As one of the World Trade Center towers burns after being hit by a hijacked jet, another jet approaches the second tower, obscured behind the first. A split second later, the second tower erupted into a fire ball. Many people jumped to their deaths before the towers collapsed.

FREE PRESS NEWS SERVICES

In the worst attack ever on the United States, terrorists struck Tuesday at the symbols of American financial and military might, using hijacked jetliners as suicide missiles to level the twin towers of the World Trade Center in New York City and blast into the Pentagon outside Washington, D.C.

Not since Pearl Harbor has a day suggested such infamy. A red-eyed President George W. Bush went before the nation Tuesday night to mourn the victims and promise justice.

The day was filled with horror from the moment television broke into morning programs to tell viewers that an airplane had struck a tower at the World Trade Center. Then, with a stunned nation watching, a second plane struck the second tower. An hour later, with cameras focused on the burning buildings, one of the towers collapsed; 30 minutes later, the second one followed.

At no time in the nation's history had such a calamity been so instantly shared with the entire country, which watched riveted.

Cities came to virtual standstills as office workers and schoolchildren saw the disasters unfold on television.

Reports began to course through news circuits that the Pentagon had been attacked, that the State Department and White House were being evacuated, and that the U.S. Capitol may be a target.

In an unprecedented move, the government ordered all commercial flights grounded.

By 2:15 p.m., only military aircraft and Air Force One were in the air.

When Bush's plane landed at a military base in Nebraska, he told the National Security Council: "We will find these people and they will suffer the consequences of taking on this nation. We will do what it takes. No one is going to diminish the spirit of this country."

The stunning attacks led to an evacuation of key government buildings

Please see TERROR, Page 13A

15 PAGES OF COVERAGE IN SECTION A

PLUS WHAT YOU CAN DO. 1C

NO TIME FOR GAMES. 1D

KNIGHT RIDDER

INFORMATION FOR LIFE

1 Amerikas schwärzester Tag

2 Die Terroristen werden zur Strecke gebracht, verspricht Bush der Nation

3 Schockwellen

4 Andrang auf Benzin

5 Mitch Albom

6 Die Geschichte eines Überlebenden

7 Die Wirtschaft

8 Flüge gestoppt

9 Leitartikel

DETROIT FREE PRESS
WWW.FREEP.COM
USA, DETROIT (MICHIGAN)

ATTACK ON AMERICA: A 32-PAGE SPECIAL REPORT

The Dallas Morning News

Texas' Leading Newspaper | Dallas, Texas, Wednesday, September 12, 2001 | DallasNews.com | 50 cents

War at home

Shaken nation awaits tally from Pentagon, Trade Center attacks; Bush vows to track down terrorists and 'bring them to justice'

DOUG KANTER/Agence France-Presse

New York's World Trade Center towers were reduced to rubble by hits from two hijacked jets. Another jet smashed into the Pentagon in Washington, and a fourth went down near Pittsburgh. No one immediately claimed responsibility.

'Today our nation saw evil, the very worst,' president says

By VICTORIA LOE HICKS
Staff Writer

Americans found themselves at war Tuesday with a shadowy enemy whose ruthless precision raised fears that more – or even worse – might lie ahead.

A grim-faced President Bush vowed to find those responsible for flying hijacked airliners into the World Trade Center and the Pentagon – claiming perhaps thousands of lives – and to "bring them to justice."

"Today our nation saw evil, the very worst of human nature," Mr. Bush said.

Earlier, at a Pentagon briefing, Army Gen. Hugh Shelton, chairman of the Joint Chiefs of Staff, said he would not discuss any possible military response, "but make no mistake about it, our armed forces are ready."

The suicide missions by the terrorists left Americans deeply shaken, as they watched the most potent symbols of the nation's financial and military might disintegrate, sickeningly, in billows of black smoke.

A fourth airliner also crashed Tuesday, going down in a field near Pittsburgh. Some authorities speculated that it had been preparing to hit the presidential retreat at Camp David, Md.

A woman on the streets of New York captured the enormity in a single word: "Armageddon."

See **SYMBOLS** *Page 14A*

A Day of Terror

The four airliners had 266 people aboard; there were no known survivors.

At the Pentagon, about 100 people were believed dead.

An estimated 300 firefighters died in rescue efforts at the World Trade Center – where 50,000 people worked. At least 78 police officers died and about 30 are missing.

Air travel throughout the nation ceased, stranding thousands of passengers.

Trading on Wall Street was shut down.

A guide to *The Dallas Morning News'* full coverage of the tragedy appears on **2A**

For continuing coverage today, visit **DallasNews.com** and tune in to WFAA (Ch. 8) and TXCN.

EDITORIAL
America the resilient

During the early, dark days of World War II, when Britain stood virtually alone against Adolf Hitler's war machine, Prime Minister Winston Churchill took his advisers to a bombed-out quarter of London. Several houses stood amid the rubble. Smoke curled from the houses' chimneys. Mr. Churchill pointed to the smoke and told them that it signified the indomitable spirit of the British people who were still carrying on with their lives despite daunting difficulties, fear and uncertainty. He urged them to take heart from this example of bravery.

By that very same token, Americans must be united, not intimidated, by the terrorist attacks in New York and Washington on Tuesday, in which thousands of people died. The great generosity and spirit of the American people were evident by midday as they rushed to donate blood and attended special prayer services around the country.

In the post-Cold War world, the most likely threat for the United States now comes from enemies operating surreptitiously, employing unconventional means and taking advantage of the openness of American society. With all possible speed, our country should pursue a homeland defense that gives the greatest emphasis to the kinds of attacks that turned the World Trade Center and the Pentagon into fiery hecatombs.

Until then, all citizens should dedicate themselves to addressing the immediate needs of the victims and their loved ones. The nation mourns grievously for the departed and their families; we have only begun to absorb the dimensions of this tragedy.

This moment is a test of our country's character. President Bush and Congress have put aside all partisan interests and now must respond with the same fortitude of Londoners 60 years ago. Our leaders must bind "we the people" together, mend and console the survivors, and call upon our great stock of moral strength.

The United States of America must continue to epitomize the values of democracy. Americans know we are a resilient people. Now, through our courage and resolve, we must remind the world of how precious freedom is and how relentlessly we will defend it.

CARMEN TAYLOR/ KHBS/KHOG-TV | CARMEN TAYLOR/KHBS/KHOG-TV | JERRY TORRENS/Associated Press

Left: A jetliner heads toward a World Trade Center tower, about 20 minutes after another plane crashed into its twin. Center: A fireball explodes from the second tower. Right: That tower collapses; 40 minutes later, the other falls.

'The whole world's changed today'

Sadness, anger grip a nation that has lost all sense of security

By TODD J. GILLMAN and MARK WROLSTAD
Staff Writers

Everything changed Tuesday. At work, home and school, Americans struggled to make sense of the horror.

"It's something I just can't imagine," said 16-year-old Erica Ward, a high school junior in Garland. "It's like the world is coming to an end."

The devastation – of a nation's symbols of security and prosperity – gripped everyone, with a strong undertow of emotions: Shock. Disbelief. Anger. Fear. The flash of explosions, the downing of airliners, the collapse of skyscrapers shook Americans' sense of safety to the core.

In Dallas and across the country, the mood of the people grew somber, dark and complex. In offices, colleagues gathered in a hush to watch the TV reports. In classrooms, teachers consoled weeping students. In airports, business executives and tourists tried to call home to let loved ones know they were all right.

Parents raced to pull their sons and daughters from school – then wondered how to explain the attacks to them. Others grew outraged and compared the attacks to Pearl Harbor, to the Kennedy assassination, to the Oklahoma City bombing.

Cindy Smith, a mother in Mansfield, put it simply: "The whole world's changed today."

See **AMERICANS** *Page 15A*

7 83197 00001

III+

©2001, The Dallas Morning News

1 Krieg zu Hause

2 Erschütterte Nation erwartet Abrechnung nach den Anschlägen auf das Pentagon und das World Trade Center; Bush schwört die Terroristen zur Strecke zu bringen und »sie vor Gericht zu stellen«

3 »Heute hat sich die ganze Welt verändert«

4 Unverwüstliches Amerika

12

THE DALLAS MORNING NEWS
REPRINTED WITH PERMISSION OF THE DALLAS MORNING NEWS
USA, DALLAS (TEXAS)
WWW.DALLASNEWS.COM

EDIÇÃO SÃO PAULO
Concluída à 0h30

FOLHA DE S.PAULO

80 ANOS

São Paulo, quarta-feira, 12 de setembro de 2001

DIRETOR DE REDAÇÃO: OTAVIO FRIAS FILHO ★ UM JORNAL A SERVIÇO DO BRASIL ★ ALAMEDA BARÃO DE LIMEIRA, 425 ★ ANO 81 ★ Nº 26.460 ★ R$ 1,70

GUERRA NA AMÉRICA

EUA SOFREM MAIOR ATAQUE DA HISTÓRIA

Spencer Platt/Getty Images

Choque de Boeing-767 provoca segunda explosão em torre do World Trade Center (esq.) por volta das 10h, em Nova York; pouco antes outro avião havia alvejado a torre norte do prédio de 110 andares; ambas ruíram entre 11h e 11h30

★ *Torres do World Trade Center e parte do Pentágono são destruídas*

★ *Milhares de pessoas morrem em atentados de autoria desconhecida*

★ *Bolsas param, petróleo dispara e aumenta temor de recessão global*

Aviões de carreira sequestrados por terroristas destruíram ontem o World Trade Center, em Nova York, e parte do Pentágono, nos arredores de Washington, no maior atentado da história. Não há números oficiais, mas policiais ouvidos pela **Folha** falam em 10 mil mortos, um sexto de todos os americanos vitimados pela Guerra do Vietnã (1961-1975).

O ataque que destruiu dois dos principais símbolos do poderio econômico e militar dos Estados Unidos foi o primeiro ao país desde Pearl Harbor, em 1941.

O presidente dos EUA, George W. Bush, prometeu em pronunciamento à nação caçar e punir "os terroristas que cometeram esses atos e aqueles que os abrigam".

O principal suspeito é o terrorista saudita Osama bin Laden, refugiado no Afeganistão. O Taleban, grupo extremista islâmico que controla quase todo o país, nega.

O ataque começou por volta de 8h45 (9h45 no horário de Brasília), momento em que um Boeing-767 foi jogado contra uma das torres de 110 andares do World Trade Center. Bombeiros tentavam esvaziar os prédios quando a segunda torre foi atingida, causando pânico.

As TVs, que transmitiam ao vivo, mostraram pessoas se jogando de alturas superiores a 200 metros, antes que as torres desabassem, entre 11h e 11h30 (horário brasileiro). Pouco antes, um terceiro avião atingia o Pentágono, sede do Departamento de Defesa dos EUA.

Pelo menos 266 foram mortos nos quatro aviões sequestrados, dois da American Airlines e dois da United —os três que atingiram alvos e um que caiu na Pensilvânia, por motivo ainda desconhecido.

Pela primeira vez na história, todos os vôos no país foram suspensos. A sede da ONU e todos os prédios públicos de Washington, incluindo a Casa Branca e o Congresso, foram esvaziados. As fronteiras com o México e Canadá, fechadas. Seguradoras calculam um prejuízo de US$ 5 bilhões só no World Trade Center.

O ataque foi condenado pelo líder palestino Iasser Arafat e por opositores dos americanos, como governantes do Oriente Médio, da China e da Rússia. Em países árabes, a população saiu às ruas para comemorar.

Como consequência dos atentados, a Bolsa de Nova York e a Nasdaq suspenderam as operações e anunciaram que não abrirão hoje. Em todo o mundo, houve uma corrida dos investidores para comprar ouro. O preço do petróleo disparou. O dólar atingiu o recorde do Real: chegou a R$ 2,677 e fechou a R$ 2,66.

À noite, a polícia de Nova York prendeu três pessoas, supostamente relacionadas ao atentado. **Págs. A4 a A37**

AVISO

A Folha circula hoje com outra organização de seus cadernos e seções em razão da cobertura especial sobre o ataque terrorista aos Estados Unidos.

OPINIÃO

EDITORIAIS

Leia "Guerra na América", sobre os atentados; e "Economia sob ataque", analisando as perspectivas. **Pág. A2**

Esta edição tem **84** Páginas
447.003 exemplares

ISSN 1414-5723
9 771414 572049 26460

Associated Press

Pedestres cobertos de fuligem deixam a área em que desabou o World Trade Center

Um cheiro embrulha o estômago

SÉRGIO DÁVILA
DE NOVA YORK

A ponte que ligava as duas torres está a dez metros de distância, sobre dois carros da polícia e quatro caminhões dos bombeiros. Enfermeiros carregam uma maca com o corpo de um bombeiro decapitado.

O ar está tomado por uma mistura de pó branco com fumaça preta. É meio-dia, mas está escuro como a noite. No que sobrou do asfalto, um tapete de papel picado. Há um cheiro doce de queimado, que embrulha o estômago. Os alarmes se juntam às sirenes. Não há ordem aparente. **Pág. A9**

"Defesa parece um queijo suíço"

MARCIO AITH
DE WASHINGTON

"A defesa dos EUA tem tantos buracos como um queijo suíço", afirma Brian Jenkins, especialista em terrorismo. "Não é preciso um ataque externo para explorá-los. O perigo interno é maior."

William Cohen, secretário de Defesa durante o governo Bill Clinton, disse que a vulnerabilidade do Pentágono sempre foi evidente. Para Marious Deeb, da American University, "houve falha de inteligência, de segurança nos aeroportos e de proteção do espaço aéreo do Pentágono". **Pág. A5**

FOLHA DE S. PAULO
WWW.FOLHA.COM.BR
BRASILIEN, SÃO PAULO

1 Krieg in Amerika

Die USA erleiden den größten Angriff ihrer Geschichte

2 • Die Türme des World Trade Centers und Teile des Pentagons sind zerstört • Tausende Menschen sterben bei Attentaten von unbekannten Tätern • Die Börsen schließen, der Erdölpreis steigt, die Furcht vor einer globalen Rezession wächst

3 Der Einschlag der Boeing 767 verursacht gegen 10.00 Uhr die zweite Explosion im Turm des World Trade Centers (links) in New York; kurz davor hatte ein erstes Flugzeug auf den Nordturm des 110-stöckigen Gebäudes gezielt; beide Türme stürzten zwischen 11.00 und 11.30 Uhr ein

4 Ein Geruch schlägt auf den Magen

5 »Die Verteidigung ähnelt einem Schweizer Käse!«

Tausende Tote in Amerika! Die Welt in Angst! Gibt es Krieg?

7 Sonder-Seiten

Großer Gott, steh uns bei!

AHW ★★★★

Mittwoch, 213/37
12. September 2001, 80 Pf

Bild

UNABHÄNGIG · ÜBERPARTEILICH

www.bild.de

Dänemark 4,50- dkr, Finnland 7,50 FM, Norwegen 10,50 nkr, Schweden 12,- skr, Spanien 140 Pta., Can. Ins. 150 Pta.

Kommentar

Kriegserklärung an die Menschheit

Von Kai Diekmann

Nichts wird mehr so sein, wie es war.

Trümmer, Blut, Tote inmitten von Amerika. Das gab es in den Vereinigten Staaten noch nie – auch nicht in beiden Weltkriegen.

Der Krieg fand in Europa und Asien statt. Jetzt brennt Manhattan.

Das World Trade Center, zwei Wolkenkratzer von 110 Stockwerken, Staub und Ruine.

Das Pentagon, die militärische Schaltstelle einer Weltmacht, in Brand gesetzt.

Alle Regierungsbehörden in den USA evakuiert.

Das Unvorstellbare, die Horrorvision von Hollywood, ist 2001 Wirklichkeit geworden. Keine Außerirdischen waren dafür nötig, sondern eine Hand voll irdischer Fanatiker waren genug.

Ein neues Pearl Harbor. Doch diesmal ist nicht die Flotte der USA getroffen worden, sondern Amerika, seine Bürger, seine Häuser.

Wer redet da noch von Terror? Das ist eine Kriegserklärung aus dem Dunkel.

Amerika wird sich wehren, muss sich wehren, wenn es sich nicht aufgeben will.

Mit dem Anschlag auf New York und Washington nehmen die Fanatiker Rache an Amerika und allem, wofür die westliche Führungsmacht steht.

Die Welt von London über Paris, Berlin bis Moskau trauert um die Opfer des 11. September und wird sich gegen die Täter zusammenschließen.

Es ist der schlimmste Terroranschlag in der Geschichte der Menschheit

Wir alle haben Angst! Gestern um 8.48 Uhr Ortszeit attackierten Terroristen das Herz der freien Welt. Kamikaze-Piloten steuerten zwei entführte Passagiermaschinen in die 411 Meter hohen Türme des World Trade Center im Zentrum von New York. Panik. Chaos. Menschen sprangen aus den Türmen. Viele tausend Tote. Minuten später stürzte ein drittes gekapertes Flugzeug ins Verteidigungsministerium in Washington. Das Weiße Haus wurde evakuiert. Die US-Regierung zog in den Atombunker. Kriegsschiffe und Bodentruppen sollen jetzt die USA mit Raketenabwehr-Systemen schützen. Als Drahtzieher der Anschläge gilt der saudische Terror-Chef Osama bin Laden. Entsetzen, Trauer, Wut vereinen die restliche Welt. US-Präsident Bush: „Eine nationale Tragödie. Ein unvorstellbarer Verlust an Menschenleben... Wir werden den Terroristen den Kampf ansagen." In Berlin rief Bundeskanzler Schröder den Krisenstab ein. Er bezeichnete die Terroranschläge als „Kriegserklärung gegen die gesamte zivilisierte Welt".

Die entführte Boeing rast in das World Trade Center

Das Unfassbare geschieht: Eine entführte Boeing 757 der American Airlines rast auf das bereits brennende World Trade Center zu...

...und explodiert in einem Feuerball. Glühende Teile regnen auf die belebten Straßen von Manhattan, die Erde bebt

Der Moment, in dem die Welt den Atem anhielt: Der zweite Turm des World Trade Centers fällt in einer riesigen Staubwolke in sich zusammen

Von Staub und Trümmern gejagt, rennen die Menschen in panischer Angst durch die Straßen von Manhattan

Bild
www.bild.de
Deutschland, Hamburg

12

Frankfurter Allgemeine

ZEITUNG FÜR DEUTSCHLAND

Mittwoch, 12. September 2001, Nr. 212/37 R * | Herausgegeben von Dieter Eckart, Jürgen Jeske, Berthold Kohler, Günther Nonnenmacher, Frank Schirrmacher | 2,30 DM D 2955 A

Angriff auf Amerika

World Trade Center zerstört / Tausende Tote / Großbrand im Verteidigungsministerium / Weißes Haus und Kapitol geräumt / Bush: Nationale Tragödie

Fotos AP

Von unserem Washingtoner Korrespondenten Leo Wieland

WASHINGTON, 11. September. Die Vereinigten Staaten von Amerika sind am Dienstag zum Ziel beispielloser Terroranschläge geworden. Zunächst stürzten zwei möglicherweise entführte Flugzeuge in der Hand von mutmaßlichen Selbstmordattentätern in das World Trade Center in New York und explodierten. Die beiden brennenden Türme stürzten wenig später ein. Dann brach in der Hauptstadt Washington aus zunächst noch ungeklärter Ursache – abermals wurde ein Flugzeug- oder Hubschrauberattentat vermutet – ein Großbrand im Verteidigungsministerium aus. Ein Teil des Pentagons stürzte ein. Aus Pennsylvania wurde der Absturz eines weiteren Passagierflugzeuges gemeldet. In New York wurde mit zehntausend Toten gerechnet.

Die amerikanische Bundespolizei FBI bestätigte, daß insgesamt vier Flugzeuge entführt worden seien. Die beiden American-Airlines-Flugzeuge, die ins World Trade Center stürzten, hatten insgesamt 156 Personen an Bord. Die Fluggesellschaft United Airlines teilte mit, sie vermisse außer dem bei Pittsburgh abgestürzten ein weiteres Flugzeug. Es wurde vermutet, daß dieses auf das Verteidigungsministerium gestürzt sei. Zwei der entführten Flugzeuge waren von Boston aus gestartet. Der New Yorker Bürgermeister Giuliani ordnete die Evakuierung des südlichen Manhattan an. Alle Brücken und Tunnels, die in das Stadtzentrum führten, blieben auf Stunden gesperrt. In Washington wurden das Weiße Haus und das Kapitol – dort wurde in der Nähe der „Museumsmeile" der National Mall ebenfalls ein Feuer gemeldet – geräumt. Alle Flughäfen des Landes wurden vorübergehend geschlossen, alle internationalen Flüge mit einem Ziel in den Vereinigten Staaten nach Kanada umgeleitet. Die New Yorker Börse stellte nach der Attacke auf das Welthandelszentrum ihren Handel ein, ebenso wie alle anderen Börsen im Land. In Chicago wurde das höchste Gebäude, der Sears Tower, geräumt. In Washington waren nach dem Weißen Haus und dem Kapitol auch verschiedene Ministerien geräumt worden. In New York wurde das Hauptquartier der Vereinten Nationen geschlossen.

Mit Entsetzen verfolgten die Amerikaner im Fernsehen die Bilder der Zerstörung, ohne Hinweise auf die Urheber der Tat oder die Zahl der Opfer zu kennen. Allein in dem 110 Stockwerke zählenden World Trade Center, aus dessen Trümmern Flammen und dichte schwarze Rauchwolken quollen, arbeiten an einem Wochentag mehr als fünfzigtausend Menschen. Im südlichen der beiden Türme konnten vor dem Einsturz nach Angaben von Rettungskräften nur 33 Stockwerke evakuiert werden.

Präsident George W. Bush, der sich am Vormittag in Florida aufhielt und dort in einer Schule in Sarasota Kindern eine Geschichte vorlas, wurde wenige Minuten nach neun Uhr vormittags (Ortszeit) von seinem Stabschef Andrew Card unterbrochen. Card flüsterte ihm die Nachricht von dem ersten Einschlag eines Flugzeuges im World Trade Center zu. Der bald darauf folgende Anflug eines zweiten Flugzeuges auf den Nordturm war dann schon live im Fernsehen zu beobachten. Erschüttert trat Bush danach mit einer kurzen Stellungnahme vor die Kameras und beklagte eine „nationale Tragödie".

Am Nachmittag wandte sich der Präsident dann vom Bundesstaat Louisiana aus ein zweites Mal über das Fernsehen an die Bevölkerung und sagte: „Die Freiheit selbst wurde an diesem Morgen von einem gesichtslosen Feigling attackiert. Sie wird aber verteidigt werden." Er sagte, daß die amerikanischen Streitkräfte im Land und außerhalb in „hohe Alarmbereitschaft" versetzt worden seien. Zuvor war bekanntgeworden, daß zwei Kriegsschiffe und Einheiten der Nationalgarde zur Hilfe bei der Rettung und Bergung von Opfern nach New York entsandt worden waren. Bush, der mit der Kongreßführung und ausländischen Politikern Kontakt aufnahm, versicherte den Amerikanern, daß alle Vorkehrungen getroffen worden seien, damit „die Regierung weiter funktioniert". Der Präsident versprach, die Urheber der Attentate „zu fassen und zu bestrafen". Er schloß mit einer Aufforderung zu einem Gebet und fügte hinzu: „Die Entschlossenheit unserer großen Nation wird geprüft. Wir werden der Welt zeigen, daß wir diese Prüfung bestehen." Einzelheiten über erste Reaktionen und Vergeltungs- oder Gegenmaßnahmen nannte er nicht.

Später reiste Bush auf eine entlegene Luftwaffenbasis, um mit seinen engsten Beratern zu sprechen. Bush wolle zwar so schnell wie möglich nach Washington zurückkehren, er halte sich aber aus Sicherheitsgründen zunächst im Bundesstaat Nebraska auf, sagte ein Sprecher. Auf der Basis gibt es unteriridische Kommandobunker. Unklar war, ob Vizepräsident Dick Cheney und der Krisenstab das Weiße Haus verließen oder im Bunkerkeller berieten. Die Führung des Kongresses sei an einen „sicheren Platz" gebracht worden, hieß es. Erste Fragen, die gestellt wurden, betrafen unter anderem die ausgebliebenen Luftabwehrmaßnahmen in dem dafür vorbereiteten Pentagon.

Es gab unmittelbar keinerlei Bekennerbriefe oder substantielle Hinweise auf die Urheber der Anschläge. Die ersten Spekulationen richteten sich auf „hausgemachten" Terrorismus nach dem Vorbild des Anschlags auf ein Regierungsgebäude in Oklahoma und auf nahöstliche Terroristen, eventuell unter der Führung des saudischen Millionärs Usama Bin Ladin. (Fortsetzung und weitere Berichte Seite 2, siehe Seite 3, Wirtschaft und Rhein-Main-Zeitung.)

Panik und Kurseinbrüche an den Finanzmärkten

F.A.Z. FRANKFURT, 11. September. Der Angriff auf die Vereinigten Staaten hat an den Finanzmärkten der Welt zu Panik und Kursstürzen geführt. Amerika befinde sich im Kriegszustand, hieß es unter Händlern. Der Aktienhandel kam zeitweise zum Erliegen. Der Ölpreis stieg um zeitweise mehr als zwölf Prozent. (Siehe Wirtschaft und Finanzmarkt.)

Frankfurter Allgemeine

F.A.Z. im Internet: www.faz.de

FRANKFURTER ALLGEMEINE ZEITUNG GMBH ■ POSTANSCHRIFT: 60267 FRANKFURT AM MAIN ■ TELEFON: (069) 75 91-0 ■ ANZEIGEN FAX: (069) 75 91-23 33; TELEFON: (069) 75 91-33 44 ■ REDAKTION FAX: (0 69) 75 91 - 17 43; E-MAIL: REDAKTION@FAZ.DE; BRIEFE AN DIE HERAUSGEBER: LESERBRIEFE@FAZ.DE ■ VERTRIEB FAX: (069) 75 91-21 80; E-MAIL: VERTRIEB@FAZ.DE ■ ABONNENTEN-SERVICE: 01 80 - 2 34 46 77 ■ PROBE-ABONNEMENT: 01 80 - 2 52 52 ■

4 390295 502300 30037

Raus, raus, raus!

Schreie, Rufe, Trampeln: Die Minuten nach dem Angriff in New York / Von Alfons Kaiser

NEW YORK, 11. September. „Schauen Sie", sagt Taxifahrer Mahmood Khalid und reicht sein Fahrtenbuch herüber. „Acht nach acht! Acht nach acht!" Fein säuberlich steht in seinem Buch: „8.08 Uhr, WTC." Um die Uhrzeit hat er eine Kundin am World Trade Center abgesetzt. „Zum Glück habe ich mich nicht in die Schlange der anderen Taxis gestellt, sondern bin wieder hoch nach Midtown gefahren!" Nicht viel später, um kurz vor neun Uhr, stürzte das erste Flugzeug in den nördlichen Turm, achtzehn Minuten später das zweite in den südlichen. Jetzt fährt er wieder hinunter, aber nicht über die Avenue. „Da ist zuviel los!" Rettungswagen, Polizei, Feuerwehr fahren über den Broadway, über die Avenues, über den West Side Highway am Hudson entlang Richtung Katastrophe. An der Straße stehen die Menschen und schauen auf die Rauchbälle, die aus den beiden Türmen quillen und immer größer werden.

Mahmood Khalid biegt nach rechts ab, nimmt den Umweg über den Meatpacking District. Halb zehn. Vor der Metzgerei Louis Zucker stehen die Männer mit ihren blutverschmutzten Kitteln und schauen ungläubig auf die qualmenden Türme. Mahmood Khalid dreht das Radio laut, Präsident Bush spricht mit bebender Stimme von einer „nationalen Tragödie", von einem „offensichtlich terroristischen Anschlag", verspricht eine „vollständige Untersuchung". An der Straße stehen zehn, zwölf Menschen um einen Landrover, dessen Türen offenstehen, und verfolgen still die Ansprache. Die meisten schauen weiter zu den Türmen, zwei Frauen schauen auf den Boden. Der Präsident: „Gott segne die Opfer, ihre Familien und Amerika!"

Dann wissen die Sprecher im Radio nicht weiter. Einer sagt: „Das sieht aus wie ein riesiger Tornado, der wütet." Vor den öffentlichen Telefonen stehen die Leute Schlange. Im Radio wird bekanntgemacht, daß die Börse evakuiert wird, die meisten Gebäude in Lower Manhattan. Auch die Mitarbeiter der Vereinten Nationen werden in Sicherheit gebracht. George-Washington-Brükke gesperrt, Holland-Tunnel gesperrt. Dann die erste Straßensperre in der Hudson Street. Mahmut Khalid kommt mit dem Taxi nicht weiter. Alle Fahrzeuge, die nicht an der Rettung beteiligt sind, müssen zurück. Khalid dreht um und fährt wieder nach Midtown hoch.

Zu Fuß kommt man weiter die Hudson Street hinunter. Hier riecht es schon verbrannt. Polizisten halten Schaulustige ab, die mit Kameras und Videokameras Richtung Tribeca stürmen wollen. „Gehen Sie nach Norden! Gehen Sie nach Norden!" Ein Polizist pfeift laut. Ein dritter Polizist schreit dreimal, immer lauter: „Bewegt euch, Jungs!" Eine Polizistin drückt nacheinander mehrere Personen eigenhändig die Straße hoch. Schreit sie an, schlägt auf sie ein.

In der Church Street springen die Menschen zur Seite, weil jetzt wieder Einsatzfahrzeuge kommen, Lastwagen des New York Police Department mit Absperrungen auf der Ladefläche und Männern, die die Gitter festhalten. Einige der Polizeiautos fahren nicht nur mit Sirene. (Fortsetzung Seite 2.)

Ins Herz

Von Klaus-Dieter Frankenberger

Zwei Flugzeuge stürzen in die Türme des World Trade Center, es kommt zu gewaltigen Explosionen, Flammen schlagen aus den oberen Stockwerken, die Wolkenkratzer brechen zusammen – diese Bilder aus dem Herzen Amerikas stammen nicht aus einem Katastrophenfilm. Was am Dienstag in New York geschehen ist, war furchtbare Wirklichkeit. Entführte, abstürzende Flugzeuge, Feuer im Pentagon, Feuer im Außenministerium. Präsident Bush nennt es eine nationale Tragödie.

Es handelt sich um einen Akt des Terrorismus von monströsen Ausmaßen. Aber es ist mehr als Terrorismus: Es ist ein Krieg gegen Amerika. Diese koordinierten und präzise ausgeführten Anschläge richten sich gegen die Vereinigten Staaten – gegen eines der imponierenden Symbole seiner wirtschaftlichen Vitalität in New York, gegen die militärische Zentrale der Supermacht in Washington, gegen symbolträchtige Einrichtungen der amerikanischen Politik und Gesellschaft. Und die Drohung gegen das daraufhin evakuierte Weiße Haus manifestiert mehr als alles andere, um was es denen ging, die hinter den Anschlägen stehen: ein Land lahmzulegen, es in Panik zu stürzen, an den Abgrund zu treiben.

Nach diesem Dienstag wird nichts mehr sein wie zuvor. Die Verwundbarkeit Amerikas durch den Terrorismus ist für jedermann sichtbar geworden. Seit Jahren haben Fachleute gesagt, daß der Terrorismus und die von nichtstaatlichen terroristischen Gruppen ausgehenden Gefahren die großen Bedrohungen des 21. Jahrhunderts sein werden. In vielen Fällen sind die Warnungen nicht ernst genommen worden; in Amerika, das schon leidvolle Erfahrungen mit dem Terrorismus gemacht hat, noch mehr als in anderen Ländern. Wie abgeschmackt klingen heute die Suggestionen, der Terrorismus sei meist eine Einbildung, eine Wahnvorstellung derer, die angeblich ohne politisches Feindbild nicht auskommen. Nun hat ein Anschlag jede Einbildungskraft übertroffen.

Die Gleichzeitigkeit der Angriffe auf verschiedene Punkte deutet darauf hin, daß die Täter über eine funktionstüchtige Organisation und sehr gute Kenntnisse verfügten, über technologische Raffinesse, über den kaltblütigen Willen zum Massenmord, über den Fanatismus zum Selbstmord. Dieser Typ von Tätern, der Antrieb und Motive aus einer kruden Mischung von politischem Extremismus und religiösem Fundamentalismus schöpft, ist eine Gefahr in jeder Hinsicht, eine Gefahr für jede Gesellschaft. Einer offenen Gesellschaft wie der der Vereinigten Staaten fällt es besonders schwer, sie unschädlich zu machen.

Wer sind die Täter? Wer steckt dahinter? Wer rechnet auf Gewinn, während er, vielleicht Tausende Kilometer entfernt, in einem amerikanischen Sender das terroristische Erdbeben im Herzen des mächtigsten Staats der Erde verfolgt? Zusieht, wie die Türme des World Trade Center einstürzen, wie sich Rauch und Staub über die Stadt ausbreiten, wie die Zahl der mutmaßlichen Opfer höher und höher steigt?

Es muß nicht so sein, daß die ersten Vermutungen, die Täter seien in den Reihen des islamischen Terrorismus zu suchen, tatsächlich zutreffen. Amerika hat viele Gegner, die ihm seine überragende Stellung und die Leistungsfähigkeit seiner Wirtschaft neiden, die ihm die Prägekaft seiner Gesellschaft und die populäre Kultur übelnehmen und sich durch die amerikanische Demokratie bedroht fühlen. Doch wer die Amerikanisierung der Welt mißbilligt, wird dadurch nicht zum Massenmörder. Wird man zum Massenmörder, wenn man sich in einer Art Zivilisationskrieg auf der Seite des Gerechten, Überlegenen, Reinen gegen die Mächte der Finsternis, gegen angebliche Vulgarisierung und Dekadenz sieht? Zum Massenmörder werden auch Kriminelle.

Amerikanische Regierungsstellen haben seit einiger Zeit gewußt, daß sich etwas zusammenbraut. Sie haben den Nahen und Mittleren Osten in den Blick genommen, jenen Raum, in dem in den letzten Wochen und Monaten die Stimmung gegen Amerika hochgeschlagen ist. Im Visier ist der Islamist Ibn Ladin. Ob er dahintersteckt, weiß man noch nicht. Gewiß ist nur: Der High-Tech-Terrorismus ist kein Spezialfach für die Kriminalistik oder für Thriller-Autoren. Es gibt ihn wirklich, als Mittel des Kriegs im 21. Jahrhundert.

FRANKFURTER ALLGEMEINE ZEITUNG
12.09.2001
WWW.FAZ.NET
DEUTSCHLAND, FRANKFURT

12

Süddeutsche Zeitung

MÜNCHNER NEUESTE NACHRICHTEN AUS POLITIK, KULTUR, WIRTSCHAFT UND SPORT

BAYERN-AUSGABE | BN | München, Mittwoch, 12. September 2001 | 57. Jahrgang / 37. Woche / Nr. 210 / 2,20 DM

Das Streiflicht

(SZ) Ob so schnell noch jemand einen Horrorfilm wird drehen wollen? Weil – in halbwegs friedlichen, also langweiligen Zeiten – das menschliche Grundbedürfnis nach Panik, nach Strömen von Blut nicht genug befriedigt werden kann, hat die Filmindustrie ja immer ihr Möglichstes getan, diesem Bedürfnis gerecht zu werden. Immer neue, immer schrecklichere Katastrophen hat sich Hollywood ausgedacht: *Godzilla* hießen dann die Erfolgs-Filme, *Mars Attacks!* oder *Independence Day*, und immer waren es Monster oder Grauen erregende Nicht-Menschen aus dem Weltall, die New York zerstörten und Amerika in die Knie zwingen wollten und meist im letzten Moment noch an der völligen Vernichtung der Welt gehindert wurden.

Und nun wissen wir, dass wir keine Marsmenschen, keine Monster mehr brauchen: Wir haben ja die Menschen dafür. Wenn es noch eine Illusion über die Sicherheit in unseren gegen alles versicherten westlichen Gesellschaften gegeben hat, wenn noch jemand davon geträumt haben sollte, es könnte ein weltweites Einverständnis geben über Mindeststandards der Zivilisation, dann ist das alles nach diesem unglaublichen Dienstag vorbei: Es kann, hat sich herausgestellt, nicht nur alles passieren, was wir uns in unseren Albträumen ausmalen könnten, es gibt auch keine Möglichkeit, diese Schrecken zu verhindern. Wer künftig sagt, die Welt sitze auf einem Pulverfass, wird sich als Verharmloser beschimpfen lassen müssen: Das Wort Pulver hat so etwas Gemütliches. Warum sollte im nächsten Akt – als Antwort auf den Vergeltungsschlag der USA vielleicht – nicht ein Flugzeug mit einer Atombombe an Bord auf New York stürzen (oder auf Paris oder auf Berlin)? Es ist genug Hass auf der Welt, um sie explodieren zu lassen.

Es ist jetzt klar, was wir bisher nur ahnen konnten, wenn wir nach Palästina, nach Spanien, nach Nordirland gesehen haben: dass es, auch wenn kein Krieg erklärt ist, keine verbindlichen Regeln mehr gibt; dass es keines auch nur erkennbaren politischen Zieles mehr bedarf, um – ohne jede Rücksichtnahme auch auf das eigene Leben – tausende, zehntausende von Unschuldigen hinzumetzeln; dass Brutalität und Rache und die Vergeltung von Racheakten die Welt der Zukunft beherrschen werden. Nicht einmal ahnen konnten wir bisher freilich, dass die Gewissenlosen, die Hasser, die Verbrechertrupps über soviel Geld, über soviel technische Möglichkeiten, über soviel Macht verfügen könnten, dass ihnen die bestgerüsteten, reichsten Staaten geradezu hilflos ausgeliefert sind. Nur Hollywood wusste es besser, seine Produzenten, seine Drehbuchautoren. Und die müssen nun keine Kulissen mehr brennen lassen, keine Computer mehr animieren; sie haben jetzt eindrucksvolles Dokumentar-Material.

HEUTE IN DER SZ

Umfang dieser Ausgabe: 68 Seiten BY

Süddeutsche Zeitung, Sendlinger Straße 8, 80331 München / Redaktion: Tel. 089/2183-0, Fax 2183-787 / Anzeigen: Tel. 089/236080, Fax 2183-795 / Abo-Service: Tel. 0180/2324747
Internet: http://www.sueddeutsche.de

Verheerende Anschläge in New York und Washington

Terror-Krieg gegen Amerika

Zwei entführte Flugzeuge rasen in das World Trade Center / Beide Türme eingestürzt / Tausende Tote befürchtet / Auch Pentagon angegriffen

Zerstörung eines amerikanischen Symbols: Der erste der Zwillingstürme des World Trade Centers in New York brach gegen zehn Uhr morgens (Ortszeit) zusammen, eine halbe Stunde später stürzte auch der zweite Turm ein. Schätzungsweise 50 000 Menschen hielten sich in dem einst 411 Meter hohen Gebäude auf. Augenzeugen berichteten, dass viele in Panik aus den brennenden Stockwerken sprangen. AP

Massenpanik in New York / Weißes Haus in Washington evakuiert / Bush: Nationale Tragödie Islamische Extremisten als Täter vermutet / US-Präsident droht mit Vergeltung

Die USA sind am Dienstag vor den Augen der ganzen Welt von einer beispiellosen Terrorwelle überrollt worden, bei der wahrscheinlich Tausende Menschen getötet wurden. Ziele waren die Symbole der amerikanischen Macht: die Millionenstadt New York und die Hauptstadt Washington. Zwei in den USA entführte Passagierflugzeuge rasten am Morgen innerhalb von 18 Minuten ins World Trade Center in New York. Beide Türme stürzten in sich zusammen. Kurz nach dem Anschlag stürzte ein Flugzeug auf das US-Verteidigungsministerium in Washington; vor dem Außenministerium detonierte eine Autobombe. Eine vierte Maschine stürzte bei Pittsburgh ab. Das Weiße Haus, das Parlamentsgebäude und wichtige Ministerien wurden nach den Anschlägen sofort evakuiert. Bürgermeister

Außerdem in dieser Ausgabe

Rudolph Giuliani ordnete die Evakuierung des südlichen Manhattan an. Alle Flughäfen in den USA wurden gesperrt, weltweit brach der Flugverkehr zusammen. Sämtliche Flüge von Deutschland nach Nordamerika wurden gestrichen. Die Nato evakuierte ihr Hauptquartier in Brüssel. Die New Yorker Börse setzte ihren Handel aus. Die US-Streitkräfte wurden weltweit in hohe Alarmbereitschaft versetzt. Auch Russland setzte die Luftabwehr in Gefechtsbereitschaft.

Wie viele Opfer diese Katastrophe forderte, war zunächst nicht bekannt. Zwischen 30 000 und 50 000 Menschen arbeiten werktags im World Trade Center, Zehntausende sind in benachbarten Häusern beschäftigt. Rettungsmannschaften befürchten, dass Tausende getötet wurden. Man müsse sich auf „einen schrecklichen Verlust von Menschenleben" einstellen, erklärte Polizeichef Howard Safir. US-Präsident George W. Bush sprach von einem „terroristischen Anschlag auf unsere Nation" und einer „nationalen Tragödie". Er sagte, die USA würden die Verantwortlichen für die Tat jagen. Wer hinter den Anschlägen steckt, war zunächst nicht bekannt. Zwei radikale Palästinensergruppen stritten jede Beteiligung ab. Die US-Regierung hält den saudischen Millionär Osama bin Laden für den Urheber. Die afghanischen radikal-islamischen Taliban, die angeblich bin Laden beherbergen, schlossen eine Beteiligung jedoch kategorisch aus

Die 411 Meter hohen Zwillingstürme des World Trade Centers gingen nach den Explosionen sofort in Flammen auf. Wrack- und Gebäudeteile flogen auf die Straße. Es herrschte völliges Chaos. Die Anschläge ereigneten sich um 8.48 und 9.06 Uhr Ortszeit. Den ersten Anschlag auf das World Trade Center beschrieb ein Augenzeuge so: „Das Flugzeug kam niedrig angeflogen. Es sah aus, als ob es in einem flachen Winkel eingeschlagen hat." Ein weiterer Augenzeuge sagte, dass Menschen voller Panik aus dem 110 Stockwerke hohen Gebäude gesprungen seien. Ein Börsenmakler rief am Telefon: „Verdammt, wir sterben!"

Die beiden entführten Maschinen in New York waren von Boston beziehungsweise Washington aus nach New York unterwegs. An Bord befanden sich insgesamt 156 Passagiere. Die *Boing 767* und *757* gehörten zur US-Fluggesellschaft *American Airlines*. Die auf das Pentagon- und in Pittsburgh abgestürzten Maschine gehörten zur Fluggesellschaft *United Airlines*. An Bord dieser beiden Maschinen befanden sich 110 Menschen.

Panik in New York: Passanten rennen um ihr Leben, als das World Trade Center brennend zusammenbricht und eine Druckwelle durch die Straßen fegt. Bürgermeister Rudolph Guiliani ließ das südliche Manhattan evakuieren. AP

Staats- und Regierungschefs aus aller Welt äußerten sich bestürzt über die Anschläge. Der russische Präsident Wladimir Putin sprach der Bevölkerung der USA seine Anteilnahme aus. Er nannte die Anschlagsserie eine „schreckliche Tragödie". Bundeskanzler Gerhard Schröder sicherte Bush die Unterstützung Deutschlands zu. Schröder verurteilte die Anschläge als „Kriegserklärung gegen die gesamte zivilisierte Welt". „Wer diesen Terroristen hilft, verstößt gegen alle fundamentalen Werte, die das Zusammenleben der Völker möglich machen" Der Kanzler berief den Bundessicherheitsrat zu einer Krisensitzung ein. Die Außenminister der EU kommen am heutigen Mittwoch zu einem Sondertreffen zusammen.

Die radikale Palästinensergruppe „Demokratische Front für die Befreiung Palästinas" (DFLP) stritt jede Beteiligung an dem Terroranschlag auf das World Trade Center ab. Der Chef der Organisation im Westjordanland, Kais Abdel Karim, sagte der Deutschen Presse Agentur, er wisse nicht, woher entsprechende Berichte über eine Beteiligung der DFLP stammten. „Wir haben mit dem Attentat absolut nichts zu tun", meinte der Stellvertreter des in Damaskus lebenden Führers der Organisation Naif Hawatme. Zahlreiche Palästinensern in den Flüchtlingscamps in Südlibanon und in Beirut feierten die Terrorserie und feuerten Freudenschüsse in die Luft. Palästinenserpräsident Jassir Arafat verurteilte die Anschläge hingegen „auf das Schärfste".

Die Börsen befanden sich weltweit im freien Fall. In New York, Lissabon und Mexiko City wurde der Handel ausgesetzt. Die London Stock Exchange wurde evakuiert. Wegen einer Bombendrohung wurde auch die Deutsche Börse in Frankfurt evakuiert.

SÜDDEUTSCHE ZEITUNG
WWW.SUEDDEUTSCHE.DE
DEUTSCHLAND, MÜNCHEN

12

die tageszeitung

LE MONDE diplomatique In 2 Tagen in der taz.

DM 1,90 ÖS 22 FF 9 LUF 46 — MITTWOCH, 12. SEPTEMBER 2001 — NR. 6547 37. WOCHE 23. JAHRGANG AUSGABE Berlin

Krieg gegen die USA

Die schlimmsten Terroranschläge der Geschichte erschüttern die USA: Flugzeuge rasen ins New Yorker World Trade Center und ins Pentagon. Tausende von Toten befürchtet. Massenevakuierungen in New York und Washington. Taliban verurteilen Terrorismus

New York: Eine gigantische Staubwolke steigt auf, als das der erste Turm des World Trade Center kollabiert. Der zweite folgt ihm gleich darauf. Die Zahl der Toten und Verletzten bleibt zunächst unklar. FOTO: AP

NEW YORK/WASHINGTON *dpa/afp/rtr/taz* ■ Die USA wurden gestern von den schwersten Terroranschlägen in ihrer Geschichte erschüttert. Innerhalb von nur 18 Minuten rasten gegen 9 Uhr morgens Ortszeit zwei Passagierflugzeuge in das World Trade Center in New York. Eine halbe Stunde später stürzte eine dritte Maschine, ein Boeing 747 Jumbo-Jet, aufs Pentagon, das US-Verteidigungsministerium in Washington. Fast gleichzeitig explodierte vor dem US-Außenministerium eine Autobombe. Beide Türme des World Trade Centers stürzten innerhalb der nächsten zwei Stunden in sich zusammen. Tausende von Menschen, so die Befürchtung, wurden unter den Trümmern begraben.

In einer ersten Reaktion nur Minuten nach den ersten Anschlägen, als die Hochhäuser noch standen, sprach US-Präsident George W. Bush, der sich gerade in einer Grundschule in Florida aufhielt, von einer „nationalen Tragödie" und einem „offensichtlichen Terroranschlag".

Mindestens eines der Flugzeuge, die das World Trade Center rammten, war laut CNN zuvor in Boston entführt worden. Doch seltsamerweise ist nicht bekannt, dass die Flugsicherheit oder die Airlines vor den jeweiligen Abstürzen über solche Entführungen informiert hätten.

Das gesamte südliche Manhattan, alle größeren Gebäude der USA und das Regierungsviertel in Washington wurden komplett evakuiert, alle Flughäfen des Landes geschlossen. Alle Flüge in die USA wurden zurückbeordert oder nach Kanada umgeleitet. Dort durften sie landen, bis auch Kanada alle Flughäfen schloss.

Zwei weitere Flugzeugabstürze stehen offenbar im Zusammenhang mit der Anschlagsserie: American Airlines und United Airlines bestätigten den Verlust von insgesamt vier Zivilmaschinen. Zwei davon sollen in Pennsylvania abgestürzt sein, die beiden anderen für die Anschläge auf das Pentagon und und das World Trade Center benutzt worden sein. Woher die erste Maschine kam, die zunächst den Nordturm des World Trade Centers traf, und um was für eine Maschine es sich handelte, blieb zunächst ungeklärt.

Weltweit wurden Krisenstäbe gebildet. Israel evakuierte alle Botschaften in der ganzen Welt. Das belgische Militär verstärkte die Sicherheitsmaßnahmen rund um das Nato-Hauptquartier in Brüssel. Russland versetzte seine Luftabwehr in Gefechtsbereitschaft. Auch in Deutschland wurde der Sicherheitsrat einberufen. Der Bundestag brach seine Haushaltsdebatte ab. Bundeskanzler Gerhard Schröder sprach von einer „Kriegserklärung an die zivilisierte Welt".

In einer zweiten Stellungnahme sagte Bush gegen Mittag: „Die USA werden jene jagen und bestrafen, die für diese feigen Anschläge verantwortlich sind." Wer das aber ist, darüber wurde gestern nur spekuliert; niemand bekannte sich. Die Vermutungen weisen in Richtung des milliardenschweren saudi-arabischen Geschäftsmannes Ussama Bin Laden. Allein die Dimension des koordinierten massiven Angriffes schlössen andere militante Organisationen aus, meinten Sicherheitsexperten. Die afghanischen Taliban, bei denen Bin Laden seit Jahren Zuflucht findet, haben jede Verbindung zu dem Anschlag bestritten und den Terrorismus verurteilt. Doch der frühere US-Sonderbeauftragte Richard Holbrooke warnte auf CNN: „Jede Nation, die Leuten Zuflucht gewährt, die für diese Anschläge verantwortlich sind, muss damit rechnen, so behandelt zu werden, als wenn sie selbst den Anschlag durchgeführt hätte." Die Welt wartet auf einen Krieg. UWI/PKT

taz, Postfach 610229, 10923 Berlin

30037

4 390254 801901

der tag, der die usa veränderte

Das amerikanische Trauma

DIE TAGESZEITUNG (TAZ)
WWW.TAZ.DE
DEUTSCHLAND, BERLIN

DIE WELT

Mittwoch, 12. September 2001 213-37 WWW.WELT.DE B C 7109 Preis 2,00 DM / 1,02 Euro

Terrorangriff auf das Herz Amerikas

Entführte Passagierflugzeuge stürzen auf World Trade Center und Pentagon – Vermutlich Tausende von Toten – Freude im Westjordanland – Börsenkrach

New York – Eine Serie verheerender Terroranschläge hat die USA erschüttert. Zuerst rasten am Dienstag nach 8.30 Uhr Ortszeit im Abstand von 18 Minuten zwei entführte Passagierflugzeuge in die beiden Hochhaustürme des World Trade Center in New York. Etwas später stürzte ein Flugzeug auf das Pentagon in Washington. Alle Flugzeuge nahmen direkt Kurs auf die Gebäude. Am Außenministerium in Washington explodierte zudem eine Autobombe. Teile des Pentagon standen in Flammen und stürzten später ein.

Seiten 2 bis 6: Der Angriff auf Amerika
Seite 8: Kommentare und Leitartikel
Seite 11: IAA-Eröffnungsfeiern abgesagt
Seiten 19, 21, 23: Das Beben an den Börsen
Seite 34: Die Reaktion der Medien
Seite 37: Sicherheitsmaßnahmen in Berlin

Panik in New York: Die Menschen in Manhattan sind verzweifelt

Während die Welt schockiert ist, bricht unter palästinensischen Jugendlichen hämischer Jubel aus

Manhattan ist von Trümmern übersät. Helfer suchen nach Überlebenden

Die Zwillingstürme des World Trade Center gingen nach schweren Explosionen in Flammen auf. Hunderte Menschen flohen in Panik aus dem Gebäude. Ein Augenzeuge berichtete, er habe gesehen, wie Menschen voller Panik aus dem 110 Stockwerke hohen Gebäude sprangen. Der erste der beiden Türme stürzte gegen 10 Uhr, der zweite gegen 10.30 Uhr ein. Die amerikanischen Behörden rechneten mit Tausenden von Toten. Man müsse sich auf „einen schrecklichen Verlust von Menschenleben" einstellen, erklärte Polizeichef Howard Safir. Normalerweise arbeiten täglich rund 40 000 Menschen im World Trade Center.

Kurz nach den Anschlägen in New York überschlugen sich die Ereignisse, und die Lage war völlig chaotisch. CNN berichtete von Massenevakuierungen in New York. Das ganze südliche Manhattan sollte geräumt werden. Das Verteidigungsministerium, das Weiße Haus, das Außen- und das Finanzministerium sowie das UNO-Gebäude wurden evakuiert. US-Präsident George W. Bush sprach von einem „offenkundigen Terroranschlag auf unser Land". „Wir erleben heute eine nationale Tragödie." Bush kündigte umfassende Untersuchungen an. Die, die für diesen Anschlag verantwortlich seien, würden gejagt. Aus Geheimdienstkreisen verlautete, die Urheber seien nicht bekannt. Es handele sich aber sicher um Terror. „Das war nicht das Werk eines schlecht ausgerüsteten Feindes. Aber es ist noch zu früh, um etwas zu sagen." US-Regierungskreise haben, wie es hieß, offenbar „einige Anzeichen" dafür, dass die Drahtzieher der Anschläge aus dem Umfeld des islamistischen Terroristenführes Osama Bin Ladin kommen.

Wie es hieß, wurde mindestens eines der Flugzeuge, die in das World Trade Center rasten, in Boston entführt, das zweite offenbar in Newark, New Jersey. In den USA wurden danach alle Flugzeugstarts abgesagt. Alle Brücken und Tunnel nach Manhattan wurden geschlossen. Ein weiteres Flugzeug stürzte im Staat Pennsylvania ab. Die Flughäfen in den gesamten USA wurden geschlossen. Alle Flüge in die USA wurden nach Kanada umgeleitet. Von Frankfurt/Main starteten keine Flugzeuge mehr Richtung USA.

Rund 2000 Palästinenser in Nablus im Westjordanland hielten eine Freudenfeier ab. Die Menge feuerte Schüsse in die Luft und skandierte Slogans zu Ehren von Osama Bin Ladin. Zuvor hatten auch Palästinenser in Flüchtlingslagern im Libanon Freudenschüsse abgegeben. Die radikale Palästinenserorganisation Islamischer Dschihad bezeichnete die Terrorakte als Folge der Nahostpolitik Washingtons.

Dagegen verurteilte Palästinenserpräsident Jassir Arafat die Anschläge als „völlig inakzeptabel" und „unglaublich". Er bekundete dem amerikanischen Volk und Präsident Bush sein Beileid. Die radikal-islamische Palästinenserorganisation Hamas bestritt jede Beteiligung an den Terroranschlägen. Zuvor hatte bereits die Demokratische Front für die Befreiung Palästinas (DFLP) jede Verantwortung für die Anschläge bestritten. Die radikal-islamischen Taliban in Afghanistan wiesen Überlegungen zurück, der von ihnen beschützte saudiarabische Extremist Osama Bin Ladin könnte hinter den Anschlägen stecken.

Die deutsche Bundesregierung berief wegen der Anschläge in den USA den Bundessicherheitsrat ein. In Berlin wurden die Sicherheitsvorkehrungen massiv verschärft. Die Bundeswehr verstärkte den Schutz ihrer Einrichtungen. „Mit Entsetzen" reagierte Bundeskanzler Gerhard Schröder auf die Terroranschläge. „Meine Regierung verurteilt diese terroristischen Akte aufs Schärfste", schrieb er am Dienstag an US-Präsident George W. Bush. Der Kanzler fügte hinzu: „Das deutsche Volk steht in dieser schweren Stunde an der Seite der Vereinigten Staaten von Amerika." Die Anschläge seien eine „Kriegserklärung gegen die gesamte zivilisierte Welt".

Bundesinnenminister Otto Schily (SPD) sagte, er sehe nach den Terroranschlägen in den USA keine unmittelbare Gefahr für Deutschland. „Es gibt keine Erkenntnisse, die die Sorge rechtfertigen, dass Deutschland in den Kreis der Anschläge einbezogen wird." Die USA versetzten ihre Streitkräfte in erhöhten Alarmzustand. Die Nato beraumte für Dienstagabend eine Krisensitzung an.

Als Reaktion auf die Katastrophen stürzten die Börsen weltweit ab. *DW*

Ein zweites Flugzeug rast in den linken Turm des World Trade Center und explodiert. Beide Türme stürzten ein. Ganz Manhattan war in Rauchschwaden gehüllt. In den beiden Gebäuden arbeiten an normalen Arbeitstagen etwa 40 000 Menschen
FOTO: AP

DER KOMMENTAR

Pearl Harbor im Jahr 2001

Jacques Schuster

Pearl Harbor, die Kuba-Krise, Vietnam – kaum etwas reicht an das heran, was gestern in Amerika auf derart entsetzliche Weise geschehen ist. Nie zuvor hat es solche Terroranschläge in den Vereinigten Staaten, ja in der gesamten westlichen Welt gegeben. Beim Angriff der Japaner auf Pearl Harbor am 7. Dezember 1942 starben 3500 Menschen. Wie viele werden es heute sein? Glaubt man ersten Meldungen, Tausende, vielleicht Zehntausende mehr.

Vor allem mit dem Anschlag auf das World Trade Center ist Amerikas Herz getroffen worden. Wie kein anderes Gebäude auf dem nordamerikanischen Kontinent symbolisieren diese beiden Türme den American Way of Life. Mehr als das: Sie sind Sinnbild der Moderne, Metapher für den Wohlstand, Chiffre für die Stärke der amerikanischen Nation, ja Zeichen der westlichen Zivilisation schlechthin.

Nicht Amerika allein, der Westen insgesamt sollte mit dem Angriff auf seine Führungsmacht in New York und Washington getroffen werden. Stimmen die ersten Vermutungen, gehen die mörderischen Schläge auf das Konto arabischer, womöglich sogar palästinensischer Terroristen. Da ist er, der Kampf der Kulturen, der „Clash of Civilizations", den Samuel P. Huntington unter großem Gelächter auch vieler deutscher Wissenschaftler und Publizisten vorausgesagt hat. Vielleicht wachen sie nun endlich auf und nehmen die Gefahren ernst, die uns von den Schurken dieser Erde drohen – sei es durch Terrorattacken, sei es durch Raketenangriffe.

Amerika wird zurückschlagen – hart und schwer. Wer die Folgen von Pearl Harbor bedenkt, wird daran keinen Zweifel lassen. Krieg ist in Sicht, und es wäre fatal, sich in Deutschland mitfühlend, aber unbeteiligt zurückzulehnen. Amerika ist nicht allein verwundet worden. Es hat die westliche Welt, es hat uns alle getroffen.

Den Autor erreichen Sie unter: **schuster@welt.de**

POLITIK

Scharping gerät weiter unter Druck
Bei seiner abschließenden Befragung vor dem Verteidigungsausschuss hat der Minister nach Angaben der Opposition möglicherweise einen der wichtigsten Bündnispartner Deutschlands brüskiert: Scharping soll den Eindruck einer britischen „Verschwörung" gegen den Bundeswehr-Einsatz in Mazedonien erweckt haben. **Seite 7**

Eichel will am Sparkurs festhalten
Bei der Einbringung seines Haushaltsentwurfs 2002 stellte der Finanzminister klar, dass es mit ihm weder Steuersenkungen auf Pump noch Wahlgeschenke geben werde. **Seite 7**

Zuwanderung: SPD sucht Einigung mit Grünen
Ein Konsens zwischen den Koalitionsparteien und der Opposition in der Zuwanderungsfrage wird immer unwahrscheinlicher. **Seite 7**

SPORT

Schatten auf der Champions League
Trotz der Terror-Anschläge in den USA hielt die Uefa an der Austragung des ersten Spieltages in der Champions League fest. Nach am Abend wurde die Entscheidung heftig kritisiert. **Seite 28**

www.welt.de
www.berufswelt.de
e-mail: redaktion@welt.de
Kostenloses Probeabo:
Tel. 0800/9 35 85 37
Fax 0800/9 35 87 37

Stärke und Provokation

Mit dem World Trade Center ist ein Wahrzeichen der Hauptstadt des Kapitals ausgelöscht

Von Rainer Haubrich

New York – Eine Angst hat dieses Gebäude von Anfang an beherrscht – es war die Höhenangst. Die beiden 110-stöckigen, mit silbern glänzendem Edelstahl verkleideten Türme des World Trade Center brachten es auf eine Höhe von 415 und 417 Metern. Zwei Jahre lang waren die Twin Towers die höchsten Gebäude der Welt – mit weiteren Superlativen: 208 Aufzüge, 50 000 Arbeitsplätze, täglich 80 000 Besucher, die zur verglasten Aussichtsetage hinauffuhren, bei gutem Wetter bis aufs Dach. Ein Erlebnis nur für Schwindelfreie.

Das World Trade Center, gebaut von dem Architekten Minoru Yamasaki, war schon bald mehr als nur ein amerikanisches Symbol. Es schien die Macht, den Einfluss und die Größe der westlichen Wirtschaftszivilisation zu verkörpern. Ein aus der Skyline Manhattans herausragendes Zeichen einer Stärke, die offenbar provozierend wirkte, vor allem auf Fanatiker anderer Wirtschaftssysteme und Kulturen – wie der Bombenanschlag vom 26. Februar 1993 drastisch vor Augen führte. Sechs Menschen starben, mehr als 1000 wurden verletzt. Der pakistanisch-palästinensische Terrorist Ramsi Ahmed Jussef wurde zu 240 Jahren Haft ohne Bewährung verurteilt. Ein Geheimdienstmitarbeiter berichtete, Jussef habe geprahlt, die beiden Türme des Welthandelszentrums würden durch die Explosion aufeinander fallen und mindestens 250 000 Menschen töten.

Die Bauarbeiten begannen 1970 mit dem Aushub gigantischer Mengen von Erde und Felsgestein, die wenige Hundert Meter weiter am Ufer des Hudson River aufgeschüttet wurden. Drei Jahre später standen die beiden Türme des World Trade Center. 1977 war der gesamte sechsteilige Komplex mit einem weitläufigen Netz von Ladenpassagen fertig gestellt. Die schlichten Pfeiler erreichten nie die Popularität des Empire State Building oder des Chrysler Building, und der kahle, windige Platz von 2000 Quadratmeter Größe zu Füßen der Türme konnte sich als Treffpunkt nie durchsetzen.

Auf dem aufgeschütteten Land am Hudson River entstand Mitte der achtziger Jahre Battery Park City mit den gedrungenen Türmen des World Financial Center von Cesar Pelli. Aber die ersten Türme am Finanzplatz New York, der Welthauptstadt des Kapitals, blieben immer die beiden unverwechselbaren, silbern leuchtenden Stelen des World Trade Center.

DIE WELT, Axel-Springer-Straße 65, 10888 Berlin, Redaktion: Brieffach 2410. *Täglich weltweit in über 130 Ländern verbreitet. Pflichtblatt an allen deutschen Wertpapierbörsen.* Redaktion: Tel. 030/25910 - Fax 030/ 25911606, Anzeigen: 040/34724380 - Fax 040/34724521, Leserservice: DIE WELT, Brieffach 7661, 20350 Hamburg Tel: 0800/9 35 85 37 - Fax 0800/9 35 87 37, e-Mail: leser@welt.de

55 bfr / 55 czk / 12 dkr / PTE 280 (Cont.) / 10 F / 330 FT / 500 GRD / 3 hfl / LC 280 / 17 KN / LIT 2800 / 41 lfr / 15 nkr / 15 ÖS / 1,20 GBP / 1,60 IEP / 240 Pts / 5,80 PLZ / 14 SEK / 2,80 sfr / SIT 380 / 59 SKK / 2 000 000 TL / TD 2

Die Welt
www.welt.de
Deutschland, Berlin

12

Ausgabe OP / Preis 1,50 DM

RHEINISCHE POST

ZEITUNG FÜR POLITIK UND CHRISTLICHE KULTUR

JAHRGANG 56 | Mittwoch, 12. September 2001 | Nr. 212

Krieg gegen die Zivilisation

- ❑ Tausende Tote in New York
- ❑ Amerika im Ausnahme-Zustand
- ❑ Bush: Eine nationale Tragödie
- ❑ USA setzen Truppen in Marsch
- ❑ Arafat bedauert, Palästinenser jubeln
- ❑ Nach Mitternacht: Raketen auf Kabul

Inferno in Amerika: Um kurz nach 10 Uhr morgens, New Yorker Uhrzeit, stürzt der erste Turm des World Trade Centers in sich zusammen. Foto: ap

Das Attentat

S.2: Osama bin Laden – Der Sponsor des Terrors
S.2: Das Reich des Bösen
S.2: Welt wurde verändert
S.3: Kamikaze über Manhattan – Eine Reportage von Thomas Spang (USA)
S.3: Die Chronik des Infernos
S.4: „Amerika bekommt, was es verdient“, sagen Araber
S.4: Wie Berlin auf den Anschlag reagiert, berichten unsere Korrespondenten
S.5: Man kann sich nirgends sicher fühlen. Ein Katastrophen-Experte im Gespräch
S.5: Wie bei uns die Sicherheit verstärkt wird
S.6: World Trade Center – der Tod eines Wahrzeichens
S.6: Angst der Banken um ihre Mitarbeiter
Wirtschaft: Der Crash
Fernsehen: Immer draufhalten
■ **News Ticker:** *www.rheinische-post.de*

ZUSTELL-SERVICE
01 80 - 2 30 31 32 / 12 Pfennig je Verbindung
Mo. bis Fr. 6.30 bis 8.30, Sa. 6.30 bis 14 Uhr

30037
4 390587 311505

War es Osama bin Laden?

DÜSSELDORF (RP). 0.03 Uhr. Nach dem brutalsten Anschlag in der amerikanischen Geschichte seit Pearl Harbour: Fernsehbilder von Raketenangriffen auf Kabul. Ein Vergeltungsschlag? In Afghanistan werden die Hintermänner der mörderischen Anschläge auf Ziele mitten in den USA vermutet. Das Weiße Haus erklärt jedoch, Washington habe nichts mit den Angriffen zu tun. Möglicherweise stehe die afghanische Opposition dahinter, heißt es. Rätselraten.

Neun Stunden zuvor, 9 Uhr Ortszeit in Manhattan: Zwei von Terroristen gekaperte Passagiermaschinen fliegen mitten ins Symbol des amerikanischen Traums von Wohlstand und Nationalstolz. Und widerlegen in Minuten die Illusion einer unverwundbaren Zivilisation.

Die ganze Welt im Ausnahmezustand: Schröder spricht von einer Kriegserklärung gegen die zivilisierte Welt. Britanniens Blair und Frankreichs Chirac verurteilen die Anschläge. Belgiens Ministerpräsident Verhofstadt betont die Entschlossenheit der Europäer, „diesen Terrorismus mit allen zur Verfügung stehenden Mitteln zu bekämpfen“. Der russische Präsident Putin spricht den Amerikanern sein Mitgefühl aus. Palästinenserpräsident Arafat kondoliert. In europäischen Hauptstädten werden Krisenstäbe gebildet.

Der Terror kommt aus heiterem Himmel. Ohne Vorwarnung rasen zwei Flugzeuge in die Zwillingstürme des World Trade Centers. Mit beinahe 20 Minuten Abstand, als sollte die Welt zum Zuschauen gezwungen werden. Explosionen erschüttern die hochaufragenden Gebäude. Wenig später sind sie aus der Skyline von New York verschwunden. Im Zentrum der Finanz- und Wirtschaftsmacht USA bricht Chaos aus. Panik auf den Straßen, Ausnahmezustand in den Krankenhäusern. Der Bürgermeister ordnet die Evakuierung von Süd-Manhatten an, spricht von einer gewaltigen Zahl von Toten. Am Ende werden es wohl Zehntausende sein.

Boeing rast ins Pentagon

In Washington rast eine Boeing 767 ins Pentagon. Ein viertes entführtes Flugzeug – Ziel Camp David? – stürzt im Bundesstaat Pennsylvania ab. In allen vier Maschinen sterben 285 Menschen. Das Weiße Haus und die Ministerien werden geräumt. In New York schließt das Gebäude der Vereinten Nationen, in Chicago der riesige Sears-Tower. Alle Flughäfen werden gesperrt, die Grenzen nach Kanada und Mexiko geschlossen.

Präsident Bush zeigt sich entschieden; ordnet die Mobilisierung aller Reserven an, um die Täter zu finden; die US-Streitkräfte werden in höchsten Alarmzustand versetzt. Feiglinge hätten die USA auf die Probe gestellt, sagt Bush, aber: „Wir werden der Welt zeigen, dass wir diesen Test bestehen.“ Hauptverdächtiger: der saudiarabische Terrorist Osama bin Laden. Ihm trauen internationale Experten zu, über die finanziellen und logistischen Mittel zu verfügen.
Fassungslosigkeit in Deutschland. Der Bundestag bricht die Haushaltsdebatte ab, Kanzler Schröder ruft umgehend den Bundessicherheitsrat zusammen. Überall werden die Sicherheitsvorkehrungen für amerikanische und israelische Einrichtungen sowie für die Flughäfen verschärft. Alle Flüge mit dem Ziel USA werden gestoppt. Innenminister Schily ordnet bundesweit Trauerbeflaggung an. Bis zum späten Abend gibt es keine Hinweise, dass Deutsche unter den Terror-Opfern sein könnten.

Entsetzen weltweit. Israel räumt rund um den Globus sämtliche Botschaften und andere öffentliche Einrichtungen. Die Luftwaffe wird in Bereitschaft gesetzt, um israelische Bergungsexperten in die USA fliegen zu können. Russland versetzt seine Flugabwehr in Gefechtsbereitschaft. Die Finanzmärkte werden weltweit ins Chaos gestürzt. Palästinenser in den Flüchtlingscamps in Südlibanon feuern Freudenschüsse ab.

Wenn der Terror kein Action-Film aus Hollywood mehr ist, sondern Realität wird: Zwei Frauen brechen weinend zusammen, kurz nachdem der erste Turm des World Trade Centers eingestürzt ist. Schreiend laufen andere durch die Straßen und rufen: „Wir werden sterben.“ Trauer und Angst neben Erleichterung. Der Mann mit dem Koffer ist dem Tod entronnen. Der Anschlag trifft Amerika ins Mark: Manhattan ist das Symbol schlechthin, wohl für die gesamte westliche Zivilisation. Wohlstand, Kreativität. Nirgendwo auf der ganzen Welt leben und arbeiten Menschen aus so vielen Nationen (weitgehend) friedlich zusammen. Foto: rtr

Rheinische Post
www.rp-online.de
Deutschland, Düsseldorf

Neues Deutschland

56. Jahrgang / Nr. 213
Berlin-Ausgabe 0323-4940
Einzelpreis: Inland **1.80 DM**
Tschechien 45.00 CZK
Österreich 15,00 ÖS
Slowak. Rep. 55,00 SKK
Dänemark 8,50 DKK
Polen 4,10 PLZ
Ungarn 310 FT
Postvertriebsst. Entgelt bez.
www.nd-online.de

SOZIALISTISCHE TAGESZEITUNG · GEGRÜNDET 1946 — Mittwoch, 12. September 2001

● Im Ratgeber: Mobilfunk und Gebühren. Mietrecht und Betriebskosten. Grundstück und Wegerecht. Euro, Giro und Versicherung

● NS-Zwangsarbeit Opfer aus Westeuropa aussortiert – Bundesregierung operiert mit dubiosem Positionspapier. Seite 5

● Etat der Hoffnung Der Bundesetat 2002 will weniger neue Schulden – ob Eichels Rechnung aufgeht, ist allerdings fraglich. Seite 6

● Scharping-Affäre Der Minister brüskiert die Briten. Opposition im Bundestag sieht endgültigen Anlass zur Entlassung. Seite 6

● A.I. – ein Film Odyssee eines Roboterkindes. Steven Spielbergs neuer Film »A.I. – Artificial Intelligence« sucht den Erfolg. Seite 9

Terrorkrieg gegen die USA Tausende Tote in New York

Attentäter steuerten entführte Flugzeuge auf das World Trade Center und in Washington auf das Pentagon / 411 Meter hohe Türme völlig eingestürzt / US-Verteidigungsministerium in Flammen / Bush: »Wir werden die Attentäter jagen«

Die schrecklichsten Terroranschläge der Geschichte haben am Dienstag die Wirtschafts- und Machtzentren der USA getroffen und Tausende von Menschenleben gefordert. Mit in den USA entführten Passagierflugzeugen brachten die Attentäter das berühmte New Yorker World Trade Center zum Einsturz. Am Morgen (Ortszeit) waren innerhalb von 18 Minuten zwei Flugzeuge in die Zwillingstürme gerast. In Washington wurden das Verteidigungsministerium mit einem weiteren Flugzeug teilweise zerstört, das Außenministerium mit einer Autobombe angegriffen. Eine vierte entführte Maschine stürzte bei Pittsburgh ab.

New York/Washington (ND/Agenturen). Kurz nach den Anschlägen in New York und Washington überschlugen sich die Ereignisse. Die Lage in beiden Städten war völlig chaotisch. Im USA-Außenministerium brach Feuer aus. Das Parlamentsgebäude auf dem Capitol Hill und das Weiße Haus wurden ebenso evakuiert wie das UNO-Gebäude in New York, die Börse in der Wall Street und alle Flughäfen und Grenzen der USA geschlossen.

Die Zwillingstürme des World Trade Center, in denen täglich 50000 Menschen arbeiten, gingen nach den schweren Explosionen in Flammen auf. Rund eine Stunde nach den ersten beiden Angriffen auf die Türme, die das zweithöchste Gebäude der Welt bilden, ereignete sich im südlichen Turm eine weitere schwere Explosion. Daraufhin stürzte der obere Teil des 411 Meter hohen Gebäudes ein. Nur wenig später fiel auch der zweite Turm in sich zusammen. CNN berichtete von Massenevakuierungen in New York. Die Behörden der Stadt gehen offiziell von Tausenden von Toten aus, teilte ein Sprecher der Polizei am Dienstagabend mit.

Die Fluggesellschaft American Airlines bestätigte den »Verlust« von zwei Flugzeugen. Dabei habe es sich um eine Boeing 767 gehandelt, die mit 92 Menschen besetzt auf dem Weg von Boston nach Los Angeles war. Das zweite Flugzeug, eine Boeing 757 mit 64 Insassen, war auf dem Flug von Washington nach Los Angeles. CNN berichtete unter Berufung auf einen Sprecher von United Airlines zusätzlich vom Verlust einer Boeing, die auf dem Weg von Newark bei New York nach San Francisco war und offenbar in der Nähe von Pittsburgh abstürzte. Eine zweite United-Boeing, die auf dem Weg von Boston nach Los Angeles war, wurde ohne nähere Angaben als abgestürzt gemeldet.

USA-Präsident George W. Bush sprach am Morgen von einer »nationalen Tragödie« und versprach später in einer Fernsehrede: »Wir werden die Täter zur Strecke bringen und bestrafen.« Der Senator von Utah, Orrin Hatch, berichtete nach Gesprächen mit dem FBI und Vertretern der Geheimdienste von einem Verdacht gegen den saudischen Millionär und mutmaßlichen Terroristenführer Osama bin Laden. Die in Afghanistan regierenden Taleban schlossen eine Beteiligung von bin Laden jedoch kategorisch aus. Dieser habe nicht die Mittel für derart präzise geplante Terroranschläge. Auch radikale Palästinensergruppen verneinten jede Beteiligung an den Terrorakten. Zahlreiche Palästinenser in den Flüchtlingscamps in Südlibanon und in Beirut sollen dennoch die Anschläge gefeiert und Freudenschüsse abgefeuert haben.

Die Terrorakte lösten weltweit Entsetzen aus. Palästinenserpräsident Yasser Arafat verurteilte die Anschläge »aufs Schärfste«. Der russische Präsident Wladimir Putin sprach dem amerikanischen Volk sein tiefes Mitgefühl aus. Gleichzeitig wurden in Russland die Sicherheitsmaßnahmen verschärft, das russische Militär setzte die Luftabwehr im gesamten Land in Gefechtsbereitschaft. NATO-Generalsekretär Robertson rief zum gemeinsamen Kampf gegen den Terrorismus auf. Auch die EU, Frankreich, Großbritannien, Kuba und viele andere Staaten verurteilten die Terrorangriffe in den USA. Papst Johannes Paul II. betete für die Opfer. Der britische Premierminister Tony Blair ließ den zivilen Flugverkehr über dem Zentrum Londons einstellen.

In Deutschland verurteilte Bundeskanzler Gerhard Schröder die Anschläge als »Kriegserklärung gegen die gesamte zivilisierte Welt«. Wer diesen Terror unterstütze, verstoße gegen die Gesetze der zivilisierten Welt, sagte Schröder nach der Sitzung des Bundessicherheitsrates am Dienstagabend in Berlin. Der Kanzler will heute eine Regierungserklärung abgeben. Der Bundestag brach am Nachmittag seine Haushaltsdebatte ab. Es wurde nicht damit gerechnet, dass die Etatdebatte in dieser Woche erneut aufgenommen wird. Die deutschen Parteien zeigten sich entsetzt. Auch PDS-Vorsitzende Gabi Zimmer reagierte bestürzt und warnte vor Gegenschlägen, die die Terrorwelle nur weiter anheizen würden.

Die Lufthansa stornierte alle Flüge in die USA. Auf dem Weg dorthin befindliche Flugzeuge wurden teilweise zurückgerufen.

Die verheerenden Anschläge stürzten die Finanzmärkte rund um den Globus ins Chaos. Die Börsen an der New Yorker Wall Street als auch die Rohstoff- und Terminmärkte in Chicago blieben geschlossen. In Deutschland stürzte der Deutsche Aktienindex DAX zeitweise um rund neun Prozent unter 4200 Punkte, der Euro stieg steil auf über 0,90 US-Cents, der Öl-Preis sprang nach den Terroranschlägen auf mehr als 31 US-Dollar pro Barrel.

Berichte, Reaktionen und Hintergründe auf den Seiten 2, 3, 15 und 18

Wer stoppt den Ritt in die Apokalypse?

Man glaubte bislang, so etwas sei nur in Action-Thrillern aus Hollywood möglich. Doch die Wirklichkeit hat den Film eingeholt, grausam wie ein Albtraum. Und kein Bruce Willis war da, um New York zu retten. In Echtzeit starben unschuldige Menschen vor den entsetzten Augen der Fernsehwelt. Wie viele, wird man vielleicht erst in einigen Wochen wissen. Zwischen Hanoi und Belgrad können Tausende und aber Tausende den unendlichen Schmerz nachvollziehen, der in diesen Stunden über den Vereinigten Staaten liegt.

Von einem zweiten Pearl Harbour ist die Rede. Als apokalyptische Reiter haben Terroristen demonstriert, wie verletzlich auch und gerade die letzte Supermacht ist. Das Lieblingswort der 90er Jahre scheint auf bisher kaum vorstellbare Art und Weise für das beginnende 21. Jahrhundert gültig – Wahnsinn. Keine politischen oder religiösen Motive können solche Taten rechtfertigen. World Trade Center, Pentagon, State Department – die Ziele der verheerenden Anschläge mögen Symbole eines verhassten USA-Imperialismus für Leute wie den islamistischen Extremisten Osama bin Laden sein. Sie sind aber auch Leuchttürme eines nicht weniger gehassten, vermeintlich allgegenwärtigen Staates bei militanten rechten Radikalen vom Schlage Timothy McVeighs, der mit einem Attentat in Oklahoma Hunderte Menschen in den Tod bombte.

»Heilige Krieger«, welcher Couleur auch immer, fallen nicht vom Himmel. Ihr Nährboden ist sehr irdisch. Die Sprache der Gewalt ist keine Erfindung von Terroristen. So wenig wie Allmachtsfantasien. Wir erleben im Nahen Osten, wie Tag für Tag Gewalt neue Gewalt gebiert. In Washington könnte diese Spirale nun weltpolitisch weiter angezogen werden – in Richtung Abgrund. Wo sind die politisch Verantwortlichen, die ein anderes Szenarium schreiben?

Olaf Standke

Die zusammenstürzenden Türme des World Trade Center in New York (o.), auch das Pentagon, das US-Verteidigungsministerium in Washington, stand in Flammen (l.). Foto: dpa

4 398662 501802 30037

NEUES DEUTSCHLAND
WWW.ND-ONLINE.DE
DEUTSCHLAND, BERLIN

FINANCIAL TIMES
DEUTSCHLAND

WWW.FTD.DE | 177/37 | MITTWOCH, 12. SEPTEMBER 2001 | C50937 | DM 2,50

Terroranschläge auf die Vereinigten Staaten von Amerika

++ Zwei Passagierflugzeuge rammen **World Trade Center** ++ Beide Hochhaustürme fallen zusammen ++ **Tausende Tote** und Verletzte ++ Weitere Maschine stürzt auf **Pentagon** ++ Weißes Haus und Kapitol evakuiert ++ Schlimmster Terroranschlag aller Zeiten ++ **Panik** in New York und Washington ++ **Präsident Bush:** Vereinigte Staaten werden Täter „zur Strecke bringen" ++ Amerikanische Truppen weltweit in höchster **Alarmbereitschaft** ++ Verdacht fällt auf Islamisten ++

„Das ist ein zweites Pearl Harbor"

Terroristen zerstören World Trade Center und Teile des Pentagon · Verdacht richtet sich auf islamische Gruppen · Panik an den Weltmärkten

MEMPHIS HI: 85° LOW: 63° CLOUDY

Angriff auf das Wahrzeichen des amerikanischen Kapitalismus: Eine entführte Boeing 767 schlägt in das World Trade Center ein. Das getankte Kerosin explodiert sofort

Von unseren Korrespondenten

Mit einer Serie verheerender Anschläge auf die Macht- und Finanzzentren der USA in New York und Washington haben Terroristen die Supermacht in Alarmbereitschaft versetzt. Innerhalb weniger Minuten rammten gestern früh zwei Passagierflugzeuge wie Kamikaze-Flieger das World Trade Center in New York. Beide Türme, die zu den höchsten Gebäuden der Welt gehören, fielen wenig später vollständig in sich zusammen. In Washington stürzte fast gleichzeitig ein Flugzeug auf das US-Verteidigungsministerium und setzte Teile des Pentagon in Brand. Ein weiteres Flugzeug stürzte bei Pittsburgh in der Nähe des Flughafens ab.

Über die Zahl der Opfer gab es auf Grund der enormen Zerstörungen in New York nur Spekulationen. Sie dürfte in die Zehntausende gehen. Im World Trade Center in Manhattan arbeiten bis zu 50 000 Menschen. Allein in den vier Flugzeugen, die vor den Anschlägen auf US-Flughäfen entführt worden waren, starben mehr als 260 Menschen.

Völlig im Dunkeln blieben bis zum Abend auch Täter, Motive und Hintergründe. Alle in Frage kommenden islamischen Terrororganisationen distanzierten sich von den Anschlägen. Der Hauptverdacht richtete sich gleichwohl auf den saudischen Millionär und mutmaßlichen Terroristenführer Osama Bin Laden. Doch auch die in Afghanistan regierende Taliban, die Bin Laden Asyl gewährt, verurteilte die Anschläge und erklärte, Bin Laden könne dafür nicht verantwortlich sein.

Wenn sich der Verdacht bestätigen sollte, dass Bin Laden oder eine islamische Organisation hinter den Anschlägen steht, gilt es als sicher, dass die USA mit Militäraktionen im Nahen Osten reagieren werden.

US-Präsident George W. Bush sprach von einer nationalen Tragödie und setzte die Streitkräfte in höchste Alarmbereitschaft. Die USA riegelten ihre Grenzen zu Mexiko und Kanada ab und schlossen ihren Luftraum komplett. Das Weiße Haus in Washington, das Pentagon und alle weiteren Regierungsgebäude wurden evakuiert. „Das ist ein zweites Pearl Harbor", sagte Senator Chuck Hagel in Anspielung auf den Überraschungsangriff der Japaner vor 60 Jahren, mit dem der Zweite Weltkrieg im Pazifik begann. US-Präsident Bush sagte am Abend in einer zweiten Fernsehansprache: „Wir werden die Täter zur Strecke bringen und bestrafen." Bush enthielt sich aber jeglicher Anspielungen auf mögliche Täter oder Gegenreaktionen der USA.

„Wir erleben heute eine nationale Tragödie"
US-Präsident Bush

Die deutsche Bundesregierung, alle europäischen Regierungen und Russlands Präsident Wladimir Putin verurteilten die Anschläge und bekundeten den USA ihre volle Solidarität. Bundeskanzler Gerhard Schröder sagte: „Dies ist eine Kriegserklärung gegen die gesamte zivilisierte Welt." Er habe US-Präsident Bush seine uneingeschränkte Solidarität zugesichert. Die Frage, ob es sich bei den Angriffen um einen Bündnisfall handle, beantworteten Vertreter der Regierung ausweichend. Im Nato-Vertrag sichern sich alle Mitgliedsstaaten gegenseitigen Beistand nach einem bewaffneten Angriff zu. Noch am Abend wollte sich der Nato-Rat in Brüssel treffen. In Berlin setzte der Bundestag erstmals die Generaldebatte zum Haushalt ab, die morgen vorgesehen war.

Geschockt äußerte sich auch der palästinensische Präsident Jassir Arafat: „Wir verurteilen diesen sehr gefährlichen Anschlag völlig", sagte Arafat. Auch die Regierungen in Ägypten, Jordanien und Libanon verurteilten den Anschlag. Auf den Straßen in einigen Städten der palästinensischen Gebiete feierten allerdings viele Menschen die Meldungen von den Anschlägen.

Terrorismus-Experten sind sicher, dass die mit äußerster Präzision ausgeführten Anschläge nur von einer straff geführten Organisation verübt werden konnten. Pilotenvereinigungen wiesen darauf hin, dass die Täter die entführten Flugzeuge selbst geflogen haben müssten. Kein Pilot würde ein Passagierflugzeug in ein Hochhaus steuern.

Gegen 8.40 Uhr war das erste Flugzeug in den nördlichen Turm des 1973 gebauten World Trade Center geflogen. Währen die Live-Bilder von dem brennenden Hochhaus um die Welt gingen, rammte eine zweite Maschine den südlichen Turm. Dutzende Menschen sprangen in Panik aus den 405 Meter hohen Häusern. Nach einer halben Stunde sackte der südliche Turm in sich zusammen und hüllt das südliche Manhattan in eine riesige Wolke aus Trümmern und Staub. Wenige Minuten später kollabierte der zweite Turm. Kurz davor waren noch zahlreiche Feuerwehrleute in das Gebäude eingerückt, um Menschen zu retten.

Der Verkehr in Manhattan brach zusammen, der südliche Teil der Insel wurde evakuiert. Einzig die berühmte U-Bahn-Linie „A-Train" blieb in Betrieb und brachte Menschen in Sicherheit. Bürgermeister Rudolph Giuliani entkam der Katastrophe nur knapp. Er hielt sich in einem Nebengebäude auf. In New York und Washington wurde der Notstand ausgerufen.

An den weltweiten Finanz- und Rohstoffmärkten reagierten die Anleger mit Panikkäufen bei Gold, Öl und Basismetallen. Dagegen brachen die Aktienbörsen ein. Die Kurse von Rentenpapieren stiegen stark, da viele Anleger deutliche Zinssenkungen als Reaktion der Zentralbanken erwarten. Der Kurs des US-Dollar brach gegenüber den wichtigsten Weltwährungen ein. Während die US-Börse nicht öffnete, gaben an den europäischen Börsen die Kurse der Versicherer und Banken besonders stark nach.

In Frankfurt wurde nur der Handel in US-Aktien für eine Stunde ausgesetzt. Die Wertpapierbörse und die deutsch-schweizerische Terminbörse Eurex beendeten den Handel 45 Minuten früher um 19.15 Uhr. Zeitgleich musste die Frankfurter Börse, in der sich noch der Parketthandel befindet, wegen einer Bombendrohung geräumt werden.

Am Devisenmarkt herrschte nach Angaben von Händlern teilweise Panik. „Jeder versucht, seine Dollar-Bestände loszuwerden, egal zu welchem Kurs", war zu hören. Der Euro kletterte um 1,52 Cent nach oben und notierte gegen 22 Uhr bei 0,915 $. Zum Yen verbilligte sich 1 $ bis zur gleichen Zeit auf 119,11 Yen. Am späten Montag hatte ein Greenback noch 120,94 Yen gekostet. Der Schweizer Franken, in unsicheren politischen Zeiten ein bevorzugter sicherer Hafen, gewann beinahe 5 Rappen. Gegen 21 Uhr MESZ kostete 1 $ nur noch 1,6410 Franken. „Der Markt ist aus den Fugen, und es kann durchaus einige Zeit dauern, bis wir zu normalen Verhältnissen zurückkehren", sagte ein Händler.

An den Rentenmärkten schichteten viele Anleger Kapital aus den USA in Märkte in Europa um. Zweijährige Bundesanleihen schlossen 39 Basispunkte unter Vortagesniveau bei 3,57 Prozent. Nach dem Schock, den die Bilder der Katastrophe bei vielen Händlern ausgelöst hatte, diskutierten sie vor allem, ob die Anschläge Auswirkungen auf das Wirtschaftswachstum in den USA haben werden. Das Vertrauen in den US-Markt dürfte auf jeden Fall leiden und damit die US-Notenbank zu weiteren Zinssenkungen zwingen.

Die Fed und die Europäische Zentralbank (EZB) werden nach Ansicht der Marktteilnehmer mit Leitzinssenkungen auf die Einbrüche an den Aktienmärkten und die Belastungen für die Wirtschaft reagieren. Die US-Notenbank erklärte, ihre Systeme für die Liquiditätsvergabe an Banken seien offen und funktionierten. Die EZB sagte, sie stünde bereit, das normale Funktionieren der Märkte zu unterstützen.

Nach dem Absturz eines weiteren Verkehrsflugzeugs brennt das **Pentagon in Washington**. Ein Hubschrauber beobachtet das Feuer.

4 395093 702501 30037

REDAKTIONSSCHLUSS DIESER AUSGABE: 22.30 UHR

DAX (XETRA) ↘ 4273,53 Schluss · DOW JONES Handel ausgesetzt · EURO in DOLLAR ↗ 0,9146

	11.9.	10.9.	% Änd.		11.9.	10.9.	Änd.
Dax	4273,53	4670,13	-8,49	30J US-T	5,437	5,441	-0,004
Stoxx*	3220,27	3440,65	-6,41	10J Bund	4,772	4,853	-0,080
Nemax**	875,06	939,33	-6,84	3-M-Euribor	4,242	4,242	0,000
Nikkei	10292,95	10195,69	0,95	Brent Öl	28,87	27,27	1,60
DJIA	geschl.	9605,51	-	€ in $	0,9146	0,8994	0,0152
Nasdaq	geschl.	1695,65	-	$ in ¥	119,11	120,94	-1,84

* EuroStoxx 50; **Nemax All Share

ONLINE FINANZTOOL: WWW.FTD.DE/CHARTS

BERICHTE ZU DEN ANSCHLÄGEN

Heftiger Schlag gegen Finanzsystem
Das World Trade Center in New York galt als Herzstück des internationalen Finanzsystems. Ein Drittel aller Zahlungen in den USA wird über den Financial District in Manhattan abgewickelt. Seite **13**

Terror auch in Deutschland denkbar
Anschläge mit entführten Flugzeugen auf Hochhäuser sind nach Angaben der Deutschen Flugsicherung hier zu Lande ebenfalls möglich. Flugabwehrsysteme würden im Einzelfall keine große Hilfe darstellen. Seite **13**

Verdacht
Der saudische Millionär Osama Bin Laden war gestern für US-Experten der Hauptverdächtige für die Anschläge in New York und Washington. Vor drei Wochen soll er mit einem Angriff gedroht haben. Seite **9**

Versicherer
Die Versicherungsbranche rechnet mit Schäden in Milliardenhöhe als Folge der Terrorangriffe. Viele Unternehmen sind selbst betroffen, weil sie Büros im World Trade Center hatten. Seite **13**

Weltbörsen
Dax
Index in Punkten
19.20 Uhr 4273,53 · 4600 · 4300 · 4000 · 9Uhr 12Uhr

Investoren haben gestern mit Panikkäufen von Gold und Öl reagiert. Die Kurse von Rentenpapieren stiegen, Aktien gaben weltweit kräftig nach. Zahlreiche Börsen setzten den Handel aus. Seite **17**

Krisensitzung im Berliner Kanzleramt
Bundeskanzler **Gerhard Schröder** ist mit den Partei- und Fraktionschefs zusammengetroffen. Er hatte die terroristischen Akte zuvor verurteilt. Dies sei eine Kriegserklärung gegen die zivilisierte Welt. Seite **9**

Amerika ist im Schockzustand
Das politische Washington und ganz Amerika befinden sich im Schockzustand. Präsident George W. Bush erklärte, man werde die Täter suchen und zur Verantwortung ziehen. Seite **9**

Kommentar: Suche nach dem Feind
Die Terroranschläge lösen eine neue Debatte über die Rolle Amerikas in der Welt aus. Es ist nur schwer vorstellbar, dass die USA je wieder so sein werden wie vor der Attacke. Seite **27**

Leitartikel: Die Folgen des Anschlags
Nach dem verheerenden Attentaten ist es wichtig, dass US-Präsident George W. Bush bedächtig handelt. Das Land darf sich keinesfalls in die internationale Isolation treiben lassen. Seite **27**

Touristikbranche besonders betroffen
Reiseunternehmen und Fluggesellschaften waren gestern ebenfalls von den Ereignissen betroffen. Tausende Reisende konnten ihren Flug nicht antreten. Die Aktienkurse von Preussag und Lufthansa sackten ab. Seite **3**

Weitere Informationen im Netz
Die Folgen des Anschlags sind noch nicht absehbar. Politiker diskutieren rund um die Uhr mögliche Reaktionen. Über den aktuellen Stand informieren wir Sie unter **www.ftd.de**

NAMEN- UND FIRMEN-INDEX SEITE 2

25,00 ös · 3,00 sfr · 70,00 bfr · 590 ft · 13,00 FF · 4,00 hfl · 71 Kc · 70,00 lfr · 4600 Lit · 400,00 Ptas (Spanien) · 430 Ptas (Kanarische Inseln) · 450,00 Esc (cont) · 88 Sk · 3 150 000 TL · 1,5 £ · 4600 Lit

ABONNENTENSERVICE 01802 30 40 20 DM 0,12/Anruf

Financial Times Deutschland
www.ftd.de
Deutschland, Hamburg

12

www.handelsblatt.com

Handelsblatt

DIE WIRTSCHAFTS- UND FINANZZEITUNG

Mittwoch, 12. 9. 2001 B

EU-Asylpolitik sorgt in Berlin für Streit
SEITE 7

Neues Profil für den Kuschelkanal
SEITE 22

Ringe werfen mehr Geld ab
SEITE 44

Nr. 176 / 37 - DM 3,00 - G 0 2531

Airlines streichen nach Anschlag Flüge

Infos für Reisende

FLUGGESELLSCHAFTEN:
Deutsche Lufthansa: 0800/100 94 99, Internet: www.lufthansa.com
American Airlines: 01803/24 23 24, Internet: www.aa.com
United Airlines: 001-800-9 32-85 55, Internet: www.ual.com

BAHN:
Deutsche Bahn: 01805/99 66 33, Internet: www.bahn.de
Besonderheit: Flugkunden können kostenlos auf die Bahn umsteigen.

REISEVERANSTALTER:
Thomas Cook: 01803/100 380; Internet: www.thomascook.com
Preussag/TUI: 0511/5 67 89 00; Internet: www.tui.de
Besonderheit: Bis Freitag sind nahezu sämtliche USA-Flugreisen abgesagt.

Weitere Informationen auf Seite 2 (Auswärtiges Amt: 01888/174600)

Beispiellose Serie von Terroranschlägen in New York und Washington – Tausende von Toten befürchtet

Angriff auf Amerika

Flammen schlugen aus beiden Türmen des World Trade Centers, bevor sie kurz danach einstürzten.

Eine beispiellose Terrorserie hat am Dienstag die Machtzentren der USA getroffen. Innerhalb von 18 Minuten rasten zwei Flugzeuge ins World Trade Center in New York, wenig später schlug eine Maschine im Pentagon in Washington ein.

HANDELSBLATT, 12.9.2001

HB NEW YORK. Der internationale Terrorismus hat am Dienstag der Supermacht USA mit den schrecklichsten Anschlägen der Terrorismus-Geschichte den Krieg erklärt. Die mit großer Präzision ausgeführten Selbstmordangriffe auf Macht- und Finanzzentren in New York und Washington mit entführten Passagierflugzeugen als fliegende Bomben kosteten nach Schätzungen der Behörden mehrere Tausend Menschenleben.

Als Urheber vermuten US-Geheimdienste nach Angaben eines amerikanischen Senators den saudischen Millionär und mutmaßlichen Terroristenführer Osama bin Laden. Er hatte nach israelischen Medienberichten vor kurzem mit einem „beispiellosen Angriff" auf die USA wegen ihrer Unterstützung Israels gedroht.

Bei den Terroranschlägen sind das World Trade Center in New York vollständig und das US-Verteidigungsministerium Pentagon in Washington zum Teil zerstört worden. Zwei Passagierflugzeuge rammten innerhalb weniger Minuten die beiden Hochhaus-Türme des World Trade Centers im Herzen von Manhattan. Nach mehreren Explosionen stürzten beide Türme in sich zusammen. Man müsse sich auf „einen schrecklichen Verlust von Menschenleben" einstellen, erklärte Polizeichef Howard Safir.

In den Zwillingstürmen des Welthandelszentrums sowie den dazugehörenden Gebäuden waren etwa 50 000 Menschen beschäftigt. New Yorks Bürgermeister Rudolph Giuliani rief den Notstand über die Stadt aus. Auch das Pentagon in Washington wurde von Explosionen erschüttert, das Gebäude stürzte zum Teil ein und wurde ebenso evakuiert wie das Außenministerium. Der US-Fernsehsender CNN berichtete von einem Feuer in dem Ministeriumsgebäude.

Bush spricht von einer nationalen Tragödie

Die US-Flugbehörde FAA bestätigte den Verlust von vier Passagierflugzeugen. Zwei Maschinen der United Airlines sowie zwei weitere der American Airlines würden vermisst. Alles deute darauf hin, dass es sich bei zwei der Maschinen um die Flugzeuge handelt, die offenbar von Terroristen entführt und anschließend in das World Trade Center geflogen worden seien. Eine weitere Maschine stürzte auf das Pentagon, die vierte stürzte in Pennsylvania ab. Nach Angaben der Fluggesellschaften befanden sich 266 Menschen an Bord der Flugzeuge.

US-Präsident George Bush sprach von einer „nationalen Tragödie". Es handele sich um einen „offensichtlichen Terroranschlag". Er kündigte an, die USA würden den Verantwortlichen für den Anschlag jagen. Nach Angaben aus US-Regierungskreisen stehen hinter den Anschlägen möglicherweise Personen um den international gesuchten saudi-arabischen Terroristen Osama bin Laden. Einige Anzeichen sprächen dafür, dass mit bin Laden oder seiner Organisation El Kaeda in Verbindung stehende Personen verantwortlich sein könnten. Die in Afghanistan herrschende radikalislamische Talibanmiliz bestritt nach Angaben eines Taliban-Sprechers jede Verwicklung bin Ladens in die Terroranschläge. Auch die Palästinenserorganisation „Demokratische Front für die Befreiung Palästinas" (DFLP) wies jede Verantwortung für die Anschläge zurück. Israel hat nach Angaben von CNN weltweit seine Botschaften evakuiert.

Sicherheitsexperten völlig überrascht

Sicherheitsexperten in Washington reagierten zunächst völlig überrascht und ratlos. Es habe keinerlei Vorwarnung gegeben, sagten sie. Kurz nach den Anschlägen in New York überschlugen sich die Ereignisse auch in Washington. Teile des Pentagons stürzten ein, auch im Außenministerium brach Feuer aus. Das Parlamentsgebäude und das Weiße Haus wurden ebenso evakuiert wie das Uno-Gebäude in New York und die Börse. Alle Flughäfen in den USA wurden geschlossen, der gesamte Flugverkehr im Land und über den Atlantik wurde eingestellt. Die Deutsche Lufthansa AG hat alle Flugzeuge auf dem Weg in die USA umgeleitet oder zurückgerufen.

Bundeskanzler Gerhard Schröder (SPD) hat die Terroranschläge in den USA verurteilt und US-Präsident George Bush des Mitgefühls und der Solidarität Deutschlands versichert. Die Bundesregierung rief unmittelbar nach den Anschlägen den Bundessicherheitsrat ein. Palästinenserpräsident Jassir Arafat hat die Anschläge „aufs Schärfste" verurteilt. Arafat sagte: „Wir verurteilen diese schrecklichen Taten ohne Einschränkung. Wir sind alle schockiert. Es ist unvorstellbar." Der russische Präsident Wladimir Putin bezeichnete den Anschlag als „terroristischen Akt". Nato-Generalsekretär George Robertson forderte, dass die internationale Gemeinschaft und die Mitglieder der Nato ihre Kräfte für den Kampf gegen Terrorismus bündeln müssten. Bei der Nato-Zentrale wurde der höchste Alarmzustand ausgerufen.

TOP-THEMA: **TERROR IN DEN USA**

Kritik am Sicherheitssystem
Nach den Anschlägen wird Kritik am US-Geheimdienst laut. Die Sicherheitssysteme hätten versagt, so der Vorwurf. SEITE 2

Terrorist im Visier
Nach Anschlägen gegen US-Einrichtungen fällt der erste Verdacht regelmäßig auf Osama bin Laden. Er gilt als einer der gefährlichsten Terroristen weltweit und steht auf den Fahndungslisten von FBI und CIA ganz oben. SEITE 3

Deutsche Politiker bestürzt
Bundeskanzler Schröder will heute eine Regierungserklärung abgeben. SEITE 4

Das Unfassbare ist geschehen
Die Attentate beweisen: Auch eine Supermacht kann sich vor Terroranschlägen nicht schützen. SEITE 11

Chaos in Manhattan
Das öffentliche Leben in den USA war wie gelähmt. In New York herrschten Chaos und Verzweiflung. SEITE 12

WIRTSCHAFT UND POLITIK

Eichel sieht Risiken für Haushalt 2002

Die Bundesanstalt für Arbeit kann im nächsten Jahr mehr Geld vom Bund erwarten als die bisher zugesagten 1,2 Mrd. DM. Dies kündigte Bundesfinanzminister Eichel bei der Einbringung des Haushalts 2002 an. Er sehe aber noch „einige Risiken" für den Finanzplan des kommenden Jahres, so der SPD-Politiker. Nach den Terroranschlägen in den USA entschied der Bundestag, die für heute geplante Generalaussprache über den Haushalt zu verschieben. SEITEN 4 und 11

Die Steuereinnahmen in Bund und Ländern werden nach Berechnungen des Deutschen Instituts für Wirtschaftsforschung 2001 um rund 5 Mrd. DM geringer ausfallen als im Mai prognostiziert. Das bedeutet ein Minus von rund 3 % gegenüber dem Vorjahr. SEITE 4

Verteidigungsminister Scharping hat am zweiten Tag seiner Anhörung vor dem Bundestags-Verteidigungsausschuss für einen Eklat gesorgt. Nach Handelsblatt-Informationen erklärte er, dass Großbritannien versucht habe, den deutschen Aufmarsch in Mazedonien zu behindern. Die Opposition erwägt, einen Entlassungsantrag zu stellen. SEITE 5

Die Tobin-Steuer findet immer mehr Anhänger. Die IG Metall und die Gewerkschaft Verdi riefen Bundeskanzler Schröder auf, bis zum Jahresende auf eine gemeinsame EU-Position zur Einführung einer Steuer auf Devisenspekulationen hinzuwirken. SEITE 5

Norwegen wird angesichts unklarer Mehrheiten nach den Parlamentswahlen wohl noch länger auf eine neue Regierung warten müssen. Der Chef der konservativen Partei Høyre, Petersen, erklärte, die Norweger hätten für die Wende gestimmt. Er nehme den Auftrag an. SEITEN 7 und 11

Die Wirtschaftsleistung im Euro-Raum ist nach Einschätzung von Bankvolkswirten im zweiten Quartal dieses Jahres gegenüber dem ersten kaum gewachsen. Vom Handelsblatt befragte Experten gehen von einem Plus von höchstens 0,2 % aus. Zum Jahresende sei aber mit einer Besserung zu rechnen. Grund für den Optimismus sind aktuelle Wirtschaftsdaten aus Frankreich. SEITE 9

Japan will die Einnahmen aus Kfz- und Kraftstoffsteuern nicht länger ausschließlich für den Bau neuer Straßen verwenden. Das Geld solle vielmehr auch allgemeinen Posten des Budgets zufließen können, erklärte Ministerpräsident Koizumi. SEITE 9

UNTERNEHMEN UND FINANZMÄRKTE

Neuer VW-Chef will Markenprofil schärfen

Der designierte Volkswagen-Chef Pischetsrieder strebt ein klareres Profil der Konzernmarken an. Die Produktpolitik müsse künftig besser abgestimmt werden, sagte der frühere BMW-Manager dem Handelsblatt. Wenn es dem Gesamtkonzern diene, werde er die Freiheit der Konzerntöchter auch mal etwas einschränken, so Pischetsrieder. Von der Idee, VW durch Aktienverflechtungen vor feindlichen Übernahmen zu schützen, hält er nichts. SEITE 13

Nokia wartet mit guten Nachrichten auf. Der finnische Handyhersteller hält trotz eines befürchteten Umsatzrückgangs um 5 % an seiner Gewinnprognose für das dritte Quartal dieses Jahres fest. SEITEN 13 und 22

Die Deutsche BA musste gestern wegen eines Warnstreiks ihrer Piloten 14 Flüge ausfallen lassen. Der Pilotenvereinigung Cockpit zufolge wollen die Flugzeugführer Gehaltserhöhungen von mindestens 20 % durchsetzen. SEITEN 17 und 22

FAG Kugelfischer lehnt das Übernahmeangebot des Konkurrenten INA ab. Die Offerte stehe in keinem akzeptablen Verhältnis zu Ertragskraft und Wertperspektive des Unternehmens, teilte der Vorstand des Wälzlager-Herstellers mit. SEITE 17

KPN wird seine deutsche Mobilfunktochter E-Plus nicht verkaufen. „E-Plus ist eines unserer bedeutendsten Assets", sagte der designierte Vorstandschef des niederländischen Telekomkonzerns, Scheepbouwer, dem Handelsblatt. SEITE 20

Das TV-Kabelnetz der Telekom in Baden-Württemberg gehört nun mehrheitlich der US-amerikanisch-britischen Callahan-Gruppe. Nach Angaben aus Verhandlungskreisen zahlte Callahan 1,2 Mrd. € für 60 % an der Kabelregionalgesellschaft. SEITE 21

Die Commerzbank bleibt Gegenstand von Übernahmespekulationen. Wie das Handelsblatt erfuhr, sind große Investment-Fonds bereit, Aktien des Instituts aus ihrem Portfolio mit 30 % Kursaufschlag an einen potenziellen Übernahmekandidaten zu verkaufen. SEITEN 22 und 23

Die Bankgesellschaft Berlin steht trotz der geplanten Kapitalerhöhung vor einer ungewissen Zukunft. Der Berliner Senat warte weiter auf ein Gesamtkonzept von NordLB und Sparkassenorganisation, sagte eine Sprecherin der Berliner Finanzsenatorin Krajewski. SEITEN 22 und 34

Die Folgen der schweren Anschläge

Nach den schweren Terroranschlägen in New York und in Washington berichtet Handelsblatt.com über die Reaktionen in der Politik und auf den Finanzmärkten. Ein Special beleuchtet die Hintergründe der Attentate. Wie wird die US-Regierung reagieren? Welche Auswirkungen haben die Terrorakte auf die Märkte?

Handelsblatt.com

Notenbanken wollen Finanzsystem notfalls stützen – Opec stoppt Höhenflug des Ölpreises – Goldpreis klettert auf höchsten Stand des Jahres

Aktienkurse brechen weltweit ein

HANDELSBLATT, 12.9.2001

HB FRANKFURT/M. Weltweit reagierten die Finanzmärkte gestern geschockt auf die Nachricht von den Terroristenattacken in New York und Washington. In ganz Europa fielen die Indizes der Aktienbörsen in Minutenschnelle. Die Wall Street, in unmittelbarer Nähe des zerstörten World Trade Centers gelegen, blieb geschlossen.

Als krisenfest geltende Anlageformen profitierten von der Flucht aus Aktien: So stiegen Anleihekurse, und der Goldpreis kletterte auf den höchsten Stand des Jahres. Der Ölpreis zog zwischenzeitlich um mehr als zehn Prozent an. Als Grund nannten Händler Sorgen, dass Nahost-Terroristen für die Anschläge verantwortlich sein könnten und US-Bestrafungsaktionen den Ölpreis bald nach oben treiben. Doch die Organisation Erdöl exportierender Staaten (Opec) stoppte den Preisanstieg am Abend. Die Opec werde die Märkte weiter ausreichend mit Öl versorgen, erklärte der Generalsekretär der Organisation, Ali Rodriguez.

Der Dollar fiel gegenüber dem Euro und anderen Währungen. „Die erste Reaktion war, Dollar zu verkaufen", sagte Ian Stannard, Analyst bei BNP Paribas in London.

Der Deutsche Aktienindex (Dax) fiel um mehr als acht Prozent; andere europäische Märkte verloren ähnlich stark. Der Handel in US-Werten an der Frankfurter Börse wurde zeitweise ausgesetzt. Wegen einer Bombendrohung wurde der Handel gegen 19.15 Uhr vorzeitig beendet. An der Londoner Börse lief das Geschäft trotz Evakuierung weiter.

Unter den Händlern in Frankfurt herrschte regelrecht Panik, berichteten Marktteilnehmer. Diese Katastrophe sei unvergleichlich, meinte Michael Pohn, Analyst bei der DG Bank. Die politischen Folgen und die ökonomischen Auswirkungen auf die USA seien nur schwer abschätzbar. Daher könne niemand die Konsequenzen für die Finanzmärkte vorhersagen.

Die US-Notenbank kündigte an, notfalls Geld in das amerikanische Bankensystem zu pumpen. Sie sei voll funktionsfähig und könne kurzfristig reagieren. Die Erklärung ähnelt jener, mit der sie auf den Börsencrash von 1987 reagierte. Das Eurosystem erklärte in einer gemeinsamen Stellungnahme in Frankfurt, es stehe bereit, die Funktionstüchtigkeit der Märkte zu unterstützen. Bei Bedarf werde Liquidität zur Verfügung gestellt. Alle Marktfunktionen würden heute voll durchgeführt. Der Schweizer Nationalbank zufolge muss das internationale Finanzsystem trotz der verheerenden Ereignisse in den USA vorerst nicht gestützt werden. SEITE 23

4 390253 103006 30037
Verlagsgruppe Handelsblatt GmbH, Postfach 10 11 02, D-40002 Düsseldorf, Internet: http://www.handelsblatt.com, Telefonzentrale: 0211/887-0; Fax: 0211/887-2980
Weitere Servicenummern finden Sie auf Seite 14

Handelsblatt
www.handelsblatt.com
Deutschland, Düsseldorf

12

Lübecker Nachrichten

Lübecker General-Anzeiger

LN Telefon: (04 51) 14 40
Anzeigen-Service: 1 44-11 11
Leser-Service 1 44-18 00

Überparteilich, unabhängig

S. · 1,30 DM / 0,66 €
Mittwoch, 12. September 2001
Nr. 217 / 37. Woche / 55. Jahrgang

Angriff auf Amerika

Terroristen steuern Flugzeuge ins World Trade Center

Tausende Tote in New York und Washington

Jet stürzt direkt aufs Pentagon

Höchste Alarmstufe für US-Armee

Bilder, die die Menschen in der ganzen Welt fassungslos machten: Während der nördliche Turm des World Trade Centers schon brennt, rast ein Passagierjet auf den südlichen zu . . . und schlägt ebenfalls im oberen Teil des 411 Meter hohen Gebäudes ein. Wenige Minuten später brechen die Türme zusammen und begraben zahllose Opfer unter sich. Fotos: DPA

NEW YORK/WASHINGTON – Die Welt steht unter Schock: Eine beispiellose Serie von Terroranschlägen in den USA hat tausende Tote und zahllose Verletzte gefordert. Ziel der Angriffe, bei denen drei entführte Flugzeuge im Kamikaze-Stil auf Symbole Amerikas gestürzt wurden, waren das World Trade Center in der Millionenstadt New York und das US-Verteidigungsministerium in der Hauptstadt Washington. Die 411 Meter hohen Zwillingstürme des World Trade Centers in Manhattan – hier arbeiteten normalerweise bis zu 50 000 Menschen – brachen etwa eine Stunde nach dem Angriff zusammen.

„Wir erleben heute eine nationale Tragödie", sagte US-Präsident George W. Bush in einer ersten Reaktion. Er setzte die Streitkräfte in Washington und New York in Alarmbereitschaft.

Die Anschlagserie begann kurz vor 9 Uhr Ortszeit, zur Zeit des morgendlichen Berufsverkehrs. Millionen Menschen weltweit verfolgten die Bilder des Terrors voller Entsetzen live im Fernsehen. Zuerst stürzten im Abstand von 18 Minuten zwei Passagierflugzeuge der American Airlines mit insgesamt 156 Menschen an Bord in die beiden Hochhaustürme des World Trade Centers (WTC). Wenig später sprangen Menschen in Panik aus den Hochhaustürmen. Etwa eine Stunde später stürzte zunächst einer, dann auch der zweite Turm ein. Die Staubwolke hüllte ganz Manhattan ein. „Wir werden vermutlich eine horrende Zahl an Opfern haben", sagte der New Yorker Bürgermeister Rudolph Giuliani. Er sprach am Abend von mehr als 2100 Verletzten. Ein Polizeisprecher ging von tausenden Toten aus. Auch deutsche Banken unterhielten Büros im WTC; sie haben offenbar keine Opfer zu beklagen.

Zur gleichen Zeit stürzte ein Flugzeug auf das Pentagon, das danach ebenfalls Feuer fing und teilweise einstürzte. Dort gab es offenbar rund 100 Opfer; der Jet stürzte auf einen Trakt, der gerade renoviert wurde und deshalb nicht so stark frequentiert war wie sonst. In der Nähe von Pittsburgh in Pennsylvania stürzte eine Boeing 767 ab. Diese vierte, ebenfalls entführte Maschine sollte offenbar im Kamikaze-Angriff auf den Präsidentenlandsitz Camp David gelenkt werden. Diese beiden Maschinen gehörten der United Airlines. An Bord starben insgesamt 110 Menschen.

Pentagon, Weißes Haus und alle weiteren Regierungsgebäude wie Außen- und Finanzministerium wurden evakuiert. Allein 20 000 Menschen verließen das Pentagon. Die USA schlossen die Grenzen. „Das ist ein zweites Pearl Harbor", sagte Senator Chuck Hagel unter Bezug auf den Überraschungsangriff der Japaner vor 60 Jahren im Pazifik. Bush sprach von einem „offenkundigen Terroranschlag auf unser Land". Die Verantwortlichen würden gejagt. Bush, der sich gestern an einem „sicheren Ort" im Bundesstaat Nebraska aufhielt, versetzte die Streitkräfte in den USA und Übersee in höchste Alarmbereitschaft. Die Marine entsandte Flugzeugträger und Kriegsschiffe mit Raketenabwehrsystemen Richtung New York und Washington.

Die Reste des World Trade Centers: Vom glanzvollen Wirtschafts- und Bankencenter sind nur noch rauchende Trümmer geblieben. Foto: REUTERS

Mit Entsetzen und Empörung reagierten Bundesregierung und Opposition auf die Terrorwelle. Bundeskanzler Gerhard Schröder nannte nach einer Sitzung des Bundessicherheitsrates die Anschläge eine „Kriegserklärung gegen die gesamte zivilisierte Welt". Schröder und Bundespräsident Johannes Rau sprachen US-Präsident Bush ihr Mitgefühl aus. Politiker sämtlicher europäischer Staaten sowie Russlands, der EU und der UN zeigten sich fassungslos und kondolierten dem amerikanischen Volk. Im Westjordanland dagegen feierten tausende Palästinenser.

Die Finanzmärkte rund um den Globus stürzten ins Chaos. In Deutschland brach der Dax stark ein, der Euro dagegen stieg auf über 0,90 US-Cents. Die US-Börsen bleiben heute geschlossen.

Fluglinien auf der ganzen Welt haben Flüge in die USA abgesagt, zurückbeordert oder umgeleitet. Auf europäischen Flughäfen kam es zu massiven Behinderungen. Die Lufthansa gab bekannt, ihre Flüge von und nach Nordamerika seien „bis auf weiteres" gestrichen. Zahlreiche deutsche Reiseveranstalter sagten ihre Reisen in die USA ab. dpa/AP

Berichte und Analysen auf den Seiten 2, 3, 4, 8 sowie Lübeck

KOMMENTAR

Ein Tag, der die Welt verändert

Bilder, bei denen der Atem stockt, die fassungslos machen, auch Angst. Die man sich wieder und wieder anschaut und nicht glauben will, dass das die Realität sein soll. Passagierflugzeuge mit ahnungslosen, unschuldigen Menschen an Bord, die in riesige Büro-Gebäude gesteuert werden, in denen wiederum unschuldige Menschen, Mütter, Väter, lieb gewordene Freunde, Opas und Onkels, Tanten, die Geliebte, der Ehemann, ihrer Arbeit nachgehen. Sie alle sind tot.

Es wird schwer, sehr, sehr schwer werden, diesen beispiellosen Akt der Barbarei, dieses gnadenlose Massaker angemessen zu beantworten, ohne dabei die Maßstäbe und Werte der zivilisierten Welt aus den Augen zu verlieren. George W. Bush wird diese Antwort für uns alle zu geben haben, eine Aufgabe, um die er nicht zu beneiden ist.

Er, der US-Präsident, ist gleichsam darauf vereidigt, die Bürger der Vereinigten Staaten überall auf der Welt zu beschützen. Dass sie gestern noch nicht einmal im Pentagon sicher waren, im Verteidigungsministerium der USA also, macht deutlich, welche Dimension die Provokation hat, mit der sich die einzig verbliebene Supermacht der Erde seit gestern konfrontiert sieht. Und es lässt ahnen, welche immensen Folgen die furchtbaren Ereignisse des 11. September 2001 auch für den Rest der Welt haben werden. **Uli Exner**

USA rätseln: War es bin Laden?

Experten erkennen Handschrift des Top-Terroristen – Explosionen in Kabul

NEW YORK – Niemand wollte sich zu den Anschlägen bekennen – doch für US-Terror-Experten gab es nur einen, dem ein Verbrechen dieser Dimension zugetraut wurde: Osama bin Laden, 44-jähriger Millionär und für die USA Staatsfeind Nummer eins. „Das trägt seine Unterschrift", sagte der republikanische Senator von Utah, Orrin Hatch, nach einer Unterredung mit dem FBI und den US-Geheimdiensten.

Der arabische Journalist Adb el-Bari Atwan, Herausgeber der in London erscheinenden Zeitung „Al Quds al Arabi", sagte, Osama bin Laden habe bereits vor drei Wochen einen noch nie dagewesenen Anschlag auf amerikanisches Gebiet angekündigt. Und ein Experte des Militärfach-Informationsdienstes „Jane's" in London meinte, es gebe nur „eine Handvoll Terrorgruppen", die zu solch einem Anschlag in der Lage sei. „An der Spitze dieser Liste würde ich Osama bin Laden nennen."

Doch Beweise gibt es nicht. Sowohl die radikalen Palästinenser-Gruppen „Demokratische Front für die Befreiung Palästinas" (DFLP) als auch die „Volksfront zur Befreiung Palästinas" (PFLP) wiesen jede Verantwortung von sich. Die afghanische Taliban-Führung, die Osama bin Laden Unterschlupf gewährt, verurteilte die Anschläge in den USA ebenso wie die radikal-islamische Hamas. Deren Sprecher Abdel Asis Rantisi sagte: „Wir wissen nicht, wer hinter diesen Anschlägen steckt."

● Kurz nach Mitternacht unserer Zeit wurde Kabul, die Hauptstadt Afghanistans, von Explosionen erschüttert. CNN zeigte Bilder eines Brandes und berichtete von Flugabwehrfeuer. Die Ursache der Explosionen blieb vorerst unklar.

Berlin wurde zur Festung

Sicherheitsstufe eins in Deutschland – Frankfurt lässt Hochhäuser räumen

BERLIN – Das Ziel des Terrors waren die Vereinigten Staaten – doch die Wellen des Bebens waren bis nach Berlin und Kiel zu spüren. Als Reaktion auf die Anschläge von New York und Washington berief Bundeskanzler Gerhard Schröder gestern den Bundessicherheitsrat ein, in Innen- und Verteidigungsministerium tagten die Krisenstäbe. In Deutschland galt Sicherheitsstufe eins.

Überall wurden amerikanische und jüdische Einrichtungen besonders geschützt, teilweise sogar abgeriegelt. Die US-Botschaft in Berlin wurde von der Polizei hermetisch abgeschirmt, gepanzerte Fahrzeuge fuhren auf. Selbst Passanten, die Blumensträuße ablegen wollten, kamen nicht durch.

In Schleswig-Holstein wurde der Schutz jüdischer Einrichtungen verstärkt, Ministerpräsidentin Heide Simonis rief am Abend Teile des Kabinetts zusammen, um weitere Maßnahmen zu beraten. Amerikanische Einrichtungen, die man schützen könnte, gibt es im nördlichsten Bundesland nicht. Die Hamburger Rathausparteien stoppten ihren Bürgerschaftswahlkampf.

Hinter allem schwang die Frage mit: Kann so etwas auch bei uns passieren? Klar ist: Auf Anschläge dieser Größenordnung wäre auch eine deutsche Hochhausmetropole wie Frankfurt nicht vorbereitet. „Diese Dimension haben wir nicht einmal in unseren Planspielen erreicht", sagte Frankfurts Feuerwehrchef Reinhard Ries.

Die hessische Landesregierung empfahl gestern Abend, die größten Hochhäuser in Frankfurt sofort zu räumen. Zur Begründung verwies Innenminister Volker Bouffier auf mögliche Nachahmungstäter. „Es gibt im Augenblick niemanden, der ein verlässliches Lagebild zeichnen könnte", sagte er. Mit anderen Worten: Niemand weiß, wie groß die Gefahr tatsächlich ist. nes/cri/dpa

12

LÜBECKER NACHRICHTEN
WWW.LN-ONLINE.DE
DEUTSCHLAND, LÜBECK

Der Terror gegen Amerika auf 8 Sonderseiten

Neue Presse

Mittwoch, 12. September 2001 ▪ Nr. 213 ▪ 37. Woche ▪ Preis 1,50 DM

Gewettert

Im Norden hält der Herbst Einzug. Regenschauer und kühle Temperaturen bestimmen das Wetter der nächsten Tage. Der Mittwoch bleibt wechselhaft. Die Tageshöchsttemperaturen liegen bei 17 Grad, so der Deutsche Wetterdienst. Seite 8

heute 16°/9° · morgen 14°/9° · übermorgen 16°/9°

Die Welt ist gelähmt

Chaos und Entsetzen in den USA, die Welt in Angst vor der Apokalypse: Zwei Passagierflugzeuge waren gestern morgen um 8.50 Uhr (Ortszeit) in das New Yorker World Trade Center in New York gerast, wenige Minuten später stürzte eine Maschine auf das Pentagon in Washington. Millionen waren wie gelähmt am TV-Schirm dabei, als die beiden 411 Meter hohen Türme des Wolkenkratzers kurze Zeit später in einer riesigen Staubwolke in sich zusammenfielen. Da war die Vermutung längst zur Gewissheit geworden: Die furchtbare Katastrophe, der vermutlich tausende von Menschen zum Opfer gefallen sind – das Werk von Terroristen. US-Präsident George W. Bush drohte: „Wir verden die Täter jagen und bestrafen."Bundeskanzler Schröder erklärte geschockt: „Eine Kriegserklärung gegen die zivilisierte Welt."

Wie die Welt auf Anschläge reagierte Seite 2
Wie der Nahe Osten reagierte Seite 3
Das Grauen in New Yorks Trade Center Seite 4
Flammen in Washingtons Pentagon Seite 5
Furchtbare Stunden in Manhattan Seite 6
Reichstag in Berlin geräumt Seite 7
Wut und Trauer in Hannover Seite 8

Neue Presse
www.neuepresse.de
Deutschland, Hannover

WESER KURIER
TAGESZEITUNG FÜR BREMEN UND NIEDERSACHSEN
H 7166
28189 Bremen
57. Jahrgang · Nr. 213 | Mittwoch, 12. September 2001 | Einzelpreis Mo.-Fr. 1,95 DM (1 €), Sa. 2,35 DM (1,20 €)

Terror trifft ins Herz Amerikas

World Trade Center zerstört / Pentagon in Flammen / Tausende Todesopfer / Welt ist geschockt

New York/Washington (dpa/ap). Der internationale Terrorismus hat der Supermacht USA den offenen Krieg erklärt: Die mit großer Präzision um 9 Uhr Ortszeit ausgeführten Selbstmordangriffe in New York und Washington haben wahrscheinlich Tausende von Menschen getötet.

Mit zwei in den USA entführten Passagierflugzeugen brachten Selbstmordattentäter die berühmten Zwillingstürme des World Trade Center in New York zum Einsturz. Wenige Minuten später war auch das Verteidigungsministerium, das Pentagon in Washington, Ziel einer Kamikaze-Attacke mit einem entführten Flugzeug. Eine vierte gekaperte Maschine stürzte bei Pittsburgh ab. Sie sollte vermutlich Camp David, den Landsitz des US-Präsidenten, zerstören.

Kurze Zeit nach der Terrorserie wurden der gesamte Flugverkehr eingestellt und öffentliche Gebäude – auch das Weiße Haus

Zum Thema:

- **Chaos an den Finanzmärkten**
  Berichte auf Seite 2
- **Experten weisen auf den Nahen Osten**
  Berichte auf Seite 3
- **Bremer sind fassungslos**
  Berichte auf Seite 9

– evakuiert. Präsident George W. Bush verbrachte den Abend an einem „sicheren Ort" in Nebraska. Die Armee setzte Elite-Einheiten zum Schutz der Hauptstadt in Marsch. Die US-Marine sicherte die Häfen.

Der sichtlich geschockte US-Präsident sprach von einer „nationalen Tragödie". In einer Fernsehrede versicherte Bush: „Wir werden die feigen Täter zur Strecke bringen und bestrafen." Aus aller Welt trafen in Washington Beileidsbekundungen ein. Bundeskanzler Gerhard Schröder und Bundespräsident Johannes Rau kondolierten für die Bundesrepublik. Schröder sprach von einer „Kriegserklärung gegen die gesamte zivilisierte Welt".

Bis zum Abend bekannte sich niemand zu den Anschlägen. PLO-Chef Jassir Arafat und mehrere radikale Palästinenserorganisationen distanzierten sich von den Anschlägen. Im Westjordanland feierten allerdings Tausende Palästinenser die Terrorwelle. US-Geheimdienstkreise vermuten den radikalsten Terroristenchef der Welt, Osama bin Laden, als Drahtzieher.

In Deutschland wurden die Sicherheitsvorkehrungen für amerikanische und jüdische Einrichtungen verschärft. Zahlreiche Gebäude wurden von der Polizei hermetisch abgeriegelt.

Kurz vor dem Aufprall: Eine Boing 767 wird in den zweiten Turm des World Trade Centers gelenkt. Der andere Turm steht bereits in Flammen, nachdem ein Passagierflugzeug in eines der beiden Wahrzeichen New Yorks gerast war. Durch die Explosionen stürzten die Gebäude ein. Foto: CNN

Kommentar

Kriegserklärung

Ensetzen, Empörung, Abscheu, Ekel. Zu schwache Worte. Was am Dienstag in New York und Washington geschehen ist, entzieht sich jeder Beschreibung. Jeder aufrechte, zivilisierte Mensch steht in dieser Stunde an der Seite der Amerikaner.

Bundeskanzler Schröder hat es richtig gesagt. Dieser Terrorismus ist eine Kriegserklärung. Eine Kriegserklärung an die Demokratien dieser Welt. Die Gräueltaten vom Dienstag zielen auf das System, nach dem wir unser gesellschaftliches Leben regeln.

Der Welt größte Demokratie, die USA, ist stellvertretend für uns Ziel dieser hasserfüllten, menschenverachtenden Wahnsinnigen geworden. Unsere tiefe Trauer gilt den Getöteten, unser ganzes Mitgefühl der amerikanischen Nation.

Die Welt ist seit gestern nicht mehr dieselbe. Schon jetzt werden die Stimmen nach Vergeltung laut. Die Beziehungen des Westens zur islamisch-arabischen Welt werden sich verschlechtern. Die unter dem Eindruck der Anschläge geschlossene amerikanische Nation wird nicht zögern, Schuldige zu bestrafen. Innerhalb von Stunden hat sich gestern die Weltlage verändert, ist der Weltfriede in Gefahr geraten.

Nirgendwo auf der Welt dürfen Terroristen Schlupflöcher finden. Nirgendwo darf Stillschweigen über ihr Tun herrschen. Nirgendwo dürfen sie geduldet werden. Jeder Staat, der Terrorismus auch nur heimlich billigt, muss mit Konsequenzen rechnen.

Angesichts der Ungeheuerlichkeit der gestrigen Anschläge fällt es schwer, besonnen zu bleiben. Wir müssen uns aber auf unsere Stärke besinnen. Wahnsinnige dürfen uns nicht dazu bringen, wahllos Rache zu üben. Wir handeln nicht unmenschlich, nicht menschenverachtend. Dennoch müssen wir ihnen ihr blutiges Handwerk legen.

Die westlichen Demokratien sind am Dienstag herausgefordert worden. Es gibt keinen Zweifel, dass unser politisches System auch dies gestärkt überstehen wird, weil das Recht auf unserer Seite ist. Gegen die kriminelle Energie und die selbstmörderische Entschlossenheit von Terroristen wird man sich nicht schützen können. Der Rechtsstaat gestattet keine blinde und ungezügelte Vergeltung. Gleichwohl ist er kein willfähriges Opfer. Wer unsere Zivilisation in Frage stellt und über Leichen geht, hat jedes Anrecht auf Gnade verwirkt.

Volker Weise

Entsetzen über Anschlagsserie

Blair sieht im Terrorismus „Teufel in unserer Welt"

Berlin/London (dpa). Die beispiellose Terrorserie in den USA hat weltweit blankes Entsetzen und tiefe Trauer ausgelöst. Bundespräsident Johannes Rau schrieb in einem in Berlin veröffentlichten Brief an US-Präsident George W. Bush: „Was in New York und Washington geschehen ist, ist unfassbar. Ich spreche Ihnen, den Hinterbliebenen der Opfer und dem ganzen amerikanischen Volk mein tief empfundenes Beileid aus."

NATO-Generalsekretär George Robertson verurteilte die Anschläge scharf. „Diese barbarischen Akte stellen eine nicht zu tolerierende Aggression gegen die Demokratie dar und unterstreichen die Notwendigkeit, dass die internationale Gemeinschaft und die Mitgliedsstaaten der Allianz ihre Kräfte vereinigen, um die Geißel des Terrorismus zu bekämpfen", erklärte er.

Ähnlich äußerte sich die Europäische Union. Der Außenpolitische Vertreter der EU, Javier Solana, erklärte: „Keine Worte können meine Antwort auf diese barbarischen Akte des Terrorismus ausdrücken." Der russische Präsident Wladimir Putin verfolgte die Ereignisse am Fernsehen und zeigte sich schockiert.

Der französische Staatspräsident Jacques Chirac sicherte den Vereinigten Staaten Solidarität und Freundschaft Frankreichs zu. Der britische Premierminister Tony Blair sagte in London, der Terrorismus sei der „neue Teufel in unserer heutigen Welt".

Der palästinensische Generaldelegierte in Deutschland, Abdallah Frangi, verurteilte die Terroranschläge auf die USA. „Dieser Tag ist ein schwarzer Tag für die Welt", sagte er in der ARD. Er werde das Gesicht der Welt verändern. Auch die in der Bundesrepublik lebenden Muslime haben die Anschläge in den USA „auf das Schärfste" verurteilt. Die Anschläge seien ein barbarischer Akt und weder durch religiöse noch ideologische Motive zu rechtfertigen, erklärte das Zentralinstitut-Islam-Archiv-Deutschland in Bremen.

CSU-Chef Edmund Stoiber sprach von einer „Quasi-Kriegserklärung gegen die USA und damit die freie Welt." Die CDU-Vorsitzende Angela Merkel äußerte ihre Fassungslosigkeit und versicherte ihre Solidarität mit den Amerikanern. FDP- Fraktionschef Wolfgang Gerhardt erklärte, an diesem Tag spürten freiheitliche Gesellschaften, welchen Bedrohungen sie ausgesetzt seien. Die-Grünen-Fraktionschefs Kerstin Müller und Rezzo Schlauch sagten, die Anschläge „haben eine unvorstellbare und noch nie da gewesene Dimension". Die Evangelische Kirche in Deutschland und die Deutsche Bischofskonferenz reagierten mit Fassungslosigkeit.

■ Niedersachsen hat nach den Anschlägen eine Hotline für Angehörige von Bürgern in den USA eingerichtet. Die Nummer beim Landeskriminalamt lautet 0511/330 22 22. Die Hotline des Auswärtigen Amtes ist unter 0 18 88-174 600 zu erreichen.

Das Wetter

Höchsttemperatur am Tag: 17
Tiefstwerte in der Nacht: 10
Ausführliche Informationen auf unserer Wetterkarte
Seite 8

30037
4 394176 301952

„Krieg! Krieg! Wer greift uns an?"

Augenzeugen können das Grauen kaum fassen / New York versinkt im Chaos

New York. Es ist ein strahlender Spätsommermorgen, der sich binnen weniger Minuten in unvorstellbares Grauen verwandelt. Menschen flüchten blutüberströmt und mit Asche bedeckt aus den beiden brennenden Wolkenkratzern des World Trade Centers. Tausende stehen weinend und schreiend vor Angst um Angehörige an den Absperrungen und wollten Auskünft – über Männer und Frauen, die in den Türmen gearbeitet haben, und über Kinder aus den umliegenden Schulen. Dann geschieht das Unfassbare: Die beiden 411 Meter hohen Türme, Stolz fast jeden New Yorkers, brechen in sich zusammen.

Die Anschlagserie trifft die Zentren der Macht und stürzt die mächtigste Nation der Welt in Panik. „Krieg! Krieg! Wer greift uns an?", schreit eine weißhaarige Frau. Die Millionenstadt versinkt im Chaos. Alle Flughäfen werden gesperrt, öffentliche Gebäude wie der Hauptsitz der Vereinten Nationen und die Börse evakuiert, alle Zufahrtsstraßen und Tunnels verbarrikadiert. Kein Zug fährt mehr, kein Bus und keine U-Bahn. Überall gellen die Sirenen von Feuerwehren, Ambulanzen und Polizeifahrzeugen.

Clyde Ebanks, Vizepräsident einer Versicherung, nimmt gerade an einer Sitzung im 103. Stock des Südturms des World Trade Center teil, als sein Chef sagt: „Sieh dir das an." Ebanks dreht sich um und sieht, wie ein Flugzeug in den Nachbarturm fliegt. Zusammen mit seinen Arbeitskollegen stürmt er die Treppen hinab. Im 70. Stock fühlen sie, wie der Turm erbebt, von dem zweiten Flugzeug getroffen. „Ich sorge mich noch um einige meiner Kollegen", sagt er später, tränenüberströmt und über und über mit grauer Asche bedeckt.

„Alle schreien, weinen, rennen, Polizisten, Feuerwehrmänner, alle Menschen", sagt der Feuerwehrmann Mike Smith. „Das ist wie ein Kriegsgebiet." John Axisa, der auf dem Weg zu seinem Arbeitsplatz im Trade Center ist, berichtet später von brennenden Menschen, die aus den zerfetzten Türmen fallen. Er rennt weg von dem Gebäude, dann hört er eine zweite Explosion und spürt eine Hitzewelle auf seinen Rücken.

Das Grauen kommt urplötzlich: Geschäftsleute rennen um ihr Leben – nur weg vom World Trade Center, das es wenig später nicht mehr geben sollte. Foto: ap

Als sich Rauch und Staub lichten, starren Passanten und Überlebende fassungslos auf die Trümmer. Die Umgebung ist von einer zehn Zentimeter dicken Schicht aus Staub, Glas und Trümmern bedeckt. Über der Stadt treiben Kilometer weit Papierbögen, die aus dem zerfetzten Wolkenkratzer geweht worden sind. Ihr Präsident verspricht den verstörten US-Bürgern, „die Leute zu jagen, die diese Tat begangen haben". Seine Nation vermag George Bush's Ankündigung an diesem Tag nicht zu trösten. Das ganze Ausmaß der beispiellosen Terrortat bleibt unabsehbar. „Selbst in Wochen können wir nicht alle Opfer ausgegraben, die unter diesen Trümmern liegen", sagt ein verzweifelter Feuerwehrmann.

Helen O'Neill (ap) / Gisela Ostwald (dpa)

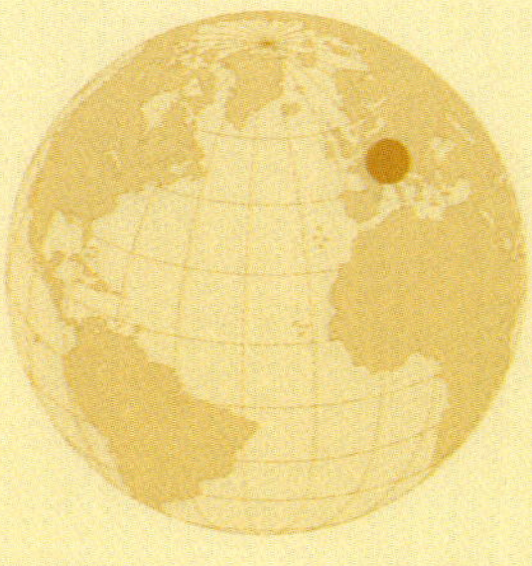

WESER KURIER
WWW.WESER-KURIER.DE
DEUTSCHLAND, BREMEN

12

MECKLENBURGISCHE ZEITUNG

Schweriner Volkszeitung

Unabhängige Tageszeitung für das Land Mecklenburg-Vorpommern • Nr. 213/56 • 1,30 DM (0,66 Euro)

MITTWOCH, 12. SEPTEMBER 2001

www.svz.de

Höchste Auflage in Westmecklenburg

Redaktion, Verlag, Druck
19061 Schwerin
Gutenbergstr. 1
(0385) 63 78-0
Fax (0385) 3 97 51 40 Redaktion
Fax (0385) 6 37 84 31 Anzeigen
E-Mail: svz@svz.de

Die Welt ist schockiert – Krieg gegen die Zivilisation

So entwickelte sich das Inferno: Der eine Turm des World Trade Center brennt schon. Wenig später rast ein zweites Flugzeug in den anderen Turm und explodiert. Fotos: dpa

Die menschliche Tragödie widerspiegelt sich in den Gesichtern der New Yorker.

Punkte 5000 4800 4600 4400 4200
DAX 4275,10
September 5. 6. 7. 10. 11.

NEMAX50 818,53 (905,93)
DOW JONES – (9603,36)
EURO 0,8964 Dollar (0,9047)
11. 9. 2001 • 19.00 Uhr Vortagswerte in Klammern

IN DIESER AUSGABE

RASTOW **Volkstanzgruppe stellt sich beim diesjährigen Erntefest erstmals vor**
Beim Erntefest in Rastow, das vom 21. bis 23. September stattfindet, stellt sich die neugegründete Volkstanzgruppe erstmals vor. Die Mitglieder übten in den Monaten zuvor fleißig. ....Seite 17

RASTOW **Volkstanzgruppe stellt sich beim diesjährigen Erntefest erstmals vor**
Beim Erntefest in Rastow, das vom 21. bis 23. September stattfindet, stellt sich die neugegründete Volkstanzgruppe erstmals vor. Die Mitglieder übten in den Monaten zuvor fleißig. ....Seite 17

WIRTSCHAFT **Hamburg will Ost-Firmen bremsen**
Handwerker der Hansestadt protestierten gegen Dumpingpreise aus dem Osten. Baufirmen in MV wehren sich. ....Seite 6

TELEGRAMM

Einen Eklat beschwor Bundesverteidigungsminister Scharping (SPD) gestern im Verteidigungsausschuss herauf. Nach Angaben der Opposition brüskierte er mit Aussagen Großbritannien.

Nach Bürgerprotesten hat die Kölner Generalstaatsanwaltschaft weitere Ermittlungen zu den verschwundenen Kanzleramtsakten aus der Amtszeit Helmut Kohls (CDU) gefordert.

Der EU-Gerichtshof hat Deutschland wegen Verstößen gegen das Umweltrecht verurteilt. Fünf Bundesländer haben zu wenig Naturschutzgebiete nach der EU-Richtlinie ausgewiesen.

Wegen der hohen Arbeitslosigkeit wird der Bund der Bundesanstalt für Arbeit dieses Jahr mehr Geld als die geplanten 1,2 Milliarden Mark überweisen. Eine Summe wurde nicht genannt.

Von einem Frachter gerammt wurde im Nord-Ostsee-Kanal das größte Schiff der deutschen Marine. Der Versorger „Frankfurt/Main" erlitt aber keine Schäden.

FUSSBALL

UEFA-CUP, 1. Hauptrunde, Hinspiel
SMK Puchov – SC Freiburg 0:0

CHAMPIONS LEAGUE, 1. Spieltag
Schalke 04 – Panathinaikos Athen 0:2
Dynamo Kiew – Borussia Dortmund 2:2

WETTER

Heute: Anfangs noch einzelne Frühnebelfelder, tagsüber Wechsel von Sonne und Wolken, Werte 15 bis 18 Grad
Morgen: Viele Wolken und immer wieder Regenschauer, Temperaturen am Nachmittag um 16 Grad

New York/Washington (dpa/AP) • Der internationale Terrorismus hat gestern die Supermacht USA mit den schrecklichsten Anschlägen der Terrorismus-Geschichte herausgefordert. Die Selbstmordangriffe auf Macht- und Finanzzentren in New York und Washington kosteten wahrscheinlich Tausende Menschenleben.

Bis kurz vor Mitternacht (MESZ) wurden 600 Schwerverletzte geborgen. Bürgermeister Giuliani sagte über die Zahl der Opfer: „Es sind sicher mehr als sich irgendjemand ausmalen kann." In den vier entführten Flugzeugen starben 266 Menschen. Als Urheber vermuten die Geheimdienste den saudischen mutmaßlichen Terroristenführer Osama bin Laden.

Mit zwei in den USA entführten Passagierflugzeugen brachten Selbstmordattentäter das New Yorker World Trade Center zum Einsturz. In Washington wurde das Verteidigungsministerium mit einem weiteren Flugzeug teilweise zerstört, das Außenministerium mit einer Autobombe angegriffen. Eine vierte Maschine stürzte bei Pittsburgh ab.

Keine Terrororganisation bekannte sich bis zum Abend zu den Anschlägen, die weltweit Entsetzen auslösten. US-Präsident Bush, der auf einen Luftwaffenstützpunkt in Nebraska gebracht wurde, sprach von einer „nationalen Tragödie" und versicherte: „Wir werden diejenigen, die für diese feigen Taten verantwortlich sind, zur Strecke bringen und bestrafen." Die Zwillingstürme des World Trade Center, in denen täglich 50 000 Menschen arbeiten, gingen nach den schweren Explosionen in Flammen auf. Rund eine Stunde nach den ersten beiden Angriffen auf die Zwillingstürme, die das zweithöchste Gebäude der Welt bilden, ereignete sich im südlichen Turm eine weitere schwere Explosion. Daraufhin stürzte der obere Teil des 411 Meter hohen Gebäudes ein. Nur wenig später fiel auch der zweite Turm in sich zusammen.

Die apokalyptischen Szenen haben auch Deutschland geschockt. In Berlin berief Bundeskanzler Schröder den Bundessicherheitsrat ein. Der Bundestag brach seine Haushaltsdebatte ab. Am Reichstag wurden die Fahnen auf Halbmast gesetzt. In ganz Deutschland wurden die Sicherheitsvorkehrungen für Einrichtungen der USA und Israels sowie auf den Flughäfen verschärft. Die Finanzmärkte rund um den Globus wurden ins Chaos gestürzt.

Zwei radikale Palästinensergruppen bestritten jede Beteiligung an den Terrorakten. Die afghanischen radikal-islamischen Taliban, die angeblich bin Laden beherbergen, schlossen ebenfalls eine Beteiligung kategorisch aus.

Zahlreiche Palästinenser in den Flüchtlingscamps in Südlibanon und in Beirut feierten die Terrorserie und feuerten Freudenschüsse in die Luft. Palästinenserpräsident Jassir Arafat verurteilte die Anschläge hingegen „auf das Schärfste". Die EU, Frankreich, Großbritannien, Russland und viele andere Staaten verurteilten die Terrorangriffe.

Berichte, Kommentar und Meinungen auf den Seiten 2 und 3

8.46 Uhr
(Ortszeit)
Ein Flugzeug rast in die oberen Stockwerke eines der Türme des World Trade Centers in New York. Dicker schwarzer Rauch dringt aus den Fenstern des 110-stöckigen Gebäudes.

9.49 Uhr
Die Flugsicherheitsbehörde streicht alle Starts in den USA.

10.00 Uhr
Eine weitere Explosion erschüttert das World Trade Center. Kurz darauf stürzt einer der Türme ein. Alle größeren Regierungsgebäude werden evakuiert.

9.40 Uhr
Behörden bestätigen, dass es sich bei einem der Flugzeuge um eine in Boston entführte Maschine gehandelt habe.

9.43 Uhr
Ein Flugzeug stürzt auf einem Hubschrauberlandeplatz am Verteidigungsministerium Pentagon ab. Der Westflügel des Weißen Hauses wird wegen einer Terrordrohung evakuiert.

9.49 Uhr
Die Flugsicherheitsbehörde streicht alle Starts in den USA.

10.00 Uhr
Eine weitere Explosion erschüttert das World Trade Center. Kurz darauf stürzt einer der Türme ein. Alle größeren Regierungsgebäude werden evakuiert.

10.23 Uhr
Eine Autobombe explodiert neben dem US-Außenministerium.

10.29 Uhr
Der zweite Turm des World Trade Centers stürzt nach einer weiteren Explosion ein.

10.34 Uhr
Die Fluggesellschaft American Airlines bestätigt die Entführung und den Absturz einer ihrer Maschinen.

10.37 Uhr
Der Flughafen Pittsburgh bestätigt den Absturz einer großen Verkehrsmaschine im Westen von Pennsylvania.

10.39 Uhr
Weitere Explosion im World Trade Center.

11.23 Uhr
American Airlines bestätigt den Verlust zweier Flugzeuge mit insgesamt 156 Menschen an Bord.

11.33 Uhr
United Airlines bestätigt den Absturz eines Flugzeuges bei Pittsburgh. Die Maschine war am Flughafen von Newark entführt worden. Sie sollte den Präsidenten-Urlaubssitz in Camp David treffen.

AUS NEW YORK

Mutti, ich lebe!

Mutti, mir geht's gut, ich lebe. Aber wir stehen hier alle unter Schock! Das World Trade Center gibt es nicht mehr. Ich kann es gar nicht glauben. Letzte Woche hatte ich selbst dort zu tun. Von der Katastrophe habe ich heute früh nicht mal gleich etwas mitbekommen. Ich war noch vor 9 Uhr in unserem Büro. Später kamen die ersten Anrufe aus Deutschland und der Schweiz. Unsere Partner dort wollten wissen, wie es uns geht, ob alles in Ordnung ist.
Dann habe ich die Nachrichten im Radio gehört. Ich hab' auch versucht, ins Internet zu kommen, aber das bricht immer wieder ab, zu viele werden das wohl versuchen. Auch das Handynetz ist vollkommen überlastet. Ich kann per Handy im Augenblick gar nicht telefonieren. Wenn ich auf die Madison Avenue hier in Manhatten runtersehe, da laufen die Menschen aufgeregt herum und alle telefonieren mit ihren Handys. Die vielen gelben Taxis sind jetzt gar nicht mehr zu sehen. Das ist ganz ungewohnt.

Susanne Pilz

Ich mache mir immer mehr Sorgen um Julia. Sie ist noch nicht im Büro, hat auch nicht angerufen. Mit ihrem Freund wohnt sie ganz in der Nähe des World Trade Centers, nur zwei Straßen weiter. Und ihr Freund arbeitet bei einer Bank in der Wall Street. Die hat auch Büros im World Trade Center...!
Eben hat auch meine Chefin aus Princeton angerufen und gesagt: „Susanne, geh' schnell Lebensmittel einkaufen. Die Geschäfte werden bald leergefegt sein!" Jetzt einkaufen? Doch ich sehe ja, dass viele Leute jetzt tatsächlich in die Geschäfte gehen. Und im Rundfunk haben sie gesagt, dass alle Brücken und Tunnel nach Manhattan gesperrt worden sind.
Jim macht sich auf den Weg. Er sagt, er wird einkaufen und das Auto voll laden. Da ist dann auch für mich was dabei.
Viele Freunde aus Deutschland haben auch schon angerufen, jeder will wissen, wie es mir geht... Ich kann es nicht fassen, dass es das World Trade Center nicht mehr gibt...
Susanne Pilz (24), Studentin aus Schwerin, absolviert zurzeit ein Praktikum in New York.
Ihre Mutter, unsere Redakteurin, Ute Pilz, telefonierte um 16.43 Uhr (MESZ) mit ihr.

SWH-01A

Schweriner Volkszeitung
www.svz.de
Deutschland, Schwerin

12

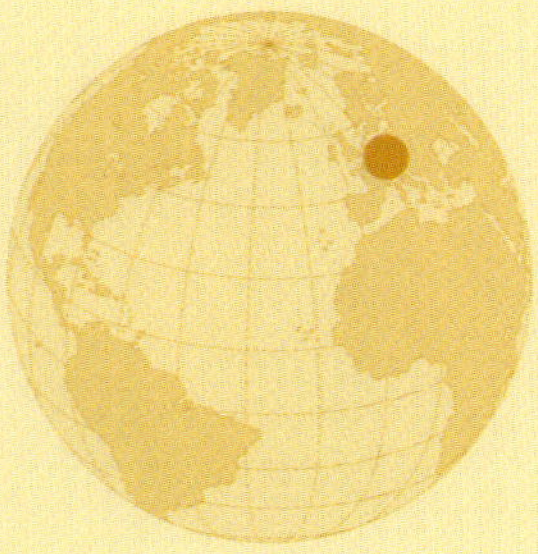

Märkische Allgemeine

Heute mit MAZab

Mittwoch, 12. September 2001 ZEITUNG FÜR DAS LAND BRANDENBURG Nr. 213, 56. Jg. PDM – A 09411 1,20 DM

Potsdamer Tageszeitung

„Stadtspuren“ als Vorbild

Städte nutzen Potsdamer Projekt nach

Mehrere Kommunen im Land Brandenburg wollen die Erfahrungen des Potsdamer Arbeitskreises „Stadtspuren“ nachnutzen. In dem Projekt hatten sich 1996 sieben Potsdamer Wohnungsunternehmen zusammen geschlossen, um Planungen und Bauvorhaben zu koordinieren. → 15

IQ-Test für Kinder

Universität entwickelt Prüfmethode

Unter der Regie eines Professors der Universität Potsdam wird ein Intelligenztest für Kinder im Alter zwischen drei und neun Jahren entwickelt. Derzeit finden im ganzen Bundesgebiet sowie in der Schweiz und Österreich Probetests statt. → 18

Protest in Tremsdorf

Initiative für Sperrung des Fresdorfer Wegs

In Tremsdorf regt sich Widerstand gegen den Autoverkehr auf dem Fresdorfer Weg, weil viele Fahrzeuge die nicht ausgebaute Straße als Zufahrt zur Autobahn benutzen. Eine Bürgerinitiative fordert jetzt die Sperrung der Straße. → 21

VfL im Mannschaftsfoto

MAZ stellt Regionalliga-Handballer vor

Die Handballer des 1. VfL Potsdam starten am nächsten Sonnabend mit einem Auswärtsspiel in Köthen in die neue Regionalligasaison. Heute stellt die MAZ Spieler, Trainer und Vereinschef des Titelaspiranten vor. → 26

KURZ & KNAPP

Scharping weiter unter Druck

BERLIN ■ Verteidigungsminister Rudolf Scharping (SPD) hat Oppositionspolitikern aus dem Verteidigungsausschuss einen Bruch der Vertraulichkeit vorgeworfen. → 4

Beratung über Bundeshaushalt 2002

BERLIN ■ Mit gegenseitigen Schuldvorwürfen von Regierung und Opposition begannen gestern im Bundestag die Beratungen über den Haushalt 2002. Bundesfinanzminister Hans Eichel (SPD) verteidigte seinen Konsolidierungskurs. → 4

Hoffnung für Bootsflüchtlinge

CANBERRA ■ Nach wochenlangem Tauziehen hat ein australisches Gericht die Regierung in Canberra zur Aufnahme der mehr als 400 Bootsflüchtlinge von Bord des Frachters „Tampa“ verpflichtet. → 4

Gemetzel auf der Weide

POTSDAM ■ Der Pferderipper von Kietz (Havelland) soll ein weiteres Tier verwundet haben – 500 Meter von der Koppel entfernt, auf der in der Nacht zum Sonntag sechs Stuten getötet wurden. Der Polizei fehlt eine heiße Spur. → 7

Eröffnung der Automesse IAA abgesagt

FRANKFURT/MAIN ■ Die für gestern Abend geplante offizielle Eröffnung der Internationalen Automobilmesse (IAA) in Frankfurt am Main wurde nach den Terroranschlägen in den USA aus Sicherheitsgründen kurzfristig abgesagt. Auf der Messe präsentieren sich rund 1100 Automobilhersteller aus 40 Ländern. → 9

Geistiger Vater von Pirx und Tichy

POTSDAM ■ Seine Werke wurden in 31 Sprachen übersetzt und oft verfilmt. Stanislaw Lem gilt als der erfolgreichste Schriftsteller Polens. Heute wird der Autor 80 Jahre alt. → 11

Auswärts-Remis und Heimniederlage

GELSENKIRCHEN/KIEW ■ Trotz einiger Proteste, wegen der Terroranschläge in den USA die Fußballspiele im Europacup abzusetzen, wurde gestern Abend gespielt. Dabei erreichte Borussia Dortmund in der Champions League bei Dynamo Kiew ein 2:2 (0:2). Der FC Schalke 04 musste sich zu Hause Panathinaikos Athen mit 0:2 (0:0) geschlagen geben. Im UEFA-Cup spielte der SC Freiburg beim SKM Puchov (Slowakei) 0:0.

AUS DEM POLIZEIBERICHT

Gestohlenes Auto verbrannte

TELTOW ■ Zwei mutmaßliche Autodiebe haben am frühen Dienstagmorgen ein von ihnen gestohlenes Fahrzeug in Teltow (Kreis Potsdam-Mittelmark) in einen Graben gefahren. Zuvor waren sie durch ein Baustellentor gefahren, teilte die Polizei in Potsdam mit. Die Männer haben anschließend die Flucht ergriffen. → 6

4 390941 101208 30037

Nach dem verheerenden Anschlag auf das World Trade Center in New York: Der Stadtteil Manhattan versinkt hinter dicken Rauchschwaden. FOTO: DPA

Terroranschläge erschüttern die USA

Flugzeuge rammten World Trade Center / Weltweites Entsetzen

NEW YORK/BERLIN ■ Die USA sind gestern von einer Terrorwelle ohne Beispiel erschüttert worden. Zwei Flugzeuge rammten innerhalb weniger Minuten die beiden Türme des World Trade Center in New York, das daraufhin vollständig in sich zusammenstürzte. Nach Angaben des Fernsehsenders CNN raste auch in das US-Verteidigungsministerium bei Washington ein Flugzeug. Am Nachmittag stürzte bei Pittsburgh eine Boeing 747 ab.

Es werden tausende Tote befürchtet, genaue Angaben lagen aber zunächst nicht vor. Auch die Hintergründe waren unklar. US-Präsident George W. Bush sprach nach den Anschlägen von einem „terroristischen Anschlag auf unsere Nation“. Die amerikanische Regierung vermutete am Abend, dass die Terrororganisation des Moslem-Extremisten Osama Bin Laden hinter den Anschlägen stehen könnte.

Nach den Kollisionen gingen beide Türme des World Trade Center in Flammen auf. Normalerweise arbeiten täglich bis zu 50 000 Menschen allein im World Trade Center. Ein Turm stürzte nach einer halben Stunde in sich zusammen, der zweite gegen Mittag. Aus den Trümmern des Gebäudes stiegen dichte Rauchwolken auf, vor Ort waren unzählige Rettungskräfte.

Die mörderische Attacke des zweiten Flugzeugs. FOTOS: REUTERS

Das Weiße Haus und mehrere Ministerien wurden ebenso evakuiert wie der Hauptsitz der Uno in New York und der Sears Tower in Chicago. Die USA versetzten alle diplomatischen Vertretungen in Alarmbereitschaft, weltweit brach der Flugverkehr zusammen. Alle Flüge von Deutschland nach Nordamerika wurden gestrichen. Bereits abgeflogene Lufthansa-Maschinen, die Grönlands noch nicht erreicht hatten, kehrten zurück.

Die US-Luftfahrtbehörde verlor nach eigenen Angaben „die Kontrolle“ über mehrere Flugzeuge im US-Luftraum. Die US-Fluggesellschaft American Airlines meldete den Verlust von zwei Flugzeugen mit insgesamt 156 Insassen. Nach FBI-Angaben wurden die beiden Maschinen entführt, ebenso eine Maschine der United Airlines. Eines der Flugzeuge, die in das World Trade Center gerast waren, war ein Jet von United Airlines.

Die Anschläge wurden weltweit mit Bestürzung und Entsetzen aufgenommen. Bundeskanzler Gerhard Schröder (SPD) sprach den USA in einem Kondolenztelegramm an Bush sein Beileid und seine „uneingeschränkte Solidarität“ aus. Die Regierung richtete einen Krisenstab ein, der die Sicherheitsmaßnahmen in Deutschland koordinieren soll. Brandenburgs Landesregierung hat die Polizeipräsenz im Land verstärkt. Für heute ist Trauerbeflaggung angeordnet. Ministerpräsident Stolpe drückte sein Mitgefühl mit den USA aus. Es sei wichtig, Solidarität zu zeigen. Stolpe bezeichnete die gestrigen Anschläge als „Kampfansage an uns alle“. *AFP/dpa* → 2, 3 und 9

ZUM TAGE

Der Schock

KLAUS ROST

Dem großen Entsetzen, zum ersten Mal buchstäblich „live“ im Fernsehen miterleben zu müssen, wie eine Passagiermaschine in den noch unbeschädigten Zwillingsturm des World Trade Centers knallt und sich im Feuer auflöst, folgt die Erkenntnis, wie verletzlich hochzivilisierte, hochtechnologisierte Staaten sind. Der Preis der Freiheit, dass jeder sich bewegen kann, wohin er will, ist teuer. Vielen Amerikanern wird er gestern zu teuer gewesen sein. Man kann aber die Prinzipien einer freiheitlichen Demokratie nicht auf dem Altar des Terrorismus opfern. Trotz der Einsicht in die Verletzlichkeit, in die Tatsache, dass es keine absolute Sicherheit gibt, ist das Ausmaß der Angriffe – die Fähigkeit der Terroristen, so koordiniert und konzentriert zuzuschlagen – mehr als beunruhigend. Zugleich stellt dieser Anschlag den westlichen Geheimdiensten ein vernichtendes Zeugnis aus. Denn dass es eine latente Bedrohung gibt, wissen sie. Und dass sie trotzdem bei einer logistischen Operation dieser Größe nicht ein einziges Warnsignal empfangen oder ernstgenommen haben – das ist schockierend.

Momentaufnahmen nach der Katastrophe: Menschen flüchten in panischer Angst, ein erschütterter Präsident Bush. FOTOS: REUTERS, DPA

Märkische Allgemeine
www.maerkischeallgemeine.de
Deutschland, Potsdam

12

DER GRÖSSTE TERRORANSCHLAG DER GESCHICHTE

DER TAGESSPIEGEL

RERUM COGNOSCERE CAUSAS

BERLIN, MITTWOCH, 12. SEPTEMBER 2001 / 57. JAHRGANG / NR. 17 526 — 1,30 DM BERLIN UND BRANDENBURG / 1,50 DM AUSWÄRTS / TSCHECHIEN 35 CZK / POLEN 4,30 PLZ / SCHWEIZ 1,50 CHF / ÖSTERREICH 12 ATS / DÄNEMARK 7 DKK / SPANIEN 190 PTAS / ITALIEN 2500 LIT / UNGARN 400 HUF / A6622

Angriff auf Amerika

Tausende Tote in Manhattan / Entführte Flugzeuge rasen in World Trade Center und Pentagon / Bush: Wir werden die Täter zur Strecke bringen

New York / Berlin (Tsp). Die USA sind am Dienstag Ziel des schlimmsten Angriffs seit der japanischen Attacke auf Pearl Harbor im Zweiten Weltkrieg geworden. In die beiden Hochhaustürme des World Trade Center in New York rasten zwei zuvor entführte Passagierflugzeuge und explodierten. Die mehr als 400 Meter hohen Türme fielen wenig später in sich zusammen und begruben möglicherweise mehrere tausend Menschen unter sich. Kurze Zeit später stürzte ein weiteres Zivilflugzeug auf das Verteidigungsministerium in Washington. Präsident Bush sprach von einer nationalen Tragödie und kündigte an, die USA würden die Verantwortlichen „zur Strecke bringen". In US-Regierungskreisen hieß es, vermutlich seien Personen um den saudiarabischen Extremisten Osama bin Laden die Drahtzieher. In Deutschland berief Kanzler Schröder den Bundessicherheitsrat ein. Schröder verurteilte die Anschläge als „Kriegserklärung gegen die gesamte zivilisierte Welt".

Das ganze Ausmaß der Tragödie war auch Stunden später noch nicht absehbar. Von den beiden 110 Stockwerke hohen Gebäuden, die die Skyline von New York bestimmten, waren nur Schuttberge geblieben. Kurz vor 9 Uhr Ortszeit, zu Beginn der Bürostunden, war zunächst ein Flugzeug in einen der beiden Türme gerast und hatte ein riesiges Loch gerissen. Knapp 20 Minuten später durchschlug ein zweites Flugzeug den anderen der 110 Stockwerke hohen Zwillingstürme und setzten ihn in Brand. In der Nacht fiel ein Nachbargebäude zusammen.

In Washington wurde am Nachmittag auch das Verteidigungsministerium mit einer weiteren gekidnappten Passagiermaschine teilweise zerstört. Eine vierte entführte Zivilmaschine stürzte aus noch unbekannten Gründen bei Pittsburgh ab. Sie sollte angeblich auf den Präsidenten-Urlaubssitz Camp David gelenkt werden. Zwischenzeitlich hatte es aus den USA geheißen, dass sogar acht Zivilflugzeuge entführt werden sollten.

Die Anschläge versetzten die USA in einen Schockzustand. Der frühere Außenminister Kissinger verglich die Lage mit dem Trauma von Pearl Harbor, als die japanischen Streitkräfte im Zweiten Weltkrieg einen großen Teil der US-Flotte zerstörten. Damals kamen 2280 US-Soldaten und 68 Zivilisten ums Leben. Die USA müssten wie damals antworten und die Attentäter so enden, wie die Angreifer von Pearl Harbor. Das Pentagon versetzte die Streitkräfte in höchste Alarmbereitschaft: „Alle militärischen Einrichtungen weltweit sind in Alarmstufe Delta."

Explosionen in Kabul

Die afghanische Hauptstadt Kabul wurde am frühen Mittwochmorgen von mehreren Explosionen erschüttert. Der US-Sender CNN zeigte Bilder von Angriffen, Gewehrsalven waren zu hören. Die USA hatten die Taliban-Miliz wiederholt zur Auslieferung des Moslemextremisten Osama bin Laden aufgefordert. Die USA vermuten bin Laden auch hinter der jüngsten Anschlagserie.

Die deutsche Botschaft in den USA hat nach den Anschlägen einen Krisenstab eingesetzt. Der Stab ist unter den Telefonnummern 001-202-471-5528 / 001-202-298-4350 / 001-202-471-5527 / 001-202-298-4365 erreichbar. Auch das Auswärtige Amt in Berlin richtete einen Krisenstab mit den Nummern 030/5000-4600 und 01888/17-4600 ein.

WIR BERICHTEN

Verlag Der Tagesspiegel GmbH • Postanschrift: 10876 Berlin • Hausanschrift: Berlin-Tiergarten, Potsdamer Straße 77–87. Telefon Redaktion und Verlag (030) 2 60 09-0 • Anzeigenservice (030) 2 60 09-700, Fax (030) 2 60 09-777; Abonnentenservice (030) 2 60 09-500 • Sammel-Telefax (030) 2 60 09-332

4 394256 001307 30037

APOKALYPSE IN NEW YORK. Nachdem zwei Flugzeuge hineingerast sind, stürzen die beiden Türme des World Trade Center in sich zusammen. Auf den Straßen herrscht Panik, Passanten und Beschäftigte aus den Nachbargebäuden rennen um ihr Leben.

Fotos: Hubert Bösl, dpa / Suzanne Plunkett, AP

TRAUER UND FRAGEN

Das ist wie Krieg

VON GERD APPENZELLER

Das ist ein Krieg, und es ist ein Krieg gegen die zivilisierte Welt. Amerika leidet unter Terroranschlägen unvorstellbaren Ausmaßes und mit den Amerikanern leiden Menschen auf der ganzen Erde. Diese Anschläge werden die Welt verändern. Wenig wird so sein wie vorher. Entführte Passagiermaschinen als fliegende Bomben, von Kamikazepiloten mitten in Hochhäuser gesteuert, brennende, in sich zusammenstürzende Wolkenkratzer, im Zentrum New Yorks, im Herzen der Vereinigten Staaten. Amerika ist tief verwundet. Was jetzt ist, ist wie nach Pearl Harbor, dem Überfall der japanischen Luftwaffe auf die amerikanische Pazifikflotte – vielleicht schlimmer. Viel spricht dafür, dass die Amerikaner das, was gestern geschah, als Kriegserklärung annehmen und entsprechend beantworten werden – mit jener Entschlossenheit, die sie in Situationen äußerster Bedrohung immer zeigen.

Noch weiß man nicht, wer für die Verbrechen verantwortlich ist. Einiges spricht für einen extremen arabischen Hintergrund. Es gab Drohungen aus dieser Richtung, Geheimdienstwarnungen. Amerikabesucher wurden von jüdischen Gesprächspartnern immer wieder auf mögliche neue Terroranschläge angesprochen. Dass die Krise des Nahen Osten in die USA abstrahlen würde, war vorhersehbar, gerade, weil sich Präsident George W. Bush im Gegensatz zu seinem Vorgänger weitgehend aus der aktuellen Vermittlungsdiplomatie zurückgezogen hatte. In dem Maße, in dem Selbstmordanschläge den Krieg aus den besetzten palästinensischen Gebieten in den jüdischen Staat hineintrugen, wuchs die Gefahr, dass die Eskalation des Terrors die Grenzen der Region überschreiten würde. Vor vorschnellen Schlussfolgerungen muss man dennoch warnen, obwohl die Signale aus der arabischen Welt gestern widersprüchlich waren. Gespenstischer Jubel in den Palästinenserlagern. Eine PLO, die sich distanzierte. Im Namen einer anderen, extremistischen, Organisation wurde zunächst die Verantwortung übernommen, wenig später gab es Dementis. Aber auch Osama bin Laden, die Taliban, könnten den religiös-fundierten Hintergrund bilden. Und es gibt noch einen dritten Verdacht. Der Anschlag von Oklahoma hat gezeigt, wozu amerikanische Terroristen bereit sind. Wer immer jedoch dahinter steht – dies war ein genauso infames wie perfektes Zusammenspiel verschiedener Täter, durch den fanatischen Willen zur Vernichtung verbunden.

Entsprechend wird die Reaktion Amerikas sein, sobald Klarheit über die Hintergründe besteht. Die Europäer haben den Amerikanern immer wieder Hysterie unterstellt. Aber die schlimmsten Befürchtungen der USA trafen alle ein, Bombenanschläge auf Botschaften und Schiffe und nun der Stoß mitten in das Herz der Zivilgesellschaft. Über die Raketenabwehr im Weltall, über National Missile Defense, wird nun erneut diskutiert werden. NMD hätte, was gestern geschah, nicht verhindert. Dennoch werden die Amerikaner alles tun, das „Böse", wie sie es nennen, auszurotten, ob sie seine Wurzeln nun im Nahen Osten oder in Afghanistan ausmachen.

Die diplomatische Pause, die der neue Präsident seinem Land verordnet hatte, ist auf furchtbare Art beendet worden. Die Lehre daraus ist bitter. Die einzige verbliebene Weltmacht wird zum Opfer des Terrors, weil sie Weltmacht ist, und weil sie sich einmischt. Und sie wird zum Opfer, wenn sie sich herauszuhalten sucht. Die Konsequenz für die USA wie für deren Verbündete ist eindeutig. Terror, gerade staatlich tolerierter Terror, muss rechtsstaatlich und gleichzeitig mit absoluter Konsequenz bekämpft werden. Diese Konsequenz kann bis zu einem Krieg reichen.

Die Menschen in Berlin aber, die den Amerikanern in ihrer jüngeren Geschichte so viel verdanken, trauern mit ihnen. Auf eine sehr bittere Weise kehrt sich jetzt ein großer Satz um: Heute sind wir alle New Yorker.

Der Tagesspiegel
www.tagesspiegel.de
Deutschland, Berlin

12

Mitten im Krieg – Amerika unter Schock: *Seite 3*

Berliner Zeitung

Mittwoch, 12. September 2001 Nr. 213 HA · 57. Jahrgang   www.berliner-zeitung.de   1.20 DM Berlin/Brandenburg · 1.50 DM Auswärts****

Verheerender Terrorangriff erschüttert die Welt
Tausende Tote nach Anschlägen in New York und Washington

Terroristen schlagen mit beispielloser Brutalität im Herzen Amerikas zu: World Trade Center und Teile des Pentagon liegen in Schutt und Asche
Präsident Bush spricht von „nationaler Tragödie" und kündigt Vergeltung an / US-Truppen in Alarmbereitschaft / Schröder versichert Deutschlands Solidarität

DPA/HUBERT MICHAEL BÖSL

Die Skyline Manhattans wenige Minuten nach dem mörderischen Anschlag. Die beiden Türme des World Trade Centers sind zusammengestürzt. Mehrere tausend Menschen starben in den Trümmern.

NEW YORK, 11. September. Die USA sind am Dienstag von einer beispiellosen Terrorwelle überrollt worden. Zunächst rasten am Morgen (Ortszeit) innerhalb von 18 Minuten zwei entführte Flugzeuge mit 156 Menschen an Bord ins World Trade Center in New York. Die beiden weltbekannten Zwillingstürme des Wirtschaftszentrums stürzten wenig später ein und begruben wahrscheinlich tausende Menschen unter sich. Fast gleichzeitig stürzte eine weitere, ebenfalls entführte Maschine auf das Verteidigungsministerium in Washington. In der Gegend von Pittsburgh im US-Bundesstaat Pennsylvania verunglückte eine Boeing 767. Es war unklar, ob auch sie entführt wurde und Kurs auf Washington genommen hatte. Eine andere Vermutung lautete, dass sie zum Landsitz des Präsidenten in Camp David gelenkt werden und abstürzen sollte. An Bord der vier Maschinen waren 285 Passagiere.

Verdacht auf Osama Bin Laden

In Washington hieß es, vermutlich stünden Personen um den saudiarabischen Extremisten Osama Bin Laden hinter den Anschlägen. Andere Experten erklärten, es könne sich auch um die Tat amerikanischer Rechtsextremisten handeln. US-Präsident George W. Bush sagte, es handele sich um eine „nationale Tragödie". „Die USA werden die Verantwortlichen für diese feigen Taten jagen und bestrafen." Die US-Streitkräfte auf der ganzen Welt seien in hoher Alarmbereitschaft. „Wir werden der Welt zeigen, dass wir diese Prüfung bestehen", kündigte er an.

Am frühen Mittwochmorgen ist die afghanische Hauptstadt Kabul von mehreren Explosionen erschüttert worden. Der US-Nachrichtensender CNN berichtete von Angriffen auf die Stadt. Fernsehbilder zeigten Flammen, Gewehrsalven waren zu hören. Die USA hatten die Taliban-Miliz wiederholt zur Auslieferung Osama bin Ladens aufgefordert, dessen Aufenthalt in Afghanistan vermutet wird.

Kurz nach den Anschlägen in New York und Washington hatten sich die Ereignisse überschlagen. Teile des Pentagon stürzten ein, auch im Außenministerium brach nach der Explosion einer Autobombe Feuer aus. Das Parlamentsgebäude und das Weiße Haus in Washington wurden ebenso evakuiert wie das UN-Gebäude in New York, die Börse geschlossen. Der Süden Manhattans wurde evakuiert. Über New York und Washington wurde der Ausnahmezustand verhängt. Bush, der sich auf einer Reise durch den Süden des Landes befand, wollte aus Sicherheitsgründen zunächst nicht nach Washington zurückkehren. „Das ist das zweite Pearl Harbor", sagte Senator Chuck Hagel.

Die Zwillingstürme des World Trade Center, in denen täglich 40 000 Menschen arbeiten, gingen nach den schweren Explosionen in Flammen auf. Hunderte Menschen flohen in Panik aus dem Gebäude. Rund eine Stunde nach den beiden Angriffen ereignete sich im südlichen Turm eine schwere Explosion. Daraufhin stürzte der obere Teil des 411 Meter hohen Gebäudes ein. Nur wenig später fiel auch der zweite Turm in sich zusammen. Stunden später stürzte ein weiteres zu dem Komplex gehörendes Gebäude ein. Bei den beiden Maschinen von New York handelte es sich um kurz zuvor entführte Passagiermaschinen der American Airlines.

Unmittelbar nach dem Aufprall der ersten Maschine waren die Gebäude so weit wie möglich evakuiert worden. Dem deutschen Generalkonsulat in New York lagen bis zum Abend keine Hinweise darauf vor, ob Deutsche unter den Opfern sind. Im World Trade Center haben fünf deutsche Firmen Vertretungen, unter anderem die Deutsche Bank.

Rau bricht Staatsbesuch ab

Alle Parteien in Deutschland stehen nach den Worten von Bundeskanzler Gerhard Schröder nach der schrecklichen Terrorserie in den USA jetzt fest an der Seite der Amerikaner. Die Deutschen seien uneingeschränkt solidarisch mit dem Bündnispartner, sagte der Kanzler am Dienstagabend nach einem Treffen mit den Partei- und Fraktionsvorsitzenden in Berlin. Zuvor hatte der Bundessicherheitsrat getagt. Bundespräsident Johannes Rau brach seinen Staatsbesuch in Finnland ab.

Schröder will an diesem Mittwoch eine Regierungserklärung zu den Terroranschlägen vor dem Bundestag abgeben. Er teilte mit, dass er darüber bereits auch mit den Präsidenten Frankreichs und Russlands, Jacques Chirac und Wladimir Putin, sowie dem britischen Premier Tony Blair gesprochen habe. Schröder kündigte an, er wolle versuchen, auf EU-Ebene entsprechende Schritte zu organisieren. Nach Angaben des Kanzlers liegen den Sicherheitsbehörden derzeit keine konkreten Hinweise für mögliche Anschläge in Deutschland vor.

Der Nato-Rat trat am Dienstagabend zu einer Dringlichkeitssitzung zusammen. Für die Zentrale in Brüssel und das europäische Hauptquartier in Mons war die höchste Alarmstufe ausgerufen worden. Die Außenminister der 15 Mitgliedsstaaten der Europäischen Union waren für diesen Mittwoch nach Brüssel gerufen worden. Dabei soll beraten werden, wie die Vereinigten Staaten in dieser Situation unterstützt werden könnten.

Palästinenserpräsident Yasser Arafat verurteilte die verheerenden Anschläge in den USA als „völlig inakzeptabel" und „unglaublich". Vor Journalisten in Gaza sagte Arafat, er bekunde „dem amerikanischen Volk, US-Präsident George W. Bush und seiner Regierung" sein Beileid. Zwei radikale Palästinensergruppen bestritten jede Beteiligung an den Terrorakten. Der Chef der „Demokratischen Front für die Befreiung Palästinas", Kari Abdel Karim, erklärte in Ramallah, die DFLP habe mit dem Attentat „absolut nichts zu tun". Zuvor hatte der TV-Sender von Abu Dhabi gemeldet, ein angebliches Mitglied der DFLP habe sich im Namen seiner Organisation telefonisch zu dem Anschlag bekannt. Ein hochrangiger Vertreter der Volksfront für die Befreiung Palästinas erklärte im arabischen Nachrichtensender ANN, auch seine Organisation habe nichts mit den Terrorakten zu tun. Zahlreiche Palästinensern in den Flüchtlingscamps in Südlibanon und in Beirut feierten die Terrorserie und feuerten Freudenschüsse in die Luft.

Das World Trade Center war schon im Februar 1993 Ziel eines verheerenden Anschlags. Damals wurden sechs Menschen getötet und mehr als 1 000 verletzt. Als Urheber gilt der in den USA inhaftierte islamische Geistliche Scheich Omar Abderrahman.

Mehrere seiner Komplizen wurden zu hohen Haftstrafen verurteilt. Einige der schwersten Anschläge auf US-Einrichtungen wurden in den letzten Jahren dem mutmaßlichen Terrordrahtzieher Osama Bin Laden zur Last gelegt. Der in Afghanistan lebende saudiarabische Millionär gilt als Drahtzieher von

Fortsetzung auf Seite 2

Berliner Verlag GmbH & Co., 10171 Berlin
Redaktion: (030) 23 27 -9, Fax -54 30
Leser-Service: (030) 23 27 -77, Fax -76
e-mail: abo@berlinonline.de
Anzeigen: (030) 23 27 -50 Fax: -66 97
www. berliner-zeitung.de nur bei
BerlinOnline – Berlin auf einen Klick!
e-mail: leserbriefe@berlinonline.de

Belgien 37 BEF · Bulgarien 2,50 Lev · Dänemark 8 dkr · Italien 2 000 Lit · Kanaren 200 Ptas · Österreich 11 ÖS · Schweiz 1,40 Sfr · Slowakei 45 Sk · Spanien 180 Ptas · Tschechien 38 Kc · Türkei 1 400 000 TL · Ungarn 290 Ft

WEITERE BEITRÄGE

Berliner Zeitung
www.berlinerzeitung.de
Deutschland, Berlin

12

MITTWOCH,
12. SEPTEMBER 2001
NR. 249 / 37.W. / A2471A
H / 1,20 DM

www.berliner-morgenpost.de

BERLINER MORGENPOST

BERLINER ALLGEMEINE

Angriff auf Amerika

Zwei Flugzeuge schlugen gestern Morgen wie Kamikaze-Flieger in das World Trade Center in New York ein: Rauch strömt aus einem Turm, ein Feuerball umhüllt den anderen dahinter. FOTO: AP/ABC

Angriff auf Amerika – Berichte auf den Seiten 2 bis 12

Wirtschaft Seite 15
Politik Seite 16
Sport Seiten 22, 23

4 390247 101209 30037

BELGIEN BEF 32 / DÄNEMARK DKK 7 / GRIECHENLAND GRD 450 / ITALIEN LIT 2500 / MAROKKO DH 12 / ÖSTERREICH ÖS 12 / POLEN PLZ 4,00 / PORTUGAL PTE 260 (CONT.) / SCHWEIZ CHF 1,50 / SPANIEN PTS 225 / SCHWEDEN SEK 11 / SLOWAKISCHE REPUBLIK SKK 38 / TSCHECHIEN CZK 32,00 / TÜRKEI TL 1 500 000 / UNGARN FT 230

„Kriegserklärung gegen zivilisierte Welt“

Bei der schwersten Serie von Terroranschlägen in der Geschichte sind in den USA gestern vermutlich tausende Menschen getötet worden. Bei präzisen Selbstmordattacken mit entführten Passagierflugzeugen als fliegenden Bomben wurden das Finanzzentrum New York und die politische Zentrale Washington getroffen. Innerhalb weniger Minuten rammten zwei Flugzeuge die Zwillingstürme des New Yorker World Trade Center, das daraufhin vollständig in sich zusammenstürzte. Wenig später raste auch in das US-Verteidigungsministerium bei Washington ein Flugzeug. Kurz darauf stürzte bei Pittsburgh eine Boeing 757 ab. Sie sollte offenbar im Kamikaze-Angriff auf den Präsidentenlandsitz Camp David gelenkt werden. Die USA versetzten ihre Streitkräfte im In- und Ausland in erhöhte Alarmbereitschaft. Bei der Nato wurde der höchste Alarmzustand ausgerufen, über Washington und New York der Ausnahmezustand verhängt. Als Drahtzieher der Anschläge wurde der Moslemextremist Osama bin Laden verdächtigt. US-Präsident George W. Bush sagte, die USA würden die „Täter jagen und bestrafen“. Er äußerte sich in dem Luftwaffenstützpunkt Barksdale im Bundesstaat Louisina. Aus Sicherheitsgründen wollte er zunächst nicht nach Washington zurückkehren. Bundeskanzler Gerhard Schröder bezeichnete die Anschläge als „Kriegserklärung gegen die gesamte zivilisierte Welt“. Der südliche Turm des World Trade Center stürzte gegen 10 Uhr (Ortszeit) zusammen, der nördliche wenig später. In den beiden mehr als 400 Meter hohen Gebäuden arbeiten täglich bis zu 50 000 Menschen, darunter auch Mitarbeiter deutscher Firmen. In New York und Washington liefen Menschen in Panik durch die Straßen. Das Weiße Haus und mehrere Ministerien wurden evakuiert. Die US-Flugbehörde verbot alle Flüge. Weltweit brach der Flugverkehr zusammen. Im Nahen Osten veranstalteten tausende Palästinenser Freudenfeiern.

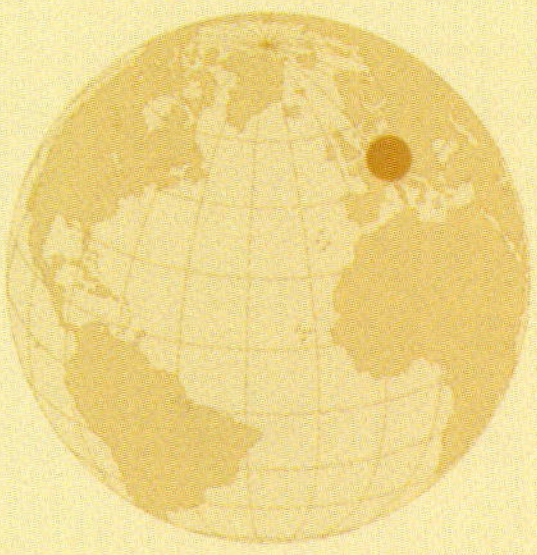

BERLINER MORGENPOST
12.09.2001
WWW.BERLINERMORGENPOST.DE
DEUTSCHLAND, BERLIN

12

Quittung: Henry Kissinger soll vor Gericht Seite 9

www.jungewelt.de

Die Tageszeitung

junge Welt

Gegründet 1947

Mittwoch, 12. September 2001 · Nr. 213 · 1,80 DM/17 öS · **PVSt A11002** · Entgelt bezahlt

2 Braune Garde
Rechte in Brandenburgs Polizei: Interview mit dem innenpolitischen Sprecher der SPD

4 Unterlassene Hilfe
Berlins Sozialämter wollen Arztkosten für Sozialhilfeempfänger nicht übernehmen

6 Rasendes Karussell
ATTAC, Gewerkschaften und Misereor: Breites Bündnis fordert Einführung einer Devisenumsatzsteuer

10 Transformiertes Land
Die Bertelsmann-Stiftung ehrt polnische Politiker für ihre Verdienste im Kampf gegen den Kommunismus

Anschläge auf öffentliche Gebäude und Regierungsinstitutionen in New York und Washington. *jW-Bericht*

Kriegserklärung an die USA

Die USA sind am Dienstag von der schwersten Terrorwelle in der Geschichte des Landes überrollt worden. Im Abstand von wenigen Minuten stürzten zwei Passagierflugzeuge in die beiden Hochhaustürme des World Trade Centers in New York. Wie es hieß, waren die Flugzeuge zuvor in Boston entführt worden. Das World Trade Center gilt als eines der Wahrzeichen der USA, damit kommt den Anschlägen auch eine hohe symbolische Bedeutung zu. Bereits 1993 war auf das Gebäude ein Anschlag mit mehreren Toten Anschl worden. Kurze Zeit nach bolis gestrigen Anschlag stürzten die Türme des Centers ein.

Der Anschlag ereignete sich kurz vor 9 Uhr Ortszeit, zur Zeit des morgendlichen Berufsverkehrs. Über die Zahl der Opfer war bis zum Nachmittag zunächst nichts bekannt. Normalerweise halten sich in dem Gebäude etwa 40 000 Menschen auf. Verschiedene Meldungen sprachen von zahlreichen Toten und Tausenden Verletzten. Laut Berichten aus New York ereigneten sich weitere Explosionen in der Stadt. Unter der Bevölkerung brach Panik aus, alle Brücken und Tunnel nach Manhattan wurden geschlossen.

Auch das Pentagon nahe Washington wurde von Explosionen erschüttert. Wie es in einigen Berichten hieß, wurde auch über dem Verteidigungsministerium ein Flugzeug zum Absturz gebracht. In dem Gebäude brachen Brände aus.

Das Außenministerium in Washington wurde ebenfalls zum Ziel eines Anschlags. Vor dem Gebäude explodierte eine Autobombe. Allerdings war das Ministerium nach den ersten Anschlägen bereits evakuiert worden. Nach Fernsehberichten wurde auf Anordnung des US-Geheimdiensts auch das Weiße Haus in Washington geräumt, ebenso wie der Sears Tower in Chicago und andere wichtige US-Gebäude.

In seiner ersten Reaktion auf die Anschläge hat US-Präsident George W. Bush von einem »offensichtlichen Terroranschlag auf unser Land« gesprochen. »Heute hatten wir eine nationale Tragödie«, erklärte der sichtlich bewegte Präsident in Sarasota im US-Staat Florida, wo er eine Rede zum Thema Bildung halten sollte. Er wollte sofort nach Washington zurückkehren. Ferner kündigte Bush an, »die Leute, die diese Tat begangen haben, zur Strecke zu bringen«.

Zu befürchten steht damit, daß die USA ihrerseits als Reaktion auf die Anschlagsserie zu Gewalt greifen. Washington hatte in der Vergangenheit wiederholt Staaten bombardiert, die nach seiner Meinung für Terrorismus verantwortlich sind.

Nach den Terroranschlägen in den USA wurde am Dienstag auch für die deutschen Sicherheitsbehörden die höchste Alarmstufe ausgerufen. Wie ein Sprecher des Bundesinnenministeriums am Dienstag in Berlin sagte, sei ein Krisenstab eingerichtet worden. Sicherheitsmaßnahmen würden eingeleitet. Vorrangiges Ziel sei der Schutz amerikanischer und deutscher Einrichtungen. Bundeskanzler Gerhard Schröder berief für den Abend den Bundessicherheitsrat ein.

Weltweit wurden die Anschläge scharf verurteilt. Die belgische EU-Ratspräsidentschaft zeigte sich schockiert. Der französische Präsident Jacques Chirac verurteilte die »monströsen Attentate« in einer Fernsehansprache an die Nation. Der russische Präsident Wladimir Putin sprach von einer »schrecklichen Tragödie«.

Nach den Terroranschlägen in den USA hat eine Schockwelle international die Börsenkurse in die Tiefe gerissen. In New York, Lissabon und Mexiko City wurde der Handel ausgesetzt. Die London Stock Exchange wurde evakuiert, der Handel aber fortgesetzt. Der Deutsche Aktienindex (DAX) stürzte unmittelbar nach den Meldungen aus New York ab und verlor bis gegen 17 Uhr mehr als sechs Prozent, war zuvor teilweise jedoch bei einem Minus von mehr als acht Prozent. Auch an den anderen Börsen in Europa gingen die Kurse auf Talfahrt. In Paris verlor der Aktienindex CAC 40 mehr als 200 Punkte oder über fünf Prozent.

Ein Experte des Militärfachinformationsdienstes *Jane's* in London bezeichnete die Anschläge als den »kühnsten Terrorangriff, der sich jemals auf der Erde ereignet hat«. Ein derartiger Anschlag bedürfe einer einmaligen logistischen Operation«, erklärte der Luftfahrtexperte Chris Yates. »Nur eine sehr kleine Handvoll von Terrorgruppen« stehe auf der Liste von Organisationen, die dazu fähig seien. »An der Spitze dieser Liste würde ich Osama bin Laden sehen.« *(Siehe auch Seite 3)*

Morgen in der jW:
Weltwirtschaft vor dem Absturz? Von Winfried Wolf

AP/DOUG MILLS

US-Präsident George W. Bush am Dienstag in der Emma-E.-Booker-Grundschule in Sarasota

4 398625 901809 30037

Junge Welt
www.jungewelt.de
Deutschland, Berlin

12

+++ Letzte Meldung: Bomben auf Afghanistan +++

EXPRESS

Mittwoch, 12. September 2001 80 Pf

Köln, Jahrgang 39, Nr. 212 K ** G 3079

Bin Laden: Sein Terror erschüttert die Zivilisation

Krieg gegen Amerika

...und Palästina lacht und feiert

Das Inferno von Amerika – Stundenbuch des Terrors – Seite 2/3

Super-Model Heidi Klum – Ich sah die Katastrophe – Seite 2

Welt am Rande des Krieges – Bush droht mit Vergeltung – Seite 4

Wut, Trauer, Hamsterkäufe – Deutschland in Terror-Angst – Seite 4

Peter Scholl-Latour – Wir sind völlig schutzlos – Seite 5

Osama Bin Laden – Drahtzieher des Terrors – Seite 6

Die Welt weint – Stimmen zum Terror-Anschlag – Seite 7

Köln trauert – Wie wir mit den Opfern fühlen – Seite 34, 35, 36

Der Bürger-Anwalt – Norbert Burger kümmert sich um die Sorgen der Leser – Seite 33

Das Wetter – 15° – Wolkig, örtlich etwas Regen – Noch mehr Wetter: Seite 13

Meine Sterne heute – Seite 30

Die Börse – * Stand: 17 Uhr

DAX*	4273,53	-396,60
Dollar	2,1619 DM	-0,0229
Euro	0,9047 $	+0,0095

Der TV-Tipp – Zauberhafte Hexen – Serie, PRO 7, 20.15 Uhr – Das TV-Programm auf Seite 13/14

XNA01AXK/2

Express
www.express.de
Deutschland, Köln

NRZ **NEUE RUHR ZEITUNG**

MITTWOCH, 12. SEPTEMBER 2001 · 54. Jahrgang, Nr 212 - DG - Montag-Freitag 1,40 DM - Samstag 1,70 DM · MEINUNGSFREUDIG - UNABHÄNGIG - BÜRGERNAH

www.nrz.de

51

Die Welt unter Schock
Krieg gegen die USA

TERROR / Flugzeuge rasen in New Yorker World Trade Center. Türme stürzen ein, Behörden befürchten tausende Tote. Anschlag auch gegen das Verteidigungsministerium in Washington. Weiterer Absturz eines Jumbo in Pittsburgh. Palästinenser bestreiten Beteiligung. Israel evakuiert Botschaften. Am späten Abend fallen Bomben auf Kabul.

NEW YORK. Bei den schwersten Terroranschlägen aller Zeiten sind gestern in den Wirtschafts- und Schalt-Zentralen Amerikas wahrscheinlich tausende Menschen gestorben. Mit vier in den USA offenbar entführten Passagierflugzeugen - als fliegende Bomben - brachten unbekannte Selbstmord-Attentäter unter anderem das World Trade Center in New York zum Einsturz, wo bislang täglich bis zu 50 000 Menschen arbeiteten. In Washington wurde das Verteidigungsministerium mit einem weiteren Flugzeug angegriffen. Eine vierte Maschine, die laut Medienberichten am Präsidenten-Sitz Camp David niedergehen sollte, stürzte bei Pittsburgh ab. An Bord der Flugzeuge befanden sich 266 Passagiere. US-Präsident Bush kündigte an, Amerika werde die Täter „zur Strecke bringen und bestrafen" und versetzte die US-Streitkräfte weltweit in höchste Alarmbereitschaft. Am späten Abend wurde die afghanische Hauptstadt Kabul Ziel schwerer militärischer Angriffe. Ob es sich dabei um US-Vergeltungsschläge handelte, war bis Redaktionsschluss unklar.

Dutzende Menschen sprangen aus den Fenstern

Kurz vor neun Uhr Ortszeit rasten innerhalb von 18 Minuten zwei Flugzeuge in das World Trade Center. Augenzeugen zufolge sprangen Dutzende von Menschen in Panik aus den Fenstern. Das Symbol der Finanzmacht USA an der Südspitze Manhattans mit den beiden 411 Meter hohen Zwillingstürmen ging in Rauch und Flammen auf und stürzte nach einer Stunde in sich zusammen. Später folgte ein 47 Stockwerke zählendes Nebengebäude. Die Zahl der Opfer war gestern Abend unklar. Die Behörden rechnen mit vielen tausend Toten und Verletzten. Nach den Anschlägen war die Lage in New York und Washington chaotisch. Es spielten sich apokalyptische Szenen ab. Ältere US-Bürger fühlten sich an die japanischen Überraschungsangriffe auf Pearl Harbor (Hawaii) 1942 im Zweiten Weltkrieg erinnert. Das Parlamentsgebäude auf dem Kapitol und das Weiße Haus wurden evakuiert, ebenso das UN-Gebäude in New York und die Börse in Wall Street. Fernsehsender berichteten von Massen-Evakuierungen und panisch flüchtenden Menschen.

Die Nato evakuierte ihr Hauptquartier in Brüssel, Israel ließ Auslandsvertretungen räumen. In Deutschland wurden US-Einrichtungen, öffentliche Gebäude und Flughäfen gesondert gesichert. Die Finanzmärkte reagierten weltweit mit Kursabstürzen, wichtige Handelsplätze wurden geschlossen.

Die Hintergründe der Terrorwelle, zu der sich bislang niemand bekannte, sind unklar. Palästinensergruppen bestritten jede Beteiligung. PLO-Chef Arafat verurteilte die Attentate scharf. US-Geheimdienste sehen als Drahtzieher den saudi-arabischen Millionär Osama Bin Laden, der mit Anschlägen auf US-Botschaften 1998 in Verbindung gebracht wurde. Bin Laden wird in Afghanistan vermutet. (dpa/ap/NRZ)

▪ Mehr Informationen unter www.nrz.de/terror

Ein Bild wie im Krieg: Die Skyline von New York nach dem Anschlag auf die beiden Türme des World Trade Centers. Wenige Minuten später brach auch der zweite Turm und stürzte in sich zusammen. Tausende fanden in den Trümmern den Tod. (Foto: ap)

DAS WETTER

Heute: Einige Regenschauer.
Morgen: Anfangs Regengüsse, später freundlich, bis 17°.

FUSSBALL AKTUELL

CHAMPIONS LEAGUE, VORRUNDE, HINSPIELE

FC Schalke - Panath. Athen	0:2
Dynamo Kiew - Bor. Dortmund	2:2

KURZ GEMELDET

Wende bei der Zuwanderung. In der rot-grünen Regierungskoalition gibt es Überlegungen, bei der Zuwanderung nicht länger den Konsens mit der Union zu suchen. ▪ NACHRICHTEN

Olympia im Blick. Ministerpräsident Clement legte das Sportstättenkonzept für die Bewerbung vor. Manche Orte sind noch umstrtitten. Fest steht, dass Rheinfire-Manager Leibkind Geschäftsführer der Olympia GmbH wird. ▪ NRW - DAS LAND

Verlag und Redaktion: Friedrichstraße 34-38, 45128 Essen, Telefon (0201) 8 04-0, Telefax (0201) 8 04-2021, E-Mail redaktion@nrz.de

Panik im 30. Stock! Wie viele Kollegen leben noch?

NRZ-EXKLUSIV / Dennis Reuther aus Arnsberg entkommt der Feuerhölle und berichtet von den Explosionen im Wolkenkratzer.

PASCAL BRÜCKMANN

NEW YORK. Es war erst sein zweiter Arbeitstag im World Trade Center „Two". Dennis Reuther (27) aus Arnsberg saß gerade vor seinem Computer im 30. Stock des Hochhauses, als er aufgeschreckt wurde. „Es prasselte gegen die Scheiben, ich dachte im ersten Moment an starken Regen." Dann sah der junge Mann, der bei der Siemens-Tochter STS im World Trade Center ein Praktikum absolviert, brennende Teile an seinem Fenster vorbeifliegen.

Kollegen tot getrampelt?

Einen Knall habe es aber nicht gegeben. „Niemand wusste was los war, es gab keinen Alarm. Als ein Kollege meinte, es sei besser zu gehen, liefen wir ins Treppenhaus." Langsam zog stechender Rauch in die Gänge. Doch die Panik brach erst aus, als das zweite Flugzeug in das World Trade Center krachte. „Es gab einen fürchterlichen Knall. Jeder rannte um sein Leben, möglicherweise sind dabei sogar einige meiner Kollegen totgetrampelt worden."

Vor dem Gebäude erblickte Dennis Reuther brennende Autos, sah schreiende Menschen. „Polizisten winkten uns aus dem Gebäude heraus, wir mussten in Intervallen herauslaufen, um nicht von den herabstürzenden Trümmern getroffen zu werden", berichtet der junge Mann im Gespräch mit der NRZ.

LESEN SIE IM INNERN

„Da keine U-Bahn mehr fuhr, rannten wir nordwärts. Im Hintergrund rauchten die Gebäude wie zwei gigantische Schornsteine. Dann stürzte alles zusammen." Dennis Reuther konnte sich rechtzeitig in Sicherheit bringen. Bei dem Telefonat mit der NRZ steht er total unter Schock. „Mir zittern die Knie, ich kann das alles noch nicht glauben." Gleichzeitig berichtet er von ersten Panikkäufen in der Stadt. Seine Eltern konnte er telefonisch nicht erreichen. Diesen Dienst übernimmt die NRZ für ihn.

Erlösende Botschaft für die Eltern

In Arnsberg hatte man bereits mit dem Schlimmsten gerechnet. Unter Tränen vernehmen die Eltern die erlösende Botschaft.

• Um 10.29 Uhr Ortszeit zerfällt das Gebäude in Staub, das für Reuther ein Ort der Hoffnung sein sollte - und für ihn und Zentausende andere zum Alptraum wurde. (NRZ)

Das Unfassbare erfährt US-Präsident George W. Bush in dieser Sekunde durch seinen Stabschef Andrew Card (links). (Foto: ap)

Neue Ruhr Zeitung
www.nrz.de
Deutschland, Essen

12

Zeitung für Sachsen-Anhalt · Gegründet 1890

Magdeburger Volksstimme

Mittwoch, 12. September 2001 — **Magdeburgische Zeitung · Magdeburger Lokalanzeiger** — Nr. 212

Heute mit:

Oldienacht steigt mit fünf Live-Bands

HAVELBERG. „Musik ohne Grenzen" ist das Motto der Oldienacht in Havelberg, bei der am 29. September fünf Bands aus fünf Partnerstädten spielen. In Verden stieß die Erstauflage auf große Resonanz.

Probleme mit der Beratungsstelle lösen

STENDAL. Wenn Jugendliche Probleme haben, können sie sich an die Jugendberatungsstelle bei der Polizei wenden.

Schwerer Unfall in der Seekurve

KAMERN. Drei Verletzte, darunter ein Kind, hat gestern Nachmittag ein schwerer Verkehrsunfall in der Seekurve bei Kamern gefordert. Zwei Pkw waren frontal zusammen gestoßen.

Freiburg nach 0:0 mit guten Chancen

PUCHOV. Mit einem 0:0 beim slowakischen Club SKM Puchov hat sich Fußball-Bundesligist SC Freiburg gute Chancen auf das Erreichen der zweiten Runde im UEFA-Cup erhalten.

16° 9°
Wechselnd bewölkt, zeitweise Schauer, nur wenig Sonne

LOKALES

Abriss sollte schnell erfolgen

Sandau. Der Abriss des einsturzgefährdeten Hauses an der Einmündung der Breiten Straße in die Poststraße sollte beschleunigt werden. Das forderte der stellvertretende Bürgermeister Dieter Schulenburg auf der jüngsten Ratssitzung. Das Fachwerkhaus steht unmittelbar an der Bundesstraße und stelle somit eine Gefährdung dar.

Schmucke Häuser im Ortsteil

Hohenkamern. Im Kamernschen Ortsteil Hohenkamern sind viele schmucke Einfamilienhäuser zu finden. Die Einwohnerzahl beträgt 73. Hohenkamern ist mit seinen rund 150 Jahren der jüngste Teil Kamerns. Er entstand als Rittergut derer von Katte. Die Einwohner fühlen sich wohl, so zum Beispiel Gottfried Richter, dessen Hobby das Schnitzen ist.

LOKAL-SPORT

1. FC hat nur geringe Chancen

Stendal. Fußball-Landesligist 1. FC Stendal sind nur geringe Chancen einzuräumen, dem Abspruch von insgesamt zwölf Siegpunkten aus den bisherigen vier Spielen zu entgehen. Nach dem SV Irxleben hat nunmehr auch Kontrahent Fermersleben Einspruch eingelegt.

Billberger auf Spitzenrängen

Billberge. Schönebeck erwies sich für die Motorrad-Biathleten vom CJD Billberge als gutes Pflaster. Beim 7. Lauf zur Landesmeisterschaft gab es für sie Platzierungen im Vorderfeld. Und beim Drei-Stunden-Rennen gab es zwei altmärkische Siege.

DEUTSCHLAND

Charterflüge in USA abgesagt

Berlin. Unmittelbar nach den Anschlägen in New York und Washington haben zahlreiche deutsche Reiseveranstalter ihre Reisen in die USA abgesagt. Bis Freitag gebuchte Flüge werden kostenlos storniert. Urlauber, die ihre Reise in den kommenden 14 Tagen antreten wollten, können kostenlos umbuchen, hieß es. (dpa)

Höppner: Weniger Erwerbslose

Magdeburg. Obwohl Sachsen-Anhalt weiter die höchste Arbeitslosenquote in Deutschland hat, sieht Ministerpräsident Reinhard Höppner (SPD) Anzeichen für eine positive Entwicklung. Die Zahl der Erwerbslosen ging seit August 2000 um 14 700 auf 256 000 zurück. Der Rückgang sei stärker als in anderen Ländern. (dpa)

Mehr Honorar für Ost-Ärzte?

Köln. Gesundheitsministerin Ulla Schmidt (SPD) will noch in dieser Legislaturperiode die Einkommenssituation der Ärzte in den neuen Bundesländern verbessern. Das Geld soll dorthin fließen, wo die Menschen behandelt werden. Dadurch würden die Honorare der Ost-Ärzte um ca. 170 Millionen Mark aufgewertet. (ddp)

Berlin will längere Ladenöffnung

Berlin. Knapp sechs Wochen vor der Landtagswahl in Berlin will der rot-grüne Senat die Debatte über längere Ladenöffnungszeiten neu beleben. Angekündigt wurde eine Bundesrats-Initiative, mit der Öffnungszeiten an allen Werktagen von 6 bis 22 Uhr ermöglicht werden sollen, vor allem am Samstag. (AP)

DIE WELT

Israel beschießt Flüchtlingslager

Jerusalem. Israels Armee hat gestern das große Flüchtlingslager am Rande der autonomen Palästinenserstadt Dschenin unter Beschuss genommen. Dabei wurden nach palästinensischen Angaben mindestens acht Menschen zum Teil lebensgefährlich verletzt. Einheiten legten einen Belagerungsring um Dschenin. (dpa)

Flut illegaler Einwanderer

Athen. Griechenland scheint immer mehr zum Einfallstor für Afghanen oder Kurden zu werden, die illegal in anderen Ländern der Europäischen Union ihr Glück suchen wollen. Allein in den letzten zehn Tagen nahm die Polizei auf der ägäischen Touristeninsel Kos 570 Menschen ohne gültige Papiere fest. (dpa)

Börse Dax: 4273 (Schlusskurs) — Dow Jones: Kein Handel

Tausende Tote in New York und Washington / US-Präsident Bush: „Nationale Tragödie"

Weltweit Entsetzen nach beispielloser Terror-Serie

Der internationale Terrorismus hat die USA mit den schrecklichsten Terroranschlägen der Geschichte herausgefordert. Mit zwei entführten Flugzeugen brachten Selbstmord-Attentäter das New Yorker World Trade Center zum Einsturz. Das Verteidigungsministerium in Washington wurde mit einem weiteren Flugzeug teilweise zerstört. Die Angriffe kosteten Tausende Menschen das Leben.

Von **Gabriele Chwallek** und **Herbert Winkler**, dpa

9.08 Uhr Ortszeit: Ein entführtes Flugzeug rast in den nördlichen Turm des World Trade Centers in New York. Foto: dpa

Washington. Die Terroranschläge gegen die Supermacht USA kamen aus heiterem Himmel. Ohne Vorwarnung rasten zwei Flugzeuge in die Zwillingstürme des World Trade Centers in New York: Feuerbälle stiegen auf, dunkler Qualm verdunkelte den blauen Himmel, beide Türme stürzten teilweise ein. Die Szenerie wirkte wie einem Katastrophenfilm entnommen.

Ein weiteres Flugzeug, eine Boeing 767, raste in das Verteidigungsministerium in Washington. Ein Teil des Gebäudes wurde verwüstet. Bei Pittsburgh stürzte eine Boeing 747 ab, zunächst aus unbekannten Gründen.

Das Weiße Haus und die Ministerien wurden evakuiert, zahlreiche andere Gebäude geschlossen. In New York wurde das Gebäude der Vereinten Nationen geräumt. Alle Flughäfen wurden gesperrt. Mehrere Flugzeuge wurden vermisst – möglicherweise entführt und in terroristische „Waffen" verwandelt.

Ein todernster Präsident George W. Bush musste der schockierten Bevölkerung von einer „nationalen Tragödie" berichten. Die Polizei sprach von einem „unvorstellbaren Verlust an Menschenleben". Bush und gab sich stark: „Wir werden Terrorismus gegen unser Land nicht zulassen."

Doch es war klar: Mit den beiden Türmen des Trade Centers kippte auch das Selbstbewusstsein der USA, dem Terror Herr zu werden. Allen Vorsichtsmaßnahmen und allen Anti-Terror-Strategien zum Trotz hatte ein unsichtbarer Feind die Großmacht ins Herz getroffen.

Sie war gewarnt – durch den Bombenanschlag von 1993 auf das World Trade Center mit sechs Toten und über 1000 Verletzten, durch Bombenanschläge auf die US-Botschaften in Kenia und Tansania im August 1998 mit 224 Toten. Seit Jahren jagte sie vergebens den saudi-arabischen Millionär Osama bin Laden, das mutmaßliche Hirn vieler Terrorangriffe.

Und doch wirkten die USA wie gelähmt, als ein Schlag dem anderen folgte. Das schlug rasch in Panik und Alarm um. In New York suchten die Menschen schreiend Schutz, als riesige Trümmerstücke von den einstürzenden Türmen auf die Straßen fielen. Passanten lagen blutüberströmt auf dem Pflaster. Die Krankenhäuser waren total überfordert.

Das Ausmaß der menschlichen Tragödie verdrängte zunächst das laute Nachdenken über die politischen Folgen, die dieser terroristische Mehrfachschlag haben wird.

Weitere Informationen:

- SEITE 3: Die Tragödie um das World-Trade-Center in New York.
- SEITE 4: Reaktionen in der Welt und in Sachsen-Anhalt.
- SEITE 5: Schockwelle an den Börsen und Chronik des Terrors.

Diese Serie von Anschlägen hat in den USA verheerende Schäden angerichtet.

US-Präsident Bush

„Wir werden die Feiglinge jagen"

Washington (oli). US- Präsident George W. Bush setzte die US-Streitkräfte sofort nach dem Anschlag weltweit in hohe Alarmbereitschaft. Er kündigte an, die „unbekannten Feiglinge, die für die Taten verantwortlich sind, zu jagen und zur Strecke zu bringen". Er habe mit Politikern in aller Welt telefoniert. „Wir werden zeigen, dass wir diesen Test bestehen", so der Präsident.

Kanzler Schröder

„Kriegserklärung gegen die Welt"

Berlin (oli). Schröder sagte nach ersten Beratungen des Bundessicherheitsrates: „Dies ist eine Kriegserklärung gegen die gesamte zivilisierte Welt." Das deutsche Volk stehe „in dieser Stunde fest an der Seite der Vereinigten Staaten von Amerika". Der Kanzler sicherte dem amerikanischen Präsidenten in einem Schreiben die „uneingeschränkte Solidarität" der Bundesrepublik zu.

Präsident Jassir Arafat

„Wir sind alle schockiert"

Gaza (oli). Palästinenser-Präsident Jassir Arafat zeigte sich betroffen. Er nahm im Gazastreifen Stellung zu den Anschlägen: „Wir verurteilen diese schrecklichen Taten ohne Einschränkung. Wir sind alle schockiert." Es sei unvorstellbar, was passiert ist. Der Führer der Palästinenser sprach „der US-Regierung und dem amerikanischen Volk" das Beileid aller Palästinenser aus.

Experte Roland Jacquard

„Bin Laden traf Terrorgruppen"

Paris (oli). Der Terrorismusexperte Roland Jacquard sieht den arabische Millionär Osama bin Laden als Drahtzieher hinter den Anschlägen. bin Laden, der in Afghanistan lebt, habe in diesem Jahr extremistischen Palästinensergruppen getroffen. Ziel sei eine gemeinsame Strategie gegen die USA gewesen. Der Experte glaubt, bin Laden habe allein gehandelt. Er verfüge über die entsprechenden Mittel.

KOMMENTAR

Unter Feuer

Von Steffen Honig

Entsetzen paart sich mit Trauer, Ohnmacht mit Wut: Seit gestern ist klar, wozu Terroristen wirklich im-Stande sind. Die einzig verbliebene Weltmacht USA wurde ins Mark getroffen – und mit ihr die gesamte westliche Welt. Die Killer-Kommandos haben ihr Ziel erreicht.

Da sind der Tod und das Leid hunderttausender Menschen, da drohen unabsehbare Folgen – wirtschaftlich, politisch und kulturell. Der börsenabhängige globale Markt geriet sofort aus den Fugen. Die Vereinigten Staaten haben sich verwundbar gezeigt. Das wird Washington nicht hinnehmen. Es steigt die Gefahr eines Krieges in Nahost, vor den Toren Europas.

Denn der Terror wurzelt offenbar im tiefen Hass radikaler islamischem Fundamentalisten auf die Werte westlicher Demokratie. Die Hoffnung auf mögliche Brückenschläge ist in Feuer und Tod begraben worden.

Volksstimme
www.volksstimme.de
Deutschland, Magdeburg

Sächsische Zeitung

MITTWOCH, 12. SEPTEMBER 2001 · **Dresden** · www.sz-online.de · 56. Jahrgang · Nr. 213 · 1,40 DM/ 0,72 Euro

Politik
Probleme beim Sparen: Minister Eichel will dennoch Kurs halten S.5

Kultur
Vertane Chance: Jüdisches Museum als Ort der Beliebigkeiten S.13

Ratgeber
Die Euro-Frage: Was wird sich bei der Kreditkarte ändern? S.21

Panorama
Liebe Leser, Sie finden „Sieben Richtige" heute auf der Seite 24

Katastrophe

Inferno in den USA: Verheerende Terror-Welle mit Tausenden Toten

Entführte Flugzeuge stürzen auf Pentagon und New Yorker World Trade Center – die Zwillingstürme brechen nach schweren Explosionen zusammen / Weißes Haus evakuiert / Bush spricht von nationaler Tragödie / Jubel in Palästinenser-Lagern / Berichte über Explosionen in Kabul

Sekunden des Grauens um 9.08 Uhr New Yorker Ortszeit. Nachdem 18 Minuten zuvor der erste Turm des World Trade Centers von einem Flugzeug vom Typ Boeing 767 getroffen worden war, nähert sich plötzlich eine Boeing 757 dem zweiten Turm, trifft ihn und löst eine riesige Explosion aus. Kurze Zeit später brechen die Türme in sich zusammen und begraben vermutlich Tausende unter sich. Foto: AP

Der internationale Terrorismus hat gestern die Supermacht USA mit den schrecklichsten Anschlägen der Geschichte herausgefordert. Die gezielten Selbstmordangriffe auf Macht- und Finanzzentren kosteten wahrscheinlich Tausende Menschenleben.

NewYork/Washington/Berlin. Mit zwei in den USA entführten Passagierflugzeugen brachten mehrere Selbstmordattentäter das New Yorker World Trade Center zum Einsturz. In Washington wurden das Verteidigungsministerium (Pentagon) mit einem weiteren Flugzeug teilweise zerstört. Eine vierte entführte Maschine stürzte bei Pittsburgh ab. Sie sollte ursprünglich offenbar auf den Präsidentenlandsitz Camp David gelenkt werden.

Zunächst bekannte sich keine Terrororganisation zu den Anschlägen, die weltweit Entsetzen und verschärfte Sicherheitsvorkehrungen auslösten. US-Sicherheitskreise gehen unterdessen davon aus, dass der saudische Millionär und Terroristenführer Osama bin Laden Urheber der Tragödie ist. US-Präsident George W. Bush sprach zunächst von einer „nationalen Tragödie" und versprach später in einer Fernsehrede: „Wir werden die Täter zur Strecke bringen und bestrafen."

Kurz nach den Anschlägen in New York und Washington überschlugen sich die Ereignisse. Die Lage in beiden Städten war völlig chaotisch. Auch im amerikanischen Außenministerium brach Feuer aus. Das Parlamentsgebäude auf dem Kapitol und das Weiße Haus wurden ebenso evakuiert wie das Uno-Gebäude in New York und die Börse in der Wall Street. Alle Flughäfen in den USA wurden geschlossen.

**

Die Zwillingstürme des World Trade Centers, in denen täglich etwa 50 000 Menschen arbeiten, gingen nach den schweren Explosionen in Flammen auf. Hunderte Menschen flohen in Panik aus dem Gebäude. Unmittelbar nach dem Aufprall der ersten Maschine waren die Gebäude so weit wie möglich evakuiert worden.

Die apokalyptischen Szenen aus den USA haben auch Deutschland schockiert. In Berlin berief Bundeskanzler Gerhard Schröder (SPD) den Bundessicherheitsrat ein. Der Bundestag brach seine Haushaltsdebatte ab. In ganz Deutschland wurden die Sicherheitsvorkehrungen für Einrichtungen der USA und Israels sowie auf den Flughäfen verschärft. Tausende nahmen gestern Abend bundesweit an Trauergottesdiensten teil.

WEITERE BERICHTE

Bin Laden unter Verdacht S.2
Verzweiflung in New York S.3
Deutschland ist vorsichtig S.4
Kommentar S.5
Medienecho S.13
Sport-Reaktionen S.18

Weltweit wurde der Flugverkehr teilweise eingestellt.

Viele Palästinenser in den Flüchtlingslagern in Südlibanon und in Beirut feierten die Terrorserie und feuerten Freudenschüsse ab. Palästinenserpräsident Jassir Arafat verurteilte die Anschläge hingegen „auf das Schärfste". Zwei radikale Palästinensergruppen bestritten jede Beteiligung an den Terrorakten. Der Chef der Demokratischen Front für die Befreiung Palästinas (DFLP), Kari Abdel Karim, erklärte in Ramallah, seine Organisation habe mit dem Attentat „absolut nichts zu tun". Zuvor hatte sich die DFLP angeblich dazu bekannt. Auch ein hochrangiger Vertreter der Volksfront für die Befreiung Palästinas (PFLP) erklärte, seine Volksfront stehe nicht hinter den Terrorakten. Die afghanischen Taliban, die angeblich bin Laden beherbergen, schlossen ebenfalls eine Beteiligung kategorisch aus.

Die afghanische Hauptstadt Kabul ist am frühen Mittwochmorgen (Ortszeit) von schweren Explosionen erschüttert worden. Wie der amerikanische Nachrichtensender CNN aus Kabul berichtete, war auch Flugabwehrfeuer zu hören. Es wurde nicht ausgeschlossen, dass es sich um erste Vergeltungsschläge der USA handeln könnte. Jedoch wiesen die USA derartige Vermutungen zurück. (dpa/AP)

■ Das Auswärtige Amt hat eine Hotline eingerichtet: 01888 /17 46 00

Chronik der Katastrophe am 11. September 2001

■ **8.50 Uhr:** Eine Maschine der Fluggesellschaft American Airlines rast in die oberen Stockwerke des nördlichen Turms des World Trade Centers in New York. Dicker schwarzer Rauch dringt aus den Fenstern des 110-stöckigen Gebäudes. Das Flugzeug war zuvor auf dem Weg von Boston nach Los Angeles entführt worden; an Bord befanden sich 92 Menschen.

■ **9.05 Uhr:** US-Präsident George W. Bush wird informiert.

■ **9.08 Uhr:** Eine zweite Maschine der American Airlines rast in den südlichen Turm. Das gekidnappte Flugzeug wollte mit 64 Menschen an Bord von Washington nach Los Angeles fliegen.

■ **9.24:** Bush spricht in Sarasota (Bundesstaat Florida) von einer „nationalen Tragödie". Es handele sich „offensichtlich" um eine terroristische Attacke.

■ **9.30 Uhr:** Ein Flugzeug stürzt auf einem Hubschrauberlandeplatz am Verteidigungsministerium Pentagon ab, in dem viele militärische Führungskräfte ihren Sitz haben sollen. Ein Teil des Gebäudes stürzt ein. Im Pentagon arbeiten rund 20 000 Menschen. Der Westflügel des Weißen Hauses wird wegen einer Terrordrohung evakuiert.

■ **9.49 Uhr:** Die Flugsicherheitsbehörde streicht alle Starts in den USA.

■ **9.50 bis 10.30 Uhr:** Beide Türme des World Trade Centers stürzen ein. Alle größeren Regierungsgebäude in Washington und der Sitz der Vereinten Nationen in New York werden evakuiert.

■ **10.00 Uhr:** Eine Maschine der Fluggesellschaft United Airlines stürzt 130 Kilometer südöstlich von Pittsburgh unter ungeklärten Umständen ab. An Bord befanden sich 45 Menschen. Später wird über erste Vermutungen berichtet, wonach die Maschine ursprünglich auf den Präsidenten-Landsitz Camp David stürzen sollte.

US-Botschaft

Dank für große Anteilnahme

Berlin. Die Botschaft der USA in Berlin hat sich für die große Anteilnahme und die zahlreichen Hilfsangebote deutscher Bürger nach der Serie von Terroranschlägen bedankt. Ein Botschaftssprecher sagte, sein Haus habe zurzeit keinen Hinweis auf Drohungen oder Attentate. Es gebe allerdings noch keine Entscheidung, ob die diplomatische Vertretung aus Sicherheitsvorkehrungen heute geschlossen bleibe. Falls die Botschaft öffne, arbeite sie mit einer Notbesatzung. Die Sicherheitsmaßnahmen innerhalb Deutschlands seien im nötigen Umfang verstärkt worden. (AP)

Wirtschaft

Furcht vor weltweiter Krise

New York/Berlin. Nach den Terrorangriffen sind gestern alle US-Finanzmärkte geschlossen worden. Ein Drittel aller US-amerikanischen Finanztransaktionen wird über New York geleitet. Damit wird die Katastrophe mit Sicherheit enorme Auswirkungen auf die US-Wirtschaft und wahrscheinlich auf die Weltwirtschaft haben. In Deutschland stürzte der Dax zeitweise um rund neun Prozent unter 4 200 Punkte. Der Euro stieg steil auf über 0,90 US-Cents, der Öl-Preis auf über 31 US-Dollar pro Barrel. Nach Ankündigung der OPEC, den Markt stabilisieren zu wollen, kostete der Barrel 29,25 Dollar. Die Frankfurter Börse wurde am Abend nach einer Bombendrohung geräumt. Zum angedrohten Zeitpunkt erfolgte keine Explosion. Der Handel wurde um 19.15 Uhr geschlossen. (dpa)

BÖRSE

Stand 11.9., 20 Uhr	Punkte	Veränderung
Dax	4 273,53	-396,60
Nemax	841,07	- 71,15
EuroStoxx	3 220,27	-220,38
Dow Jones	geschlossen	
Euro-Kurs	1 Euro = 0,9047 USD	

WETTER

Heute setzt sich das unbeständige Wetter fort. Bei wechselnder bis starker Bewölkung muss man mit Schauern und Regen rechnen. Temperatur: 12 bis 15 Grad. Panorama

INHALT

KONTAKT

Abo-Service/Zustellung	☎01802 328 328 (12 Pfennig pro Gespräch)
Mo–Fr 7–19 Uhr; Sa 8–12 Uhr	0351-48 64 28 11
Kleinanzeigenannahme	☎0351-840 444
Mo–Fr 8–19 Uhr	0351-48 64-24 39
Tickettelefon	☎0351-84 04 20 02
Leserreisentelefon (Mo–Fr 9–19 Uhr)	☎01803-234 143
E-Mail-Adressen	redaktion@dd-v.de
anzeigen@dd-v.de	abo@dd-v.de
SZ-Lesertelefon	☎0351-48 64 22 73
SZ-Redaktion Fax	0351-48 64 23 54

Ausland: 35 Kc / 40 Sk / 13 öS / 220 pts / esc 250,00 cont / 250 pts (Kanaren) / 490 Dr / 255 Ft / 3,00 BGL

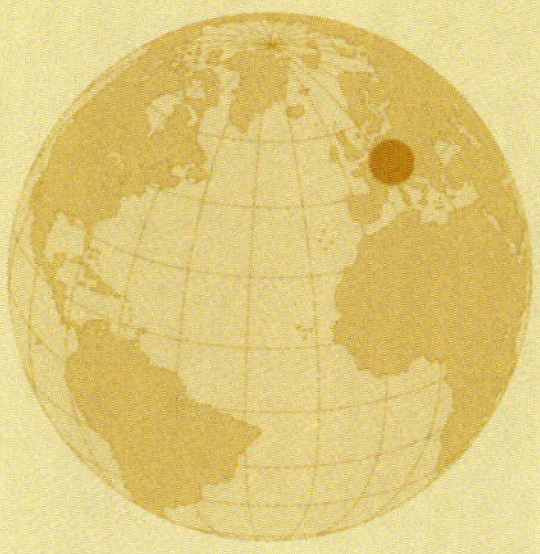

12

SÄCHSISCHE ZEITUNG
WWW.SZ-ONLINE.DE
DEUTSCHLAND, DRESDEN

TLZ Weimar

Thüringische Landeszeitung

TLZ-EXTRA: Acht Seiten zum Terror-Anschlag

Online-Special: unter: www.TLZ.de

Nummer 213 · 57. Jg. · 37. Woche · F 04286 UNABHÄNGIG · WELTOFFE… UNDEN Mittwoch, 12. September 2001 · Preis: 1,40 DM / 0,70 €

Kriegserklärung gegen die Welt

Terror-Welle in Amerika – Tausende Tote – Auch Thüringen trauert

New York/Washington/Berlin. (tlz) Eine „Kriegserklärung gegen die zivilisierte Welt" – so hat Bundeskanzler Gerhard Schröder (SPD) die schrecklichsten Anschläge in der Terrorismus-Geschichte genannt. Tausende von Menschen starben in New York und Washington: Der internationale Terrorismus hat die Supermacht USA wie nie herausgefordert.

Die mit großer Präzision ausgeführten Selbstmordangriffe auf Macht- und Finanzzentren in New York und Washington mit entführten Pas-

- **Seite 2:** Kommentar: Intellekt statt Rache
- **Seite 3:** Der Krieg: Wer greift uns denn an
- **Seite 4:** Gebete für die Opfer der Anschläge
- **Seite 5:** Das ist wie ein zweites Pearl Harbour

sagierflugzeugen als fliegende Bomben lähmten die freie Welt. Als Urheber verdächtigen US-Geheimdienste den saudischen Millionär und mutmaßlichen Terroristenführer Osama bin Laden. Er hatte vor kurzem mit einem „beispiellosen Angriff" auf die USA wegen ihrer Unterstützung Israels gedroht.

Mit zwei entführten und vermutlich von Terroristen gesteuerten amerikanischen Passagierflugzeugen brachten die Attentäter das berühmte New Yorker World Trade Center zum Einsturz. In Washington wurden das Verteidigungsministerium mit einer weiteren gekidnappten Passagiermaschine teilweise zerstört. Das Außenministerium wurde in Brand gesetzt.

Eine vierte entführte Zivilmaschine stürzte aus unbekannten Gründen bei Pittsburgh ab.

Um die Angriffsziele spielten sich apokalyptische Szenen ab, die ältere US-Bürger an die japanischen Überraschungsangriffe auf Pearl Habour (Hawaii) 1942 im Zweiten Weltkrieg erinnerten.

Präsident George W. Bush sprach von einer „nationalen Tragödie" und sagte: „Wir werden diejenigen, die für diese feigen Taten verantwortlich sind, zur Strecke bringen und bestrafen." Die US-Streitkräfte wurden weltweit in Alarmzustand versetzt, Kriegsschiffe nach New York in Marsch gesetzt.

In Berlin berief Bundeskanzler Gerhard Schröder den Bundessicherheitsrat ein und versicherte den USA Solidarität.

In Erfurt ließ Ministerpräsident Bernhard Vogel die amerikanische Flagge mit Trauerflor vor der Staatskanzlei hissen.

Passagiermaschinen als fliegende Bomben auf das Welthandelszentrum in New York: Zwei von Selbstmord-Attentätern entführte Flugzeuge rasen in beide Türme des World Trade Centers. Kurz danach stürzt das Gebäude zusammen und begräbt Tausende von Menschen unter sich. Amerika ist noch Stunden nach den Anschlägen wie gelähmt. Foto: dpa

Hotline gibt Auskunft über Angehörige

Frankfurt/Berlin. (tlz) Wer sich um Angehörige in den USA sorgt, kann sich über verschiedene Telefonnummern informieren: Das Auswärtige Amt und American Airlines haben Hotlines für Angehörige in Deutschland eingerichtet. Reisende in die USA sollten sich bei den Fluggesellschaften oder Reisebüros über die Möglichkeiten informieren.

i American Airlines: 069/ 50 98 50 70; Lufthansa: 0800 / 100 94 99; Hotline Auswärtiges Amt: 01888/17 46 00.

„Ein neues Zeitalter des Terrorismus"

Jena. (tlz/mar) Ein „Zeitalter des Terrorismus" fürchtet der Jenaer Politikwissenschaftler Professor Helmut Hubel auf die Welt zukommen. Er bezeichnete die Anschläge auf die Symbole der US-Weltmacht als ein „zweites Pearl Harbour". Sie hätten „die Hilflosigkeit und die Unfähigkeit der Staaten gezeigt, die Zivilbevölkerung aktiv zu schützen." In der Dimension verglich er die Ereignisse von New York und Washington mit der Kuba-Krise. Die Folgen dieser Ereignisse seien derzeit noch nicht absehbar.

Liebe Leser,
die TLZ hat wegen der Anschläge in den USA die Seiten-Struktur geändert.

Kondolenzliste für alle in der Staatskanzlei

Glockenläuten, Friedensgebete, Blumen und Anteilnahme

■ Von H. Hoffmeister, H. Kaczmarek und N. Block

Erfurt/Jena. (tlz) Thüringen trauert. Glocken läuten in der Kirchenprovinz Sachsen, zu der Erfurt gehört. In Jena wird für heute zu Friedensgebeten geladen. Vor dem Erfurter Rathaus werden Blumen niedergelegt. In vielen Thüringer Kirchen beten die Menschen spontan für die Opfer der Terror-Anschläge in Amerika. Ministerpräsident Bernhard Vogel (CDU) forderte die Thüringer auf, in den nächsten Tagen auf alle Feste und Feiern zu verzichten. In der Staatskanzlei liegt von heute morgen, 8 Uhr, ein Kondolenzbuch aus, in das sich alle Bürger eintragen können.

Fassungslosigkeit und Entsetzen machte sich nach Bekanntwerden der schrecklichen Nachrichten aus New York in ganz Thüringen breit. Viele Bürger des Freistaates haben Kontakte in die USA. Es existieren zahlreiche Partnerschaften von Städten, Schulen und Vereinen.

Thüringen sei unter den ostdeutschen Ländern Amerika in besonderer Weise zu Dank verpflichtet, sagte Wirtschaftsminister Franz Schuster (CDU) im TLZ-Gespräch. Die Amerikaner bauten hier nach der Wende 35 Unternehmen mit 6734 Arbeitsplätzen auf – mehr als jede andere Nation. Schuster: „Amerika hat sich hier als besonders engagierter Investor gezeigt. Wir stehen jetzt an der Seite der Amerikaner. Wir müssen ihnen helfen, mit dieser Situation fertig zu werden." Schuster vermutet, dass der Welthandel nun eine Phase der Neuorientierung durchleben werde – nach einer derartigen Provokation und Herausforderung.

Tiefe Betroffenheit auch beim evangelischen Landesbischof Christoph Kähler. Seine Gedanken seien besonders bei den umgekommenen Frauen, Kindern und Männern und deren Angehörigen.

Schutt und Asche sowie ein paar Gebäudeteile sind nach dem Anschlag vom World Trade Center übrig geblieben. Foto: dpa

Thüringische Landeszeitung
www.tlz.de
Deutschland, Weimar

12

„Eine nationale Tragödie": US-Präsident George W. Bush. Foto: AP

NÜRNBERGER Nachrichten

57. Jahrgang
B 5393

Ausgabe A

Unabhängige Zeitung für Politik, Lokales, Wirtschaft, Kultur und Sport

Einzelpreis: 1,80 DM / 0,92 € Mittwoch, 12. September 2001 Nummer 212

Das World Trade Center gibt es nicht mehr: Chaos und Entsetzen nach beispielloser Terrorserie in den USA

Die Welt steht unter Schock

Attacken auf amerikanische Symbole: Pentagon und Weißes Haus evakuiert — Vier Flugzeuge brachten Tod und Verderben — Präsident Bush: „Nationale Tragödie" — Osama bin Laden als Drahtzieher? — Die Finanzmärkte in Aufruhr

Heute lesen Sie

DAX ⇩ Dow-Jones ⇘ Dollar/DM ⇗

DAX-Index (Ffm)	4273,53	(—396,60)
Dow-Jones	—geschlossen—	
1 Dollar in DM	2,1819	(+0,0200)
1 Euro in Dollar	0,8964	(—0,0083)
Goldfixing London	287,00	(+15,50)

31137
4 390539 301805

http://www.nn-online.de
http://www.nordbayern.de

Der internationale Terrorismus attackiert die Macht- und Finanzzentren der Vereinigten Staaten: Das World Trade Center gibt es nicht mehr. Nach der Attacke durch zwei Flugzeuge stürzten die weltberühmten Zwillingstürme in New York in sich zusammen. Foto: AP

NEW YORK (AP/dpa/rtr) — Chaos und tiefes Erschrecken in den USA und in der ganzen Welt: Vor den Augen einer entsetzten Öffentlichkeit ist die Supermacht von einer offenkundig minutiös koordinierten Terrorkampagne überrollt worden, die vermutlich Tausende von Menschen das Leben kostete.

Ziel der Angriffe, bei denen entführte Flugzeuge im Kamikaze-Stil — möglicherweise von eigens dafür ausgebildeten Piloten — auf die Symbole Amerikas gestürzt wurden, waren New Yorks Finanzzentrum und die Hauptstadt Washington. „Wir erleben heute eine nationale Tragödie", sagte US-Präsident George W. Bush.

Gebannt verfolgten Millionen von Menschen auf der ganzen Welt die Bilder von den Terroranschlägen live auf ihren Fernsehschirmen. Zuerst bohrten sich im Abstand von 18 Minuten zwei Passagierflugzeuge der American Airlines mit 156 Menschen an Bord in die beiden Hochhaustürme des World Trade Center in New York, in denen etwa 50 000 Menschen arbeiten. Beide Türme fielen später in sich zusammen.

Nur kurz danach stürzte ein Flugzeug auf das Pentagon, das dann ebenfalls in Flammen stand und teilweise zerstört wurde. Eine vierte Maschine, die angeblich den Präsidenten-Urlaubssitz Camp David treffen sollte, stürzte bei Pittsburgh in Pennsylvania ab. Gegen Mitternacht fiel auch noch ein Nebengebäude des World Trade Center in sich zusammen.

Das US-Verteidigungsministerium, das Weiße Haus und alle weiteren Regierungsgebäude waren kurz nach den Anschlägen evakuiert worden, darunter alleine 20 000 Menschen, die im Pentagon arbeiten. In Washington wurden Truppen in Marsch gesetzt. Die USA schlossen ihre Grenzen. „Das ist ein zweites Pearl Harbor", sagte Senator Chuck Hagel unter Bezug auf den Überraschungsangriff der Japaner vor 60 Jahren, mit dem der Zweite Weltkrieg im Pazifik begann.

Arafat „fassunglos"

Bush sprach von einem „offenkundigen Terroranschlag auf unser Land". Er kündigte an, man werde die Verantwortlichen für die Anschlagsserie jagen: „Das war nicht das Werk eines schlecht ausgerüsteten Feindes." Als Drahtzieher vermuten die Geheimdienste den saudischen Terroristen Osama bin Laden.

Tausende von Palästinensern feierten im Westjordanland die Terroranschläge. Der palästinensische Präsident Jassir Arafat äußerte sich hingegen fassungslos. „Wir verurteilen diesen sehr gefährlichen Angriff völlig. Ich übermittle mein Beileid dem amerikanischen Volk, dem amerikanischen Präsidenten und der amerikanischen Regierung, nicht nur in meinem Namen, sondern auch im Namen des palästinensischen Volkes." Mehrere palästinesische Gruppen und auch die Taliban in Afghanistan erklärten, sie hätten damit nichts zu tun. Um Mitternacht wurden aus der afghanischen Hauptstadt Kabul mehrere Explosionen gemeldet. Offen blieb, ob es sich um einen Vergeltungsschlag handelte.

Bundeskanzler Gerhard Schröder sprach nach einer eilig einberufenen Sitzung des Bundessicherheitsrates von einer „Kriegserklärung gegen die gesamte zivilisierte Welt". Er sicherte den USA die „uneingeschränkte Solidarität" Deutschlands" zu.

Auch die internationalen Finanzmärkte wurden durch die Nachrichten aus den USA ins Chaos gestürzt. Die Börsen an der New Yorker Wall Street und die Rohstoff- und Terminmärkte blieben geschlossen. An der Frankfurter Börse ging eine Bombendrohung ein.

Erstmals in seiner Geschichte wird der Bundestag wegen der Tragödie in den USA die auf mehrere Tage angesetzte Etat-Debatte absagen. Viele Veranstaltungen, die für die nächste Zeit geplant waren, werden ausfallen oder nur in eingeschränkter Form stattfinden.

Tag des Terrors

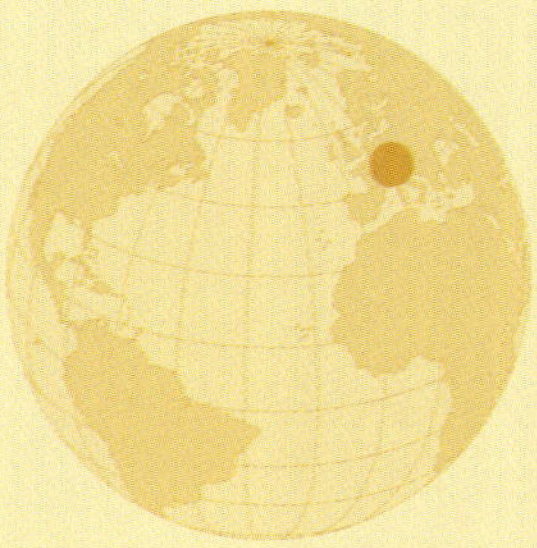

NÜRNBERGER NACHRICHTEN
WWW.NN-ONLINE.DE
DEUTSCHLAND, NÜRNBERG

12

Exklusiv-Interview mit Würzburgs Basketball-Star Dirk Nowitzki SEITE A 10

Das Wetter
Heute
10 bis 15° Celsius
Morgen
11 bis 17° Celsius

MAIN POST
WÜRZBURGER NEUESTE NACHRICHTEN

Finanzen
DAX
Dienstag: 4273,53
Montag: 4670,13
Euro
Dienstag: 0,8964
Montag: 0,9047
(zum US-Dollar)

57. Jahrgang, Nr. 210 ★ Mittwoch, 12. September 2001 ★ Preis 1,90 DM

Aus dem Inhalt

Redaktion: Telefon (09 31) 60 01-0
E-Mail: redaktion@mainpost.de
Anzeigen: Telefon (01801) 678 678
E-Mail: service.center@mainpost.de
Abo-Service: Telefon (01801) 567 567
E-Mail: service.center@mainpost.de

4 394268 601908 30037

Terror - die Welt unter Schock

Tausende von Toten bei Anschlägen in New York und Washington befürchtet

NEW YORK (DPA/AP/RTR) Der internationale Terrorismus hat am Dienstag die Supermacht USA mit den schrecklichsten Anschlägen der Terrorismus-Geschichte herausgefordert. Die mit großer Präzision ausgeführten Selbstmordangriffe auf Macht- und Finanzzentren in New York und Washington kosteten wahrscheinlich Tausende von Menschenleben.

Als Urheber vermuten die Geheimdienste nach Angaben eines ranghohen US-Senators den saudischen Millionär und mutmaßlichen Terroristenführer Osama bin Laden. Auch israelische Sicherheitsexperten nannten bin Laden, aber auch Iran oder die Hisbollah als mögliche Urheber.

Mit zwei in den USA entführten Passagierflugzeugen brachten mehrere Selbstmord-Attentäter das berühmte New Yorker World Trade Center zum Einsturz. In Washington wurden das Verteidigungsministerium mit einem weiteren Flugzeug teilweise zerstört, das Außenministerium mit einer Autobombe angegriffen. Eine vierte entführte Maschine stürzte bei Pittsburgh ab.

Keine Terrororganisation bekannte sich bis zum Abend zu den Anschlägen, die weltweit Entsetzen und verschärfte Sicherheitsvorkehrungen auslösten. Der Senator von Utah, Orrin Hatch, berichtete nach Gesprächen mit dem FBI und Vertretern der Geheimdienste von deren Verdacht gegen bin Laden. US-Präsident George W. Bush sprach von einer „nationalen Tragödie" und versprach später in einer Fernsehrede: „Wir werden die Täter zur Strecke bringen und bestrafen."

Zunächst rasten am Morgen (Ortszeit) innerhalb von 18 Minuten zwei Flugzeuge ins World Trade Center in New York. Das Symbol der Finanzmacht USA an der Südspitze Manhattans mit den beiden 110 Stockwerke hohen Zwillingstürmen ging in Rauch und Flammen auf und stürzte etwa eine Stunde später in sich zusammen. Die Behörden in New York rechneten mit Tausenden von Toten. In Washington zerstörte eine weitere abstürzende Maschine teilweise das US-Verteidigungsministerium (Pentagon).

Das vierte entführte Passagierflugzeug sollte offenbar im Kamikaze-Angriff auf den Präsidenten-Landsitz Camp David gelenkt werden. Das sagte der Kongressabgeordnete James Moran nach einer Krisensitzung mit dem Führungsstab der Marineinfanterie, der US-Elite-Einheit, am Dienstag in Washington. Der United-Airlines-Flug 93 war mit 45 Menschen an Bord 160 Kilometer südöstlich von Pittsburgh im US-Staat Pennsylvania abgestürzt. In der Nähe liegt der Staat Maryland, in dem sich Camp David befindet. Die Absturzstelle befindet sich fast auf einer Linie zwischen Washington und New York.

Kurz nach den Anschlägen in New York und Washington überschlugen sich die Ereignisse. Die Lage in beiden Städten war völlig chaotisch. Im amerikanischen Außenministerium brach Feuer aus. Das Parlamentsgebäude auf dem Kapitol und das Weiße Haus wurden ebenso evakuiert wie das UN-Gebäude in New York. Die Börse in Wall Street und alle Flughäfen in den USA wurden geschlossen. Weltweit wurde der Flugverkehr teilweise eingestellt. Die Finanzmärkte rund um den Globus wurden durch die Nachrichten aus den USA ins Chaos gestürzt.

Die Zwillingstürme des World Trade Center, in denen täglich allein 50 000 Menschen arbeiten, gingen nach den schweren Explosionen in Flammen auf. Hunderte Menschen flohen in Panik aus dem Gebäude. Rund eine Stunde nach den ersten beiden Angriffen auf die Türme, die das zweithöchste Gebäude der Welt bilden, ereignete sich im südlichen Turm eine weitere Explosion.

Daraufhin stürzte der obere Teil des 411 Meter hohen Gebäudes ein. Nur wenig später fiel auch der zweite Turm in sich zusammen. Unmittelbar nach dem Aufprall der ersten Maschine waren die Gebäude so weit wie möglich evakuiert worden.

Die Kliniken wurden vom Ansturm der Verletzten überrollt. Ein Arzt im Vincent's-Krankenhaus sagte: „Hunderte Menschen haben Verbrennungen am ganzen Körper". New Yorks Bürgermeister Rudolph Giuliani sprach von einer „gewaltigen Zahl" an Toten. Er ordnete die Evakuierung von Süd-Manhattan an und rief die Bürger auf, sich in Sicherheit zu bringen.

Zwei radikale Palästinensergruppen bestritten jede Beteiligung an den Terrorakten. Der Chef der „Demokratischen Front für die Befreiung Palästinas", Kari Abdel Karim, erklärte in Ramallah, die DFLP habe mit dem Attentat „absolut nichts zu tun". Auch ein hochrangiger Vertreter der Volksfront für die Befreiung Palästinas (PFLP) erklärte im arabischen Sender ANN, auch seine Organisation stehe nicht hinter den Terrorakten. Palästinenserpräsident Jassir Arafat verurteilte die Anschläge „auf das Schärfste". Die EU, Frankreich, Großbritannien, Russland und viele andere Staaten verurteilten die Terrorangriffe in den USA.

Nach dem Einsturz des World Trade Centers versinkt ganz Manhattan in einer Staubwolke. FOTO DPA

Menschen fliehen in Panik vor der Katastrophe in New York. FOTO AP

Kommentare, weitere Meldungen und Hintergründe zu der Anschlagserie in den USA auf den Seiten A 2, A 3, A 5 und „Das Thema" Seite B 1.

Bush: Eine nationale Tragödie

Schröder sichert den USA Solidarität zu

WASHINGTON/BERLIN (AP/RTR) In seiner ersten Reaktion auf den Anschlag auf das World Trade Center hat US-Präsident George W. Bush am Dienstag von einem „offensichtlichen Terroranschlag auf unser Land" gesprochen. „Heute hatten wir eine nationale Tragödie", erklärte der sichtlich bewegte Präsident in Sarasota im US-Staat Florida, wo er eine Rede zum Thema Bildung halten wollte.

Er kündigte an, „die Leute, die diese Tat begangen haben, zur Strecke zu bringen. Wir werden die Verantwortlichen für die Anschläge jagen und bestrafen". Bush wörtlich: „Die Entschlossenheit unserer großen Nation wird geprüft. Aber es besteht kein Zweifel daran: Wir werden der Welt zeigen, dass wir diese Prüfung bestehen. Anschließend bat Bush die Anwesenden, einen Moment inne zu halten und gemeinsam mit ihm im Stillen für die Opfer des Anschlags zu beten. Gleichzeitig teilte Bush mit, dass die Streitkräfte der USA nach den Terroranschlägen in New York und Washington in erhöhten Alarmzustand versetzt worden sind.

Derweil verurteilte in Berlin Bundeskanzler Gerhard Schröder die Anschläge in den USA als „Kriegserklärung gegen die gesamte zivilisierte Welt". „Wer diesen Terroristen hilft oder sie schützt, verstößt gegen alle fundamentalen Werte, die das Zusammenleben der Völker möglich machen", sagte Schröder am Dienstagabend. Er sicherte US-Präsident George W. Bush die uneingeschränkte Solidarität Deutschlands zu: „Die Anteilnahme aller Deutschen gilt den Opfern und den Angehörigen der Opfer." Er stehe in Verbindung mit seinen europäischen Amtskollegen und, soweit in der gegenwärtigen Lage möglich, auch mit der US-Regierung, sagte Schröder weiter.

Nach einem Treffen mit den Fraktionschefs des Deutschen Bundestages am Abend ergänzte der Kanzler, aus dieser Runde teilten alle seine Einschätzung, dass es sich um einen Angriff auf die gesamte zivilisierte Welt handele. Schröder sagte, die Bundesregierung habe verstärkte Sicherheitsvorkehrungen angeordnet. Dies betreffe vor allem die Transportwege, den Luftverkehr und Einrichtungen der USA in Deutschland. Es bestehe aber kein Anlass für weitergehende Beunruhigung, sagte der Regierungschef.

Laut Schröder liegen den Sicherheitsbehörden derzeit keine konkreten Hinweise für mögliche Anschläge in Deutschland vor. Zudem bot der Kanzler an, die Opposition ständig über neue Erkenntnisse der Sicherheitsbehörden zu informieren. Eine für Freitag geplante Reise nach Stockholm sagte Schröder ab.

Trauerbeflaggung in ganz Deutschland

Regierungserklärung zur Katastrophe in den USA - Feste abgesagt

BERLIN (EPD/AP/DPA) In Deutschland haben Regierung und Sicherheitsbehörden auf die Anschläge in den USA reagiert. Bundeskanzler Gerhard Schröder berief den Bundessicherheitsrat ein und informierte die Vorsitzenden der Bundestagsfraktionen und die Vorsitzenden der Bundestagsparteien über die Geschehnisse in den USA. An diesem Mittwoch wird Schröder im Bundestag eine Regierungserklärung abgeben. Der Bundesinnenminister ordnete für Dienstag und Mittwoch bundesweite Trauerbeflaggung an. Und während auch die beiden großen Kirchen in Deutschland mit Bestürzung auf die Ereignisse reagierten, sagten die FDP, die Grünen und die CSU wegen der Anschläge für Dienstagabend geplante Feste ab. CSU und bayerische Landesregierung hatten zum „Berliner Auftakt des Münchner Oktoberfestes" eingeladen, Grüne und FDP zu Sommerfesten. Auch der für den heutigen Mittwochabend vorgesehene Empfang wie auch die Eröffnungsfeier der Internationalen Automobilausstellung (IAA) in Frankfurt am Donnerstag wurden abgesagt. Die Veranstaltung selbst wird aber vom 13. bis 23. September stattfinden. Dagegen ist nach Ansicht des Münchner Oberbürgermeisters Christian Ude ungewiss, ob das Oktoberfest - vorgesehen vom 22. September bis 7. Oktober - in der bayerischen Landeshauptstadt veranstaltet werden kann.

MAIN-POST
WWW.MAINPOST.DE
DEUTSCHLAND, WÜRZBURG

12

4 Sonderseiten zum verheerendsten Anschlag der Geschichte

Rhein-Zeitung

Mittwoch, 12. September 2001

UNABHÄNGIGE TAGESZEITUNG

56. Jahrgang · Nr. 212 · G 5919
Einzelpreis DM 1,80 · Ausgabe RD · Diez

Tausende Tote: Terror-Angriff auf die USA versetzt die Welt in Angst

Entführte Flugzeuge stürzen auf World Trade Center und Pentagon – Präsident Bush will Verantwortliche „zur Strecke bringen"

Die berühmte Skyline von Manhattan in Flammen: Gestern Morgen starteten Selbstmordattentäter eine unfassbare Serie von Terroranschlägen. In der Metropole New York brach Panik aus, die Stadt stürzte ins Chaos. Ein zweiter Anschlag galt dem Verteidigungsministerium in Washington. Foto: ap

Weltweit Entsetzen, Fassungslosigkeit, Kriegsangst: Der internationale Terrorismus hat gestern die Supermacht USA mit den schrecklichsten Anschlägen der Geschichte herausgefordert.

NEW YORK/WASHINGTON. Die Welt trauert mit den USA um Tausende von Toten – wehrlose Opfer von Selbstmordangriffen auf Macht- und Finanzzentren in New York und Washington. Als Urheber vermuten die US-Geheimdienste den saudischen Millionär und mutmaßlichen Terroristenführer Osama bin Laden. US-Präsident George W. Bush, der zunächst zu einer sicheren Kommandobasis in Nebraska gebracht wurde, sprach von einer „nationalen Tragödie" und kündigte an, die Verantwortlichen „zur Strecke zu bringen". Die US-Streitkräfte wurden weltweit in höchste Alarmbereitschaft versetzt.

Mit zwei in den USA entführten Passagierjets brachten mehrere Selbstmordattentäter das New Yorker World Trade Center zum Einsturz. Am Abend brach auch noch ein drittes Hochhaus zusammen. In Washington wurde das Verteidigungsministerium (Pentagon) mit einem dritten Flugzeug teils zerstört, das Außenministerium mit einer Autobombe angegriffen. Eine vierte entführte Maschine stürzte bei Pittsburgh ab. Sie sollte offenbar den Präsidentenlandsitz Camp David zerstören. Kurz nach den Anschlägen in New York und Washington überschlugen sich die Ereignisse. Die Lage in beiden Städten war völlig chaotisch. Im amerikanischen Außenministerium brach Feuer aus. Das Parlamentsgebäude auf dem Kapitol und das Weiße Haus wurden ebenso evakuiert wie das UN-Gebäude in New York und die Börse in der Wall Street. Alle US-Flughäfen wurden geschlossen.

+++ THEMA DES TAGES +++

Kriegs-Szenen mitten in New York

Augenzeugen erlebten den blanken Horror

US-Standorte sind alarmiert

▶ Alles auf 4 Sonderseiten

Die apokalyptischen Szenen aus den USA haben auch Deutschland geschockt. Bundespräsident Johannes Rau schickte dem US-Präsidenten Bush ein Beileids-Telegramm. In Berlin berief Bundeskanzler Gerhard Schröder den Bundessicherheitsrat ein. Der Bundestag brach seine Haushaltsdebatte ab. In ganz Deutschland wurden die Sicherheitsvorkehrungen für Einrichtungen der USA und Israels sowie auf den Flughäfen verschärft. Die Finanzmärkte rund um den Globus wurden durch die Nachrichten aus den USA ins Chaos gestürzt. Die Börsen an der New Yorker Wall Street und die Rohstoff- und Terminmärkte in Chicago blieben geschlossen. Zwei radikale Palästinensergruppen bestritten jede Beteiligung an den Terrorakten. Der Chef der „Demokratischen Front für die Befreiung Palästinas", Kari Abdel Karim, erklärte etwa in Ramallah, die DFLP habe mit dem Attentat „absolut nichts zu tun". Auch die afghanischen radikalislamischen Taliban, die angeblich bin Laden beherbergen, schlossen ebenfalls eine Beteiligung kategorisch aus.

Viele Palästinenser im Südlibanon und in Beirut feierten die Terror-Serie und gaben Freudenschüsse ab. Palästinenserpräsident Jassir Arafat verurteilte die Anschläge hingegen „auf das Schärfste"

▶ Seite 2: Leitartikel

Amerika bis ins Mark erschüttert

Menschen weinten oder trauerten stumm

NEW YORK. Die Amerikaner sind fassungslos – und mit ihnen die ganze Welt. „Das ist das zweite Pearl Harbor", sagte US-Senator Chuck Hagel schockiert. Augenzeugen sprachen von Szenen wie aus einem Horrorfilm. Der New Yorker Bürgermeister Rudolph Giuliani befürchtet eine „furchtbare" Zahl von Opfern.

Das ganze Ausmaß der beispiellosen Terrortat blieb unabsehbar. „Selbst in Wochen können wir nicht alle Opfer ausgraben, die wohl unter diesen Trümmern liegen", sagte ein verzweifelter Feuerwehrmann. Im ganzen Land weinten die Menschen vor den Fernsehern oder saßen einfach nur stumm da, weil ihnen die Worte für das Grauen fehlten. Auf den Straßen vieler Städte war es kurzzeitig gespenstisch still, während New York und Washington im Chaos versanken.

In vielen Teilen der Welt herrschte Trauer, wurde der Opfer gedacht. Auch Papst Johannes Paul II. war bestürzt. Ein enger Mitarbeiter: „Vom ersten Moment an hat er für den ewigen Frieden der zahlreichen Opfer gebetet."

Szenen wie im Krieg: Verletzte Menschen fliehen in nackter Panik und rennen um ihr Leben. Für Tausende New Yorker kam jede Hilfe zu spät. Foto: ap

BÖRSE AKTUELL: +++ Heftiger Absturz +++ Schluss-DAX: 4273,53 (–396,60) +++ Versicherer unter Druck +++

Lokales

20 Diezer bangen um die „Rescue 1"

Das Schicksal der New Yorker Elite-Einheit „Rescue 1" ist ungewiss: Gestern hatten die Feuerwehr-Profis Einsatz im Inferno von Manhattan. 20 Männer der Freiwilligen Feuerwehr Diez/Freiendiez sind besonders in Sorge. Noch vor vier Jahren hatten sie mit ihren amerikanischen Kollegen auf dem World-Trade-Center gestanden. ▶ Seite 15

Sozialhilfe zahlt nun die VG

Die Würfel für die Sozialhilfe-Regelung in der Verbandsgemeinde Katzenelnbogen sind gefallen. Die VG übernimmt ab Januar 2002 den 25-Prozent-Anteil der Ortsgemeinden für Sozialhilfe-Beiträge, nachdem die Orte zunächst einzeln über das Für und Wider abgestimmt hatten. ▶ Seite 21

Sport

Champions League, erster Spieltag

Schalke 04	Panathinaikos Athen	0:2
Dynamo Kiew	Borussia Dortmund	2:2

UEFA-Cup, erste Runde, Hinspiel

SK Matador Puchov	SC Freiburg	0:0

▶ Seite 11

Volleyballer zahlen Lehrgeld

Drei Niederlagen in drei Spielen kassierten die deutschen Volleyballer bei der EM in Ostrau. Trotzdem ist Bundestrainer Stelian Moculescu vor den Spielen gegen Ungarn und Jugoslwien nicht unzufrieden. ▶ Seite 11

Panorama / Kultur

Chirurg operierte trotz Hepatitis

Ein Aachener Chirurg soll 20 seiner Patienten mit Hepatitis B angesteckt haben. Deshalb muss er sich vor Gericht verantworten. Die Staatsanwaltschaft wirft ihm vor, auch als sich die Infektionen in der Klinik gehäuft hätten, keine Konsequenzen gezogen zu haben. Wie dies geschehen konnte, lesen Sie auf Panorama. ▶ Seite 27

Der polnische Autor Lem wird 80

„Der Mensch ist ein Affe, dem es gelingt, das schärfste Rasiermesser zu schaffen, um einem anderen Affen die Kehle durchzuschneiden" – diese Sentenz hat der polnische Science-Fiction-Autor Stanislaw Lem verfasst. An die Stelle des einstigen Fortschrittglaubens ist bei ihm, der heute 80 Jahre alt wird, längst tiefe Skepsis getreten. ▶ Seite 28

Grafik des Tages

Attentate im Herzen der USA

USA
New York
Washington
Ein Großraumflugzeug stürzt nahe Pittsburgh ab.
Zwei Flugzeuge fliegen in die beiden Türme des World Trade Centers – beide Türme fallen später in sich zusammen.
New York
Pittsburgh
Washington
Ein Flugzeug stürzt auf das Pentagon. Teile des US-Verteidigungsministeriums sind zerstört.
ATLANTIK
500 km
12.9.2001

Der verheerende Terrorschlag in den USA: Zwei Flugzeuge prallten in das World Trade Center, ein Jet stürzte auf das Pentagon in Washington, ein weiterer stürzte ab.

Auf einen Blick

Wir für Sie

Vertrieb: 0261/892-123
Anzeigen: 0261/892-8
Redaktion: 0261/892-777

Rhein-Zeitung
www.rhein-zeitung.de
Deutschland, Koblenz

Trierischer Volksfreund

ST NR. 212/126. JAHRGANG
TRIERER ZEITUNG

Unabhängig • Überparteilich • Gegründet 1875

MITTWOCH, 12. SEPTEMBER 2001
EINZELPREIS 1,90 DM/45 LuF/BeF

RHEINLAND-PFALZ

Kampf der „Zerspargelung“: CDU macht gegen Windkraft mobil. S. 6

LOKALES

Konkurrenz belebt das Geschäft: Basten und Kaster wollen für Triers CDU in den Bundestag. S. 7

SPORT

Körbeweise Absagen: HERZOGtel-Basketballer suchen noch immer einen Namenssponsor. S. 15

KULTUR

Genie aus der Kornflasche: Janssen-Radierungen in der Akademie Kues. S. 21

TERRORISMUS

Die Welt unter Schock

Schreckliche Anschläge in den USA fordern tausende Todesopfer

WASHINGTON/BERLIN/TRIER. (dpa/sey/wy) Der internationale Terrorismus hat die Supermacht USA mit den schrecklichsten Anschlägen der Geschichte herausgefordert. Die mit großer Präzision ausgeführten Selbstmordangriffe in New York und Washington kosteten Tausende von Menschenleben. Als Urheber vermuten die Geheimdienste den saudischen Millionär und Terroristenführer Osama bin Laden.

Mit zwei in den USA entführten Passagierflugzeugen brachten mehrere Selbstmordattentäter das berühmte New Yorker World Trade Center zum Einsturz. In Washington wurde das Verteidigungsministerium mit einem weiteren Flugzeug teilweise zerstört, die Explosion einer Autobombe vor dem Außenministerium wurde offiziell nicht bestätigt. Eine vierte entführte Maschine stürzte bei Pittsburgh ab. US-Präsident George W. Bush sprach von einer „nationalen Tragödie“ und versprach: „Wir werden die Täter zur Strecke bringen und bestrafen.“ Die Anschläge lösten weltweit Entsetzen und verschärfte Sicherheitsvorkehrungen aus.

Gilt als Terror-Drahtzieher: Osama bin Laden.

Zunächst rasten am Morgen (Ortszeit) innerhalb von 18 Minuten zwei Flugzeuge ins World Trade Center in New York. Das Symbol der Finanzmacht USA an der Südspitze Manhattans mit den beiden 110 Stockwerke hohen Zwillingstürmen ging in Rauch und Flammen auf und stürzten etwa eine Stunde später in sich zusammen. Die Behörden in New York rechneten mit tausenden Toten. In Washington zerstörte eine weitere abstürzende Maschine teilweise das US-Verteidigungsministerium (Pentagon). Die Lage in beiden Städten war völlig chaotisch.

Die apokalyptischen Szenen aus den USA haben auch Deutschland geschockt. In Berlin berief Bundeskanzler Gerhard Schröder den Bundessicherheitsrat ein. Der Bundestag brach seine Haushaltsdebatte ab. Am Reichstag wehten die Fahnen auf Halbmast. In ganz Deutschland wurden die Sicherheitsvorkehrungen für Einrichtungen der USA und Israels sowie auf den Flughäfen verschärft. Auf der US-Airbase Spangdahlem ordneten die Militärs die höchste Alarmstufe („Delta“) an. Für die Finanzmetropole Frankfurt empfahl die hessische Landesregierung für heute die Schließung der „symbolträchtigen“ Hochhäuser. Zahlreiche Flüge in die USA wurden gestrichen. Aus dem Bundesamt für Verfassungsschutz verlautete, es gebe keine Hinweise auf geplante terroristische Angriffe in Deutschland.

Bundeskanzler Gerhard Schröder verurteilte die Anschläge als „Kriegserklärung gegen die gesamte zivilisierte Welt“.

Pendler nach Luxemburg sollten ab sofort wieder ihre Personalausweise bei sich tragen – im Großherzogtum muss mit verstärkten Kontrollen gerechnet werden.

Angriff auf das World Trade Center in New York: Der hintere der beiden Zwillingstürme ist bereits von einem Flugzeug getroffen und steht in Flammen, die zweite Maschine rast heran (links) und bohrt sich Sekunden später in den zweiten Tower. Fotos: dpa/Pentagon

Mehrere radikale Palästinensergruppen bestritten jede Beteiligung an den Terrorakten. Die afghanischen radikal-islamischen Taliban, die angeblich bin Laden beherbergen, schlossen ebenfalls eine Beteiligung kategorisch aus und bestritten jeden Kontakt mit dem angeblichen Terroristenchef. Zahlreiche Palästinenser in den Flüchtlingscamps in Südlibanon und in Beirut feierten die Terrorserie und feuerten Freudenschüsse in die Luft. Palästinenserpräsident Jassir Arafat verurteilte die Anschläge „auf das Schärfste“.

Nach den Anschlägen hat das Auswärtige Amt in Berlin eine Hotline für Angehörige eingerichtet. Die Nummer lautet 01888-174600. Auch die Fluglinie American Airlines hat ein Notruftelefon in Deutschland eingerichtet. Unter der Nummer 069/50 98 50 70 könnten sich Angehörige von Passagieren oder Mitarbeitern mit der Fluggesellschaft in Verbindung setzen.

KOMMENTAR SEITE 2
THEMEN DER ZEIT SEITEN 3,4
@ www.intrinet.de/aktuell

DIE BÖRSE

DAX	Euro
4273,53	0,8964 $
Vortag 4670,13	Vortag 0,9074

Der Schock über die Terroranschläge in den USA hat an der Deutschen Börse zu den großen Verlusten geführt. SEITEN 5

INHALT

LESERSERVICE

Telefon 0651/7199-0
TV-Abo-Service: 0651/7199-998
TV-Anzeigenannahme: 0651/7199-999
Internet: www.intrinet.de

WETTER

15 / 10

FUSSBALL

Schalker Fehlstart

GELSENKIRCHEN. (red) Der FC Schalke 04 hat in der Champions League eine böse Überraschung erlebt. Der Fußball-Bundesligist verlor sein erstes Spiel in der „Königsklasse“ überraschend mit 0:2 gegen Panathinaikos Athen. Revier-Rivale Borussia Dortmund schaffte dagegen nach einem 0:2-Rückstand bei Dynamo Kiew noch ein 2:2. Im Uefa-Cup erreichte der SC Freiburg ein 0:0 beim slowakischen Vertreter SK Matador Puchow und wahrte damit die Chance auf das erstmalige Erreichen der zweiten Runde.

SPORT SEITE 15

KERNENERGIE

Bangen in Cattenom

Grund für Reaktorschäden noch immer unklar

CATTENOM. (wy) Wenn Block drei der vier Atomreaktoren im lothringischen Cattenom beim Ankoppeln an das elektrische Netz am Wochenende wieder Probleme macht, wird er abgeschaltet.

Diese Zusicherung gab der Direktor der Anlage, Dominique Minière, gestern vor Journalisten in Cattenom. Block drei war Ende Januar zu einer Zehnjahres-Revision abgeschaltet worden. Dabei war festgestellt worden, dass 26 Brennstäbe beschädigt und einer gebrochen war. Die Behebung der Schäden hatte sich als so schwierig herausgestellt, dass der Reaktor vier Monate länger als geplant abgeschaltet blieb. Die Schäden sollen durch Vibrationen im Reaktor-Kern entstanden sein. Der Grund dafür ist trotz umfangreicher Untersuchungen noch nicht bekannt. Minière bestätigte Meldungen des *TV*, wonach es Anzeichen gebe, dass auch in Block vier mit beschädigten Brennstäben zu rechnen sei. Dieser Block wird Ende November zum Austausch von Brennelementen abgeschaltet.

KOMMENTAR SEITE 2
RHEINLAND-PFALZ SEITE 6

TV-SERIE

Klagen: Ja Krise: Nein

TRIER/FRANKFURT. (bl) Über 80 Prozent der Funktionen in Sportvereinen werden durch ehrenamtliche Mitarbeiter besetzt. „Das Ehrenamt ist unersetzbar“, sagt deshalb Christoph Niessen, Geschäftsführer des Sportbunds Rheinland. Trotz der Klagen vieler Sportvereine, Hilfskräfte, Vorstandsmitglieder oder Übungsleiter zu finden, will Manfred von Richthofen, Präsident des Deutschen Sportbundes, nicht von einer Krise sprechen. Im *TV*-Gespräch plädiert er aber für verbesserte Rahmenbedingungen im Ehrenamt.

SPORT SEITE 17

HAUSHALT

Rot-Grün hält an Sparkurs fest

BERLIN. (dpa) Die rot-grüne Bundesregierung hält unvermindert an ihrem strikten Sparkurs fest. Bundesfinanzminister Hans Eichel (SPD) wies bei der Einbringung des Haushalts 2002 die Forderung der Opposition nach neuen Steuersenkungen auf Pump zurück. Die Opposition warf der Bundesregierung vor, fast alle ihre haushaltspolitischen Zahlen liefen in die falsche Richtung. Der Haushalt gerate aus den Fugen. Die Beratungen wurden wegen der Terroranschläge in den USA am Nachmittag unterbrochen.

BERICHT/KOMMENTAR SEITE 2

FLUG-AFFÄRE

Schweres Geschütz gegen Scharping

Minister soll bei Mazedonien-Einsatz Großbritannien brüskiert haben – Eklat vor Verteidigungsausschuss

BERLIN. (dpa) Verteidigungsminister Rudolf Scharping (SPD) hat sich offenbar erneut selbst unter Druck gebracht. Bei seiner abschließenden Befragung vor dem Verteidigungsausschuss kam es zu einem Eklat.

Nach Angaben der Opposition hat Scharping im Ausschuss außenpolitische Informationen vorgetragen und damit möglicherweise einen der wichtigsten Bündnispartner Deutschlands, Großbritannien, brüskiert. Scharping seinerseits wirft der Opposition nun Bruch der Vertraulichkeit vor.

„Scharping hat heute das i-Tüpfelchen gesetzt. Die Affäre gewinnt eine außenpolitische Dimension“, sagte der CDU-Verteidigungspolitiker Paul Breuer. Der Minister sei nun endgültig nicht mehr haltbar. Die Opposition erwägt noch in dieser Woche einen Entlassungsantrag. Wegen der Geheimhaltung wollte Breuer keine Einzelheiten über den Auftritt Scharpings nennen, der auch bei anderen Mitgliedern des Ausschusses für Empörung sorgte.

Scharping soll vor dem Ausschuss ohne Aufforderung berichtet haben, dass sich der deutsche Aufmarsch in Mazedonien verzögert habe, weil Großbritannien zwar Hilfestellung zugesagt, diese dann aber nicht gewährt habe. Auf Fragen, ob dies eine „Verschwörung“ der Briten gegen die Deutschen gewesen sei, habe Scharping ausweichend geantwortet, hieß es in Teilnehmer-Kreisen. Den ersten Hinweis auf Probleme mit den Briten soll im Ausschuss Generalinspekteur Harald Kujat gegeben haben. Scharping habe dann gesagt, er wolle offen darüber reden, hieß es. Der Staatssekretär im Verteidigungsministerium Walther Stützle habe Kujat anschließend vor der Tür wegen des Vorgangs „angeschrien“.

Scharping warf nun seinerseits Oppositionspolitikern aus dem Verteidigungsausschuss einen Bruch der Vertraulichkeit vor. Es müsse für dem Verteidigungsminister möglich sein, „in einer vertraulichen Sitzung auch vertrauliche Informationen zu geben“, sagte Scharping am Dienstag.

Dem Fernsehmagazin „Spiegel TV“ warf er noch einmal „üble Manipulation“ vor. Es habe für einen Beitrag über eine Pressekonferenz des Ministers in Mazedonien Abläufe verändert und Bilder zusammengeschnitten, sagte Scharping. Er habe dem Ausschuss die ungeschnittenen Bilder gezeigt. Die Manipulation werde Konsequenzen haben. „Spiegel TV“ wies die Vorwürfe zurück. Es seien weder Abläufe verändert noch Zitate des Ministers zusammengeschnitten worden. Die Darstellung werde auch durch die Berichte anderer Medien bestätigt.

Trierischer Volksfreund
www.trierischervolksfreund.de
Deutschland, Trier

12

Frankfurter Rundschau

Unabhängige Tageszeitung

Mittwoch, 12. September 2001 · Jahrgang 57 · Nr. 212/37 · www.fr-aktuell.de · *D-Ausgabe · Preis 2,00 DM · D 2972

5 Seiten zur Eröffnung der IAA — Sonderseiten A 1 – A 5

Diesel-Kraftstoff soll genauso besteuert werden wie Benzin, fordert Andreas Troge, Präsident des Umweltbundesamtes, im *FR*-Interview. Ökologische Gründe für den Rabatt gebe es nicht. — Interview, Sonderseite A 3

Sachsens CDU, einst vom Erfolg verwöhnt, ist in zwei Lager gespalten. Auf dem Parteitag wird nun abgerechnet: Milbradt, der Herausforderer, gegen Flath, das Werkzeug Biedenkopfs. — Aus den Bundesländern, Seite 7

Transatlantische Irritationen: Während die deutschen Hochschulen auf amerikanische Effizienz getrimmt werden, triumphiert in den USA das Humboldtsche Bildungsideal. — Feuilleton, Seite 17

Freie Aussprache	8
Wirtschaft	9 – 14
Sport	15, 16
Feuilleton	17 – 19
Roman	19
Fernsehen und Funk	21, 22
Hessen	27, 28
Kino	A 8

Heute mit den Rubriken:
Automarkt
Wohnungs- und Immobilienmarkt
Stellenanzeigen

Verheerende Terrorserie erschüttert die USA

World Trade Center und Pentagon mit entführten Flugzeugen zerstört / Tausende Tote befürchtet

Die USA sind am Dienstag von den schwersten Terroranschlägen ihrer Geschichte erschüttert worden. Dabei wurden die beiden Türme des World Trade Centers in New York völlig und das US-Verteidigungsministerium in Washington teilweise zerstört. New Yorks Bürgermeister Rudolph Giuliani sprach von einer „gewaltigen Zahl von Toten" und rief die Einwohner auf, das südliche Manhattan zu verlassen. Zunächst war nicht bekannt, wer hinter den Anschlägen steckt. US-Präsident George W. Bush machte Terroristen verantwortlich und kündigte Vergeltung an. Das Weiße Haus, alle Schlüsselministerien und andere wichtige Gebäude in den USA wurden evakuiert, sämtliche Flughäfen und Grenzen geschlossen.

WASHINGTON/NEW YORK. 11. September (ap/afp/dpa/rtr). Zwei vermutlich entführte Passagierflugzeuge rasten am Dienstag gegen 9 Uhr morgens (Ortszeit) im Abstand von 18 Minuten in die Zwillingstürme des World Trade Centers. Die 411 Meter hohen Gebäude gingen nach schweren Explosionen in Flammen auf und stürzten etwa eine Stunde später in sich zusammen. Über die Zahl der Toten und Verletzten gab es zunächst keine Angaben; sie kann in die Tausende gehen. Wahrscheinlich seien außer den Insassen der Flugzeuge zahlreiche Menschen innerhalb der beiden Wolkenkratzer getötet und tausende weitere verletzt worden, hieß es. In den beiden Türmen arbeiteten normalerweise rund 50 000 Menschen.

Der US-Sender CNN berichtete von Massenevakuierungen in New York. Alle Brücken und Tunnel nach Manhattan wurden geschlossen. Giuliani rief die Einwohner auf, „Ruhe zu bewahren und so weit sie können Süd-Manhattan zu verlassen". In Manhattan explodierte offenbar ein weiteres Gebäude.

Vermutlich waren beide Maschinen, die das World Trade Center rammten, zuvor entführt worden. Nach US-Angaben handelte es sich bei einer Maschine um eine Boeing 767, die in Boston gestartet war. Das zweite Flugzeug wurde offenbar in Newark (New Jersey) entführt. American Airlines bestätigte den Verlust zweier Maschinen mit insgesamt 156 Passagieren an Bord, und United Airlines meldete den Absturz zweier weiterer Maschinen mit insgesamt 131 Passagieren an Bord. Eine davon ging in der Nähe von Pittsburgh (Pennsylvania) zu Boden, über die zweite gab es keine näheren Angaben.

Weitere Berichte auf den Seiten 2, 3 und 4, Kommentar Seite 3

Kurz nach den Anschlägen auf das World Trade Center stürzte ein Flugzeug auf das Verteidigungsministerium (Pentagon) in Washington. Es war zunächst nicht klar, ob es sich um eines dabei der beiden United Airlines-Flugzeuge handelte. Vor dem Außenministerium in Washington explodierte nach Angaben der Polizei eine Autobombe. CNN berichtete von einem Feuer im Ministeriumsgebäude.

Nach den Anschlägen wurden sämtliche Flughäfen in den USA geschlossen. Der Luftraum über New York wurde gesperrt. Alle Transatlantik-Flüge in die USA wurden nach Kanada umgeleitet.

Präsident George W. Bush sprach in einer ersten Reaktion von einem „offenkundigen Terroranschlag auf unser Land". In Sarasota (Florida) sagte er: „Wir erleben heute eine nationale Tragödie." Bush kündigte Vergeltung an. Die USA würden die für die Tat Verantwortlichen jagen und „die Leute, die diese Tat begangen haben, zur Strecke bringen". Er versetzte das US-Militär im In- und Ausland in erhöhte Alarmbereitschaft.

Nach Angaben von Journalisten will Bush vorerst nicht nach Washington zurückkehren. Er habe beschlossen, die Hauptstadt zunächst zu meiden. Den Angaben zufolge flog er nach Louisiana.

Zunächst war nicht bekannt, wer hinter den Anschlägen steckt. Die palästinensischen Gruppen DFLP (Demokratische Front für die Befreiung Palästinas), PFLP Volksfront für die Befreiung Palästinas und die radikal-islamische Hamas teilten mit, ihre Organisationen hätten nichts mit den Terrorakten zu tun. Aus US-Geheimdienstkreisen verlautete, die Urheber der Taten seien nicht bekannt.

Aus US-Regierungskreisen war zu hören, einiges spreche dafür, dass es sich um Personen handle, die mit dem saudi-arabischen Extremisten Osama bin Laden in Verbindung stehen. Nach Angaben des Journalisten Abdel Bari Atwan von der in London erscheinenden Zeitung *El Kuds es Arabi* steht bin Laden hinter den Anschlägen auf das World Trade Center. Bin Laden habe vor etwa drei Wochen angekündigt, in den USA einen noch nie dagewesenen Anschlag zu verüben. Atwan hatte bin Laden mehrmals interviewt und steht in engem Kontakt zu dessen Anhängern. Die radikal-islamischen afghanischen Taliban bestritten eine Verwicklung bin Ladens.

New York am Dienstag: Einer der Türme des World Trade Centers bricht zusammen. Kurz darauf stürzt auch der zweite ein. (Bild: ap/ABC)

Schröder wertet Anschläge als „Kriegserklärung"

Weltweit Bestürzung über Terror/Nato sieht Angriff auf Demokratie/Freude bei Palästinensern

Mit großer Bestürzung haben westliche Staaten und Russland auf die Anschläge in den USA reagiert. Bundeskanzler Gerhard Schröder berief den nationalen Sicherheitsrat ein und bezeichnete die Anschläge als „Kriegserklärung gegen die gesamte Welt". Weltweit sagten Fluglinien ihre Flüge in die USA ab. In den Flüchtlingslagern in Libanon feuerten Palästinenser Freudensalven in die Luft. Palästinenserpräsident Yassir Arafat verurteilte die Anschläge. Israel räumte weltweit seine Botschaften.

FRANKFURT A. M., 11. September (dpa/rtr/afp/ap). Die Europäische Union äußerte sich schockiert über die Anschläge. Der EU-Ratsvorsitzende, Belgiens Ministerpräsident Guy Verhofstadt, verurteilte am Dienstag im Namen der EU „mit allem Nachdruck diese grausamen Taten, denen unschuldige Menschen aus der Zivilbevölkerung zum Opfer fallen".

Nato-Generalsekretär George Robertson verurteilte die Anschläge. „Diese barbarischen Akte stellen eine nicht zu tolerierende Aggression gegen die Demokratie dar und unterstreichen die Notwendigkeit, dass die internationale Gemeinschaft und die Mitgliedstaaten der Allianz ihre Kräfte vereinigen, um die Geißel des Terrorismus zu bekämpfen", erklärte Robertson in Brüssel. Für das US-Militär in Europa gilt die höchste Sicherheitsstufe.

Bundesaußenminister Joschka Fischer versicherte seinem US-amerikanischen Amtskollegen Colin Powell Mitgefühl für die Opfer. „Wir fühlen mit den Opfern und ihren Angehörigen. Deutschland steht angesichts dieses furchtbaren Verbrechens fest an der Seite des amerikanischen Volkes", hieß es in einem Schreiben an Powell. Auch Bundespräsident Johannes Rau bekundete in einem Schreiben an US-Präsident George W. Bush sein Mitleid.

Bundeskanzler Gerhard Schröder (SPD) will am heutigen Mittwoch eine Regierungserklärung zu den Terrorakten abgeben, anschließend kommt der Sicherheitsrat erneut zusammen. Das kündigte eine Sprecherin der Bundesregierung an. Der Bundestag brach am Nachmittag seine Beratungen über den Haushalt 2002 ab und setzte die für Mittwoch geplanten weiteren Beratungen von der Tagesordnung.

Alle Flüge von Deutschland mit Ziel USA wurden vorläufig gestoppt. Das teilte die Flugsicherung in Frankfurt am Main mit. Eine Sprecherin sagte, die Bundesregierung habe den Flugstopp angeordnet.

Russlands Präsident Wladimir Putin sprach der Bevölkerung der USA seine Anteilnahme aus und bezeichnete die Anschläge als „terroristischen Akt". Das russische Militär versetzte die gesamte Flugabwehr in Gefechtsbereitschaft, berichtete die Nachrichtenagentur Interfax.

In den Flüchtlingslagern in Libanon gaben Palästinenser Freudenschüsse ab. Viele Menschen schossen in die Luft, als sie die Nachrichten von den Explosionen in den USA hörten, wie ein Korrespondent der Agentur afp meldete. Palästinenserpräsident Arafat verurteilte die Anschläge: „Wir waren völlig geschockt. Es ist unglaublich." Auch Ägyptens Präsident Hosni Mubarak verurteilte den Terror.

Israel räumte nach den Anschlägen sämtliche Botschaften und andere öffentliche Einrichtungen. Israel sperrte seinen Luftraum für ausländische Flugzeuge.

Die afghanische Taliban-Führung bezeichnete die Anschläge der pakistanischen Nachrichtenagentur AIP zufolge als „terroristischen Akt".

Zuwanderungsgesetz

Justizressort wendet sich gegen Schilys Entwurf

vgo BERLIN, 11. September. Bundesinnenminister Otto Schilys Entwurf für ein Zuwanderungsgesetz stößt auf massive Vorbehalte im Bundeskabinett. In einer 80-seitigen Stellungnahme kritisiert das Justizministerium etliche Regelungen des Vorhabens als „verfassungsrechtlich bedenklich" und „nicht europatauglich". In seiner amtlichen Stellungnahme, die der *FR* vorliegt, stuft das Ressort unter anderem als fragwürdig ein, dass nach Schilys Plänen der Umfang der Arbeitsmigration allein von der Regierung und ohne Parlamentsbeteiligung festgelegt werden soll.

Bei einem Treffen zwischen Fachpolitikern von SPD, Grünen und dem Innenministerium gab es am Dienstag keine Annäherung. Die Zahl der zu klärenden Punkte sei sogar „einvernehmlich erhöht" worden, so ein Teilnehmer. Der parlamentarische Geschäftsführer der SPD-Fraktion, Wilhelm Schmidt, schloss ein Scheitern des Reformplans nicht mehr aus. Die Grünen-Landtagsfraktion in Nordrhein-Westfalen beschloss ihr Nein zum Schily-Entwurf. Demnach müsste sich NRW im Bundesrat der Stimme enthalten.

Kommentar Seite 3, Bericht Seite 5

Rabins Tochter wirbt für Dialog

Israels Vize-Verteidigungsministerin setzt auf Verhandlungen

Israels Vize-Verteidigungsministerin Dalia Rabin-Pelosoff hat eingeräumt, dass mit militärischen Optionen allein kein Ausweg aus dem Nahost-Konflikt zu finden ist. In einem – vor der Katastrophe in den USA geführten – *FR*-Interview sagte die Politikerin der Arbeitspartei, in Israel „ist man sich inzwischen bewusst, dass es keine militärische Lösung in diesem Konflikt gibt".

JERUSALEM, 11. September (geg/ap/rtr/afp). Letztendlich sei eine Lösung des Konflikts mit den Palästinensern „nur in der politischen Arena zu finden", sagte Rabin-Pelosoff. Insofern unterstütze sie ein Treffen zwischen Außenminister Schimon Peres und Palästinenserpräsident Yassir Arafat, um das sich seit Wochen auch EU-Politiker bemühen. Die stellvertretende Verteidigungsministerin warf Arafat zwar vor, den palästinensischen „Terror zu dirigieren". Aber man könne sich den Führer der Palästinenser nicht aussuchen.

Nach einem israelischen Panzervorstoß in der Nacht zum Dienstag auf die autonome Stadt Dschenin sagten Palästinenser ein für den Abend geplantes Treffen zwischen Arafat und Peres zunächst ab. Eine generelle Absage sei aber nicht zu erwarten, hieß es. Bei dem Panzereinsatz seien acht Palästinenser verletzt worden, teilte eine Klinik mit. Nach Angaben der israelischen Armee diente die Aktion dazu, palästinensische Selbstmordattentäter von Anschlägen in Israel abzuhalten.

FR-INTERVIEW

Konfliktlösung braucht einen Dialog, sagt Rabin-Pelosoff. Auf Seite 6.

Palästinenser erschossen im Norden Israels zwei Israelis. Ein weiterer Israeli wurde bei der Schießerei in der Nacht zum Dienstag nahe dem Kibbuz Magal verletzt, wie der israelische Militärrundfunk weiter meldete. Der Angriff auf die Israelis fand in der Nähe der Demarkationslinie zum Westjordanland nördlich der autonom verwalteten Palästinenserstadt Tulkarem statt.

Märkte nach den Attentaten

Kurse stürzen, Öl teurer

msy FRANKFURT A. M., 11. September. Auch an den Börsen haben die Anschläge in den USA Entsetzen ausgelöst. Die Kurse fielen weltweit deutlich. In New York blieb der Aktienhandel den gesamten Tag geschlossen. Der Deutsche Aktienindex verlor binnen Minuten mehr als ein Zehntel und notierte kurz vor Handelsende mit einem Tagesminus von acht Prozent bei 4275 Zählern. Der Euro stieg, weil die Unsicherheit über die Entwicklung in den USA Dollarverkäufe im großen Stil auslöste. Die europäische Gemeinschaftswährung kletterte um weit mehr als einen Cent auf über 0,91 Dollar.

Auch die Preise für Öl und Benzin zogen sofort kräftig an. Für ein Barrel (159 Liter) der Nordsee-Ölsorte wurden 29,60 Dollar verlangt – 2,15 Dollar mehr als vor den Anschlägen. Mit Benzinpreiserhöhungen ist nach Aussage eines Esso-Sprechers zu rechnen. *Bericht Wirtschaft*

D 2972

Ihr Sieg vor Gericht bringt die Flüchtlinge Australien noch nicht näher

Bundesrichter gibt „Tampa"-Asylsuchenden Recht auf Einreise – doch vorerst sind sie weiter unterwegs nach Nauru

Von Boris B. Behrsing (Canberra)

Die mehr als 400 Flüchtlinge vom Frachter „Tampa" dürfen nach Australien einreisen. Das entschied ein Bundesgericht in Melbourne am Dienstag gegen den Willen der australischen Regierung. Canberra legte umgehend Berufung ein. Unterdessen hielt der Marinetransporter „Manoora" mit den überwiegend afghanischen Flüchtlingen Kurs auf die Pazifikinsel Nauru.

Nicht einmal Stehplätze gab es noch im Sitzungssaal des australischen Bundesgerichts in Melbourne, als Richter Tony North am Dienstag sein mit Spannung erwartetes Urteil im Falle der Flüchtlinge vom norwegischen Frachter „Tampa" verkündete. Quintessenz des Richterspruchs: Die Regierung des konservativen Premierministers John Winston Howard handelte illegal, als sie die Flüchtlinge nicht auf der zu Australien zählenden Weihnachtsinsel an Land ließ. Die „Tampa" hatte die Menschen am 26. August von einem sinkenden indonesischen Schiff gerettet. Australiens Regierung nahm sie auf dem Frachter in Haft, ließ sie von 45 schwer bewaffneten Soldaten bewachen und auf die „Manoora" bringen. Dagegen klagten Menschenrechtsgruppen vor dem Bundesgericht.

Richter North sagte in seiner Urteilsbegründung: „Es ist ein altes Recht des Gerichts, Menschen vor Inhaftierung zu schützen, die ohne gesetzliche Autorität erfolgt." Hunderte von Menschenrechts-Aktivisten jubelten auf den Straßen Melbournes nach der Verkündung.

Nach dem Urteil muss die Regierung die Asylsuchenden bis Freitag, 17 Uhr Ortszeit, nach Australien bringen. Der australische Truppentransporter „Manoora" hat indes einen Großteil seiner Reise zu dem kleinen pazifischen Eiland Nauru hinter sich gebracht. Für ein Hilfspaket im Wert von umgerechnet 22 Millionen Mark hat sich die Inselrepublik bereit erklärt, die in Australien unerwünschten Flüchtlinge vorübergehend aufzunehmen. Frei sein werden sie allerdings auch dort nicht: Australien liefert auf dem Luftweg Drahtzäune, die um die Unterkünfte aufgestellt werden sollen.

Canberra kritisierte die Entscheidung des Bundesgerichts scharf und legte Berufung ein. Die „Manoora" werde nicht umkehren, erklärte Einwanderungsminister Philip Ruddock. Verteidigungsminister Peter Reith sagte, es sei das Recht jeder Regierung, darüber zu entscheiden, wer einreisen dürfe. Die Flüchtlinge hätten viel Geld bezahlt, um australisches Recht zu brechen. Das Urteil ist ein schwerer Schlag gegen die von der Regierung Howard eingeschlagene unerbittlich harte Politik der Absperrung Australiens gegenüber Asylsuchenden.

Ursprünglich sollten die Flüchtlinge nach Papua-Neuguinea gebracht und mit Flugzeugen nach Neuseeland und Nauru transportiert werden. Nun soll es, wie am Dienstag aus dem Verteidigungsministerium verlautete, direkt nach Nauru gehen. Voraussichtlich werden die Flüchtlinge aber noch auf dem Marineschiff bleiben müssen, bis über die Berufung entschieden ist.

Auf der „Manoora" befinden sich seit dem Wochenende mehr als 200 weitere Flüchtlinge, die auf hoher See gestoppt und an Bord gebracht wurden. Zudem lief vor der australischen Nordküste am Dienstag ein indonesisches Fischerboot mit etwa 130 Menschen an Bord auf ein Riff. Auch bei ihnen soll es sich Agenturangaben zufolge um afghanische Flüchtlinge handeln. Australien bemühte sich, das Boot wieder seetauglich zu machen und nach Indonesien zurückzuschicken. Sollte das misslingen, würden auch diese 130 Asylsuchenden nach Nauru gebracht, sagte Außenminister Alexander Downer.

Das Wetter

Meist regnerisch

FRANKFURT A. M., 11. September (FR). Überwiegend bedeckt mit Regen und Schauern, im Norden und Osten teils sonnig. Höchsttemperaturen bis 18 Grad. Weitere Aussichten: regnerisch. *Siehe Seite 8*

Frankfurter Rundschau
60266 Frankfurt am Main
Telefon 069/21991, Fax 069/2199-3421
Anzeigenannahme Telefon 0800/2020100
Anzeigenannahme Fax 069/1310030
Vertrieb-Leserservice:
Tel. 069/21993478, Fax 069/2199-3264
Internet: www.fr-aktuell.de

Frankfurter Rundschau
www.f-r.de
Deutschland, Frankfurt

12

Wenn Roboter zu sehr lieben – Spielbergs Film „A. I.“ / *Seite 29*

STUTTGARTER ZEITUNG

Nr. 211 – 37. W. / 57. Jahrgang – E 4029 | F | MITTWOCH, 12. SEPTEMBER 2001 | DM 1,80 sfr 2,20 / öS 16 / Ft 260 / Lire 2700 / ffr 9 / bfr 50 / hfl 2,70 Ptas 230 / TD 1,90 / KN 12 / Esc 280 (cont.) / Dr 450 / TL 1 650 000

DER ANSCHLAG

Jagd auf die Schuldigen

Augenzeugen sprechen von der Apokalypse. Der Anschlag auf das World Trade Center ist Teil einer Kette grausigen Ausmaßes. Die Terrorakte rauben der Weltmacht Amerika binnen weniger Stunden das Gefühl der Unverletzlichkeit. Die USA haben den Wettlauf mit dem Terror verloren. Seite 3

Der Anschlag von 1993

Auf das World Trade Center ist schon einmal ein Anschlag verübt worden. Ende Februar 1993 sind durch einen Bombenanschlag von Islamisten sechs Menschen getötet und über tausend verletzt worden. Seite 5

Symbol in Trümmern

Die Zwillingstürme im Herzen von New York waren eine Stadt für sich. Mehr als 50 000 Menschen arbeiteten in den beiden Gebäuden. Die schlanke Silhouette der hoch aufragenden Türme galten weltweit als Symbol für Amerika. Seite 5

Die Chronik der Katastrophe

Um 14.56 Uhr kündigt die Deutsche Presse-Agentur die Katastrophe mit einer Eilmeldung an. Vierzig Minuten später spricht Präsident Bush von einem „terroristischen Anschlag auf unsere Nation“. Dann geschieht das Unfassbare: Beide Türme stürzen ein. Seite 5

Qualm über Manhattan: Ein beispielloser Terrorakt vernichtet das World Trade Center im Zentrum von New York Foto AP

Angriff auf Amerika: Tausende Tote in New York

Flugzeuge treffen World Trade Center und Pentagon – Präsident Bush nennt Terroranschläge eine „nationale Tragödie“

NEW YORK (AP/dpa/rtr). Eine beispiellose Terrorserie hat gestern die Wirtschafts- und Machtzentren der USA erschüttert. Innerhalb von 18 Minuten rasten zwei Flugzeuge ins New Yorker World Trade Center, wenig später eine weitere Maschine ins Verteidigungsministerium. Die beiden Türme des World Trade Center stürzten ein. Die Behörden rechnen mit tausenden von Toten.

Kurz nach den Anschlägen überschlugen sich die Ereignisse, die Lage war völlig chaotisch. Teile des Pentagons stürzten ein, auch im Außenministerium brach Feuer aus. Das Parlamentsgebäude und das Weiße Haus wurden evakuiert, ebenso das Gebäude der Vereinten Nationen in New York. Die Börse und sämtliche Flughäfen in den Vereinigten Staaten wurden geschlossen. Der Fernsehsender CNN berichtete von Massenevakuierungen in New York. Bei dem Flugzeuganschlag ist nach Angaben des New Yorker Bürgermeisters Rudolph Giuliani eine „gewaltige Zahl von Menschen“ ums Leben gekommen.

Die Anschläge mit zumindest einem entführten Verkehrsflugzeug lösten weltweit Entsetzen aus. Präsident George Bush sprach in seiner ersten Reaktion von einem Terrorakt. Es handle sich um eine „nationale Tragödie“, sagte Bush, der zum Zeitpunkt des Attentats in Sarasota (Florida) weilte. Nato-Generalsekretär George Robertson hat die Anschläge in den USA als barbarische Akte und nicht hinnehmbaren Angriff auf die Demokratie verurteilt. Die Attentate zeigten, dass die internationale Gemeinschaft und die Mitglieder der Nato ihre Kräfte für den Kampf gegen Terrorismus vereinen müssten.

Die weltbekannten Zwillingstürme des World Trade Center, in denen täglich 40 000 Menschen arbeiten, gingen nach schweren Explosionen in Flammen auf. Hunderte Menschen flohen in Panik aus dem Gebäude. Eine Stunde nach den ersten Angriffen auf die beiden Hochhäuser erschütterte eine weitere schwere Explosion den südlichen Turm. Daraufhin stürzte der obere Teil des 411 Meter hohen Bauwerks ein. Nur wenig später fiel auch der zweite Turm in sich zusammen. Unmittelbar nach dem Aufprall der ersten Maschine waren die Gebäude so weit wie möglich evakuiert worden.

Bei einer der beiden Maschinen, die in das Attentat von New York verwickelt waren, handelt es sich nach Angaben der Luftfahrtbehörde um eine Boeing 737 der Fluggesellschaft United Airlines. Laut FBI wurde die Maschine entführt. Nach den Anschlägen hat die Fluggesellschaft American Airlines den Verlust von zwei Flugzeugen mit insgesamt 156 Menschen an Bord gemeldet. Die US-Luftfahrtbehörde hatte eigenen Angaben zufolge „die Kontrolle“ über ein oder mehrere Flugzeuge im Luftraum über den USA verloren.

Radikale Palästinensergruppen bestritten jede Beteiligung an den Terrorakten. Der Chef der Demokratischen Front für die Befreiung Palästinas, Kari Abdel Karim, erklärte in Ramallah, seine Organisation habe mit den Anschlägen „absolut nichts zu tun“. Zuvor hatte der TV-Sender von Abu Dhabi gemeldet, ein angebliches Mitglied der Demokratischen Front habe sich telefonisch zu dem Attentat in den USA bekannt.

Ein hochrangiger Vertreter der Volksfront für die Befreiung Palästinas versicherte im arabischen Nachrichtensender ANN, auch seine Organisation habe nichts mit den Terrorakten zu tun. Zahlreiche Palästinenser in Flüchtlingscamps feierten die Terrorserie und feuerten Freudenschüsse in die Luft. Palästinenserpräsident Jassir Arafat verurteilte die Anschläge „aufs Schärfste“. Er sagte vor Journalisten: „Wir verurteilen diese schrecklichen Taten ohne Einschränkung. Wir sind alle schockiert. Es ist unvorstellbar!“ Arafat sprach der US-Regierung und dem amerikanischen Volk das Beileid aller Palästinenser aus.

In Deutschland berief Bundeskanzler Gerhard Schröder den Sicherheitsrat ein. Für den Abend war ein Treffen mit den Fraktionsvorsitzenden im Bundestag geplant. Der Bundestag brach seine Haushaltsdebatte nach dem Anschlag ab. Im Auswärtigen Amt wurde ein Krisenstab eingerichtet. Bundespräsident Johannes Rau und Kanzler Schröder haben US-Präsident Bush kondoliert. Rau schrieb von „Entsetzen und großer Erschütterung“, die er bei der Nachricht empfunden habe. Schröder nannte die Anschläge „verabscheuungswürdig“, er sprach von einer „Kriegserklärung gegen die gesamte zivilisierte Welt“. Das deutsche Volk „steht in dieser schweren Stunde an der Seite der Vereinigten Staaten“.

Das World Trade Center war schon im Februar 1993 Ziel eines verheerenden Anschlags gewesen. Damals wurden sechs Menschen getötet und mehr als 1000 verletzt. Als Urheber gilt der in den USA inhaftierte islamische Geistliche Scheich Omar Abderrahman.

HEUTE

Drogerien steigen aus

Deutschlands Drogeriehändler kehren reihenweise dem grünen Punkt den Rücken. Die Unternehmen wollen ihre Verpackungen – billiger – über ein eigenes System entsorgen.

Wirtschaft Seite 11

Zetsche zuversichtlich

Der Chrysler-Chef Zetsche gibt sich im Interview mit der StZ zuversichtlich: „Das Schlimmste ist vorbei.“

Wirtschaft Seiten 12, 13

Wetter: bewölkt, 16° Seite 25

30337 4 390402 901804

Schockwelle an den internationalen Börsen

Handel in Vereinigten Staaten ausgesetzt – Aktienkurse stürzen weltweit ab

Von Klaus Dieter Oehler

NEW YORK/FRANKFURT. Die internationalen Finanzmärkte haben auf die Anschlagwelle in den USA schockiert reagiert. Innerhalb von Minuten stürzten die Aktienkurse weltweit in den Keller. Anleger flüchteten in Rentenpapiere, und die europäische Gemeinschaftswährung Euro legte gegenüber dem US-Dollar zu. Die Börsen an der New Yorker Wall Street als auch die Rohstoff- und Terminmärkte in Chicago blieben geschlossen.

An zahlreichen europäischen Börsenplätzen hieß es zunächst, der Handel solle zumindest vorübergehend unterbrochen werden. In Frankfurt wurden die US-amerikanischen Aktien vorerst vom Handel ausgesetzt. Der Deutsche Aktienindex (Dax) verlor zeitweise rund neun Prozent und fiel unter die Marke von 4200 Punkten. Der Euro stieg steil auf über 0,90 US-Cents, der Öl-Preis sprang nach den Terroranschlägen auf mehr als 31 US-Dollar pro Barrel.

In London brach der Leitindex FTSE-100 binnen Minuten um mehr als 200 Punkte ein. In der britischen Hauptstadt wurde die Börse geräumt, der Handel sollte allerdings weitergehen. Die Dreiländerbörse Euronext für Paris, Amsterdam und Brüssel dementierte unterdessen Berichte, der gesamten Handel solle unterbrochen werden. Zuvor war der CAC-40 der wichtigsten französischen Aktien, um 4,25 Prozent eingebrochen. Der Euro-Stoxx-50 für die 50 wichtigsten Aktien innerhalb der Euro-Zone verlor rund fünf Prozent auf 3267 Zähler. In Mexiko schloss die Börse nach den Schreckensmeldungen in den USA vorzeitig ihre Pforten. An der Frankfurter Börse verloren vor allem Versicherungswerte deutlich an Wert, weil die Unternehmen möglicherweise mit drastischen Schadenzahlungen belastet werden. Die Aktien des Münchner Versicherungsriesen Allianz sackten innerhalb weniger Minuten um mehr als zehn Prozent ab, die Münchner Rückversicherung verlor sogar knapp 14 Prozent. Auch die Titel der Lufthansa gerieten stark unter Druck. Sie notierten am Nachmittag mit 12,7 Euro gut 17 Prozent niedriger.

Analysten meinten, die Kursverluste entsprächen nicht den zu erwartenden wirtschaftlichen Folgen für die Unternehmen. Einige Börsianer jedoch waren pessimistischer. Sollte die Lage eskalieren, seien bei einer Wiederaufnahme des Börsenhandels in New York Kurseinbrüche um 2000 bis 3000 Punkte für das Börsenbarometer Dow Jones denkbar, hieß es. Andere Börsenhändler bezeichneten dies jedoch als übertrieben.

Kurz nach den Anschlägen hat Präsident Bush dem Terrorismus den Kampf angesagt. Foto AP

Der Westen unter Schock

Den Krieg erklärt

Von Adrian Zielcke

Luftangriffe auf das World Trade Center! Die Türme stürzen ein. Sie haben tausende Menschen unter sich begraben. Angriffe auf das Pentagon, auf das Außenministerium; das Weiße Haus wird evakuiert! Das ist eine Kriegserklärung an Amerika! Schon einmal sind die Vereinigten Staaten mitten im Frieden überfallen worden. Das war in Pearl Harbour 1941. Damals konnte der Feind, Japan, unter Anspannung aller Kräfte geschlagen werden. Gestern aber war es kein Staat, der Amerika den Krieg erklärte. Gestern ist ein Verbrechen verübt worden, das nicht mehr zu überbieten ist. Es muss von teuflisch-genialen Hirnen ausgedacht, geplant und durchgeführt worden sein. Hinter den Planern muss eine große militärisch geschulte Organisation stehen. Flugzeuge auf das Pentagon, entführte (!) Flugzeuge gegen das World Trade Center – das war bisher allenfalls ein Stoff für schlechte Katastrophenfilme. Jetzt aber ist der Albtraum Wirklichkeit geworden. Panik herrscht nicht nur in den Straßenschluchten New Yorks und in Washington. Dieser Anschlag löst auf der ganzen Welt Angst und Entsetzen aus.

Die Terrorflüge mit entführten Maschinen sind ein Angriff auf Amerika selbst. Das World Trade Center war ein Symbol New Yorks und damit der Weltmacht Amerika – die freie westliche Welt ist folglich mitten ins Herz getroffen worden. Man hat sich in den vergangenen Jahren an die Kleinkriege auf dem Balkan, im Nahen Osten, in Afghanistan gewöhnt. Die großen Auseinandersetzungen schienen überwunden zu sein. Auch der erste Anschlag auf das World Trade Center von 1993 geriet bereits in Vergessenheit – ebenso wie die Thesen des Professors Samuel Huntington, der zu Beginn der neunziger Jahre vor einem gewaltsamen Zusammenstoß der Kulturen gewarnt hatte. Die Warnungen des Pentagons vor neuen Gefahren, vor terroristischen Schurken und ihren Staaten wollte niemand so recht hören. Schwarzmalerei, um mehr Geld fürs Militär zu erhalten, so schien es! Die Tragödie von New York und Washington zeigt auf bestürzende Weise, dass die amerikanischen Ängste vor Terroristen nie grundlos waren – sie zeigt auch, dass es keinen wirklichen Schutz vor Terrorangriffen gibt. So verständlich der Wunsch der Weltmacht ist, unverwundbar zu werden, so unrealistisch ist er offensichtlich.

Damals, vor sechzig Jahren, kannten die USA ihren Feind. Sie wussten, wie sie ihn schlagen konnten. Heute steht Amerika ohnmächtig vor den Trümmern seiner stolzen Symbole. Osama bin Laden, islamischer Fundamentalist und Terrorist, hat seit Jahren von solchen Anschlägen gesprochen. Hat er die apokalyptischen Szenen bewirkt? Er findet Unterstützung bei den afghanischen Taliban-Kämpfern, bei den palästinensischen Selbstmordattentätern. Die islamistischen Terroristen finden in vielen Ländern der Welt Unterstützung. Sie müssen sich um ihren Nachwuchs keine Sorgen machen. Dieser Feind ist schwerer zu bekämpfen, als es das mächtige Japan einst war. Amerika ist der Erzfeind schlechthin für die Verbrecher, die sich als Gotteskämpfer verstehen. Amerika steht für westliche Zivilisation, für Globalisierung, und nicht zuletzt ist Amerika Garant der Existenz Israels. Die Opfer des gestrigen Infernos haben friedlich gelebt, geliebt, gearbeitet. Aus der Sicht der Terroristen war es ihr Verbrechen, Amerikaner zu sein. Deshalb mussten sie sterben. Es ist unfassbar.

Der 11. September dieses Jahres wird als schwarzer Tag in die Geschichte der Menschheit eingehen. Vielfältige Versuche, im Zeitalter der Globalisierung Konflikte und Gegensätze unterschiedlicher Kulturen und Zivilisationen friedlich zu überwinden, sind gescheitert. Nicht nur die Vereinigten Staaten, sondern die ganze freie Welt steht jetzt vor der Frage, wie die westliche Zivilisation künftig zu schützen ist. Denn schlagartig ist gestern klar geworden: Amerika und der Westen haben Todfeinde! Es herrscht Krieg, auch wenn es kein konventioneller Krieg ist. Auch Europa ist von diesem Krieg betroffen. Europa kann nicht so tun, als gehe es der Terror jenseits des Atlantiks nichts an. Denn die transatlantische Welt wächst immer mehr zusammen, und die Terroristen haben ihre Stützpunkte in vielen Ländern. Es wäre naiv anzunehmen, dass sie ihren Kampf auf Amerika beschränkten.

Mitgefühl und Trauer gelten am Tag nach der schrecklichen Tat den Opfern, ihren Angehörigen, den Amerikanern. Die Weltmacht Amerika hat an diesem 11. September 2001 einen schweren Schock erlitten. Aber Amerika wird stark genug sein, auch diese entsetzliche Tragödie zu überwinden. Und der Westen insgesamt wird stark genug sein, Freiheit, Demokratie und die Errungenschaften der Aufklärung zu verteidigen – im vollen Bewusstsein, dass er verwundbar ist, dass er keinen absoluten Schutz gegen den Terror garantieren kann.

Stuttgarter Zeitung
www.stuttgarter-zeitung.de
Deutschland, Stuttgart

Wien
Mittwoch, 12. September 2001
Nr. 251 / S 10,– (0,73 €)
www.kurier.at

KURIER

UNABHÄNGIGE TAGESZEITUNG FÜR ÖSTERREICH

Nach Kamikaze-Terror USA im Kriegszustand

► Luftangriffe auf New York, Washington

► Tausende Todesopfer in den Ruinen

► Terror-Pate Bin Laden im Verdacht

► Weltweite Panik in der Wirtschaft

Unvorstellbarer Schock für die USA und die Welt: Terroristen griffen New York und Washington an. Die Folgen sind unabsehbar. **SEITEN 2–7 und 9**

AP, AP/TODD HOLLIS

Live im TV vor Millionen fassungsloser Seher: Der erste Turm des World Trade Centers ist schon getroffen, dann kracht der nächste Jet in den zweiten Turm und explodiert

Krieg

Selbstmordanschläge. Seit Monaten erschüttert diese perverse Form des religiös-politischen Terrorismus den Nahen Osten. Die schrecklichen Bilder begleiten monoton immer neue Schreckensnachrichten. Bis zur Abstumpfung gegenüber dem Leid: Zerfetzte Attentäter, verstümmelte Leichen, Schwerstverletzte, weinende Opfer, brennende Wracks – und fanatische Bekenner, die zynisch Menschen als tödliche Waffe verwenden.

Der eigene Körper als Waffe, die Auslöschung des Attentäters als Einsatz im Kampf gegen einen verhassten Feind. Der Bombentod des Täters als die Verheißung des Paradieses.

Unmenschlich, unvorstellbar – und an Grauen nicht mehr zu überbieten. Und doch brachte die Kombination aus politischem und religiösem Fanatismus die unbegreifbare Steigerung: Vier Jets mit insgesamt 266 Menschen an Bord von Selbstmordkommandos gekapert und gezielt als Bomben eingesetzt.

Das ist Krieg. Krieg gegen die Menschheit und jegliche Menschlichkeit. *- FFW*

ÜBERBLICK

Verheugen unter Druck

Das Nein des EU-Kommissar zu einer Ausstiegskonferenz für Temelin wird in Österreich heftig kritisiert. **SEITE 8**

Inspektor für Tunnels

Bis Ende September soll ein Inspektor eingesetzt werden, der die heimischen Tunnels kontrollieren soll. **SEITE 12**

Sojajogurt für Europa

Die heimischen Molkereien punkten auf dem europäischen Markt mit innovativen Produkten. **SEITE 21**

Magnetfeld auf Rezept

Wegen unseriöser Werbung sollen Magnetfeldgeräte bald nur noch nach Verschreibung erhältlich sein. **SEITE 33**

Wolken und Regen

Der Nordwestwind bringt dichte Regenwolken. Nur im Süden Sonne. **SEITE 14**

9024 7170
Erscheinungsort: Wien, Verlagspostamt 1070 Wien, P.b.b. ● 01Z021634K;
Lit 3200,–, DM 3,–, sfr 2,80, Dr 550,–, Pts 260,–, Kanaren 300,–, HUF 300,–, KC 25,–, SK 30,–, KN 15,–, SIT 340,–, TL 2,500.000,–

Redaktion: 1070 Wien, Seidengasse 11, Tel. (01) 52 100/0, Fax (01) 52 100/2263, 2265, eMail Redaktion: leser@kurier.at; **Abo-Service:** Tel. (01) 521 30 29 71, eMail Abos: kurier-abo@mediaprint.at

KURIER
WWW.KURIER.AT
ÖSTERREICH, WIEN

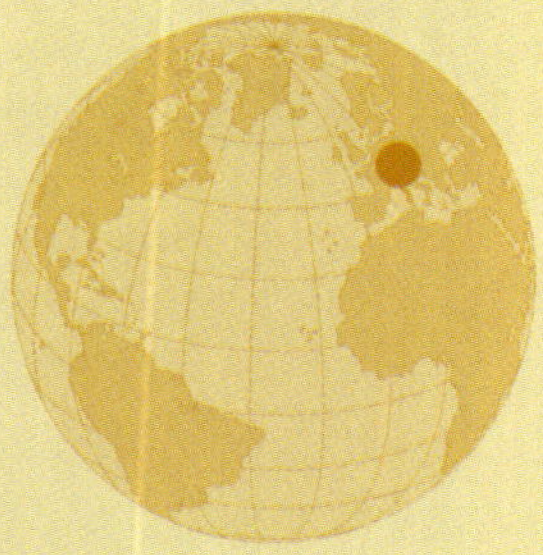

12

DER STANDARD

MI., 12. SEPTEMBER 2001 | ÖSTERREICHS UNABHÄNGIGE TAGESZEITUNG | HERAUSGEGEBEN VON OSCAR BRONNER | € 1,09 / S 15,–

Rauchwolken verdunkelten am Dienstag Manhattan, als die beiden von zwei Flugzeugen getroffenen Türme des World Trade Centers brannten und dann kollabierten. *Foto: EPA/Boesl*

Terror gegen USA erschüttert die Welt

HEUTE

Kopf des Tages Landesrat Günther Platter stellt sich einer Kampfabstimmung um die Spitze der Tiroler ÖVP. **Seite 44**

Volksbegehren Christgewerkschafter Fritz Neugebauer unterstützt das Sozialstaats-Volksbegehren. **Seite 12**

Voest-Alpine Der Aufsichtsrat der Voest-Alpine Stahl bestellte Franz Struzl zum neuen Vorstandsvorsitzenden. **S. 13**

Kommentar der anderen: „Sozialstaat durch Engagement!" – ein Plädoyer von Alfred J. Noll. **43**

Abo-Hotline 0810 20 30 40

BÖRSE

New York (DJ)	ausgesetzt
Frankfurt (DAX, Schluss)	4273,34 –
Wien (ATX, Schluss)	1153,89 –
€ (in US-$, 17.00)	0,9147 +
S-Anleiherendite:	4,607 +
Gold, London (in US-$)	287,40 –
Börsenkurse auf	S. 16 + 18

WETTER

Meist ist es stark bewölkt und regnerisch, nur im Süden kann es auflockern. Die Schneefallgrenze liegt bei 1400 m. Höchstwerte erreichen 10 bis 18 Grad. **Seite 10**

■ Tausende Tote bei Attentat auf World Trade Center in New York befürchtet
■ Pentagon in Flammen – Bush: Werden Verantwortliche jagen und bestrafen

New York/Washington – Die USA wurden Dienstag von den schrecklichsten Terroranschlägen der Geschichte getroffen. Mit entführten US-Passagierflugzeugen brachten unbekannte Selbstmordattentäter das New Yorker World Trade Center zum Einsturz. Die Behörden befürchteten Tausende, wenn nicht Zehntausende von Toten. In Washington wurden das Verteidigungsministerium und das Außenministerium mit einem weiteren Flugzeug und einer Autobombe angegriffen. Eine vierte Maschine stürzte bei Pittsburgh ab.

Die Anschläge lösten weltweit Entsetzen und verschärfte Sicherheitsvorkehrungen aus. Die EU, Frankreich, Großbritannien, Russland und viele andere Staaten verurteilten die Terrorangriffe. US-Präsident George Bush sprach von einer „nationalen Tragödie". Die Börsen reagierten mit Kursabstürzen.

„Die USA werden die Verantwortlichen für diese feigen Taten jagen und bestrafen. Und wir haben alle erforderlichen Sicherheitsvorkehrungen getroffen, um das amerikanische Volk zu schützen", sagte Bush vom US-Luftwaffenstützpunkt Barksdale im Bundesstaat Louisiana aus. Am Dienstagabend kehrte er, nach einem Zwischenstopp im Hauptquartier der strategischen Luftstreitkräfte in Nebraska, nach Washington zurück. „Unsere Streitkräfte auf der ganzen Welt sind in hoher Alarmbereitschaft", sagte der US-Präsident. Die Grenzen der USA wurden geschlossen. Am Nachmittag (Ortszeit) wurden Flugzeugträger und andere Kriegsschiffe vor die Ostküste entsandt.

Die Urheber der Terroranschläge könnten nach US-Einschätzung Verbindungen zum saudi-arabischen Extremistenführer Osama Bin Laden haben, der sich in Afghanistan versteckt hält. Ein Sprecher der in Afghanistan herrschenden Taliban hat am Dienstag eine Verwicklung ausgeschlossen. „Osama Bin Laden kann so etwas nicht machen, auch wir nicht", sagte Abdul Hai Mutmaen in Kandahar.

Palästinenserpräsident Yassir Arafat sagte vor Journalisten: „Wir verurteilen diese schrecklichen Taten ohne Einschränkung. Wir sind alle schockiert. Es ist unvorstellbar." Auch andere Palästinenserführer distanzierten sich von den Anschlägen. Allerdings feierten zahlreiche Palästinenser in den Flüchtlingscamps im Südlibanon und in Beirut die Terrorserie.

Die Flugzeuge, die auf die Gebäude stürzten, sind nach Ansicht von Terrorismusexperten von eigens dafür ausgebildeten Piloten geflogen worden. Kein Pilot, nicht einmal mit einer Pistole am Kopf, würde in die Türme fliegen.

Der gestern nach Wien gekommene frühere US-Vizepräsident Al Gore hat die Terrorwelle als „unsagbar bösen Akt" verurteilt und Präsident Bush seiner Unterstützung versichert. (red)

12 Seiten Berichte, Fotos, Kommentar

Hassobjekt USA

Wer bringt eine so immense kriminelle Energie für eine solche Horrortat auf? Jedenfalls jemand mit einem unbändigen Hass auf die einzige verbliebene Supermacht, auf die mächtigste Demokratie der Geschichte, auf die globale militärische, wirtschaftliche und kulturelle Hegemoniemacht. Eine radikale palästinensische Splittergruppe? Oder der Erzterrorist Osama Bin Laden? Oder doch rechtsextreme Gruppen am „verrückten Rand" der US-Gesellschaft? Die USA sind die überwältigende Macht dieser Welt. Ebenso überwältigend ist offenbar der Hass in der Welt gegen sie. Absurde Verschwörungstheorien und Vorwürfe mit Hauch von Realität, die arrogant wirkende und wohl auch arrogante Vorgangsweise der Regierung George W. Bush (Absage an Kioto-Pakt, *go it alone* mit der Raketenabwehr), daneben die amerikanische Popkultur als Weltkultur, der tiefe Hass besonders im islamischen Fundamentalismus gegen den „großen Satan" und seinen Lebensstil – das vermengt sich zu einem Motiv für legitimen Protest einerseits und massenmörderische Aggression andererseits. Palästinenser tanzten jubelnd in den Straßen. Die USA sind das reale Symbol der Globalisierung. Das ist der erste Globalisierungskrieg.

RAU

Terrorwelle löst Schock in Österreich aus

Wien – Einen Schock hat in Österreich die Terrorwelle gegen die USA ausgelöst. Bundespräsident Thomas Klestil und Bundeskanzler Wolfgang Schüssel schickten Kondolenztelegramme an US-Präsident Bush. Klestil sprach von einem „Anschlag auf die Menschlichkeit". Die Spitzen der Regierung traten zu einer Krisensitzung zusammen. Schüssel hielt auch Kontakt mit den Oppositionschefs. Die Sicherheitsmaßnahmen für Einrichtungen der USA wurden verschärft, alle jüdischen Einrichtungen evakuiert. Im Kanzleramt wurde unter der Telefonnummer 0800-211 212 eine kostenlose Hotline für Anfragen nach der Anschlagserie eingerichtet. (red)

ZN: 141256W88E · P.b.b. Verlagspostamt 1010 Wien · Nr. 3866 · Adresse: 1010 Wien, Herrengasse 19–21 · Tel. 01/531 70 · http://derStandard.at · DM 3.–/sfr 2,50/Ft 250/SK 40/KC 40/Lit 3200/Drs 240/bfr 100/TL 1,000.000

12

DER STANDARD
WWW.DERSTANDARD.AT
ÖSTERREICH, WIEN

Photo: ap

ZWÖLF SEITEN SONDERBERICHTE ÜBER DEN TERROR GEGEN DIE USA

Wie kam es zu den Anschlägen, wer steckt dahinter, was sind die Folgen? Fakten, Analysen, Reportagen und Kommentare

SEITEN 1 – 10, 17, 19

Die Presse

UNABHÄNGIGE TAGESZEITUNG FÜR ÖSTERREICH

AKTUELLE KURSE

Dow Jones	kein Handel
DAX Frankfurt	4273,53 ▽
ATX Wien	1153,89 ▽
Euro zu Dollar	0,8964 $ ▽
Gold (2. Goldfixing London)	287,00 △

Alle Börsenkurse ab Seite 20

Mi 37 / Nr. 16.070 / 14 Schilling (1,02 Euro) *Vormals* Neue Freie Presse *Gegründet 1848* Mittwoch, 12. September 2001

Amerika hilflos gegen Frontalangriff des Terrorismus Weltweit höchste Alarmbereitschaft für US-Streitkräfte

Eine „nationale Tragödie" erschüttert Amerika und die freie Welt: World Trade Center durch zwei Flugzeuge zerstört; Angriffe auch gegen Pentagon und State Department; alle Führungszentralen evakuiert; gesamter Flugverkehr gestoppt.

NEW YORK / WASHINGTON. Die Vereinigten Staaten erlitten am Dienstag den größten Schock ihrer Geschichte: Eine unvorstellbare Terrorwelle forderte Tausende, möglicherweise Zehntausende Opfer und zeigte die mächtigste Nation der Welt in absoluter Hilflosigkeit gegenüber dem Terrorismus. Die US-Streitkräfte wurden am Abend weltweit in höchste Alarmbereitschaft versetzt. „Alle militärischen Einrichtungen weltweit sind in Alarmstufe Delta", teilte ein Sprecher des durch ein Attentat ebenfalls zum Teil zerstörten Pentagon mit. In der Hauptstadt wurden Truppen-Konvois beobachtet.

Über die Hintermänner der unvorstellbaren Serie von Selbstmordanschlägen wird vorerst nur spekuliert. Alle Vermutungen richten sich jedenfalls gegen verschiedene islamische Gruppierungen: In Frage kommen sowohl die Palästinenser, die in letzter Zeit zunehmend zu Selbstmordanschlägen Zuflucht genommen haben, wie auch Afghanistan, wo das Taliban-Regime intensiv mit den radikalen antiwestlichen Gruppierungen kooperiert. Der US-Sicherheitsrat vermutet Osama bin Laden hinter den Anschlägen.

In den USA kam das gesamte öffentliche Leben zum Erliegen, der zivile Flugverkehr bleibt bis Mittwoch gestoppt. Weltweit herrscht Entsetzen. Auch in Österreich wurde die für Donnerstag angesetzte Nationalratssitzung abgesagt.

Die zwei Türme des World Trade Center stürzten ein. In kurzem Abstand waren zwei gekidnappte Flugzeuge gegen die Zwillingstürme gekracht, die bald darauf einstürzten: Normalerweise befinden sich bis zu 50.000 Menschen in dem Gebäude. Selbst Verteidigungs- und Außenministerium in Washington wurden Ziele von Anschlägen. Ein viertes entführtes Flugzeug wurde von den Streitkräften abgeschossen. Ein zweiter Anschlag auf das Verteidigungsministerium ist in letzter Minute verhindert worden. In New York stürzte am Abend ein weiteres Hochhaus ein, Folge der Anschläge auf das World Trade Center.

US-Präsident George W. Bush kehrte am Abend nach Washington zurück und richtete eine Rede an das amerikanische Volk. Bush sprach von einer „nationalen Tragödie".

Es berichten E. Male, A. Rohrer (beide USA), W. Böhm (Brüssel), S. Knaul (Tel Aviv), G. Braune (Ottawa), B. Imhasly (New Delhi), K. El-Gawhary (Kairo), B. Bischof, C. Domforth, K. Ettinger, A. Fieber, M. Fritzl, W. Greber, G. Hofer, M. Koch, H. Kronspieß, M. Kugler, F. Leibl, M. Lohmeyer, I. Luttenberger, P. Martos, R. Nowak, P. Percher, N. Rief, H. W. Scheidl, F. Schellhorn, H. Schmidt, S. Schöffl, H. Schneid, W. Schneider, A. Schwarz, M. Seeh, R. Seyfried, E. Sittinger, K. Stöger, M. Stuhlpfarrer, C. Ultsch, T. Vieregge, G. Walterskirchen, E. Witzmann

Die Tragödie: Der erste Turm des World Trade Centers in New York stürzt ein, der andere folgt wenig später, tausende Menschen verlieren ihr Leben. Photo: ap

37
9 015580 990338
DM 3,00, sfr 2,70, Lit 3200, bfr 100, SIT 350, HRK 14, KČ/SK 40, Ft 240, TL 1.000.000
„Die Presse", 1015 Wien, Parkring 12a; PF 6. ☎ 5 14 14. Fax: DW 400 (Redaktion); DW 251 (Anzeigen). Abonnement: ☎ 795 00 DW 50, Fax: DW 55. Verlagspostamt: 1010 Wien, P.b.b. Zulassungsnummer: 01Z023038K
www.diepresse.at

Schock an Börsen, Angst vor Ölkrise steigt

An den Aktienmärkten in Europa brach Panik aus, weltweit wird nun mit einer weiteren Abschwächung der Konjunktur gerechnet.

WIEN/LONDON. Panik herrschte unmittelbar nach Bekanntwerden der Tragödie in New York an den europäischen Aktien- und Rohstoffmärkten. Der Rohölpreis schossen innerhalb weniger Minuten in die Höhe. Die Händler gehen vorerst zwar noch von Panikkäufen aus, es könnte aber auch durchaus zu einer neuen Ölkrise kommen. Preise von bis zu 40 Dollar je Faß werden bereits wieder für möglich gehalten. Im Gefolge steigender Ölpreise und panikartiger Verkäufe an den Aktienmärkten wird auch eine weitere Abschwächung der Konjunktur weltweit befürchtet.

Zu schweren Verlusten kam es an den europäischen Wertpapiermärkten gekommen. In London und Frankfurt brachen die Kurse regelrecht ein. Alle europäischen Indizes rutschten deutlich ins Minus, der Frankfurter DAX verlor bis zu acht Prozent. Kaum besser ging es der Londoner Börse, deren Hauptgebäude evakuiert wurde, während der Handel fortgesetzt wurde. Stark gestiegen sind die Kurse für Anleihen und Gold. An der Wall Street wurde der Handel kurz nach Bekanntwerden der Tragödie eingestellt, auch die Technologiebörse Nasdaq blieb vorerst geschlossen.

HEUTE

Benzin soll teurer werden. Die EU-Kommission überlegt, die Harmonisierung und Anhebung von Treibstoff-Abgaben. Österreich wäre massiv betroffen: Die Abgaben könnten um ein Viertel erhöht werden. *Seite16*

Die Reformländer brauchen selbst Zuwanderer, so Sozialforscher Münz, Geburtenraten gehen zurück. *East*conomist *Seite 25*

Studiengebühren. Alle Hände voll zu tun haben die Studienabteilungen wegen der Überweisungen der Studienbeiträge. Diese sind in Euro vorgeschrieben. *Bildung Seite 27*

Sport. Comeback von Michael Jordan eine so gut wie beschlossene Sache. – Fußball-EM-Kandidatur 2008: „Bei Uefa-Inspektion muß Euphorie her!" *Seiten 31, 32*

Die Apokalypse

VON ANDREAS SCHWARZ

Es gibt Bilder, für die versagt jede Beschreibung: Flugzeuge, die die berühmtesten Wolkenkratzer der Welt zum Einsturz bringen, die Zerstörung der militärischen Schaltzentrale der USA, erzwungene Flugzeugabstürze, Autobomben, Tod, Verwüstung. Wer geglaubt hat, alles über die vernichtenden Möglichkeiten des Terrorismus zu wissen, ist am Dienstag eines Schlechteren belehrt worden. Wo der Haß ein Ziel hat, ist offenbar jede Steigerung möglich.

Die USA waren immer schon Ziel meist nahöstlichen Terrors, aber sie sind noch nie so ins Mark getroffen worden. Bomben im Libanon oder in Afrika, Entführungen, selbst der bisherige Terror auf amerikanischem Boden wie der Autobombenanschlag auf das jetzt zerstörte World Trade Center – das alles war Terror, der die Vereinigten Staaten traf, der sie oft zu harten Reaktionen gegenüber den mutmaßlichen Drahtziehern veranlaßte; das war aber auch Terror, der zwar wie eine Art unvermeidliche internationale Kriminalität via CNN und Co. in die amerikanischen Wohnzimmer getragen wurde, aber an Amerika irgendwie auch vorbeiging.

Ein konzertierter Angriff aber, ein massenmörderischer Akt, der in wenigen Minuten Tausende und Abertausende Menschen in den Tod reißt und dramatisch die Verwundbarkeit der einzigen Supermacht der Welt aufzeigt – das ist für die Vereinigten Staaten wie Krieg, den es in der Neuzeit auf seinem Boden nie erleben mußte.

Fanatiker, die Amerika das Verderben wünschen, gibt es genug. Die Vereinigten Staaten, die sich – nicht immer uneigennützig, aber zumeist zum Wohl der freien Welt – für eine undefinierte Weltordnung aus Demokratie und Menschenrecht engagieren, haben sich von Libyen über den Irak bis zu krausen islamischen Fundamentalisten der Marke Osama bin Laden mehr Feinde gemacht als jeder andere Staat der Welt.

Daß sie einmal von apokalyptischen Bildern heimgesucht werden würden, wie sie jeden Hollywood-Schinken unglaubwürdig machen, hat in den USA aber niemand für möglich gehalten. Amerika wird sich, wie schnell immer der Krieg gegen die Drahtzieher aufgenommen wird, so schnell nicht davon erholen. Gestern hat in der Tat der Terror gesiegt.

Die Presse
www.diepresse.com
Österreich, Wien

Mittwoch, 12. Sept. 2001 / Nr. 14.849, S 10,-

Wien Krone

Kronen Zeitung

UNABHÄNGIG

www.krone.at

Wien 19, Muthgasse 2, ☎ 01/36 011-0

ABONNENTEN-SERVICE: ☎ 01/52130-2971

Terrorangriff auf Amerika!

„Krone"-Augenzeugenbericht von Hans Janitschek

Kronen Zeitung
www.krone.at
Österreich, Wien

12

George W. Bush: „Wir werden die Täter finden und bestrafen"

trenkwalder EDV-DIENSTE Besuchen Sie uns in der Halle 10 Stand 10516.

NR. 1458 – MITTWOCH, 12. SEPTEMBER 2001 P.B.B. VERLAGSPOSTAMT 1100 WIEN – 376300W95E – REDAKTION: 1100 WIEN, DAVIDGASSE 79, TEL.: 919 19-0, FAX: 602 28 58. S 20,– / € 1,45

Wirtschafts Blatt

www.wirtschaftsblatt.at

ÖSTERREICHS ERSTE TAGESZEITUNG FÜR WIRTSCHAFT & FINANZEN

Experten warnen vor weiterem Dollarabsturz und langfristigem Rückschlag für die internationale Konjunktur

Terror erschüttert die Weltwirtschaft

Die USA verlieren nach den gestrigen Anschlägen ihren Nimbus als unangreifbare Wirtschaftsmacht. Die Folgen des Terrors reichen bis Europa: Die Börsen reagierten mit dramatischen Kurseinbrüchen. Die Wall Street sperrte erst gar nicht auf, der Dollar sackte ab, Öl und Gold schnellten in die Höhe.

A2/3, B1/2/5/6

Die Katastrophe in New York (re. o.) und Betroffenheit im Handelsraum der Bank Austria

WIRTSCHAFTSBLATT
WWW.WIRTSCHAFTSBLATT.AT
ÖSTERREICH, WIEN

12

Reisen

Mittwoch, 12. September 2001

Tages-Anzeiger

• Die unabhängige schweizerische Tageszeitung Auflage 268 179 109. Jahrgang, Nr. 211 WWW.TAGESANZEIGER.CH Fr. 2.20 (inkl. 2,4% MwSt.)/Lit. 3800/DM 3.-/Pts. 350/Dr. 700/£ CYP 1.10/ÖS 22.-/FF 15.-/Kan. Ins. Pts. 375

Der Angriff auf Amerika

Eine gigantische Staubwolke über Manhattan kündet nach dem Einsturz der beiden Türme des World Trade Center von den Terroranschlägen.

BILD HUBERT MICHAEL BOESL/EPA

Nach den schwersten Terroranschlägen der Geschichte fragt die Welt in einem Zustand von Entsetzen und Schock: Wer hat das getan?

Von **Victor Breu, New York und Ignaz Staub, Washington**

Nach 15 Uhr Schweizer Zeit am Dienstag werden Millionen von Menschen in der ganzen Welt Zeugen eines unglaublichen Geschehens: Ein Flugzeug war um 14.46 Uhr (8.46 Uhr in New York) in einen Turm des World Trade Center gerast. Während Rauchwolken aus dem Gebäude dringen und Livekameras auf den symbolträchtigen Bau im Süden Manhattans gerichtet sind, ist plötzlich ein zweites Flugzeug zu sehen, das in den zweiten Turm des Komplexes prallt, in dem an Werktagen 50 000 Personen arbeiten.

Nur eine Stunde nach den ersten beiden Anschlägen bekommt die Terrorserie einen zweiten Schauplatz: Aus Washington wird gemeldet, dass ein drittes Flugzeug auf das Pentagon gestürzt sei und Teile des Verteidigungsministeriums in Flammen stünden. In New York fällt derweil, kurz nach 16 Uhr Schweizer Zeit, der erste Turm in sich zusammen. Kurz danach, aus Washington wird eben eine Explosion vor dem Aussenministerium gemeldet, bricht auch der zweite Turm ein. Nochmals fünf Stunden später wird das zum World-Trade-Komplex gehörende 47-stöckige Bürogebäude Nummer 7 ebenfalls zusammenbrechen.

Es ist 16.30 Uhr, als American Airlines und United Airlines den Verlust von vier Passagierflugzeugen bestätigen. Die vierte Maschine war bei Pittsburgh abgestürzt, offenbar entführt und auf dem Weg zu einem weiteren Anschlag.

Unmittelbar nach dem ersten Anschlag hatte sich Präsident George Bush, auf Besuch in einer Schule in Florida, zu Worte gemeldet und im Fernsehen von einem Terroranschlag gesprochen. Es wurde angekündigt, er werde sofort ins Weisse Haus zurückkehren. Doch dann überwiegen Sicherheitsbedenken, und die Maschine des Präsidenten wird auf eine Militärbasis in Louisiana umgeleitet. Von dort erklärt Bush: «Wir werden alles tun, um Amerika und das amerikanische Volk zu schützen.» Später fliegt er nach Nebraska und am Abend nach Washington.

Während in New York und Washington der Notstand ausgerufen wird und die Bergung von Opfern anläuft, beginnt die Suche nach Experten, die das Geschehen erklären und mögliche Urheber benennen können. Am häufigsten wird in den ersten Stunden nach den Anschlägen der Name des mutmasslichen Terroristen Osama Bin Laden genannt. Die USA machen den aus Saudiarabien stammenden Millionär für Bombenanschläge auf US-Botschaften in Kenya und Tansania im Jahr 1998 verantwortlich. Am Abend weisen die in Afghanistan regierenden Taliban solche Mutmassungen zurück. Die USA versetzen ihre Streitkräfte in höchste Alarmbereitschaft. Die Marine entsendet Flugzeugträger und Kriegsschiffe mit Raketenabwehrsystemen Richtung New York und Washington.

Bis am späten Dienstagabend gab es keine verlässlichen Schätzungen über die Zahl der Opfer. New Yorks Bürgermeister Rudolph Giuliani spricht von einer «horrenden Zahl von Toten».

Leuenberger ringt nach Worten

In der ganzen Welt melden sich Regierungschefs zu Wort und geben ihrer Abscheu über die Terrortat Ausdruck. In Bern sagt ein geschockter Moritz Leuenberger: «Es gibt keine Worte für die politische und menschliche Katastrophe apokalyptischen Ausmasses.» Die Finanzmärkte reagieren mit Kurseinbrüchen.

KOMMENTAR

Krieg der Zivilisationen

Von **Philipp Löpfe**

Dies könnte der Tag sein, an dem die USA ihr Glück aufgebraucht haben», erklärte der Polizeichef von New York am Dienstag. Das Ausmass der Zerstörung begann sich zu diesem Zeitpunkt erst abzuzeichnen. Die düstere Prophezeiung des Polizeichefs ist leider realistisch. Noch bevor klar wird, wie viele Menschenleben die Angriffe auf das World Trade Center und das Pentagon gekostet haben, steht fest, dass die politischen Konsequenzen immens sein werden.

Die perfiden Attacken von bisher unbekannten Terroristen werden eine politische Kettenreaktion mit unbekanntem Ausgang nach sich ziehen. Der Schock über Vorgänge, die bisher höchstens in billigen Horrorfilmen zu sehen waren, wird der Trauer über Tausende von Opfern weichen – und dann dem Hass. Präsident George W. Bush hat bereits unmissverständlich erklärt, dass die USA «die für diese Tat Verantwortlichen jagen und bestrafen werden». Bei dieser Jagd werden sie keine Halbheiten dulden und absolute Loyalität verlangen. Erste Kommentare auf CNN waren eindeutig: «Wer nicht für uns ist, ist gegen uns», lautet der Tenor.

Nicht nur der hohe Blutzoll beeinflusst die Stimmung. Dass gerade das symbolträchtige World Trade Center und das Pentagon Ziel der Attacken waren, trifft die Amerikaner in ihrem Stolz. Die ohnehin schon patriotische Nation wird mit einer massiven Welle von Patriotismus reagieren. Das Klima in den USA wird sich ändern. Multikulturelle Toleranz wird darunter leiden. Washington hat den Notstand ausgerufen, die USA befinden sich mental im Krieg.

Nach dem Fall der Berliner Mauer schreckte Samuel P. Huntington die Welt mit einem apokalyptischen Szenario auf, dem «Krieg der Zivilisationen». Die Menschheit werde sich entlang von religiösen und ethnischen Grenzen selbst zerfleischen, warnte der Harvard-Professor. Wirtschaftsboom und Interneteuphorie haben diese Warnungen verblassen lassen. Die abscheulichen Anschläge in New York und Washington haben sie schockartig wieder ins Bewusstsein gerufen.

Der «Krieg der Zivilisationen» ist seit gestern wieder eine Option geworden. Wer immer hinter dem feigen Terroranschlag steht, er hat der Welt bewiesen, dass ihm jedes Mittel recht ist, diesen Krieg loszutreten. Der Westen und vor allem die USA können diesen Krieg verhindern: wenn sie sich auf die Werte ihrer humanistischen Zivilisation besinnen.

Abo-Service: Mo–Fr: 01/404 64 64, Sa/So: 0800 80 80 15, Fax: 01/248 69 04, Verlag: 01/248 41 11,
Inserate: Tel. Annahme: 01/248 41 41 (7.30–20.00 Uhr), Fax: 01/248 41 91, Internet: e-inserat.ch,
E-Mail: inserat@tamedia.ch; Redaktion: 01/248 44 11, Fax: 01/248 44 71;
E-Mail: redaktion@tages-anzeiger.ch; Werdstrasse 21, 8004 Zürich, Briefe: Postfach, 8021 Zürich, AZA

9 771422 999005 01211

Tages-Anzeiger
www.tages-anzeiger.ch
Schweiz, Zürich

DER TERROR-WAHNSINN AUF 9 SEITEN

TAUSENDE VON TOTEN

Mittwoch, 12. September 2001 Fr. 1.50

Blick

UNABHÄNGIGE SCHWEIZER TAGESZEITUNG

Redaktion: 01/259 62 62 Abos: 062/746 43 43 AZ 4800 Zofingen Nr. 211
Fax: 01/262 29 76 Internet: http://www.blick.ch 41. Jahrgang ★★

L 3200; Pta. 250; Kan. Inseln Pta. 275; fFr. 12.–; OeS 20.–; DM 1.80; £ 1.50; $ 2.60; Dr. 550; C£ 1.–; Esc. 400; TRL 2550000; Ft 300

Das trifft uns alle!

Krieg gegen Amerika

FOTO AP

- World Trade Center zerstört
- Das Pentagon in Flammen
- Weisses Haus und Capitol evakuiert
- Panik in Manhattan: Millionen Menschen auf der Flucht
- 4 Flugzeuge entführt
- Alle Flughäfen geschlossen
- Notstand in ganz Amerika

Blick
www.blick.ch
Schweiz, Zürich

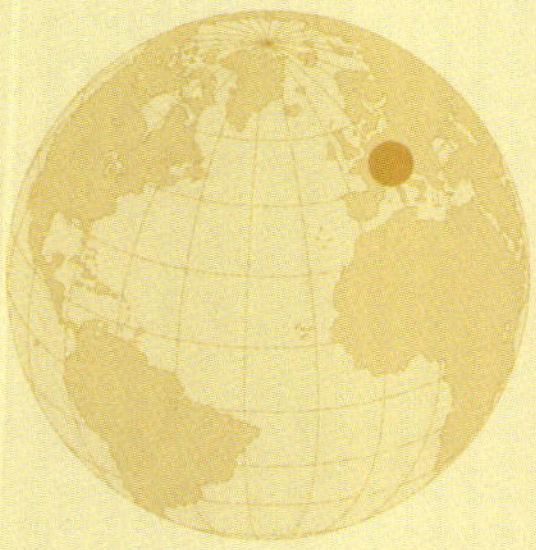

Fr. 1.50 (TVA 2,4% incluse) FF 6.50/Lires 4000/Ptas 400 MERCREDI 12 SEPTEMBRE 2001 N° 255 www.lematin.ch

Le Matin

le quotidien romand

www.lematin.ch
24 heures sur 24

TERREUR SUR L'AMÉRIQUE

20 PAGES SPÉCIALES

Postcode 1 JA 1000 Lausanne 1

1 Terror über Amerika

2 20 Seiten Spezial

Le Matin
www.lematin.ch
Schweiz, Lausanne

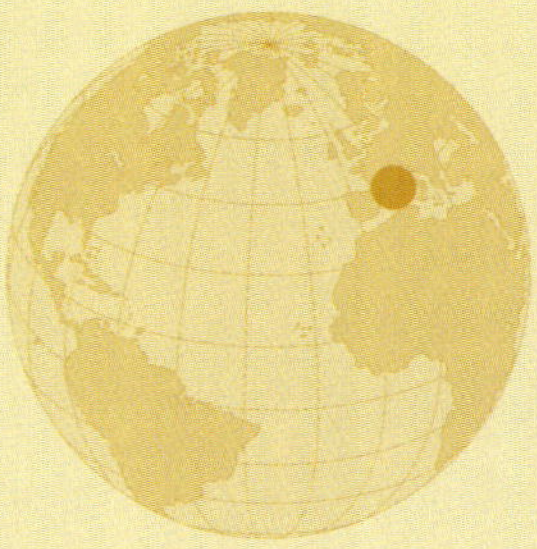

12

MERCREDI 12 SEPTEMBRE 2001

Libération

11 SEPTEMBRE 2001

1,14 euro France métropolitaine
www.liberation.com
M 0135-912-7,50 F-1,14 €

1 11. September 2001

(Zeitungsumschlag; erste und letzte Seite)

Libération
www.liberation.fr
Frankreich, Paris

12

Diário de Notícias

www.dn.pt

DIRECTOR: MÁRIO BETTENCOURT RESENDES | DIRECTOR ADJUNTO: ANTÓNIO RIBEIRO FERREIRA | PREÇO (IVA INCLUÍDO) 100$ - 0.5 EURO | ANO 137.° N° 48 385 QUARTA-FEIRA, 12 DE SETEMBRO DE 2001

Guerra

Explosões no aeroporto de Cabul

■ Atentados suicidas destroem as duas torres do World Trade Center em Nova Iorque e atingem o Pentágono em Washington ■ Terroristas desviaram aviões comerciais e provocaram um número indeterminado de vítimas ■ Reportagem nos EUA, crónicas das principais capitais mundiais e opiniões de especialistas em estratégia ■ Perfil dos principais suspeitos, a memória das ficções e a história de edifícios emblemáticos

Páginas 2 a 23 e 56

1 **Krieg**

2 Explosionen im Flughafen von Kabul

3 • Selbstmordattentäter zerstörten die beiden Türme des World Trade Centers in New York und griffen das Pentagon in Washington an • Terroristen entführten Passagierflugzeuge und verschuldeten eine unbestimmte Anzahl von Opfern • Reportagen aus den USA, Berichterstattung aus den wichtigsten Hauptstädten der Welt und Meinungen von Strategen • Profil der Hauptverdächtigen, Gedenken an Geschichten und Geschichte der symbolträchtigen Gebäude

DIÁRIO DE NOTICIAS
WWW.DN.PT
PORTUGAL, LISSABON

50p
Wednesday
September 12 2001
Published in London
and Manchester
guardian.co.uk

The Guardian

A declaration of war ❶

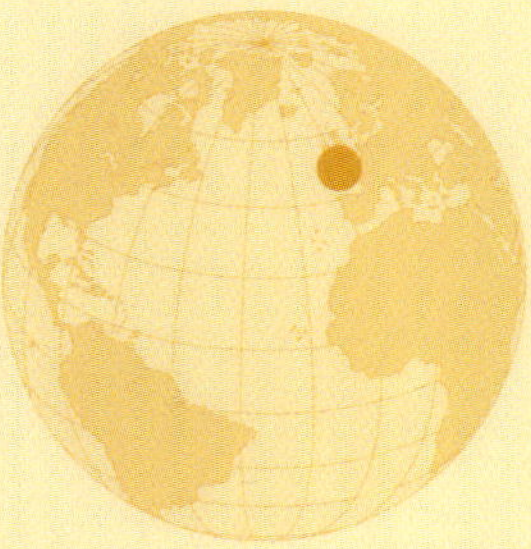

❶ Eine Kriegserklärung

© The Guardian
www.guardian.co.uk
Grossbritannien, London

12

THE Mirror

Wednesday September 12 2001

32p

WAR ON THE WORLD

❶ Krieg gegen die Welt

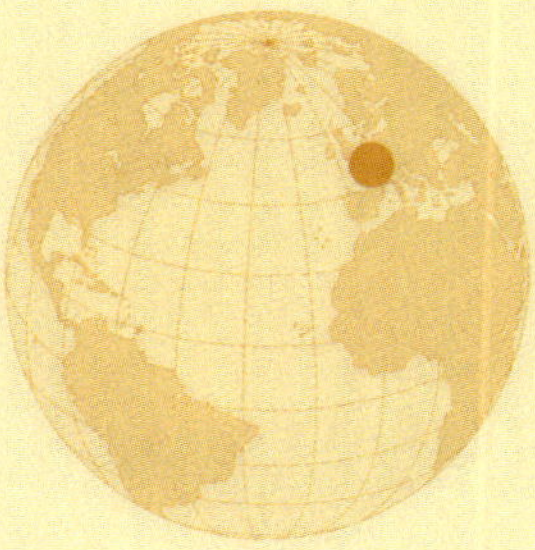

The Mirror
www.mirror.co.uk
Grossbritannien, London

12

Scotland's Business, Financial & Political Daily

Wednesday 12 September, 2001 www.businessam.co.uk

SCOTTISH NEWSPAPER OF THE YEAR

business a.m.

Todd Hollis/AP

Attack on America

Terror from the skies
Hijackers strike at the heart of the US with attacks on the Twin Towers and the Pentagon Page 4

Markets in turmoil
Fears about the impact of the attacks on the global economy send shares plunging Page 2

Ian Bell
For America or against? That could become the only question relevant in the 21st century Page 3

Profile of a terrorist
The world's most wanted man, Osama bin Laden, has emerged as the chief suspect Page 34

Security failures claim
Security at US airports has a alarming failure rate, according to a Congress investigation Page 35

Subscriptions Tel: 084504 55355

80p

No 246

Business a.m.
www.businessam.co.uk
Grossbritannien, Edinburgh

1 Das Grauen fiel vom Himmel

Flugzeugentführer treffen die USA mit Angriffen auf die Zwillingstürme und das Pentagon mitten ins Herz

2 Märkte in Aufruhr

Besorgnis über die Auswirkungen der Angriffe auf die Weltwirtschaft bewirkt Kursverfall

3 Profil eines Terroristen

Der meistgesuchte Mann der Welt, Osama bin Laden, erscheint als Hauptverdächtiger

4 Sicherheit

Die Sicherheit von US-Flughäfen weist laut Untersuchungen des Kongresses erschreckende Mängel auf

12

'We are poised at what is arguably one of the most dangerous, uncontrollable moments in history'

The photographs the world will never forget: 8-page special section

The Herald

219th year No 196 — Wednesday September 12, 2001 — 48p

TERRORISTS' INFERNO: Flames and smoke erupt at the World Trade Centre, after hijacked planes slammed into the twin towers, bringing terror to the heart of Manhattan. The towers collapsed, causing an untold number of deaths. Picture: Allsport UK

The war of the worlds

IAN BRUCE
GEOPOLITICS EDITOR

www.theherald.co.uk

WEATHER 12 • FEATURES 18 • ARTS 19 • COMMENT 20/21 • LETTERS 21 • FAMILY ANNOUNCEMENTS 22 • BUSINESS 23 • CROSSWORD 40 • SPORT 33/40

THE HERALD
WWW.THEHERALD.CO.UK
GROSSBRITANNIEN, GLASGOW

❶ **Krieg der Welten**

❷ »Wir stehen am Rande eines der wohl gefährlichsten und unkontrollierbarsten Augenblicke der Geschichte«

Die Bilder, die die Welt niemals vergessen wird

12

NORTHWEST INDIANA'S NEWSPAPER

THE TIMES

RIDGE FINAL

An edition of The Times serving Munster, Highland, Griffith and Calumet Township

WEDNESDAY SEPTEMBER 12, 2001

SPECIAL REPORT

5 SECTIONS, 54 PAGES

www.thetimesonline.com

Newsstand: 50 cents

DAY OF TERROR

UNCOUNTABLE DEAD IN 'SECOND PEARL HARBOR'

SHAWN BALDWIN / ASSOCIATED PRESS

UNITED STATES UNDER ATTACK | COMPLETE COVERAGE INSIDE

IN WASHINGTON

PRESIDENT SPEAKS: Bush says the United States will punish those behind the deadliest attack in U.S. history. **A3**

IN NEW YORK

THE SCENE: It was the image of a nightmare: people on fire jumping from the World Trade Center towers before the buildings collapsed. **A4**

IN CHICAGO

CITY SHUTS DOWN: An eerie silence filled the Loop as many buildings were evacuated and somber workers hurried home. **A8**

AT AIRPORTS

PLANES GROUNDED: Airports in Chicago, the south suburbs, and Lake and Porter counties are ordered closed. **A10-11**

AT WORSHIP

CLERGY REACT: Local clergy try to make sense of the tragedy, offer words of comfort to faithful in churches, synagogues. **B1**

AT SCHOOL

EXTRA PRECAUTIONS: High school students wonder if it's war, while teachers shield younger children from the news. **B2**

The Times is printed with soy color inks, exclusively on recycled paper.

INDEX

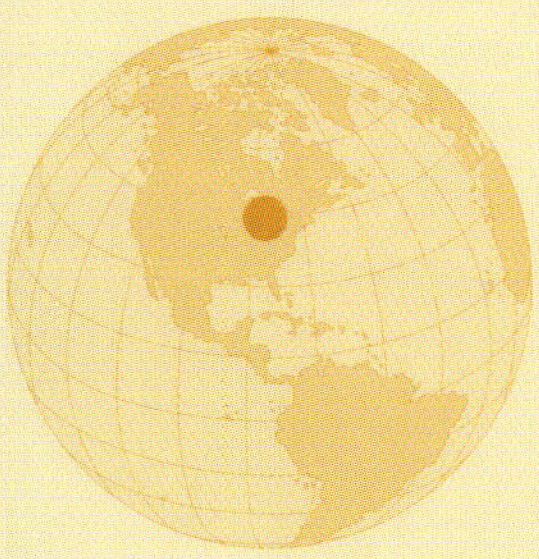

1 **Tag des Terrors**

2 Zahllose Tote im »zweiten Pearl Harbor«

3 Angriff auf die Vereinigten Staaten • Ausführliche Berichterstattung im Innenteil

THE TIMES
WWW.THETIMESONLINE.COM
USA, MUNSTER (INDIANA)

12

woensdag
12 september 2001

ƒ 2,00
€ 0,91
56e JAARGANG NO. 115, WEEK 37
ADRESSEN EN TEL. NRS. PAGINA 2
WEBSITE: www.ad.nl

Algemeen Dagblad

België Bfr. 60 · Can. Eil. Pts. 365 · Cyprus C£ 1,50 · Duitsland Dm 4,00 · Frankrijk Ffr. 13,00 · Gr. Brit. £ 1,60 · Griekenl. Drs. 750 · Hongarije Huf 500 · Italië Lire 4000 · Luxemburg Fr. 60 · Madeira Esc. 450 · Malta LM 1,10 · Marokko D. 22,00 · Oostenr. Osch. 28 · Polen Zl. 10,70 · Portugal Esc. 425 · Spanje Pts. 350 · Thailand Baht 150 · Tsjechië Kr. 75 · Tunesië M. 2.400 · Turkije TL 3.200.000

Vrijwel droog, 16-18 °C
Wind: matig tot vrij krachtig W
Weerkaart en overzicht 24

KRANT · MAGAZINE · WEBSITE

OORLOG TEGEN VS

Foto Michael Boesl

• Pentagon in brand • World Trade Center weggevaagd • Honderden doden

Bush: We laten ons niet intimideren

Van onze redactie buitenland

New York - President Bush heeft vannacht in een toespraak tot een diepgeschokte natie de inlichtingen- en opsporingsdiensten opdracht gegeven de daders van de zwaarste aanslag in de geschiedenis op te sporen en voor de rechter te brengen. De Verenigde Staten zullen daarbij geen onderscheid maken tussen de terroristen, die het land in het hart getroffen hebben en landen die terroristen herbergen. „De daders van deze laffe aanslagen kunnen onze gebouwen vernietigen, maar niet de grondvesten van dit grootse land", aldus Bush vanuit het Witte Huis. Hij benadrukte dat de overheidsdiensten, het zakenleven en de samenleving zich niet laten intimideren.

Met zware aanslagen op symbolen van de macht van Amerika, het World Trade Center en het Pentagon, heeft een onbekende terreurorganisatie de VS gisteren diep en hard geraakt. Vermoedelijk zijn in New York en Washington honderden mensen om het leven gekomen.

De aanvallen worden door analisten toegeschreven aan de terrorist-miljonair Osama bin Laden, die onderdak heeft gevonden in Afghanistan. De Afghaanse hoofdstad Kaboel werd gisteravond getroffen door een serie explosies, maar het Witte Huis ontkende met klem dat de VS achter die aanvallen zit.

Het drama begon aan het eind van de ochtendspits. Om tien voor negen plaatselijke tijd boorde een gekaapte Boeing 767 zich in een van de twee wolkenkrabbers van het New Yorkse World Trade Center. Binnen 20 minuten ramde een ander lijntoestel de tweede toren. Ruim een half uur later volgde de derde aanval, in Washington. Een vliegtuig stortte neer op het Pentagon, het ministerie van Defensie, dat voor een deel werd verwoest. De torens van het WTC stortten later in. 's Avonds begaf ook een bijgebouw het. Een vierde vliegtuig, vermoedelijk gekaapt door dezelfde groep terroristen, stortte kort na het opstijgen neer op zo'n 130 kilometer van Pittsburgh. Een passagier meldde via zijn mobieltje dat het vliegtuig in handen van kapers was gevallen. Het Witte Huis en andere gebouwen van de federale overheid waren toen al geëvacueerd. Aan het einde van de dag keerde de president, die op het moment van de aanvallen in Florida was, terug in het Witte Huis. Onduidelijk is of er Nederlanders onder de slachtoffers zijn. Volgens de Nederlandse consul-generaal in New York, Bob Hiensch, werkten in het WTC acht Nederlanders. Volgens het Nederlands Bureau voor Toerisme zijn er dagelijks 3 à 4000 Nederlanders in de stad. Burgemeester Giuliani sprak van zeker 2000 gewonden, zijn politie van 78 vermiste agenten. Vermoedelijk kwamen in New York ten minste 200 brandweerlieden om.

Op pagina 2
Bush zweert wraak

Het tweede vliegtuig staat op het punt zich in een toren van het World Trade Center te boren. De andere toren staat dan al in brand. *Foto AP*

Manhattan een oorlogszone

Door onze correspondent Marc Guillet

New York - De aanslag door terroristische kamikazepiloten verandert het zuiden van Manhattan in een oorlogszone. De ochtendspits wordt een nachtmerrie. Het financiële district, dat tot het fatale moment van de eerste zelfmoordaanslag schitterde in een zee van zonlicht, ziet er uit als de straten van Beiroet na zware bombardementen. Roetwolken verduisteren de zon.

Kort nadat twee gekaapte vliegtuigen zich in de torens van het World Trade Center hebben geboord, lijkt het alsof een sneeuwstorm heeft gewoed. Straten, auto's, bomen en gebouwen liggen onder een dikke laag stof en as. Huilende en gillende mensen rennen verdwaasd weg van de rampplek. Bloed stroomt van hun gezichten. Hun ogen drukken angst en paniek uit.

Ontelbare sirenes van politie, brandweer en ambulances echoen tegen de wolkenkrabbers.

Voor winkels en kantoren, die in allerijl gesloten zijn, liggen de stille getuigen van de paniek: een vertrapte lichtblauwe damesblazer, een zwarte herenschoen.

De terroristen hadden uit publicitair oogpunt geen beter doelwit kunnen kiezen. De Twin Towers bepalen de skyline van Manhattan en behoren tot de belangrijkste symbolen van New York.

Van alle kanten komen hulpverleners aangestormd. Ambulancepersoneel deelt stofkapjes uit aan brandweerlieden. Uitgeputte en met stof bedekte politieagenten happen naar adem. FBI-agenten met semi-automatische wapens bemannen kruispunten. Een huilende agente, totaal overstuur, wordt door collega's omarmd. Diverse mensen staan dubbelgevouwen voorover en braken stof uit. Lichtgewonden worden provisorisch verbonden en krijgen het advies zich zo snel mogelijk uit de voeten te maken.

Deryck, een slanke zwarte man, die werkt voor de bank Credit Suisse in het World Trade Center, is zo wit dat het lijkt of hij een baal meel over zich heen heeft gekregen. „Toen het eerste vliegtuig zich in de toren had geboord, rende iedereen naar buiten. Ik schreeuwde: God, spaar mijn leven." Hij is buiten adem en hapt naar lucht.

Op pagina 5
'Laten we bloed geven'

Gewonden vluchten uit het World Trade Center *Foto AP*

• COMPLETE BERICHTGEVING OP PAG. 2, 3, 5, 7, 9, 11, 13 • SPORT 17, 19 • BINNENLAND 20 • ECONOMIE 21 • KUNST/MEDIA 22 • RADIO/TV 23 • WEER 24

Algemeen Dagblad
www.ad.nl
Niederlande, Rotterdam

1 **Krieg gegen die USA**

2 • Pentagon in Flammen • World Trade Center zerstört • Hunderte Tote

3 Bush: Wir lassen uns nicht einschüchtern

4 Manhattan ein Kriegsgebiet

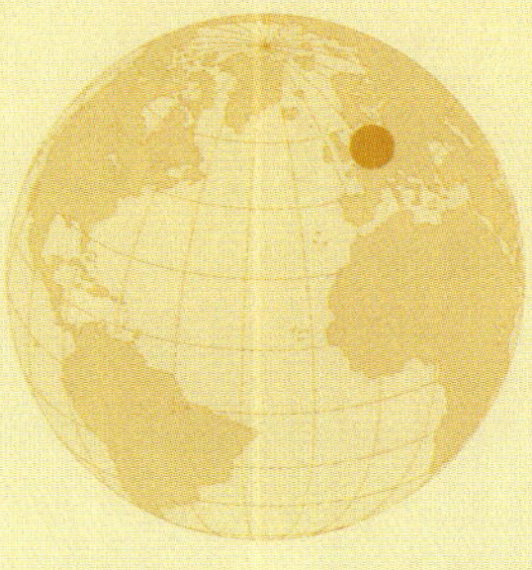

de Volkskrant

WOENSDAG 12 SEPTEMBER 2001

28 PAGINA'S

● Kamikaze-acties terroristen ● World Trade Center vernietigd ● Explosies in Kabul

Bush zweert wraak voor aanval

Van onze correspondent
Bert Lanting
WASHINGTON

De Verenigde Staten zijn gisteren het doelwit geworden van een terroristisch Armageddon. Terroristen lieten twee gekaapte vliegtuigen te pletter vliegen tegen het World Trade Center in New York, het symbool van Amerika's welvaart. Ook lieten zij een vliegtuig neerstorten op het Pentagon. Een vierde toestel stortte neer even buiten Pittsburgh. Bij de aanslagen zijn vermoedelijk duizenden mensen omgekomen. De Amerikaanse president Bush zwoer wraak. Kort na middernacht waren er explosies te horen in de Afghaanse hoofdstad Kabul.

Wolken stof en rook verrijzen boven Manhattan als beide torens van het World Trade Center instorten.

Pagina 2:
- WTC was symbool Amerikaans kapitalisme
- Kok vraagt VS om 'waardige' reactie

Pagina 3:
- Schurkenstaat minder gevaarlijk dan terrorist
- Bin Laden voert oorlog tegen alles wat westers is
- Aanslagen vuurproef voor president VS

Pagina 4:
- Amerikanen weten urenlang niet waar Bush is
- Wereld reageert met walging op aanslagen

Pagina 5:
- Financiële markten storten in
- New York zal nooit meer hetzelfde zijn

Pagina 7:
- Commentaar

Pagina 5V:
- Alleen Yorin blijft comedy uitzenden

Stroom:
- NOS tevreden, RTL 4 en 5 snel

105 minuten terreur

'Ik zie de mensen springen'

Van onze medewerker
Elsbeth Tiedemann
NEW YORK

❶ **Bush schwört Rache für Anschlag**

❷ • Kamikaze-Terror • World Trade Center zerstört • Explosionen in Kabul

❸ »Ich sehe die Menschen springen«

❹ 105 Minuten Terror

De Volkskrant
www.volkskrant.nl
Niederlande, Amsterdam

HET FINANCIEELE DAGBLAD

'Al het geene tot het financieele eenige betrekking heeft' – sinds 1796

ZORG OM COLLEGA'S
Verzekeraars vinden de materiële schade even niet belangrijk. 'Op dit moment heb ik meer aandacht voor de menselijke kant'
► PAGINA 3

RECESSIEGEVAAR
De aanslag op de Verenigde Staten kan het laatste zetje zijn dat de wereld in een recessie duwt
► PAGINA 3

EEN TWEEDE PEARL HARBOR
Ook in de afgelopen eeuw hebben de VS laten zien dat, op momenten waar het er echt om gaat, het beste naar boven komt
► PAGINA 15

VANDAAG OP DE SITE
► Marktreacties op golf aanslagen VS
► Cijfers Heineken, SNT, GTI, Altadis
► Frankrijk, Spanje: inflatie (cpi) augustus

WOENSDAG 12 SEPTEMBER 2001 — 30 PAGINA'S ♦ NR 215

❶ **Terreuraanslagen raken VS in het hart**

❷
- Gecoördineerde terreuractie
- Veiligheidsmaatregelen verscherpt
- Bush belooft jacht op daders

AMSTERDAM — Bij aanslagen op het World Trade Center (WTC) in New York en het Pentagon in Washington zijn gisteren waarschijnlijk duizenden mensen om het leven gekomen. De verantwoordelijkheid voor de terreuraansladen was bij het sluiten van deze krant niet opgeëist.

NEW YORK — Ook de tweede toren van het World Trade Center stort volledig in.

❸ **Angst raast door financiële markten**

AEX-INDEX

NIEUWSOVERZICHT

❹ **Wereld verbijsterd na aanvallen op VS**

MARKTEN

❺ **Newyorkers lopen verdwaasd rond in oorlogszone**

Reddingswerkers rennen bij het World Trade Center uit.

❶ **Terroranschläge treffen die USA ins Herz**

❷ • koordinierte Terrorhandlung
- Sicherheitsmaßnahmen verschärft
- Bush verspricht Jagd auf den Täter

❸ Angst rast durch Finanzmärkte

❹ Angriffe auf die USA erschüttern die Welt

❺ New Yorker laufen geschockt durch Kriegsgebiet

Het Financieele Dagblad
www.fd.nl
Niederlande, Amsterdam

Het PAROOL

VRIJ, ONVERVEERD

WOENSDAG 12 SEPTEMBER 2001 LAATSTE EDITIE HET PAROOL. OPGERICHT IN HET OORLOGSJAAR 1940 61STE JAARGANG NR 17343 / TEL. 020-562.9333 PRIJS: fl 2,10 (€ 0,95)

NEGEN PAGINA'S EN PS OVER HET INFERNO.

Laatste nieuws steeds op **www.parool.nl**

2 **Reacties:** de wereld is totaal verbijsterd.
3 **Beelden:** een terreurdaad en de gevolgen.
4 **Kamikaze-piloten**: de daders vlogen zelf.
5 **Major attack:** er is steeds voor gewaarschuwd.
6 **Botsende culturen:** het Westen en de islam.

● Na een eeuw van barbaarse oorlogen en een tijdperk van nucleaire gijzeling waanden we ons eindelijk redelijk veilig. Die illusie zijn we kwijt.

Oorlogsverklaring

• Duizenden doden • Hart Manhattan weggevaagd • Honderden vermist in Pentagon

FOTO DOUG KANTER/EPA

Arnold Heertje

TERRORISME moet worden bestreden, merkte premier Kok op. Golda Meir, de enige vrouwelijke premier van Israël, trok die conclusie in de jaren zeventig, toen de terreur was beperkt tot aanvallen op Israëlische doelen, ambassades en vliegtuigen.

De wereld heeft niet naar haar geluisterd.

Dat terreur eerst joden, maar uiteindelijk de gehele mensheid treft, wilde niemand geloven. De wereld is gisteren op een verschrikkelijke manier door schade en schande wijs geworden. De les is geleerd dat het verbale geweld van de laatste jaren en maanden de dwingende voorbode is van het onvoorstelbare.

Door de technologie treffen de beelden de netvliezen van iedereen, wereldwijd en zonder vertraging. Ook de netvliezen van kinderen in het begin van hun pubertijd, die door de loop der dingen hun jeugd overslaan. Zij zien wat een paar misdadigers een onbestemd aantal mensen aandoen. Klimmende cijfers gaan over in veranderende kwaliteit.

De wereld na 11 september 2001 is voorgoed gescheiden van de geschiedenis ervoor. Veel te vroeg ontmoeten de kinderen van vandaag het door mensen georganiseerde onmenselijke kwaad. Hun verwerkte ervaring vertalen ze op termijn in door verdraagzaamheid gedreven eenheid in verscheidenheid. In deze donkere uren het enige lichtpunt.

Bin Laden brein achter aanslagen

(Van onze redactie buitenland)
AMSTERDAM – Washington is ervan overtuigd dat Osama bin Laden het brein is achter de terreuraanslagen in New York en Washington. In Boston, waar twee vliegtuigen zijn gekaapt voor de aanslagen, heeft de politie vijf Arabische mannen op het oog.

Het gaat onder meer om twee broers met paspoorten van de Verenigde Arabische Emiraten; één van hen is piloot. In een parkeergarage van het Bostonse vliegveld stond een auto met een Arabische vlieghandleiding.

Het aantal slachtoffers van de aanslag gisteren kan pas over weken worden vastgesteld, maar loopt volgens president George Bush in de duizenden. Onder de slachtoffers zijn in elk geval driehonderd brandweerlieden en 85 politiemensen in New York, die omkwamen toen de beide torens van het World Trade Center instortten, en de 266 passagiers en bemanningsleden van de vier gekaapte vliegtuigen. In het Pentagon zouden honderd tot achthonderd doden zijn gevallen.

Bush was vannacht de eerste die een slachtofferaantal noemde. "Duizenden levens werden plotseling beëindigd door het kwaad," zei hij in een toespraak tot de natie.

Volgens Washington dragen de aanslagen alle kenmerken van Osama bin Laden. Als de VS bewijzen tegen hem levert, zal de Taliban-regering in Afghanistan uitlevering van Bin Laden overwegen, aldus de Afghaanse ambassadeur in Pakistan.

Volgens een Pakistaanse krant heeft Osama bin Laden echter elke betrokkenheid bij de aanslag ontkend.

LAMBIEK BERENDS

Illusie van veiligheid ligt nu aan scherven

DE WERELD IS een barre en bizarre plek voor mensen. Gisteren was die wereld getuige van 'terreur in de maak', een angstaanjagend specimen van reality-tv. We keken er met ongeloof en verbijstering naar. Wel, we waren er uiteraard van op de hoogte dat het soms ongeciviliseerd toegaat her en der, en als televisiekijker zijn we redelijk gehard. En toch was dit opnieuw schokkend, buitengewoon schokkend, onvoorstelbaar schokkend.

Waarom? Misschien omdat we ons na een eeuw met een reeks barbaarse oorlogen en een tijdperk van nucleaire gijzeling eindelijk redelijk veilig waanden. Dat was dus een illusie.

Misschien omdat de beelden van een naakte onmenselijkheid waren. Misschien omdat genadeloos de kwetsbaarheid werd blootgelegd van een samenleving die zich afficheert en wordt geafficheerd als de enig overgebleven supermacht.

Maar misschien vooral omdat de omgeving zo vertrouwd was, zo banaal eigenlijk: het marktplein van onze *global village*. Omdat het zo onbehouwen rechtstreeks was, recht voor z'n raap, geen beeld gemanipuleerd, geen sequentie in scène gezet. Een passagiersvliegtuig dat een gebouw binnenvliegt in een stad, waarvan in elk geval de contouren van de skyline de meesten vertrouwd voorkomen. Gebouwen die als een stier in de arena door de knieën gaan, hulpeloos, reddeloos, zonder recht op genade. Mensen die voor hun leven rennen, als figuranten in een horrorfilm.

Maar het waren geen figuranten en het was geen Hollywoodproductie.

Het is bovenal ook onthutsend dat dit kon gebeuren in het land dat zo furieus tekeergaat tegen *rogue states*, dat al jaren internationaal terrorisme beschouwt als de grootste bedreiging, nu het voormalige 'rijk van het kwaad' niet meer de aartsvijand is. Dat daar een raketschild in de ruimte tegen wil bouwen. Dat beschikt over een enorm veiligheidsapparaat, over het geld en de technologie om dat op de been te houden en te perfectioneren.

Een land ook dat als brein achter deze nachtmerrie vrijwel onmiddellijk de man aanwijst die het sinds jaren openlijk als zijn grootste vijand beschouwt.

Maar in dat land is het mogelijk in een verbluffend gecoördineerde actie vier lijntoestellen te kapen, waarvan twee op dezelfde luchthaven, en daar dood en verderf mee te zaaien. Waartoe diende gisteren de militaire overmacht van de Verenigde Staten, nu het symbool daarvan, het Pentagon, zelf doelwit werd van terreur?

Moet de pessimistische conclusie luiden dat tegen het internationale terrorisme geen kruid gewassen is? Dat het kan toeslaan waar en wanneer het wil, ook al staan de technische en financiële middelen van geen enkele terreurgroep in geen enkele verhouding tot die van het slachtoffer?

• Vervolg op pagina 4

Vrees voor dood Nederlanders

DEN HAAG – Het ministerie van Buitenlandse Zaken gaat ervan uit dat er 'zeker' Nederlanders onder de slachtoffers van de aanslagen zijn. Vanmiddag was er nog geen duidelijkheid over het aantal vermiste Nederlanders. "Er zijn dagelijks duizenden landgenoten op Manhattan. Sommigen melden zich bij het Nederlandse consultaat in New York." Bij het informatienummer 0800 1205 kwamen tot vanmiddag ruim duizend telefoontjes binnen.

INHOUD

8 710371 001002

❶ **Kriegserklärung**

❷ Tausende Tote • Herz Manhattans weggefegt • Hunderte im Pentagon vermisst

❸ Nach einem Jahrhundert der barbarischen Kriege und einem Zeitalter der nuklearen Geiselnahme wähnten wir uns endlich einigermaßen sicher. Diese Illusion ist weg

❹ Bin Laden führender Kopf hinter den Anschlägen

❺ Illusion der Sicherheit zerschmettert

❻ Angst um niederländische Opfer

Het Parool
www.parool.nl
Niederlande, Amsterdam

12

NRC HANDELSBLAD

www.nrc.nl — WOENSDAG 12 SEPTEMBER 2001

Opnieuw buien

Amerikanen kwetsbaar maar vastberaden • Pagina 3

Tekst toespraak president Bush • Pagina 3

Financiële markten in mineur • Pagina 17

Pagina 2, 3, 4, 5 • Nieuws en achtergronden
Pagina 9 • Commentaren en hoofdartikel
Pagina 17, 18, 19 • Economische gevolgen
Pagina 27 • TV-verslaggeving
www.nrc.nl • Dossier, nieuws en achtergronden

Aanval op VS, Bush wil vergelding

Islamieten veroordelen aanval op VS

EU en NAVO ferm tegen terreur

Nederlander vreest voor aanslagen

Europees voetbal afgelast

Swiss Re verwacht megaclaim

Snel ingrijpen door bedrijfsleven

ECB biedt hulp

'Zoals toen Kennedy werd vermoord'

Om negen uur had de ramp in New York nog iets overzichtelijks. Maar dat was snel voorbij. „Dit is Pearl Harbor II", riepen mensen. „World War III." We moesten het benoemen.

Aanslagen met vliegtuigen op WTC en Pentagon

Aanslag psychologische klap wereldeconomie

Omdat de wereldeconomie al balanceerde op de rand van een recessie, komt de vertrouwensschok die volgt op de aanslagen in New York en Washington op het slechtst denkbare moment.

NRC HANDELSBLAD — Vier weken op proef voor ƒ 22,50 (10,21 euro)

1 Angriff auf die USA. Bush will Vergeltung

2 »So wie damals, als Kennedy ermordet wurde«

3 Anschlag psychologischer Schlag gegen die Weltwirtschaft

4 Amerikaner verletzbar, aber entschlossen

5 Ansprache von Präsident Bush, Originaltext

6 Finanzmärkte im Minus

7 Muslime verurteilen Angriff auf USA

EU und NATO geschlossen gegen Terror

Niederlande befürchten ebenfalls Anschläge

Fußballturnier in Europa abgesagt

Swiss Re erwartet Mega-Forderungen

Schnelle wirtschaftliche Interventionen

EZB bietet Hilfe an

NRC Handelsblad
www.nrc.nl
Niederlande, Rotterdam

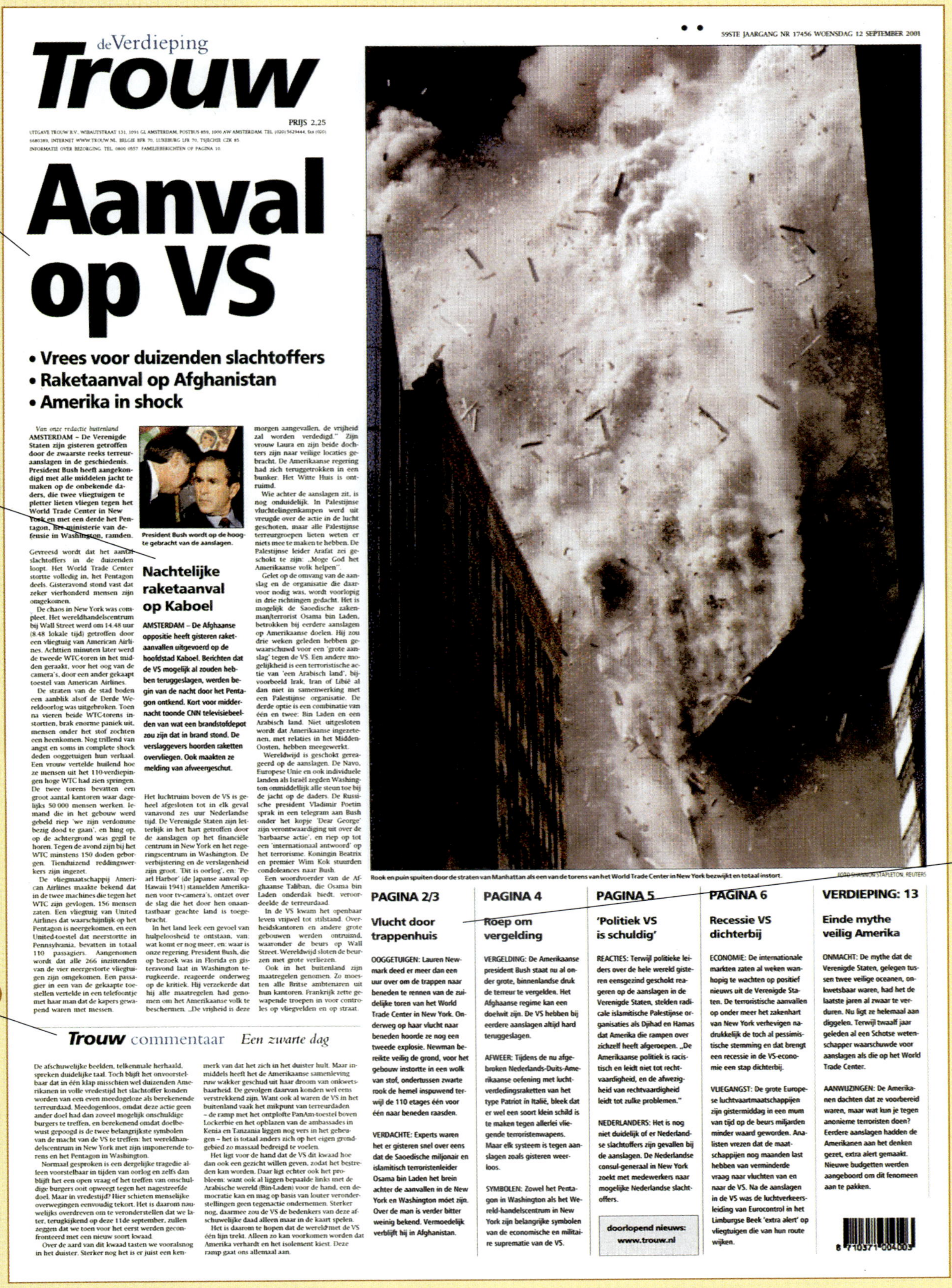

deVerdieping

Trouw

59STE JAARGANG NR 17456 WOENSDAG 12 SEPTEMBER 2001

PRIJS 2,25

Aanval op VS

- Vrees voor duizenden slachtoffers
- Raketaanval op Afghanistan
- Amerika in shock

President Bush wordt op de hoogte gebracht van de aanslagen.

Nachtelijke raketaanval op Kaboel

AMSTERDAM – De Afghaanse oppositie heeft gisteren raketaanvallen uitgevoerd op de hoofdstad Kaboel. Berichten dat de VS mogelijk al zouden hebben teruggeslagen, werden begin van de nacht door het Pentagon ontkend. Kort voor middernacht toonde CNN televisiebeelden van wat een brandstofdepot zou zijn dat in brand stond. De verslaggevers hoorden raketten overvliegen. Ook maakten ze melding van afweergeschut.

Het luchtruim boven de VS is geheel afgesloten tot in elk geval vanavond zes uur Nederlandse tijd. De Verenigde Staten zijn letterlijk in het hart getroffen door de aanslagen op het financiële centrum in New York en het regeringscentrum in Washington. De verbijstering en de verslagenheid zijn groot. 'Dit is oorlog', en: 'Pearl Harbor' (de Japanse aanval op

Trouw commentaar *Een zwarte dag*

Rook en puin spuiten door de straten van Manhattan als een van de torens van het World Trade Center in New York bezwijkt en totaal instort.

FOTO SHANNON STAPLETON, REUTERS

PAGINA 2/3

Vlucht door trappenhuis

OOGGETUIGEN: Lauren Newmark deed er meer dan een uur over om de trappen naar beneden te rennen van de zuidelijke toren van het World Trade Center in New York. Onderweg op haar vlucht naar beneden hoorde ze nog een tweede explosie. Newman bereikte veilig de grond, voor het gebouw instortte in een wolk van stof, ondertussen zwarte rook de hemel inspuwend terwijl de 110 etages één voor één naar beneden raasden.

VERDACHTE: Experts waren het er gisteren snel over eens dat de Saoedische miljonair en islamitisch terroristenleider Osama bin Laden het brein achter de aanvallen in de New York en Washington móet zijn. Over de man is verder bitter weinig bekend. Vermoedelijk verblijft hij in Afghanistan.

PAGINA 4

Roep om vergelding

VERGELDING: De Amerikaanse president Bush staat nu al onder grote, binnenlandse druk de terreur te vergelden. Het Afghaanse regime kan een doelwit zijn. De VS hebben bij eerdere aanslagen altijd hard teruggeslagen.

AFWEER: Tijdens de nu afgebroken Nederlands-Duits-Amerikaanse oefening met luchtverdedingsraketten van het type Patriot in Italië, bleek dat er wel een soort klein schild is te maken tegen allerlei vliegende terroristenwapens. Maar elk systeem is tegen aanslagen zoals gisteren weerloos.

SYMBOLEN: Zowel het Pentagon in Washington als het Wereld-handelscentrum in New York zijn belangrijke symbolen van de economische en militaire suprematie van de VS.

PAGINA 5

'Politiek VS is schuldig'

REACTIES: Terwijl politieke leiders over de hele wereld gisteren eensgezind geschokt reageren op de aanslagen in de Verenigde Staten, stelden radicale islamitische Palestijnse organisaties als Djihad en Hamas dat Amerika die rampen over zichzelf heeft afgeroepen. „De Amerikaanse politiek is racistisch en leidt niet tot rechtvaardigheid, en de afwezigheid van rechtvaardigheid leidt tot zulke problemen."

NEDERLANDERS: Het is nog niet duidelijk of er Nederlandse slachtoffers zijn gevallen bij de aanslagen. De Nederlandse consul-generaal in New York zoekt met medewerkers naar mogelijke Nederlandse slachtoffers.

doorlopend nieuws: www.trouw.nl

PAGINA 6

Recessie VS dichterbij

ECONOMIE: De internationale markten zaten al weken wanhopig te wachten op positief nieuws uit de Verenigde Staten. De terroristische aanvallen op onder meer het zakenhart van New York verhevigen nadrukkelijk de toch al pessimistische stemming en dat brengt een recessie in de VS-economie een stap dichterbij.

VLIEGANGST: De grote Europese luchtvaartmaatschappijen zijn gistermiddag in een mum van tijd op de beurs miljarden minder waard geworden. Analisten vrezen dat de maatschappijen nog maanden last hebben van verminderde vraag naar vluchten van en naar de VS. Na de aanslagen in de VS was de luchtverkeersleiding van Eurocontrol in het Limburgse Beek 'extra alert' op vliegtuigen die van hun route wijken.

VERDIEPING: 13

Einde mythe veilig Amerika

ONMACHT: De mythe dat de Verenigde Staten, gelegen tussen twee veilige oceanen, onkwetsbaar waren, had het de laatste jaren al zwaar te verduren. Nu ligt ze helemaal aan diggelen. Terwijl twaalf jaar geleden al een Schotse wetenschapper waarschuwde voor aanslagen als die op het World Trade Center.

AANWIJZINGEN: De Amerikanen dachten dat ze voorbereid waren, maar wat kun je tegen anonieme terroristen doen? Eerdere aanslagen hadden de Amerikanen aan het denken gezet, extra alert gemaakt. Nieuwe budgetten werden aangeboord om dit fenomeen aan te pakken.

1 Angriff auf die USA

• Tausende von Opfern befürchtet • Terror fegt das WTC hinweg • Ausnahmezustand in amerikanischen Städten

2 Ferngespräch aus dem WTC-Gebäude: »Wir sterben gerade«

3 Trouw Kommentar: Ein schwarzer Tag

4 Flucht durchs Treppenhaus

Ruf nach Vergeltung

»US-Politik ist schuld«

USA kommen der Rezession näher

Mythos vom sicheren Amerika ist zu Ende

12

Trouw
www.trouw.nl
Niederlande, Amsterdam

Aftenposten

Morgenutgave. Onsdag 12. september 2001. Uke 37. Nr. 418. 142. årg. Kr. 12,00. Fly/ekspr.: Vest-/Midt-Norge kr. 13,00. Nord-Norge kr. 14,00

Terrorkrig mot USA

Inferno. *Manhattan i flammer etter terrorangrepene på USA i går.* FOTO: HUBERT MICHAEL BOESL/EPA

Tusenvis ble drept da USA ble angrepet av terrorister i går. 50 000 personer hadde sin arbeidsplass i World Trade Center. President Bush forsikrer at de ansvarlige vil bli jaget og straffet.

Mange land i Europa har iverksatt omfattende sikkerhetstiltak i frykt for flere terrorangrep. Mistankene går først og fremst mot den saudi-arabiske geriljalederen Osama bin Laden.

Kaos, gråt og frykt

Sirener. – Mennesker overalt. Kaos. Det føles hinsides at noe slikt kan skje – terrorangrep mot USA mens jeg befinner meg i møte i den norske FN-delegasjonen. Jeg går mot China Town – folk overalt. Røyk overalt. Mange gråter. Sirener hyler, ambulansene står, skriver Aftenpostens reporter i New York. I kaoset av løpende mennesker står en uteligger helt stille på 40. gate. – God bless you, sier han.

Øyenvitne. Et øyenvitne som jobber på Wall Street, fem kvartaler unna World Trade Center, forteller hva han så: – På kontoret i 25. etasje merket jeg at det begynte å riste voldsomt. Da jeg så ut gjennom vinduet, så jeg fly nummer to komme. Det kjørte rett inn i det andre tårnet. Med mine egne øyne så jeg folk hoppe ut fra World Trade Center, forteller mannen.

Hjelpeløse. *To kvinner holder rundt hverandre mens de ser World Trade Center kollapse etter terrorangrepet.* FOTO: ERNESTO MORA/AP

92 ombord. *Et fly styres inn i det ene av de to 110 etasjer høye tårnene på World Trade Center på Manhattan. Flyet hadde 81 passasjerer og en besetning på elleve.* FOTO: AP

64 ombord. *Verden glemmer aldri bildene (over) som viser øyeblikket da fly nummer to styres inn i det andre tårnet. 64 mennesker var om bord.*

Bildet av Frihetsgudinnen som løfter sin fakkel mot et Manhattan innhyllet i flammer og støv, vil brenne seg inn i verdens bevissthet. Verden vil aldri bli den samme etter dette.

Aftenposten på kommentarplass

Side 2, 3, 4, 5, 6, 17 (leder), 29 og 32

7 039781 201637

1 Terrorkrieg gegen die USA

2 Tausende wurden getötet, als die USA gestern von Terroristen angegriffen wurden; 50 000 Personen hatten ihren Arbeitsplatz im World Trade Center; Präsident Bush versichert, dass die Verantwortlichen verfolgt und bestraft werden. Viele europäische Länder haben aus Furcht vor weiteren Terrorangriffen umfassende Sicherheitsmaßnahmen ergriffen. Der Verdacht richtet sich in erster Linie gegen den saudi-arabischen Guerilla-Führer Osama bin Laden

3 Chaos, Tränen und Furcht

4 Das Bild der Freiheitsgöttinnen, die ihre Fackeln gegen ein in Flammen und Staub gehülltes Manhattan erheben, wird sich ins Bewusstsein der Welt einprägen. Nach diesem Ereignis wird die Welt nie wieder dieselbe sein

5 92 an Bord. Ein Flugzeug steuert in einen der beiden 110 Stockwerke hohen Türme des World Trade Centers in Manhattan. Das Flugzeug hatte 81 Passagiere und 11 Besatzungsmitglieder an Bord

64 an Bord. Die Welt wird die Bilder (siehe oben) nie vergessen, die den Augenblick zeigen, als Flugzeug Nummer zwei in den zweiten Turm steuerte. 64 Menschen waren an Bord

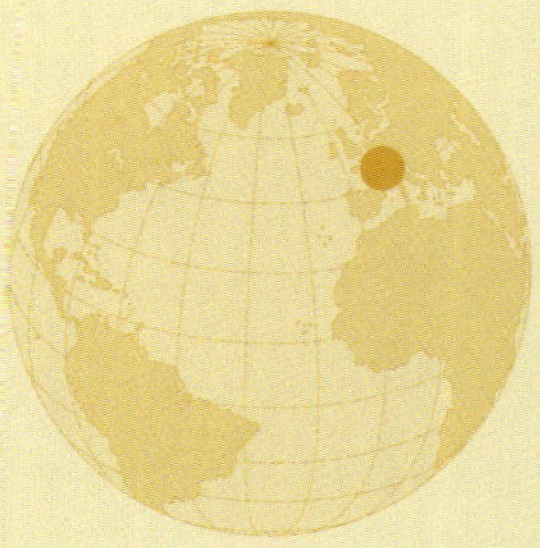

Aftenposten
www.aftenposten.no
Norwegen, Oslo

SVERIGES STÖRSTA MORGONTIDNING

NUMMER 247
VECKA 37 • 6

DAGENS NYHETER.

ONSDAG 12 SEPTEMBER 2001

www.dn.se — VARDAGAR 10:– LÖRDAG/SÖNDAG 11:– TEL: 08-738 10 00

World Trade Center kollapsade. Två kapade flygplan flög rakt in i de två tornen i skyskrapan World Trade Center mitt på Manhattan i New York. Kort senare rasade de båda 412 meter höga tvillingtornen samman. Omkring 40 000 människor hade sin arbetsplats i World Trade Center. Hur många som dödats och skadats är ännu oklart.

FOTO: AP/ABC

ATTACKEN MOT USA

Krigstillstånd råder i praktiken i USA sedan landet utsatts för den största terroristattacken någonsin. Ett mycket stort antal människor dödades och skadades, hur många är ännu okänt.

FÖRSVARSHÖGKVARTERET Pentagon utanför Washington och World Trade Center i New York attackerades på tisdagen med kapade flygplan. Bara i de två 110 våningar höga World Trade Center-tornen arbetade cirka 40 000 människor. Ett fjärde plan störtade utanför Pittsburgh i Pennsylvania. Innan planet störtade ringde en passagerare larmnumret och ropade: "Vi är kapade, vi är kapade."

President George W Bush avbröt omedelbart ett besök i Florida. Bush sade i ett uttalande att USA ska "spåra upp och straffa de människor som utförde denna handling".

Landets militär sattes i högsta beredskap, gränserna mot Kanada och Mexiko stängdes och det blev omöjligt att ta sig in i eller ut ur landet. Samtliga federala byggnader stängdes i Washington, kontorsbyggnaderna evakuerades och efter ett par timmar var Washington en tömd spökstad. Vita huset och kongressbyggnaden spärrades av och vaktades av k-pistbeväpnade federala agenter.

Vid midnatt hördes explosioner och sågs flygande robotar i Afghanistans huvudstad Kabul. Enligt amerikanska talesmän rörde det sig dock inte om ett anfall från USA.

Terrorattacken mot USA, A4–A11, C1

USA
Boston
NEW YORK
Washington
0 100 km

1. 08.45 kraschar en Boeing från American Airlines i World Trade Centers norra torn i New York.
2. 09.05 kraschar ett av United Airlines Boeingplan i det södra tornet.
3. 09.43 kraschar ett flygplan i försvarshögkvarteret Pentagon i Washington.
4. 10.10 kraschar United Airlines flight 93 sydöst om Pittsburgh i Pennsylvania.

GRAFIK: DN

"Det var som en mardröm"

DN i New York
Lennart Pehrson

DET HAR HUNNIT GÅ några timmar sedan katastrofen inträffade, men hans kropp skakar fortfarande.

– Det var som en mardröm. Gatan där vi tog oss ut var fylld av kroppsdelar som vi tvingades kliva över, berättar han.

När den första explosionen kom hade Jeff Angione just kommit till jobbet på börsgolvet på American Stock Exchange i en lägre byggnad bara ett par hundra meter från World Trade Center och de höga torn som lite senare kollapsade.

Jeff Angione gick ut på gatan med sina kolleger och stannade tillräckligt länge för att på nära håll se hur flygplan nummer två kraschade in i det andra tornet i en "stor eldboll och enorma rökmoln". När han en stund senare lämnade nedre Manhattan med den sista tunnelbanan som gick såg området ut som en krigszon med kaos och panikslagna människor.

Svart rök och flygande föremål fyllde gatorna åtskilliga kvarter bort när delar av skyskraporna föll. En del klarade sig ut ur de byggnaderna genom att springa i trapporna 50 eller 70 våningar ned. Men många dog när flygplanen kraschade in i byggnaderna, andra satt fast när de lite senare föll samman.

Målen för attackerna hade knappast valts av en tillfällighet.

World Trade Center var inte bara ett jättelikt kontorskomplex där närmare 40 000 människor arbetar. Byggnaderna har också sedan 70-talet varit en symbol för New York, en central del i Manhattans skyline, en del av det mäktiga finansdistriktet runt Wall Street och en stolt påminnelse om New York som "världens huvudstad".

Dessutom har World Trade Center varit en av New Yorks populäraste destinationer för turister som kunnat beskåda en vidunderlig utsikt från taket på en av byggnaderna.

Fortsättning på sidan A 8

"Ett krig mot demokratin" Ledare, A 2

"Det finns ingen plats att ta vägen" Debatt, A 4

USA förlamad supermakt Sidan A 7

Misstankar riktas mot bin Ladin Sidan A 10

Skärpt säkerhet i Sverige Sidan A 11

Världsekonomins grundvalar skakas Sidan A 11

DN.se Läs senaste nytt om attacken mot USA • Webb-tv • Rörlig grafik • Länkar • www.dn.se

VÄDER, A 18
Halvklart och någon skur. Sydostlig vind. Cirka 16 grader.

MILJÖMÄRKT TRYCKSAK

7 388101 001007

❶ Attacke gegen die USA

❷ In den USA herrscht nach der größten Terrorattacke überhaupt praktisch der Kriegszustand. Eine sehr große Anzahl von Menschen wurde getötet oder verletzt; wie viele es waren, ist noch unbekannt

❸ Es war wie ein Albtraum

❹ Ein Krieg gegen die Demokratie

Es gibt keinen Platz zur Flucht

USA – gelähmte Supermacht

Verdacht richtet sich gegen bin Laden

Verschärfte Sicherheit in Schweden

Grundfeste der Weltökonomie erschüttert

Dagens Nyheter
www.dn.se
Schweden, Stockholm

DEL 1
LEDARE 2
DEBATT 3
POLITIK 14
EKONOMI 14
NAMN 27
VÄRLDENS GÅNG 29

DEL 2
ALLMÄNT 32
UTLAND 34
GÖTEBORG 36
LOKALT 38
VÄSTSVERIGE 43
SPORT 45
KONSUMENT 50

Göteborgs-Posten

www.gp.se

Månadens fyr: HANÖ

ONSDAG 12 SEPTEMBER 2001 • NR 248 • VECKA 37 • 143:E ÅRGÅNGEN • PRIS 12 KRONOR • VÄXEL 031-62 40 00 • PRENUMERATION 031-80 47 00 • PRIVATANNONSER 031-80 06 00

New York 2001-09-11

Bild: DOUG KANTER

WORLD TRADE CENTER I RUINER. Förödelsen vid World Trade Center var i det närmaste total. Först kollapsade de två Twin Tower-byggnaderna sedan flygplan kraschat rakt in i dem. Senare på kvällen rasade även ett 47-våningshus i området.

Historiens värsta terrordåd hittills

Tre skyskrapor i ruiner efter attacken i New York

■ USA är ett land i chock. Gårdagens terrorattack är den värsta som världen hittills skådat. Klockan nio lokal tid i går morse kraschade ett trafikflygplan rakt in i World Trade Centers norra skyskrapa på Manhattan. 18 minuter senare kom ett betydligt större trafikflygplan, och kraschade mot den södra skyskrapan. En dryg timma senare hade de båda 110 våningar höga byggnaderna kollapsat.

En stund senare kom nästa attack, denna gång mot försvarshögkvarteret i Pentagon. Även här var det en självmordsattack med flygplan och fem våningar rasade samman på byggnaden.

Senare under kvällen rasade en tredje byggnad, 47 våningar hög, vid World Trade Center. Ytterligare ett höghus på Manhattan höll på rasa i morse sedan det brunnit i tio timmar.

Totalt kapades under gårdagen minst fyra trafikflygplan av terrorister, ett vapen som användes var kniv.

Hur många offer dåden krävde var i natt oklart men det handlar om tusentals offer bara i New York.

Omkring 200 brandmän och uppemot 100 poliser, som deltog i räddningsarbetet på Manhattan, befarades ha omkommit eller saknades tidigt i morse.

EXTRA

Bush lovar leta upp de skyldiga

Halv tre i natt, svensk tid, höll president George W Bush ett kort, men känsloladdat tv-tal till det amerikanska folket.

Han betonade att USA inte låter sig knäckas av terrordåd.

Alla officiella institutioner ska i dag hålla öppet som vanligt.

Han lovade också att leta upp terroristerna och ställa dem inför rätta.

– Jag gör ingen skillnad på de som utförde dådet och de som skyddar dem, sade han.

Folk kastade sig ut i panik

■ Fruktansvärda scener utspelade sig i samband med självmordsattackerna mot World Trade Center. Folk kastade sig i panik ut från skyskraporna, samtidigt som ett regn av glassplitter föll ner mot marken.

Ett sjukhus i närbelägna Greenwich Village sade sig ha "tagit emot hundratals människor med brännskador från topp till tå".

Reino Björk från Göteborg blev ögonvittne till katastrofen.

– Efter ett tag hördes ett enormt dunder och ett av tornen kollapsade. Det följdes av ett stort rökmoln och människor på gatan skrek rakt ut.

Han pekas ut som ansvarig

■ Vem ligger bakom terrorattackerna i USA?

Det är frågan som hela USA nu ställer sig. De starkaste misstankarna riktas mot den saudifödde Usama bin Ladin.

Den omkring 45-årige bin Ladin har fått skulden för att ha organiserat och finansierat bombningarna av de amerikanska ambassaderna i Kenya och Tanzania i augusti 1998. Då dog över 200 människor. Som bestraffning bombade USA påstådda utbildninggsläger för terrorister i Afghanistan samt en fabrik i Sudan, som bin Ladin sades vara delägare i.

I natt skakades Afghanistans huvudstad Kabul av en robotattack. USA förnekade dock att de har något med robotanfallet att göra.

Terrorattacken mot USA, sidorna 2, 3, 4, 5, 6, 7, 8, 9, 10, 11, 12, 13 och www.gp.se

7 388111 001202

1 **Schlimmster Terrorangriff in der Geschichte**

2 Drei Wolkenkratzer in Schutt und Asche nach der Terrorattacke in New York

3 Die Ruinen des World Trade Centers
Die Zerstörungen am World Trade Center waren nahezu total. Zuerst kollabierten die beiden Haupttürme des World Trade Centers, nachdem die Flugzeuge direkt in sie hineingeflogen waren. Später am Abend stürzte dann noch ein 47-geschossiges Wohnhaus in sich zusammen

4 Bush verspricht die Schuldigen aufzuspüren

5 Er wird als Verantwortlicher genannt

6 Menschen stürzten sich aus Panik in die Tiefe

Göteborgs-Posten
www.gp.se
Schweden, Göteborg

12

ISSN 1406-0981

EESTI PÄEVALEHT

Postimees

Viking Lotto oodatav jackpot 9 miljonit krooni.
Võidutase 5+1 on kasvanud üle 500 000 krooni!
www.eestiloto.ee

6 krooni | Kolmapäev, 12. september 2001 | Nr. 211 (3276)

TERROR USAs

AP

1 Terror in den USA

Postimees
www.postimees.ee
Estland, Tartu

LA STAMPA

MERCOLEDÌ 12 SETTEMBRE 2001. ANNO 135. N. 251. L.1.500 / € 0,77 (PREZZI ESTERO IN ULTIMA) • SPEDIZIONE ABB. POSTALE 45% ART. 2 COMMA 20/B LEGGE 662/96 - TO • www.lastampa.it

TERRORE NEL CUORE DI NEW YORK, MIGLIAIA DI VITTIME. BUSH: SAPREMO RISPONDERE E PUNIRE I COLPEVOLI

ATTACCO ALL'AMERICA

Quattro aerei di linea dirottati e usati come missili
Due colpiscono le Twin Towers che crollano
le vittime forse ventimila, in azione 55 kamikaze
Jet sul Pentagono, un altro cade vicino a Pittsburgh

Sospesi i voli, bloccate le frontiere e il porto
Chiusi gli spazi aerei di Israele, Londra e Bruxelles
Stato di allerta in Europa e nelle basi militari Usa
Si segue la pista del terrorista Osama Bin Laden

Stop a Wall Street, crack nelle Borse europee
in un giorno bruciati 810 mila miliardi
Greenspan e la Bce: pronti a intervenire
Il petrolio a 29 dollari, l'oro balza ai massimi

UNA GUERRA SENZA NEMICI

Marcello Sorgi

L'ATTACCO all'America, come lo abbiamo seguito in diretta, in un clima di allarme da guerra che s'è rapidamente diffuso in tutto il mondo, era talmente impensabile fino a ieri che neppure i film più spietati e spettacolari lo avevano mai descritto così. Le torri del World Trade Center, edifici simbolo del progresso e del commercio mondiale, erano già state oggetto di un'azione terroristica; ma non avremmo mai pensato di vederle crollare sotto i colpi di aerei pilotati da kamikaze, in una nuvola di fumo che avvolge tutt'a un tratto vite, storia, presente, futuro, soccorritori inermi, fili telefonici e antenne satellitari, la Casa Bianca, il Pentagono, il Congresso, l'efficientissimo sistema di sicurezza americano.

Anche per chi la guerra non l'ha vissuta e l'ha studiata sui libri di scuola, la sensazione, l'atmosfera ricordano Pearl Harbor sessant'anni fa. Ma è una Pearl Harbor senza Giappone, una guerra senza nemico, contro la quale non serve l'atomica e neppure lo scudo spaziale.

E nel silenzio tetro del dopo, un silenzio rotto solo dal rombo lontano e solitario dell'aereo presidenziale di George W. Bush, che per un giorno ha cercato in cielo la salvezza sua e degli Stati Uniti, non c'è solo la debolezza di un paese ferito, della maggiore democrazia al mondo, dell'avversario primo e unico, talvolta, del terrorismo mondiale. No: a ben vedere è la democrazia nel suo insieme che accusa il colpo; è il mondo globalizzato, che vede infrangersi l'illusione di una ricchezza diffusa fondata su un più forte regime di scambi; è l'idea stessa di frontiere più aperte, migrazioni più libere, società più evolute, che si scontra col sorgere di nuovi muri.

L'Italia certo - ma non solo l'Italia - è chiamata a una nuova speciale solidarietà con gli Stati Uniti, alleati che nel ruolo di guardiani dei diritti violati, di avversari delle sopraffazioni, di combattenti delle cause perdute, hanno sempre fatto la parte più importante. Non c'è più spazio per ambiguità come quelle che in passato accompagnavano le manifestazioni ad Aviano, per il Cermis o contro la pena di morte; per le spallucce fatte più di recente a cospetto della chiusura dell'ambasciata americana a Roma, dopo un allarme terrorismo; per le indulgenze di questi giorni del movimento antiglobal verso la violenza di strada. La ripugnanza per lo schiavismo del Settecento denunciata dalla conferenza di Durban può diventare una comoda scappatoia, se non è altrettanto chiaro l'atteggiamento verso i crimini contemporanei.

Il mondo intero appare vittima di una desolazione in cui, per dirla con Carlo Levi, «Cristo non è arrivato, né vi è arrivato il tempo, né la speranza, l'anima individuale, il legame tra le cause e gli effetti, la ragione, la storia». Ma beninteso, questo non può essere un alibi.

L'esplosione causata dall'attacco suicida su una delle Twin Towers. L'altra è già in fiamme. Entrambe crolleranno pochi minuti dopo.

LA TESTIMONIANZA DI UN GIORNALISTA DE LA STAMPA

«Ho visto corpi cadere dalle torri in fiamme»

Glauco Maggi
inviato a NEW YORK

«Ero davanti alle Torri quando tutto è successo. Ho visto la prima persona volare dall'alto. Erano le 9,11. Sembrava già morta mentre ondeggiava cadendo dalla torre in fiamme. Poi altre, alcune parevano ancora vive. Ne ho contate una decina, con i miei occhi. Le ho viste cadere accompagnate dal lamento straziato della folla nelle strade del Sud di New York. Una folla che guardava verso l'alto, dove ieri si immaginava l'agonia, la carneficina: come in un mondo rovesciato, l'inferno. L'appuntamento con la fine è per le 9,52. La prima torre crolla in una nuvola alta cento metri, che tutto avvolge» A PAGINA 3

DA PAGINA 2 A PAGINA 17

IL DIARIO DI MANHATTAN, «DOWNTOWN SEMBRA POMPEI»
Chiusi i telefonini, i profughi sul ponte di Brooklyn in fila per donare il sangue: «E voi europei, che cosa fate?»
Gianni Riotta A PAGINA 5

COME REAGIRE: E' LA PROVA PIU' DIFFICILE PER GLI USA
Per orrenda che sia l'offesa, la linea giusta è colpire soltanto quando si è certi dell'identità dell'avversario
Boris Biancheri A PAGINA 17

IL GIGANTE FERITO NON RESTERA' IN GINOCCHIO
Questa tragedia poteva forse essere evitata se gli americani si fossero subito fatti carico della crisi del Medio Oriente
Igor Man A PAGINA 9

CIAMPI: L'ITALIA E' IN LUTTO, IL MONDO CIVILE SI RIBELLA
Messaggio del Presidente al paese: «Offesa l'intera comunità internazionale. Serve una lotta senza quartiere al terrorismo»
Aldo Cazzullo A PAGINA 13

COSSIGA: «DA NOI QUALCUNO DIRÀ CHE HANNO FATTO BENE»
«Chi pensa che l'ordine costituito si possa rovesciare con violenza troverà, con le debite proporzioni, giustificazioni all'accaduto»
Mario Calabresi A PAGINA 15

1 **Anschlag auf Amerika**

2 Terror im Herzen von New York, tausende Todesopfer.
Bush: Wir werden zu antworten wissen und die Schuldigen bestrafen

3 Ein Krieg ohne Feinde

4 Zeugenaussage eines Journalisten der Stampa
»Ich habe Menschen aus den brennenden Türmen fallen sehen«

La Stampa
www.lastampa.it
Italien, Turin

12

Fondato nel 1876

CORRIERE DELLA SERA

MERCOLEDÌ 12 SETTEMBRE 2001
ANNO 126 - N. 216
Lire 1.500

IL PIU' GRAVE ATTO DI GUERRA DAL 1945. IL MONDO SCONVOLTO E PARALIZZATO, ESERCITI IN ALLERTA. BUSH: PUNIREMO

Manhattan avvolta da fumo e polvere dopo il crollo delle Torri. Qui sopra, il profilo dell'isola con i due grattacieli ancora intatti

Attacco all'America e alla civiltà

Aerei di linea dirottati dai terroristi si schiantano contro i grattacieli di New York e sul Pentagono a Washington
Crollano le Torri gemelle, forse ventimila morti. Sospettati gli islamici di Bin Laden, nella notte bombe su Kabul

SIAMO TUTTI AMERICANI
di FERRUCCIO DE BORTOLI

Il secondo aereo sta per colpire la seconda torre, mentre la prima è già in fiamme

Una persona si lancia nel vuoto da uno dei grattacieli colpiti e incendiati

LA POTENZA VULNERABILE
di SERGIO ROMANO

IL NEMICO INVISIBILE
di FRANCO VENTURINI

IL RACCONTO DI UNA TESTIMONE / «Un boato, sono corsa in strada, le Torri erano in fiamme»

«Ho visto decine di persone lanciarsi dalle finestre»

di MARIA TERESA COMETTO

ALL'INTERNO

LA METROPOLI – La fuga dei sopravvissuti «Calpestavano i neonati» – Alessandra Farkas

LE COMUNICAZIONI – Dal Pacifico a Londra voli fermi e telefoni muti – Mangiarotti e Montefiori

LA NAZIONE – Lo choc di una Pearl Harbor «E' il giorno del giudizio» – Goffredo Buccini

NEI PAESI ARABI – Applausi e feste per le strade di Beirut e Gerusalemme – Maria Grazia Cutuli

L'ECONOMIA – Wall Street resta chiusa Paura nelle Borse europee – De Rosa e Radice

A ROMA – Berlusconi incontra Ciampi e rilancia lo scudo stellare – Breda, Di Caro, Saulino

Corriere della Sera
www.corriere.it
Italien, Mailand

1 **Angriff auf Amerika und die Zivilisation**

Von Terroristen entführte Linienflugzeuge zerschellen gegen die Wolkenkratzer von New York und das Pentagon in Washington. Die Zwillingstürme stürzen ein, vielleicht 20 000 Tote. Die Islamisten um bin Laden unter Verdacht, in der Nacht fielen Bomben auf Kabul

2 Die schwerste Kriegshandlung seit 1945. Die Welt ist erschüttert und gelähmt. Militär in Alarmzustand. Bush: Wir werden die Schuldigen bestrafen

3 Wir sind alle Amerikaner

4 Die verwundbare Macht

5 Der unsichtbare Feind

6 Der Bericht eines Augenzeugen: »Ein Donnern, ich lief auf die Straße, die Türme standen in Flammen«
»Ich habe etwa zehn Personen gesehen, die sich aus den Fenstern stürzten«

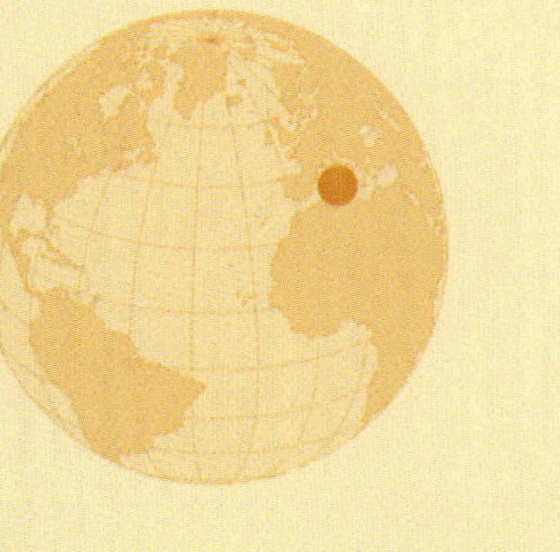

L'OSSERVATORE ROMANO

Via del Pellegrino 00120 CITTÀ DEL VATICANO - Segreteria di Redazione 0669883461 / 0669884442 - fax 0669883675
Servizio fotografico 0669884797 - Marketing e Diffusione 0669899470 - fax 0669882818 - ABBONAMENTI 0669899483
0669899480 - fax 0669885164 - e-mail: ornet@ossrom.va
WWW.VATICAN.VA/news_services/or/home_ita.html
SPEDIZIONE IN ABBONAMENTO POSTALE - ROMA
CONTO CORRENTE POSTALE N. 649004

GIORNALE QUOTIDIANO POLITICO RELIGIOSO
UNICUIQUE SUUM NON PRAEVALEBUNT

Copia L. 1.500 - € 0,78
Copia arretrata L. 2.500 - € 1,30

Anno CXLI - N. 208 (42.846) CITTÀ DEL VATICANO Mercoledì 12 Settembre 2001

CRIMINALE SEQUENZA DI ATTACCHI TERRORISTICI CONTRO GLI STATI UNITI D'AMERICA

La follia del terrore

La follia del terrore ha colpito oggi gli Stati Uniti. Il disastro riaccende nella memoria quello di Pearl Harbor.

Un'ora di follia sembra essersi impossessata del mondo. Orrore, sgomento, angoscia attanagliano l'intera comunità internazionale.

Menti diaboliche hanno attuato e stanno perseguendo crimini mostruosi che fanno sprofondare l'umanità in un inimmaginabile clima di guerra.

NEW YORK, 11.

Attacco terroristico al cuore degli Stati Uniti: due aerei di linea sono stati dirottati e lanciati contro il World Trade Center di New York, un altro contro il Pentagono. Nella capitale federale sono stati sgomberati la Casa Bianca, la sede del Congresso e i ministeri, a New York il Palazzo di Vetro dell'Onu e i grattacieli di Manhattan. Un altro velivolo, con 93 passeggeri a bordo, si è schiantato al suolo nei pressi dell'aeroporto di Pittsburgh, in Pennsylvania. Un altro aereo dell'«United Airlines» — riporta l'Ansa — è caduto in una località per ora sconosciuta.

Gli Stati Uniti sono al centro di quello che appare come il più grave attacco terroristico mai subito sul proprio territorio. Il Presidente, George W. Bush, — che secondo fonti Nato sarebbe stato condotto in luogo sicuro — ha parlato di «tragedia nazionale», confermando che quello in corso ha tutte le caratteristiche di «un attacco terroristico al nostro Paese», mentre il Segretario di Stato, Colin Powell, attualmente a Lima, ha assicurato che «lo spirito della democrazia non morirà mai». Non ci sono indicazioni per il momento sul numero dei morti, anche se il sindaco di New York, Rudolph Giuliani — che ha ordinato lo sgombero della parte Sud di Manhattan e di tutte le scuole della città — ha parlato di un «enorme numero di vittime».

Il primo aereo ha colpito una delle torri gemelle del World Trade Center, simbolo di New York, poco prima delle 9 (le 15 in Italia). Mentre era in corso lo sgombero del complesso e sul posto accorrevano i mezzi di soccorso, alle 9.15 un secondo aereo, dirottato subito dopo il decollo da Boston, si è schiantato contro l'altra torre. Sono seguite varie esplosioni. Le due torri sono crollate travolgendo e mettendo in fuga i soccorritori.

A Manhattan si è diffuso il panico, con la parte meridionale dell'isola avvolta in una nuvola di fumo e i grattacieli della città sgomberati in fretta dal personale. Ponti e tunnel sono stati chiusi, il traffico è rimasto paralizzato. Wall Street ha rinviato a tempo indeterminato l'apertura delle contrattazioni.

Le comunicazioni telefoniche stanno incontrando grandi difficoltà all'interno degli Stati Uniti, sulla scia degli attacchi terroristici delle ultime ore. Sia la rete telefonica fissa che quella cellulare hanno gravi problemi, soprattutto nelle comunicazioni tra New York e Washington. Restano per il momento regolarmente funzionanti le linee all'interno di New York per le chiamate urbane. Tutti i voli transatlantici per gli Usa sono stati dirottati sul Canada.

Gli esperti che stanno valutando le caratteristiche degli attentati a New York e a Washington segnalano che essi hanno evidentemente, per i terroristi che li hanno organizzati, un preciso valore simbolico. Con questi due attentati infatti si è voluto colpire gli Usa come potenza economico-finanziaria (attaccando le torri gemelle del World Trade Center, nel quartiere della più importante borsa del mondo) e come potenza militare (investendo direttamente il Pentagono).

La preghiera e la vicinanza del Papa in questo oscuro e tragico momento

The Hon. George W. Bush
President of the United States of America
The White House
WASHINGTON DC

Shocked by the unspeakable horror of today's inhuman terrorist attacks against innocent people in different parts of the United States I hurry to express to you and your fellow citizens my profound sorrow and my closeness in prayer for the Nation at this dark and tragic moment. Commending the victims to Almighty God's eternal mercy, I implore his strength upon all involved in rescue efforts and in caring for the survivors. I beg God to sustain you and the American People in this hour of suffering and trial.

IOANNES PAULUS PP. II

All'On. George W. Bush
Presidente degli Stati Uniti d'America
Casa Bianca
WASHINGTON DC

Colpito dall'indicibile orrore degli inumani attacchi terroristici compiuti oggi contro persone innocenti in differenti parti degli Stati Uniti mi urge esprimere a lei e ai suoi concittadini il mio profondo dolore e la mia vicinanza, nella preghiera, alla Nazione in questo oscuro e tragico momento. Raccomandando le vittime all'eterna misericordia di Dio Onnipotente imploro la sua forza su quanti sono impegnati nelle operazioni di soccorso e nelle cure ai sopravvissuti. Prego Dio di sostenere lei e il popolo americano in questa ora di sofferenza e di prova.

GIOVANNI PAOLO PP. II

George W. Bush: «Una tragedia nazionale»

WASHINGTON, 11.

«Questo è un momento difficile per l'America: oggi, abbiamo avuto una tragedia nazionale»: con queste parole, il Presidente degli Stati Uniti, George W. Bush, che era in Florida, s'è oggi rivolto al Paese in televisione. Il Presidente ha parlato prima che gli attacchi terroristici colpissero anche Washington. George W. Bush ha detto: «Due aeroplani si sono schiantati contro il World Trade Center in un apparente attacco terroristico contro il nostro Paese».

Il Presidente americano ha aggiunto: «Ho parlato col vice Presidente, con il Governatore di New York, con il Direttore dell'Fbi. Ho ordinato che tutte le risorse del Governo federale vadano ad aiutare le vittime e le loro famiglie e servano a condurre un'indagine a tutto campo per dare la caccia e trovare la gente che ha compiuto questi atti».

«Il terrorismo contro il nostro Paese non pagherà» ha quindi concluso George W. Bush. E, chiedendo un momento di silenzio ai presenti, ha pregato: «Possa Dio benedire le vittime, le loro famiglie e l'America».

Orrore, sgomento, angoscia in tutto il mondo

NEW YORK, 11.

Orrore, sgomento, angoscia. Sono i sentimenti che si sono impadroniti della scena mondiale non appena l'eco della tragedia consumatasi nel cuore degli Stati Uniti ha cominciato a diffondersi.

Sgomberate e messe sotto stretta sorveglianza tutte le Ambasciate americane nel mondo, in particolare quella in Albania — Paese considerato dalla CIA come una delle basi operative di Osama Bin Laden, accusato di aver compiuto numerosi attentati contro strutture americane —, mentre caccia militari si sono alzati in volo nei cieli degli Stati Uniti per intercettare eventuali altri aerei dirottati immediatamente dopo l'inaudita serie di attentati che ha sconvolto il Paese.

Sconcerto, incredulità ed orrore intanto si diffondevano nel mondo. Tutti i Capi di Stato o di Governo che per motivi diversi si trovavano in viaggio o comunque lontani dalle loro sedi, sono rientrati o stanno rientrando per seguire da vicino l'evolversi della situazione. Numerosissimi governi hanno dato la loro disponibilità per qualsiasi tipo di aiuto di cui gli Stati Uniti dovessero avere bisogno in questo drammatico momento.

Tra le prime reazioni internazionali da registrare l'immediata convocazione da parte del Presidente russo, Vladimir Putin, del Ministro degli esteri, Igor Ivanov, per «consultazioni sugli attentati terroristici nelle città americane». Putin tramite il suo portavoce ha fatto immediatamente pervenire le sue condoglianze al Presidente degli Stati Uniti «per l'immensa tragedia». Sempre dalla Russia l'ex leader sovietico Mikhail Gorbaciov ha definito l'attacco come «una tragedia non solo nazionale americana, ma per tutta l'umanità» ed ha espresso l'auspicio che «tutti gli Stati ed i popoli si uniscano contro questa follia del terrorismo». Gorbaciov ha anche chiesto l'immediata riunione del Consiglio di Sicurezza dell'Onu per affrontare l'emergenza del terrorismo. «Quelli che sono dietro questi atti — ha aggiunto Gorbaciov — devono essere portati in tribunale e castigati nel modo più severo».

Il Presidente dell'Autorità Palestinese Yasser Arafat rivolgendosi ad un gruppo di giornalisti ha voluto esprimere «le mie condoglianze — ha detto — e le condoglianze del popolo palestinese al Presidente statunitense per questo terribile atto». «Condanniamo totalmente — ha concluso Arafat — questa grave operazione... Siamo completamente sconvolti».

Scioccato il Premier britannico Tony Blair. Raggiunto dalla notizia mentre stava per incontrare rappresentanti sindacali inglesi ha annullato l'impegno ed è rientrato a Londra. Blair, dopo aver espresso il suo cordoglio, ha sollecitato uno «sforzo congiunto per sradicare il male del terrorismo di massa» e ha definito gli attacchi «i più terribili e scioccanti eventi negli Stati Uniti». «Questo nuovo terrorismo di massa — ha aggiunto — è il nuovo male del mondo di oggi. Dobbiamo sradicare questo male tutti insieme».

«Sostegno assoluto al popolo statunitense» ha assicurato il Presidente francese Jacques Chirac che, interrotto bruscamente un impegno ufficiale in Bretagna, è rientrato a Parigi. Chirac ha anche dichiarato che «con immensa commozione la Francia apprende la notizia di questi mostruosi attentati» ed ha assicurato al Presidente Bush il pieno sostegno del popolo francese.

Anche il Cancelliere tedesco Schroeder ha scritto al Presidente degli Stati Uniti George W. Bush esprimendo a nome del Governo tedesco sgomento e dolore. «Il mio Governo — ha detto — condanna nel modo più veemente questi attentati terroristici» ed è vicinissimo al popolo e al Governo statunitense. «Si tratta — ha aggiunto il Cancelliere — di una dichiarazione di guerra al mondo civile».

Il Presidente della Repubblica Italiana Ciampi in un messaggio a reti televisive unificate ha espresso esecrazione, orrore e sgomento del popolo italiano di fronte agli attentati compiuti contro gli Stati Uniti. «L'Italia è in lutto — ha detto il Presidente —. È necessaria una lotta senza quartiere contro il terrorismo». Ciampi aveva immediatamente inviato un messaggio di solidarietà al Presidente Bush: «L'Italia — aveva scritto — ed il popolo italiano sono vicini a Lei e a tutti gli americani nel lutto, nel dolore e nell'esecrazione. L'Italia è al fianco degli Stati Uniti. La comunità internazionale deve rispondere compatta a questi atti esecrandi». Commentando la tragedia Ciampi aveva detto che: «Non vi sono parole che possano esprimere il mio sgomento ed il mio orrore nell'apprendere dei devastanti attentati che hanno colpito gli Stati Uniti, ma che offendono e chiamano in causa tutta l'umanità».

Il Ministro degli esteri Ruggiero al rientro dalla Croazia, ha detto che quanto è accaduto negli Stati Uniti «può cambiare i destini del mondo in cui viviamo».

Condanna e cordoglio hanno espresso anche l'Unione Europea e la Nato il cui Segretario generale George Robertson ha duramente condannato l'attacco agli Usa come «un atto barbarico».

Reazioni si sono avute naturalmente anche ad altri livelli.

Massima allerta è stata decretata in tutte le basi militari della Nato e i più grandi aeroporti internazionali sono stati messi sotto strettissimo controllo. Israele ha dichiarato lo stato di massima allerta

Ripercussioni anche su tutte le borse le quali per frenare il crollo improvviso seguito al diffondersi delle drammatiche notizie hanno chiuso su tutte le Piazze.

1 Der Wahnsinn des Terrors

2 Verbrecherische Serie von terroristischen Anschlägen gegen die Vereinigten Staaten von Amerika

3 Das Gebet und der Beistand des Papstes in diesem dunklen und tragischen Moment

4 George W. Bush: Eine nationale Tragödie

5 Entsetzen, Bestürzung, Kummer auf der ganzen Welt

12

L'Osservatore Romano
www.vatican.va/news_services/or
Vatikanstadt

ΤΑ ΝΕΑ

ΤΕΤΑΡΤΗ 12 ΣΕΠΤΕΜΒΡΙΟΥ 2001 ΔΡΧ. 300 - ΕΥΡΩ 0,88

ΤΡΟΜΟΣ ΠΑΝΩ ΑΠ’ ΤΟΝ ΚΟΣΜΟ

“ΓΙΑΤΙ αν η έντρομη αμερικανική κοινή γνώμη αυτή την ώρα βρίσκεται σε πλήρη σύγχυση... ΠΟΙΟΣ αμφιβάλλει ότι η αντίδραση του βαριά πληγωμένου αμερικανικού γοήτρου θα εκδηλωθεί... ΚΑΙ ποιος μπορεί να προβλέψει τις συνέπειες ενός πιθανού φαύλου κύκλου της βίας... ΕΙΣ βάρος της παγκόσμιας ειρήνης και ιδίως – είναι τάχα ασύνηθες; – εις βάρος άλλων αθώων σε μια τυφλή αντιτρομοκρατική φρενίτιδα”

Από τις ΡΙΠΕΣ (σελ. 3)

1 Terror über der Welt

2 »Auch wenn sich die öffentliche Meinung der erschrockenen Amerikaner zu dieser Stunde in völliger Verwirrung befindet ... Wer zweifelt daran, dass eine Reaktion auf die tiefe Verletzung des amerikanischen Prestiges folgen wird ... Und wer kann die Konsequenzen eines wahrscheinlichen Teufelskreises der Gewalt vorhersehen ... zu Lasten des Weltfriedens und besonders – ist das so ungewöhnlich? – zu Lasten anderer Unschuldiger in einem blinden antiterroristischen Wahnsinn«

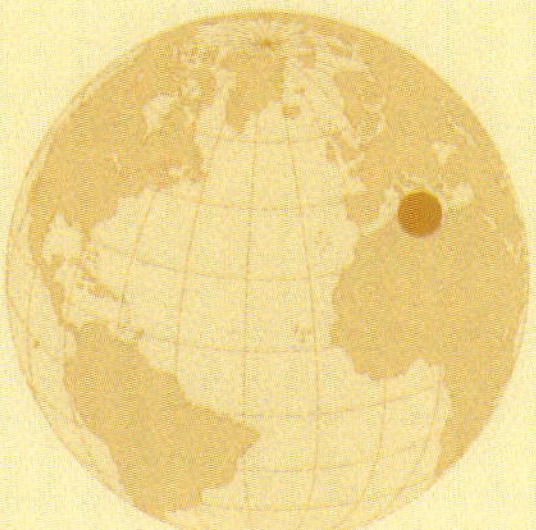

Ta Nea
http://ta-nea.dolnet.gr
Griechenland, Athen

12

12 stran mimořádného zpravodajství

www.lidovky.cz
24 hodin aktuálních zpráv

LIDOVÉ NOVINY

Konta pomoci a spojení na humanitární organizace
Strana 8

Čtvrtek 13. září 2001 * * NEZÁVISLÝ DENÍK ZALOŽENÝ 1893 Cena 8,50 Kč

BUSH: JE TO VÁLKA

Den po apokalypse: Tisíce mrtvých. Hlavním podezřelým zůstává bin Ládin

VLAJKA NAD ROZVALINAMI. Hasiči vztyčují americkou vlajku na troskách zničeného newyorského Světového obchodního centra
Foto AP

USA chystají teroristům tvrdou odpověď

AMERICKÁ TRAGÉDIE
- Amerika počítá mrtvé
- Mezi zraněnými je česká studentka
- Jak došlo k únosu letadel a k zřícení mrakodrapů
- Cena benzinu roste

Čtěte na stranách 1 až 12

Spojené státy se včera vzpamatovávaly ze šoku po úterním teroristickém útoku, který si vyžádal tisíce obětí. Americké úřady pátrají po organizátorech tohoto největšího teroristického činu v historii.

WASHINGTON - „Vražedné útoky proti naší zemi byly víc než teroristické činy - byly válečným aktem," prohlásil včera americký prezident George W. Bush v mimořádném televizním projevu věnovaném úterním útokům proti Světovému obchodnímu centru v New Yorku a ministerstvu obrany ve Washingtonu. Přesný počet obětí útoků zatím není znám. Americké úřady ho odhadují na tisíce. Podle dostupných informací není mezi mrtvými žádný občan ČR.

Bílý dům má podle svého vysoce postaveného představitele „závažné informace", které spojují úterní útoky s teroristou Usámou bin Ládinem. Prezident podle téhož zdroje zvažuje různé možnosti vojenského zásahu proti bin Ládinovi a případně i proti Afghánistánu, kde se skrývá.

Ministr zahraničí USA Colin Powell je přesvědčen, že vyšetřování v dohledné době odhalí, kdo útoky provedl. „Odpovíme, jako když se jedná o válku. Bude to dlouhodobý zápas," upřesnil ministr.

Riziko dalších útoků kleslo

Z trosek budovy newyorského obchodního centra včera záchranáři vyprostili několik vážně zraněných lidí a desítky mrtvých. Naděje, že se podaří ještě zachránit další z několika tisíc zasypaných osob, stále žije. V budově washingtonského Pentagonu je ale podobná naděje mizivá. Počet obětí se tam odhaduje až na osm set.

Aktuální riziko dalších útoků zřejmě pokleslo. „Věříme, že pachatelé splnili svůj plán, a tudíž se riziko výrazně snížilo," řekl mluvčí Bílého domu Ari Fleischer. **Pavel Máša**

V troskách jsou stále živí lidé, někteří volají z mobilu

NEW YORK, 11 hodin místního času **(od zvláštního zpravodaje LN v USA)** - Trosky Světového obchodního centra (WTC) pohřbily zřejmě tisíce lidí. Je ale velká šance, že pod troskami jsou stále živí. Tisíce záchranářů prohledávají zbytky zřícených budov. Je pro ně připraveno na deset tisíc jídel. Celý Manhattan je pokrytý vrstvou prachu a trosek.

Úřady oznamují, že ve zřícené budově zůstalo kromě tisíců zaměstnanců a návštěvníků WTC na tři sta hasičů a asi 85 policistů. Mnozí jsou naživu a komunikují se záchranáři pomocí mobilních telefonů. „Odstraňování trosek je krutě pomalé," komentuje situaci jeden ze záchranářů. Přes noc se podařilo vyprostit devět lidí, kteří přežili.

Na záchranné práce nasazují hasiči těžkou techniku. Většinu míst ale musejí pro jejich nedostupnost prohledávat pouze za pomoci příruční techniky. *Pokračování na straně 3*

Petr Zavadil
zvláštní zpravodaj LN v USA

Lidové noviny ▪ Číslo 214 ▪ Ročník XIV ▪ CENA V ZAHRANIČÍ: öS 15 - DM 2,50 - SFR 2,50 - Lit 2200 - Dr 400 - Kn 9 - EUR 1,28 ▪ INTERNET: www.lidovky.cz

1 **Bush: Das ist Krieg**

2 12 Seiten Extraausgabe

3 USA sichern den Terroristen eine harte Antwort zu

4 Amerikanische Tragödie

5 Die Flagge über den Trümmern. Feuerwehrleute hissen die amerikanische Flagge auf den Trümmern des vernichteten New Yorker Welthandelszentrums

LIDOVÉ NOVINY
WWW.LIDOVKY.CZ
TSCHECHISCHE REPUBLIK, PRAG

WARSZAWA

ŚRODA
12 września 2001
NR 213. 3817
NAKŁAD 572 TYS. WAW 2,00 zł
9 W TYM 7% VAT
REDAKTOR PROWADZĄCY
MARCIN BOSACKI
WYDAJE AGORA SA
NUMER INDEKSU 350141
www.gazeta.pl

gazeta
WYBORCZA

REKLAMA
AMERYKA W OGNIU
Newsweek
WYDANIE SPECJALNE
JUŻ W KIOSKACH!

WOJNA Z USA

Po uderzeniach dwóch samolotów, o 10 czasu lokalnego zawaliła się pierwsza wieża World Trade Center, o 10.30 – druga (ten moment na zdjęciu). Setki tysięcy ludzi uciekały w panice (zdjęcie poniżej)

Atak terrorystów na Amerykę. *Tysiące ofiar. Zburzone wieże World Trade Center*

W precyzyjnej operacji nieznani terroryści użyli czterech porwanych samolotów łącznie z 266 pasażerami. Wszyscy zginęli. Dwa samoloty przebiły na wylot obie wieże World Trade Center. Mówi się nawet o ponad 10 tys. ofiar – w biurowcach i na ulicach Manhattanu. Trzeci samolot uderzył w Pentagon w Waszyngtonie. Czwarty, zapewne zmierzający na rezydencję prezydenta w Camp David, spadł w lesie pod Pittsburghiem. Jednej z pasażerek udało się zadzwonić: – Porwali nas, zadźgali członka załogi, lecimy w dół.

Ewakuowano ONZ, Kapitol, Biały Dom, budynki federalne w całych USA. Zamknięto przestrzeń powietrzną nad krajem. Przed północą naszego czasu zawalił się trzeci budynek World Trade Center.

Kto za tym stoi? Przedstawiciele CIA mówią, że dowody wskazują na osławionego terrorystę Osamę ben Ladena, który z terenu Afganistanu sterował wieloma zamachami.

Z ostatniej chwili. O północy czasu polskiego agencje poinformowały o wybuchach 20 km od stolicy Afganistanu Kabulu. Wydawało się, że to akcja odwetowa USA. Już po kwadransie Pentagon zaprzeczył. Zasugerował, że ostrzał prowadzi opozycja afgańska. BW

DLA GAZETY

RICHARD HOLBROOKE

były ambasador USA przy ONZ, negocjator pokoju w Bośni

Ten widok powinien poruszyć nie tylko Amerykanów, ale i Francuzów, Rosjan, Polaków... Terroryzm jest zagrożeniem dla wszystkich demokratycznych państw. Mam nadzieję, że po tym, co się stało, pokonamy przeszkody i zjednoczymy się w walce z terrorystami. Aby ukarać ludzi, którzy dokonali zbrodni, potrzebujemy współpracy polityków, wojskowych i służb specjalnych od Rosji po Kanadę. *not.* BW

WWW.GAZETA.PL/ATAK
na żywo 24 godziny na dobę

1 Krieg gegen die USA

2 Angriff der Terroristen auf Amerika. Tausende von Opfern. Zertrümmerte Türme des World Trade Centers. Vom letzten Moment: Raketen auf Kabul. USA: Das waren wir nicht

GAZETA WYBORCZA
WWW.GAZETA.PL
POLEN, WARSCHAU

NOWA MATURA z „Rzeczpospolitą”

Przez cały tydzień drukujemy pytania egzaminacyjne

Dziś A12 – 13

język angielski – pytania
matematyka – odpowiedzi
jutro: język niemiecki – pytania, język angielski – odpowiedzi
www.rp.pl/matury

RZECZPOSPOLITA

Dziś MOJA KARIERA

Umowy terminowe i kontrakty są wciąż zjawiskiem marginalnym na rynku pracy

www.rzeczpospolita.pl | Środa, 12 września 2001 roku | NR 213 (5986) cena 2,00 zł (w tym 7% VAT)

Nowy Jork i Waszyngton w ogniu • Wieżowce World Trade Center zrównane z ziemią • Tysiące ofiar śmiertelnych • Podejrzany – Osama bin Laden

Atak na Amerykę

We wtorek o godzinie 8.56 nieznani na razie terroryści przypuścili zmasowany bezprecedensowy atak na Stany Zjednoczone.

W nowojorskie World Trade Center i siedzibę Departamentu Obrony w Waszyngtonie uderzyły porwane i pilotowane najwyraźniej przez terrorystów samoloty pasażerskie. Dwa wieżowce World Trade Center się zawaliły. Pentagon stanął w płomieniach.

Nowy Jork i Waszyngton zostały całkowicie sparaliżowane. Liczba ofiar śmiertelnych może sięgać wielu tysięcy. Takiego wstrząsu Ameryka nie przeżywała od czasu zaskakującego japońskiego ataku na Pearl Harbor podczas II wojny światowej. Do późnych godzin wieczornych nie było informacji o ewentualnych ofiarach wśród Polaków w Nowym Jorku.

Prezydent George W. Bush zarządził specjalne śledztwo i zapowiedział odwet.

Sekretarz generalny NATO lord Robertson wezwał kraje sojuszu do „zjednoczenia sił w walce z przekleństwem terroryzmu”. Rada Ambasadorów sojuszu oceni, czy należy zastosować artykuł 5. traktatu założycielskiego NATO, zgodnie z którym po ataku zbrojnym przeciwko państwu członkowskiemu pozostałe kraje NATO wesprą „zaatakowaną stronę, podejmując działania, jakie uznają za stosowne, łącznie z użyciem sił zbrojnych”.

Najpierw Nowy Jork, potem Waszyngton

Zaczęło się od ataku na jeden z dwóch 110-piętrowych wieżowców nowojorskiego World Trade Center na Manhattanie, w którym siedziby mają wielkie instytucje finansowe. Doszło do niego tuż przed 9.00 czasu lokalnego, gdy tysiące ludzi rozpoczynały tam pracę. Samolot pasażerski, który wystartował z Bostonu i został porwany przez terrorystów na trasie do Los Angeles, uderzył w północny wieżowiec. Samolot, na którego pokładzie było przypuszczalnie 92 pasażerów, eksplodował, a budynek stanął w płomieniach.

Kilkanaście minut później w drugi wieżowiec WTC uderzył inny samolot pasażerski, porwany z waszyngtońskiego lotniska Dullesa, skąd miał lecieć do Los Angeles. Przewoził najprawdopodobniej 64 pasażerów.

Kilkadziesiąt minut później zaatakowany został Waszyngton. Kolejny porwany samolot pasażerski uderzył w budynek Pentagonu. W zachodnim skrzydle tego największego w USA budynku biurowego powstała wielka wyrwa. Pentagon stanął w płomieniach.

Po dwóch godzinach zawalił się pierwszy z wieżowców WTC, potem drugi. Terrorystom udało się sparaliżować pracę wiodących instytucji finansowych świata. Koło Pittsburgha rozbił się czwarty samolot, który leciał z Newark do San Francisco. Być może terroryści chcieli go skierować na Biały Dom. W Waszyngtonie ewakuowano wszystkie budynki rządowe. Miasto uległo kompletnemu paraliżowi.

Kto za tym stoi?

Najwięcej podejrzeń pada na ukrywającego się obecnie w Afganistanie Osamę bin Ladena – wroga Ameryki numer jeden. Ponosi on odpowiedzialność za ataki bombowe w 1998 roku na ambasady USA w Kenii i Tanzanii, w których wyniku zginęły 224 osoby. Bin Ladena uważa się za głównego sponsora terrorystów islamskich.

Bin Laden kilka tygodni temu zapowiadał, że dojdzie do „poważnego ataku przeciwko interesom amerykańskim”.

W nocy z wtorku na środę doszło do wielu wybuchów w Kabulu, stolicy Afganistanu, co niektórzy uznali za efekt akcji odwetowej USA. Władze amerykańskie zaprzeczyły jednak, jakoby lotnictwo USA dokonało ataku na Afganistan. Porywacze samolotu, który spadł potem na budynek Pentagonu, byli uzbrojeni w noże. Informacja ta pochodzi od Barbary Olson, dziennikarki telewizji CNN, która leciała tym samolotem i przed katastrofą połączyła się telefonicznie z mężem.

Oburzenie świata

Prezydent Aleksander Kwaśniewski oświadczył, że w pełni solidaryzuje się z narodem amerykańskim. Stwierdził, że mamy do czynienia z niewyobrażalnym aktem terrorystycznym.

Premier Jerzy Buzek powiedział, że w stan pogotowia postawione zostały policja, brygady antyterrorystyczne i straż pożarna. Wzmocniono ochronę ambasad, granic i lotnisk.

Polscy dyplomaci w NATO powiedzieli, że Polska na pewno wywiąże się z obowiązków sojuszniczych. – Stosujemy zasadę muszkieterów: wszyscy za jednego i jeden za wszystkich – powiedział jeden z dyplomatów.

W stan pogotowia zostały postawione służby wywiadowcze wszystkich krajów NATO.

– Te nieludzkie akcje nie mogą pozostać bezkarne – powiedział prezydent Rosji Władimir Putin, który wyraził współczucie narodowi amerykańskiemu i wezwał społeczność międzynarodową do wspólnej walki z terroryzmem.

Atak potępił również papież Jan Paweł II.

D.Z.

- Korespondencje Anny Rogozińskiej-Wickers z Nowego Jorku i Krzysztofa Darewicza z Waszyngtonu A2 – 3
- Osama bin Laden – sylwetka – deklaracja wojny A4
- Europejczycy wspierają Amerykanów A5
- Komentarze Jadwigi Staniszkis i Rafała Ziemkiewicza A6
- Reakcje giełd A7

Solidarność z Ameryką

MACIEJ ŁUKASIEWICZ

W ciągu kilkunastu minut wydarzyły się rzeczy niesłychane: zawaliły się wieże nowojorskiego World Trade Center, w ogniu stanął Pentagon. Ewakuowano Biały Dom, Kapitol, Departament Stanu, CIA, Skarb Federalny, Giełdę, gmach ONZ, dziesiątki innych obiektów. Kompletnie sparaliżowane zostały instytucje, stanowiące symbol politycznej, militarnej i gospodarczej potęgi USA. W szaleńczych samobójczych atakach, o zorganizowanie których podejrzewany jest jeden człowiek — wróg numer 1 Ameryki, Osama bin Laden — zginęło prawdopodobnie tysiące niewinnych ludzi — w obiektach na ziemi i w porwanych samolotach. Najbardziej wymyślne filmy katastroficzne nie przewidziały takiego scenariusza. W przeciwieństwie do nich, nie będzie niestety happy endu.

Stany Zjednoczone, jedyne naprawdę globalne mocarstwo, które wyszło niedawno zwycięsko z zimnej wojny, dysponujące nieprawdopodobnymi technologiami, przygotowujące programy obrony kosmicznej, zostało skonfrontowane z nową wojną. Totalną wojną terrorystyczną, wobec której okazuje się bezbronne. To, co wydarzyło się w Nowym Jorku i Waszyngtonie, byłoby zapewne nowym Pearl Harbor, powodem do deklaracji wojny, gdyby przeciwnikiem było państwo czy grupa państw. Mamy jednak do czynienia z wrogiem, przeciwko któremu nie jest możliwa ani wojna konwencjonalna, ani nuklearna, ani nawet partyzancka. Nie wiemy bowiem dokładnie, kto konkretnie zaplanował i wykonał wczorajsze zamachy, ale wszystko wskazuje na terrorystów z kręgu islamu, prowadzących wojnę nie z USA, ale z całą zachodnią cywilizacją i jej wartościami, której tylko symbolem w oczach religijnych fanatyków pokroju bin Ladena czy ludzi Hezbollahu są Stany Zjednoczone.

Reakcje licznych państw świata zachodniego świadczą o tym, że prawda ta wreszcie zaczyna do nich docierać. Możemy nie być bezradni w tej wojnie, pod warunkiem że skończy się tolerancja dla wszelkiego terroryzmu, motywowana czy to sympatiami dla jego deklarowanych celów, interesami politycznymi i wygrywaniem ich przeciwko interesom innych, czy wreszcie korzyściami gospodarczymi. Terroryści nie działają w politycznej próżni — najwyższy czas, aby się w niej znaleźli.

W tej dramatycznej konfrontacji jesteśmy po stronie wartości, które zostały z całą bezwzględnością zaatakowane w Nowym Jorku i Waszyngtonie. Dziś głęboko współczujemy i solidaryzujemy się z Ameryką.

Panika na giełdach • Wyprzedaż akcji • Zdrożało złoto i ropa naftowa

Zamach na nowojorskie World Trade Center wywołał panikę na światowych rynkach akcji. Główne indeksy giełd europejskich straciły po około 5 proc. Największe straty zanotowali posiadacze walorów banków i firm ubezpieczeniowych.

W USA zamknięto wczoraj wszystkie giełdy. Zamach wydarzył się na pół godziny przed otwarciem giełdy na Wall Street. Wiadomość o zamachu spowodowała zwyżkę cen ropy naftowej o 20 proc. W górę poszło też złoto.

W Polsce przed atakiem terrorystów za dolara płacono 4,20 zł, potem złoty osłabł wobec dolara o 5 groszy. Zagraniczni inwestorzy zaczęli wyprzedawać także masowo polskie akcje, w rezultacie czego WIG20 stracił 2,8 proc.

G. BR.

SZERZEJ A7

Redaktor prowadzący: Jerzy Paciorkowski

Kurs NBP		Kantory średnio	Stopy proc.
USD	4,2165 zł ▲ 0,37%	4,2097 zł ▼ 0,22%	NBP 17 – 18,5
EUR	3,7851 zł ▼ 0,39%		WIBOR(3M) 14,98
WIG	12 634,98 ▼ 1,76%		OBROTY 215,335 ▲ 69,7%
WIG20	1 115,41 ▼ 2,79%		(rynek akcji, w mln zł)

R W3 nakład 245 321 egz.; 35063 X

1 **Angriff auf Amerika**

2 New York und Washington in Flammen • Wolkenkratzer World Trade Center dem Erdboden gleichgemacht • Tausende von Todesopfern • Der Verdächtige – Osama bin Laden

3 Am Dienstag um 8.56 Uhr haben vorläufig unbekannte Terroristen einen beispiellosen Massenanschlag auf die USA verübt

4 Panik an den Börsen • Ausverkauf von Aktien • Devisen und Erdöl teurer geworden

5 Solidarität mit Amerika

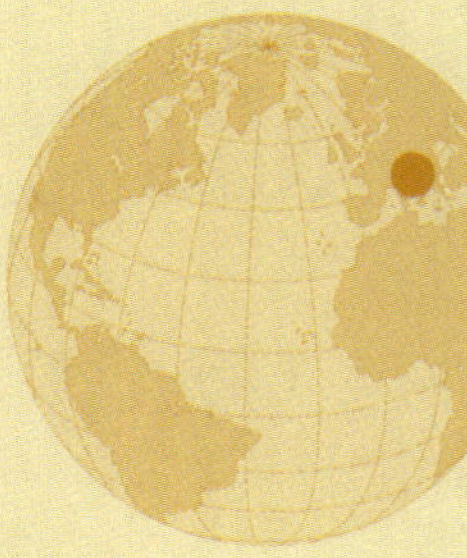

12

RZECZPOSPOLITA
WWW.RZECZPOSPOLITA.PL
POLEN, WARSCHAU

Cena 1 zł (w tym 7 proc. VAT)

Środa
12 września 2001

Nr 213 (16 717) Nakład 29 799 A B C
Ind. 350 419 PL ISSN 0137-9291

Dziś po południu specjalne wydanie „Słowa" a w nim aktualne wiadomości z USA

SŁOWO POLSKIE

Dolnośląska gazeta codzienna www.slowopolskie.pl

● Największy atak na Stany Zjednoczone od czasu Pearl Harbor ● Zginęło około 15 tysięcy osób

Zamach na Amerykę

Porwany samolot pasażerski na chwilę przez uderzeniem w wieżę World Trade Center w Nowym Jorku.

Kula ognia po uderzeniu samolotu. W chwilę potem obie wieże zawaliły się.

Samoloty pasażerskie opanowane przez terrorystów ugodziły we wtorek około dziewiątej rano czasu miejscowego w 110-piętrowe budynki World Trade Center na nowojorskim Manhattanie i w Pentagon w Waszyngtonie. Szacuje się, że zginęło około 15 tysięcy osób.
Przed północą czasu polskiego rozpoczęło się bombardowanie stolicy Afganistanu – Kabulu. Biały Dom zaprzeczył, że to USA dokonały ataku.

Budynki WTC, jeden z najbardziej znanych na świecie symboli amerykańskiej potęgi, stanęły w ogniu i po dwóch godzinach runęły.

„Zaczęła się szalona gonitwa po wszystkich alejach na zachodniej stronie Manhattanu. Ludzie wpadli w histerię, wołając »Umrzemy«. Wielka chmura dymu i pyłu przesunęła się wzdłuż alei, zdawało się, że pochłonie każdego" – tak reporterka Reutera Marjorie Olster zapamiętała zawalenie się pierwszego budynku w ponad godzinę po uderzeniu samolotu.

Wszystkie lotniska zamknięto. Ewakuowano wiele gmachów publicznych, w tym siedzibę ONZ i giełdę. Policja zablokowała wszystkie drogi dojazdowe do miasta i wszystkie tunele. Nie kursowały pociągi ani metro, nie działała komunikacja autobusowa, telefony stacjonarne.

Godz. 8.50 (14:50 czasu polskiego). – Samolot American Airlines (lot nr 11 z Bostonu do Los Angeles), porwany po starcie w Bostonie, uderza w północną wieżę World Trade Center w Nowym Jorku. Na pokładzie samolotu były 92 osoby.

Godz. 9:08 (15:08). – Samolot American Airlines (lot 77 z Waszyngtonu do Los Angeles) uderza w południową wieżę World Trade Center. Na pokładzie samolotu były 64 osoby.

Godz. 15:30. – Samolot spada na Pentagon w Waszyngtonie, niszcząc część gmachu. Na razie nie wiadomo, jaki lot odbywała maszyna. Linie United Airlines podały jednak, że w nieznanym miejscu rozbił się ich samolot z 65 osobami na pokładzie (lot 175 z Bostonu do Los Angeles).

Godz. 9:50-10:30 (15:50-16:30). – Zawalają się obie wieże World Trade Center.

Godz. 10:00 (16:00). – Samolot United Airlines (lot 93 z Newark do San Francisco) rozbija się niedaleko Pittsburgha. Na pokładzie samolotu było 45 osób.

Godz. 10:00-11:30 (16:00-17:30). – Trwa ewakuacja m.in. Kapitolu i Białego Domu. Amerykańska dyrekcja lotnictwa cywilnego zamyka wszystkie lotniska w kraju.

Godz. 23.55 (czasu polskiego). – Spadły bomby na Kabul. W Afganistanie ukrywa się Osama bin Laden - terrorysta podejrzewany o zorganizowanie zamachów na Nowy Jork i Waszyngton.

Więcej strony 2 – 6 ▶

1 Der Anschlag auf Amerika

2 • Der größte Anschlag auf die USA seit Pearl Harbor • 15 000 Menschen sind ums Leben gekommen

3 Die Passagierflugzeuge, die von Terroristen gelenkt wurden, haben am Dienstag früh gegen 10 Uhr Ortszeit die 110-stöckigen Türme des World Trade Centers und das Pentagon in Washington getroffen. Man schätzt, dass etwa 15 000 Menschen ums Leben gekommen sind. Vor Mitternacht polnischer Zeit begann die Bombardierung der afghanischen Hauptstadt Kabul. Das Weiße Haus stritt ab, dass die USA angegriffen hätten

Słowo Polskie
www.slowopolskie.pl
Polen, Breslau

1 **Armageddon**

2 Großes Land. Großes Leid. Große Trauer

3 Amerikanische Tragödie

4 »Ich bin tief betroffen von den Nachrichten über die heutigen tragischen Geschehnisse in den USA. Die Serie der barbarischen terroristischen Anschläge ist gegen unschuldige Menschen gerichtet und ruft in uns Betroffenheit und Unverständnis hervor. Ich richte mein herzliches Beileid an die Verwandten der Verstorbenen und an alle Betroffenen, aber auch an das ganze amerikanische Volk. Wir verstehen ihr Leid und ihren Schmerz gut. Das russische Volk kennt den Schrecken des Terrorismus aus eigener Erfahrung. Ohne Zweifel dürfen ähnliche unmenschliche Aktionen nicht unbestraft bleiben. Alle internationalen Bündnisse müssen sich im Kampf gegen den Terrorismus vereinen.« Präsident W. Putin

5 Im Namen Allahs

6 »Und er versammelte sie auf dem Platz, der auf Jüdisch ›Armageddon‹ hieß. Es gab Blitze, Donner, Stimmen und ein großes Erdbeben, wie es die Menschheit noch nie erlebt hatte. Die große Stadt zerfiel in drei Teile.« Prophet Joann Bogoslav

Izvestia
www.izvestia.ru
Russland, Moskau

12

«**В Америке сесть в самолет так же просто, как в автобус.** А чтобы попасть носом самолета в здание, не обязательно быть асом. Достаточно пройти недельные курсы» **стр. 6**

Подписка!
подписной индекс газеты «Коммерсантъ»
50060

Среда
12 сентября 2001
№ 165 (№ 2295 с момента возобновления издания)

Коммерсантъ

Газета Издательского дома «Коммерсантъ»
Издается с 1909 года
С 1917 по 1990 год не выходила по не зависящим от редакции обстоятельствам
С 1990 года выходит в еженедельном режиме
С 1992 года — в ежедневном

Официальные курсы ЦБ России на 12.09.01

Австралийский доллар	15,14	Белорусский рубль**	19,92	Греческая драхма**	77,83	Евро	26,44	Казахский тенге***	19,93	Норвежская крона*	33,11	Украинская гривна*	55,18	Шведская крона*	27,67
Австрийский шиллинг*	19,21	Бельгийский франк***	65,54	Датская крона*	35,56	Испанская песета***	15,89	Канадский доллар	18,83	Португальское эскудо***	13,19	Финская марка*	44,47	Швейцарский франк	17,44
Английский фунт	42,82	Голландский гульден	12,00	Доллар США	29,44	Итальянская лира**	13,68	Немецкая марка	13,52	Турецкая лира****	20,67	Французский франк*	40,31	Японская иена***	24,22

*За 10. **За 1000. ***За 100. ****За 1000000. По данным агентства Reuters

Индексы ведущих фондовых бирж на 11 сентября (пунктов)

Nikkei-225	10292,95 (+97,26)	DAX-30*	4204,97 (-465,16)
FTSE-100	4759,3 (-274,4)	DJIA**	9605,51 (-0,34)
CAC-40	4059,75 (-325,99)	NASDAQ Composite**	1695,38 (+7,68)

*На 20.00. **На 10.09.01. По данным агентства Reuters

Третья мировая

Вчера главные города США Нью-Йорк и Вашингтон подверглись массированному удару с воздуха. Самой мощной мировой державе была, по сути, объявлена война со стороны международного терроризма. Война тут же стала мировой: в нее оказались вовлечены все ведущие государства мира.

В 8.45 утра, когда жители Нью-Йорка спешили на работу, крупнейший город и деловой центр Америки потряс мощнейший взрыв. В небо взметнулся огромный шар огня, после чего Манхэттен заволокло черным дымом. На головы прохожих с неба летели куски бетона и дождь из осколков стекла. Спустя 18 минут — новый удар, от которого содрогнулась земля. Первой о том, что произошло, сообщила британская телекомпания SkyNews: два «боинга», 767-й и 737-й, один за другим протаранили архитектурную гордость Нью-Йорка — состоящее из двух башен 110-этажное здание Всемирного торгового центра (как стало известно позднее, один из самолетов был захвачен террористами-камикадзе, когда вылетел из Бостона. Второй был захвачен в Нью-Джерси, в аэропорту Ньюарк). В первой башне находится всемирно известный ресторан «Окна на мир». В другой — две смотровые площадки на 107-м и на 110-м этажах. В торговом центре располагается множество престижных ресторанов и офисов различных компаний, а также отель мирового класса.

Все это перестало существовать в считанные минуты.

(Окончание на стр. 6)

Чем провинились США

США — не единственное государство, ведущее борьбу с терроризмом, но именно США в глазах террористов всех мастей олицетворяют вселенское зло. При этом в отличие от других государств США всегда открыто называют международные террористические организации и страны—спонсоры терроризма и принимают против них наиболее жесткие санкции.

Госдеп ежегодно публикует черный список, в который входит около 50 террористических организаций, действующих в мире. Около 20 из них можно отнести к исламистским. Причем более половины этих организаций базируются на Ближнем Востоке.

К числу стран—спонсоров терроризма США традиционно относят Ирак, Иран, КНДР, Кубу, Ливию, Сирию и Судан. В последние годы в докладах отмечается, что центр международного терроризма смещается в Афганистан (в основном благодаря Осаме бен Ладену (Osama bin Laden), которого приютили талибы). Однако Афганистан не входит в число стран-спонсоров, поскольку США не признают режим талибов. Это, впрочем, не помешало правительству США ввести санкции против движения «Талибан».

Санкции против террористических организаций и стран-спонсоров включают замораживание активов, запрет на контакты американских компаний, отказ в выдаче виз выявленным членам террористических организаций, судебное преследование всех, кто оказывает им какую-либо помощь.

Наиболее известная акция возмездия США против террористов — ракетный удар по территории Судана и Афганистана после взрывов американских посольств в Кении и Танзании в августе 1998 года.

Небоскребы похоронили под собой все рынки

Начало серии террористических актов в США точно совпало по времени с моментом открытия финансовых рынков страны. После первых же взрывов было объявлено об отмене торгов на крупнейших американских торговых площадках NYSE, NASDAQ, NYMEX. Фактически парализованным оказался фондовый рынок страны: ведь в зданиях Международного торгового центра (WTC) расположились офисы десятков крупнейших инвестиционных компаний мира. Основным же арендатором, по данным агентства Bloomberg, был один из крупнейших инвестиционных банков мира Morgan Stanley Dean Witter & Co., снимавший 12% площадей.

Трагедия дала повод для начала спекулятивной игры на финансовом рынке. Американский доллар резко (на 1,5–2%) ослабел по отношению к остальным мировым валютам, в результате курс евро превысил уровень в $0,91.

(Российское население отреагировало очень оперативно и бурно. Перед обменными пунктами стали выстраиваться очереди из желающих сдать валюту. Курс покупки наличного доллара резко упал. К 22.00 в Москве было крайне сложно продать доллар дороже 25 руб., в Санкт-Петербурге — дороже 24 руб.)

Падение доллара в Европе могло оказаться и более глубоким, если бы известия из-за океана не вызвали обвала котировок на всех биржах. Европейские индексы сразу же рухнули на 6–9%, хотя до этого наблюдался рост в пределах 2%. Многие фондовые и товарные биржи закрылись раньше времени.

(Окончание на стр. 6)

Тяжелый страховой случай

Серия беспрецедентных терактов в США имеет все шансы стать самым крупным в истории страховым случаем. Западные аналитики оценивают ущерб, нанесенный вчерашней катастрофой страховому рынку в миллиарды долларов. Хотя точных цифр сейчас, конечно, не берется назвать никто. «Это обернется для иностранных страховщиков еще большими убытками, чем ураган в Западной Европе два года назад,— заявил „Ъ" председатель Всероссийского союза страховщиков Игорь Юргенс.— Тогда страховые выплаты превысили $6 млрд».

В результате теракта погибли тысячи людей, разрушены здания деловых центров и прилегающие к ним территории. Все эти последствия являются страховыми случаями, за которые будут расплачиваться американские страховщики. Долгое время они не страховали от стихийных бедствий, терактов и т. п. Однако после взрыва в одном из зданий торгового центра в Нью-Йорке (того самого, который вчера снова стал мишенью террористов) в 1993 году страховка последствий теракта стала в США довольно распространенным явлением.

Кроме того, страховщикам придется оплатить перерывы в работе деловых центров, которые влекут за собой целый ряд страховых случаев. Кроме американских компаний огромные убытки понесут и страховые компании других стран — крупные риски, как правило, перестраховываются. «Это будет сильным потрясением для страхового рынка США и мирового рынка в целом»,— заявил „Ъ" директор «Ресо-Гарантия» Игорь Иванов. Впрочем, страховщики все равно расплатятся. Известно, что страховой рынок США аккумулирует треть инвестиций страны и его активы оцениваются в триллионы долларов.

ЛИЗА ГОЛИКОВА

Armageddon Now

Выступление президента Джорджа Буша на базе ВВС в Барксдейле, штат Луизиана

11 сентября 2001 года

Сегодня сама свобода подверглась нападению со стороны безликого труса, и свобода будет защищена. Я хочу вновь заверить американский народ, что все ресурсы федерального правительства задействованы для помощи местным властям, для спасения жизней и для помощи жертвам этих атак. Не сомневайтесь: Соединенные Штаты найдут и накажут тех, кто несет ответственность за эти трусливые действия.

Я находился в постоянном контакте с вице-президентом, министром обороны, службой национальной безопасности и моим кабинетом. Мы приняли все необходимые предосторожности для обеспечения безопасности для того, чтобы защитить американцев. Наши военные у нас дома и по всему миру находятся в состоянии полной боевой готовности, и мы приняли все меры безопасности, необходимые для продолжения работы нашего правительства.

Мы находились в контакте с лидерами конгресса и с мировыми лидерами для того, чтобы заверить их, что мы сделаем все, что будет необходимо для того, чтобы защитить Америку и американцев.

Я прошу американский народ присоединиться ко мне в выражении благодарности всем, кто изо всех сил боролся ради спасения наших сограждан, и присоединиться ко мне в молитве за жертвы и их семьи.

Решимость нашей великой нации подвергается испытаниям. Но будьте уверены: мы покажем миру, что выдержим это испытание. Да благословит Господь.

Заявление президента России Владимира Путина по поводу террористических актов в США

11 сентября 2001 года

Сегодня США столкнулись с беспрецедентным актом агрессии со стороны международного терроризма.

Прежде всего я выражаю искреннее глубокое соболезнование всем пострадавшим и семьям погибших.

Сегодняшнее событие в Соединенных Штатах выходит за рамки национальных границ. Наглый вызов всему человечеству, по крайней мере всему цивилизованному человечеству. И то, что произошло сегодня, лишний раз подчеркивает актуальность предложения России объединить усилия международного сообщества в борьбе с террором, этой чумой XXI века.

Россия не понаслышке знает, что такое террор. И поэтому мы лучше всего понимаем чувства американского народа, и, обращаясь от имени России к народу Соединенных Штатов, хочу сказать, что мы с вами, мы целиком и полностью разделяем и чувствуем вашу боль. Мы поддерживаем вас.

Всемирный торговый центр уже взрывали

Первый террористический акт в здании Всемирного торгового центра в Нью-Йорке произошел 28 февраля 1993 года. Ровно в полдень в подземном гараже одного из небоскребов была взорвана бомба. Шесть человек погибли, более тысячи получили ранения. Нанесен материальный ущерб на сумму свыше $500 млн. Ответственность за взрыв взяла на себя арабская террористическая организация «Пятый батальон армии освобождения».

В организации взрыва обвинили египтянина Омара Абдель Рахмана (Omar Abdel Rahman) и пакистанца Рамзи Ахмед Юсефа (Ramzi Ahmed Yousef), имевших связи с Осамой бен Ладеном (Osama bin Laden). Омар Абдель Рахман был арестован в США в 1993 году, Рамзи Ахмед Юсеф — в Пакистане в 1995 году. Обоих приговорили к пожизненному заключению.

В Нью-Йорке помнят и трагический случай, когда 28 июля 1945 года бомбардировщик B-25 Mitchell в тумане задел крылом Empire State Building, в тот момент самое высокое здание в мире. Пострадал 79-й этаж небоскреба. Под обломками самолета и рухнувшими на землю бетонными глыбами погибли 14 человек.

главные новости

Назначен новый зампред «Газпрома» по финансам
Им стал глава банка «МЕНАТЕП Санкт-Петербург»
стр. 4

Госдума хочет читать бюджет задом наперед
А фракция ОВР — начать с нулевого чтения
стр. 2

Владимир Путин отметил боевые заслуги журналистов
48 человек получили ордена и медали
стр. 7

Банки начали войну за право работать через почту
стр. 4

Эдуард Лимонов остался в «Лефортово»
стр. 3

Талибы перешли в наступление
Их противники ищут замену Ахмад-шаху Масуду
стр. 8

В Ленске возбуждены уголовные дела по фактам хищения средств, отпущенных на восстановление города
стр. 3

Итальянские матросы устроили поножовщину в Новороссийске
стр. 9

Майкл Джордан возвращается в баскетбол
стр. 11

«Локомотив» не дотянул до победы

Вчера московский «Локомотив» в своем первом матче в групповом турнире Лиги чемпионов сыграл вничью с бельгийским Anderlecht. «Железнодорожники» имеют все основания быть недовольными счетом 1:1, поскольку упустили массу возможностей одержать победу.

Команды начали матч практически без разведки. В первые минуты инициатива была на стороне «Локомотива», но до серьезных угроз воротам гостей дело не доходило. А бельгийцы использовали первую же возможность. На 15-й минуте последовал навес с левого фланга в штрафную «железнодорожников», Жиль де Бильд (Gilles de Bilde) отпасовал головой на Марка Хендрикса (Marc Hendrikx), и тот открыл счет. Защитники «Локомотива» безвольно наблюдали за происходящим.

Но уже три минуты спустя «Локомотив» разыграл блестящую комбинацию. Максим Бузникин технично ушел от опеки защитника, дал пас назад по диагонали Владимиру Маминову, и тот неотразимо пробил с линии штрафной площадки. Гол вдохновил «Локомотив». Российские футболисты заиграли быстрее, и не очень молодым игрокам гостей было трудно за ними поспевать. Будь подопечные Юрия Семина поточнее, «Локомотив» ушел бы на перерыв, ведя в счете с разницей в один, а то и в два мяча. Один только Маминов мог забить дважды. Особенно близок был успех после его удара на 45-й минуте, и только перекладина спасла гостей.

Второй тайм начался куда более вяло: сказывалась усталость. Ведь игроки «Локомотива» еще не успели восстановиться после игры с Tirol, а футболисты Anderlecht на высоких скоростях играть не умеют вовсе. Но даже несмотря на утомление, «Локомотив» имел массу возможностей забить. Марат Измайлов, Маминов, Джакоб Лекхето (Jakob Lekheto), вышедший вместо Максима Бузникина Неман Вуйчевич (Neman Vujcevic), Руслан Пименов — все они могли принести «Локомотиву» победу.

АФСАТИ ДЖУСОЙТИ

4 601865 000011 30037

1. **Der Dritte Weltkrieg**
2. Welche Schuld trifft die USA?
3. Die Wolkenkratzer haben die Finanzmärkte unter sich begraben
4. Schwerer Versicherungsfall
5. »In den USA ist es genauso einfach, sich in ein Flugzeug zu setzen wie in einen Bus. Um die Nasenspitze des Flugzeugs in ein Gebäude zu lenken, muss man kein professioneller Pilot sein. Es genügt, einen Wochenkurs zu machen.«
6. Die Taliban sind zum Angriff übergegangen
7. Der Auftritt des Präsidenten George Bush beim Sender BBC in Barxdeyle, Louisiana
8. Der Antrag des russischen Präsidenten Wladimir Putin zum Thema Terroranschläge in den USA
9. Auf den Weltfinanzmarkt wurden schon einmal Anschläge verübt

Kommersant
www.kommersant.ru
Russland, Moskau

الأهرام الدولي
Al-Ahram - INTERNATIONAL

٢٢ صفحة

www.ahram.org.eg
E-mail:ahram@ahram.org.eg

12 Sep. 2001

No. 41918

الفزع يجتاح أمريكا تحت رعب الانفجارات الرهيبة

هجمات انتحارية بالطائرات على البنتاجون ومركز التجارة العالمى بنيويورك

طائرتان تصطدمان عمدا بمركز التجارة وثالثة بالبنتاجون وحريق غامض بالبيت الأبيض

أعداد مهولة من القتلى والمصابين فى نيويورك وواشنطن ونداءات للتبرع بالدم

إعلان حالة التأهب القصوى بين القوات والقواعد العسكرية الأمريكية فى العالم

إيقاف جميع الرحلات الجوية من وإلى الولايات المتحدة لأول مرة فى التاريخ

ردود فعل عالمية غاضبة:

بلير يطالب بتكاتف دولى لمواجهة الإرهاب

تضارب شديد بشأن الجهة المسئولة عن الحوادث الإرهابية

بوش عقب الهجوم:

الهجوم على المركز التجارى العالمى عمل إرهابى وأتعهد بتعقب منفذى الهجمات

داخل العدد

1 **Die Angst fällt ein – Amerika in Angst vor schrecklichen Explosionen**

2 Selbstmordanschläge mit Flugzeugen auf das Pentagon und das World Trade Center in New York

3 Zwei Flugzeuge rasen vorsätzlich in das Handelszentrum, ein drittes ins Pentagon, ein rätselhafter Brand im Weißen Haus

4 Eine schreckliche Anzahl von Toten und Verwundeten in New York und Washington, Aufrufe zur Blutspende; Verkündung des äußersten Alarmzustands bei den Truppen und den amerikanischen Militärstützpunkten in der Welt

5 Starke Widersprüche hinsichtlich der Stelle, die für die Terroranschläge verantwortlich ist

Al Ahram International
www.ahram.org.eg
Ägypten, Kairo

Allgemeine Zeitung

N$ 2,00 (inkl. MwSt.)
ISSN 1560-9421

Älteste Tageszeitung Namibias

85. Jahrgang, Nr. 178
Mittwoch, 12. September 2001

Postfach 86695, Omurambaweg 11, Windhoek, Telefon: +264-61-225822, Fax: +264-61-220225, Fax: +264-61-245200, www.az-namibia.de - E-Mail: aznews@iway.na

Heute

Hausbau

Das Ministerium für Regional- und Kommunalverwaltung und Wohnungsbau hat Lüderitzbucht mehr als N$ 70 Millionen bewilligt. • *Seite 3*

Wachstum

Die Anzahl der Fahrzeuge wird in Deutschland weiterhin steigen. Besonders Frauen und Senioren treiben die Motorisierung voran. • *Seite 2*

Ausbildung

Kleinfarmer haben eine Schulung erhalten, um das Etunda-Bewässerungsprojekt voranzutreiben. Mehr dazu auf der Farmerseite • *Seite 4*

2. Bundesliga

Eintracht Frankfurt bleibt nach dem 3:2-Sieg am Montagabend gegen den KSC weiterhin an der Tabellenspitze. • *Seite 6*

Wetter

Teilweise bewölkt im Nordosten, sehr warm im Landesinneren. Im Süden wird es wieder kälter.

Katima Mulilo	15/35°
Rundu	18/35°
Okaukuejo	16/33°
Ongwediva	17/34°
Grootfontein	18/31°
Windhoek	09/24°
Gobabis	10/25°
Mariental	07/22°
Keetmanshoop	04/16°
Walvis Bay	09/20°
Lüderitzbucht	11/20°
Oranjemund	12/19°

Der Spruch

Fanatismus besteht im Verdoppeln der Anstrengung, wenn das Ziel vergessen ist.

George Santayana
amerik. Philosoph

Schwarzer Tag für Amerika

„America under Attack" - Terrorangriffe treffen die Supermacht USA ins Herz

New York/Berlin (dpa) - Der internationale Terrorismus hat gestern der Supermacht USA mit den schrecklichsten Anschlägen der Terrorismus-Geschichte den Krieg erklärt. Die mit großer Präzision ausgeführten Selbstmordangriffe auf Machtzentren in New York und Washington mit entführten Passagierflugzeugen als fliegende Bomben kosteten mehrere Tausend Menschenleben.

Als Urheber vermuten US-Geheimdienste den saudischen Millionär und mutmaßlichen Terroristenführer Osama bin Laden. Er hatte nach israelischen Medienberichten vor kurzem mit einem „beispiellosen Angriff" auf die USA wegen ihrer Unterstützung Israels gedroht. Mit zwei entführten und möglicherweise von Terroristen gesteuerten amerikanischen Passagierflugzeugen brachten die Attentäter das berühmte World Trade Center zum Einsturz. In Washington wurden das Verteidigungsministerium mit einer weiteren gekidnappten Passagiermaschine teilweise zerstört und das Außenministerium mit einer Autobombe in Brand gesetzt. Eine vierte entführte Zivilmaschine stürzte aus unbekannten Gründen bei Pittsburgh ab.

Keine Terrororganisation bekannte sich bis zum Abend zu den Anschlägen, die weltweit Entsetzen und verschärfte Sicherheitsvorkehrungen auslösten. Der Senator von Utah, Orrin Hatch, berichtete nach Gesprächen mit dem FBI und Vertretern der Geheimdienste von deren Verdacht gegen bin Laden. US-Präsident George W. Bush sprach von einer „nationalen Tragödie" und sagte später in einer Fernsehrede: „Wir werden diejenigen, die für diese feigen Taten verantwortlich sind, zur Strecke bringen und bestrafen." Die US-Streitkräfte wurden weltweit in Alarmzustand versetzt, Kriegsschiffe nach New York in Marsch gesetzt.

Zunächst rasten morgens um 08.42 Uhr und 09.00 Uhr (15.00 Uhr MESZ) innerhalb von 18 Minuten zwei Flugzeuge in die 411 Meter hohen Bürotürme des World Trade Center. Das Symbol der Finanzmacht USA an der Südspitze Manhattans mit den beiden 110 Stockwerke hohen Zwillingstürmen ging in Flammen auf und stürzten etwa eine Stunde später in sich zusammen. Die Behörden in New York rechneten mit Tausenden von Toten.

In Washington zerstörte um 09.35 Uhr eine weitere abstürzende Maschine teilweise das US- Verteidigungsministerium (Pentagon), in dem sich Verteidigungsminister Donald Rumsfeld aufhielt. Die vierte entführte Maschine stürzte um 10.29 Uhr ab und sollte nach Fernsehmeldungen angeblich auf den Präsidenten-Urlaubssitz Camp David gelenkt werden.

Kurz nach den Anschlägen in New York und Washington überschlugen sich die Ereignisse. Die Lage in beiden Städten war völlig chaotisch. Im amerikanischen Außenministerium brach Feuer aus. Das Parlament und das Weiße Haus wurden ebenso evakuiert wie das UN-Gebäude in New York und die Börse in Wall Street. Alle Flughäfen in den USA wurden geschlossen. In New York und Washington wurde der Notstand ausgerufen.

Die Finanzmärkte rund um den Globus wurden durch die Nachrichten aus den USA ins Chaos gestürzt. In islamischen Staaten, vor allem in Libanon und den Palästinensergebieten, zeigten die Menschen offene Freude über die Ereignisse. Ägypten und Palästinenserpräsident Jassir Arafat verurteilten hingegen die Anschläge.

Die afghanischen radikalislamischen Taliban, die bin Laden beherbergen, schlossen ebenfalls eine Beteiligung kategorisch aus.

Eine palästinensische Frau im Flüchtlingslager in Beirut jubelt, als sie von dem Angriff auf die USA erfährt. • *Foto: dpa*

Um 9.03 Uhr wird gestern auch der zweite Turm des World Trade Centre von einem Flugzeug getroffen. • *Foto: Reuters*

US-Präsident George W. Bush legt eine Gedenkminute ein. Es werden zehntausende Tote vermutet. • *Foto: dpa*

Allgemeine Zeitung
www.az-namibia.de
Namibia, Windhoek

12

Cumhuriyet kitapları
YZB SELAHATTİN'İN ROMANI 1-2
İlhan Selçuk
Cumhuriyet kitap kulübü
Çağ Pazarlama A.Ş. Türkocağı Cad. No: 39/41 (34334) Cağaloğlu-İstanbul Tel: (212) 514 01 96

Cumhuriyet

Cumhuriyet kitapları
DÜŞÜNÜYORUM ÖYLEYSE VURUN
İlhan Selçuk
Cumhuriyet kitap kulübü
Çağ Pazarlama A.Ş. Türkocağı Cad. No: 39/41 (34334) Cağaloğlu-İstanbul Tel: (212) 514 01 96

78. YIL SAYI: 27734 / 500.000 TL (KDV içinde) — KURUCUSU: YUNUS NADİ (1924-1945) BAŞYAZARI: NADİR NADİ (1945-1991) — 12 EYLÜL 2001 ÇARŞAMBA

DÜNYA SARSILIYOR

Tarihin en büyük terörü, süper devlet ABD'yi vurdu. İntihar saldırıları yaşamı durdurdu; on binlerce kişi öldü. ABD savaş hali ilan etti. Herkes korku içinde...

✔ New York'taki Dünya Ticaret Merkezi'nin ikiz kulelerine düzenlenen iki ayrı saldırıyla başlayan kâbusu, tüm dünya televizyonlardan dehşet içinde izledi. Saldırılar ABD'liler tarafından "2. Pearl Harbour" olarak nitelendirildi.

✔ Başkent Washington'da olağanüstü durum ilan edildi. DTM'den sonra Pentagon, Dışişleri Bakanlığı'ndaki patlamalar ABD'de paniğe neden oldu. Japon Kızıl Ordu örgütü katliamları üstlendi.

Petrol ve altın fiyatları yükseldi, dolar değer yitirdi

Saldırı, ekonomi piyasalarını vurdu

✔ Saldırı haberleri, piyasaları sarstı. Petrol ve altın fiyatları fırladı, Dünyada dolar Euro karşısında değer yitirdi, Türkiye'de yükseldi.

✔ Altın 20 dolar birden yükselirken saldırının ardından Euro 91 senti geçti. New York borsası kapandı. Avrupa borsaları altüst oldu.

✔ Frankfurt DAX endeksi kapatılmadan önce yüzde 9'lara ve Paris CAC 40 endeksi de yüzde 6'lara geriledi. Londra borsasında da bir ara işlemler durduruldu.

Dehşet anları

15.56 (TSİ): New York'taki Dünya Ticaret Merkezi'nin ikiz kulelerinden birine uçak çarptı.
16.14: İkinci kuleye de bir uçak çarptı.
16.40: Başkan George Bush, "Görünen o ki bu bir terörist saldırıdır" dedi.
16.50: Beyaz Saray boşaltıldı.
16.53: ABD Dışişleri Bakanlığı boşaltıldı.
16.53: Pentagon'da 2 patlama.
17.00: ABD'deki bütün ticari uçuşlar iptal edildi.
17.05: İkiz kulelerden biri yıkıldı.
17.28: İkinci kule de yıkıldı.
17.38: ABD Dışişleri Bakanlığı'nın içinde bomba yüklü bir araç patladı.
17.55: Kaçırılan bir uçağın rotası Pentagon'a çevrildi.
18.17: Ve panik... Manhattan'ın güneyi terk ediliyor.
18.34: Bir Boeing, Pennsylvania yakınına düştü.
18.38: 2 American Airlines uçağı 156 yolcusuyla kayboldu.
18.48: Taleban saldırıları kınadı.
19.11: Havadaki ikinci uçak da düştü.
19.25: Müthiş iddia: Fransız haber ajansı (AFP) saldırıları, Japon Kızıl Ordu örgütünün üstlendiğini duyurdu.
20.10: Fox televizyonu, ölü sayısını en az on bin olarak duyurdu.

ABD Başkanı Bush: Cezalandıracağız

ABD Başkanı George Bush, Amerika'yı ve Amerikan halkını korumak için gereken her şeyin yapılacağını söyledi. Yaşananların büyük bir trajedi olduğunu belirten Bush, terörist saldırıların sorumlularının mutlaka yakalanarak cezalandırılacağını söyledi.

Filistinliler kutladı

ABD'ye yönelik korkunç saldırının ardından Filistin ve Lübnan'da binlerce Filistinli sevinç gösterileri yaptı; terörist Usame bin Ladin'e övgüler yağdırdı. Filistinliler, "Bin Ladin, Tel Aviv'i bombala", "Bin Ladin başladı ve biz devam edeceğiz" diye bağırdılar.

ABD'de terör
HİKMET ÇETİNKAYA ■ 7. Sayfada

Terörün coğrafyası yok
MUSTAFA BALBAY ■ 14. Sayfada

Üçüncü Dünya Savaşı budur
YALÇIN DOĞAN ■ 11. Sayfada

Ders bu kadar acı mı olmalıydı?
HİKMET BİLA ■ 14. Sayfada

Savaş gibi
DENİZ SOM ■ 17. Sayfada

EN BÜYÜK TERÖR OLAYININ HABER VE FOTOĞRAFLARI *3,4,5,6,12 ve 13. Sayfalarımızda*

1 Die Welt erschüttert

2 Der größte Terroranschlag der Geschichte traf die Supermacht USA. Selbstmordattentate forderten zehntausende von Toten. Die USA erklären den Krieg. Alle schweben in Angst

3 Der Anschlag hat den Wirtschaftsmarkt getroffen

4 Augenblicke des Schreckens

5 US-Präsident Bush: Wir werden bestrafen

6 Palästinenser feierten

12

Cumhuriyet
www.cumhuriyet.com.tr
Türkei, Istanbul

Milliyet
BASINDA GÜVEN
www.milliyet.com.tr
12 Eylül 2001 Çarşamba

DÜNYANIN KALBİNE KAMİKAZE

İKİNCİ PEARL HARBOR

Amerika tarihinin en ağır saldırısına uğradı

Amerikan ordusu savaş alarmına geçti

Dolar düştü petrol ve altın fiyatları fırladı. Büyük kentler boşaltıldı

Ünlü ikiz kuleler bu saldırılardan sonra çöktü

Teröristler kaçırdıkları uçaklarla intihar eylemleri yaptılar

Hedefler, New York Dünya Ticaret Merkezi Pentagon Kongre ve Dışişleri binasıydı

1. Das zweite Pearl Harbor
2. Amerika wurde dem größten Terroranschlag der Geschichte ausgesetzt
3. Die amerikanische Armee läutet die Glocken für den Krieg
4. Dollar ist gesunken, Erdöl- und Goldpreise explodieren. Große Städte wurden evakuiert
5. Die berühmten Zwillingstürme eingestürzt
6. Die Terroristen verübten mit entführten Flugzeugen Selbstmordattentate
7. Ziele waren das New Yorker World Trade Center, das Pentagon, das Kongressgebäude und das Außenministerium
8. Kamikazeangriffe auf das Herz der Welt

Milliyet
www.milliyet.com.tr
Türkei, Istanbul

12 EYLÜL 2001 ÇARŞAMBA

Türkiye

GÜNLÜK SİYASİ GAZETE

MARK 665.000
DOLAR 1.430.000
EURO 1.290.000

ALTIN, BORSA VE EKONOMİ HABERLERİ 9,10 ve 11. SAYFALARIMIZDA

Dünya şokta

Dünya Ticaret Merkezi'nin ikiz kuleleri ve Pentagon 'un bir bölümü uçak saldırıları sonucu yerle bir oldu. Şehirler tahliye edildi, ABD'de hayat durdu

Süper güç Amerika tarihin en büyük terör saldırısına maruz kaldı

İki saldırı birden

● Dünyanın en güçlü devleti Amerika Birleşik Devletleri, dün peşpeşe gerçekleşen inanılmaz terör saldırılarıyla sarsıldı. İlk saldırı sabah saatlerinde New York'taki Dünya Ticaret Merkezi'nde meydana geldi. İkiz kulelerden küçük olana bir nakliye uçağı intihar saldırısında bulunurken, bundan 18 dakika sonra 156 yolcu bulunan Boeing tipi bir yolcu uçağı diğer kuleye göbekten girdi.

Türkler de var

● Her iki binada peş peşe meydana gelen patlamaların ardından, kulelerin büyük olanı ikiye bölünerek tamamen çöktü. 50 bin çalışan ile 70 bin ziyaretçinin bulunduğu binada çok sayıda ölü ve yaralının olduğu bildirildi. 1. kulenin yerle bir olmasının ardından ikinci kule de tamamen çöktü. Kulelerde 10'dan fazla da Türk vatandaşının bulunduğu kaydedildi.

Savaş alarmı!

● Beyaz Saray, bir uçak saldırısı ihtimali üzerine tamamen boşaltıldı. Bu arada, Pennsylvania eyaletine bağlı Pittsburg şehrindeki bir havaalanına da kaçırılan bir uçağın düştüğü öğrenildi. Ülke genelinde savaş alarmı verilirken, resmi binaların tümündeki insanlar tahliye edildi. New York ve Washington'dan insanlar diğer şehirlere gönderilmeye başlandı. 19

BUSH: İntikam alacağız

Sesi titriyordu

● Saldırı haberini Florida'da alan ABD Başkanı Bush, ülkesine yapılan saldırılar üzerine sert açıklamalarda bulundu. Canlı yayında ağlamaklı bir sesle konuşan Bush, "Saldırıyı yapanları kesinlikle bulacağız ve ABD'ye yapılanları kesinlikle karşılıksız bırakmayacağız" dedi. 18

Pentagon da vuruldu

Dünyanın en iyi korunan binası saldırı sonucunda yerle bir oldu

● Pentagon'un vurulması üzerine ABD Ordusu en yüksek düzeyde alarma geçti. "Yaşayan şehir" denilen Pentagon'un bir bölümü, patlamanın 20 dakika sonrasında çöktü. İkinci bir saldırı ihtimaline karşı bina boşaltıldı. Pentagon'dan sonra Senato binası, alışveriş merkezi Washington Mall, Ticaret Bakanlığı ve Dışişleri Bakanlığı'nda da peş peşe saldırılar gerçekleşti. Amerikan Federal Sivil Havacılık Bürosu bütün uçuşları yasakladı. 18

DURUM

Yılmaz ÖZTUNA

Pax Americana'ya saldırı

Yazımı dün akşam saat 18'deki bilgilere göre kaleme alıyorum. Tarihin en büyük terörist saldırısı, New York ve Washington şehirlerini alt üst etti. Panik, Birleşik Amerika'dan Avrupa'ya sıçradı.

E - mail: yilmaz.oztuna@ihlas.net.tr

1 **Die Welt steht unter Schock**

2 Die Zwillingstürme des World Trade Centers und ein Teil des Pentagons wurden durch die Flugzeugangriffe vernichtet. Die Städte wurden evakuiert; in den USA steht die Zeit still

3 Die Supermacht Amerika wurde dem größten Terroranschlag der Geschichte ausgesetzt

4 Zwei Angriffe auf einmal

5 Es waren auch Türken dabei

6 Kriegsalarm!

7 Bush: Wir werden uns rächen – seine Stimme zitterte –

8 Das Pentagon wurde auch angegriffen – die bestgesicherten Gebäude der Welt wurden durch einen Angriff vernichtet

9 Angriff auf Pax Americana

TÜRKIYE
WWW.TURKIYEGAZETESI.COM
TÜRKEI, ISTANBUL

THE JERUSALEM POST

www.jpost.com

VOLUME LXIX, NUMBER 20990 WEDNESDAY, SEPTEMBER 12, 2001• 24 ELUL 5761 • 24 JAMAD II 1422 NIS 6.00 (EILAT NIS 5.10)

1 **AMERICA UNDER ATTACK**

2 Thousands die as two hijacked planes destroy World Trade Center

Pentagon also hit by seized plane 3

Bulletin

Early this morning, CNN reported bombings taking place in Kabul, the capital of Afghanistan.

Smoke, flames, and debris erupt from one of the World Trade Center towers as an airliner (right) strikes it yesterday morning. The first tower was already burning after a first plane hit it minutes earlier. (AP, Reuters)

Inside

12/9/2001

By JERRY SCHWARTZ

NEW YORK (AP) – Mounting an audacious attack against the United States, terrorists crashed two hijacked airliners into the World Trade Center and brought down the twin 110-story towers yesterday morning. A jetliner also slammed into Washington's Pentagon as the seat of government itself came under attack.

Hundreds were apparently killed aboard the jets, and untold numbers were feared dead in the rubble. Thousands were injured in New York alone.

A fourth jetliner, also apparently hijacked, crashed in Pennsylvania.

President George W. Bush ordered a full-scale investigation to "hunt down the folks who committed this act."

Rescue workers had been trying to evacuate those who work in the twin towers when the glass-and-steel skyscrapers came down in a thunderous roar within about 90 minutes after the attacks, which took place minutes apart around 9 a.m. But many people were thought to have been trapped. About 50,000 people work at the Trade Center and tens of thousands of others visit each day.

American Airlines said two of its planes, both hijacked, crashed with a total of 156 people aboard, but said it could not confirm where they went down. Two United airliners with a total of 110 aboard also crashed – one outside Pittsburgh, the other in a location not immediately identified. Altogether, the planes had 266 people aboard.

People on fire leaped from the windows to certain death, including a man and a woman holding hands. Some jumped from as high as the 80th floor as the planes exploded into fireballs. People on the ground screamed and dived for cover as debris rained down. Dazed office workers covered in dirt wandered around like ghosts, weeping, trying to make sense of what happened.

Donald Burns, 34, who had been at a meeting on the 82nd floor of One World Trade Center, saw four severely burned people on the stairwell. "I tried to help them but they didn't want anyone to touch them. The fire had melted their skin. Their clothes were tattered," he said.

For the latest updates throughout the day from an Israeli perspective, click on www.jpost.com

"People were screaming, falling, and jumping out of the windows," from high in the sky, said Jennifer Brickhouse, 34, of Union, New Jersey, who was going up the escalator into the World Trade Center.

By early afternoon, the downtown area was cordoned off and a rescue effort was under way. Hundreds of volunteers and medical workers converged on triage centers, offering help and blood. Paramedics waiting to be sent into the rubble were told that "once the smoke clears, it's going to be massive bodies," said Brian Stark, a former navy paramedic who volunteered to help.

He said the paramedics had been told that hundreds of police and firefighters are missing from the ranks of those sent in to respond to the first crash.

Within the hour after the attack in New York, the Pentagon took a direct, devastating hit from a plane. The fiery crash collapsed one side of the five-sided structure.

"This is perhaps the most audacious terrorist attack that's ever taken place in the world," said Chris Yates, an aviation expert at Jane's Transport in London. "It takes a logistics operation from the terror group involved that is second to none. Only a very small handful of terror groups is on that list. ... I would name at the top of the list Osama bin Laden."

The president put the military on its highest level of alert. Authorities in Washington immediately called out troops, including an infantry regiment, and the navy sent aircraft carriers and guided missile destroyers to New York and Washington.

The White House, the Pentagon, and the Capitol were evacuated along with other federal buildings in Washington and New York. The president was taken to Offutt Air Force Base in Nebraska, headquarters for the Strategic Air Command, the nation's nuclear strike force, the White House said.

Security was tightened along the Canadian border and at naval installations and other strategic points. All commercial air traffic across the country was halted until at least noon today.

"This is the second Pearl Harbor," said Sen. Chuck Hagel, a Nebraska Republican. "I don't think that I overstate it." The December 7, 1941, Japanese attack on Pearl Harbor killed nearly 2,400 people and drew the United States into World War II.

Sen. John McCain, an Arizona Republican, said: "These attacks clearly constitute an act of war."

A Virginia congressman, Rep. James Moran, said the intended target of the plane that crashed in Pennsylvania was apparently Camp David, the presidential retreat in Maryland.

The crash site is 135 kilometers northwest of there. Moran spoke after attending a briefing in Washington.

In June, a US judge had set this Wednesday as the sentencing date for a bin Laden associate for his role in the 1998 bombing of a US Embassy in Tanzania. The sentencing had been set for the federal courthouse near the World Trade Center. No one from the US Attorney's Office could be reached yesterday to comment on whether the sentencing was still on.

Afghanistan's hard-line Taliban rulers condemned the attacks and rejected suggestions that bin Laden was behind them, saying he does not have the means to carry out such well-orchestrated attacks. Bin Laden has been given asylum in Afghanistan.

Abdel-Bari Atwan, editor of the *Al-Quds al-Arabi* newspaper, said he received a warning from Islamic fundamentalists close to bin Laden, but did not take the threat seriously. "They said it would be a huge and unprecedented attack but they did not specify," Atwan said in a telephone interview in London.

In Nablus, thousands of Palestinians celebrated the attacks, chanting "God is Great" and handing out candy.

In New York, Mayor Rudolph Giuliani said 2,100 people were injured – 1,500 "walking wounded," and 600 others who were taken to area hospitals, 150 of them in critical condition. It could take weeks to dig through the rubble for victims.

See ATTACK, Page 14

Sharon declares day of mourning 4

By HERB KEINON

The fight against terror is an "international struggle of the free world against the forces of darkness, who seek to destroy our liberty and way of life," Prime Minister Ariel Sharon said after midnight last night, in a brief announcement during which he declared today a day of national mourning.

"On behalf of the people of Israel, I wish to send our deepest condolences and heartfelt sympathy to the American people, President Bush, and the entire US government following the terror attacks against the US and our common values," Sharon said.

"At this most difficult hour," he said, "all Israelis stand as one with the American people. Our hearts are with you, and we are ready to provide any assistance at any time." Sharon said the government has declared today a day of mourning.

Magen David Adom has asked that Israelis with Type O blood donate today at MDA stations in Jerusalem, Haifa, and Tel Hashomer. The blood will be flown to the United States.

1 **Angriff auf Amerika**

2 Tausende sterben, nachdem zwei entführte Flugzeuge das World Trade Center zerstören

3 Auch das Pentagon von gekapertem Flugzeug getroffen

4 Sharon erklärt Trauertag

THE JERUSALEM POST
WWW.JPOST.COM
ISRAEL, JERUSALEM

12

1 **Die Regierung Bush glaubt sich mit einem Kriegszustand konfrontiert und deutet einen Militärschlag an. Washington: Eine Gruppe von Selbstmordattentätern hat sich in Amerika zu Piloten ausbilden lassen**

2 Libanesen unter den Opfern der Explosion der entführten Flugzeuge

3 … und die beiden Türme sind verschwunden

4 Die europäischen Geheimdienste glauben, dass eine Verbindung zwischen bin Laden und den Selbstmordanschlägen besteht

5 Die Kongressabgeordneten äußern sich zu ihrem Versagen: »Fiasko der nachrichtendienstlichen Organe«

6 Abu Dhabi: Es gibt keine Bürger der Vereinigten Arabischen Emirate in den entführten Flugzeugen

Al Anwar
www.alanwar.com
Libanon, Beirut

الشرق الأوسط

ASHARQ AL-AWSAT

جريدة العرب الدولية

The Leading Arabic International Newspaper

أميركا تحترق .. وبوش يتوعد بالانتقام

الضحايا بالآلاف وتأهب في القوات الأميركية وواشنطن ونيويورك تعيشان أجواء حرب عالمية

هجمات بطائرات مختطفة على مركز التجارة العالمي والبنتاغون وسيارة مفخخة تنفجر في وزارة الخارجية

السعودية تأسف وتدين انفجارات المدن الأميركية

متحدثان يزعمان مسؤولية منظمة فلسطينية والجيش الأحمر الياباني

Asharq Al-Awsat
www.asharqalawsat.com
Grossbritannien, London
(Saudi-arabische Zeitung)

1 **Amerika wird angegriffen und es gibt Tausende von Opfern. Bush droht mit Vergeltung**

2 Alarmzustand in den amerikanischen Streitkräften. Washington und New York erleben eine Weltkriegsstimmung. Luftangriffe durch zivile Flugzeuge auf das World Trade Center und das Pentagon. Ein beladenes Auto explodiert im Außenministerium. Schließung der Flughäfen

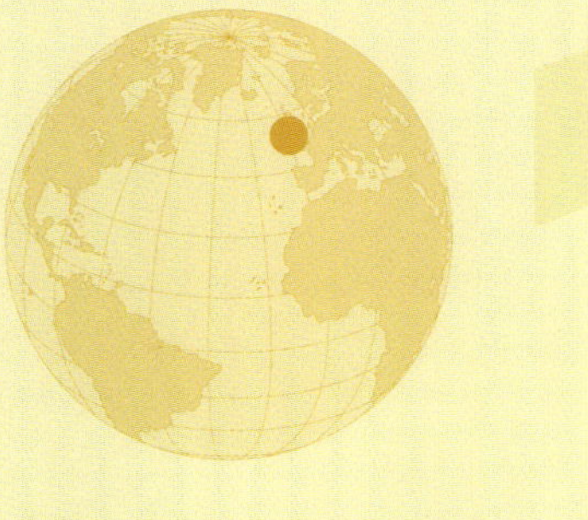

12

Havoc as airlines suspend flights to US, page 2

Read The Independent IN arab news

The first English language newspaper in Saudi Arabia now brings you news from the leading British daily — The Independent.

arab news

SAUDI ARABIA'S FIRST ENGLISH LANGUAGE DAILY

Published simultaneously from Jeddah, Riyadh and Dammam

DANAO Juice milk

Double good health, double good taste!

Good health tastes great.

www.arabnews.com VOL. XXVI NO. 289 WEDNESDAY, SEPTEMBER 12, 2001 — JAMAD AL-THANI 24, 1422 A.H. 20 PAGES 2 RIYALS e-mail: arabnews@arabnews.com

Terror strikes US

Thousands die as planes crash into WTC towers

By Muhammad Sadik
Salah Awad
& Molouk Y. Ba-Isa

NEW YORK/WASHINGTON — In the worst attack on American soil since Pearl Harbor, three hijacked planes slammed into the Pentagon and New York's landmark World Trade Center yesterday, demolishing the two 110-story towers that symbolize US financial might.

Horrific scenes of terrified people fleeing the mayhem flashed across TV screens as the mighty twin towers located near the tip of Manhattan imploded one at a time, sending a massive plume of dust and smoke billowing over the city.

No death toll was immediately available but officials feared the number could climb into the thousands, as more than 40,000 people worked in the steel and glass Trade Center. New York officials said hundreds of firefighters and police may have perished trying to save others.

The attacks presented President George W. Bush with the sternest test of his eight-month presidency. He cut short a trip to Florida and flew to a Offutt Air Force Base in Nebraska, after stopping briefly in Louisiana where he vowed to bring those responsible to justice. "Make no mistake, the United States will hunt down and punish those responsible for these cowardly acts," the president said.

Related reports on Pages 2, 14, 15 & 16

Explosions lit up the night sky in Kabul, Afghanistan, CNN reported early today. The Cable News Network showed footage of a series of flashes and flames in the Afghan capital. However, US officials said that President Bush had not ordered the attacks.

The US attacks, which involved the hijacking of four commercial planes — two from Boston, one each from Newark and Dulles, outside Washington — brought normal life across the United States to a standstill, turning the major cities of the nation into eerie ghost towns. All financial markets were closed, millions of workers sent home early, all flights around the nation were canceled and all airports shut in an unprecedented move. Markets will remain closed today.

It began shortly before 9:00 a.m. when the first plane slammed into the north tower in the heart of New York's financial district, opening a massive hole near the top. With TV stations showing the scene live, a second plane followed 15 minutes later, scoring a direct hit on the south tower.

Minutes later came the report of a third kamikaze attack on the Defense Department in North Virginia, across the Potomac River from Washington. That building, too, burst into flames. Defense Secretary Donald Rumsfeld was in the building and tried to assist the victims before being evacuated.

Then came the deadliest blow of all — the death of the twin towers., which caved in one after the other. Authorities evacuated key landmarks like the White House, the fire-damaged Pentagon, the Sears Tower in Chicago, the CIA building and the Walt Disney theme parks. All baseball games were canceled.

It was the worst attack on American soil since Japanese war planes bombed the US fleet at Pearl Harbor on Dec. 7, 1941, killing 2,280 soldiers and 68 civilians and forcing the United States into World War II.

There were a total of 266 people on board the day's four hijacked planes — two that crashed into the twin towers, one that slammed into the Pentagon and a fourth that crashed in a wooded area near Pittsburgh, Pennsylvania.

"I wouldn't want to say what the death toll could be. It will be a horrible number. I saw people dropping out of windows," a shaken New York City Mayor Rudolph Giuliani told ABC News, adding that 200 firefighters were missing.

Yesterday's attacks triggered scenes of panic, disbelief and heroism in the largest US city, where police and firefighters risked their lives to save people from the 110-story twin towers before their 200,000 tons of steel frame came smashing down, covering lower Manhattan in a shower of soot. "It's nuts, there is debris and dust everywhere, and it looks as though a volcano erupted down there," said Michael DeVita, who was working on the 84th floor of World Trade Center Building No. 2 when the first plane hit Building No. 1. Hospitals in New York were overwhelmed as a black cloud billowed into the blue skies over Manhattan where the city skyline had been dramatically and permanently altered. "Hundreds of people are burned from head to toe," said Dr. Steven Stern at St. Vincent's Hospital in the Greenwich Village neighborhood of lower Manhattan. Rescue workers used commuter ferries to carry victims across the Hudson River to safety in Hoboken, New Jersey, where the scene resembled a war zone.

Disaster relief agencies said they were working with the military to rush thousands of pints of blood to New York City and Washington to treat an untold number of injuries from aerial hijack attacks in those cities.

At 11 a.m. yesterday morning Americans in the Gulf were alerted by the State Department that over the last several months, the US Government had learned that US citizens and interests abroad might be at increased risk of a terrorist action from extremist groups. In addition the notice mentioned the American military in Korea and Japan were also potential targets. The alert also stated that there was still a concern with information received by the US government in May 2001 that American citizens might be the target of a terrorist threat from extremist groups with links to Osama Bin Laden's Al-Qaida organization.

Major cities turn into eerie ghost towns

New Yorkers run for their lives as one of the World Trade Center towers collapses on Tuesday. (AFP)

Bush vows revenge as US denies Kabul attack

Two women console each other in the streets of New York. (Reuters)

Kingdom denounces 'inhuman' attacks

RIYADH — Saudi Arabia yesterday denounced the "regrettable and inhuman" attacks on the World Trade Center and the Pentagon in the United States, and reiterated its commitment to fight all forms of terrorism.

"Saudi Arabia strongly denounces these kinds of acts, which are against religious values as well as cultural and human norms," an official Saudi source said. The official conveyed the Kingdom's sincere condolences to the families of the victims, US President George W. Bush and American people.

Western European leaders broke off their normal business to return to their capitals for crisis meetings and expressed solidarity with the United States. From every corner of Europe, leaders condemned attacks they branded horrendous, abominable, disgusting, monstrous and abhorrent.

The European Union said it was the worst attack on America since Pearl Harbor 60 years ago and was "one of those few days in life that one can actually say will change everything". "This is an act of war by madmen," EU External Relations Commissioner Chris Patten said.

Norway called it the worst terrorist attack in history. Russian President Vladimir Putin expressed deep sympathy to the American people "in connection with this terrorist act, this terrible tragedy".

(Continued on Page 14)

DESTRUCTION OF NEW YORK S LANDMARK TOWERS

Attacks leave America in shock, disbelief

NEW YORK — Thousands of panicked New Yorkers poured into the streets of Manhattan yesterday, choking on white ash that billowed through a 20-block radius around of the World Trade Center. Two passenger planes, the first around 8:45 a.m. (1245 GMT) crashed into the landmark 110-story towers where thousands work, destroying the foundation of the 28-year-old concrete buildings, both of which later crumbled to the ground.

"I looked outside and saw a big chunk of the World Trade Center missing," said Verizon employee Ellen Leon. "Fifteen minutes later I saw people jumping out of the building. Bodies were flying out. I don't know if they were already dead or if they were just going to die."

From the decimated Wall Street district to Times Square to the Upper West Side, New Yorkers were stunned and shocked. Sirens blared as ambulances, police cars and fire engines raced through the streets of the nation's most densely populated city of 8 million. Public transportation including subways and bus services were halted.

"Some guy came out of the World Trade Center and his skin was falling off," one bystander told news channel CNN. "It was horrific." "I lived in Portland, Oregon, when Mount St. Helens blew and it's the only thing I can compare it to — volcanic ash," said a Reuters reporter at the scene in downtown Manhattan.

The city was under siege, with tens of thousands of employees stranded in their office buildings. All tunnels like the Midtown, Lincoln and Holland tunnels were closed, according to the New York Police Department. Only the Manhattan Bridge and the Queensboro Bridge were open for people to leave the island of Manhattan. LaGuardia, Kennedy and Newark Airports were closed.

With most cellular phone service out — their antennas were fixed atop the World Trade Center — dozens of weeping people lined up to use pay phones. In midtown Manhattan, crowds gathered around the Empire State building, where in 1945 a B-25 bomber plowed into the side of the art Deco building, killing 14 people.

People gathered around cars listening in stunned silence to live reports on car radios of the attacks and the pandemonium. "Stay clam, stay at home," New York City Mayor Rudolph Giuliani told CNN. "If you are south of Canal Street, get out. Walk slowly and carefully. If you can't figure what else to do, just walk north."

Extreme shock, anger and dismay overtook hundreds of Americans and tourists who stood stunned in Times Square after multiple attacks shook the country's confidence. New Yorkers stared in disbelief at the giant video screens in Times Square that showed heavy white smoke obliterating Manhattan's lower skyline.

"It's crazy," said James Price, 33, who works at a nearby law firm in midtown Manhattan, just a few miles north of where the attacks took place. "That's what makes the city go. And now they're gone. It seems like anything can happen to us. We're not protected at all," Price said.

Chris Savino, a 41-year-old filmmaker, looked up at the ABC News video screen and said: "This is like Pearl Harbor. I never knew in my lifetime I would see this. It's unfathomable."

Construction workers at a site for a new Toys 'R Us store on Broadway hung signs saying "Pray for families & victims" and "God Bless America," prompting a wave of clapping. At Colombia University in the Upper West Side of Manhattan, students gathered in foyers of the various buildings to watch television. "Everyone is in shock. People are still on campus. Everyone has

(Continued on Page 14)

1 Terror trifft die USA

2 Tausende sterben, nachdem Flugzeuge ins World Trade Center einschlagen

3 Metropolen verwandeln sich in unheimliche Geisterstädte

4 Bush schwört Vergeltung, USA streiten Angriff auf Kabul ab

5 Saudi-Arabien verurteilt »unmenschliche« Angriffe

6 Angriffe versetzen Amerika in Schock und Unglauben

12

Arab News
www.arabnews.com
Saudi-Arabien, Jeddah

14 WEDNESDAY, SEPTEMBER 12, 2001 — Terror Strikes US — arab news

A part of a tower can bee seen after the collapse of the first World Trade Center Tower in New York on Tuesday. The worst terrorist attack of all time struck at the economic and political heart of the United States in a bloody, coordinated assault that razed New York's giant World Trade Center, collapsed parts of the Pentagon and sent shock waves across the world. (AFP)

CHRONOLOGY

Events that followed quickly in the US terrorist attacks:

— 7:58 a.m. United Airlines Flight 175 departs Boston's Logan Airport to Los Angeles with 65 people on board.

— 7:59 a.m. American Airlines Flight 11 departs Boston for Los Angeles with 92 people on board.

— 8:45 a.m. A plane crashes into the South Tower of the 110-story World Trade Center building in lower Manhattan, New York City.

— 9:03 a.m. A plane crashes into the North Tower of the World Trade Center building.

— 9:30 a.m. President George W. Bush addresses nation from Florida and calls explosions an "apparent terrorist attack".

— 9:40 a.m. The Federal Aviation Administration closes all US airports.

— 9:45 a.m. A plane crashes into the Pentagon, headquarters of the Department of Defense, causing a massive explosion, just outside Washington, D.C.

— 10:00 a.m. The South Tower of the World Trade Center collapses into the Financial District of New York.

— 10:10 a.m. A portion of the Pentagon collapses.

— 10:48 a.m. United Airlines reports the crash south of Pittsburgh, Pennsylvania, of Flight 93 bound from Newark, New Jersey, to San Francisco with 45 passengers aboard.

— 11 a.m. The second World Trade Center tower collapses.

— 11:18 a.m. American Airlines confirms that two of its jetliners were hijacked and lost. (DPA)

World condemns 'mass terrorism'

(Continued from Page One)

Kuwait and Qatar yesterday condemned a series of terrorist attacks against key trade and military installations in New York and Washington, offering sympathy to the people of the United States.

"Kuwait, which rejects all forms of terrorism, condemns these terrorist acts and expresses its deep sympathy to the people of the United States," the Kuwaiti Cabinet said.

In a statement carried by the official KUNA news agency, the Cabinet said it "followed with deep concern the acts of sabotage against key US installations."

In Doha, Qatari Foreign Minister Sheikh Hamad ibn Jassem Al-Thani condemned "the terrorist attacks and their serious consequences for global security."

"Qatar condemns terrorism of all forms and whatever its origin," Sheikh Hamad said, quoted by the official QNA news agency. He expressed his sympathy to the "friendly" American people and offered condolences to the families of the victims.

"France has always condemned terrorism, condemns it without reserve and thinks we must fight terrorism by all means," President Jacques Chirac said as he broke off a regional tour to rush back to Paris.

British Prime Minister Tony Blair expressed his disgust before racing back to London from a conference. "This mass terrorism is the new evil in our world today. It is perpetrated by fanatics who are utterly indifferent to the sanctity of life," he said. Queen Elizabeth expressed "total shock".

"The German people stand by the United States of America at this difficult hour," Chancellor Gerhard Schroeder wrote in a letter to Bush in which he pledged "unlimited solidarity". Parliament in Berlin suspended normal business. Air traffic authorities said all flights leaving Europe to the United States had been suspended. Spanish Prime Minister Jose Maria Aznar called the string of attacks a "terrorist frenzy".

Ordinary people also were horrified. "It's crazy — and if it's the US today it'll be us tomorrow, you can bet. These people are crazy," said a stunned butcher in Paris.

"I send my condolences, the condolences of the Palestinian people to American President Bush and his government and to the American people for this terrible act," Palestinian President Yasser Arafat told reporters in Gaza. "We completely condemn this serious operation...We were completely shocked. It's unbelievable, unbelievable, unbelievable."

"It's simply a terrible thing," he said. "These tragic actions contradict all human and religious values," Lebanese Prime Minister Rafik Hariri said.

Mexico's President Vicente Fox said: "We reiterate our total, categorical rejection of all forms of violence, of all forms of terrorism."

Britain, one of the United States' closest allies, offered all the help at its disposal to bring the perpetrators to justice. EU leaders said fighting guerrilla attacks would now top the agenda indefinitely.

"It's certainly going to mean that the fight against international terrorism is going to dominate the international agenda until it's won," the EU's Patten said.

"The international community must respond together to these disgusting acts," said Italian President Carlo Azeglio Ciampi.

"It is probably the largest attack we have ever seen against an open democracy and therefore an issue for the entire democratic world," said Sweden's Prime Minister Goran Persson. "All democratic forces must form a united front." (Agencies)

World on alert after terror attacks

PARIS — Countries worldwide went on maximum alert yesterday and US officials clamped down on security at home and abroad after a string of bloody terrorist attacks rocked the US East Coast.

Security was heightened at US installations and airports the world over and trans-Atlantic air travel halted after attackers hijacked four planes, crashing two into the World Trade Center and also striking at the Pentagon and the State Department.

The death toll was initially impossible to estimate, but would include more than 250 passengers on the commercial airliners and large numbers of victims in the targeted buildings and on the ground.

US President George W. Bush said from Shreveport, Louisiana, that "our military at home and around the world is on high alert status." The New York National Guard was called in to help New York City police after the collapse of the World Trade Center's two towers, Mayor Rudolph Giuliani told CNN television.

As police evacuated panicked and stunned workers from lower Manhattan and downtown Washington, and the United States closed its border with Mexico, security was stepped up at US military bases and embassies around the world.

The US State Department called on all diplomatic posts worldwide to take "necessary security precautions". The department's headquarters in Washington was evacuated along with the White House, Congress and other government buildings.

All airports in the United States and Canada were shut down after the attacks. All European flights to the United States were suspended. Train travel between Boston and Washington was also put on hold.

Two Royal Jordanian planes which were heading yesterday to the United States have landed at Shannon airport in Ireland following the spate of attacks in New York and Washington, an aviation official said.

The US-Canada border was expected to be closed, CBC television reported from Canada. NATO evacuated its headquarters in Brussels and tightened measures at four alliance bases in Italy after the wave of attacks, including the base at Aviano, one of the principal US airbases in Europe.

US authorities also boosted surveillance around the US base in Incirlik, southern Turkey, but a spokesman would not specify the level of alert to which troops at the base were posted.

The Israeli air force was placed on high alert, Israeli public television reported.

Thai authorities threw up a security cordon around the US embassy in Bangkok, the second biggest in the world, with a 100-member SWAT team deployed around the mission.

China stepped up security outside the embassy in Beijing.

The US embassy in Lithuania was shut down, as was the embassy in Sarajevo. The three US diplomatic missions in Turkey — in Ankara, Istanbul and Adana — will be closed today.

The US embassy in Paris urged US nationals to take heightened security precautions in the wake of the attacks. Officials in Finland urged Americans to "maintain a low profile, and vary routes and times for any required travel."

French Interior Minister Daniel Vaillant said after meeting Prime Minister Lionel Jospin that security would be boosted at airports, train stations, the underground metro network in Paris, as well as at all public buildings.

Governments hastily convened top Cabinet meetings in the wake of the attacks.

Germany went on high alert and the Cabinet met to coordinate security measures across the country. European Union foreign ministers were due to meet early today, at 0800 GMT.

The American University in Cairo said the Egyptian government was providing it with extra security.

In Germany, police, some with dogs and others on horseback, stepped up their presence around the Reichstag parliament building, where a session debating the 2002 budget was canceled.

The German Federal Chancellery put up its automatic security gates. The government said it would step up protection of US and Israeli interests in the country.

India ordered additional security at the US embassy in the capital. Police patrols spread across New Delhi and barricades were hastily erected at government buildings as the federal Cabinet committee on security began an emergency meeting at Prime Minister Atal Behari Vajpayee's home.

Japan ordered its military to tighten security for the huge US bases scattered across the country and US Marines went on maximum alert after yesterday's aircraft attacks on the World Trade Center and the Pentagon. (Agencies)

A rescue helicopter surveys damage to the Pentagon Building as fire fighters battle flames after an apparent terrorist airplane crashed into the US military Headquarters outside of Washington on Tuesday. (Routers)

American Muslims urged to donate blood, help victims

WASHINGTON — Joining the Muslim community around the country, the Washington based American Muslims for Jerusalem (AMJ) is appalled and strongly condemns the terrorist attacks in New York, Washington, and other parts of the country.

AMJ sends out its deepest condolences to the families of the victims of these cowardly attacks.

As Muslims we utterly deplore these heinous and barbaric acts and hope for the quick apprehension and swift applications of justice of those responsible.

We also urge the media to exercise restraint, act responsibly when reporting, and not rush to judgment. Until the perpetrators are identified and brought to justice, all media reports should be accurate, show restraint, and be sensitive.

AMJ calls on Muslims nationwide to offer every assistance they can to help the victims of today's terrorist attacks in New York and Washington, DC.

Muslims in local communities should take the following immediate actions:

— Muslim medical professionals are asked to go to the scenes of the attacks to offer aid and comfort to the victims.

— Muslim relief agencies should contact their counterparts to offer support in the recovery efforts.

— Individual Muslims should donate Red Cross. (Call 1-800-GIVE-LIFE.) They should also send donations to those relief agencies that are on the scene of the attacks.

Millions of callers jam phone lines, turn to Internet

(Continued from Page One)

their cell phones out," said graduate student Lida Poletz, adding that all classes were canceled.Doctors and nurses crowded around televisions in Cornell's Upper East side hospital, one doctor said. Patients stood outside, watching the dust clouds plume above New York's once majestic skyline.

Millions of callers jammed telephone lines across the United States, but despite the clogged lines the US national telephone networks continued to operate. With phone lines jammed, scores of Americans turned to the Internet to e-mail friends and relatives alerting them that they are all right.

"We're experiencing double call volume of a normal busy day, which is generating network congestion. The network is fine. There's just too many calls," said Dave Johnson, a spokesman for AT&T Corp. the nation's biggest long-distance carrier. (Agencies)

History of the World Trade Center

NEW YORK — The World Trade Center (WTC) took seven years to build and was completed in 1973 at a cost of $750 million. It officially opened for business in 1975.

— The Port Authority of New York and New Jersey placed the seven-building complex on 16 acres of land in lower Manhattan, making it then the largest commercial complex in the world,

— It was designed by Minoru Yamasaki and Emery Roth in stainless steel and glass.

— One World Trade Center tower was 1,368 feet tall (417 meters) and Two WTC was 1,362 feet tall (415 meters). The two 110-story towers briefly served as the world's tallest buildings until the Sears Tower in Chicago surpassed it in 1973 at 1,407 feet (433 meters). Now Petronas Tower 2 in Kuala Lumpur, Malaysia, is the tallest building in the world.

— The complex had 435 tenants from 26 countries that employed 40,000 office workers.

— Beneath the WTC complex lay an enormous underground shopping center, as well as the New York City Metropolitan Transit Authority Subway trains N,R,A,C and E, the 1 and 9 trains and New Jersey PATH commuter trains, serving some 150,000 daily commuters.

— There were 70 stores and restaurants in the complex. The famous restaurant and nightclub, Windows on the World, was at the top of One WTC.

— Feb. 26, 1993: A terrorist car bomb attack killed six people, injured more than 1,000 and caused $300 million in damage.

— Jan. 8, 1998: Ramzi Yousef was convicted of the 1993 bombing and sentenced to prison.

— July 2001: the Port Authority turned the complex to the private sector by leasing it for 99 years to Silverstein Properties Inc. and Westfield America Inc. for $3.2 billion. (R)

WTC, one of most potent US symbols

By Catherine Pepinster
Special to Arab News

NEW YORK — The attack on the World Trade Center was an assault on one of the most potent symbols of American prestige and economic power — its twin towers were big, brash, and smart places to do business. From the top of Manhattan Island to the bottom, from the bridges linking it to the outer boroughs to the far shore of Brooklyn, New Yorkers and tourists alike saw them for what they were — among the great architectural and engineering achievements of the last 30 years.

But the designers behind the Center were hired by the owners, the New York and New Jersey Port Authority, to build more than something that made an architectural statement. They also had to think the unthinkable — how to build skyscrapers which could withstand the most dramatic assaults, including a bomb, or even a small plane crashing into them.

But it is hard to believe that any building would have withstood yesterday's terrorist attack on the twin towers. For not only were the aircraft so much bigger than the designers imagined might possibly hit the buildings, but either by accident or design, the jets hit the buildings just where they would have done the most damage.

To understand what brought down one of the World Trade Center towers, and why the same buildings withstood a bomb in one of the basements eight years earlier, you have to realize that buildings are like trees. The bottom of a building, close to the foundations, is like the solid trunk, but the upper floors are as fragile as branches. So when the terrorists had the planes crash into the towers near the top of the buildings, they hit them at their most vulnerable points.

The series of traumas — first the planes' impact, then the fires caused by aviation fuel, followed by an explosion — was too much for them to bear — literally.

High-rise buildings have a very complex system of construction compared to any other type of building. Like all buildings, they must be flexible, otherwise they would snap, but their height means they have to be particularly strong in order to withstand wind and impact. That means the designers have to produce a building which is able to absorb the shock of huge amounts of energy. But the force with which objects as powerful as 737s flying at speed hit the skyscrapers was so enormous that one building came tumbling down.

The WTC's twin towers are unusual in that the outer cladding of the buildings actually bear some of the load for the structures. In most skyscrapers, internal pillars provide the strength, and the walls merely keep the wind out. John MacArthur, of structural engineers Arup, said: "They are steel perimeter frame buildings and they are designed to withstand wind, with what is effectively a steel tube going around the building, with beams also made out of steel at every floor level. The towers were designed with the impact of a plane in mind. Buildings like these are designed to be flexible. As they deflect an impact, they absorb more energy, they sway more and creak. But it gets to the stage where a building can absorb no more. You can't design a building to absorb every single type of impact. Nobody could have ever considered something of the magnitude of this event." Gordon Masterton, chairman of the Institute of Civil Engineers' structural and building board, said: "Engineers will be studying the terrible events at the World Trade Center very closely. When they work on buildings of this kind, they try to make them as robust as possible. But there is a limit. If we designed buildings to withstand the impact the World Trade Center suffered, you would have no choice but to make every building a nuclear bunker. There is a limit to what we can really contemplate. People couldn't work or live in buildings like that, nor could they afford to build them." When they were completed in 1974, the 417-meter and 415-meter World Trade Center towers were the tallest in the world, two imposing monuments to America's spirit of free enterprise. Totaling 12m square feet, around 55,000 people worked in the twin towers, for hundreds of companies on 107 floors. Its owners, the New York and New Jersey Port Authority first wanted a single 150-story tower for its new business center, but discarded this due to an excessive scale. It brought in Minoru Yamasaki, who was morbidly afraid of heights, as architect, with Emery Roth and Sons, which created more than 60 skyscrapers in New York since the end of the Second World War, were the associate architects, handling production and collaborating on design.

Structural engineers Skilling, Helle, Christiansen and Robertson produced two towers which were akin to tubes of steel and glass, with 23m deep foundations, seven story high entrance lobbies, 23 express and 72 other elevators as well as 43,600 windows in the towers.

Steel prefab pieces came from yards in Seattle, Los Angeles, and St. Louis. They were held across the river at a Penn Central yard and trucked through the Holland Tunnel as needed. Eight cranes were constructed in Australia specifically for the center. Called Kangaroo cranes, they sat atop the buildings and rose as the buildings went higher.

Disaster first hit the center on Feb. 26, 1993, when a bomb exploded, killing six people, injuring around 1,000 others, and disrupting its businesses to the extent that 43 per cent went out of business. Four men were convicted and imprisoned for the bombing in 1996. Despite the attack, it was decided that the observation decks of WTC 2 at 107th and 110th floors should stay open. Until yesterday, they were still being visited every day by 80,000 people. (The Independent)

Arab News
www.arabnews.com
Saudi-Arabien, Jeddah

1. Die Welt verdammt den »Massen-Terrorismus«
2. Die ganze Welt ist nach Terrorangriffen in Alarmbereitschaft
3. Amerikanische Muslime rufen zu Blutspenden und zur Hilfe für die Opfer auf
4. Millionen Anrufer blockieren die Telefonleitungen und gehen ins Internet
5. Die Geschichte des World Trade Centers
6. Das World Trade Center: eines der mächtigsten Symbole der USA

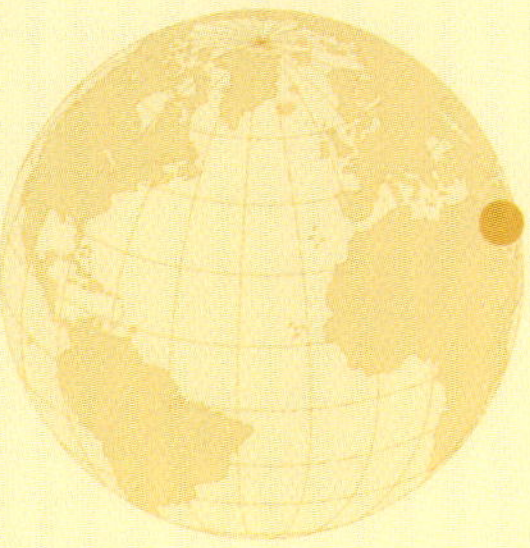

Terror Strikes US

WEDNESDAY, SEPTEMBER 12, 2001 15

Nationwide call for blood donations

New York hospitals overwhelmed by Trade Center victims

By Ian Driscoll
and David Howard Sinkman

NEW YORK — Casualties from the World Trade Center attacks poured into New York hospitals yesterday and the death toll at emergency rooms began mounting, hospital officials said.

At St. Vincents Hospital in lower Manhattan, 209 victims had been admitted by about 2 p.m. EDT (1800 GMT) and three had died there. Another 18 were in critical condition, said Mark Ackermann, chief of the hospital's corporate services.

At St. Vincents and elsewhere, emergency medical officials put out calls for volunteer nurses and doctors. An emergency call for blood donations also went out.

Bellevue Hospital had taken in 125 casualties, between 30 and 40 of whom were described as having major injuries, including broken bones, broken hips, internal problems and burns. Two victims were dead on arrival, hospital officials told Reuters in early afternoon.

No official casualty tolls from the attacks were available and New York Mayor Rudolph Giuliani said at a news conference such numbers would not be known for a day or two.

"The number of casualties will be more than any of us can bear, ultimately," Giuliani said.

"There are over 300 doctors here and they have been divided up into four trauma teams," said Dr. Luis Marcos, president of New York Health and Hospitals Corp., which includes Bellevue and 10 other New York hospitals.

"The numbers keep growing as we speak. This is something that gives you nightmares, something you see in the movies," said Marcos.

Victims from the attack on the World Trade Center — many suffering from extensive burns — began arriving at nearby hospitals about an hour after two planes slammed into the twin towers.

As the first victims came, about 50 or 60 doctors and nurses were standing in scrubs and uniforms waiting for the next wave of ambulances. The first wave arrived around 10 a.m. EDT (1400 GMT), doctors said.

The entire entrance to the emergency room was lined with stretchers covered with white sheets.

The first plane struck the north tower of the landmark complex in lower Manhattan, and the building was soon engulfed in flames. Moments later a second plane struck the south tower.

Both towers of the complex collapsed.

"I expect we will be working nonstop for at least the next 24 hours," Dr. Bernd Reisbeck, a physician at St. Vincents, said.

Meanwhile, Washington area hospitals geared up for a flood of casualties yesterday after an airplane crashed into the Pentagon, leaving dozens feared killed from the jetliner and at least 40 injured people from the Pentagon, according to early reports.

The aircraft, apparently a deliberately diverted scheduled flight, sliced into the building at a time when the offices and corridors would be bustling with people.

"All hospitals are in their emergency response mode and they are all prepared to receive victims transported to them," said Robert Malson, president of the D.C. Hospital Association. "All of the hospitals are on maximum alert."

Virginia Hospital Center Arlington admitted 30 victims by 2 p.m. (1900 GMT), said spokeswoman Kathryn Hughes. Those patients were suffering from a variety of injuries, including burns, cuts and shortness of breath. Some were in surgery, she added.

At Washington Hospital Center, seven victims had been admitted by mid-day, most suffering burn injuries of varying degrees, a spokeswoman said.

And at George Washington University Hospital, just blocks from the White House, two Pentagon victims, a mother and an infant, were brought to the emergency room. Hospital spokeswoman Linda Dent said both were in stable condition.

The airplane that crashed into the Pentagon yesterday morning followed shortly after two aircraft smashed into the twin towers of New York's World Trade Center, demolishing the landmark. A fourth crashed in Pennsylvania.

An FBI official at the scene said he believed the plane was an American Airlines plane that had been bound from Washington Dulles Airport for Los Angeles.

The airline said it was unable to account for a Boeing 757 with 58 passengers, four flight attendants and two pilots that had been flying that route.

Malson said his organization consisted of the 16 hospitals in Washington as well as a hospital at Andrews Air Force Base and the National Naval Hospital in Bethesda, Maryland.

Georgetown University Hospital also received one victim, a spokeswoman said, adding she had no details on the patient's injuries or condition.

She said Virginia Hospital Center was likely receiving most victims from the Pentagon. Some burn victims would likely be transported to the Washington Hospital Center in Washington, she said.

****Call for blood donations****

Disaster relief agencies said they were working with the military yesterday to rush thousands of pints of blood to New York City and Washington to treat an untold number of injuries from aerial hijack attacks in those cities.

The American Red Cross, which collects about half of the country's blood, said it has 60,000 units in various East Coast cities ready to ship to New York City hospitals, and to the Washington area where the extent of damage and injuries from the attacks were less devastating.

"We're working with the military in New York and New Jersey so we can get the blood in the appropriate hospitals," Red Cross Vice President Dr. Jerry Squires said in an interview.

"We stand ready to ship more to those areas if they are needed," Squires said.

With rail and auto traffic into Manhattan halted and all US commercial air traffic grounded, shipping the blood supplies to their destinations would be difficult if not impossible without help from the military.

The National Association of Community Blood Centers, which supplies 70 percent of the blood in New York City, said it sent about 15,000 pints to New York City immediately after the World Trade Center attacks, by far the most devastating, and is coordinating with the military to ship more.

"Some hospitals are running out of blood," a spokeswoman for the association said. "We need people to donate blood in Washington, New York and northern New Jersey."

To avoid chaos and overcrowding at blood donation centers, the Red Cross urged potential donors to call 800-GIVELIFE to schedule appointments.

"There are people lining up at our blood centers all across the United States, all the way out to Los Angeles," said Squires. "Over the next week or two we're going to need donors to continue to come in to replenish those inventories."

Officials said the most needed blood types are 0 positive and 0 negative, the so-called universal blood types that can be transfused into anyone in an emergency.

Although the Red Cross was not calling for emergency blood donations, the National Association of Community Blood Centers was urging donors to come forward. The New York Blood Center announced a blood emergency for the greater New York/New Jersey metropolitan area.

"There are a lot of burn victims," an association spokeswoman said. "They'll need platelets, plasma and red blood cells. That's why it's so important for people to give blood."

The Federal Emergency Management Agency said it was working closely with the White House and other federal agencies to coordinate relief efforts.

For the first time, the Department of Health and Human Services said it had activated a nationwide medical disaster response. It said it was prepared to send out its 80 disaster medical assistance teams. (R)

The remaining tower of New York's World Trade Center, Tower 2, dissolves in a cloud of dust and debris about a half hour after the first twin tower collapsed early on Tuesday. (Reuters)

Rescue workers remove a man from one of the World Trade Center towers in New York City, early on Tuesday.

People walk away from the World Trade Center tower in New York City on Tuesday morning. (Reuters)

One of the two World Trade Center towers falls to the ground after a plane crashed into it early Tuesday. (Reuters)

People watch as smoke billows from the two World Trade Center towers after planes crashed into each tower, in New York early on Tuesday. (Reuters)

A police officer (right) and others walk in the streets covered in debris near the World Trade Center towers on Tuesday morning. (AFP)

US President George W. Bush talks on the phone with New York Mayor Rudy Guiliani and Gov. George Pataki aboard Air Force One. Bush gave a statement about the two planes that crashed into the World Trade Center in New York City and one that crashed into the Pentagon in Washington DC earlier on Tuesday. (AFP)

Emergency personnel battle a fire at the Pentagon in Washington, DC, earlier Tuesday after an airplane crashed into it. At the same time, two passenger planes were crashed into the twin towers of the World Trade Center in new York City. Both towers collapsed. (AFP)

1 **New Yorker Krankenhäuser überlastet mit den Opfern des World Trade Centers**

2 Landesweiter Aufruf zur Blutspende

Arab News
www.arabnews.com
Saudi-Arabien, Jeddah

THE BANGLADESH OBSERVER

REGD. NO. DA 5 | DHAKA WEDNESDAY SEPTEMBER 12, 2001 | BHADRA 28, 1408 | JAMADIUS SANI 23, 1422 | 16 PAGES : PRICE TAKA 7.00

NEW YORK CITY: Smoke and fire surround the upper floors of the World Trade Center in New York City on Tuesday in this image from television, after a second plane crashed into the building. Planes crashed into the upper floors of both World Trade Center towers minutes apart in a horrific scene of explosions and fires that left gaping holes in the 110-story buildings (1). People in front of New York's St. Patrick's Cathedral react with horror as they look down Fifth Ave towards the World Trade Center towers and President Bush said the crashes were apparently the work of terrorists (2). President Bush looks down as he makes a statement regarding the terrorist acts upon the World Trade Center on Tuesday during a brief statement in Sarasota, Fla. (3). –AP

Bush orders to hunt down perpetrators

Terrorists crash four hijacked planes into WTC, Pentagon, Pennsylvania

NEW YORK/WASHINGTON, Sept 11:–Three hijacked planes crashed into major U.S. landmarks today, destroying both of New York's mighty twin towers and plunging the Pentagon in Washington into flames in an unprecedented assault on key symbols of U.S. military and financial power, reports Reuters.

Loss of life was expected to be catastrophic from the collapse of the giant towers of the World Trade Center where about 50,000 people work. The two enormous edifices both fell in a huge cloud of smoke and fire two hours after the initial impacts.

New York Mayor Rudolph Giuliani said there had been a "tremendous number of lives lost" in the assault on his city.

The attacks, the worst on the U.S. mainland in modern history, plunged the country into chaos and panic, paralysing communications, closing markets and forcing the evacuation of key buildings.

Another plane crashed south of Pittsburgh. It was not clear if this was another attempted hijacking. As international flights were diverted to Canada, the Federal Aviation Authority said it had yet to account for a number of planes.

President George W. Bush cut short a visit to Florida and rushed back to Washington to face the greatest crisis of his young presidency.

He called the deliberate aerial assaults an "apparent terrorist attack", and ordered a full-scale investigation. Early speculation about the source of the attack centered on Saudi-born guerilla leader Osama Bin-Laden.

Palestinian gunmen at refugee camps in Lebanon fired into the air to celebrate news of the attacks on major U.S. landmarks and government offices.

"Hundreds of people are burned from head to toe," said Dr. Steven Stern at St. Vincent's Hospital in the Greenwich Village neighbourhood of lower Manhattan.

"The whole of lower Manhattan is coated in half an inch of dust," Reuters reporter Daniel Sternoff said.

The attacks forced the evacuation of all government buildings in Washington, including the White House and other tall buildings around the country, cut cell phone communications on the East Coast and grounded all commercial planes in the United States.

Early reports said all three planes used in the attacks were hijacked, one of them from Boston and one from Washington. It was not immediately known who flew the planes and what happened to them.

The day of horror began around 9 a.m. (1300 GMT) in New York when the first plane

See Page 15 Col 2

Security around US Embassy reinforced

Staff Correspondent

The US embassy in Dhaka reinforced its security bulwark following terrorist assaults on a number of American establishments including the World Trade Centre in New York, Washington and Pennsylvania on Tuesday.

The mission has also advised American citizens in Bangladesh to remain alert and stay in safety to avoid any possible embarrassing situation.

The Caretaker Government, meanwhile, beefed up security measures in and around the diplomatic enclaves at Baridhara in view of the situation.

World leaders shocked

LONDON, Sept 11:–Astonishing terrorist strikes in the United States quickly reached a global audience Tuesday, with many around the world watching live coverage of an aircraft hitting the World Trade Center, says AP.

Audiences were transfixed by the awful images from New York, where both World Trade Center towers collapsed.

Key indexes sank on world stock markets and some European airlines canceled flights to the United States and recalled planes already in the air.

Russian President Vladimir Putin expressed his condolences to the American people over the ter-

(See Page 15 Col 4)

Khaleda shocked

BNP Chairperson Begum Khaleda Zia last night expressed her deep shock and anguish over the terrorist attack in American institutions in Washington and New York, reports BSS.

In an instant reaction she expressed her solidarity with the bereaved Americans and called for resistance against barbaric attack which cost many lives and property.

Army deployment

CA's plea after Khaleda's demand evokes reaction

Staff Correspondent

Chief Adviser to the Caretaker Government Justice Latifur Rahman's formal request to the President on Saturday to make early deployment of Army to quell polls related violence has evoked sharp reactions from the different political quarters.

No sooner had the BNP Chairperson Begum Khaleda Zia demanded deployment of Army at her public meeting in Khulna on Saturday, then the Chief Adviser rushed to the President to get it approved. Latif's mad rush to the President to get the Army deployment okayed from the President was nothing but a naked demonstration of his favour to a particular political party, commented, the political observers.

It was earlier decided that Army would be deployed in the district headquarters as rapid striking forces from September 26 just six days ahead of the October 1 election. But the sudden move of the Chief Adviser to make early deployment of Army for the election purpose was considered by the political quarters as a blue print of a particular political party. The present Caretaker Government is more interested in appeasing certain political forces instead of holding fair and free election– the constitutional responsibility of the government, the political observers said.

Commenting on the early deployment of Army, former President and Jatiya Party Chairman H.M. Ershad who was once Chief of Army Staff said that such move would make the Army controversial. He believed that there was no need for deployment of Army at the moment as police and paramilitary BDR had yet not failed. It was the duty of the nation to keep the Army above any political controversy in the national interest.

Bangladeshis in NY safe

With the US under a veritable armageddon in terrorist attacks, most of the Bangladeshis living in New York are safe but rushing to the stores to get essentials, messages reaching Dhaka said, reports UNB.

Farzana Ahmed, a Bangladeshi living in New York, said, "The NY City is totally closed. Thousands of people are feared killed. But I am stuck in my office because there is no communication".

A frightened Farzana said, "whatever is going on in and around the World Trade Center, I don't know the details about it, most of Bangladeshi people living in Queens and they are okay".

Farzana, keeping constant touch with the newsroom of UNB in Dhaka on the cybernet termed the incident an attack on humanity.

CEC endorses army deployment

Staff Correspondent

Going one step ahead of the President and the Chief Adviser, Chief Election Commissioner MA Syed on Tuesday endorsed immediate deployment of army to quell the fomenting violence unleashed by the troublemakers.

"I want army deployment right at the moment. The Caretaker Government has taken a good decision, a sensibly right step," he told reporters at the Election Commission, talking about Monday's decision to call out army on September 22 on election purposes.

In a rebuttal to the suspicion on polls, the CEC confidently ex-

(See Page 15 Col. 5)

Inside

NAMAZ TIMINGS

September 12
Zohr: 11:58 am
Asr: 4:21 pm
Magrib: 6:09 pm
Esha: 7:23 pm
Tomorrow's Fajr 4:29 am
Source: Islamic Foundation

Weather

Day temperature is likely to remain nearly unchanged over the country.

Light to moderate rain or thunder-shower accompanied by temporary gusty or squally wind is likely to occur at most places over Rajshahi division and at many places over Dhaka, Khulna and Barisal divisions and at a few places over Chittagong and Sylhet divisions with moderately heavy to heavy fall at places over Rajshahi, Khulna and Barisal divisions.

The maximum temperature recorded in Dhaka on Tuesday was 32.4 degrees Celsius (90.3 degrees Fahrenheit) and the minimum 24.6 degrees Celsius (76.3 degrees Fahrenheit).

The percentage of humidity recorded on Tuesday was 77 in the morning and 93 in the evening.

The highest temperature recorded on Tuesday was 34.6 degrees Celsius (93.9 degrees Fahrenheit) at Srimongal and the lowest 24.0 degrees Celsius (75.2 degrees Fahrenheit) at Barisal, Khepupara and Syedpur.

	Sun rises	Sun sets
September 11		6:07 pm
September 12	5:44 am	

Election rally at Ctg Polo Ground

Remain alert against taking away your votes with money, gun: Hasina

CHITTAGONG, Sept. 11:–Foreseeing foul play, Awami League President Sheikh Hasina today (Tuesday) urged the people to remain alert so that none can take away their votes with money or guns, reports UNB.

Addressing a mammoth election rally at the Polo ground here, she alleged that BNP-Jamaat axis rejected by the people in 1996 election could perceive that they won't get vote at the October 1 polls and were now trying to foil it.

"They are creating a state of anarchy across the country killing our party leaders and workers to foil the election," Hasina said, urging the people to face with patience the situation created by "BNP terrorists."

The AL chief asked the caretaker government to combat the BNP-Jamaat-sponsored terrorism and create congenial atmosphere for neutral elections.

"It is the main responsibility of caretaker government to remain neutral and create conditions for a neutral election," Hasina said.

Amidst cheers and thunderous slogans from her audience, the former Prime Minister said people would not accept results of any rigged election under a "blueprint" by BNP-Jamaat clique.

"The Awami League is the hot favourite in the October 1 election... Mass tide has been created for boat and victory is ours," she told her audience.

Hasina was however critical of the administration for taking no action against BNP terrorists. She said although a "jihad" was declared against Joynal Hazari, it did not take any action against VP Joynal of BNP.

Braving torrential rain, thousands of people converged on the Polo ground shouting: "boat-boat".

Hasina asked her party workers to campaign door-to-door for Awami League and ensure that people could vote peacefully.

If reelected, the former PM said her party would take further steps to turn the port city into commercial capital and install Chittagong-Cox's Bazar rail line.

Referring to her party's election manifesto, she said the number of women seats in Parliament would be increased to 60 through the amendment of the Constitution, registered

See Page 15 Col 2

Hasina condemns terrorist attack in US

Former Prime Minister Sheikh Hasina last night strongly condemned the "terrorist attack" on World Trade Centre, Pentagon and State Department of the United States in an unprecedented blitzkrieg on any capital in human history, reports UNB.

The Awami League president called for building world opinion against the "inhuman dastardly attack".

In her instant reaction, Hasina said Awami League had always been protesting world terrorism and heinous attack on common people.

"We must build up world opinion against subversive acts," said Hasina, who is now on election tour of the country's south-eastern part.

The former Prime Minister expressed solidarity with US President George Bush and people of the United States.

Addresses public meetings in Jessore, Kaliganj

Khaleda urges President to deploy army immediately

KALIGANJ, Sept 11:–BNP Chairperson Khaleda Zia today (Tuesday) urged the President to immediately deploy Army to recover illegal arms and arrest terrorists, reports UNB.

"You (President) are in charge of Defense, deploy army immediately, otherwise, you will be held responsible for killing of any BNP workers... You are not above accountability," she said in her strongly worded speech at a huge election rally here.

Khaleda also urged the Chief Adviser to take practical steps to create condition for free and fair election. Otherwise, she said, "we will understand that you do not want to hold a fair election."

"The Caretaker Government will have to bear the responsibility of all consequences," she warned addressing the rally at Naltola Bhusan Pilot High School-ground in Kaliganj (Jhenidah-4) in favour of BNP candidate Shahiduzzaman Beltu.

She said Awami League has a huge store of arms, which will influence the election.

The BNP Chief also accused Awami League of creating chaos and anarchy through terrorism across the country to foil the election sensing a massive election debacle.

She said the people will reject AL as it had unleashed a reign of terror in the country during its five-year rule besides misappropriating public money.

"Awami League has to be kept out of power as they came to power in 1996 after 21 years and grabbed food for next 40 years," she said.

She sought votes for the BNP-led four-party alliance candidates to free the country from corruption and terrorism.

On her way to Kaliganj from Jessore, thousands of people greeted the BNP Chief chanting slogans with bunches of "sheaf of paddy", election symbol of BNP, in their hands.

Our correspondent from Jessore adds: BNP Chairperson Begum Khaleda Zia today reiterated her election pledge to build a corruption and terrorism free country if voted to

See Page 15 Col 6

Political violence claims 12 lives in last two days

Staff Correspondent

At least twelve people were killed and hundred others injured in a series of political violence at different parts of the country during the last two days.

The rival political activists, particularly BNP and Awami League, locked in clashes centering election campaign in Dhaka, Munshiganj, Mymensingh, Feni, Barisal and Bhola.

Of the eleven victims, four were killed on Tuesday and seven on Monday. The four deaths, two were reported from Feni and one each in Munshiganj and Mymmensigh on Tuesday, were identified as Awami League activists. On Monday, two were killed in Bhola, two in Munshiganj and Feni one in Dhaka.

A BNP leader was killed when a group of miscreants attacked his house and shot him from a point blank range at Begunbari under Tejgaon thana on Monday night. He was identified as Abdullah Khokan alias Mama Khokan, general secretary of ward 37 unit of BNP.

Our Feni Correspondent reports: Two Awami League workers were killed and 25 injured in the political violence in the district on Tuesday. The activists—Abul Kashem and Abu Yusuf Kiron—were abducted and killed allegedly by BNP supporters in Dhalia and Kemamotia.

According to police, some armed BNP activists abducted Awami League activist Abul Kashem when he was pasting poster of Awami League candidate Mahbubul Alam Tara at Dhalia bus stand at 10.30 a.m. Police rescued him from Balua Chowmuhani and sent him to Sadar Hospital where he succumbed to his injuries at 2.30 p.m. Doctors said he bore marks of injury by sharp weapons. After the incident Awami League supporters attacked BNP workers leaving 10 people injured.

Awami League leader Abu Yusuf Kiran (25) who was abducted reportedly by BNP supporters from Kazirhat of Lokkar Tek in Mangalkandi union, succumbed to his injuries at Chittagong Medical College Hospital on Tuesday morning.

A police constable Abul

See Page 15 Col 7

ETV coverage

BNP leaders exchange hot words with CEC

Staff Correspondent

Some leaders of BNP had a wordy duel with Chief Election Commissioner MA Syed over the coverage of election results by electronic media, including private television channel ETV.

The serious difference of opinion that turned into hot exchange of words arose when the CEC was briefing the representatives of Awami League and BNP on the process of announcing the election results at the Election Commission Secretariat on Tuesday.

BNP leaders, especially bureaucrat-turned-politician Mofazzal Karim, insisted on airing the initial unofficial results only on Bangladesh Television instead of allowing private TV channels separately. BNP's opposition to ETV came understandably as the party considered the country's first

See Page 15 Col 3

1 Vier von Terroristen gekaperte Flugzeuge stürzen ins World Trade Center, auf das Pentagon und auf Pennsylvania

2 Bush befiehlt Jagd auf die Täter

3 Sicherheitsvorkehrungen rund um die amerikanische Botschaft verstärkt

4 Staatsoberhäupter auf der ganzen Welt sind geschockt

5 Khaleda ist erschüttert

6 Hasina verurteilt terroristische Attacken in den USA

THE BANGLADESH OBSERVER
WWW.BANGLADESH.NET
BANGLADESCH, DHAKA

THE HINDU
INDIA'S NATIONAL NEWSPAPER
Printed at Chennai, Coimbatore, Bangalore, Hyderabad, Madurai, Delhi, Visakhapatnam, Thiruvananthapuram and Kochi
32 Pages Rs. 3
CHENNAI, WEDNESDAY, SEPTEMBER 12, 2001
ISSN 0971 - 751X Vol. 124. No. 217
Internet: www.hindugrouponnet.com & www.hinduonnet.com

America under attack

● World Trade Center collapses ● Part of Pentagon destroyed ● White House evacuated ● Thousands feared killed

DIGEST

All SP MLAs in U.P. quit

Woman without veil attacked

Assembly dissolved

Israel, India next?

Did terrorists have their own pilots?

Smoke, shock spread over New York

WORLD TRADE CENTER, NEW YORK

The second tower of the World Trade Center as it caves in. (Right): A TV grab shows clouds of smoke and dust spreading over New York as the tower comes down after having an aircraft crash into it on Tuesday. Both the towers of the Center have since come down. — Reuters, AFP

Video-grabs taken from Russian TV channel NTV and US Fox TV showing the second plane that smashed against one of the twin towers of the World Trade Center in New York on Tuesday in an apparent terrorist attack. — AFP

AMERICA IN AGONY: Women unable to control themselves, console one another, as they watch the World Trade Center crashing down on Tuesday. — AP

India shocked: Page 13
Osama hand suspected: Page 16

1 Angriff auf Amerika

2 • World Trade Center eingestürzt • Teil des Pentagons zerstört
• Weißes Haus evakuiert • Tausende Tote befürchtet

3 Hatten die Terroristen ihre eigenen Piloten?

4 Rauch und Schrecken verbreiten sich über New York

THE HINDU
WWW.HINDUONNET.COM
INDIEN, CHENNAI

12

حمله موشکی نیروهای ائتلاف شمال افغانستان به فرودگاه کابل

در حمله موشکی به فرودگاه کابل، دو فروند هواپیما به کلی نابود شدند و به یک مخزن مهمات نیز آسیب وارد شده است

اطلاعات

مراسم سالگرد آیت الله العظمی گلپایگانی (ره) فردا برگزار می شود

رئیس جمهوری درگذشت آیت الله خاتم یزدی راتسلیت گفت

چهارشنبه ۲۱ شهریور ۱۳۸۰ - ۲۳ جمادی الثانی ۱۴۲۲ - ۱۲ سپتامبر ۲۰۰۱ - شماره ۲۲۲۹۳ - ۲۰۰ ریال - همراه با ۱۶ صفحه نیازمندیهای روزنامه اطلاعات

جهان حمله تروریستی به مراکز حساس سیاسی، نظامی و اقتصادی آمریکا را محکوم کرد

هولناکترین فاجعه تروریستی تاریخ در قلب آمریکا

هزاران تن زیر آوارهای ساختمان تجارت جهانی مدفون شده‌اند

برخورد دو هواپیمای مسافربری با دو برج ۱۱۰ طبقه‌ای مرکز تجارت جهانی در نیویورک، هزاران کشته و زخمی برجا گذاشت

نشست فوق العاده اتحادیه اروپا برای بررسی انفجارهای آمریکا آغاز به کار کرد

رئیس جمهوری آمریکا طی سخنانی اعلام کرد: ما تفاوتی میان تروریست‌ها و کسانی که به آنها پناه داده‌اند قائل نخواهیم شد

انفجار بمب، ساختمان‌های کاخ سفید، وزارت امور خارجه و کنگره آمریکا را به لرزه درآورد

تمامی مراکز مالی آمریکا تا اطلاع ثانوی تعطیل شدند

«یاسر عرفات» حملات تروریستی به ساختمان مرکز تجارت جهانی در نیویورک و پنتاگون در واشنگتن را محکوم کرد

طالبان حمله به مرکز تجارت جهانی و وزارت دفاع آمریکا را محکوم کردند

در پیام رئیس جمهوری اسلامی ایران

ملت و دولت ایران عملیات تروریستی در آمریکا را محکوم کردند

خاتمی: تأسف عمیق و همدردی خود را با ملت آمریکا به ویژه آسیب دیدگان و خانواده قربانیان حادثه اعلام می‌دارم

تروریسم محکوم است و جامعه جهانی باید ریشه ها و ابعاد آن را بشناسد و برای خشکاندن آن گامهای اساسی بردارد

گزارش: برای ایجاد امنیت ترافیکی، باید «فرهنگ ترافیک» را بشناسیم و رعایت کنیم

نظرها و اندیشه ها: دولت این عاشقان پاینده باد — غلامعلی رجایی

فروش استثنائی سایپا

آگهی مزایده مرکبات — شرکت سهامی کشت و صنعت جیرفت

آگهی مناقصه عمومی خرید لوله تیپ — شرکت سهامی کشت و صنعت جیرفت

فراخوان

دستورالعمل و تقویم ثبت نام پذیرفته شدگان آزمون سراسری سال ۱۳۸۰

پایان عملیات اجرایی، افتتاح و واگذاری ۲۰۰۰ واحد مسکن استیجاری (اجاره به شرط تملیک) در شهرهای کاشان، گلپایگان، شهرضا، فولادشهر، نجف آباد، خمینی شهر، مبارکه، شاهین شهر و بهارستان - شهریور ۱۳۸۰

روابط عمومی سازمان مسکن و شهرسازی استان اصفهان

1 Grausames terroristisches Attentat im Herzen Amerikas

2 Die Welt verdammt das terroristische Attentat auf das militärische, politische und wirtschaftliche Zentrum von Amerika

3 Die iranische Nation und Regierung verurteilen den Terroranschlag in Amerika

Ettelaat
www.ettelaat.com
Iran, Teheran

12

FOUNDED BY QUAID-I-AZAM MOHAMMAD ALI JINNAH

DAWN

http://DAWN.com Vol. LV No. 250 Karachi, Jamadi-us-Saani 23, 1422 Wednesday, September 12, 2001 28 PAGES Rs 13.00

•US closes air traffic •full emergency alert ordered •office complexes evacuated

Thousands dead as planes crash into WTC, Pentagon

By Masood Haider

NEW YORK: Smoke billows up after the first of the two towers of the World Trade Center collapsed on Tuesday.—AFP

NEW YORK, Sept 11: In what is said to be the most devastating attack on the United States since the Pearl Harbour bombing during the Second World War, unknown men launched a simultaneous air attack against US political and financial centres on Tuesday, with two hijacked aircraft slamming into the World Trade Center in New York, one crashing into the Pentagon, and a fourth in Pennsylvania.

Related reports, pictures on Pp 15, 16

Bush vows to hunt down and punish terrorists

Taliban rule out Osama's hand

By Our Staff Reporter

It is crime against humanity, says Arafat

Continued on Page 3

Security tightened in Islamabad

By Our Reporter

Oil prices up by $4 a barrel

Aircraft diverted to other airports

Musharraf condemns attacks

Shape of Washington's retaliation awaited

By Tahir Mirza

❶ Tausende Tote, nachdem Flugzeuge in das World Trade Center und auf das Pentagon stürzen

❷ • USA schließen Flugverkehr • Höchste Alarmbereitschaft angeordnet • Bürogebäude evakuiert.

❸ Bush schwört, die Terroristen zur Strecke zu bringen und zu bestrafen

❹ Taliban schließen »Osamas Hand« aus

❺ Sicherheitsvorkehrungen in Islamabad verschärft

❻ Arafat spricht von einem Verbrechen gegen die Menschheit

❼ Flugzeuge auf andere Flughäfen umgeleitet

❽ Musharraf verurteilt Angriffe

❾ Ölpreise steigen um vier Dollar pro Barrel

❿ Ausmaß der Washingtoner Vergeltung erwartet

DAWN
WWW.DAWN.COM
PAKISTAN, KARATSCHI

Rabu, 12 September 2001

SUARA PEMBARUAN

Memperjuangkan Harapan Rakyat Berdasarkan Pancasila

Harga Eceran Rp 1.500,-

Hiburan: **Buku Koleksi Permata** — Bintang film Elizabeth Taylor menulis buku tentang koleksi permatanya yang menurut rencana diterbitkan tahun depan, 8

Kesra: **Waspada Mengonsumsi Ikan Asin** — Telinga, hidung, dan tenggorokan (THT) adalah lokasi yang rentan terhadap kanker nasofaring. Kanker ini muncul pada mereka yang mengonsumsi ikan asin sehingga perlu diwaspadai, 9

Nusantara: **Tuntut Penempatan Tugas** — Ratusan pegawai eks Kanwil Departemen Penerangan Jawa Tengah menuntut gubernur di daerah ini untuk menempatkan mereka ke tempat tugas. Sejak 6 September 2001, mereka "dirumahkan", 16

EKSKLUSIF

Indonesia Transito Imigran (3)

Yang Digebuk dan Yang Dipungli

Dua Pesawat Tabrak Gedung WTC New York

Serangan Teroris Paling Berani di Dunia

DITABRAK PESAWAT – *Api membubung tinggi pada dua menara World Trade Center, Manhattan, New York, Amerika Serikat, Selasa (11/9) pagi waktu setempat, akibat ditabrak dengan sengaja oleh dua pesawat terbang yang dibajak teroris. Presiden Amerika George Bush mengatakan, tragedi tersebut, hingga berita ini diturunkan, mengakibatkan enam orang tewas dan 1.000 orang luka-luka.*

Markas Besar AB di Pentagon Juga Terbakar Hebat

KPU Siap Laksanakan Pemilihan Presiden Langsung Tahun 2004

Dana IMF US$ 395 Juta Cair

Luar Biasa, Indonesia Sabet 10 Emas

Penebangan Lontar di Timor Kian Mengkhawatirkan

Perolehan Medali

PEROLEHAN MEDALI HINGGA SELASA (11/9) Pukul 21.30 WIB

	Emas	Perak	Perunggu
1. Malaysia	39	26	32
2. Indonesia	25	21	27
3. Thailand	23	23	28
4. Vietnam	17	17	23
5. Filipina	12	24	23
6. Singapura	9	8	13
7. Myanmar	6	8	18
8. Brunei	0	0	3
9. Laos	0	0	2
10. Kamboja	0	0	2

1 **Der gewagteste Terroranschlag der Welt**

2 Zwei Flugzeuge prallen gegen das WTC in New York

3 Airbus stürzt auf das Pentagon und entfacht ebenfalls einen weitläufigen Brand

Suara Pembaruan
www.suarapembaruan.com
Indonesien, Jakarta

人民日報

RENMIN RIBAO

2001年9月12日 星期三

今日12版（华东、华南地区16版）

人民网网址：http://www.people.com.cn

http://www.peopledaily.com.cn

国内统一刊号：CN11-0065

第19422期（代号1-1）

人民日报社出版

江泽民主席致电布什总统

就美一些地方受到严重袭击，代表中国政府和人民，向布什总统并通过布什总统，向美国政府和人民表示深切的慰问，并对死难者家属表示哀悼

中华人民共和国主席 江泽民

2001年9月11日于北京

江主席对我在美人员安全深表关心

中国政府已于当夜指示中国驻美大使馆、驻美各总领事馆、常驻联合国代表团立即采取措施，给所有受到伤害的同胞提供一切必要的帮助

外交部发言人发表谈话

● 美国纽约和华盛顿地区一些地方9月11日受到严重袭击，造成重大人员伤亡，我们对此深感震惊

● 中国政府一贯谴责和反对一切恐怖主义的暴力活动

美国纽约华盛顿受到严重袭击

接连遭到飞机撞击而引发爆炸

纽约世界贸易中心和华盛顿五角大楼

九运会火炬传递点火起跑仪式举行

江泽民点燃主火炬 胡锦涛出席 李岚清致辞

朱镕基总理会见普京总统

宾主进行了亲切友好的交谈

八月份我国工业生产快速增长

面向市场 依靠科技

我国农业结构调整取得明显成效

加快推进农业结构战略性调整

本报评论员

新加坡总统纳丹

今起对我国进行国事访问

人物介绍

今日导读

❶ **Präsident Jiang Zemin sendet Beileidstelegramm an Präsident Bush**

❷ Aufgrund der schweren Angriffe an einigen Orten in Amerika übermittelt Präsident Jiang im Namen der chinesischen Regierung und des chinesischen Volkes Präsident Bush, der amerikanischen Regierung und dem amerikanischen Volk sein tief empfundenes Mitleid, zudem den Familienangehörigen der Getöteten und Verwundeten sein Beileid

❸ Präsident Jiang Zemin ist sehr besorgt über die Sicherheit des chinesischen Personals in Amerika

❹ Die chinesische Regierung hat bereits in der Nacht veranlasst, dass die chinesische Botschaft und die Konsulate sowie die chinesischen Abgeordneten der ständigen Vertretung der UNO sofort Maßnahmen ergreifen, um den Landsleuten alle notwendige Hilfe zu erteilen

❺ Erklärung des Sprechers des Auswärtigen Amtes in China

❻ Schwere Anschläge in New York und Washington

Renmin Ribao
www.peopledaily.com.cn
VR China, Peking

工人日報

WORKERS' DAILY

2001年9月12日 星期三 农历辛巳年 七月廿五 (今日八版)

国内统一刊号:CN11—0002 代号:1—5 第13802期

江泽民就美受到严重袭击致电布什

并对我在美人员安全深表关心

外交部发言人就美受到严重袭击发表谈话

江泽民点燃九运会主火炬

九运会火炬传递点火起跑仪式隆重举行

胡锦涛出席 李岚清致辞

纽约华盛顿遭受严重袭击

纽约世贸中心"双子"大楼被炸塌，五角大楼一角被炸毁，国务院、国会附近也发生爆炸，布什说撞击事件可能是恐怖分子所为并下令美军处于高度戒备状态

朱镕基总理会见普京总统

《中俄总理第六次定期会晤联合公报》公布

大力推进产业结构调整

云南千万巨奖揽才攻关

取缔非法矿窿和选矿厂行动启动

南丹炸封非法矿窿

新闻分析

地铁成为新的商业带

开放式基金热卖

Gongren Ribao – Workers' Daily
VR China, Peking

1 Schwere Anschläge in New York und Washington

2 »Zwillingstürme« des World Trade Centers explodiert und eingestürzt, ein Teil des Pentagons zerstört, Explosionen auch in der Nähe des State Departments und beim amerikanischen Parlament. Präsident Bush spricht von wahrscheinlich terroristischen Anschlägen und versetzt die amerikanischen Streitkräfte in höchste Alarmbereitschaft

3 Staatspräsident Jiang Zemin sendet nach den schweren Anschlägen in Amerika ein Beileidstelegramm an Präsident George W. Bush

4 Zudem zeigt sich Jiang Zemin tief besorgt über die Sicherheit des chinesischen Personals in Amerika

5 Rede des Regierungssprechers des Auswärtigen Amtes nach den schweren Anschlägen in Amerika

朝日新聞
2001年9月12日
米テロ死者 数千人
大統領 報復の決意明言
乗っ取り計4機
3機激突 1機墜落
日本企業17人未確認
都内早大生 搭乗名簿に
テロ関連ニュース
株1万円割れ
TOPIXも一時990台
日経平均9600円台
テレビ・ラジオ16・17面 天気18面
夢も折り込みます
0120-76-4611
公務員
全日制
10/10開講
ガリガリの人達
―症状にもいろいろあるんです―
あつがり 虚弱体質の方に
さむがり 冷え症の方に
いたがり 胃腸の弱い方に
いやがり 食欲のない方に
ころがり 疲れやすい方に
つよがり 血色の悪い方に
やみあがり 病中病後の方に
薬用養命酒が効きます。
説明書をさしあげます
薬用養命酒

1 **Terror in den USA fordert mehrere tausend Tote**

2 Vier Maschinen wurden entführt – Drei schlugen ein, eine stürzte ab

3 Sorge um 17 vermisste Mitarbeiter eines japanischen Unternehmens – sie sind laut Passagierliste in Washington an Bord gegangen

4 Präsident spricht von »entschlossener Vergeltung«

5 Aktienkurse unter die Marke von 10 000 gerutscht. Auch Topix-Index in der ersten Stunde auf 990 Punkte gefallen. Nikkei-Index bei 9600 Punkten

The Asahi Shimbun
www.asahi.com
Japan, Tokio

NEWSPAPER OF THE MOST IMPORTANT CITY IN NEW ZEALAND

SECOND EDITION

The Evening Post

LATEST

www.stuff.co.nz — WEDNESDAY, SEPTEMBER 12, 2001 — 80c Airfreight: 51 incl gst

AMERICA UNDER ATTACK

Hijacked airliners slam into World Trade Center, Pentagon

DEATH TOLL UP TO 10,000

Massive rescue under way

Explosions in Afghanistan

Air traffic chaos

THREE HOURS OF TERROR

12.56am (NZ time): An airliner hits one of the 110-storey World Trade Center towers in New York, exploding in a fireball and punching a hole in the building s facade.

1.14am: A second plane hits the second of the World Trade Center s Twin Towers, the impact raining debris on to the streets below. "There was a glimpse of its broad, silver fuselage head-on as it ducked and snaked and then flew directly at the second tower. It seemed to vanish and the fireball spewed from one side," said witness Mark Wood.

6 PAGES INSIDE

1.40am: US President George W Bush, in Sarasota, Florida, calls the blasts "an apparent terrorist attack" and vows to find "those folks who committed these acts".

1.53am: A third airliner ploughs into the Pentagon in Washington DC, turning a section of the world s largest office building into an inferno.

2.05am: As thousands of workers flee the building, one of the World Trade Center s two towers collapses in a cloud of dust that coats lower Manhattan. Many workers were trapped in the building when it fell. Onlookers watch in horror as people throw themselves from the building from as high as the 80th floor. A man and woman hold hands as they fall.

2.28am: The second tower of the World Trade Center – once the world s tallest building – collapses "like a house of cards". Thousands of New Yorkers evacuate Manhattan island on foot. A massive rescue operation swings into action.

3.34am: A fourth airliner, travelling from Newark to San Francisco, crashes in western Pennsylvania. A passenger on the plane dialled 911 before the crash saying: "We are being hijacked. We are being hijacked." Officials speculate the commandeered plane was en route to the Presidential retreat at Camp David.

Authorities predict a death toll of 10,000 in New York alone.

Reuters

CALL US
Post reporters 474-0444; Post fax 474-0237; Money, Business 474-0253; Sport, Racing 474-0073; Features 474-0048; Editor s office 474-0105; Porirua reporter 237-2954; Hutt reporters 570-2288; Kapiti reporter 296-1412; Photographs 474-0102; Classified 473-9999; Accts, other dpts 474-0222; Deliveries 474-0100

WEATHER
Mainly fine: Another out-and-about day tomorrow. A few cloud patches but mainly fine, with a northerly breeze. **Page 44**

Wed Sep 12 12:31:39 2001

1 **Angriff auf Amerika**

2 Entführte Passagierflugzeuge schlagen ins World Trade Center und das Pentagon ein

3 Bis zu 10 000 Todesopfer

4 Intensive Rettungsaktion angelaufen

5 Explosionen in Afghanistan

6 Chaos im Luftverkehr

The Evening Post
www.stuff.co.nz
Neuseeland, Wellington

12

+++ Feuerwehrleute und Rettungskräfte hissen eine US-Fahne in dem riesigen Trümmerberg.

+++ Mitglieder des New York Police Departments patrouillieren durch den abgesperrten Bezirk der Ruine des WTCs.

+++ Zwei Feuerwehrmänner tragen eine Leiche, die in einen Plastiksack gehüllt ist.

13. September

Nr. 38 13. September 2001 56. Jahrgang www.zeit.de C 7451 C Preis 5,50 DM

DIE ZEIT

dkr 32,00 - fmk 35,00 - ptas 675,00 (Inseln 700,00) - FF 28,00 - hfl 7,50 - öS 45,00 sfr 5,50 - Lire 7400,00 - dr 1600,00 - bfr 136,00 - esc (Cont.) 900,00 - lfr 136,00

WOCHENZEITUNG FÜR POLITIK • WIRTSCHAFT • WISSEN UND KULTUR

Krieg gegen die USA

Der monströse Massenmord eint die Welt im Widerstand gegen die Internationale des Schreckens

Die Zielscheibe: Unsere Zivilisation

Terror total und global

Von Josef Joffe

Das World Trade Center ausradiert, das Pentagon in Flammen, das Weiße Haus, das Capitol, die Ministerien evakuiert: Amerika, das mächtigste Land auf Erden, ist das Opfer der fürchterlichsten Terrorattacke seiner Geschichte geworden. Ungezählt sind die Toten, die Verwundeten. Wie im Krieg herrscht das Gesetz der Triage: Die Retter helfen sofort nur denen, die zwischen Tod und Leben schweben. Die anderen warten oder sterben. Für die USA ist es das historische Trauma schlechthin. Selbst die beiden Weltkriege hat dieses Land weit vor seinen Küsten erlebt; fremde Mächte haben zuletzt im „Krieg von 1812" auf seinem Territorium gewütet, als die Briten Washington niederbrannten.

Seitdem galt die Prophezeiung von Alexandre de Tocqueville, dessen Buch *La démocratie en Amérique* auch fast zwei Jahrhunderte später noch immer der klügste Kommentar zu dem einzigartigen politischen Gebilde namens USA ist. „Die Vereinigten Staaten", schrieb Tocqueville, „ist eine Nation ohne Nachbarn." Ihre historische Erfahrung ist die der absoluten Sicherheit, die kein europäischer Staat je genießen durfte: „Inmitten eines riesigen Kontinentes bleibt die Union abgeschottet vom Rest der Welt, als wären all ihre Grenzen von Ozeanen umschlungen."

„America under attack", melden die amerikanischen TV-Sender in stummen, starren Lettern, während die Bilder des Grauens abrollen. Tocqueville ist passé, Amerika hat den letzten Teil seiner weltpolitischen Unschuld verloren, der Riese ist nun wahrhaftig zum Opfer eines Terrors geworden, dem gewiss das Etikett „international" gebührt. Der erste Angriff auf das World Trade Center im Jahre 1993 war mit sechs Toten noch halbwegs glimpflich verlaufen, Oklahoma City mit seinen 168 Opfern war das Mordwerk des Amerikaners Timothy McVeigh. Grundsätzlich aber hat es sich die Internationale des Terrors nie getraut (oder nie geschafft), Amerika so systematisch daheim zu attackieren wie in dieser Woche. Die Liste früherer Anschläge ist lang: Beirut 1983, Lockerbie 1988, Nairobi/Daressalam 1998, Aden 2000 ... Aber das war weit weg und vereinzelt, keine strategische Offensive, die ein Generalstab nicht hätte teuflischer aushecken können.

Pearl Harbor – sechzig Jahre danach

Nur mit dem japanischen Überfall auf Pearl Harbor am 7. Dezember 1941 lässt sich das Massaker dieser Woche vergleichen. Die Japaner versenkten die halbe US-Pazifikflotte, aber auch Hawaii war seinerzeit noch kein amerikanischer Bundesstaat, überdies 4500 Kilometer vom Festland entfernt. Und doch: 19 Schiffe und 2500 Tote waren genug, um Amerika nach diesem „Tag der Niedertracht" (Roosevelt) in den totalen Krieg gegen Tokyo zu katapultieren.

Und nun, nach dem monströsen Massenmord, der Amerika ins Herz treffen sollte? Das Pentagon ist das zentrale Symbol amerikanischer Militärmacht; das World Trade Center mitten im Wall Street *financial district* ist nicht bloß das symbolische Zentrum amerikanischer Wirtschaftsmacht. Denn hier laufen die Fäden (genauer: die Glasfaserkabel) einer globalen Wirtschaftsordnung zusammen. Diese Zielscheibe war nicht allein eine amerikanische; die Terroristen wollten nicht nur Amerika, sondern das Herz einer westlichen Zivilisation treffen, die sie mit mörderischer Inbrunst hassen. Ein vergleichbarer Zivilisationsbruch lässt sich nur an den Namen Hitler, Stalin und Pol Pot festmachen.

Damals wurde der Horror von Menschen vernichtenden säkularen Heilslehren getrieben. Heute sind die Schuldigen noch nicht identifiziert; möglich, dass die paranoiden Erben und Rächer von McVeigh dem eigenen Land den Krieg erklärt haben. Plausibler ist freilich die islamistische Variante, inszeniert von jenen „Gotteskämpfern", die Amerika und Israel nicht nur als „Ungläubige", sondern auch als Speerspitze der Moderne und der westlichen Zivilisation verteufeln. Sie hassen den freien Markt, die liberale Ordnung, das interessengeleitete Individuum, die Freiheit zur Selbstbestimmung, die Trennung von Kirche und Staat, die Europa erst nach Jahrhunderten blutiger Religionskriege verwirklichen konnte. Dass jedermann nach seiner Fasson selig werden möge, dieses Prinzip ist den Taliban, den bin Ladens, den Hizbullahi, den Hamas-Selbstmördern so fremd, wie es uns bis zum Dreißigjährigen Krieg gewesen ist.

In dieser Woche scheint der Harvard-Politologe Samuel Huntington mit seinem viel gescholtenen *Kampf der Kulturen* (1995) auf schrecklichste Weise Recht zu bekommen. Nicht mehr Staaten wie im 19. Jahrhundert, nicht mehr Ideologien wie im 20. kämpfen um die Vorherrschaft, sondern politisch formierte, hoch bewaffnete Glaubenslehren. Wohin man auch blickt, ob nach Bosnien, Tschetschenien, Nordirland, Nahost, Sudan oder Indonesien, lauert hinter der Blutrunst, hinter dem Kampf um Identität und Land die Gnadenlosigkeit eines Glaubens, der neben seinem Gott keinen anderen duldet. Vor allem nicht eine westliche Zivilisation, die angeblich nur dem einen Gott, dem Mammon, huldige. Wer diesen unter dem Gemäuer seines Tempels begraben will, legt folgerichtig das Symbol allen Übels, das World Trade Center, in Schutt und Asche.

Doch weil Amerika in offener Feldschlacht nicht zu besiegen ist, wird der Krieg „asymmetrisch" geführt: geheim, gemein, ohne Flagge und Absender. Der Terrorismus „mag zwar unsinnig sein", schrieb ein russischer Minister der Zarenzeit, „doch ist es eine giftige, ja furchtbare Idee, aus dem Unvermögen Macht zu schöpfen". Die Anarchisten, die seinerzeit Bomben warfen, mussten sich zeigen, schleuderten noch im Sterben ihre politischen Parolen in die Menge. Doch hat der moderne Terrorismus weder Stimme noch Identität. Sein Mittel ist der Zweck: der nackte Terror, der aus dem Dunkeln heraus Angst und Schrecken verbreitet.

Mithin: Wer sich nach dieser „Kriegshandlung" (so der frühere UN-Botschafter Richard Holbrooke) mit der Hortortat brüstet, wird's nicht gewesen sein; wer's getan hat, wird schweigen. Jedenfalls haben die „üblichen Verdächtigen" wie Taliban, Hamas und Dschihad jegliche Schuld abgestritten – während die Palästinenser auf der Straße ihren Hass auf Amerika mit Freudentänzen zelebrierten. Denn schnell und schrecklich wäre die amerikanische Vergeltung. Doch Vergeltung gegen wen? „Asymmetrische Kriegführung" bedeutet, dass man der erdrückenden Militärmacht des Opfers die Zielscheibe entzieht – dessen beste Waffen entwertet, weil er nicht weiß, gegen wen er sie richten soll.

Ist das Monstrum auf heimischem Boden gewachsen, wird der FBI es rasch finden. War's bin Laden, wie Washington glaubt, könnte er eine so ausgeklügelte strategische Operation nicht ohne Hilfe eines oder mehrerer Staaten eingefädelt haben. Deren Führung wird nicht mehr ruhig schlafen können – zu Recht. Denn es ist kein gesichtsloser Terrorakt, sondern ein Krieg, der gegen Amerika entfesselt worden ist: Pearl Harbor 60 Jahre danach. Dieser Zivilisationsbruch wird nicht ungestraft bleiben. Doch lassen George Bushs besonnene öffentlichen Auftritte hoffen, dass Amerikas heiliger Zorn nicht in heillose Wut umschlagen wird. Dabei müssen die Verbündeten helfen, gerade auch jene Staaten, die im Angesicht des Terrors so häufig beschwichtigt, ja auf eigene Rechnung gearbeitet haben. Je wärmer der Beistand von außen, desto kühler bleibt der politische Verstand im Inneren der Vereinigten Staaten.

Es geht aber nicht nur um Bündnissolidarität, sondern um die Abwehr von Zivilisationsbrüchen. Gerade weil den Terroristen ihr Leben nichts wert ist, müssen die zivilisierten Nationen zeigen, dass ihre Art zu leben ihnen sehr viel wert ist. Es geht folglich um den gemeinsamen Kampf gegen jene Verblendung, die der Attentäter François Babeuf vor zwei Jahrhunderten bewies, als er sich wegen eines Anschlags auf das „Direktorium" der Französischen Revolution vor Gericht verantworten musste: „Kein Mittel ist verbrecherisch, wenn es einem heiligen Zweck dient." Doch entheiligen Verbrechen wie die vom 11. September *jeden* Zweck.

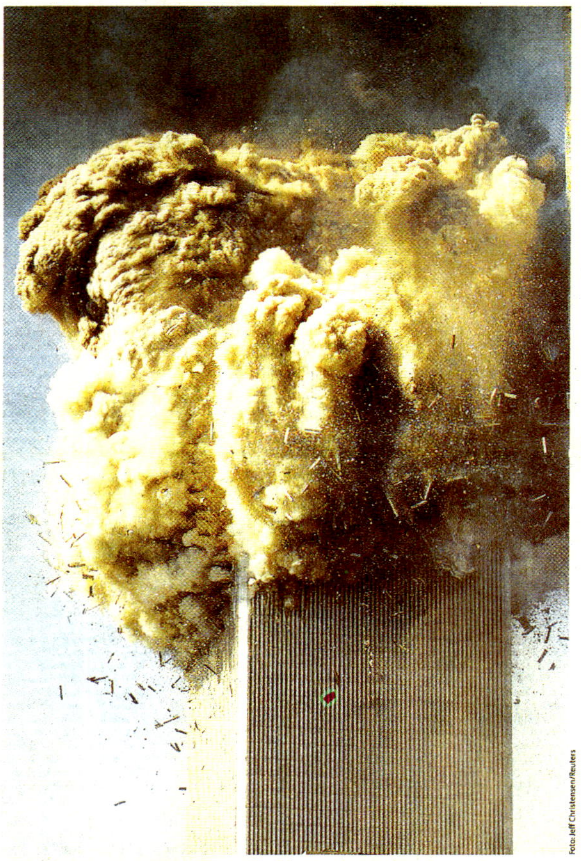

World Trade Center in New York: Angriff auf das Herz der amerikanischen Macht

Ein Teil der Auflage der ZEIT ist bereits am Mittwoch, den 12. September 2001, erschienen

Das Mammut-Verbrechen

Solidarität mit Amerika

Von Helmut Schmidt

Wer nach dem Ende des Hitlerschen Weltkrieges und den Zerstörungen Deutschlands die amerikanische Marshall-Hilfe im Gedächtnis hat, wer sich an die vielerlei ausländischen Hilfen bei der Abwehr des deutschen Terrorismus erinnert, wer um die entscheidende Hilfe der USA zur Wiedervereinigung Deutschlands weiß, aber ebenso jeder, der sein Bekenntnis zu den Menschenrechten und zur Nächstenliebe ernst gemeint hat: Wir alle empfinden heute ungeteilte Solidarität mit der amerikanischen Nation.

Das Ausmaß und die Vielfalt der fast gleichzeitigen Terroranschläge auf das Leben von Zehntausenden Amerikanern und auf die Führungs- und Nervenzentren des Staates sind nicht ohne eine weit gespannte Organisation, nicht ohne eine größere Zahl von Selbstmordattentätern, nicht ohne eine größere Zahl von Helfern und Sympathisanten und nicht ohne viel Geld denkbar. Deshalb wird es wahrscheinlich nicht lange dauern, bis die Urheberschaft dieses Mammutverbrechens geklärt ist.

Bis zu diesem Zeitpunkt ist es sowohl für die USA als auch ebenso für die europäischen Regierungen notwendig, nicht auf Gerüchte hereinzufallen und falsche Schuldige auszumachen. Die enorme Aufregung kann manch einen und in manchen Orten der ganzen Welt zu hysterischen Reaktionen verleiten. Deshalb gilt für alle Regierungen und für alle Politiker als erste Verhaltensregel: Kühle, abwägende Vernunft bewahren.

Für alle Regierungen gilt zweitens, auf eine mögliche Fortsetzung der Verbrechensserie gefasst zu sein und Vorsorge für die Sicherheit der ihnen anvertrauten Bürger zu treffen. Drittens und zugleich ist eine weitgreifende Spurensuche und Verbrechenserforschung geboten; dazu müssen alle Regierungen der den USA verbündeten und befreundeten Staaten der amerikanischen Regierung jedwede Hilfe leisten.

Es ist denkbar, dass wir es mit einer privaten fanatischen Terrorbande zu tun haben. Es ist auch denkbar, dass ein Staat indirekte Beihilfe geleistet hat, so wie wir es im Falle des Terrors der RAF erlebt haben. Es ist nicht völlig auszuschließen, dass es sich um eine von einem Staat ins Leben gerufene Terrororganisation handelt. In jedem dieser möglichen Fälle wird die notwendige Reaktion durch die USA und durch die von Terroristen bedrohten Staaten verschieden sein müssen. In jedem Falle werden rechtsstaatliche Regierungen ihre eigene Verfassung und die Charta der Vereinten Nationen zu wahren haben.

Sofern sich aufseiten der Terroristen ein Staat oder eine Regierung als beteiligt herausstellen sollte, so kann daraus ein Krieg entstehen. Deshalb ist umso mehr kühle Vernunft geboten. In jedem Falle werden die USA sich mit großer Kraft und all ihrer Vitalität zur Wehr setzen. Und wir Deutschen werden an ihrer Seite stehen.

Inferno in Amerika:

11. September 2001: Der Tag, an dem der Tod nach Manhattan und Washington kam

Augenzeugenberichte über die Vernichtungsflüge

Interview mit dem Harvard-Politologen Stephen Walt über die Folgen für die US-Außenpolitik

Porträt: Osama bin Laden

DOSSIER, S. 15–18

ZEIT Online GmbH: www.zeit.de
ZEIT-Stellenmarkt: www.jobs.zeit.de
Zeitverlag Gerd Bucerius GmbH & Co.,
20079 Hamburg Telefon 040 / 32 80 - 0;
E-Mail: DieZeit@zeit.de, Leserbriefe@zeit.de
Leser-Service:
Tel. 040 / 37 03 - 40 41, Fax 040 / 37 03 - 56 57
E-Mail: abo-service@guj.de

4 390745 105501 38

Die Zeit
www.zeit.de
Deutschland, Hamburg

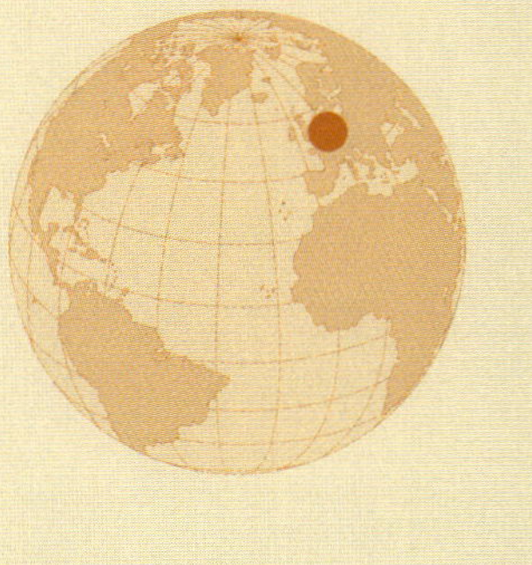

13

Hamburger Abendblatt

UNABHÄNGIG / ÜBERPARTEILICH

www.abendblatt.de — Donnerstag, 13. September 2001 · 1,20 DM

Sie wissen, wer's war

● FBI-Chef: „Entführer sind identifiziert" – Spur zu bin Laden verdichtet sich
● NATO beschließt den kollektiven Verteidigungsfall auch gegen Terroristen
● Polizei durchsucht Wohnung in der Harburger Marienstraße
● Heute um 10 Uhr Gedenkminuten in Deutschland – die Welt trauert

Peter Kruse
Hamburg

Nur 24 Stunden nach den barbarischen Terrorangriffen auf das Welthandelszentrum in New York und einen Teil des Verteidigungsministeriums Pentagon in Washington sind mehrere der Attentäter identifiziert. Das sagte der Chef der US-Bundespolizei FBI Robert Mueller gestern Abend in Washington.

US-Justizminister John Ashcroft ergänzte, die vier Flugzeuge seien von drei bis sechs Terroristen pro Maschine gekapert worden. Die Attentäter hätten Rasiermesser bei sich gehabt und mit Bomben gedroht.

Zugleich verdichtete sich der Verdacht, dass Topterrorist Osama bin Laden hinter den Terroranschlägen steht. US-Senator Orrin Hatch gab bekannt, dass der amerikanische Geheimdienst ein Gespräch zwischen zwei Männern und dem Fundamentalisten und Drahtzieher vieler Terroranschläge, Osama bin Laden, abgehört hat. Die Männer sprachen von „gelungenen Angriffen auf zwei Ziele". Bin Laden, der sich in Afghanistan versteckt haben soll, beglückwünschte die Attentäter, soll aber die Beteiligung bestritten haben.

Dass die Spur zu bin Laden führt, bestätigte jetzt auch das Kanzleramt in Berlin. Das Auswärtige Amt erklärte, dass die USA und Deutschland alle Landsleute aus beiden Ländern aufgefordert haben, Afghanistan zu verlassen.

Insgesamt glaubt das FBI, fünf Namen auf den Listen der Boston-Flüge gefunden zu haben, bei denen es sich um Attentäter handeln könnte. Mindestens einer von ihnen ist ein ausgebildeter Pilot. Zwei von ihnen waren Brüder. Sie waren am Dienstagmorgen von Portland, Maine, nach Boston geflogen. Ihr Leihwagen wurde inzwischen am Flughafen Portland sichergestellt.

Auch am Flughafen in Boston stellte das FBI ein verdächtiges Fahrzeug sicher. Darin befanden sich zwei Plastiktüten mit Dokumenten in Arabisch, eine Flug-Anleitung für Verkehrsflugzeuge, eine Tabelle zur Berechnung des Treibstoffverbrauchs eines Flugzeuges sowie ein Koran.

Ebenfalls in Boston stürmten zwei Dutzend bewaffnete FBI-Beamte in schusssicheren Westen ein Hotelzimmer im Westin Hotel in der Back-Bay-Gegend der Stadt. Dort soll einer der Entführer übernachtet haben.

In Florida durchsuchte das FBI am West Atlantik Boulevard die Wohnung von Mohammed Atta (33). Sein Name stand auf einer der Passagierlisten. Ein Bruder oder Cousin von Atta, Marwan Al Shehhi, soll in Hamburg gewohnt haben. Beide sollen sich nach Aussagen eines FBI-Agenten als Deutsche ausgegeben haben.

Eine der Spuren führte auch in die Marienstraße im Hamburger Stadtteil Harburg. Dort sollen in einer Wohnung zwei Araber gelebt haben. Die Polizei sperrte die Straße gestern Abend ab.

US-Präsident George W. Bush sprach gestern von einem monumentalen Kampf des Guten gegen das Böse, den das Gute gewinnen werde. Es werde „kein Unterschied zwischen den Terroristen, die uns angriffen, und den Ländern gemacht, die ihnen Zuflucht gewähren", sagte er. Die USA würden nicht zulassen, „dass der Feind diesen Krieg gewinnt, indem wir unser Leben verändern und unsere Freiheit einschränken".

In Manhattan gab es auch gestern bei Tagesanbruch grauenhafte Bilder. Am Rande der Trümmerberge, die so hoch wie fünfstöckige Häuser sind, lagen in den Straßen Leichenteile. Immer wieder meldeten sich Verschüttete aus unterirdischen Hohlräumen über Handy.

Bis gestern Abend sind neun Lebende aus den Schutthalden geborgen worden. Die Polizei sagt, dass mit 10 000 Toten gerechnet werden muss. Ums Leben kamen auch vier deutsche Geschäftsleute. In Washington musste das Pentagon abermals geräumt werden, weil sich nach dem Angriff das Feuer wieder ausbreitete. Dort sollen 800 Beamte und Militärs umgekommen sein. 80 Tote sind bisher geborgen worden. Nach Aussage von US-Außenminister Colin Powell haben die Flugzeug-Entführer auch das Weiße Haus und die Präsidentenmaschine „Air Force One" treffen wollen.

Inzwischen hat sich die Welt mit Amerika in der Trauer um die Opfer und der Entschlossenheit zum Kampf gegen den Terror solidarisiert. Am Abend stellten die NATO-Staaten den kollektiven Verteidigungsfall gemäß Artikel 5 des NATO-Vertrags fest: Damit sind die NATO-Staaten zu gegenseitigem Beistand verpflichtet, der auch militärische Unterstützung einschließen kann. Zurzeit sind keine Militär-Aktionen geplant. .
Für den Luftraum über Deutschland sowie für amerikanische Einrichtungen wurden zusätzliche Sicherheitsmaßnahmen angeordnet. Heute um 10 Uhr werden die Menschen in allen deutschen Betrieben und Behörden fünf Minuten lang der Toten in Amerika gedenken. Gewerkschaften und Arbeitgeberverbände haben dazu aufgerufen.

Nach dem Terrorschlag ist auch in der Bundesrepublik die Stimmung gereizt. Es gebe massive Morddrohungen gegen in Deutschland lebende Muslime, sagte der Vorsitzende des Zentralrats der Muslime, Nadeen Elyas. Er warnte vor pauschaler Verurteilung der Moslems.

In Hamburg wird es heute um 17 Uhr eine Gedenkfeier auf dem Rathausmarkt geben. Bischöfin Maria Jepsen, ihr katholischer Amtsbruder Hans-Jochen Jaschke, Bürgermeister Ortwin Runde und US-Generalkonsulin Susan Ellbow werden sprechen. Der Wahlkampf zur Bürgerschaft bleibt bis Sonntag ausgesetzt.

Das ganze Ausmaß der angerichteten Schäden in den USA liegt nach einer ersten Übersicht der Versicherungskonzerne bei wenigstens 80 Milliarden Mark.

Auf den Trümmern des World Trade Centers: Drei New Yorker Feuerwehrleute hissen die amerikanische Flagge. Der Mast, der zum Gebäude gehörte, ist wie durch ein Wunder intakt geblieben. FOTO: AP

Die Täter bestrafen, die Rache zähmen

Helge Adolphsen
St. Michaelis

Ich werde diese Bilder nicht los: Die einstürzenden, brennenden Türme. Der eine Mann, der über Schutt und Trümmer läuft, voll verzweifelter Hoffnung, noch Lebende zu finden. Jubelnde Kinder im Ostteil Jerusalems mit dem Siegeszeichen. „Das kann nicht wahr sein! Das können Menschen doch nicht tun!"

Wahnsinn. Irrsinn. Schwer ist es, Worte zu finden. Trauer, Wut, Ohnmacht in uns. Ja, das ist möglich, und das ist auch gut: Mitgefühl und Solidarität zu zeigen mit den Menschen in Amerika. Über alle Gegensätze und Unterschiede hinweg sind wir mit ihnen verbunden. Wir sind auf das Menschlichste in uns zurückgeworfen. Aber wir dürfen unsere Fassungslosigkeit und Wut nicht in Rachegefühle umschlagen lassen.

Einerseits müssen die Täter bestraft werden. Andererseits müssen alle Anstrengungen darauf gerichtet sein, dass aus den jubelnden Kindern nicht neue Attentäter werden. Die entscheidende Frage für mich: Wie kann der Teufelskreis der Gewalt unterbrochen werden? Gegen den Ruf nach Rache und Vergeltung will ich den Traum des Bergpredigers Jesus von der Gewaltlosigkeit ins Spiel bringen. Traum – das klingt nach Schwärmerei.

Ich meine etwas ganz anderes: die Kinder nicht zum Hass erziehen. Ihnen reale Lebenschancen geben. In der Erziehung auf Feindbilder und auf jenen religiösen Fanatismus verzichten, der militant macht. Ihnen zeigen, dass es zum Miteinanderleben in versöhnter Verschiedenheit keine Alternative gibt. Ihnen vermitteln, dass Juden, Christen und Muslime als Nachkommen des gemeinsamen Stammvaters Abraham Brüder und Schwestern sind. Warum sagen die Mullahs und Imame nicht: „Auf Terror- und Selbstmordkommandos liegt kein Segen." Warum sagen die Rabbiner nicht: „Auf Vergeltung liegt kein Segen"? Warum sagen Christen nicht lauter: „Selig sind die Sanftmütigen, denn sie werden das Erdreich besitzen"? Sanftmütigkeit bedeutet keine Tatenlosigkeit. Sie ist Inspiration zum aktiven Handeln, zur Vorherrschaft der Politik über die Sprache der Waffen. Ein erneuertes Bewusstsein muss sich durchsetzen. Jede Mutter, die über ihr ermordetes Kind trauert, geht alle an. Und jeder Terrorist verrät die Ziele, für die er sein Leben einsetzt. In diesem Geist beginnt ein jüdisches Gebet, das in einem KZ gebetet wurde, so: „Friede sei den Menschen, die bösen Willens sind, und ein Ende sei gesetzt aller Rache. . ."

Michel-Pastor Helge Adolphsen

Liebe Leserinnen und Leser,
setzen wir ein Zeichen, dass wir mit den Amerikanern trauern! Die letzte Seite im Abendblatt ist heute ein Poster. Nehmen Sie es heraus, hängen Sie es in Ihr Fenster, in die Schaufenster, legen Sie es sichtbar in Ihr Auto.
Ihr Abendblatt

Amerikaner, wir sind bei euch

Menschlich gesehen

Er möchte helfen

„Es ist schrecklich, untätig vor dem Fernseher sitzen zu müssen und nicht helfen zu können", sagt Hamburgs Ballett-Intendant, der Amerikaner John Neumeier. Die feigen Terroranschläge auf das World Trade Center in New York und das Pentagon in Washington haben ihn so mitgenommen, dass er am liebsten in sein Heimatland fliegen möchte, um Hilfe zu leisten. Es sei typisch amerikanisch, meint er, dass seine Landsleute zu Tausenden spontan kämen, um Blut zu spenden. Er selbst würde es auch tun.

Ganz untypisch aber sei die Stille gewesen, mit der die New Yorker beispielsweise nach dem Schock auf das furchtbare Geschehen reagiert hätten: „Ich glaube, sie alle haben begriffen, dass nach diesem Anschlag nichts mehr in der Welt so sein wird, wie es mal war", sagt er. „Wir alle müssen umdenken, zusammenhalten, sonst sind wir verloren."

Gerade ist der 59-Jährige, der das Hamburg Ballett seit 1973 leitet, aus den Hamptons zurückgekommen, dem beliebtesten Erholungsgebiet der New Yorker. Und auch für ihn ist jetzt die Welt nicht mehr, wie sie war.

„Es war ein furchtbarer Schock, als ich diese Bilder sah", sagt er. Neben dem Entsetzen ist er von Trauer um die Opfer erfüllt und der Erleichterung, dass „keine schnelle Kriegsdeklaration gemacht worden ist. Unbesonnenes Handeln kann hier nur zur Eskalation führen". M.G.

Nummer 214
37. Woche / 54. Jahrgang
190 Pts · 6,50 dkr · 12,00 ÖS / C 3390 A
4 390339 001202 40037

REDAKTION: 040-347 00
Anzeigen: 040-35 10 11
Vertrieb: 040-33 39 40 11

Weitere Berichte: Seiten 2, 3, 4, 5, 6, 7, 8, 11, 13, 14, 15, 16, 17, 25, 27, 29, 30, letzte Seite

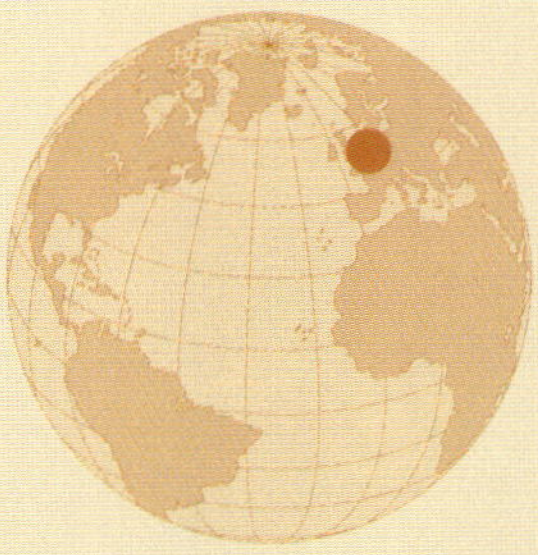

Hamburger Abendblatt
www.abendblatt.de
Deutschland, Hamburg

13

Der Anschlag und die Folgen: Sonderausgabe unserer Zeitung

Rhein-Zeitung

UNABHÄNGIGE TAGESZEITUNG

Donnerstag, 13. September 2001

56. Jahrgang · Nr. 213 · G 5912
Einzelpreis DM 1,80 · Ausgabe BK · Stadt Koblenz

Lokales

12 Koblenzer in New York vermisst

Stunden des Bangens und Zitterns, aber auch der Hoffnung, müssen Angehörige und Freunde von zwölf Koblenzern durchleben. Sie haben noch keine Nachricht und wissen nicht, ob sie dem Inferno von New York lebend entkommen konnten. Zwei Reisegruppen sind in den Staaten unterwegs. ▶ **Seite: 17**

„Und kommt jetzt der 3. Weltkrieg?"

An allen Schulen waren die Attentate von Amerika gestern Thema Nummer eins. In einer Koblenzer Grundschule legten die Kinder spontan eine Schweigeminute ein. In einer anderen Schule wurde ein arabisches Mädchen derbe angeblafft. ▶ **Seite: 19**

Sport

UEFA sagt Europacup-Spiele ab

Endlich reagierte auch die UEFA: Die Europäische Fußball-Union sagte gestern die restlichen Champions-League-Begegnungen des ersten Spieltags ab; darunter das Gastspiel der Bayern in Rotterdam und Leverkusens Heimpartie gegen Fenerbahce Istanbul. Auch die für heute terminierten UEFA-Cup-Spiele wurden verschoben. ▶ **Seite: 27**

Volleyballer können heimfliegen

Es kam, wie es kommen musste: Nach der vierten Pleite im vierten Spiel müssen die deutschen Volleyballer bei der EM in Ostrau die Koffer packen. Das Team von Trainer Stelian Moculescu verlor gegen Ungarn 0:3 und bleibt selbst im Falle eines Erfolges gegen Olympiasieger Jugoslawien heute Tabellenletzter. ▶ **Seite: 27**

Panorama / Kultur

Bilder, die sprachlos machen

New York wird nie wieder so sein, wie es einmal war. Bilder, die das ganze Ausmaß des schrecklichen Infernos zeigen; Bilder von Menschen, die nur knapp dem feigen Anschlag entkommen sind; Bilder von Angst, Wut und Trauer; Bilder, die sprachlos machen – auf Panorama. ▶ **Seite: 11**

Die Apokalypse hat viele Gesichter

Feuer schießt auf, riesige Rauchpilze steigen in den Himmel. Panik, Verzweiflung, Zerstörung auf der Leinwand. Ob „The Day after" oder „Independence Day": Aus Hollywood kamen und kommen immer wieder Katastrophenfilme. Doch die Wirklichkeit ist viel schrecklicher. Lesen Sie auf der Seite Kultur mehr zum Thema Apokalypse. ▶ **Seite: 12**

Grafik des Tages

Pentagon weiter in Flammen

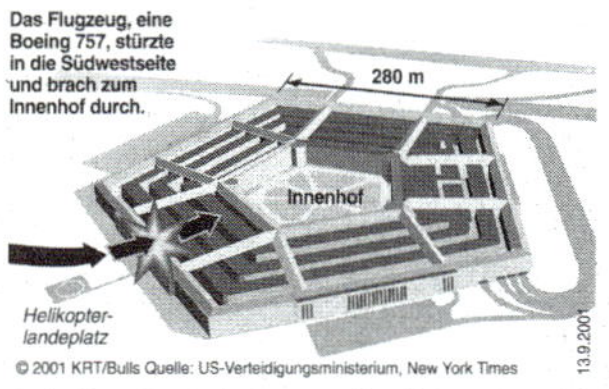

© 2001 KRT/Bulls Quelle: US-Verteidigungsministerium, New York Times

Auch einen Tag nach dem Angriff auf das US-Verteidigungsministerium breitete sich das Feuer im Pentagon weiter aus. Hoffnung auf Überlebende gibt es kaum noch.

Auf einen Blick

Wir für Sie

Vertrieb: 0261/892-123
Anzeigen: 0261/892-8
Redaktion: 0261/892-777

NATO will Terrorismus bekämpfen: Kommt Bundeswehr zum Einsatz?

Bündnis steht USA bei – Erster kollektiver Verteidigungsfall in der Geschichte der Allianz – Hinweise auf bin Laden verdichtet

Befindet sich Deutschland bald im Krieg gegen den internationalen Terrorismus? Nach dem Terror-Anschlag auf das World Trade Center und das Pentagon beschloss die NATO, an der Seite der USA gegen die Drahtzieher vorzugehen.

NEW YORK/BRÜSSEL. Erstmals in ihrer Geschichte hat die NATO am späten Mittwochabend den kollektiven Verteidigungsfall beschlossen. Der besagt, dass das Bündnis die Terror-Anschläge auf das World Trade Center in New York und das Pentagon in Washington als Angriff gegen die gesamte Allianz betrachtet, falls sie vom Ausland aus eingeleitet worden sind. Militärische Reaktionen seien jedoch zur Zeit nicht geplant, so der NATO-Generalsekretär George Robertson. Bundeskanzler Gerhard Schröder erklärte, Deutschland trage den Beschluss des NATO-Rates voll mit. Über das Ausmaß eines deutschen Beistandsbeitrags müsse allerdings noch entschieden werden. Denn bewaffneten Auslandseinsätzen der Bundeswehr muss der Bundestag zustimmen.

+++THEMA DES TAGES+++

Wein-Manager flog mit in den Tod
New York kämpft gegen das Grauen an
Osama bin Laden ist nicht zu fassen
▶ **Alles auf den Sonderseiten**

Vor der Entscheidung der NATO hatte US-Präsident George W. Bush einen „monumentalen Kampf zwischen Gut und Böse" angekündigt, in dem das Gute siegen werde. Gleichzeitig drohte er: „Wir werden keinen Unterschied machen zwischen denen, die diese Attacken ausgeführt haben, und denen, die ihnen Schutz bieten."

Ein Symbol des amerikanischen Lebenswillens: In den Trümmern des World Trade Centers in New York hissen Feuerwehrleute nach dem verheerenden Anschlag die US-Flagge. ■ Foto: ap

Die Suche nach den Drahtziehern der Terrorserie lief unterdessen auf Hochtouren – „Erfolgsmeldungen" lösten sich mit Spekulationen ab. So erklärte FBI-Chef Robert Mueller, man habe die Identität einiger Täter festgestellt. Ein hoher Regierungsbeamter versicherte, die ins Pentagon gestürzte Maschine habe ursprünglich das Weiße Haus angesteuert. In Boston im Bundesstaat Massachusetts stürmte die Polizei ein Hotel. Dort waren in der Gästeliste die Namen von fünf Personen aufgetaucht, die möglicherweise mit den Flugzeugentführungen am Dienstag zu tun hatten. Einige der Attentäter haben nach Angaben des US-Justizministeriums in den USA eine Pilotenausbildung erhalten.

Gleichzeitig verdichten sich aber die Hinweise auf den mutmaßlichen Terroristenführer Osama bin Laden als Verantwortlichen für die Anschläge. US-Ermittler gehen nach Medienberichten zu 90 Prozent davon aus, dass der in Afghanistan lebende bin Laden hinter den Anschlägen steckt. Das afghanische Taliban-Regime bot der US-Regierung Gespräche über eine mögliche Auslieferung von Osama bin Laden an.

Der Weltsicherheitsrat hat die internationale Gemeinschaft aufgerufen, ihre Anstrengungen gegen den Terrorismus zu verdoppeln. In einer einstimmig verabschiedeten Resolution erklärte sich das höchste Entscheidungsgremium der Vereinten Nationen „entschlossen, Terrorakte mit allen verfügbaren Mitteln zu bekämpfen".

Für die großen Versicherungen ist der Anschlag wahrscheinlich die kostspieligste von Menschen verursachte Katastrophe. Experten beziffern den direkten Schaden auf mindestens fünf Milliarden Dollar (elf Milliarden Mark).

▶ Seite 2: Leitartikel

Wir setzen ein Zeichen

Auch die Menschen in unserer Region stehen unter Schock. Sie trauern um die Opfer und fühlen mit deren Angehörigen. Jeder kann seine Betroffenheit öffentlich bekunden. In den Geschäftsstellen unserer Zeitung liegen von heute an Kondolenzbücher aus. Außerdem kann ein Kondolenz-Schreiben (Seite 3) unterzeichnet werden. Die terroristischen Anschläge in den USA haben unsere Zeitung zu einem weiteren Schritt bewogen: Der redaktionelle Teil erscheint heute komplett in Schwarz-Weiß – als Zeichen unseres Mitfühlens.

Gedenken im ganzen Land

BRÜSSEL/MAINZ. Die Europäer sollen an diesem Freitag um 12 Uhr mit drei Schweigeminuten den verheerenden Anschlägen gedenken. „Wir erklären den 14. September zum Tag der Trauer", sagte der belgische Außenminister und amtierende EU-Ratspräsident Louis Michel. Mit Gedenk-Gottesdiensten und Glockengeläut haben Tausende Rheinland-Pfälzer der Opfer gedacht. Ministerpräsident Kurt Beck (SPD) hat für heute, 16 Uhr, zu einem Trauermarsch aufgerufen, der vom Landtag zum Dom geht, um sich zum stillen Gedenken zu versammeln.

Kaum noch Hoffnung auf Überlebende in den Trümmern

Dutzende deutsche Touristen vermisst – Aufräumarbeiten unter Hochdruck

NEW YORK/WASHINGTON. Die Rettungsteams in New York versuchen fieberhaft, Überlebende unter den Trümmern zu bergen. Im Pentagon haben Helfer jedoch die Hoffnung aufgegeben, in dem brennenden und zerstörten Gebäude noch auf Verletzte zu stoßen. Allein dort wird mit bis zu 800 Toten gerechnet.

Noch entsetzlicher fällt die Bilanz in New York aus. „Vermutlich sind in jedem der beiden eingestürzten Türme des World Trade Centers mehrere tausend Menschen gestorben", befürchtet Bürgermeisters Rudolph Giuliani. Bislang sind erst 45 Leichen aus den Trümmern geborgen, neun Menschen gerettet worden. Giuliani kündigte an, dass an der Stelle der zusammengestürzten WTC-Zwillingstürme ein neues Welthandelszentrum aufgebaut werden soll. Nach Schätzungen der US-Ratingagentur Moody's ist durch die Anschläge ein Versicherungsschaden von bis 32,4 Milliarden Mark entstanden.

Dutzende deutscher Touristen gelten bislang als vermisst. Das Generalkonsulat sowie die UN-Mission der Bundesrepublik in New York „sind intensiv bemüht, dem Schicksal von deutschen Vermissten nachzugehen", hieß es. Es gebe bisher keine konkrete Hinweise darauf, dass außer fünf Deutschen in den zum Absturz gebrachten Flugzeugen tatsächlich weitere Bundesbürger ums Leben gekommen seien. Mitarbeiter von deutschen Firmen in der vom Anschlag betroffenen Gegend im Süden Manhattans konnten sich offenbar rechtzeitig in Sicherheit bringen.

BÖRSE AKTUELL: +++ Berg- und Talfahrt +++ Schluss-DAX: 4335,20 (+61,67) +++ Kein Handel mit US-Aktien +++

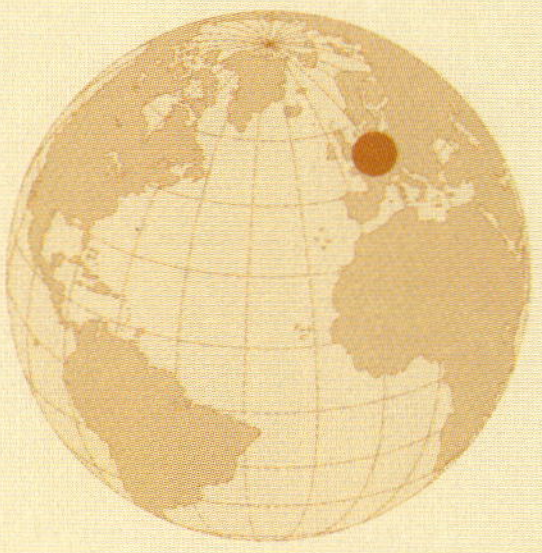

Rhein-Zeitung
www.rhein-zeitung.de
Deutschland, Koblenz

Wien
Donnerstag, 13. September 2001
Nr. 252 / S 10,– (0,73 €)
www.kurier.at

KURIER

UNABHÄNGIGE TAGESZEITUNG FÜR ÖSTERREICH

The day after

- FBI enttarnt Araber als Täter
- Verdacht erhärtet sich gegen Bin Laden
- Volle Solidarität der NATO mit USA
- Hektische Suche nach den Opfern
- Aktionen gegen Krise der Wirtschaft

Der Tag danach: Ausführliche Berichte über die Folgen der Terrorwelle in den USA auf den SEITEN 2-11, 17-21, 25-26

AP/THOMAS E. FRANKLIN

Dokument des ungebrochenen Patriotismus: Inmitten der Trümmer des World Trade Centers setzen Feuerwehrleute die US-Flagge auf Halbmast

Still

In Berlin sagten die Theater ihre Vorstellungen ab. In der Wiener Staatsoper und im Raimund-Theater wurden Trauerminuten eingehalten. In der Volksoper baten die Darsteller, auf Applaus zu verzichten. Der Musiksender VIVA setzte in den USA sein Programm aus, Konkurrent MTV sagte zumindest die Shows ab. Kurz: Auf der ganzen Welt wurde bei Unterhaltungsveranstaltungen auf die Ereignisse in den USA reagiert, für die Bezeichnungen wie „Anschläge" oder „Terrorakte" hilflos zu kurz greifen.

In der Wiener Stadthalle dagegen feierte die Gruppe Depeche Mode gemeinsam mit mehr als 10.000 Besuchern ein fröhliches Popfest. Keine Absage, kein Moment der Trauer, ja nicht einmal ein Wort des Bedauerns von der Bühne. Hier rollte die übliche, eitle Rock-Inszenierung ab, inklusive „Hello Vienna!" und „Wie geht's euch?"

Ja, das Leben soll und muss weitergehen, und dazu gehört auch die Show. Aber erst nach einem Augenblick der Stille. Und der hätte ruhig einen ganzen Abend dauern dürfen. - *GUITAR*

ÜBERBLICK

Irrweg www.anwalt.at
Wer auf „Anwalt" klickt, bekommt „bio". Die Kammer denkt über bessere Internet-Auftritte nach. SEITE 13

Unsichere ORF-Wahl
Ob die Wahl des neuen ORF-Generaldirektors heuer überhaupt stattfinden darf, soll ein Gutachten klären. SEITE 32

Kurze Wetterbesserung
Tagsüber Sonnenschein im ganzen Land, und es ist wärmer als zuletzt. SEITE 14

LOTTOZIEHUNG VOM 12. 9. 2001

3 5 14 24 29 42 Zusatzzahl 6

Joker: 603725 Angaben ohne Gewähr

9024 7170
Erscheinungsort: Wien, Verlagspostamt 1070 Wien, P.b.b. ● 01Z021634K;
Lit 3200,–, DM 3,–, sfr 2,80, Dr 550,–, Pts 260,–, Kanaren 300,–, HUF 300,–, KC 25,–, SK 30,–, KN 15,–, SIT 340,–, TL 2,500.000,–

Redaktion: 1070 Wien, Seidengasse 11, Tel. (01) 52 100/0, Fax (01) 52 100/2263, 2265, eMail Redaktion: leser@kurier.at; Abo-Service: Tel. (01) 521 302 971, eMail Abos: kurier-abo@mediaprint.at

KURIER
WWW.KURIER.AT
ÖSTERREICH, WIEN

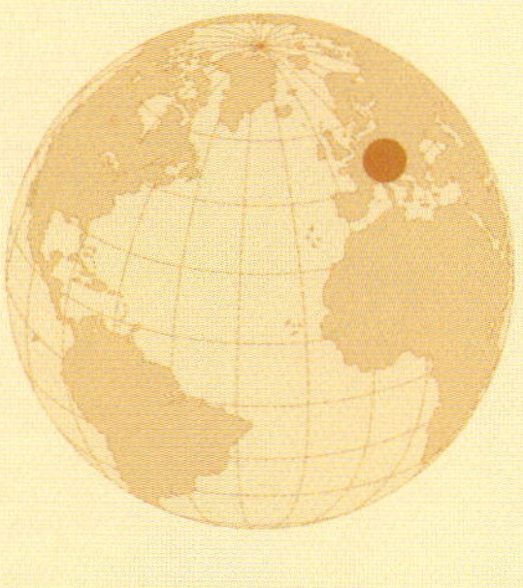

ATS 11,– /€ 0,80

WIENER ZEITUNG

NR. 177 HTTP://WWW.WIENERZEITUNG.AT / leser@wienerzeitung.at seit 1703 TELEFON: 01-206 99 – DONNERSTAG, 13. SEPTEMBER 2001

Heute auf der Homepage der „Wiener Zeitung“

Nach den Terroranschlägen in den USA hat sich das Internet als zuverlässiges Kommunikationsmedium bewiesen. Die Online-Ausgabe „*Wiener Zeitung*“ liefert die wichtigsten Links.
http://www.wienerzeitung.at

Sonderministerrat: Trauerminute heute um 10 Uhr

Die Regierungsmitglieder gedachten gestern bei einem Sonderministerrat der Opfer der USA. Für heute 10 Uhr hat Kanzler Schüssel österreichweit die Abhaltung einer Trauerminute angekündigt. Foto: APA
Seite 6

Nach „Schwarzem Dienstag“ jetzt der große Crash?

Unsicherheit über die wirtschaftlichen Folgen der verheerenden Anschläge in den USA: Während Tokios Börse auf den tiefsten Stand seit 1983 abstürzte (Bild), tendierten Europas Börsen behauptet. Foto: AP
Seite 17

Aus Trauer um die Opfer und Sorge: Viele Absagen

Aus Trauer um die Opfer, aber auch aus Sorge um die Sicherheit wurden in Österreich und in der ganzen Welt zahlreiche Veranstaltungen wie die Emmy-Verleihung und alle Europacup-Spiele abgesagt.
Seiten 4, 7, 10, 13

Spuren weisen laut Nachrichtendiensten zu Osama bin Laden – CNN meldet Festnahmen in Boston und Florida

Bush: „Ein Akt des Krieges“ Auch Hintermänner bestrafen

Washington/New York – In seiner vierten Fernsehansprache nach den Anschlägen von New York und Washington bezeichnete US-Präsident George W. Bush Mittwochnachmittag die Angriffe als „einen Akt des Krieges“, der sich gegen alle freien Menschen der Welt gerichtet habe. Der Feind versuche sich zu verstecken, er werde es aber nicht schaffen. Zuvor hatte Bush bereits angekündigt, dass die USA keinen Unterschied zwischen den Tätern und jenen, die ihnen Schutz gewähren, machen würden. Die Spuren der Attentate führen nach Meinung von US-Regierungsstellen und westlichen Geheimdiensten zu dem international gesuchten saudi-arabischen Millionär Osama bin Laden.

Unterdessen suchen die Rettungsmannschaften in Washington und New York weiter nach Opfern und Überlebenden unter den Trümmern. Aus dem völlig zerstörten World Trade Center wurden bisher neun Menschen lebend geborgen.

Die Opferbilanz könnte in die Zehntausende gehen. In der Nacht zum Mittwoch wurde bekannt, dass auch rund 300 Feuerwehrleute und 80 Polizisten, die nach dem ersten Anschlag auf das WTC dort eingetroffen waren, beim Einsturz der beiden Türme ums Leben gekommen sind.

Im Pentagon in Washington, das Mittwoch abend noch immer in Flammen stand und neuerlich evakuiert wurde, befürchtet man zwischen 100 und 800 Todesopfer. Hoffnung auf Überlebende besteht nicht mehr.

Erste Anhaltspunkte für den Ablauf der Anschläge sind die Gespräche über Mobiltelefone von zwei Passagieren und einer Flugbegleiterin, die diese kurz vor den Abstürzen geführt hatten. Sie berichteten übereinstimmend von drei bis fünf Entführern, die mit messerartigen Waffen die Gewalt über die Maschinen erzwungen hätten. Der Geheimdienst hat außerdem ein Gespräch zwischen zwei Anhängern bin Ladens abgehört, in dem von den gelungenen Angriffen auf zwei Ziele gesprochen wurde, teilte Senator Orrin Hatch mit. Fahnder berichteten von Hinweisen, wonach die Terroristen sich bewusst Langstreckenflüge ausgesucht hätten, um mit der großen Treibstoffmenge an Bord ein maximales Maß an Zerstörung zu erzielen. Nach Zeitungsmeldungen sollen die Behörden von Massachusetts, fünf Araber identifiziert haben, die in die Anschläge verwickelt sein sollen. Einer von ihnen sei ein ausgebildeter Pilot. Nach Angaben des Nachrichtensenders CNN wurden Mittwoch abend in Boston und Florida einige Männer festgenommen, die mit den Anschlägen in Verbindung stehen sollen.

In den Trümmern des eingestürzten World Trade Centers gingen die Bergungsarbeiten mit allen verfügbaren Kräften weiter. Einige der Verschütteten hatten sich per Funktelefon gemeldet. Besonders in den übrigen Gebäuden des riesigen Handelskomplexes in Süd-Manhattan, hofft man noch auf zahlreiche Überlebende. Die Behörden vermuteten, dass sich zum Zeitpunkt des ersten Flugzeugeinschlages zwischen 10.000 und 20.000 Menschen im WTC aufhielten. Bis die genaue Zahl der Toten feststeht, könne es Wochen dauern.

Seiten 2 bis 8, 10, 17, 18, 22.

Immer weniger Verletzte werden in die Spitäler eingeliefert; damit steigt die traurige Gewissheit Tausender Toten. Foto: AP

In den zum Teil noch immer brennenden Ruinen der beiden Türme des World Trade Centers suchen Feuerwehrleute und Helfer verzweifelt nach Überlebenden des unfassbaren Terroranschlags, der die USA Dienstag früh getroffen hat. Foto: EPA

Börse News

NY (Mo)	9.618,51
Frankf. (18.00h)	4.353,30↗
Wien (ATX)	1.154,45↗
Euro (in $)	0,9052↗
Gold	279,00↘

Wetter

Eine kurze Zwischenbesserung stellt sich ein. Zunächst halten sich entlang der Alpennordseite noch dichte Wolkenfelder, die allmählich dünner werden. Tagsüber scheint im ganzen Land die Sonne.

SONDERSEITEN „FREIZEIT“ UND „MEDIEN“

9 007731 000201

P.b.b. Verlagspostamt 1030 Wien/ 01Z022333 K

WIENER ZEITUNG
WWW.WIENERZEITUNG.AT
ÖSTERREICH, WIEN

13

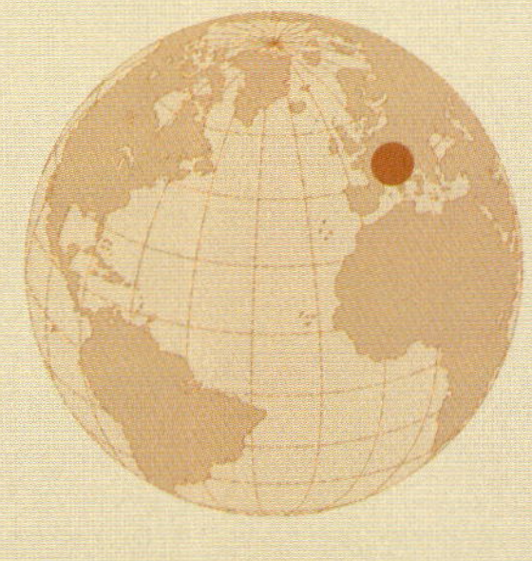

Le Monde

numéro spécial

www.lemonde.fr

57e ANNÉE – N° 17614 – 7,90 F - 1,20 EURO FRANCE MÉTROPOLITAINE – JEUDI 13 SEPTEMBRE 2001 FONDATEUR : HUBERT BEUVE-MÉRY – DIRECTEUR : JEAN-MARIE COLOMBANI

1

L'Amérique frappée, le monde saisi d'effroi

2

● Les Etats-Unis ont subi, mardi 11 septembre, la pire attaque de leur histoire ● Le nombre de victimes dépasse celui de Pearl Harbor ● Du World Trade Center au Pentagone, des terroristes défient Washington ● « La liberté se défendra », déclare le président Bush

SOMMAIRE

Ce numéro du *Monde* est en deux cahiers, le premier entièrement consacré à la tragédie du 11 septembre. *aden* est diffusé, comme d'habitude, à nos lecteurs d'Ile-de-France. Sur notre site www.lemonde.fr, suivi de l'information en continu et dossier multimédia

S. RAMSON/AP

3

Nous sommes tous Américains

DANS CE MOMENT tragique où les mots paraissent si pauvres pour dire le choc que l'on ressent, la première chose qui vient à l'esprit est celle-ci : nous sommes tous Américains ! Nous sommes tous New-Yorkais, aussi sûrement que John Kennedy se déclarait, en 1962 à Berlin, Berlinois. Comment ne pas se sentir en effet, comme dans les moments les plus graves de notre histoire, profondément solidaires de ce peuple et de ce pays, les Etats-Unis, dont nous sommes si proches et à qui nous devons la liberté, et donc notre solidarité.

ÉDITORIAL

Comment ne pas être en même temps aussitôt assaillis par ce constat : le siècle nouveau est avancé.

J.-M. C.

Lire la suite page 18

4

C'est la nuit à Manhattan, au pied des tours devenues cimetières

NEW YORK
de notre correspondant

« Attention, elle s'effondre ! » Un policier new-yorkais, en sueur, le visage écarlate, nous repousse, en courant une rue plus loin, des deux tours jumelles du World Trade Center, les célèbres *Twins*. Des hurlements, des cris : *« Oh, my God ! »* Des gens pleurent, se prennent dans les bras. Il est 10 h 10 à Manhattan, il ne reste plus qu'une tour en feu. Une épaisse fumée noire et grise enveloppe le sud de Manhattan. Le sol est jonché de papiers déchiquetés. Tout est masqué par une épaisse couche de poussière grise, très claire. Les rues, les voitures, les gens sont couverts de cette « neige » qui atténue le bruit des pas, des véhicules et rend l'atmosphère encore plus irréelle.

Au milieu des sirènes des ambulances, de la police, des pompiers, les gens ne disent pas un mot, hébétés. Ils se regardent, baissent la tête, pressent le pas pour fuir ou tentent de reprendre leur progression vers ce qui était le World Trade Center. Ceux qui n'ont pas de masque se couvrent le visage. Des blessés, choqués ou en manque d'oxygène, sont allongés sur le trottoir, entourés, réconfortés. La progression est difficile. Les policiers en nombre mais désemparés interdisent parfois de passer, et puis laissent faire, dépassés par les événements. Nous avançons encore, les rues sont désertes, seuls les pompiers sont là, abattus, découragés.

Soudain, la deuxième tour s'effondre. Nous nous réfugions en courant dans un restaurant dont le patron ouvre les portes. Tout le monde se jette sous les tables. Des pompiers, bouteille d'oxygène sur le dos et masque sur le visage, nous rejoignent. Trois secondes plus tard, la masse de gravats et de poussière s'abat. Le bâtiment tremble, quelques vitres se brisent. Puis le silence. Il fait nuit noire en plein jour. Dehors, on ne voit pas à deux mètres. Une forte odeur de brûlé se répand. L'électricité est coupée. Le patron du restaurant distribue à ceux qui retournent dans la rue des serviettes pour se couvrir le nez et la bouche. Des véhicules de police et de pompiers sortent, noircis et cabossés, du nuage de poussière. Quelques minutes plus tard, le paysage réapparaît, hallucinant. New York est mutilée. Les deux tours ont disparu. Elles ont été arrachées, emportées. Il y a une heure, elles étaient encore là, intactes, brillantes au soleil. Les immeubles de bureaux, verre et acier, autour de ce qui était le complexe du World Trade Center sont en flammes, les vitres brisées. Certains sont en partie effondrés. Explosions et détonations se succèdent à chaque minute. Des blocs de ferraille tombent encore au loin, bruits sourds, soulevant des nuages de poussière.

« Vous le croyez, vous ? La guerre en plein cœur de Manhattan... », dit un pompier épuisé en s'asseyant sur le trottoir. Un gaillard de deux mètres couvert de poussière, de boue, les yeux rougis, au bord des larmes. Il donne à son supérieur le nom des cinq camarades qui se trouvaient avec lui dans l'entrée de la tour effondrée et dont il n'a pas la moindre nouvelle.

La nuit, lorsque les *Twins* étaient éclairées, c'était un endroit magique. Aujourd'hui, c'est un cimetière.

Eric Leser

D. BONDAREFF/AP

5

DE NEW YORK À WASHINGTON

Nos reporters racontent

Nos correspondants à New York à Washington racontent la fuite des employés des tours jumelles de New York et du Pentagone dans l'affolement. Scènes de piétinement parmi les blessés, les décombres, la fumée et les secours qui affluent. Récits et témoignages de survivants. Reportages p. 4 à 7

8

Suspect numéro un

OUSSAMA BEN LADEN

LE NOM du dissident saoudien Ben Laden est fréquemment avancé lorsque les Etats-Unis évoquent les éventuels responsables des attentats. Accusé d'être l'organisateur de plusieurs actions terroristes contre les intérêts américains, il fut l'allié de Washington en Afghanistan.

Lire page 12

Allemagne, 3 DM ; Antilles-Guyane, 10 F ; Autriche, 25 ATS ; Belgique, 48 FB ; Canada, 2,50 $ CAN ; Côte d'Ivoire, 900 F CFA ; Danemark, 15 KRD ; Espagne, 250 PTA ; Gabon, 900 F CFA ; Grande-Bretagne, 1 £ ; Grèce, 500 DR ; Irlande, 1,40 £ ; Italie, 3000 L ; Luxembourg, 46 FL ; Maroc, 10 DH ; Norvège, 14 KRN ; Pays-Bas, 3,30 FL ; Portugal CON., 300 PTE ; Réunion, 10 F ; Sénégal, 900 F CFA ; Suède, 16 KRS ; Suisse, 2,20 FS ; Tunisie, 1,4 Din ; USA (NY), 2 $; USA (others), 2,50 $.

M 0147 - 913 - 7,90 F - 1,20 €

6

Erreur sur la menace

L'AMÉRIQUE vivait depuis quelque temps d'une ambition sinon d'une illusion : rendre son territoire invulnérable à toute attaque venant d'un de ces *rogue states* (Etats voyous) qui, dans la liste des menaces, venaient remplacer l'Union soviétique disparue. Les démocrates, réticents, avaient emboîté le pas aux républicains et lancé le programme de la défense antimissile avant même que le héraut de cette politique, George W. Bush, ne gagne la Maison blanche. Les idéologues du Parti républicain ne se contentaient pas du financement de quelques recherches et de quelques essais. Ils théorisaient leur obsession. Ils voyaient l'avènement dans les relations internationales d'une nouvelle ère qui ne devait plus rien avoir de commun avec la guerre froide.

Plus de dix ans après la chute du mur de Berlin, ils ne voulaient pas seulement définir de nouveaux rapports avec la Russie postcommuniste. Ils voulaient encore la convaincre du danger potentiel représenté par des Etats supposés réfractaires au jeu traditionnel des relations internationales. Ils y avaient presque réussi. Ils concentraient tous leurs efforts sur la remise en cause de traités jugés *« obsolètes »*, qui, au temps de la guerre froide, avaient figé la rivalité Est-Ouest mais avaient en même temps permis que le conflit idéologique ne débouche pas sur une confrontation armée. Ils voulaient les remplacer par des *gentlemen's agreements* entre gens de bonne compagnie et de bonne volonté. Ils mettaient en doute la dissuasion nucléaire qui, par la menace de destruction réciproque, était censée avoir retenu au bord du gouffre les plus audacieux ou les plus irresponsables (voir Nikita Khrouchtchev au moment de la crise de Cuba en 1962). Ils contestaient la qualité morale de la dissuasion nucléaire – comment justifier la mort des milliers de civils innocents ? – et son efficacité – quel président des Etats-Unis voudrait être placé devant le choix entre déclencher l'apocalypse nucléaire ou accepter la destruction de son pays ?

Le bouclier antimissile ou NMD (pour National Missile Defense) devait apporter la solution de ce dilemme. Face à des Etats en mesure de se doter d'armes de destruction massive, nucléaires, biologiques ou chimiques, mais insensibles à la logique implacable de la dissuasion, les Américains devaient être en mesure de se protéger contre toute agression.

Daniel Vernet

Lira la suite page 18

7

LA PRESSE INTERNATIONALE

« Troisième guerre mondiale »

Les médias internationaux évoquent la nouveauté d'un conflit général désormais engagé avec un terrorisme insaisissable. L'Amérique doit entièrement réévaluer son dispositif de défense, écrivent les éditorialistes américains. L'expert en stratégie François Heisbourg nomme « hyperterrorisme » la nouvelle menace. Seuls le cinéma et le roman avaient exploré de tels scénarios-catastrophes.
Notre rubrique Horizons p. 16 à 19

1 **Amerika getroffen, die Welt von Entsetzen erfasst**

2 • Die Vereinigten Staaten haben am Dienstag, den 11. September, den schlimmsten Angriff ihrer Geschichte erlitten • Vom World Trade Center bis zum Pentagon fordern die Terroristen Washington heraus • Die Zahl der Opfer übersteigt die von Pearl Harbor • »Die Freiheit wird sich verteidigen«, erklärt Präsident Bush

3 Wir sind alle Amerikaner

4 Es ist Nacht in Manhattan, am Fuße der zu Friedhöfen gewordenen Türme

5 Von New York bis Washington – unsere Reporter berichten

6 Irrtum über die Bedrohung

7 Internationale Presse – »Dritter Weltkrieg«

8 Verdächtiger Nummer eins – Osama bin Laden

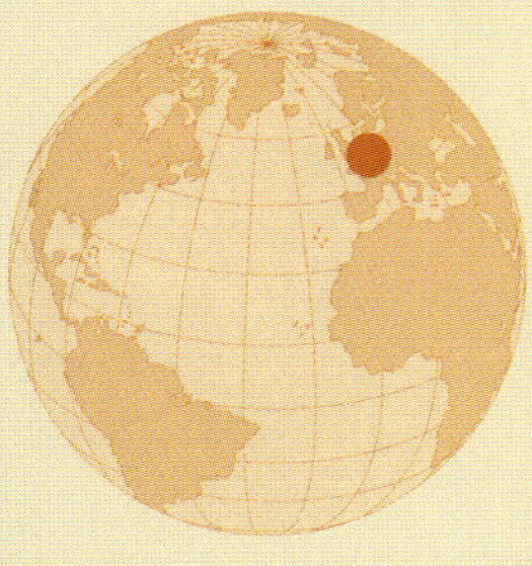

Le Monde
www.lemonde.fr
Frankreich, Paris

TORSTAINA 13. SYYSKUUTA 2001

HELSINGIN SANOMAT

USA:n Helsingin-lähetystön portinpieli täyttyi kukista ja kynttilöistä TERRORIHYÖKKÄYS C 6

- **Demokratia suojautuu vain yhteistyöllä.** Pääkirjoitus A 4
- **USA:n mahdotonta eristäytyä muusta maailmasta.** Tuomas Forsbergin Vieraskynä A 4
- **Terrorin vastainen rintama voimistui huimasti.** Kari Huhdan Näkökulma C 4
- **www.helsinginsanomat.fi Tuoreimmat uutiset ja kuvat terrorihyökkäyksestä.**

Keskiviikkona ei päässyt lentäen New Yorkiin TERRORIHYÖKKÄYS C 6

1889 2001 PÄIVÄLEHTI HELSINGIN SANOMAT

Maailmanlopun näkymä odotti newyorkilaisia keskiviikkoaamuna

MARCOS TOWNSEND / EPA

Varhain keskiviikkoaamuna World Trade Centerin pilvenpiirtäjien paikalla oli lohduton näky.

Uhriluku yhä arvoitus

▸ Poliisi etsi vahvoin voimin terrorihyökkäyksestä epäiltyjä Bostonista ja Floridasta

Jyri Raivio
HELSINGIN SANOMAT

NEW YORK. Epätoivoiset pelastustyöt uhrien löytämiseksi World Trade Centerin raunioista New Yorkissa ja puolustusministeriön yhä palavasta päämajasta Pentagonista Washingtonissa jatkuivat keskiviikkona jo toista päivää.

Tuhot olivat kuitenkin niin suuret, ettei kukaan uskaltanut esittää edes alustavia arvioita uhrien lopullisesta määrästä.

New Yorkin pormestari Rudolph Giuliani sanoi televisiossa aamupäivällä, että raunioiden raivaustyöt saattavat kestää jopa kaksi viikkoa.

Vasta niiden jälkeen voidaan sanoa jotensakin varmasti, kuinka monta uhria kahden kaapatun matkustajakoneen iskeytyminen maailman suurimpiin kuuluvan rakennuksen kahteen torniin lopulta vaati.

Epävarmuuden jatkuessa nähtiin amerikkalaisilla tv-kanavilla lohduttomia näytelmiä.

Romahtaneissa pilvenpiirtäjissä työskennelleiden omaisia ilmaantui kuvaruutuun mukanaan kadonneiden valokuvia.

He esittivät sydäntä särkeviä vetoomuksia omaistensa löytämiseksi.

Presidentti George W. Bush puhui aamupäivällä yhdysvaltalaisille. Hän maalasi puheessaan kuvan kansakunnasta, joka on sodassa varjoihin kätkeytyvää vihollista vastaan.

Mielipidetiedustelut osoittivat, että yli 90 prosenttia amerikkalaisista olisi valmis hyväksymään sodan syyllisten rankaisemiseksi.

Viranomaiset jatkoivat kuumeisesti tutkimuksiaan.

Bostonissa poliisi hyökkäsi vahvoin voimin keskikaupungin hotelliin, mutta hyökkäyksen syistä tai tuloksista ei iltaan mennessä ollut saatavissa tietoja.

Molemmat World Trade Centeriin syöksyneet koneet olivat lähteneet Bostonista.

TERRORIHYÖKKÄYS C 1 JA C 3

Taleban HS:lle: Bin Laden eristyksissä

Kaius Niemi
HELSINGIN SANOMAT

ISLAMABAD. Afganistanin Taleban-liike ilmoitti keskiviikkona, että terrorismista epäilty Osama bin Laden ei voinut suunnitella USA:n lentokoneiskuja. Hän ei ole voinut soittaa tai tavata ihmisiä eikä hänellä ole internet-yhteyksiä, talebanien suurlähettiläs selitti.

TERRORIHYÖKKÄYS C 2

Finnairin lento lykkääntymässä

▸ Suomalaisuhreja ei ole löytynyt

Kirsi Hölttä
HELSINGIN SANOMAT

▸ Finnairin torstainen lento New Yorkiin oli myöhään keskiviikkoiltana vaarassa lykkääntyä. Yhdysvaltojen oli määrä avata ilmatilansa ainakin osittain kaupalliselle liikenteelle kello 19 Suomen aikaa, mutta niin ei tapahtunut.

Yhdysvaltoihin pääsyä odottaa hotelleissa paljon matkustajia. Myös New Yorkissa paluulentoa odottaa noin 260 matkustajaa.

Tiistain terrorihyökkäys ei todennäköisesti ole vaatinut suomalaisuhreja. Ulkoministeriö ja New Yorkissa asuvien suomalaisten omaiset sekä suomalaisyritykset jatkavat tarkistuksia.

TERRORIHYÖKKÄYS C 5–C 6

Talouskaaos rauhoittui, ja kurssit nousivat paikoin

▸ Maailma odottaa New Yorkin pörssin aukenemista, öljyn hinta laski

HELSINGIN SANOMAT

▸ Yhdysvaltoihin tehtyjen terrori-iskujen vaikutukset maailmantalouteen tasaantuivat keskiviikkona. Öljyn hinta kääntyi laskuun.

Osakekaupassa oltiin varovaisia, vaikka heiluvat osakekurssit olivat paikoin nousussa. Arvopaperikaupan ennustettiin alkavan New Yorkissa jälleen tänään.

Pörssien vetovastuun ottaneessa Lontoon pörssissä työntekijät itkivät töissä ja odottivat suruviestejä New Yorkin kollegoistaan.

Tiettävästi suomalaisyhtiöillä ei ole työntekijöitä kateissa World Trade Centerin tuhon jäljiltä.

Suomalaiset vientiyhtiöt ovat antaneet lentorajoituksia työntekijöilleen. Kuitenkin vain muutama asiakas on perunut lentonsa.

Metsäteollisuus odottaa paperin kysynnän kasvavan paljon, koska sanomalehdet pulskistuvat.

Suomalaisilla vakuutusyhtiöillä ei ole korvausvastuita terrori-iskuista.

TERRORIHYÖKKÄYS C 7–C 9

New Yorkin kulttuurisesongin alku katkesi kokonaan
Manhattanin taide-elämä lamaantui. Terrori-iskussa kärsivät eniten musiikkiklubit ja galleriat.
KULTTUURI B 11

Jalkapallon kaikki europelit siirrettiin terrori-iskun takia
Euroopan jalkapalloliitto UEFA siirsi kaikki keskiviikon ja torstain Mestarien liigan ja UEFA-cupin ottelut.
URHEILU D 1

Helsingin Sanomissa taas poikkeuksellinen rakenne
Terrorihyökkäys- ja taloussivut ovat C-osassa, ruokatorstai B-osassa ja urheilu D-osassa.

Tänään 56 sivua

★ ★ ★ ★ ★ ★

1. **Zahl der Opfer noch ein Rätsel**
2. New Yorker erwarteten am Mittwochmorgen das Weltende zu sehen
3. Polizei sucht mit vollem Einsatz in Boston und Florida nach Verdächtigen des Terroranschlags
4. Finnair-Flüge werden verschoben
5. Keine finnischen Opfer gefunden
6. Wirtschaftschaos wieder beruhigt, Kurse teilweise wieder gestiegen
7. Wiedereröffnung der New Yorker Börse weltweit erwartet, Ölpreis sinkt
8. Die Taliban zu Helsingin Sanomat: bin Laden isoliert

HELSINGIN SANOMAT
WWW.HELSINGINSANOMAT.FI
FINNLAND, HELSINKI

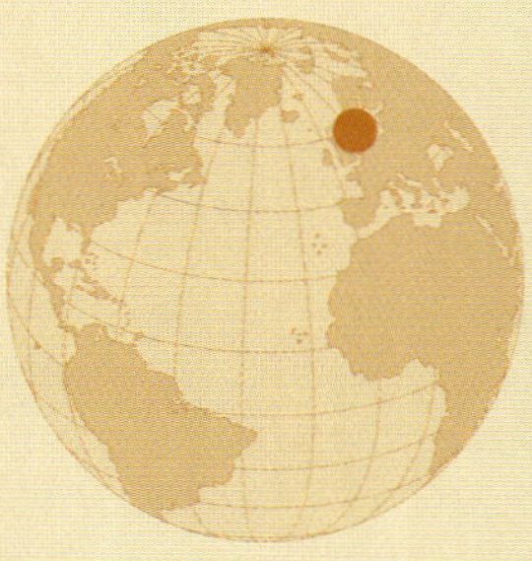

13

Prager Zeitung

Das Wochenjournal aus der Mitte Europas

Nr. 38 • Donnerstag, 20. September 2001 • 10. Jahrgang • KČ 35,- / SK 40,- / DM 2,80 / ÖS 17,- / SFR 2,- / US$ 2,-

Terror
Tschechiens Metropole nach dem Anschlag
Seite 3

Hamburg
Prag und die Hafenstadt an der Elbe
Seiten 13 bis 20

Restaurants
Thailändisches Fest im Corinthia Towers
Prager Tagblatt

Havel und Klaus fordern harte Bestrafung

Tschechien erklärt seine Solidarität und sichert den USA aktive Mitarbeit zu

Von Gerd Lemke

Der schicksalsträchtige 11. September hat auch die Tschechische Republik verändert. Am Tag nach dem größten terroristischen Anschlag seit Menschengedenken haben Staatspräsident Václav Havel, Parlamentspräsident Václav Klaus und Verteidigungsminister Jaroslav Tvrdík getagt, um über neue Sicherheitskonzepte nachzudenken. Doch genausowenig wie ihre amerikanischen Kollegen haben sie ein Patentrezept. Einstweilen wurde die Bewachung der Gebäude staatlicher Institutionen, Elektrizitätswerke, chemischer Fabriken und Flughäfen verstärkt.

Doch wie lückenhaft die Bewachung ist, beweist ein harmloser Zwischenfall während der Tagung des Sicherheitsrates. Ein geistesgestörter 26Jähriger tauchte völlig unbehelligt zwischen den Politikern auf, ließ sich wenig später ohne Widerstand abführen.

Und dann kam an die Öffentlichkeit, dass zur Stunde des Unglücks die Führungstroika der Armee im Ausland weilte, Verteidigungsminister Tvrdík in der Slowakei, sein Stellvertreter Štefan Füle in Brüssel und Generalstabschef Jiří Šedivý in Ungarn. Niemand im Lande hätte im Angriffsfall Befehlsgewalt besessen, die Armee wäre führungslos gewesen.

Der tschechische Geheimdienst BIS beruhigt in seiner Einschätzung. Tschechien sei nicht direkt gefährdet, könne aber dank der geographischen Lage als Hinterland für Terrorgruppen dienen. Außerdem wie der BIS darauf hin, dass die Kommunisten in der früheren Tschechoslowakei Gruppen, die gegen den Imperialismus kämpften, Unterschlupf und Ausbildung gewährt habe. Diese Untergrundkämpfer verfügen noch immer über eine hervorragende Kenntnis des Landes. Außerdem habe die Mitgliedschaft in der NATO das Risiko erhöht.

Weinend und fassungslos lagen sich die Menschen in den Armen, jeder suchte Trost bei dem anderen. Die Ereignisse in den Vereinigten Staaten ließen auch in Prag niemanden unberührt. *Foto: čtk*

Doch anders als im Fall der Bombardierung von Serbien vor zwei Jahren steht die Bevölkerung geschlossen hinter der NATO. Stellvertretend für das Land bekräftigt Klaus die Bereitschaft zur Mitarbeit im Bündnisfall. „Wir stehen an der Seite Amerikas ... Wir sind bereit, nicht nur moralisch zu helfen, sondern auch mit Taten. Wir wissen, dass unsere Zugehörigkeit zur demokratischen Welt für uns nicht nur bedeutet, sich an ihren Früchten zu beteiligen, sondern auch Verantwortung für ihren Schutz erfordert", schreibt er dem amerikanischen Botschafter in Prag, Craig Stapleton.

Lubomír Zaorálek (ČSSD), Vorsitzender des parlamentarischen Auslandsausschusses, würde eine Mitarbeit begrüßen. „Die größte Gefahr wäre, dass die USA die Antwort auf den Angriff alleine suchen würde." Präsident Havel forderte in einer Fernsehansprache eine harte Bestrafung. „Nach dem Verbrechen muss die Strafe folgen. Diese Strafe wird hart und muss hart sein. Es ist im Interesse der gesamten Menschheit und die Menschheit muss einen Aufruf herausgeben, dass man bestimmte Dinge nicht darf."

Ins Zwielicht ist allerdings Außenminister Jan Kavan geraten, der zwei Tage nach dem Attentat mit seinem jemenitischen Amtskollegen Abu Bakr Abdallah Kirbi über den Verkauf von Armeeausrüstung an das arabische Land verhandelt hat. Jemen hatte sich noch am 6. September geweigert, jemenitische Staatsbürger von den USA verhören zu lassen. Im vergangenen Jahr war das US-Kriegsschiff USS Cole im Hoheitsgebiet des Jemen mit Raketen angegriffen worden, 17 amerikanische Marinesoldaten kamen dabei ums Leben.

Bis zum Redaktionsschluss dieser Ausgabe wurden noch 66 tschechische Staatsbürger, die sich in New York aufhielten, vermisst.

Tschechien in Wirtschaftsprozess auf Anklagebank

Nach Prager Entscheidung gegen die Privatisierung von Becherovka droht erneut ein internationales Schiedsgerichtverfahren

Von Till Janzer

Auf die tschechische Regierung rollt bereits die dritte Anklage wegen unzureichenden Schutzes ausländischer Investitionen innerhalb der vergangenen zwei Jahre zu. Nach einem gewonnenen Schiedsverfahren mit den Vereinigten Staaten und einem verlorenen mit den Niederlanden - beidesmal war der amerikanische Unternehmer Ronald Lauder Kläger - plant der französische Likörhersteller **Pernod Ricard**, mit Hilfe seines Staates zu klagen.

Hintergrund des drohenden Prozesses ist eine Entscheidung des Prager Kabinetts vom Montag dieser Woche: Die Regierung warf Pernod Ricard praktisch aus dem Rennen um die Privatisierung von **Jan Becher - Karlovarská Becherovka** (JBKB). Sie entschied, 59 Prozent der Aktien an Becherovka vorerst unter staatlicher Verwaltung zu lassen und sie nicht zu verkaufen. Stattdessen plant das tschechische Finanzministerium zusammen mit den Kollegen aus dem Landwirtschaftsressort, die Privatisierung von Becherovka neu anzugehen.

Vor vier Jahren hatte die Pernod-Ricard-Tochterfirma **Salb** für 700 Millionen Kronen 34 Prozent der Aktien an Becherovka erworben. Damals gab Tschechien den Investoren die Zusicherung, später weitere 59 Prozent Aktienanteil aus staatlicher Hand zu erhalten. Nun wurde Salb und damit Pernod Ricard schlicht aus dem Privatisierungsgeschäft geworfen, auch ihr Anteil von 34 Prozent soll verkauft werden. Im selben Zug verlor Salb das Stimmrecht an 21 Prozent staatlicher Aktien, was das Unternehmen auch um den De-facto-Status des Mehrheitseigentümers bringt.

Beim Likörproduzenten ist man sich aber sicher: „Gemäß unserer Auffassung müssten wir in einem Rechtsstreit um den Schutz unserer Investitionen große Chancen auf Erfolg haben", ließ eine ungenannte Quelle aus der Nähe der Unternehmensleitung von Salb wissen.

Vergangene Woche war zudem bekannt geworden, dass Tschechien einen Prozess vor dem internationalen Schiedsgericht in Stockholm gegen Ronald Lauder, einen der ehemaligen Geldgeber des größten tschechischen Privatsenders **TV Nova** verloren hat. Lauder, Sohn aus der Gründerfamilie der Kosmetikfirma Estée Lauder, hatte den Staat wie im Fall Becherovka angeklagt, nicht ausreichend seine Investitionen in Tschechien geschützt zu haben. Er war laut seinen Schätzungen um rund eine halbe Milliarde Dollar gekommen, als Nova-Chef Vladimír Železný 1997 einseitig den Vertrag mit Lauders Investitionsobjekt **ČNTS** gekündigt hatte. Diesen Geldwert möchte der Amerikaner nun von der Tschechichen Republik ersetzt haben. Über die Entschädigungssumme ist allerdings in Stockholm noch nicht entschieden worden. Zudem ficht Tschechien den Rechtsspruch an, da angeblich der tschechische Teil des dreiköpfigen Schiedsgerichts nicht ausreichend beachtet worden sei.

9 771211 699000 01038

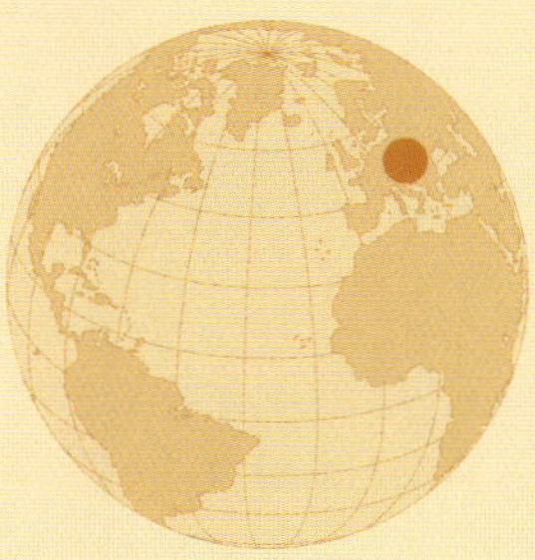

Prager Zeitung
www.pragerzeitung.cz
Tschechische Republik, Prag

13

ИЗВЕСТИЯ

13 сентября 2001 года, четверг,
№ 168 (26006)
Московский выпуск
Рекомендуемая цена — 4 р. 50 коп.
http://www.izvestia.ru
Газета выходит с марта 1917 года

Подписка продолжается.
Наш индекс: 50050

Минута молчания

Президент Российской Федерации Владимир Путин подписал указ «Об объявлении минуты молчания в знак траура в связи с трагическими последствиями террористических актов в Соединенных Штатах Америки». Публикуем полный текст Указа:

«В результате террористических актов, совершенных 11 сентября 2001 года в Соединенных Штатах Америки, имеются многочисленные жертвы и пострадавшие. Это беспрецедентное преступление против народа США и всего человечества.

Народ России разделяет скорбь американского народа и соболезнует родным и близким погибших во время этих трагических событий. Выражая солидарность с народом США, постановляю:

1. Объявить в Российской Федерации в знак траура минуту молчания 13 сентября 2001 года в 12 часов по московскому времени.

2. Приспустить 13 сентября 2001 года на всей территории Российской Федерации Государственные флаги Российской Федерации.

3. Предложить телерадиокомпаниям и учреждениям культуры приостановить 13 сентября 2001 года в 12 часов по московскому времени передачи и развлекательные мероприятия на 1 минуту.

4. Настоящий Указ вступает в силу со дня подписания».

Москва, Кремль, 12 сентября 2001 г.

ТЕМА ДНЯ: ТЕРРОР

Если не начнется полномасштабная война или не произойдут новые атаки террористов, будущее не представляется совсем уж мрачным. И в России, и в мире уже начался рост курса доллара. А ценные бумаги самых ликвидных отечественных предприятий подешевели не столь значительно, как того можно было ожидать. 2

Кадры, запечатлевшие, как на Манхэттен обрушивается чудовищный серый вал от двух рухнувших небоскребов Всемирного торгового центра, обошли весь мир. Однако далеко не все видели самую жуткую сцену — как еще до этого люди, которые оставались в здании, выходили на подоконники и поодиночке, а чаще вдвоем — взявшись за руки — бросались вниз с высоких этажей. 3

Около 400 авиарейсов совершили непредусмотренную посадку в аэропортах Галифакса, Гандера, Ванкувера, Монреаля, Торонто и других городов Канады… В торонтском аэрокомплексе «Пирсон» самолетами забито все пространство бетонного поля. Здание аэровокзала наглухо оцеплено, доступ прессе перекрыт. Всякое воздушное сообщение внутри Канады прекращено… 4

Весь мир — насилие

На каком свете мы теперь живем

Катастрофа, катаклизм, апокалипсис, Армагеддон… Все слова уже сказаны. Осталось их осознать. Сейчас на страницы газет, на экраны телевизоров выплеснется море предположений, догадок и домыслов относительно того, как это было возможно, как это могло случиться. Вместе с тем, давно уже, пожалуй, человечество не имело случая задуматься о том, куда движется цивилизация и какие опасности ее поджидают. Это уже вопросы на засыпку не одним философам. Это вопросы на засыпку обывателю.

Юрий БОГОМОЛОВ

Голливуд вроде бы накликал беду на Америку своими многочисленными худфильмами, фантазиями о транснациональных террористических организациях. Художественные призраки имеют свойство материализовываться. Но он, Голливуд, еще рассказывал о хороших парнях, которые всегда оказывались в нужное время и в нужном месте. Увы, в самом нужном месте и в самое нужное время их как раз и не оказалось. Художественные образы Добра не материализова…

Соединенные Штаты Америки. Наши дни

● Цитата дня

«В Божьем Граде разразится большой гром, братья будут разорваны Хаосом, и хотя сама крепость устоит, великий вождь будет повержен…» «Третья большая война начнется тогда, когда запылает большой город».

НОСТРАДАМУС, 1654 г.

● ХРОНИКА ПОСЛЕДНИХ СОБЫТИЙ

…

Афганское движение «Талибан», предоставившее бен Ладену убежище, заявило, что начинать переговоры о его высылке из страны «преждевременно». Прежде талибы вообще отказывались рассматривать такую возможность. Что это — намек на смягчение позиции, косвенное признание вины саудовского террориста?

Следователи, изучающие списки пассажиров угнанных самолетов, установили, что «пятеро из них арабского происхождения». Именно на этих людей отныне падает основное подозрение.

(Окончание на 3-й стр.)

Ограниченное небо

VIP-пассажиров подвергнут VIP-досмотру

Вчера вечером президент России Владимир Путин обсудил вопросы безопасности полетов с руководителями гражданской авиации. Утром этот же вопрос стал главным на расширенном заседании Комиссии РФ по делам ИКАО (Международная организация гражданской авиации), где рассматривался ход подготовки к предстоящей 33-й сессии ассамблеи. Россия подготовила к ней специальный документ, касающийся безопасности полетов. В свете последних событий в США российская инициатива может стать главным вопросом повестки дня ассамблеи.

Тимур ХИКМАТОВ

…

● Кстати

…

КУРСЫ ВАЛЮТ С 13 СЕНТЯБРЯ

ЦЕНА

ISSN 0233-4356

1 Die ganze Welt – Gewalt

In welcher Welt leben wir?

2 Thema des Tages: Terror

3 Schweigeminute

4 Grenzen im Himmel

VIP-Durchsuchung für VIP-Passagiere

5 »In Gottes Stadt geschieht ein großer Donner. Die Brüder werden durch das Chaos auseinander gerissen. Auch wenn die Festung stehen bleibt, wird der Führer getroffen. Der dritte große Krieg fängt an, wenn die Stadt in Flammen steht.« Nostradamus, 1654

Izvestia

www.izvestia.ru

Russland, Moskau

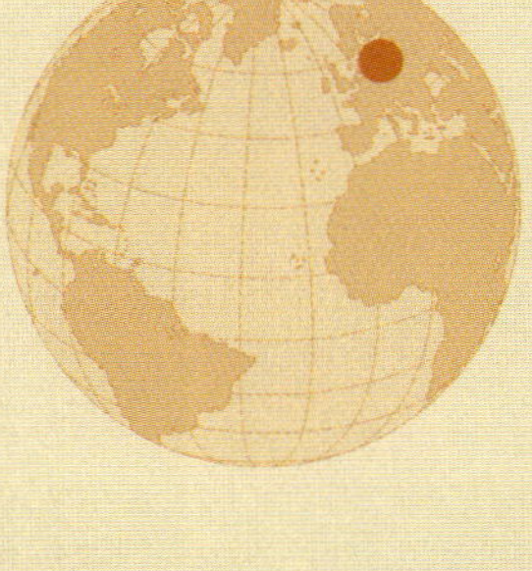

ЧЕТВЕРГ, 13 СЕНТЯБРЯ 2001 ГОДА № 178 (2790)

РОССИЙСКАЯ ГАЗЕТА

ВЫХОДИТ С 11 НОЯБРЯ 1990 ГОДА

Война миров

Американская трагедия поставила человечество на грань войны

ВЧЕРА • СЕГОДНЯ • ЗАВТРА

Минута молчания по Указу Президента

Горькие слезы Каширки и Манхэттена

Дума приняла обращение к конгрессу США

РАССКАЗЫ ОЧЕВИДЦЕВ

Он позвонил попрощаться перед смертью...

Роман ГРИНБЕРГ. Бруклин.

Моя девушка чудом спаслась

Дмитрий САБАТЕЦКИЙ. Москва.

Наш поезд поехал назад

Александр ЖУРБИН. Нью-Йорк.

После Апокалипсиса

12 сентября 2001 года мы проснулись в совершенно новом мире. Точно так же, как люди проснулись после 6 августа 1945 года, после Хиросимы. Или после 22 июня сорок первого. Пор руинами зданий в Нью-Йорке и Вашингтоне погибли наивные надежды, что новое тысячелетие будет с миром и согласием. Глобализация повернулась к нам вторым своим ликом, и этот лик страшен.

Смерть по канонам боевика

Удар почти ядерный

(Окончание на 3-й стр.)

Кабул бомбили, но не американцы

Центробанк начал проверку столичных пунктов обмена валюты

Паспортно-визовый стол на дому

В Ленск прибудет прокурорский десант

1000000 рублей принесла Приморскому краю операция "Кассовый чек"...

«ДЕЛОВОЙ ЗАВТРАК»

Рухнувшие небоскребы

Америка погребена под собственными мифами

Тамара ШКЕЛЬ.

ТАК РОЖДАЮТСЯ СЕНСАЦИИ

Березовский снимает Путина

Подробности — стр. 4

А тем временем в Америке

(ИТАР—ТАСС).

1 Krieg der Welten

Amerikanische Tragödie bringt die Menschheit an den Rand des Krieges

2 Nach der Apokalypse

3 Die gestürzten Wolkenkratzer

Amerika ist unter den eigenen Mythen begraben

4 Schweigeminute

Erlass des Präsidenten

5 Bittere Tränen in Manhattan

Rossiiskaia Gazeta
www.rg.ru
Russland, Moskau

Notre site Web : www.lematin.ma

LE MATIN

du Sahara et du Maghreb

LA PLUS FORTE AUDIENCE DES QUOTIDIENS DU MAROC

Directeur Politique Ahmed ALAOUI – Directeur Général Abdelhafid ROUISSI – Directeur de la Rédaction Hassan ALAOUI KACIMI

N. 11.193 - JEUDI 13 SEPTEMBRE 2001 - 24 JOUMADA II 1422 - 24 ELOUL 5761 - PRIX : 2,50 DH

S.M. le Roi Mohammed VI a regagné hier le Maroc après une visite officielle en Mauritanie

Volonté commune de raffermir la complémentarité

Les deux chefs d'Etat ont dénoncé et condamné les actes criminels contre les institutions publiques américaines

• **S.M. le Roi offre un dîner en l'honneur du Président Ould Taya et décore plusieurs personnalités mauritaniennes et des membres de la communauté marocaine en Mauritanie**

(Ph. LINH)

(Ph. LINH)

S.M. le Roi Mohammed VI a regagné le Royaume, mercredi à 15h05 GMT, à l'issue d'une visite officielle de trois jours en Mauritanie, à l'invitation du Président Mouâouiya Ould Sid'Ahmed Taya.

S.M. le Roi a été accueilli à son arrivée à l'aéroport de Tanger-Ibn Battouta par S.A.R. le Prince Moulay Rachid.

Le Souverain accompagné de S.A.R. le Prince Moulay Rachid, a passé en revue un détachement de la Garde Royale qui rendait les honneurs avant de saluer les couleurs nationales au son de l'hymne national.

S.M. le Roi a été salué ensuite par le Premier ministre, M. Abderrahmane Youssoufi, le Président de la Chambre des Représentants, M. Abdelouahed Radi, le Président de la Chambre des Conseillers.

Suite page 2

L'indignation gagne toutes les capitales après les attentats meurtriers de New York et Washington

Le Président Bush dénonce des "actes de guerre" contre l'Amérique

L'ambassadrice des Etats-Unis à Rabat exprime ses vifs remerciements à S.M. le Roi Mohammed VI

L'AMBASSADRICE des Etats-Unis d'Amérique à Rabat, Mme Margaret Tutwiler a exprimé mardi soir sa profonde considération et ses vifs remerciements à S.M. le Roi Mohammed VI pour les sentiments de sympathie à l'égard du peuple américain et pour sa condamnation des actes terroristes, exprimés dans le message que le Souverain a adressé au Président M. George W. Bush, suite aux attentats perpétrés contre des édifices et institutions américains. Tous les Américains, vivant aux Etats-Unis ou à l'étranger, sont attristés par la tragique perte de vies humaines innocentes, indique Mme Tutwiler dans un communiqué parvenu à la MAP. Mettant en exergue les relations d'amitié historiques ancestrales existant entre le Maroc et les Etats-Unis, Mme Tutwiler exprime, au nom de l'ambassade américaine au Maroc, sa gratitude à S.M. le Roi pour les propos contenus dans son message, et ses vifs remerciements au peuple marocain pour sa sympathie à l'égard du peuple américain.

De son côté le président George W. Bush a qualifié mercredi les attentats terroristes de mardi, qui ont fait des milliers de victimes, d'"actes de guerre" contre les Etats-Unis et promis d'en pourchasser les responsables. "Les attaques délibérées et meurtrières qui ont été menées hier (mardi) contre notre pays étaient plus que des actes de terreur. Elles étaient des actes de guerre", a déclaré le Président Bush dans une déclaration télévisée depuis la Maison Blanche. "La liberté et la démocratie ont été attaquées", a-t-il affirmé, en parlant d'un "ennemi qui essaie de se cacher mais qui ne pourra pas le faire pour toujours". "Cela va être une bataille monumentale du bien contre le mal, mais le bien l'emportera", a poursuivi le président américain en indiquant que "les Etats-Unis d'Amérique utiliseront toutes leurs ressources pour vaincre cet ennemi" qu'il n'a pas identifié. Le Président Bush a encore indiqué avoir demandé au Congrès des fonds d'urgence "afin que nous soyons prêts à dépenser ce qu'il faut pour sauver les victimes, et aider les citoyens de New York et Washington à faire face à cette tragédie".

M. Bush s'est réuni mercredi matin avec ses conseillers de sécurité nationale et devait recevoir en fin de matinée les dirigeants du Congrès.

(Ph. LE MATIN)

Le Pt Arafat a donné mercredi à Ghazza son sang pour les victimes américaines et a décrété une minute de silence dans les territoires palestiniens.

Lire pages 19 à 22

Grandeur et servitude d'une superpuissance

PERSONNE ne peut se réjouir du grand malheur qui vient de frapper les Etats-Unis d'Amérique. En tout cas, aucun musulman digne de ce nom. Aujourd'hui que les regards des inquisiteurs semblent se tourner vers le Moyen-Orient dans le but, presque avoué, d'y découvrir un nouveau bouc émissaire arabe, il faut peut-être mettre en garde contre la tentation de *"réparer"* - par la vengeance, qui plus est -, une grande injustice par une autre. Car ce qui s'est passé mardi à New York et à Washington est également cela : une injustice en même temps qu'une infamie.

Ahmed Chater

Suite page 2

Education et infrastructures dans le monde rural

Convention entre l'ONEP et la Fondation BMCE

« Nous, Marocains, savons nous rassembler sur l'essentiel », souligne M. Othman Benjelloun

(Ph. SAOURI)

Lire page 4

REDACTION : 88, boulevard Mohammed V - Casablanca - Tél : 022.30.12.71 - Fax : 022.31.75.35 - Télex : 277.94 M - ADMINISTRATION PUBLICITE - IMPRIMERIES : 88, Bd. Mohammed V - Casablanca - Tél : 022.26.88.60 - Fax : 022.26.29.69 - Télex : 022.238.45 S - Site Web http://www.lematin.press.ma

1 Wille zur Stärkung der gegenseitigen Zusammenarbeit

2 Seine Majestät König Mohammed VI. ist nach einem Staatsbesuch in Mauretanien gestern wieder in Marokko eingetroffen

3 Die beiden Staatschefs haben die kriminellen Akte gegen öffentliche amerikanische Institutionen verurteilt

4 Präsident Bush verurteilt die »kriegerischen Handlungen« gegen Amerika

5 Entrüstung breitet sich nach den mörderischen Attentaten von New York und Washington in allen Hauptstädten aus

6 Die Botschafterin der Vereinigten Staaten in Rabat äußert ihre tiefe Dankbarkeit gegenüber Seiner Majestät König Mohammed VI.

7 Größe und Last einer Supermacht

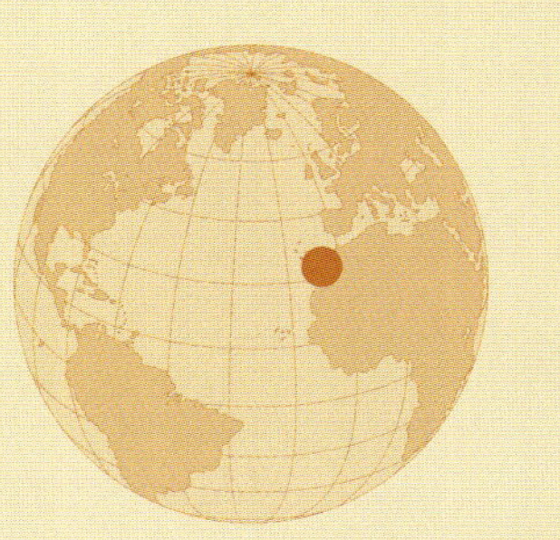

Le Matin du Sahara et du Maghreb
www.lematin.ma
Marokko, Casablanca

L'AMBASSADEUR D'ITALIE AU TOGO, LE CONSUL DU TOGO AU DANEMARK ET LES MEMBRES DE LA COMMISSION NATIONALE DES MARCHES ET DU COMITE TECHNIQUE INTERMINISTERIEL HIER A LOME II

P. 3

GRAND QUOTIDIEN NATIONAL D'INFORMATION

TOGO-PRESSE

DENYIGBA ƉƐ - ƐJAƉƐ

NUMERO 6110 PRIX 100 FRANCS Jeudi 13 Septembre 2001

HIER EN CONSEIL DES MINISTRES / APRES LES ATTAQUES TERRORISTES EN SERIE QUI ONT SECOUE LES USA

LE CHEF DE L'ETAT EXHORTE LE PEUPLE A LA VIGILANCE POUR SE PREMUNIR CONTRE LES FORCES DU MAL

● Un comité de crise mis sur pied pour suivre la situation dans ce pays

La situation catastrophique qui s'est produite mardi dernier avec la vague d'attentats dont les Etats-Unis d'Amérique ont été victimes a fortement préoccupé le conseil des ministres réuni hier sous la présidence du chef de l'Etat.

Le conseil des ministres s'est réuni ce jour mercredi 12 septembre 2001 à Lomé II, sous la présidence du chef de l'Etat, Son Excellence Gnassingbé Eyadèma.

Un seul sujet était à l'ordre du jour : la situation née de la tragédie des attentats terroristes dont les Etats-Unis ont été victimes le mardi.

Le président de la République a exprimé sa vive consternation et condamné énergiquement cet acte de barbarie qui a endeuillé la nation américaine, menaçant ainsi la paix et l'économie mondiales.

Il a réitéré au nom du peuple togolais, ses sentiments de solidarité au peuple américain et à ses dirigeants dans

(Suite P. 3)

... présidé par le président de la République Gnassingbé Eyadéma (1er à droite). C'était hier à Lomé II

Les membres du gouvernement en pleins travaux du conseil des ministres ...

LUTTE CONTRE LA CECITE

Du matériel roulant remis au ministre Agba

P. 4

1 Der Staatschef ermahnt das Volk zu Wachsamkeit, um sich gegen die Kräfte des Bösen zu wappnen

2 Gestern im Ministerrat / Nach der Serie von Terroranschlägen, die die USA aufgerüttelt haben

3 Ein Krisenkomitee wurde eingerichtet, um die Situation in diesem Land zu verfolgen

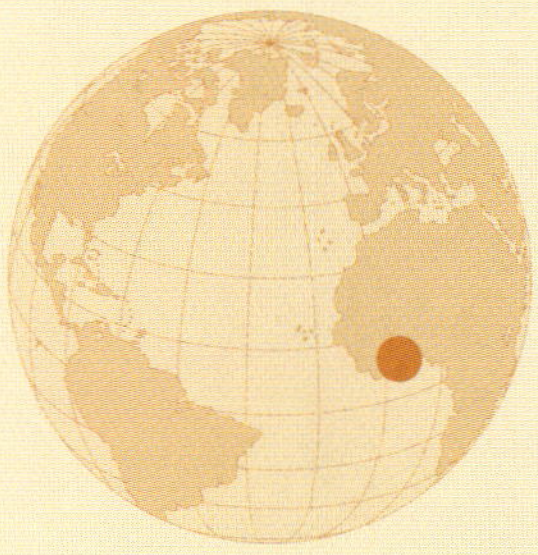

Togo-Presse
Togo, Lomé

13

1 Führende Persönlichkeiten des Staates und der Regierung begaben sich zur Botschaft der USA, um ihr Beileid auszudrücken

2 Ausdruck des tiefen Beileids für das amerikanische Volk

3 Beim Anschlag wurden keine Mongolen verletzt

4 Die amerikanische Botschaft in der Mongolei arbeitet im normalen Rhythmus

5 Kostenlose Telefongespräche mit mongolischen Bürgern in den USA

6 Kurseinbrüche

7 Die Weltöffentlichkeit ist entsetzt

Unen
www.unen.mn
Mongolei, Ulan Bator

WAR ON AMERICA

Thursday September 13, 2001

First published 1831 No. 51,176 $1.10 (incl GST)

The Sydney Morning Herald

Apocalypse now . . . a group of firefighters gaze through dust filled air at the shattered remains of the World Trade Centre, destroyed by two hijacked aeroplanes on Tuesday. There is no casualty toll yet. 'It will be more than we can bear," said New York's mayor Rudi Giuliani. Photo: Reuters/Shannon Stapleton

Bush: this means war

● Aircraft carriers guard coasts ● Six survivors found in rubble ● Fears for 50 Australians

'Half an hour into the flight to Los Angeles, the passengers must have known something was wrong. Somewhere near Albany the plane took a sharp turn and headed straight to New York City.' MARIAN WILKINSON reconstructs the fatal flights **Page 5**

'The two implosions – and a third at the Pentagon – reduced the Bush Administration to a wobbly attempt to demonstrate it still had a grip on the levers of power.' PAUL McGEOUGH on the mood in New York and America **Page 11**

Mark Riley and Gay Alcorn
Herald Correspondents
in the United States

The United States has moved onto a war footing against a still hidden enemy, as estimates of the death toll from Tuesday's catastrophic terrorist assaults on the World Trade Centre and the Pentagon climb into the thousands.

Aircraft carriers with missile defence systems were positioned off both the east and west US coasts and in the Arabian Gulf as President Bush's National Security Council and intelligence services tried to determine who was responsible and how to retaliate.

Mr Bush, facing the first crucial test of his leadership, vowed to hunt down those responsible for the "evil, despicable acts of terror", and all countries which harboured terrorists.

He made it clear that he expected friends and allies to "join forces for a war on terrorism".

The White House said it had received no warning before two hijacked aircraft slammed into the twin towers of the World Trade Centre in New York, another into the Pentagon, and another into a field in Pennsylvania.

The Minister for Foreign Affairs, Mr Downer, said 50 Australians were unaccounted for.

He said the assault would constitute an act of terrorism against Australia if any of its citizens had been killed.

No official tally of Australians working in the World Trade Centre was made available, but New York officials said they suspected it would be 100 or more.

The sophisticated and coordinated act of terror lasted less than 90 minutes but fear quickly spread throughout the country.

All flights were grounded for the first time in US history, government buildings were shut, and Mr Bush criss-crossed the country aboard Air Force One because the Secret Service feared for his safety.

The Commander of the US Atlantic Fleet, Admiral Robert Natter, said: "We have been attacked like we haven't since Pearl Harbour."

Republican and Democratic politicians said the attack was an act of war, and vowed swift revenge.

No creditable claim of responsibility had been made by yesterday, although FBI and intelligence officials said they suspected it was the work of the Saudi extremist Osama bin Laden.

"This apparently was well-planned over a number of years, planned by real pros and experts," Republican Senator Orrin Hatch said in Washington after a security briefing.

"Their belief is, at least initially, that this looks like Osama bin Laden's signature."

He said intelligence services had intercepted communications between bin Laden operatives discussing the attacks.

Bin Laden is thought to be hiding in Afghanistan, where the Taliban regime denied any knowledge of those behind the attacks.

The Taliban militia said it would consider requests for the extradition of bin Laden but would need evidence from US investigators.

A Palestinian journalist reported in Islamabad that bin Laden had congratulated the terrorists who carried out the deadly strikes, but had denied being involved.

The scenes of terror were worst in New York, the largest city in the US and the financial capital of the world.

Six survivors were found as a massive rescue operation began amid the rubble of the World Trade Centre. Emergency services reported receiving several mobile telephone calls from people trapped in the ruins.

Rescuers said they could hear screams from under the rubble. They hoped further survivors would be found in large air-pockets between the slabs of broken buildings.

Mr Bush estimated the total dead to be in the thousands.

The Mayor of New York, Mr Rudolph Giuliani, said: "I have a sense it's a horrendous number of lives lost. Right now we have to focus on saving as many lives as possible." Estimates of the death toll from the attack on the Pentagon, where 20,000 people work, ranged from 100 to 800. The 266 people in the four hijacked planes all died.

Mr Bush addressed the nation from the Oval Office late on Tuesday, declaring that the US would find and punish "those behind these evil acts", along with any country that harbours them.

"These acts shattered steel, but they cannot dent the steel of American resolve," he said.

Economists warned that the effect of the attacks on international markets could tip the already flagging US economy into recession, taking the rest of the world with it.

Regional financial markets descended into chaos, with billions of dollars wiped off the value of sharemarkets as investors rushed away from shares, corporate bonds and the US dollar in favour of government-backed bonds, gold and oil.

US stock exchanges were expected to remain closed on Tuesday. All airports in the country remained closed.

Fifteen US warships were sent to protect the west coast and Hawaii, while USS Kennedy and USS George Washington were off the east coast, protecting New York City and Washington, DC. USS Enterprise was ordered to remain in the Gulf.

As many as 50,000 people worked in the two 110-storey towers at the World Trade Centre, and an unknown number of visitors, business guests and shoppers were also inside.

The Australian property group Westfield Holdings had recently signed a $US3.2 billion, 99-year lease on the centre's shopping precinct. The company said one US-based employee remained missing from its 10-person office.

US reports said five Arabic men had been identified as suspects and that a rental car containing Arabic-language flight training manuals had been seized at Boston's Logan International Airport.

The men had boarded the two aircraft that crashed into the World Trade Centre – an American Airlines 767 and a United Airlines 767, which left Logan Airport bound for Los Angeles.

The American Airlines plane crashed into one of the towers at 8.45 am local time on Tuesday, and the other plane hit the second tower about 15 minutes later.

People ran from the towers, others were trapped inside, and some hurled themselves from the windows, before both buildings and a smaller adjoining building collapsed.

An American Airlines 757 en route from Dulles Airport near Washington to Los Angeles was flown into the Pentagon at 9.40 am.

The fourth aircraft, which crashed outside Pittsburgh – a United Airlines 757 flying from Newark, New Jersey, to San Francisco – was believed to have been heading for the White House, the Congress or the presidential retreat at Camp David.

Security officials in Massachusetts identified the five Arab men as suspects, *The Boston Herald* reported.

Two of the men, whose passports were traced to the United Arab Emirates, were brothers, one of whom was a trained pilot, said the paper. At least two other suspects had crossed from Canada and flown to Logan airport.

The paper said the suspects had no guns, but used shaving kits and other carry-on luggage to smuggle knife-like weapons.

Once in the air, the hijackers in one plane reportedly began killing flight attendants in order to lure a pilot from the cockpit.

TODAY'S COVERAGE

FULL INDEX Page 2

ISSN 0312-6315
9 770312 631049

1 Bush: Das bedeutet Krieg

2 • Flugzeugträger bewachen die Küsten • Sechs Überlebende in den Trümmern gefunden • Angst um 50 Australier

3 »Auf dem Flug nach Los Angeles müssen die Passagiere nach einer halben Stunde gemerkt haben, dass etwas nicht stimmte. Irgendwo in der Nähe von Albany machte das Flugzeug eine scharfe Kurve und steuerte gerade auf New York zu.« Marian Wilkinson rekonstruiert die tödlichen Flüge

4 »Die zwei Implosionen – und eine dritte im Pentagon – reduzierten den Handlungsspielraum der Bush-Regierung auf einen zittrigen Versuch zu demonstrieren, dass sie immer noch Zugriff auf die Hebel der Macht hatte.« Paul McGeough zur Stimmung in New York und Amerika

The Sydney Morning Herald
www.smh.com.au
Australien, Sydney

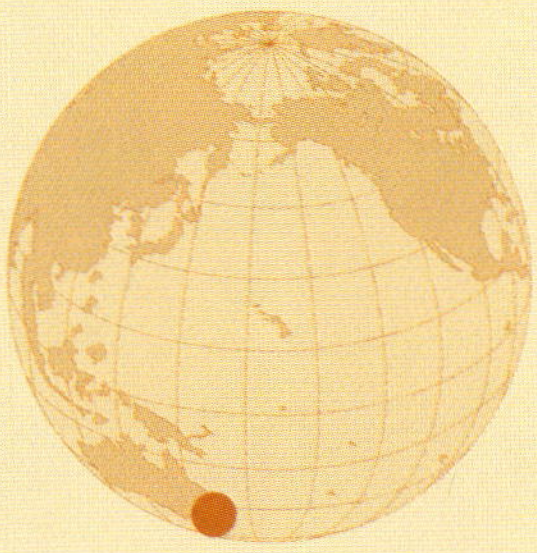

+++ Ruf nach Verstärkung: Ein Feuerwehrmann ruft verzweifelt nach weiteren Rettungskräften.

+++ Nach ihrem Einsatz verlassen erschöpfte Feuerwehrleute den Unglücksort.

+++ US-Präsident George W. Bush spricht an der Seite des Feuerwehrmanns Bob Beckwith allen Rettungshelfern seinen Dank aus.

14. September

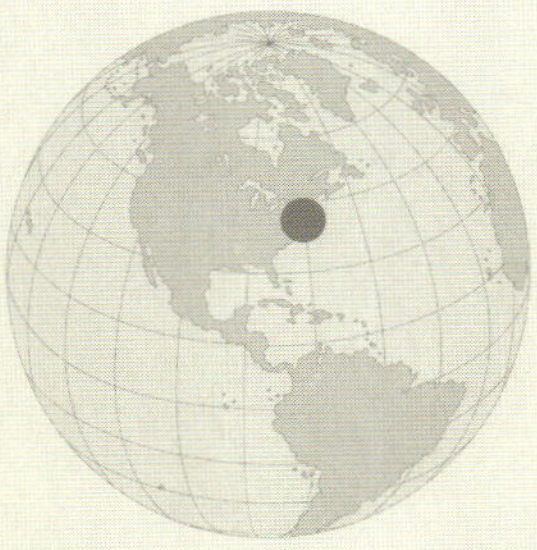

Time
www.time.com
Usa, New York (New York)

14

WOCHE-GESPRÄCH Günter Grass: „Die PDS soll mitregieren" **SEITEN 38+39**

TERROR-EXTRA 24 Seiten Analysen, Reportagen, Hintergründe, Porträts

DIE WOCHE

DEUTSCHLANDS MODERNE WOCHENZEITUNG

GEGRÜNDET 1993

POSTFACH 60 04 69 · 22204 HAMBURG · Österreich 31 öS · Schweiz 3,90 sfr · Niederlande 4,95 hfl · Belgien 95 bfr · Luxemburg 95 lfr · Frankreich 18 FF · Italien 5200 Lit · Spanien 500 Ptas · Kanaren 525 Can. Ptas · Portugal 550 Esc (Cont.) · Griechenland 1200 Dr · Finnland 22 Fmk · Ungarn 640 Ft · Slowenien 750 SIT C 3786 C

NR. 38 / 14. SEPTEMBER 2001 WWW.WOCHE.DE DM 3,90 / € 1,99

ANGST VOR DEM FLÄCHENBRAND

Weltkrieg des Terrors

Der perfide Angriff auf die USA ist das Fanal für eine neue Form blutiger Konfrontation – auch die Deutschen können Opfer der Gewaltspirale werden

VON SABINE ROSENBLADT

FOTO: AP

Was für ein Symbol! Zwei Passagierflugzeuge am heiteren Himmel über Manhattan, sie nähern sich den Zwillingstürmen des World Trade Centers, jenen hoch aufragenden Wahrzeichen des American way of life – und dann beginnt das flammende Inferno, das in unzähligen Hollywood-Katastrophenfilmen vorhergesehen, schaurig-scheußlich ausgemalt worden ist. Minuten später brennt auch das Pentagon, die Zitadelle im Herzen des Militärgiganten USA, die Schaltzentrale der mächtigsten Nation der Erde.

Fassungslos sitzen die Menschen rund um den Globus vor den Fernsehern und beobachten die Zerstörung Manhattans, mitten im Frieden. Eine mörderische Attacke aus gesichtslosem Dunkel auf die weltoffene, multikulturelle Metropole am Hudson River, ein militärisch geplanter Vernichtungsangriff auf zivile Ziele, der sich jedem historischen Vergleich entzieht. Wer, um Gottes willen, ist so kaltblütig und so fanatisch, dass er Zehntausende einfach so in den Tod reißen kann? Eine „Kriegserklärung an die gesamte zivilisierte Welt" nennt Gerhard Schröder den Terroranschlag. Und in jener zivilisierten Welt wird dies genauso empfunden – in Deutschland zumal, dem engsten Verbündeten der USA auf dem europäischen Kontinent. Angst vor dem großen, dem globalen Krieg mit einer völlig neuen Schlachtordnung kriecht in die Herzen und Hirne – Furcht davor, dass maßlose Gewalt mit ebenso maßloser Gegengewalt beantwortet werden könnte. Und dass die Deutschen in diesen Strudel hineingerissen würden, dass dies das Ende all dessen sein könnte, was in den 56 Jahren seit dem letzten Weltkrieg gewachsen ist.

Die Terrorattacke hat mit einem Schlag alle Gewissheiten der „Neuen Weltordnung" zerstört, die der Vater des amtierenden US-Präsidenten George W. Bush nach dem Ende des Kalten Krieges zu erkennen glaubte. Amerika, der „wohlwollende Hegemon" (Zbigniew Brzezinski), die „unentbehrliche Nation" (Madeleine Albright), der Weltpolizist und Wertewächter, entdeckt plötzlich zweierlei: dass es irgendwo, von irgendwem unermesslich gehasst wird. Und dass es auf ungeheuerliche Weise verwundbar ist.

Denn wozu taugen nationale Raketenabwehrsysteme, die 60 Milliarden Dollar kosten sollen, wenn eine Hand voll Selbstmordattentäter ausreicht, um Zehntausende New Yorker zu töten? Was nützen hochintelligente Cyberwar-, Raketen-, ABC-Waffen-Abwehrprogramme, wenn ein paar kaltblütige Terroristen nur Passagierjets kidnappen müssen, um sie zu fliegenden Bomben umzufunktionieren? Das Pentagon – ein Popanz? Als CNN die Bilder von den rauchenden Trümmern des militärischen Gehirns der Supermacht in alle Welt ausstrahlte, gingen in Gaza jubelnde Palästinenser auf die Straßen.

Was für ein Symbol! Der Vergleich mit Pearl Harbor, der manchen amerikanischen Politikern in den Sinn kam, wurde von Henry Kissinger, dem „grand old man" der amerikanischen Außenpolitik, als noch zu schwach beiseite gewischt: Pearl Harbor sei nur eine pazifische Militärbasis gewesen, „aber dies ist das Kernland!" Alle Kriege des vergangenen Jahrhunderts hat die Weltmacht auf fremden Territorien ausgefochten. Der Krieg daheim, vor der Haustür, in den Straßen New Yorks – das ist auf grauenhafte Weise neu für Amerika.

Dabei hatte es durchaus Vorahnungen gegeben. Samuel Huntington etwa, der Harvard-Politologe und Autor des düsteren Krisenszenarios vom „Zusammenprall der Kulturen", warnte vor zwei Jahren seine Heimat, sie sei „die einsame Supermacht" – „ein isoliertes Land, außer Tritt mit dem Rest der Welt" und von zwei Dritteln der Weltbevölkerung als Bedrohung empfunden.

LIEBE LESER

Nichts ist in der ersten Hälfte dieser WOCHE-Ausgabe so, wie Sie es gewohnt sind. Eine fundierte Berichterstattung über den Angriff gegen die USA machte es erforderlich, die übliche Blattstruktur zu durchbrechen.

Seine Sünden sind Macht, Größenwahn, Gier", schrieb Huntington damals – ein Bild, das mit der Selbstwahrnehmung der meisten seiner Landsleute nicht im geringsten übereinstimmte. Hip Hop und Coca-Cola, Baywatch und Microsoft: Waren es nicht die Segnungen der amerikanischen Zivilisation, die von Nowosibirsk bis Daressalam alle lieben, alle brauchen, alle haben wollen? Ja – und eben deshalb symbolisieren sie den Dämon der Globalisierung, der in die fernsten Ritzen dringt und Identität zerstört. Ihn zu töten heißt den Drachen zu töten. Osama Bin Laden, der schwerreiche „Pate" des islamistischen Terrors, bläst seit Jahren von Afghanistan aus zum Angriff gegen den „großen Satan" USA: Auf sein Konto gehen verheerende Anschläge in Saudi-Arabien, im Jemen, in Kenia, in Tansania.

Schon im August 1998 rächte sich Washington mit Luftschlägen auf den Sudan und Afghanistan. Dies sei „der Krieg der Zukunft", schwante US-Außenministerin Madeleine Albright damals. „Der Krieg hat begonnen", konterte Bin Laden; und aus Kairo drohte die Terrortruppe Al-Gama'a al-Islamiyya: „1 Milliarde Muslime stehen bereit, um ihre Körper in Bomben zu verwandeln."

New York, 11. September 2001: Der Krieg hat begonnen. Und sofort offenbart sich, wie verwundbar die Supermacht ist: Während die 400 Meter hohen Türme des World Trade Centers in sich zusammensacken, bricht nebenan Chaos an der Wall Street aus. Die internationalen Finanzmärkte, ihrer Leitbörse verlustig, stürzen in Turbulenzen, Öl- und Goldpreis schießen nach oben. Ist das der Stoß, den die schwächelnde Weltkonjunktur noch braucht, um endgültig in die Rezession abzukippen?

Mit infamer Präzision haben die Terroristen ins Herz der gültigen Weltordnung gezielt – und einen Volltreffer gelandet. Das Imperium americanum wankt. Es wird hart zurückschlagen gegen die Angreifer. Aber jene schweigende Mehrheit der Weltbevölkerung, die in Amerika die hässliche Fratze der Globalisierung sieht, wird es dabei nicht auf seiner Seite haben. Die „Schurken-Supermacht" (Huntington) muss erkennen, wie gefährlich ihr selbstgewisser Unilateralismus wird.

Im ersten halben Jahr seiner Amtszeit hat Präsident George W. Bush die Russen brüskiert und die Chinesen verärgert, er hat Kopfschütteln bei den Europäern und blankes Entsetzen bei den südkoreanischen Verbündeten ausgelöst. Tatenlos hat seine Regierung zugeschaut, wie sich Israelis und Palästinenser blutig ineinander verbissen. Jetzt hat er den Krieg im eigenen Land. Einen Krieg von so gewaltiger Symbolkraft, dass sich über die Folgen nur spekulieren lässt.

Der Traum der Hightech-Nation von Sicherheit und Unverwundbarkeit ist zerstoben. Nichts ist mehr so, wie es vor diesem schwarzen Dienstag war. Die Opfer der Globalisierung schlagen zurück: Wenn die Silhouette des brennenden World Trade Centers das erste Wahrzeichen für die kommenden Konflikte des 21. Jahrhunderts sein sollte, dann wird „die zivilisierte Welt" bald nicht mehr wiederzuerkennen sein.

Vielleicht haben die jugendlichen Globalisierungsgegner von Seattle, Göteborg und Genua nur früher als die westlichen Regierungschefs erkannt, dass eine Weltordnung, die wenige sehr reich, aber viele ärmer macht, auf tönernen Füßen steht. Ob eine Tobin-Steuer auf Devisenspekulationen hilft, die Macht der Finanzmärkte zu kontrollieren, ob es andere Mittel gibt, mehr globale Gerechtigkeit zu schaffen – auch darüber muss nach diesem entsetzlichen 11. September geredet werden. Die Antwort kann nicht nur mit Blut geschrieben werden.

4 390378 603900 38

DIE WOCHE im Internet: WWW.WOCHE.DE

DIE WOCHE

SEIT MÄRZ 2002 EINGESTELLT

DEUTSCHLAND, HAMBURG

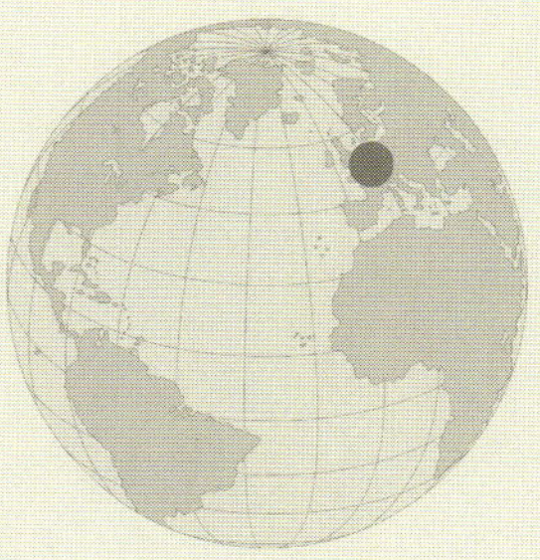

14

FREITAG,
14. SEPTEMBER 2001
NR. 251 / 37.W. / A2471A
H / 1,20 DM ☆

www.berliner-morgenpost.de

BERLINER MORGENPOST

BERLINER ALLGEMEINE

Briefe in die USA

Die Menschen in Amerika brauchen unser Mitgefühl: Schreiben Sie Karten, E-Mails oder Briefe – eine Aktion der Berliner Morgenpost

America, we stand by you!

Seite 29

Nach den Terror-Anschlägen werden allein in New York fast 5000 Menschen vermisst – US-Regierung kündigt Feldzug an

Wann schlägt Amerika zurück?

Stilles Entsetzen, schmerzende Trauer in Amerika. FOTO: REUTERS

BM **New York/Washington** – Die USA wollen die Terroranschläge von New York und Washington mit massiver militärischer Vergeltung beantworten. Vize-Verteidigungsminister Paul Wolfowitz kündigte an, es werde nicht bei einem Vergeltungsschlag bleiben: „Es wird ein Feldzug und keine einzelne Aktion." Wolfowitz sagte weiter, die USA würden die Vergeltungsaktion gegen die Verantwortlichen und deren Helfer so lange fortführen, bis der Terror aufhöre. Es gehe darum, Staaten auszulöschen, die Terrorismus unterstützten.

Zuvor hatte bereits Präsident George W. Bush eine militärische Antwort auf die Terrorangriffe angekündigt. Er sprach vom „ersten Krieg des 21. Jahrhunderts". In Gesprächen mit mehreren Staats- und Regierungschefs habe er Unterstützung für jede Art von Vergeltung erhalten, die er anordnen werde, sagte Bush. Die Nato hatte gestern bereits den kollektiven Verteidigungsfall festgestellt und den USA Unterstützung zugesagt. „Ich bin fest entschlossen, diesen gegen Amerika erklärten Krieg zu gewinnen", erklärte Bush. „Es ist eine neue Art von Krieg." Wann ein Vergeltungsschlag erfolgen könnte, ließ Bush offen. Heute will sich der Präsident in New York persönlich ein Bild vom Anschlag auf das World Trade Center verschaffen.

Erstmals nannte die US-Regierung den moslemischen Top-Terroristen Osama bin Laden als Hauptverdächtigen. Außenminister Colin Powell sagte, US-Diplomaten verhandelten derzeit mit der pakistanischen Regierung darüber, wie mit dem im Nachbarland Afghanistan lebenden bin Laden zu verfahren sei. Staatschef Pervez Musharraf hatte zuvor betont, die USA hätten Pakistans volle Unterstützung.

Nach Angaben von US-Justizminister John Ashcroft sind an den Anschlägen mindestens 18 Luftpiraten beteiligt gewesen. Zur Nationalität und Herkunft der Attentäter machte Ashcroft keine Angaben.

Nach dem ersten Entsetzen ruft die Öffentlichkeit in Amerika immer lauter nach Vergeltung. Fast 90 Prozent der Bevölkerung fordern in Umfragen, militärisch zurückzuschlagen – auch wenn es Krieg bedeutet. Selbst wenn dabei das Blut unschuldiger Zivilisten fließt, sollen die Terroristen und ihre Helfer bezahlen, meinen zwei Drittel.

Wie durch ein Wunder konnten sich gestern sechs Menschen aus den Trümmern des World Trade Center befreien. Fünf Feuerwehrleute überlebten den Einsturz der Wolkenkratzer in einem Fahrzeug. Ein sechster Mann wurde kurz darauf aus dem Schutt gezogen. Rettungsarbeiter begrüßten die Geretteten enthusiastisch mit Beifall. „Das ist die beste Nachricht seit Tagen", freute sich ein Sanitäter. „Sie gibt uns neue Kraft für die Suche nach Lebenszeichen." Trotz ihres unermüdlichen Einsatzes in den Tonnen von Trümmern hatten Rettungsmannschaften zuvor kaum noch Chancen gesehen, Überlebende unter den Tausenden von Verschütteten zu entdecken. Die Zahl der geborgenen Todesopfer stieg gestern auf rund 100. Aber nur etwa jedes zweite Opfer wurde bisher identifiziert. Fast 5000 Menschen gelten bisher offiziell als vermisst.

Beim Anschlag auf das US-Verteidigungsministerium in Washington sind nach jüngsten Angaben mindestens 190 Menschen ums Leben gekommen. Diese Schätzung schließt die Insassen der gekaperten American-Airlines-Maschine ein, die auf das Pentagon stürzte. Nach Angaben von Pentagon-Beamten gelten etwa 130 Militärangehörige und zivile Angestellte als tot. In den Trümmern des Pentagons hörten Suchtrupps Signale der „Black Box" der abgestürzten Maschine. Von der in Pittsburgh abgestürzten Passagiermaschine wurde der Flugschreiber bereits gefunden. Das Verbot kommerzieller Flüge in den USA wurde gestern teilweise aufgehoben. Die New Yorker Börse bereitet für Montag den Neustart des Aktienhandels vor.

Tägliche Lagebesprechung

BM **Berlin** – Das Kanzleramt hat ein Gremium eingesetzt, das mindestens einmal täglich über die Sicherheitslage beraten soll. Teilnehmen werden Vertreter der zuständigen Ressorts sowie des Bundeskriminalamts und der deutschen Nachrichtendienste. **Seite 2**

Zaghaft kehrt das Leben zurück

Pause für die Feuerwehr. F.: AP

New York City beginnt wieder zu leben. Langsam, zaghaft. Während am Katastrophenort im Süden Überlebende gesucht, Opfer geborgen und Trümmer beseitigt werden, spazieren Menschen wieder über die Fifth Avenue. **Seite 3**

Sind wir im Krieg?

Waren die Terroranschläge in New York und Washington wirklich eine Kriegserklärung an die USA und die westliche Welt, wie viele Politiker erklärten? Versuch einer Begriffs-Definition von Sven Felix Kellerhoff. **Seite 4**

Angst vor der Wirtschaftskrise

BM **Berlin** – Die Unsicherheiten über die wirtschaftlichen Folgen der Terroranschläge wachsen. Einige Volkswirte sprechen von drohender Rezession. Die Europäische Zentralbank sieht dagegen keine ernsthaften Auswirkungen. **Seite 9**

Schweigen in Deutschland

Gedenkminuten in der Stuttgarter Porsche-Fabrik. FOTO: AP

Deutschland und Berlin trauern. Fünf Minuten Stille. Ob im Luxuskaufhaus oder im Supermarkt, in den Betrieben oder auf der Straße. Überall in der Hauptstadt gedachten die Menschen um zehn Uhr der Opfer des Terrors. **Berlin Seite 27**

Der Sport macht weiter

BM **Berlin** – Der Automobil-Weltverband hat entschieden, trotz der Terror-Anschläge den Großen Preis von Italien am Sonntag starten zu lassen. Auch die Fußball-Bundesliga und die Deutsche Eishockey Liga laufen planmäßig. **Seiten 16, 18**

4 390247 101209 50037

BELGIEN BEF 32 / DÄNEMARK DKK 7 / GRIECHENLAND GRD 450 / ITALIEN LIT 2500 / MAROKKO DH 12 / ÖSTERREICH ÖS 12 / POLEN PLZ 4,00 / PORTUGAL PTE 260 (CONT.) / SCHWEIZ CHF 1,50 / SPANIEN PTS 225 / SCHWEDEN SEK 11 / SLOWAKISCHE REPUBLIK SKK 38 / TSCHECHIEN CZK 32,00 / TÜRKEI TL 1 500 000 / UNGARN FT 230

Eine Spur der Attentäter führt nach Hamburg

BM **Berlin** – Bei der Fahndung nach den Hintermännern der Terroranschläge in den USA haben amerikanische und deutsche Ermittler erste Erfolge erzielt. Eine heiße Spur führt dabei nach Deutschland: Offenbar lebten drei der bis zu 24 Flugzeugentführer zeitweise im Hamburger Stadtteil Harburg. Dort wurde in der Nacht zu Donnerstag ihr Unterschlupf entdeckt und ein Verdächtiger festgenommen.

In den USA läuft bei der Suche nach den Drahtziehern ein beispielloser Großeinsatz mit 7000 Beamten. Die Bundespolizei FBI hat offenbar 50 Männer im Visier, die an Planung und Ausführung der Anschläge sowie am Aufbau der Logistik beteiligt gewesen sein sollen. US-Medienberichten zufolge sind die Personen bereits identifiziert.

In Deutschland leitete Generalbundesanwalt Kay Nehm gestern ein Ermittlungsverfahren ein. Nach seinen Angaben besteht der Verdacht, dass zu Jahresbeginn in Hamburg eine terroristische Vereinigung gebildet worden sei. Dabei habe es sich um Personen mit arabischem Hintergrund und „islamisch-fundamentalistischer Grundhaltung" gehandelt. Ihr Ziel sei es gewesen, zusammen mit anderen islamischen Gruppierungen im Ausland auf „spektakuläre Weise durch Zerstörung von symbolträchtigen Gebäuden" die USA anzugreifen.

Zwei Mitglieder dieser Vereinigung sollen an Bord der Maschinen gewesen sein, die in die Türme des World Trade Centers rasten. Ein weiteres Mitglied dieser Gruppierung soll an Bord der in Pennsylvania abgestürzten Linienmaschine gewesen sein.

Fünf mutmaßliche Mitglieder der Organisation Al-Quaida des Top-Terroristen Osama bin Laden werden voraussichtlich in Frankfurt am Main vor Gericht gestellt. Der Sprecher des Frankfurter Oberlandesgerichts, Wolfgang Frank, bestätigte gestern eine entsprechende Vorankündigung der Bundesanwaltschaft. Die Männer werden der Bildung einer terroristischen Vereinigung beschuldigt und sollen um Weihnachten 2000 einen spektakulären Bombenanschlag im französischen Straßburg vorbereitet haben. Das Oberlandesgericht rechnet mit einer Klageerhebung noch in diesem Jahr. Zur Abwicklung des Prozesses werde die höchste Sicherheitsstufe eingehalten.

Bei den Beschuldigten handelt es sich um fünf Männer aus Algerien, Irak und Frankreich, die im vorigen Dezember und im April festgenommen worden waren. In einer konspirativen Wohnung in Frankfurt-Eckenheim waren diverse Waffen sowie 20 Kilo des Bombengrundstoffes Kaliumpermanganat gefunden worden. **Seite 6**

Unsere Welt war bunt!

Wie der Schrecken des Terrors auch die MTV-Generation trifft

VON KATI DEGENHARDT

Das World Trade Center fällt in sich zusammen. Es ist aber kein Film, der alle Rekorde an den Kinokassen sprengt, das ist Terrorismus.

Wird New York unsere Wirklichkeit? Für einen Moment jagen mir panische Gedanken durch den Kopf. Was, wenn diese in wenigen Augenblicken aufeinander folgenden Terrorattacken der Auftakt zu einem Krieg sind? Ilona, meine Freundin in Downtown-Manhattan sagt, als ich sie endlich erreiche, ganz leise am Telefon: „It's Krieg. Alle rennen, alle sind hysterisch. Ich habe Angst!"

Ich auch. Mir fallen Freunde ein, die in New York leben. Ihnen darf einfach nichts passiert sein. Aber darum geht es irgendwie auch nicht. Es geht nicht um persönliche Betroffenheit. Nur weil inzwischen jeder einen kennt, der einen kennt, der in New York arbeitet, oder Verwandte hat oder gerade American Airlines geflogen ist. Es geht nicht darum, dass einem der ferne Blick auf das World Trade Center zufällig vertraut ist. Dass die Sicherheitskontrollen in den Flughäfen immer lästig und überflüssig erscheinen.

Präsident George W. Bush hat gesagt, was passieren wird und worum es jetzt geht: „Die Guten müssen die Bösen bestrafen." Er malt uns ein Bild in Schwarz und Weiß. Seine Entschlossenheit beängstigt. Unsere junge Welt war immer bunt. Wenigstens in den letzten zehn, zwölf Jahren. Nicht jeder ist gleich. Sicherlich nicht. Und bunt bedeutet nicht für jeden gleich bunt. Die MTV-Generation findet Musik nicht einfach gut. Sie steht drauf: Auf Lautes, Hippes, Schnelles, Geiles. Auf Marken, auf Technik, manche auch auf Drogen. Nicht jeder 20-Jährige lebt mit MTV. Aber wir leben alle mit Fernsehen und Internet. Mit einer Flut von Informationen und von Wegen, die uns offen stehen. Angesichts der vielen Möglichkeiten, kann man sich für vieles entscheiden. Für links oder rechts, für politisches Engagement oder Desinteresse. Für Bildung, für Reisen oder für Kultur.

Kann man sich auch aussuchen, ob einen Terror interessiert?

Wir leben in Deutschland. Das Leben hier hat uns geprägt, die meisten jedenfalls. Viele sind aber zum Beispiel in Michigan zur Schule gegangen, studieren vielleicht in Hongkong, machen ihre Ausbildung in Holland oder fliegen in den Urlaub nach Kuba. Wir haben Freunde aus der Türkei, aus Korea, aus Frankreich. Globalisierung, vielleicht nicht in allen Bereichen und ihrer ganzen Tragweite, wird längst gelebt. Die Devise heißt: Alles ist möglich. Dass damit das Gute gemeint ist, ist ja wohl klar. Dass auch das Böse dazu gehört, vergisst sich leicht.

Tiefe Trauer: Berliner Schülerinnen in der Nähe der US-Botschaft. FOTO: DDP

Horrorszenarien kennt inzwischen jeder. „Das ist ja wie Independence Day, Mars Attacks!" Hollywood hat die Bilder längst gezeigt, die für einen Augenblick die nackte Angst in unser Bewusstsein gerückt haben. Meine Freundin Nina sagt: „Ich kann das nicht glauben." Etwas Ähnliches könnte im Extremfall auch die Welt bedrohen, die eben noch bunt war. Aber es wäre wohl ein Augenblick geblieben. Jetzt ist es, als lebten wir oder die Terroristen auf einem anderen Stern. Niemand kann sich vorstellen, woher die Entschlossenheit einzelner Gruppen stammt, Tausende zu töten und sich selbst mitzuopfern.

Es ist einfach unmöglich, sich Motive für diese plötzliche Verbreitung des Grauens auszumalen. Es muss doch irgendeinen Nutzen geben, den wenigstens einer, der hinter den Anschlägen steckt, aus einer derartigen Provokation ziehen kann. Was steht uns in Zukunft noch bevor?

Freunde treffen sich, diskutieren, um wenigstens ein bisschen Luft zu bekommen. Bekannte, mit denen man noch nie über Politik gesprochen hat, erzählen, dass sie früher gegen den Golfkrieg demonstriert haben. Oder in der ehemaligen DDR als Kinder Angst vor dem Ausbruch des Dritten Weltkriegs hatten. Auch die Kids der MTV-Generation stehen unschlüssig

Angst ist eine neue Erfahrung. Das eigene Gefühl, erstmals bereit zu sein, jegliche Form der Vergeltung zu akzeptieren, wenn ein Feind nur persönlich und gefährlich genug erscheint. Auch wenn man vorher überzeugter Gegner aller Gewalt war.

Die Autorin ist 23 Jahre alt und studiert Geschichte und Publizistik

BERLINER MORGENPOST
14.09.2001
WWW.BERLINERMORGENPOST.DE
DEUTSCHLAND, BERLIN

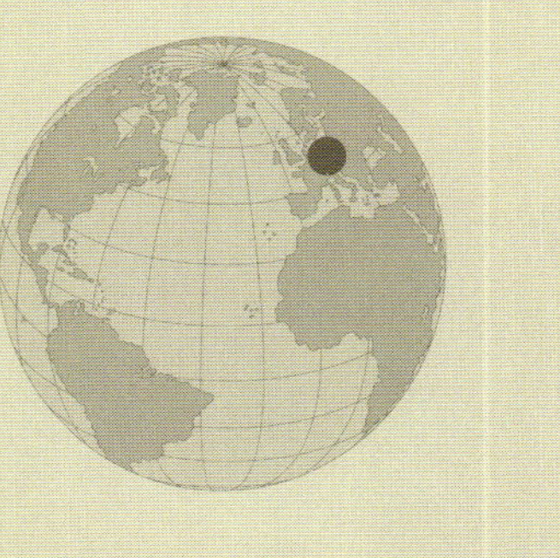

14

Der Terror und die Folgen: *Berichte auf 25 Seiten*

Berliner Zeitung

Freitag, 14. September 2001 Nr. 215 HA - 57. Jahrgang www.berliner-zeitung.de 1.20 DM Berlin/Brandenburg - 1.50 DM Auswärts**

AFGHANISTAN

Der Gastgeber Bin Ladens

VON KATJA TICHOMIROWA

Mohammed Omar trifft seine Entscheidungen allein mit Gott. Für seine Anhänger, die Taliban, ist er „Amir-el-mu'minin", der Befehlshaber der Gläubigen. Alle Aufgaben des Landes entfallen auf ihn, sagen seine Minister über den Gründer und Führer der Taliban-Bewegung. Er ist in allen Belangen des Muslimischen Emirats Afghanistan die letzte Instanz.

Allein mit seinem Gott wird Omar auch über das Schicksal des afghanischen Volkes entscheiden. Liefert er seine Schutzbefohlenen einem möglichen Angriff der USA auf das Land aus oder verhandelt er mit der amerikanischen Regierung über eine Auslieferung seines Schützlings Osama Bin Laden, seinem Gönner, Mitstreiter und Weggefährten im Kampf gegen die Ungläubigen und mutmaßlichen Urheber der Terror-Angriffe auf New York und Washington?

Irgendwo in den Bergen um Kandahar, dem Sitz der Taliban-Regierung, soll Osama Bin Laden sich verborgen halten. Er genießt das Gastrecht des Taliban-Chefs und den Ruf eines Helden, der, wie Mohammed Omar selbst, schon im Krieg gegen die sowjetischen Besatzer an der Seite der afghanischen Gotteskrieger kämpfte. Nachts soll er gelegentlich in die Stadt kommen – um seinen vielfältigen Geschäften nachzugehen und seinen Gastgeber zu treffen. Mohammed Omar ist Bin Laden eng verbunden. Die beiden Männer teilen geschäftliche Interessen und sie verfolgen ein gemeinsames Ziel: Die Durchsetzung und Ausbreitung ihres Glaubens, einer extrem puristischen Auslegung des Islam.

***Mohammed Omar** Chef der Taliban-Regierung, lässt sich nicht fotografieren*

Bin Laden zeigt sich überaus dankbar für den Schutz, der ihm gewährt wird. Die Taliban profitieren von den weit verzweigten Verbindungen Bin Ladens, die es ihnen ermöglichen, das UN-Embargo gegen Afghanistan zu umgehen. Der saudi-arabische Multimillionär gibt sein Geld, seine Kampfgefährten aus Saudi-Arabien, Ägypten und dem Sudan stellen ihr technisches Wissen in den Dienst der Taliban.

Mohammed Omar und Osama Bin Laden aber eint auch die Wahl ihrer Mittel. Nicht allein, wer sich ihnen in den Weg stellt, muss mit ihrer unnachgiebigen und skrupellosen Verfolgung rechnen. Auch wer den vorgeschriebenen Pfad verlässt, wird grausam bestraft. In seiner Eigenschaft als Vorsitzender des afghanischen Religionsrates ließ Mohammed Omar das Tanzen, Fotografieren, Fußballspielen, selbst das Halten von Kanarienvögeln verbieten. Auch das Strafmaß für alle, die sich seinen Anweisungen widersetzen, legt Omar fest. Männer, deren Bart nicht in der vorgeschriebenen Weise spriest, werden ausgepeitscht, Frauen, die Ehebruch begehen, gesteinigt, Homosexuelle lebendig begraben.

Omar wacht streng über diese „gottgegebenen Gebote". Es heißt, er sei scheu und zurückhaltend, tapfer, überaus anspruchslos und von untadeliger Moral. Auch darin soll er seinem Weggefährten Bin Laden gleichen. Ihre Anhänger wissen wenig über die beiden Männer, das wenige aber, das bekannt ist, wird zu immer neuen Legenden verwoben. Mohammed Omar ist ein Gefangener dieser Legenden. Liefert er seinen Bruder an Amerika aus, schafft er einen Märtyrer, der seinen Mythos zerstört.

Berliner Verlag GmbH & Co., 10171 Berlin
Redaktion: (030) 23 27 -9, Fax -54 30
Leser-Service: (030) 23 27 -77, Fax -76
e-mail: abo@berlinonline.de
Anzeigen: (030) 23 27 -50 Fax: -66 97
www. berliner-zeitung.de nur bei
BerlinOnline Berlin auf einen Klick!
e-mail: leserbriefe@berlinonline.de
Belgien 37 BEF · Bulgarien 2,50 Lev · Dänemark 8 dkr · Italien 2000 Lit Kanaren 200 Ptas · Österreich 11 ÖS · Schweiz 1,40 Sfr · Slowakei 45 Sk Spanien 180 Ptas · Tschechien 38 Kc · Türkei 1 400 000 TL · Ungarn 290 Ft
4 394050 501201 50037

Scharping: Wir stehen nicht vor einem Krieg
Breite Unterstützung für Nato-Beschluss

USA planen einen Feldzug gegen den Terrorismus / Eine Spur der Täter führt nach Deutschland
Millionen gedenken in Deutschland schweigend der Opfer der Anschläge

AP/BRDIGET BESAW GORMAN

Ein Feuerwehrmann sucht nach einem geeigneten Platz, um die amerikanische Fahne in den Trümmern des World Trade Centers zu befestigen.

BERLIN/BRÜSSEL/NEW YORK, 13. September. Die Bundesregierung ist Befürchtungen entgegengetreten, Deutschland stehe nach dem Beistandsbeschluss der Nato für die USA vor einem Krieg. Vor möglichen Militäraktionen auf Grund der Terroranschläge in den USA müssen nach den Worten von Verteidigungsminister Rudolf Scharping (SPD) die Ermittlungsergebnisse von Polizei und Geheimdiensten abgewartet werden. Erst auf dieser Grundlage könnten die Vereinigten Staaten und der Nato-Rat weitere Entscheidungen treffen, sagte Scharping nach Lagebesprechungen mit Bundeskanzler Gerhard Schröder in Berlin. „Wir stehen nicht vor einem Krieg, wir stehen vor einer ernsten terroristischen Herausforderung", betonte er. Darauf werde es „eine angemessene Reaktion geben". Mit einem Krieg im traditionellen Sinn habe das aber nichts zu tun, sagte er der „Berliner Zeitung".

Bush beantragt 20 Milliarden

Die USA machten gleichzeitig deutlich, dass sie die Terroranschläge auf New York und Washington mit massiver militärischer Vergeltung beantworten wollen. Der stellvertretende Verteidigungsminister Paul Wolfowitz kündigte am Donnerstag an, es werde nicht bei einem Vergeltungsschlag bleiben: „Es wird ein Feldzug und keine einzelne Aktion." Bush sprach vom „ersten Krieg des 21. Jahrhunderts". Er habe in Gesprächen mit mehreren Staats- und Regierungschefs Unterstützung für jede Art von Vergeltung erhalten, die er anordnen werde. Bush beantragte beim Kongress zusätzliche Mittel von 20 Milliarden Dollar für die Terrorismusbekämpfung.

Amerikanische und deutsche Ermittler haben bei der Jagd nach den Hintermännern der verheerenden Terroranschläge erste Fahndungserfolge erzielt. Eine heiße Spur führt dabei nach Deutschland: Möglicherweise lebten drei der bis zu 24 Flugzeugentführer zeitweise in Hamburg. Dort wurden in der Nacht zum Donnerstag Wohnungen durchsucht und zwei Verdächtige festgenommen. Einer von ihnen soll einen ägyptischem Pass besitzen und legal auf einem Flughafen gearbeitet haben.

Die Nato-Entscheidung über den kollektiven Beistand für die USA wird in Berlin von einer breiten Koalition fast aller Parteien mitgetragen. Union und FDP sicherten der Bundesregierung am Donnerstag ausdrücklich ihre Unterstützung zu. Die Grünen betonten, dass Deutschland den USA zwar Beistand leisten müsse, mahnten aber Besonnenheit an. Lediglich die PDS nahm eine generell ablehnende Haltung ein.

US-Außenminister Colin Powell bezeichnete erstmals öffentlich den moslemischen Extremisten Osama Bin Laden als Verdächtigen für die Terror-Anschläge in New York und Washington. Bin Laden hält sich in Afghanistan versteckt. Die dort regierende Taliban-Miliz hat den Fundamentalisten als unschuldig bezeichnet und seine Auslieferung an die USA strikt abgelehnt. Er werde mit dem pakistanischen Staatschef Pervez Musharraf über Bin Laden beraten, sagte Powell in Washington. Pakistan ist eines der wenigen Länder, welche die Taliban-Regierung im benachbarten Afghanistan anerkennen.

Der neue US-Botschafter Dan Coats dankte Deutschland für seine Solidarität. Nach einem Treffen mit Außenminister Joschka Fischer (Grüne) sagte Coats, Amerika erwarte, dass Deutschland und Europa die USA im Kampf gegen den Terrorismus unterstützen. Fischer erklärte, Bündnisse seien nicht nur für gute, sondern vor allem für schlechte Zeiten da. Millionen Menschen verharrten am Vormittag während einer bundesweiten Gedenkpause schweigend im Andenken an die Opfer.

In New York gelten nach dem Anschlag mehr als 4 700 Menschen offiziell als vermisst. Am Donnerstag wurden noch mehrere verschüttete Feuerwehrleute lebend geborgen. Bei dem Anschlag auf das US-Verteidigungsministerium sind etwa 190 Menschen ums Leben gekommen, darunter auch die 64 Insassen des in das Gebäude gestürzten Flugzeuges.

Die Unionsfraktion im Bundestag verlangt nach dem Terror in den USA neue Schwerpunkte in der deutschen Politik. Fraktionschef Friedrich Merz (CDU) sagte nach einer Sitzung der Fraktionsspitze, der inneren und äußeren Sicherheit sowie dem friedlichen Zusammenleben in der Bundesrepublik müsse mehr Beachtung geschenkt werden. Zugleich stellte sich die Fraktion voll hinter den Nato-Beschluss. FDP-Chef Guido Westerwelle sagte, zu der Nato-Entscheidung gebe es „keine Alternative".

PDS lehnt ab

Die Grünen unterstützten den Nato-Beschluss. Dies sei aber kein „Blankoscheck, keine Vorentscheidung" für einen Militäreinsatz der Bundeswehr, erklärten die Grünen-Vorsitzenden Claudia Roth und Fritz Kuhn. Der PDS-Fraktionsvorsitzende Roland Claus sagte der „Berliner Zeitung", seine Partei halte den Nato-Beschluss für bedenklich. Er befürchte, dass eine Spirale der Gewalt in Gang gesetzt werde, die sich nicht mehr stoppen lasse. *(po.)*

SOLIDARITÄT MIT AMERIKA

Ein Zeichen der Solidarität mit den Menschen in den USA soll an diesem Freitag von Berlin ausgehen. Die „Berliner Zeitung" veröffentlicht an dieser Stelle einen Aufruf, der von den Vorsitzenden aller im Bundestag vertretenen Parteien unterzeichnet ist:

Der 11. September 2001 hat alle Menschen in Deutschland, Europa und der ganzen Welt in tiefe Trauer und Bestürzung versetzt. Wir alle in Deutschland sind voller Abscheu über die terroristischen Anschläge in den Vereinigten Staaten von Amerika. Dies ist ein Angriff gegen die gesamte zivilisierte Welt, ein Angriff auf die Grundwerte menschlichen Zusammenlebens. Jetzt müssen alle Demokraten zusammenstehen, um den Frieden und die Freiheit in dieser Welt zu verteidigen und gemeinsam entschlossen den Terror zu bekämpfen. Unsere Solidarität gilt dem ganzen amerikanischen Volk. Unser Mitgefühl gilt den Opfern und deren Angehörigen.
Wir versammeln uns in Berlin, am Freitag, dem 14. September 2001, um 17 Uhr am Brandenburger Tor

WEITERE BEITRÄGE

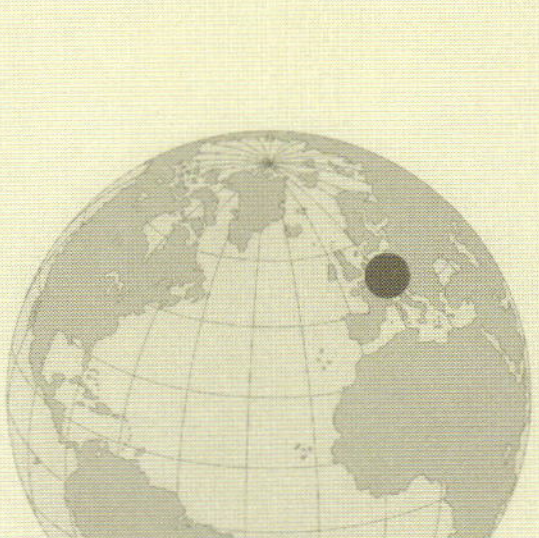

BERLINER ZEITUNG
WWW.BERLINERZEITUNG.DE
DEUTSCHLAND, BERLIN

14

Mo.-Fr. 1,40 DM – Sa. 1,70 DM

EX

WESTDEUTSCHE ALLGEMEINE

Die Zeitung des Ruhrgebiets **WAZ** Unabhängig – Überparteilich

www.waz.de Nummer 214 / 37. Woche Deutschlands größte Regionalzeitung 1 Freitag, 14. September 2001

Angst vor einem Rachekrieg

Fischer mahnt USA zur Besonnenheit - Offenbar Ultimatum an Afghanistan

WAZ Washington. Die US-Regierung ist offenbar fest entschlossen, einen Vergeltungskrieg für die Terrorangriffe in New York und Washington zu führen. In den übrigen NATO-Staaten wächst die Furcht, in einen schwer kalkulierbaren Konflikt gezogen zu werden.

US-Präsident Georg W. Bush kündigte eine militärische Antwort auf die Flugzeuganschläge vom Dienstag an und sprach vom „ersten Krieg des 21. Jahrhunderts". Der stellvertretende US-Verteidigungsminister Paul Wolfowitz erklärte, es werde eine andauernde militärische Vergeltung geben.

Derweil verdichten sich die Anzeichen, dass die USA einen Angriff auf Afghanistan planen. Dort halten die radikal-islamischen Taliban den saudiarabischen Terroristen Osama bin Laden versteckt. Er ist nach Ansicht der US-Regierung der Hauptverdächtige für die Gewaltakte.

Aus Angst vor Vergeltungsschlägen hätten nahezu alle Ausländer die afghanische Hauptstadt Kabul verlassen, berichtete die Nachrichtenagentur Reuters. Zudem hätten die USA im angrenzenden Pakistan Militärmachthaber Musharraf um Unterstützung gebeten. Gerüchten zufolge hat die US-Regierung den Taliban ein Ultimatum zur Auslieferung bin Ladens gestellt. US-Verteidigungsminister Donald Rumsfeld schwor die Truppen in einer Botschaft bereits ein: „Sehr, sehr viel wird von euch in den nächsten Wochen und Monaten verlangt werden."

Dagegen mahnte Bundesaußenminister Joschka Fischer (Grüne) das Weiße Haus zur Besonnenheit. Im Kampf gegen den Terrorismus müssten Deutschland, Europa und die USA mit Entschlossenheit, kühlem Kopf und Gelassenheit vorgehen. Verteidigungsminister Rudolf Scharping (SPD) warnte davor, nur mit militärischen Mitteln zu reagieren. „Wir stehen nicht vor einem Krieg, wir stehen vor der Frage, was ist eine angemessene Antwort", sagte Scharping. Frankreichs Staatspräsident Jacques Chirac stellte sich dagegen bedingungslos hinter Bush: Die Wahl der Mittel im Kampf gegen den Terrorismus liege jetzt bei den USA, sagte Chirac.

Die NATO hat erstmals in ihrer Geschichte den so genannten „kollektiven Verteidigungsfall" festgestellt, der alle Mitgliedsstaaten der Allianz zur Unterstützung der Amerikaner anhält - wenn der Urheber der Terrorschläge feststeht und die USA Hilfe einfordern. „Aktionen sind im Rahmen der NATO derzeit nicht geplant", versicherte jedoch der deutsche NATO-Botschafter Gebhardt von Moltke in Brüssel.

Fünf Feuerwehrleute aus Trümmern gerettet

Unterdessen gibt es über die Zahl der Opfer des Terrors weiter nur Schätzungen. Mindestens 4763 Menschen würden noch vermisst, sagte New Yorks Bürgermeister Rudolph Giuliani. Die Gerichtsmediziner hätten 94 Tote identifiziert. Zudem seien in den Trümmern des World Trade Centers zahlreiche Leichenteile gefunden worden. Fünf Feuerwehrleute wurden lebend geborgen.

Noch Wochen sollen sich Rettungskräfte mit schwerem Gerät und bloßen Händen durch die Trümmerberge graben. Der US-Kongress bewilligte Soforthilfen von 43 Mrd DM.

Erschöpft: Bill Fennelly von der Freiwilligen Feuerwehr ruht sich für einen Moment aus. Die Helfer leisten Schwerstarbeit. Am Donnerstag konnten sie fünf Kollegen aus den Trümmern retten. ap-Bild

Heute: Erst nachmittags wird es freundlicher, bis 16 Grad.

Samstag: Stark bewölkt und regnerisch, bis 16 Grad.

Sonntag: Weiterhin sehr unfreundlich, bis 15 Grad.

Spur der Terroristen führt auch nach Deutschland

Drei Flugzeugentführer lebten in Hamburg

WAZ Hamburg. Die Terrorangriffe auf die USA mit mehreren tausend Todesopfern sind offenbar auch von Deutschland aus vorbereitet worden.

In Hamburg nahm die Polizei bei mehreren Wohnungsdurchsuchungen einen Verdächtigen vorläufig fest. Der Mann mit ägyptischen Pass soll am Flughafen Fuhlsbüttel gearbeitet haben. Ferner sollen drei der für die Terrorakte Verantwortlichen in der Hansestadt gelebt und studiert haben. Seit dem gestrigen Donnerstag ermittelt das Bundeskriminalamt gegen mehrere mutmaßliche Mitglieder einer terroristischen Vereinigung.

Laut Generalbundesanwalt Nehm saßen zwei der Tatverdächtigen, die zeitweise in Hamburg lebten, in der ersten Maschine, die auf das World Trade Center stürzte. Ein Dritter saß in einem ebenfalls entführten Flugzeug, das in Pennsylvania abstürzte. In einem Gepäckstück, das einer der drei am Flughafen Boston zurückgelassen habe, seien Uniformstücke und ein Abschiedsbrief gefunden worden, erklärte der Bundesanwalt.

Insgesamt waren nach Angaben von US-Generalstaatsanwalt John Ashcroft zwölf bis 24 Personen an der Entführung der vier Flugzeuge beteiligt, von denen zwei in die Türme des New Yorker World Trade Centers rasten und eines ins Washingtoner Verteidigungsministerium stürzte. Die Täter sollen von etwa 24 weiteren Personen unterstützt worden sein.

An der gesamten Aktion waren nach Informationen aus Justizkreisen offenbar mehrere terroristische Zellen beteiligt, die Verbindungen zu arabischen Ländern wie Saudi-Arabien und Ägypten unterhalten haben sollen. In den US-Staaten Massachusetts und Florida wurden mindestens sechs Personen festgenommen.

4 394488 201407 40040

Drohungen und Übergriffe gegen Araber in USA

Washington. Nach den Anschlägen in New York und Washington sind in den USA zahlreiche Amerikaner arabischer Abstammung Opfer von Attacken geworden. In Moscheen und Läden wurden Fenster eingeschlagen und Todesdrohungen hinterlassen, islamische Zentren wurden mit hasserfüllter Graffiti beschmiert. In einem Vorort Chicagos versuchten 300 Amerikaner, eine Moschee zu stürmen. (ap)

Shelter Now fürchtet um inhaftierte Mitarbeiter in Kabul

Halle. Nach Abzug fast aller ausländischen Helfer und Diplomaten aus Afghanistan hat sich die Hilfsorganisation „Shelter Now" besorgt über einen möglichen Abbruch der Kontakte zu ihren inhaftierten Mitarbeitern geäußert. Den Inhaftierten gehe es zwar gut, sagte ein Sprecher der Organisation. Er sei sich aber nicht sicher, ob ihnen bewusst ist, dass sie derzeit fast die einzigen Ausländer in Afghanistan sind. (epd)

Verstärkte Suche nach Messern in Flugzeugen

Frankfurt. Nach den Anschlägen in den USA sind Messer und Scheren in der Flugzeugkabine nur noch in Ausnahmefällen zugelassen. Die Frankfurter Flughafengesellschaft Fraport teilte mit, ihr Personal werde auf solche Gegenstände künftig verstärkt achten. Die Flughafenbetreiber riefen die Passagiere auf, wegen verschärfter Sicherheitsvorschriften rechtzeitig zum Flughafen zu reisen. (ap)

Letzte Gedanken gelten den Liebsten

New York, der Terror, der Tod - was geschah, hat unfassbare Dimensionen. Nicht nur, weil sich die mächtigste Militärmacht aller Zeiten anschickt, mit einem Krieg Vergeltung zu üben. Nein, das Grauen zeigt sich auf furchtbare Weise in bizzarer Banalität.

Niemand kennt bisher die genaue Zahl der Toten unter den Trümmern der Türme. So hat Bürgermeister Rudolph Giuliani 6000 Leichensäcke angefordert, sicherheitshalber. Und ein Geschäft, in das bis Dienstag, Ortszeit 9 Uhr, Familien einkehrten, um Hemden und Kleider zu kaufen, ist jetzt „Lager" von Leichen - New York, der lebendige, lebenslustige Organismus, der täglich abertausenden Menschen jeden noch so ausgefallenen und luxuriösen Wunsch zu erfüllen vermag, erstarrt angesichts dieser Art Tod.

Ein tausendfacher Tod war es. Die Zahlen erschrecken; doch der Tod bleibt anonym: Zahlen sind keine Menschen.

Wie ein Stich ins Herz aber treffen schlichte, wenige Worte: „Mom, ich liebe dich so sehr!" rief Mark Bingham in sein Handy. Wie sehr sie ihren Mann liebe „und die Jungen" - nur das noch zu sagen, war auch CeeCee Lyles letzter Wunsch. Beide saßen im Jet, der bei Pittsburgh zerschellte.

Mark Bingham und CeeCee Lyles - zwei Fremde. Doch wie sich ihr Geist in Todesahnung den Liebsten zuwendet, rührt an, bringt sie uns nah'. Und mit Schmerz blickt man in die Fratze des Terrorismus; in blinde, gnadenlose Brutalität. „Vergeltung"? Danach darf sie sich nicht richten. **Rolf Potthoff**

BEILAGEN

BWZ Cocktail

Cocktail: Er hieß Puff Daddy und hatte einen peinlichen Abgang. Jetzt kehrt der HipHop-Star als P. Diddy zurück.
Treffpunkte: Die wichtigsten Termine der nächsten Woche.

TERROR GEGEN DIE FREIE WELT

Berichte, Kommentare, Analysen auf zwölf Seiten

- Seite 2: Leitartikel „Der Sommer 1914" von Uwe Knüpfer. Leitartikel „Radikale Fanatiker" von Alfons Pieper Korrespondentenbericht aus Brüssel: „Das machen die Amerikaner allein"
- WAZ Extra: Helden in den Flugzeugen, Bedrohungslage in Berlin, Fahndungserfolge, Lesermeinungen, die Taliban, Schurkenstaaten, Umgang mit den Ängsten.
- Aus dem Westen: Erlebnisbericht von Lena Ohlms.
- Kultur: Die Katastrophe jenseits von Hollywood
- Ruhrgebiet: Wie das Revier der Opfer der Terroranschläge gedenkt.
- Fernsehen: TV-Kritik.

- In der ganzen EU finden am heutigen Freitag um 12 Uhr Schweigeminuten statt. Die WAZ-Mediengruppe schließt sich mit allen Mitarbeiterinnen und Mitarbeitern an.

WWW.WAZ.DE

USA: Der Terror und die Folgen für die Welt

Wir unterrichten Sie in zwei Extras über die neuesten Entwicklungen und zeigen die aktuellsten Bilder: Klicken Sie „Nach dem Terror" sowie „WAZ-Extra". Wenn Sie Ihre persönliche Meinung äußern möchten: Unser Gästebuch ist weiterhin für Sie geöffnet.

DIE BÖRSE

Dax	NEMAX	Dow Jones	Euro
4392 (20.00) 4335 (Vort.)	**857** (20.00) 849 (Vortag)	**geschlossen** geschl. (Vortag)	0,9060 $ 0,9052 (Vort.)

Tagesgew.: Henkel VA 68,58 (+7,02%) **Verlierer: Adidas 65,89** (-3,10%)

Es gibt keinen Weg zum Frieden. Der Frieden ist der Weg. *Mahatma Gandhi*

Weithin sichtbar

Manhatten aus der Satellitenperspektive: Die Aufnahme aus 677 km Höhe vom 12. September zeigt den Rauch, der aus den Trümmern des Word Trade Centers in New York aufsteigt.

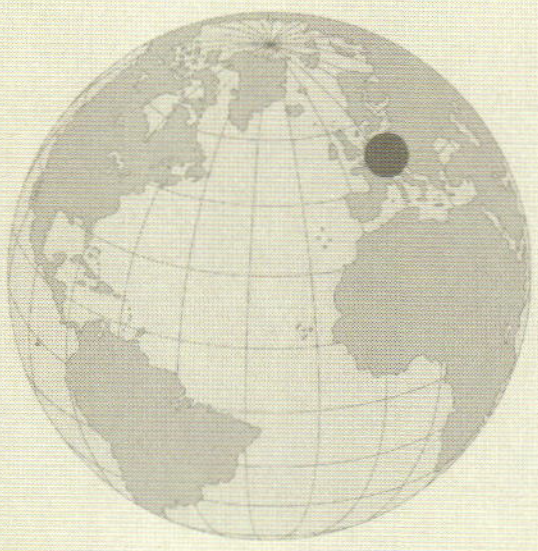

Westdeutsche Allgemeine (WAZ)
www.waz.de
Deutschland, Essen

14

Ausgabe Saarbrücken-Mitte
G 6024

Abo-Service: (06 81) 502 502
Privatanzeigen: (06 81) 502 503
Redaktion: (06 81) 502 504

INTERNET: www.sz-newsline.de

Saarbrücker Zeitung

UNABHÄNGIG GEGRÜNDET 1761 ÜBERPARTEILICH

Nr. 214 FREITAG, 14. SEPTEMBER 2001 Einzelpreis 2,30 Mark / 8,40 FF / 55 Flux / 330 Pta / 3100 Lit / 60 BEF / 1,18 Euro

Bush erklärt Terroristen den Krieg

Mehrere Selbstmord-Attentäter kamen offenbar aus Deutschland – US-Verteidigungsministerium: Wir werden ganze Staaten ausschalten

Bereit zur Vergeltung US-Präsident George W. Bush hat klargemacht, dass er in mehreren Schlägen auf den Terror-Akt von New York und Washington reagieren wird. Sein Ziel ist offenbar Osama Bin Laden. FOTO: REUTERS

Die Spur der Terroristen, die in den USA Tausende Menschen töteten, führt nach Deutschland. US-Präsident Bush will Krieg gegen die Hinterleute führen. Dabei stehen die Nato-Partner an der Seite der USA.

Washington/Karlsruhe (red). US-Präsident George W. Bush hat eine militärische Antwort auf die Terrorangriffe in New York und Washington angekündigt und vom „ersten Krieg des 21. Jahrhunderts" gesprochen. In Gesprächen mit mehreren Staats- und Regierungschefs habe er Unterstützung für jede Art von Vergeltung erhalten, die er anordnen werde, sagte Bush am Donnerstag.

„Ich bin fest entschlossen, diesen gegen Amerika erklärten Krieg zu gewinnen", erklärte Bush. Die Nato hatte am Mittwochabend erstmals in ihrer Geschichte den kollektiven Verteidigungsfall festgestellt. US-Vize-Verteidigungsminister Paul Wolfowitz kündigte an, es

Zu den Folgen der Terror-Anschläge auf die USA lesen Sie auf Seite 2: Leitartikel und Kommentar; Seiten 2, 3, 4, Wirtschaft Kultur und Lokales: Weitere Berichte.

werde nicht bei einem Vergeltungsschlag bleiben: „Es wird ein Feldzug und keine einzelne Aktion". Es gehe darum, Staaten auszuschalten („ending states"), die Terrorismus unterstützten. Als Hauptverdächtiger für die Attacken mit gekaperten Flugzeugen auf beide Türme des World Trade Centers in New York und das Pentagon in Washington sowie für den Absturz einer weiteren Maschine wird zumeist der saudische Millionär Osama Bin Laden genannt, der sich zuletzt überwiegend in Afghanistan aufhielt. Die Anschläge wurden offenbar auch von Deutschland aus vorbereitet. Die Bundesanwaltschaft ermittelt gegen eine islamistische Gruppe in Hamburg.

Feind Amerikas Der Multi-Millionär Osama Bin Laden bestreitet die Mittäterschaft an den Anschlägen. Doch die USA sehen in ihm den Drahtzieher. Schließlich hat er dem Land den Krieg erklärt. Nun will Amerika antworten. FOTO: REUTERS

SAARBRÜCKEN

SPD hofft auf Abweichler

Horst Schmeer kandidiert für das Amt des Saarbrücker Bürgermeisters, Lutz Lange für das Amt des Finanzdezernenten. Das beschlossen am Mittwoch Delegierte aus 23 Ortsvereinen der SPD mit deutlicher Mehrheit. Dabei hofft die SPD auf Stimmen von Abweichlern aus der schwarz-grünen Koalition. Nur so haben die beiden bei der Wahl eine Chance. *(Lokales, Seite L1: Bericht)*

INHALT

Saar-Wetter

Heute gibt es einen raschen Wechsel von stärkerer Bewölkung mit zum Teil kräftigem Regen und kurzen freundlichen Abschnitten.
Seite 7 +16°

Keiner steppte wie Fred Astaire

Nicht unbedingt schön, aber spritzig und elegant – so kennen Filmfans Fred Astaire. In den 30er und 40er Jahren steppte keiner so wie er. Heute stellen wir den „Leinwand-Helden" Astaire vor.
Blick in die Welt/Seite 8

THEATER ZEIT. SAAR STAATS THEATER
Oktober 2001

Das Saarländische Staatstheater informiert über die Premieren im Monat Oktober. Von Interesse ist ein dreiteiliger Schönberg-Abend, bei dem die große Sängerin Gwyneth Jones mitwirkt.
THEATERZEIT liegt der Zeitung bei.

Das Fernseh- und Hörfunkprogramm, Teletipps der Woche, Neues vom SR auf dem Halberg, Rätsel, Schach und Skat, Münzen und Briefmarken: Das finden Sie heute in unserer Beilage.

Die Gewinnzahlen und Gewinnquoten finden Sie heute auf Seite 7

Wie wir Katastrophenbilder sehen

Wie tief die Scheinwelt des Kinos in unsere Köpfe eindringt, zeigt sich jetzt, wenn die grausame Terror-Wirklichkeit die Fiktion der Katastrophen-Filme einholt. Unsere Kino-Kolumne handelt von Katastrophen-Bildern.
Kultur/Seite 6

Das aktuelle Fernsehprogramm und Hörfunktipps finden Sie heute auf Seite 13

Häkkinen hört offenbar auf

Das Ende der Formel-1-Karriere von Mika Häkkinen scheint beschlossene Sache. Nach Angabe aus Teamkreisen will der Weltmeister von 1998 und 1999 an diesem Samstag in Monza seinen Rücktritt zum Saisonende erklären.
Sport/Seite 15

New Yorker Börse öffnet am Montag

New York/Frankfurt (ap). Abwarten lautete die Devise gestern an den europäischen Aktienmärkten: Denn den dritten Tag in Folge war die New Yorker Börse wegen des Terroranschlags in den USA geschlossen. Sie wird den Handel am Montag wieder aufnehmen, wie gestern Abend in New York bekannt wurde. Entsprechend vorsichtig agierten die Investoren an den europäischen Aktienmärkten. Nach leichten Gewinnen am Vormittag lag der Dax am späten Nachmittag mit 0,65 Prozent im Minus. Der Nemax 50 verzeichnete ein Plus von 0,43 Prozent. An den Börsen in London und Paris zeigten die Kurse leicht nach unten.

4 394976 002301 60137

Die Welt trauert mit Amerika

Millionen schweigen in Deutschland zu Ehren der Opfer – 4763 Vermisste in New York

Saarbrücken/Berlin/New York (red). Die Trauer um die Toten des Terrors in den USA hat am Donnerstag Millionen Menschen in Deutschland vereint: In Betrieben, Behörden und Schulen auch im Saarland gedachten sie um zehn Uhr in fünf Schweigeminuten den Opfern der Anschläge in den USA. Busse und Bahnen standen still, Montagebänder wurden abgeschaltet, Radiosender verstummten, Glocken läuteten. Auch die Bundesregierung und Bundeskanzler Gerhard Schröder beteiligten sich an dem Aufruf des DGB und der Arbeitgeberverbände. Bundesinnenminister Otto Schily verlängerte die Trauerbeflaggung für alle Bundeseinrichtungen bis zum heutigen Freitag. Vor der amerikanischen Botschaft in Berlin versammelten sich Hunderte mit Kerzen und Blumen.

Die Zahl der nach dem Terroranschlag in New York vermissten Menschen stieg am Donnerstag auf 4763. Hoffnung auf Überlebende gab es kaum noch, auch wenn aus den Trümmern des World Trade Centers nach Angaben von Bürgermeister Rudolph Giuliani bis Donnerstag erst 94 Menschen tot geborgen wurden. Von diesen konnten höchstens 30 identifiziert werden. Einzelne Firmen vermissten Hunderte Angestellte. Allein das auf Staatsanleihen spezialisierte Finanzhaus Cantor Fitzgerald L.P. wartete auf ein Lebenszeichen von 730 der 1000 Mitarbeiter. Der Finanzdienstleister Marsh and McLennan vermisst 700 Mitarbeiter, die in den Zwillingstürmen des World Trade Centers arbeiteten. Die Geschäftsbank Keefe Bruyette and Woods, die ihre Büros im 89. und 90. Stock des Südturmes hatte, weiß bei 69 ihrer 172 Angestellten nichts über deren Verbleib. Mehr als 3000 Tonnen Trümmer und Schutt des World Trade Centers wurden zur Untersuchung zu einer ehemaligen Müllkippe nach Staten Island gebracht. US-Präsident George W. Bush will heute nach New York reisen und sich selbst ein Bild von den Zerstörungen durch die Terror-Anschläge auf das World Trade Center machen.

Bei dem Angriff auf das Verteidigungsministerium in Washington kamen nach vorläufiger offizieller Schätzung 190 Menschen ums Leben, einschließlich der 64 Menschen an Bord des als Waffe eingesetzten Passagierflugzeugs. Bis Donnerstagmittag wurden 70 Tote geborgen.

Schweigen Porsche-Mitarbeiter in Stuttgart-Zuffenhausen gedenken am Donnerstag wie Millionen andere Deutsche mit einer Schweige-Minute der Menschen, die Opfer der Terror-Anschläge in den USA wurden. FOTO: DPA

Neuer Technik-Studiengang im Saarland

Saar-Regierung unterstützt Akademie der Wirtschaft mit 1,2 Millionen Mark

Saarbrücken (pr). Das Saarland komplettiert sein Studien-Angebot: Ab Wintersemester 2002 wird an der ASW (Akademie der Saarwirtschaft) ein dreijähriger Studiengang angeboten, der zum „Diplom-Ingenieur Maschinenbau (BA Saarland)" führt. Wie Ministerpräsident Peter Müller, Kultusminister Jürgen Schreier, Walter Koch, Präsident des Verbandes der Metall- und Elektroindustrie des Saarlandes (ME Saar) und Winfried Kallenborn, Vorstandsvorsitzender der ASW, gestern in Saarbrücken vor der Presse mitteilten, wird das Studium an der Berufsakademie finanziell im Wesentlichen von 14 saarländischen Unternehmen getragen, die sich pro Student mit 80 000 bis 100 000 Mark engagieren werden. Das Saarland wird in den ersten sechs Jahren insgesamt 1,2 Millionen Mark beisteuern, um die Vorbereitungs- und Anlaufkosten zu decken. Wenn der Betrieb voll läuft, sollen insgesamt gut 150 Studenten in St. Ingbert eingeschrieben sein.

Regierung und Wirtschaft legen Wert darauf, dass der neue Studiengang nicht als Konkurrenz zu der Ausbildung an Saar-Uni oder Fachhochschule (HTW) zu sehen ist, sondern zusätzlich junge Menschen für die Naturwissenschaften gewinnt. Angesprochen werden sollen vor allem Fachabiturienten.

Für Müller ist die Einrichtung eines technischen Studienganges ein wichtiger Mosaikstein, das Saarland als Wirtschaftsstandort attraktiv zu machen. Offen ist noch die bundesweite Anerkennung des Studienganges, die durch die Kultusminister-Konferenz erfolgen muss. Darum will sich die Regierung bemühen. „Wenn es aber nicht anders geht, machen wir es allein!", so Müller. *(Seite 2: Kommentar; Seite 9: Weiterer Bericht)*

Mehr zum Thema finden Sie im SZ-Internet-Angebot: www.sz-newsline.de/kompass

KURZ

Saar-Polizei mit Trauerflor unterwegs

Saarbrücken (mju). Zum Gedenken an die Opfer der Terror-Tragödie in den USA, unter denen auch zahlreiche Rettungs- und Sicherheitskräfte sind, fahren alle Streifenwagen der Saar-Polizei bis auf weiteres mit Trauerflor. Polizisten und Feuerwehrleute stehen auch heute ab 15.15 Uhr an der Saarbrücker Ludwigskirche Spalier. Dort findet um 16 Uhr ein ökumenischer Solidaritätsgottesdienst statt, zu dem Landesregierung und Landtag eingeladen haben.

Familien-Show wird verschoben

Saarbrücken (red). Saarland Online, Saar-Shopping, energis, Schmidt-Küchen und die Saarmesse GmbH haben die Kindershow auf der Welt der Familie (Samstag und Sonntag) abgesagt. Grund: Die tragischen Ereignisse in den USA. Das komplette Programm – unter anderem mit den Fernseh-Stars Marijke Amado, Harry Wijnvoord und Matthias Krings – wird zu einem späteren Zeitpunkt nachgeholt. *(Bericht folgt in unserer Samstag-Ausgabe, siehe auch Wirtschaft)*

Zum Teil wieder Flüge über den Nordatlantik

Frankfurt (ap). Nachdem der amerikanische Luftraum am gestrigen Donnerstag wieder freigegeben wurde, haben die Fluggesellschaften United Airlines und Northwest Airlines erklärt, ihre Nordatlantikflüge würden voraussichtlich am heutigen Freitag wieder aufgenommen. Bei der Lufthansa stand die Entscheidung am Donnerstagabend noch aus. In der Nacht sollte der erste Lufthansaflug aus Kanada in Frankfurt eintreffen.

Viele Veranstaltungen im Saarland abgesagt

Saarbrücken (red). Wer in den nächsten Tagen Veranstaltungen besuchen will, sollte sich zuvor noch einmal rückversichern, ob diese auch tatsächlich stattfinden. Aufgrund der Terror-Anschläge wurden bereits viele Termine abgesagt. So beispielsweise das Richtfest für den Neubau von IDS Scheer, die Premiere Detlev Schönauers neuem Kabarett-Programm, aber auch der CDU-Landesparteitag und die Frauen-Bundesliga.

RESSORT THEMEN DES TAGES
TEL.: (0681) 502 20 51
FAX.: (0681) 502 20 59
E-MAIL: themen@sz-sb.de

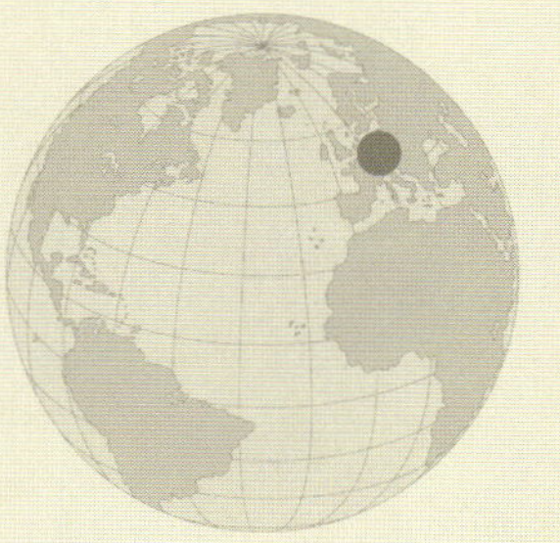

SAARBRÜCKER ZEITUNG
WWW.SZ-NEWSLINE.DE
DEUTSCHLAND, SAARBRÜCKEN

14

Foto: Reuters

LENKTE ER EINEN KAMIKAZEJET?
VERDÄCHTIGER LIESS SICH IN FLORIDA IN EINER FLUGSCHULE AUSBILDEN Seite 2

JA 48 %
NEIN 44 %

AKTION GEGEN DEN TERROR:
NUR KNAPPE MEHRHEIT DAFÜR, DASS SICH ÖSTERREICH SOLIDARISIERT Seite 18

OÖNachrichten

Nr. 212 • Freitag, 14. September 2001 — UNABHÄNGIG — www.nachrichten.at S 12.– / € 0,87

Amerika kennt die Täter, Russland nennt Drahtzieher Nato folgt USA in den Kampf

NEW YORK/HAMBURG. Amerika kennt die Namen von 50 mutmaßlichen Beteiligten an der Terror-Attacke, aber nicht die der Drahtzieher. Zwei der Selbstmord-Flugzeugentführer lebten im Hamburg.

Russische Quellen nannten gestern Osama Bin Laden, die „Islamische Bewegung Usbekistans" und das Taliban-Regime als Drahtzieher und behaupteten, Moskau habe die USA schon vor Wochen gewarnt. Die Stichhaltigkeit dieser Informationen steht nicht fest.

Gesichertes Faktum hingegen ist, dass drei Männer aus den Vereinigten Emiraten, die in Hamburg als Studenten lebten, maßgeblich am Überfall auf Amerika beteiligt waren. Zwei weils fünf Hijacker in zwei Maschinen, jeweils vier in die beiden anderen. Sie müssen laut US-Justizminister über eine mindestens Organisation mit be-Flugzeuge eingeschleust, jeweils fünf Hijacker in zwei Maschinen, jeweils vier in die beiden anderen. Sie müssen laut US-Justizminister über eine „komplexe Organisation mit bedeutender Unterstützung" verfügt haben. Mehr als 4000 FBI-Beamte sind bei der umfangreichsten Verbrecherjagd, die in den USA jemals lief, im Einsatz.

Allein in New York galten gestern 4763 Menschen als vermisst. Die Stadtverwaltung hat 11.000 „Body Bags" (Leichensäcke) bereitgestellt.

Trauertag in USA und EU

US-Präsident Bush hat den heutigen Freitag zum Trauer- und Gebetstag erklärt, sämtliche EU-Staaten schlossen sich dieser Initiative an.

Im Bemühen um internationale Solidarität hat Bush mit der formellen Beistandserklärung der europäischen Nato-Verbündeten einen ersten großen Erfolg erzielt. Der Präsident warb auch um die gemäßigte islamische Welt, indem er demonstrativ dazu aufrief, die amerikanischen Araber und Moslems mit „Respekt" zu behandeln. Das US-Verteidigungsministerium kündigte an, der Kampf gegen den Terror werde ein Feldzug, nicht ein Einzelschlag werden.

Kerzen erhellen die Dunkelheit der Trauer besser als Washingtons gleißende Lichter. Foto: AFP/EPA

Nachrichten Inhalt

Nachrichten Seiten

Wetter Nachrichten

Neue Regenschauer ziehen auf. Bis 16 Grad.
Seite 28

Nachrichten Adressen
Verlag: 4010 Linz, Promenade 23, 0732/7805-0
Anzeigenannahme: 0732/7805-500 Fax 0732/784821
Abonnenten-Service: 0732/7805-560, Fax 0732/794144
E-mail-Adressen: Redaktion@oon.at, Abo-service@oon.at, Anzeigen@oon.at
50037
9 005454 100024
P.b.b. Erscheinungsort Linz, Verlagspostamt 4020 Linz 01Z020284 K 01A020285

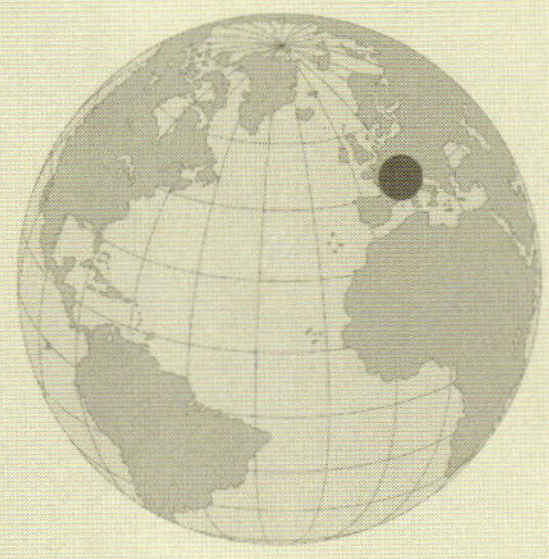

Oberösterreichische Nachrichten
www.nachrichten.at
Österreich, Linz

14

14. september 2001 ■ Årgang 117. Nr. 344 ■ www.politiken.dk • Pris 11,00 ■ Abonnementsservice 70 15 01 01

POLITIKEN

Nogen sol, men også enkelte regnbyger. Omkring 18 grader. Svag til let vind fra mellem vest og syd.

FREDAG

OVERBLIK

Værftsdirektør dømt igen

Den tidligere direktør for Svendborg Værft Per Glente fik i går halvandet års betinget fængsel. Østre Landsret mente, at han førte Skibskreditfonden bag lyset i 1986, da han var med til at overbelåne tre skibe.

Dommen er en stadfæstelse af en tidligere dom – blot med den forskel, at hele fængselsstraffen er gjort betinget, hvor den tidligere dom havde gjort tre af månederne ubetinget.

Per Glente har hele tiden erkendt, at han var med til at overbelåne de seks skibe i 1986, men han har samtidig sagt, at overbelåning var udbredt i branchen og accepteret af den siddende minister.

Den forklaring købte retten altså ikke.

1. SEKTION side 12
Ledende artikel
KULTUR & DEBAT side 4

EU-penge på vej til Femerbro

EU vil sætte en fast forbindelse over Femer Bælt på listen over de vigtigste europæiske trafikprojekter. Dermed er EU også parat til at hive de helt store pengesedler frem for at støtte byggeriet.

Det fremgår af en hvidbog om transportpolitik, som netop er offentliggjort. I hvidbogen oplyser EU, at støtten til vigtige jernbaneprojekter skal hæves til 20 procent. I forvejen støttes andre vigtige trafikprojekter med 10 procent.

Hvis medlemslandene vedtager den nye politik, kan det betyde EU-støtte på tre milliarder kroner til forbindelsen.

1. SEKTION side 11

Dåseøl rykker nærmere

Øl- og sodavandsdåser på de danske butikshylder rykkede et afgørende skridt nærmere, da EF-domstolens generaladvokat i går anbefalede, at det danske dåseforbud skal erklæres ulovligt. EF-domstolens dommere følger normalt indstillingerne fra generaladvokaten, og derfor har både bryggerierne og detailhandelen gjort alt klar til, at dåserne kan sættes på hylderne.

Miljø- og energiminister Svend Auken (S) siger, at det langtfra er givet, at EF-domstolen følger generaladvokatens indstilling.

Hos de konservative mener den politiske ordfører, Lene Espersen, at Auken skal lave en aftale med EU-kommissionen.

1. SEKTION side 14

5 708730 910150

USA udpeger bin Laden

I går oplyste de amerikanske myndigheder, at der savnes omkring 5.000 mennesker efter tirsdagens angreb. Kolleger til redningsarbejderne på billedet fik en opmuntring midt i det barske arbejde, da de reddede fem brandmænd. Det var uklart, hvor længe de fem havde været spærret inde i ruinerne af World Trade Center. – Foto: Stephen Chermin/AP

USA peger direkte på terrorlederen Osama bin Laden som den hovedmistænkte bag tirsdagens terror. I går søgte amerikanerne at sikre sig Pakistans støtte til at jagte bin Laden i Afghanistan. 5.000 frygtes dræbt.

Af Lars Halskov, Rasmus Emborg og Bjarne Schilling

USA udpegede i går for første gang officielt den kendte terrorleder Osama bin Laden som den hovedmistænkte bag attentaterne mod USA tirsdag, der anslås at have kostet omkring 5.000 mennesker livet.

USAs udenrigsminister, Colin Powell, skulle sent i går forhandle med Pakistans præsident, Pervez Musharraf, for at sikre sig støtte til at pågribe bin Laden, der menes at opholde sig i nabolandet Afghanistan. Dermed forekommer et amerikansk angreb på Afghanistan og Osama bin Laden stadig mere sandsynligt.

Der blev i går meldt om flugt fra Afghanistans hovedstad, Kabul, men lederen af det afghanske Talebanstyre, mullah Mohammad Omar, sagde ifølge nyhedsbureauet AFP, at bin Laden umuligt kunne have noget at gøre med attentaterne, fordi han ikke råder over nogen piloter og ikke havde mulighed for at træne dem, hvis han havde nogen.

Både Colin Powell og præsident George Bush har slået fast, at USA vil slå hårdt til med en gengældelse, og at de lande, der huser terrorister, risikerer angreb på lige fod med terroristerne selv. Samtidig har de dog understreget, at USA først vil slå til, når man er helt sikker på, hvem der bærer skylden.

I går rapporterede tv-stationen BBC, at Talebanstyret i Afghanistan skulle have sat bin Laden i husarrest, men sent i aftes var dette endnu ikke bekræftet.

Der er endnu ikke endegyldige beviser for, at bin Laden bærer skylden for angrebene, men i går lykkedes det forbundspolitiet, FBI, at komme et stort skridt videre i den største menneskejagt i USAs historie. FBI har kastet 7.000 medarbejdere ind i efterforskningen, og i går identificerede politiet mindst 50 personer, der sættes i forbindelse med angrebene.

Blandt de identificerede er de grupper af terrorister, i alt 18 mennesker, der kaprede de fire fly, som blev brugt ved angrebene. Samtidig jager politiet flere personer, der mistænkes for direkte at have hjulpet terroristerne på landjorden.

Tysk politi slog i går til med ransagninger i fire lejligheder i Hamburg, og to personer blev tilbageholdt. Politiet mener, at mindst en af de to mænd, der deltog som selvmordspiloter ved attentaterne, har boet i en af lejlighederne.

Sammen med en anden mand fik han flyveundervisning på en skole i Florida, og de blev identificeret, efter at der blev fundet arabisksprogede lærebøger i flyvning i en bil, som en af de to mænd havde lejet. Han optrådte også på passagerlisten til et af de kaprede fly.

Omkring 5.000 savnes

Mens efterforskningen skred hurtigt frem, gik det stadig langsomt med oprydningsarbejdet i ruindyngerne i New York og Washington, og håbet om at finde overlevende svinder.

Ifølge New Yorks borgmester, Rudolph Giuliani, savnes 4.763 personer efter attentatet mod byen, men oprydningsarbejdet er stadig overordentlig vanskeligt og farligt, fordi bygningsrester også i går styrtede ned. Redningsmandskabet havde i aftes, dansk tid, fundet 94 omkomne ved World Trade Center, men det var kun lykkedes at identificere 46. Byen har indkøbt næsten 11.000 ligposer. Ved Pentagon skønnedes tabstallet at være 190, og 70 omkomne var bragt ud af ruinerne.

Præsident George W. Bush ventes til New York i dag. Han ringede i går til borgmester Giuliani og New Yorks guvernør, George Pataki, og betegnede attentaterne som »den første krig i det 21. århundrede«.

Kongressen ventes at give præsident Bush støtte til at bruge den militære magt, han skønner nødvendig, samt bevilge 20 mia. dollar (ca. 165 milliarder kroner), som skal bruges på oprydningsarbejdet og på at styrke flysikkerheden i landet.

lars.halskov@pol.dk
rasmus.emborg@pol.dk
bjarne.schilling@pol.dk

1. SEKTION side 2-9
Ledende artikel
KULTUR & DEBAT side 4

TERROR

NATOs nye strategi
Aktiveringen af NATO-pagtens artikel 5 er en stor advarselsklokke til den, der benytter sig af terror – men også til dem, der huser terroristerne. Det siger NATOs generalsekretær i et eksklusivt interview om alliancens nye rolle.
1. SEKTION side 4

Dansker slap ud
Den danske ingeniør Peter Luke Carter var på arbejde på 72. etage, da World Trade Center blev angrebet af to fly. Trods de forfærdelige forhold bevarede de fleste roen, og det er en stor del af forklaringen på, at mange slap ud af bygningen, fortæller han.
1. SEKTION side 7

Ambivalente arabere
Mange palæstinensere i Danmark har en dobbelt holdning til bombeangrebet. På den ene side afskyer de massedrabet. På den anden side har supermagten USA høstet, som den har sået, lyder det.
1. SEKTION side 8

I kamp med kaprere
Passagererne på Flight 93 tog sagen i egen hånd og gik til modstand mod flykaprerne, da de via mobiltelefoner hørte, at World Trade Center var angrebet. Det kan være grunden til, at flyet styrtede ned i stedet for at ende som terrorbombe.
1. SEKTION side 9

EU-ledere i tæt politisamarbejde

Af Christian Lindhardt og Jens Bostrup, Bruxelles, og Kristian Klarskov

De 15 EU-lande vil i fremtiden arbejde tættere sammen for at forhindre terrorangreb som det, der forleden ramte USA. Samarbejdet skal omfatte både politi, strafferet og efterretning fremgår det af en erklæring, som der stadig sent i aftes blev arbejdet på i de 15 hovedstæder.

Erklæringen forventes udsendt her til morgen, og en talsmand for den belgiske ministerpræsident siger, at der er bred enighed blandt landene om hovedpunkterne i erklæringen. Den forventes også underskrevet af formændene for Europakommissionen og Europaparlamentet samt EUs udenrigspolitiske koordinator.

»Den vil indeholde et svar på, hvordan EU kan reagere på det, der er sket i USA, og hvordan vi kan forhindre det i fremtiden. I det svar kan man ikke udelukke hverken øget samarbejde om politi eller efterretning«, siger talsmanden.

Ifølge Politikens oplysninger forpligter regeringscheferne sig til at vedtage, at de gensidigt skal anerkende hinandens retsafgørelser, og at anholdelses- og udleveringsprocedurerne mellem landene skal forenkles. Ligesom samarbejdet om politi og efterretning er det ting, som EU-lederne tidligere har haft på dagsordenen, men med deres fælles erklæring sender de nu et markant signal om at området har særlig betydning og skal have endnu større prioritet.

Udenrigsminister Mogens Lykketoft bekræfter, at der arbejdes på en erklæring, der indeholder formuleringer om et øget samarbejde.

»Der er nogle formuleringer i den retning, men den er ikke færdiglavet endnu«, sagde han sent i aftes.

I dag vil det belgiske EU-formandskab desuden indkalde til et ekstraordinært møde i næste uge blandt EUs justits- og indenrigsministre.

christian.lindhardt@pol.dk
jens.bostrup@pol.dk

1 Die USA benennen bin Laden

2 Die USA zeigen direkt auf den Terroristen Osama bin Laden als Verantwortlichen für die Anschläge vom Dienstag. Gestern bemühten sich die Amerikaner um Pakistans Unterstützung für die Jagd auf bin Laden in Afghanistan. 5000 Tote werden befürchtet

Politiken
www.politiken.dk
Dänemark, Kopenhagen

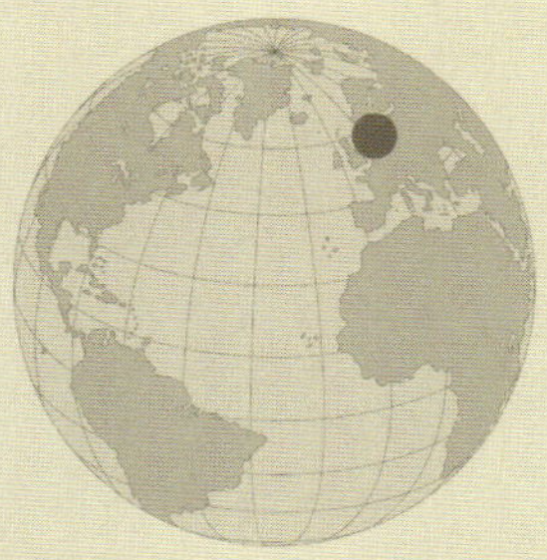

+++ Immer noch steigt Rauch auf aus den Trümmerbergen rund um das ehemalige Wahrzeichen Manhattans.

+++ Weinend betrachtet eine junge Frau am New Yorker Union Square ausgehängte Suchanzeigen von Menschen, die seit den Anschlägen vermisst werden.

+++ Rettungshelfer durchsuchen am 26. 9. 2001 ein Loch unter einem Trümmerberg in der Zone Ground Zero.

+++ Eine US-Flagge weht inmitten der Bagger und Kräne, die für die Aufräumarbeiten verwendet werden.

15. September

und die Zeit danach …

NATIONAL WEEKLY EDITION

The Washington Post

VOLUME 18, NO. 47 SEPTEMBER 17 - 23, 2001 www.nationalweekly.com $1.95

September 11, 2001

A Date Which Will Live in Infamy

DID WE THINK IT COULDN'T HAPPEN HERE?

A TEST OF BUSH'S PRESIDENCY

THE MESSAGE BEHIND THE MAYHEM

1 11. September 2001

Ein Datum, das in Schande überdauern wird

2 Haben wir gedacht, es könnte bei uns nicht passieren?

Eine Prüfung für Bushs Präsidentschaft

Die Botschaft hinter der Schreckenstat

The Washington Post,
National Weekly Edition
www.nationalweekly.com
www.washingtonpost.com
USA, Washington
(District of Columbia)

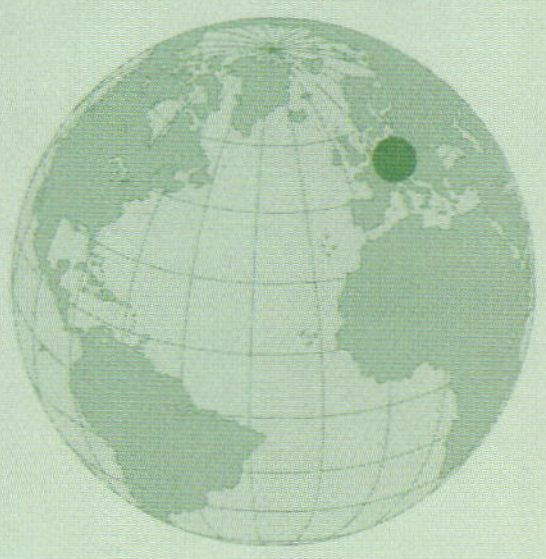

Spiegel
www.spiegel.de
Deutschland, Hamburg

Aachener Zeitung

Samstag, 15. September 2001 · 56. Jahrgang

Nummer 215 — 2,00 DM / 41,00 bfr / 2,25 hfl

AZ kompakt

Sport
Häkkinen macht ein Jahr „Babypause"
Seite 10

Kultur

Herr der alten Schule: Schauspieler Charles Regnier ist tot
Seite 7

Reise & Freizeit
Vom Barock bis zur Moderne: Wiens neue Mitte
Beilage

AZ lokal

Ulla Schmidt kandidiert erneut für den Bundestag
Aachen. Ohne Gegenstimme und ohne Enthaltung wurde Bundesgesundheitsministerin Ulla Schmidt gestern abend von den Aachener Sozialdemokraten wieder zur Bundestagskandidatin gewählt. Sie tritt gegen Dieter Bischoff an.

Das Wetter
14 / 10 — Schon am Morgen verdichten sich die Wolken, und es beginnt zu regnen.
Seite 2

Familienanzeigen
Heute im Produkt Wirtschaft und Service

Fußball aktuell

2. Bundesliga

Ahlen – Bochum	2:5
Oberhausen – Mainz	1:3
Saarbrücken – Duisburg	1:0

Telegramm

Vergeltung ja, aber ohne die Bundeswehr
Mainz. Nach den Terroranschlägen in den USA ist eine deutliche Mehrheit der Deutschen für militärische Vergeltung. Laut ZDF-Politbarometer bezeichnen 57 Prozent der Befragten Vergeltung als richtig, 35 Prozent als nicht richtig. Allerdings sind nur 37 Prozent für die Beteiligung der Bundeswehr, 57 Prozent dagegen. Unter den SPD-Anhängern befürworten 60 Prozent einen Gegenschlag, bei CDU/CSU 58, bei der FDP 54, bei den Grünen 31 und bei der PDS 43 Prozent.

AZ direkt

Zeitungsverkauf/-zustellung:
Tel. 0180 100 1400
Fax 0241/5101 790
Anzeigen-Annahme:
Tel. 0180 100 1200
Fax 0241/5101 790
Redaktion:
Tel. 0241/5101-310
Fax 0241/5101-360
Verlag:
Tel. 0241/5101-0 (Zentrale)

Die AZ im Internet:
www.aachener-zeitung.de

AZ web

4 394121 102009 60037

Geste der Betroffenheit und der Solidarität: In Aachen gedachten gestern rund 3000 Schüler aus über 20 Schulen der Opfer des Terrors in den USA. Sie stellten hunderte Grablichter auf und bildeten Menschenketten. Am Abend zogen rund 5000 Menschen schweigend durch die Innenstadt. Foto: Michael Jaspers

USA machen Weg für Vergeltung frei

● 35 000 Reservisten einberufen ● Taliban drohen mit Rache

New York/Berlin. In den USA laufen die Vorbereitungen für einen länger anhaltenden Schlag gegen Drahtzieher und Helfer der Terroranschläge auf Hochtouren. Kampfpiloten wurden in Alarmbereitschaft versetzt. Präsident George W. Bush rief am Freitag den nationalen Notstand aus und genehmigte die Einberufung von bis zu 50 000 Reservisten. Verteidigungsminister Donald Rumsfeld berief daraufhin 35 000 ein. Rumsfeld gab zu verstehen, dass man eine Kombination kurzfristiger Gegenschläge und langfristiger politischer, diplomatischer und wirtschaftlicher Maßnahmen plane. Eine einstimmig verabschiedete Resolution des US-Senats ermächtigt Bush, „alle erforderlichen und angemessenen Kräfte gegen Länder, Organisationen und Personen einzusetzen, die nach seiner Entscheidung die terroristischen Angriffe geplant, autorisiert oder unterstützt haben". Der Kongress bewilligte außerdem ein 40 Milliarden Dollar (86 Milliarden Mark) umfassendes Paket zum Kampf gegen den Terrorismus und für den Wiederaufbau. Die radikal-islamische Taliban-Regierung in Afghanistan drohte unterdessen mit Rache, sollten die USA wegen der Terroranschläge Vergeltung gegen ihr Land üben.

Lesen Sie auf Seite 3:
Die Bilder der Woche
Seite 4:
Suche nach der richtigen Strategie
Kommentar:
Die Woche des Angriffs
Seite 5:
Das Grauen holt Manhattan ein

Schwere Gewitterregen über New York behinderten am Freitag die Rettungsmannschaften und verwandelten die Trümmerberge des eingestürzten World Trade Centers in eine Schlammlandschaft. Unter den Resten der Wolkenkratzer werden noch mehr als 4700 Tote vermutet. Das Feuer im Pentagon ist inzwischen gelöscht. Dort wurde die Zahl der Opfer auf 190 geschätzt. In Washington und bei Pittsburgh wurden die Flugschreiber der dort abgestürzten Flugzeuge geborgen, von denen wichtige Daten über den Verlauf der Entführungen erwartet werden.

Auch in Deutschland geht die Suche nach Verdächtigen weiter. Ein in Hamburg festgenommener Mann wurde wieder freigelassen, weil sich der Tatverdacht nicht erhärtete. NRW-Innenminister Fritz Behrens räumte ein, es sei nicht auszuschließen, dass an den Anschlägen in den USA „Terroristen beteiligt waren, die sich früher auch in NRW aufgehalten haben". Nach einem Zeitungsbericht lebte und studierte einer der Attentäter einige Zeit in Bochum. Drei Personen aus NRW werden nach den Anschlägen in New York noch vermisst.

Millionen Europäer gedachten gestern an dem von der EU ausgerufenen „Tag der Trauer" der Terroropfer mit Schweigeminuten. In ganz Deutschland läuteten die Kirchenglocken. Die politische Führung Deutschlands gedachte am Brandenburger Tor in Berlin unter dem Motto „Keine Macht dem Terror" der Opfer. (dpa/rtr)

Sicherheit in Deutschland wird teurer

Berlin. Bundesinnenminister Otto Schily kann nach den Anschlägen in den USA mit mehr Geld für die Innere Sicherheit rechnen. Bundeskanzler Gerhard Schröder sagte gestern, alles, was Schily sinnvollerweise anfordere, „wird der Finanzminister zu bedienen haben". Finanzminister Hans Eichel signalisierte Bereitschaft, mehr Geld per Umschichtung bereitzustellen.

Als Reaktion auf die Anschläge sind unterdessen auch in Deutschland die Fluggast- und Gepäckkontrollen auf Flughäfen verschärft worden. Angesichts wachsender Furcht vor Terror-Aktionen in Deutschland wird die Gefährdung unterschiedlich eingeschätzt. Regierungssprecher Uwe-Karsten Heye betonte, man stehe „nicht vor einem Krieg". Auch Schily erklärte, es bestehe „keine aktuelle Gefahr für unser Land". Man müsse sich aber auf Veränderungen einstellen. Dabei „kann es sein, dass wir polizeiliche Ziele auch mit militärischen Mitteln zu erreichen versuchen".

Dagegen zeigte sich der Sprecher des niedersächsischen Verfassungsschutzes, Rüdiger Hesse, besorgt: „Die zentrale Sicherheitsherausforderung geht von militanten Islamisten aus." Die Innenminister Bayerns und Niedersachsens hatten Befürchtungen geäußert, Deutschland könne besonders gefährdet sein, wenn Amerika zurückschlage und sich Terrorkommandos wegen der strikten Kontrollen in den USA in Europa Ersatzziele suchten.

Sie geben nicht auf: Starke Gewitter erschwerten gestern den Rettungskräften die Arbeit in den Trümmerbergen des New Yorker World Trade Centers. Über 4700 Tote werden dort noch vermutet. Foto: dpa

Auch bei den Medien liegen Nerven blank

Falschmeldungen im Kampf um die Quote

Von unserem Korrespondenten Friedemann Diederichs

Washington/New York. Es war zunächst ein Gerücht, das umgehend den Rang einer offiziellen Meldung erhielt, Feuerwehrleute weinen und TV-Moderatoren in einer Zeit der nicht enden wollenden Hiobsbotschaften leichten Herzens sprechen ließ: Fünf Feuerwehrmänner seien, weitgehend unversehrt und in einem Geländewagen zusammengepfercht, nach über 50 Stunden aus den Trümmern des World Trade Centers befreit worden. Doch die Freude über die vermeintlich sensationelle Rettung währte nur kurz: Die Fernsehanstalten waren einer klassischen „Ente" aufgesessen und hatten – im Rennen um Quoten – keine Zeit auf Rückfragen verwendet.

Ein Rüffel vom Bürgermeister

„Ich möchte alle Journalisten bitten, sorgfältig zu arbeiten und die Quellen von Nachrichten zu verifizieren." Mit diesen Worten erteilte gestern dann auch New Yorks Bürgermeister Rudolph Giuliani den Medien einen gewaltigen Rüffel. Denn kurz zuvor hatte sich ebenfalls herausgestellt, dass am Vorabend auf den meisten Fernsehkanälen verbreitete Meldungen über einen erneuten Entführungsversuch einer American-Airlines-Maschine am John F. Kennedy Flughafen auf waghalsigen Interpretationen der Reporter beruhten. Zwar hatten bis an die Zähne bewaffnete Polizei-Eliteeinheiten den bereits zum Abflug bereitstehenden Jet gestürmt und mehrere Personen in Handschellen abgeführt. Doch gestern hieß es bei den Behörden: Es gibt keinerlei Verbindung der Festgenommenen zum Terror-Netz des mutmaßlichen Drahtziehers der Anschlags-Serie, Osama bin Laden. Man habe alle wieder freilassen müssen.

Reporter verkleiden sich als Rettungskräfte

Berichte, die im Flugzeug Überwältigten hätten Messer und andere Stichwerkzeuge am Körper getragen, stellten sich somit auch als falsch heraus. Obwohl eine derartige Bewaffnung angesichts der äußerst scharfen Sicherheitsvorkehrungen an den US-Flughäfen ohnehin kaum glaubhaft gewesen war, hatten die meisten großen Zeitungen die Meldungen verbreitet.

Man möge sich im Kreis der Medienvertreter beruhigen, forderte auch der demokratische Senator Joseph Biden, Vorsitzender des Auswärtigen Ausschusses, die Berichterstatter auf. Ein gutes Dutzend Reporter hat dazu ausreichend Zeit: Sie verbringen diese nämlich in Zellen von Polizeirevieren in New York. Sie hatten sich – im Kampf um die besten Fotos und den schnellsten Nachrichtenzugang – bei den Rettungsarbeiten als Feuerwehrmänner, Polizisten oder technische Helfer verkleidet und waren aufgefallen, weil sie mehr Zeit ihren Kameras als den Trümmerbergen des World Trade Centers gewidmet hatten.

Wir berichten auch das Wochenende über für Sie im Internet: AZ web
www.aachener-zeitung.de

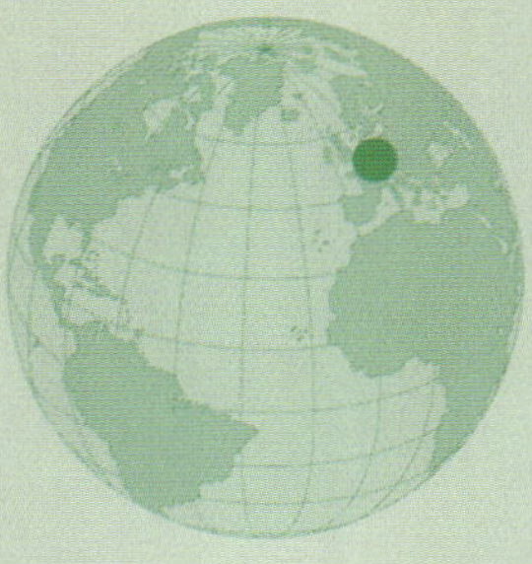

Aachener Zeitung
www.aachener-zeitung.de
Deutschland, Aachen

WESTFÄLISCHE RUNDSCHAU

WR

Mo. - Fr. 1,20 DM
Sa. 1,50 DM

Zeitung für Dortmund

General Anzeiger

D

WR-online
www.westfaelische-rundschau.de

- **Sportergebnisse:** Über 2300 Tabellen: Von der Bundesliga bis zur Kreisklasse
- **Lokal-Nachrichten:** Bilder und Berichte aus Ihrer Stadt und der Nachbarschaft

Nr. 215 37. Woche — Unabhängig - Überparteilich — Samstag, 15. September 2001

D ☆

Amerikaner zögern mit Gegenschlag - Terror-Spur nach Bochum - Viele Deutsche vermisst

Rau: Amerika steht nicht allein

Berichte auf
6 Seiten

Lesen Sie bitte heute:

- Bilddokumente: Vier Tage der Verzweiflung
- Brandenburger Tor: ein Meer von Sternenbannern
- GdP: Kontrollmängel auf den Flughäfen
- Fahndung: Verdächtige lebten unauffällig
- US-Präsident Bush: Freie Hand für die Vergeltung
- „Szenen aus der Hölle" für die Feuerwehr

WR aktuell online
www.westfaelische-rundschau.de
wr-special: Nachrichten und Bilder aus Amerika - aktuell rund um die Uhr.

G

Floris Gewinnspiel 13. Tag
Tragen Sie heute den dreizehnten Buchstaben auf Ihrer Teilnahmekarte ein. Übrigens können Sie den tagesaktuellen Buchstaben auch über unser Info-Telefon: 0 180 5/01 20 20 erfahren.

Bildschirm-Tipp

- **„Tatort" (ARD, So., 20.15 Uhr)** - Abschied von Kommissar Brinkmann (Karl-Heinz von Hassel).
- **„Antonia (1)" (SAT.1, So., 20.15 Uhr)** - Zweiteiler: Studentin heiratet einen Märchenprinzen.

Das Wetter
Im Tagesverlauf wieder Regen - 11 bis 14 Grad

4 394619 201504 60037

Überall auf der Welt - wie hier in Frankfurt - wurde gestern der Opfer des Terror-Anschlages gedacht. (ddp-Bild)

Eigener Bericht

Berlin/Washington/Bochum/Düsseldorf. (PK/dpa) Die Spuren des Terrorkrieges gegen die USA führen jetzt möglicherweise auch nach NRW.

Das Innenministerium in Düsseldorf schließt nicht aus, dass einzelne Personen, die im Land leben, Kontakt zu der Organisation von Osama bin Laden haben, möglicherweise sogar in Ausbildungslagern in Afghanistan und an der Vorbereitung der Anschläge gegen Pentagon und World Trade Center beteiligt waren. Der Verfassungsschutz habe entsprechende Erkenntnisse.

Einer der Attentäter lebte und studierte nach Informationen der „WAZ" offenbar einige Zeit in Bochum. Der Mann habe zu der Gruppe arabischer Studenten gehört, gegen die auch in Hamburg ermittelt werde. Er soll Passagier des Jets gewesen sein, der bei Pittsburgh abgestürzt ist. BKA und LKA hätten ein Lagezentrum in Bochum eingerichtet.

Das FBI hat gestern der Bundesanwaltschaft in Karlsruhe in größerem Umfang Material über die deutschen Verbindungslinien der Täter übermittelt. Hamburg gilt als Hauptstützpunkt. Hier hatte einer der Täter acht Jahre gelebt.

Unter den Trümmern des World Trade Center in New York sind wahrscheinlich noch zahlreiche Deutsche begraben. Das Auswärtige Amt dementierte zwar eine Meldung des baden-württembergischen Innenministeriums, 700 Deutsche seien vermisst. Aber es gebe Vermisstenmeldungen in erheblicher Höhe. Das Generalkonsulat in New York versucht derzeit fieberhaft, den Verbleib der Vermissten aufzuklären.

Der erwartete Gegenschlag der Amerikaner - voraussichtlich gegen Afghanistan, wo Osama bin Laden seine Operationsbasis hat - verzögert sich offenbar.

200 000 Menschen trauern in Berlin

Die USA sehen in dem saudischen Kaufmann zwar den Hauptschuldigen für die Terror-Angriffe auf New York und Washington am Dienstag. Es könnten jedoch noch andere Organisationen beteiligt sein, räumte das Weiße Haus ein. Washington will offenbar noch Genaueres über die Täter herausfinden, bevor es zur angekündigten Vergeltung kommt - zumal die Größenordnung der Unterstützung des Afghanistan benachbarten Pakistans für einen US-Militärschlag noch unsicher ist.

Mehr als 200 000 Menschen versammelten sich am Abend vor dem Brandenburger Tor in Berlin, um der Opfer des Terrors zu gedenken. Bundespräsident Johannes Rau versicherte dem anwesenden US-Botschafter Daniel Coats: „Amerika steht nicht allein".

Rettungskräfte entmutigt: „Die Zeit arbeitet gegen uns"

Die Bergung der Opfer aus den Trümmern des World Trade Center in New York hat sich gestern zu einem Wettlauf gegen die Zeit entwickelt. Die Rettungsarbeiter fühlten sich entmutigter denn je. „Die Zeit arbeitet nicht für uns", sagte der Leiter des Katastrophenschutzes, Joe Albaugh. Das Wetteramt sagte zudem starke Regenfälle und noch mehr Wind voraus. Damit wuchs die Furcht, bereits beschädigte Gebäude in der Umgebung der Einsturzstelle könnten weiter an Stabilität verlieren. 4763 Menschen gelten seit den Anschlägen als vermisst. Die Zahl der geborgenen Toten gab der New Yorker Bürgermeister Rudolph Giuliani mit 184 an. „In vielen Fällen", fügte er sichtlich bewegt hinzu, „bestehen diese 184 nur aus Leichenteilen." Nur 75 der Leichen seien vollständig, erst 35 von ihnen seien identifiziert. (dpa-Bild)

Düsseldorf, Frankfurt: Wieder US-Flüge

WR-Nachrichtendienste

Im Westen. Erstmals seit den Terroranschlägen sind gestern wieder Flüge aus Deutschland in die USA gestartet - allerdings nur von US-Fluggesellschaften.

Gestern Nachmittag startete einem Flughafen-Sprecher zufolge eine Boeing 767 der United Airlines in Düsseldorf.

Bis zum frühen Abend hatten vier Maschinen von Delta, United Airlines und American Airlines vom Frankfurter Flughafen abgehoben. Auch mehrere Maschinen aus den USA durften wieder landen.

Die Lufthansa musste dagegen alle 25 für gestern geplanten Flugpaare in die Vereinigten Staaten annullieren - aufgrund einer Entscheidung von US-Behörden. Betroffen davon seien 16 000 Fluggäste.

In der Nähe des Airport-Rhein-Main-Flughafens wurde eine Turnhalle zum Notquartier für gestrandete Passagiere umfunktioniert. Die Rückkehr eines Teils der wegen der Anschläge nach Kanada umgeleiteten Passagiere verzögerte sich. Sechs Maschinen, die im Laufe des Tages zurückerwartet wurden,ch mehrere Maschinen aus den USA durften wieder landen.

ARD: Hacker brachen in Zentral-Computer ein

WR-Nachrichtendienste

Hamburg. Hacker sind im Auftrag des TV-Magazins „ARD- Ratgeber Technik" in den Zentralcomputer einer großen Bank eingebrochen.

„Das Sicherheitssystem des deutschen Geldinstituts war so mangelhaft geschützt, dass die Kontenknacker aus Thüringen und die TV-Redakteure innerhalb von wenigen Tagen 1,5 Millionen Onlinebuchungen einschließlich Geheimnummern (PINs) und Online-Nummern in den Händen hielten", teilte der Nord-

„Das Sicherheitssystem des deutschen Geldinstituts war so mangelhaft geschützt, dass die Kontenknacker aus Thüringen und die

kommenden Sonntag zwischen 17.03 und 17.30 Uhr nicht nennen.

Die Hacker nutzten die Tatsache aus, dass die Techniker der Bank den Webserver völlig falsch konfiguriert hatten. Der Internet Information Server (IIS 4.0) von Microsoft ermöglichte damit Unbefugten einen Zugriff auf Bereiche des Bankcomputers, die sonst hart gegen einen Zugriff von außen geschützt sind.

Nach Angaben der Redaktion des ARD-Ratgebers hätten die Hacker mit Hilfe der ver völlig falsch konfiguriert hatten. Der Internet Information Server (IIS 4.0) von Microsoft ermöglichte damit Unbefugten einen Zugriff auf Bereiche des Bankcomputers, die sonst hart gegen

Westfälische Rundschau
www.westfaelische-rundschau.de
Deutschland, Dortmund

15+

ALLGEMEINE

JÜDISCHE WOCHENZEITUNG

56. Jahrgang Nr. 20 | BERLIN, DEN 26. SEPTEMBER 2001 / 9. TISCHRI 5762 | Preis DM 3

„Die Juden sind schuld!“

Der Terror in den USA und das Wiederaufleben alter Stereotypen / Von Michael Wolffsohn

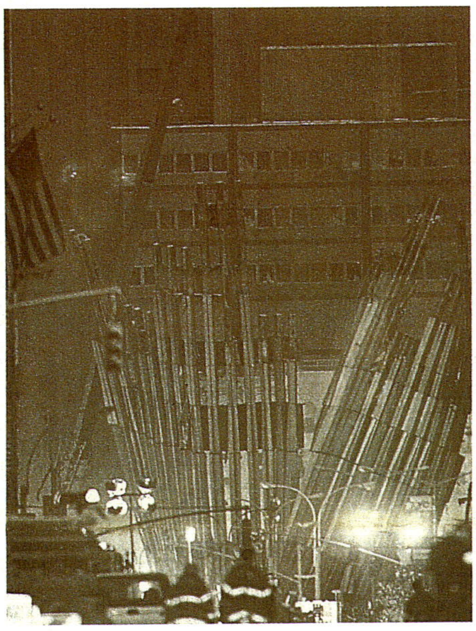

Zweierlei Maß? Wenn Amerikaner getötet werden, ist es Krieg (l. Attentat auf das World Trade Center in New York am 11. September), wenn Juden ermordet werden, ist es „nur“ Terror (r. Anschlag auf eine Pizzeria in Jerusalem am 9. August). Fotos: ddp/Isranet

„Die Juden sind schuld“, zumindest „die Juden in Israel“. In diesen apokalyptischen Tagen des sich auf den Islam berufenden Terrors ist dieses Argument von einer das Christentum praktizierenden Umwelt zu hören. Nicht weniger direkt in unserem christlich sich nennenden Deutschland stößt man auf diesen gedanken- und kenntnislosen Gedanken. Je gebildeter und geschulter die Argumentierenden, desto eher formulieren sie verklausuliert, aber wer's versteht, versteht's. Und „wir Juden“ verstehen. Mit dem Antisemitismusvorwurf sollte man dabei freilich zurückhaltend sein, denn subjektiv sind die meisten, die jene These vertreten durchaus Juden- und Israelfreunde. Objektiv müssen wir leider feststellen, daß auch viele dieser Freunde sich in ihren Tiefenschichten nicht von uralten antisemitischen Klischees befreit haben. Man wäre versucht, zu sagen, daß wir mit solchen Freunden keine Feinde mehr benötigten.

Das Denkmuster der Freunde, von den Gegnern und wahren Antisemiten ganz zu schweigen, ist schnell skizziert: Weil Israel, „die Juden“, seit Jahrzehnten eine „völlig uneinsichtige und brutale“ Palästinenserpolitik betrieben hätten, bekämen jetzt die USA als Israelfreunde und -helfer die Rechnung für Israels (vermeintliche oder tatsächliche) Mißachtung der Menschenrechte in den besetzten Gebieten, und besonders für die Methoden von Israels Ministerpräsident Scharon vorgelegt.

Daß die USA seit dem Sechstagekrieg von 1967 (aus eigenem Interesse!) eine strategische Allianz mit Israel geschmiedet haben, ist unbestreitbar. Daß sie deshalb Israels Politik insgesamt unkritisch gebilligt und nicht zu ändern versucht hätten, ist eine abenteuerliche, kenntnislose Behauptung.

Doch um Nahost geht es nur vordergründig. Das sind vorgeschobene Argumente, willkommene Anlässe, um eine grundsätzliche Distanzierung „des Westens“ von Israel zu rechtfertigen. Längst gibt es diese Distanzierung in Westeuropa, besonders in Frankreich. Nun sollen auch Deutschland und vor allem die USA folgen. Darum geht es denen, die einen unmittelbaren Zusammenhang zwischen den Terroranschlägen gegen die USA und Nahost herstellen. Sie übersehen oder wollen übersehen, daß ein derartiges Terrorinferno nur nach jahrelangen Vorarbeiten verwirklicht werden konnte. Da Scharon erst im Februar dieses Jahres zum Premier Israels gewählt wurde, scheidet schon aus zeitlich-logischen Gründen das Scharon-Argument aus. Davor, bei den Wahlen vom Mai 1999, hatten die Israelis der „Falken“-Politik Netanjahus einen Korb gegeben und Barak den Auftrag erteilt, eine friedenspolitische Offensive einzuleiten. Sie scheiterte, aus welchen Gründen auch immer, aber es gab sie. Eine Reaktion auf Israels Fortsetzung der Konfrontation kann daher weder der antiisraelische noch der antiamerikanische Terror sein, zumal Israel, genau an dem Tag, an dem die „Al-Aksa-Intifada (29. September 2000) ausbrach, die weitestgehenden Zugeständnisse in der Jerusalemfrage verkündete und im Januar 2001 sogar bereit war, fast hundert Prozent des Westjordanlandes zu räumen. Trotzdem wurden die Intifada und die Vorbereitungen der Terroranschläge fortgeführt. Sowohl Israels vermeintliche Nachgiebigkeit als auch Israels Unnachgiebigkeit scheiden deshalb als Erklärung aus. Intifada und Terror gab und gibt es unter beiden Vorgaben israelischer Politik.

Die Verbindung zwischen Israel und dem islamistischen Anti-US-Terror ist also unsinnig, weil falsch. Dieser Terror richtet sich nicht gegen Israel oder die USA, sondern gegen „den Westen“, die westlich-freiheitlich-demokratische-marktwirtschaftliche Ordnung schlechthin und letztlich natürlich auch gegen Deutschland als unbestreitbaren Teil des Westens. Israel „verantwortlich“ zu machen, bedeutet, es in die Rolle zu drängen, die traditionell „den Juden“ zugedacht war: als „Ruhestörer“ und Sündenbock für alles und jedes.

Blauäugig dachten viele Amerikaner bis zum 11. September, Außenpolitik finde weit draußen statt und gehe sie nichts an. Sie mußten leidvoll erfahren, daß Außenpolitik ihr Innenleben, ganz wörtlich, vital trifft. Sie verstanden bis zum 11. September auch nicht, daß man Terror mehr präventiv als reaktiv begegnen müsse. Deshalb lehnten sie damals die gezielte Ermordung der Väter des Terrors ab. In Deutschland und Westeuropa ist man außen- und weltpolitisch nicht mehr ganz so provinziell, hielt aber in den vergangenen Jahren den Terror weitgehend für ein innernahöstliches Problem und kritisierte heftig die gezielten Tötungen der Terrordrahtzieher. Man übersah und übersieht, daß der gegen Israel gerichtete „Terror“ eigentlich schon seit langem ein „Krieg“ ist, daß Angriffe auf und in Jerusalem oder Tel Aviv im Kern nichts anderes als jene Angriffe auf New York und Washington sind. Bei letzteren spricht man nun auch vom „Krieg“ und dort, in und gegen Israel, ist es „nur“ Terror.

Krieg ist „ein Akt, um den Gegner zur Erfüllung unseres Willens zu zwingen“ (Clausewitz, *Vom Kriege*). Jeder Krieg, das wissen wir auch vom alten Clausewitz, hat ein „ursprüngliches Motiv“, einen politischen Zweck. Krieg ist kein Selbstzweck, er „ist eine bloße Fortsetzung der Politik mit anderen Mitteln“. Israels gezielte Ermordung beziehungsweise „Liquidierung“ von Palästinensern, Politikern oder Terroristen oder beiden, ist also kein politischer, sondern ein rein kriegerischer Akt. In jedem Krieg sterben Menschen. Das ist überall und immer das schreckliche, unmenschliche Gesetz des Krieges.

Wenn Menschen - unter dem Gesetz des Krieges - sterben müssen, gibt es folgende Alternative: Sollen möglichst viele Menschen auf der anderen (im Krieg nennt man sie „feindlichen“) Seite sterben oder nur diejenigen, die einer politischen Lösung im Wege stehen und ihrerseits sogar militärisch („terroristisch“) gegen die eigene Seite vorgehen? Die Frage zu stellen, heißt sie zu beantworten, es sei denn man haßt die andere Seite insgesamt. Weil selbst die Regierung Scharon nicht aus kollektivem Haß, sondern aus politischen Zielen Palästinenser (nicht aber „die“ Palästinenser, also das palästinensische Volk) bekämpft, wählt sie die gezielte Ermordung.

Das bedeutet: Wenn schon Unmenschlichkeit durch Krieg und im Krieg, dann so wenig wie möglich, nur so viel Unmenschlichkeit wie militärisch nötig und vor allem gezielt auf Einzelne, um die politische Lösung (welche auch immer) im Kollektiv der anderen mit den dort politisch Denkenden und dann Handelnden auch eines Tages durchsetzen zu können. Nicht zuletzt deshalb bleibt Arafat verschont. Die meisten Israelis wissen nämlich: Die Arafats kommen und gehen, aber das Palästinenserproblem bleibt.

Die derzeitige Vorgehensweise der Anti-US-Terroristen und Palästinenser, ihrer Führung ebenso wie der islamischen Fundamentalisten und der weltlichen „Ablehnungsfront“, geht kollektiv vor. Ihre Aktionen richten sich blind „gegen den Westen“ und „gegen Israel“, nicht gezielt gegen bestimmte Menschen. Ihre Vorgehensweise ist deshalb durch und durch unpolitisch und ohne jede Perspektive, also - leider - dem Islam sowie dem palästinensischen Volk schädlich.

Über die Gerechtigkeit, Richtigkeit oder gar Weisheit der israelischen Politik mag man streiten, nicht jedoch darüber, daß Israel nur ein Vorwand für antiwestlichen Terror von Islamisten ist.

Den USA wird geraten, sie werden sogar gewarnt, ja nicht „alttestamentarisch“ zu reagieren. Nicht „Auge um Auge, Zahn um Zahn“, sei die Parole, sondern die „Verhältnismäßigkeit“ von Verbrechen und Strafe. Jene Warnung ist im Kern eine Warnung vor „den Juden“, denn das „Alte Testament“, die Hebräische Bibel, ist das A und B und C von Juden und Judentum. Ganz abgesehen davon besagt „Auge um Auge, Zahn um Zahn“ nichts anderes als „Verhältnismäßigkeit von Verbrechen und Strafe“. Auch wenn jüdische Museen wie Pilze aus dem Boden sprießen, die Unkenntnis über uns Juden und das Judentum ist geblieben und auch die Bereitschaft, uns als „Ruhestörer“ und „Sündenböcke“ anzusehen.

Vor einem Jahr rief Kanzler Schröder die Deutschen zum „Aufstand der Anständigen“ auf. Jetzt spricht man vom „Krieg der Anständigen“. Hoffentlich ist dieser erfolgreicher als jener - so schlimm jeder Krieg ist. Doch manchmal ist das Schlimme notwendig, um das Schlimmste zu verhindern.

4 390110 703905 20

In dieser

„Keine konkrete Gefährdung“

Gespräch mit Otto Schily

Sind jüdische Einrichtungen in Deutschland seit den Attentaten in New York und Washington besonders gefährdet?

Schily: Die Sicherheitsbehörden haben derzeit keine Hinweise, daß jüdische Einrichtungen in Deutschland konkret gefährdet sind. Dennoch haben Bund und Länder gemeinsam entschieden, vorsorglich die Schutzmaßnahmen für jüdische und israelische Einrichtungen zu verstärken.

Gibt es eine konkrete Bedrohung beispielsweise durch islamistische Extremisten?

Schily: Wir verfügen über keine konkreten Hinweise auf Terroranschläge von extremistischen Islamisten in Europa, auch nicht hier in Deutschland. Ich kann allerdings nicht ausschließen, daß sich die Lage nach einem amerikanischen Gegenschlag völlig verändert. Es ist offenkundig, daß sich ein weltweites Netz islamischer fundamentalistischer Terroristen gebildet hat, in dem es leider auch Bezugspunkte zu Deutschland gibt. Dieses Netz zu zerstören, wird eine mühselige und langwierige Aufgabe sein, die wir entschlossen angehen.

Was wird zum Schutz jüdischer Einrichtungen getan?

Schily: Die vorhandenen Sicherheitsmaßnahmen wurden erheblich verstärkt. Besonders gefährdete Objekte wie Synagogen, jüdische Schulen und Gemeindezentren werden ständig durch Polizeikräfte geschützt. Die örtliche Polizei hält Kontakt zu den Repräsentanten dieser Einrichtungen. Sie kann sofort reagieren, wenn sich die Lage verändert. Jüdische Friedhöfe werden regelmäßig von Polizeistreifen überwacht.

Wurde die Gefahr islamistischer Terroristen in der Bundesrepublik bislang unterschätzt?

Schily: Nein, Ausländerextremismus ist ein Phänomen, dem sich Verfassungsschützer und Polizei auch in der Vergangenheit intensiv gewidmet haben. Ihre Ermittlungstätigkeit war Grundlage der Verhaftung des mutmaßlichen Finanzchefs Bin Ladens in München 1998 und von vier islamistischen Terroristen im vergangenen Dezember in Frankfurt. Die Anschläge in den USA haben aber gezeigt, daß wir unsere Sicherheitsarchitektur überprüfen und nötigenfalls Gesetze ändern müssen, um diese neue Dimension des Terrorismus wirksam aufklären und bekämpfen zu können.

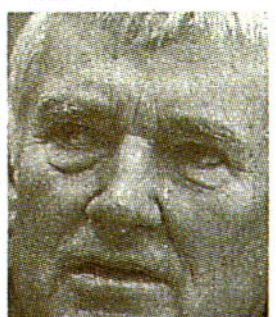

Mit dem Bundesinnenminister sprach Judith Hart/Foto: ddp

Allgemeine Jüdische Wochenzeitung
www.juedische-allgemeine.de
Deutschland, Berlin

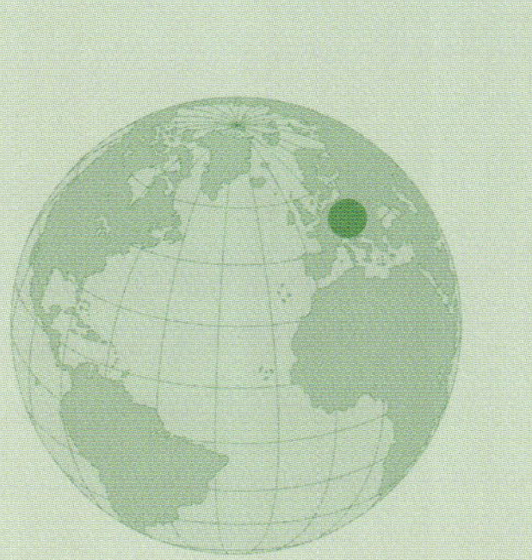

Fr. 1.50 (TVA 2,4% incluse) FF 6.50/Lires 4000/Ptas 400 MD SAMEDI 15 SEPTEMBRE 2001 N° 258 www.lematin.ch

Le Matin

le quotidien romand

SPORTS ....p. 21

ANNONCES CLASSÉES .....pp. 40-50

VIRRE

VIVRE ....p. 54

LES LARMES AVANT LA RIPOSTE

SPÉCIAL ATTENTATS

Pages 10-17

Reuters/Brian Snyder

PUB

RENAULT Des offres qui décollent! 026 662 40 84

GARAGE - CARROSSERIE FRIEDLI SA PAYERNE «vous savez, c'est là où il y a l'avion?!»

Postcode 1 JA 1000 Lausanne 1

1 Die Tränen vor dem Gegenangriff

2 Sonderausgabe Anschläge

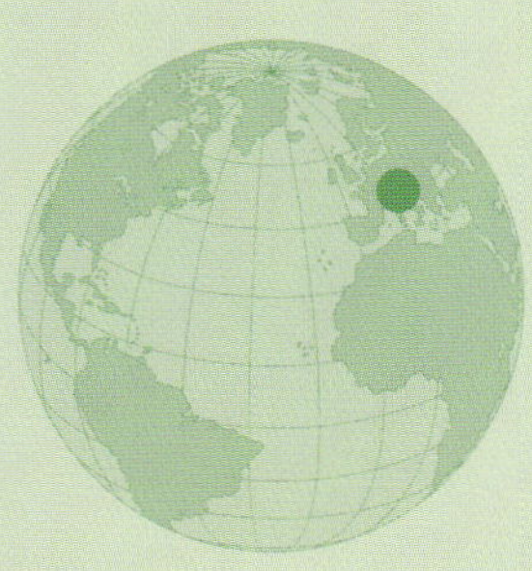

Le Matin
www.lematin.ch
Schweiz, Lausanne

Salzburger Nachrichten

Samstag / Sonntag, 15./16. September 2001 — UNABHÄNGIGE ZEITUNG FÜR ÖSTERREICH — Nr. 214, 57. Jahrgang, S 15,– € 1,09

5021 Salzburg, Karolingerstraße 40
Telefon: 0662/8373-0
Abo-Service/Zustelldienst: 0662/8373-110
Anzeigen: 0662/8373-223
E-Mail: redakt@salzburg.com
aboservice@salzburg.com
anzeigen@salzburg.com
Homepage: www.salzburg.com

Werben für Demokratie

RONALD BARAZON

Der Massenmord in den USA wird zu einer weltweiten Polizei- und Militäraktion gegen Terroristen führen.

Diese Reaktion allein kann aber das Problem nicht lösen: Die freie Welt muss sich auch mit den Motiven der Anschläge auseinander setzen und die Vorwürfe gegen die westlichen Demokratien entkräften. Die Vorwürfe der Feinde der freien Welt haben weltweit durchaus Gehör gefunden und dafür gesorgt, dass Terroranschläge nicht nur abgelehnt werden, sondern auch auf Verständnis stoßen.

Die Demokraten haben Handlungsbedarf: Sie müssen eine globale und über viele Jahre andauernde Werbe- und PR-Kampagne für Ihre Werte starten, in Radio- und Fernsehsendungen, auf Internetseiten die Vorzüge des einzigen Systems schildern, das jeden Menschen in seinen unverletzlichen Rechten respektiert.

Diese Aktionen müssen in allen Sprachen erfolgen und tatsächlich in allen Ländern zu empfangen sein. Auch darf man nicht enttäuscht sein, wenn der Erfolg auf sich warten lässt. Eine umfassende Informationstätigkeit für die Demokratie ist das beste Instrument zur Verteidigung der freien Welt und verursacht einen Bruchteil der Kosten des Militärs.

Vorwurf Nummer eins: Die Reichen würden immer reicher, die Armen immer ärmer, die Globalisierung sei das Instrument, um diese Entwicklung voranzutreiben.

Die Behauptung ist nachweisbar falsch. Die Globalisierung hat vor allem Arbeitsplätze in den Industrieländern vernichtet. Entwicklungsländer, die die Industrialisierung angenommen haben, verzeichnen durch die Globalisierung einen bislang nicht gekannten Wohlstand. In Armut verharren allerdings jene Länder, die die moderne Wirtschaft ablehnen.

Vorwurf Nummer zwei: In der freien Welt zähle nur der Profit, man habe keine Ideale, der Mensch werde verachtet.

Das Gegenteil ist der Fall. Die westlichen Demokratien sind in der Geschichte der Menschheit die ersten Gesellschaften, die allen Mitgliedern, ohne Beachtung des Geschlechts, der Rasse, der Religion, der sozialen Stellung, des Einkommens, alle Staatsbürgerrechte einräumen und in der Not Sozialhilfe bieten. In den islamischen Staaten, von denen die schärfste Kritik an der freien Welt ausgeht, zählt der Mensch nur, wenn er den Vorstellungen der religiösen Machthaber entspricht.

Vorwurf Nummer drei: Die USA, und mit ihnen die europäischen Verbündeten, würden die Welt beherrschen.

Eine Verkennung der Tatsachen. Die USA haben noch nie einen Eroberungskrieg geführt und die Europäer haben sich längst aus den ehemaligen Kolonien zurückgezogen. Selbstverständlich darf man nicht übersehen, dass die USA zur Absicherung ihrer Interessen mit Verbrecherregimes paktieren und die Europäer in der Kolonialzeit die Menschenrechte verletzt haben. Diese nicht zu entschuldigenden Verfehlungen stellen aber nicht den Wert der Menschenrechte und der Demokratie in Frage.

Vorwurf Nummer vier: Der amerikanische Weg, die Mischung aus Freiheit des Individuums, Wettbewerb und Fernsehunterhaltung beherrsche auch ohne politischen und militärischen Druck die Welt,. Die Lebensweise sei unmoralisch und müsse bekämpft werden.

Ob der angeblich lockere Umgang mit Moral im Westen stärker verurteilt gehört als die Unterdrückung der Frauen im Islam, ist eine persönliche Entscheidung. Auch, ob man sich der ständigen Diskussion über alles und jedes, dem Zweifel, stellt, oder eine Religion vorzieht, die dem Einzelnen verbietet, Fragen zu stellen.

Die Wahl zwischen den verschiedenen Kulturen muss jeder Einzelne, jede Gesellschaft, jeder Staat treffen. Die Tatsache, dass es sich hier um eine Wahl, eine freie Entscheidung handelt, muss die zentrale Botschaft der geforderten Werbekampagne für die Demokratie sein.

Die Grausamkeit des Terrors manifestiert sich in Tausenden Einzelschicksalen: Wie diese junge Frau, die ihren Verlobten vermisst, suchten unzählige New Yorker in den Tagen nach den Anschlägen ihre Angehörigen. Zerrissen zwischen Hoffnung und Verzweiflung. Mit jeder Stunde wird deutlicher, dass kaum noch Aussicht auf die Bergung von lebenden Personen aus den Trümmern des World Trade Centers besteht. Inzwischen laufen die Vorbereitungen für den Vergeltungsschlag auf Hochtouren.
Berichte und Hintergründe auf den Seiten 2-6, 9, 17, 18. Bild: SN/AP

WOCHENENDE SPEZIAL

DM, 2,20; GRD 600; KN 14; BEF 80; L, 3000; HUF 400; SIT, 350;
9015 6274
P.b.b. Erscheinungsort Salzburg
Verlagspostamt 5020 Salzburg, 007020097 K

DER STANDPUNKT

Die US-Politik muss trotz des Leides kühlen Kopf bewahren

VIKTOR HERMANN

Die Öffentlichkeit in aller Welt wartet nach den furchtbaren Terroranschlägen auf New York und Washington auf die Reaktion der Supermacht USA. Die amerikanische Öffentlichkeit fordert unüberhörbar Vergeltung, Rache, zumindest die Bestrafung der Schuldigen.

Jetzt muss eine umfassende polizeiliche Jagd nach allen Terroristen der Welt beginnen, nach ihren Helfern und Zuträgern, nach ihren Unterstützern. Viele dieser Verbrecher sind in den Ländern, in denen sie Unterschlupf gefunden haben, den Geheimdiensten bekannt. Bisher hat man sie oft aus politischen Gründen toleriert und lediglich beobachtet. Damit muss Schluss sein.

US-Politiker unterliegen aber nun der Versuchung, dem psychologisch verständlichen Wunsch nach Rache nachzugeben. Ja, manche von ihnen haben bereits Worte gewählt, die die Stimmung noch anheizten. Die Rede ist von einem „Kriegszustand", man will die Terroristen finden und bestrafen – gemeint ist töten –, Unterstützer und Paten ebenso.

Politiker, die nicht nur an die nächste Wahl denken, sondern an die Verantwortung für die nächste Generation und – im Fall der USA – an das Schicksal der ganzen Welt, sind aber aufgerufen, kühlen Kopf zu bewahren, auch wenn das angesichts des unermesslichen Leides der Opfer und ihrer Familien wahrlich schwer fällt. Die Verlockung ist groß, Afghanistan in Grund und Boden zu bomben, weil dieses Land dem Terroristen Osama Bin Laden als Basis dient. Und es gibt Stimmen, die gleich noch in den anderen „Schurkenstaaten" aufräumen wollen – Nordkorea, Sudan, Iran, Libyen ... Diesen Ländern unterstellt Washington seit langem, sie seien Brutstätten des internationalen Terrorismus und eine Gefahr für den Weltfrieden.

Doch bedenken wir die Folgen: Eine Militäraktion, wie die USA sie schon in früheren Fällen durchgeführt haben, nähme unweigerlich den Tod von ungezählten unschuldigen Zivilisten in jedem dieser Länder in Kauf. Damit wäre mit einem Schlag zunichte gemacht, worauf wir in Europa und in Nordamerika uns viel zugute halten. Demokratie und Menschenrechte müssten zu hohlen Phrasen verkommen, wenn aus purer Rache Menschen massakriert würden. Das Leid Tausender Familien, die in New York und Washington Angehörige verloren haben, würde um nichts gelindert durch das Leid Tausender afghanischer Familien.

Ein weiterer Grund, auf einen undifferenzierten Racheakt zu verzichten, ist die Frage nach dem politischen Nutzen solchen Vorgehens. George W. Busch sagt, Amerika befinde sich in einem Krieg. Doch noch kann niemand den Kriegsgegner identifizieren. Uind: Es ist ein Krieg, der nicht zu gewinnen ist. Denn jede Militäraktion gegen Osama Bin Laden und seine mörderischen Helfershelfer hätte vor allem einen Effekt, der dem Terroristen ins Konzept passt. Die Anschläge von Dienstag sollen eine Reaktion der USA provozieren, die so hart ist und von den Betroffenen als so grausam empfunden wird, dass den Terroristen neue Sympathisanten zufliegen. Sollte George W. Busch jetzt massiv und hart reagieren, dann folgt er jenem Drehbuch, das der Terrorist Osama Bin Laden geschrieben hat.

Salzburger Nachrichten
www.salzburg.com
Österreich, Salzburg

THE WEEK THAT SHOOK THE WORLD

14 PAGES OF NEWS AND ANALYSIS • PLUS 14-PAGE SPECIAL EDITION OF THE REVIEW

THE INDEPENDENT

SATURDAY EDITION

No 4,580 www.independent.co.uk SATURDAY 15 SEPTEMBER 2001 (IR£1) 90p

A silent world, united in grief

BY PAUL VALLELY

ACROSS THE globe yesterday millions of people stood, united in silence. Their heads were bowed. The only sounds were those of muffled sobs; the only movements were the discreet raising of hands to wipe away the tears.

It was a silence that reverberated across Europe, through Asia and as far away as Australia, echoing far louder than the explosions that destroyed the twin towers of the World Trade Centre in New York. An estimated 800 million people observed three minutes of quiet reflection for the victims of Tuesday's terrorist massacres, in which more than 5,000 people are now believed to have died.

All over the world – in some 43 countries – at the stroke of 11am, shops, offices, schools, factories, railway stations, airports and city centres fell quiet. Television and radio stations suspended programmes. Stock exchanges ceased trading. Court cases were halted. Buses and trains stopped. Pubs, which were due to open, kept their doors closed.

Throughout Britain, in the biggest outpouring of public grief since the death of Diana, Princess of Wales, millions stopped to pay their respects to the victims, among whom it is feared some 500 Britons number. It was a gesture that unified the nation. The Queen and the Prime Minister took part, as did taxi drivers, shop assistants and suspects awaiting criminal trials.

At Buckingham Palace the gates were closed so that no one could enter or leave during the period of mourning. And at the House of Commons, which was in emergency session to discuss the crisis, Michael Ancram, the new shadow Foreign Secretary, was interrupted by the Speaker, Michael Martin, in the middle of his speech, for the unprecedented three-minute tribute.

MPs – including the Prime Minister, Tony Blair, the new Tory leader, Iain Duncan Smith, and the Liberal Democrat leader, Charles Kennedy – stood between the benches of the chamber as the chimes of Big Ben sounded outside. Some of the politicians looked near to tears as the clock ticked away the seconds.

Outside, tourists and other pedestrians stopped and turned to face the great clock tower. Traffic too came to a halt until a muted peel of bells from Westminster Abbey marked the end of the silence.

It was an image that was repeated across Europe. In Brussels, the president of the European Commission, Romano Prodi, joined thousands of EU officials to observe the silence in the heart of the administrative district of the city. Alongside them stood Richard Morningstar, the outgoing US ambassador to the EU. Flanking him were the European foreign policy high representative, Javier Solana, and the EU commissioner for external affairs, Chris Patten, with a host of other European dignitaries.

In Berlin, a sign had been laid on the pile of white roses and carnations placed in front of the American embassy. It harked back to the words of solidarity President John F Kennedy delivered in 1963 to residents in the city, then divided by the Cold War. "Ich bin ein Berliner," he said then. "We're all New Yorkers," the sign said yesterday.

In Paris the bells of Notre Dame cathedral rang out across the French capital then fell silent on the same stroke of noon. At the Place de la Concorde the great Ferris wheel set up for millennium celebrations had come to a halt. Drivers on the Metro stopped their trains and asked passengers, over the intercom, to join three minutes of "homage to the victims".

All the television screens in the Virgin Megastore on the Champs-Elysées were switched to a picture of the American flag at half-mast. Customers and staff stood to attention and, when the silence ended, John Lennon's pacifist anthem "Imagine" was played over the loudspeakers.

Elsewhere in France – in the National Assembly, in airports, offices, shops and in churches and in a service attended by President Jacques Chirac in the courtyard of the Elysée Palace – the silence was scrupulously observed.

In Italy, at the motor racing track at Monza, Formula One drivers, engineers and fans stood silent in the pit lane, and for another nine minutes no engines were turned on. For tomorrow's Grand Prix, the Ferrari team's cars will abandon their traditional red colours, they will not carry sponsorship, and drivers will be clad in black and white.

Fiumicino airport in Rome, the scene of a Palestinian terrorist attack in the early Eighties, was eerily silent as loudspeakers were turned off and conveyor belts came to a halt. The stillness was broken only by the sobbing of some American tourists still unable to return home.

Elsewhere new friends added their tribute to that of America's old allies. Outside the US embassy in Moscow yesterday hundreds of bunches of flowers were piled up, many of them laid the day before when Russia held its minute of silence. All flags on government buildings were flown at half-mast, a symbol of President Vladimir Putin's pledge to increase co-operation with Nato after Tuesday's attacks.

It was a promise which clearly was endorsed in the hearts of the ordinary Russian. A steady flow of people arrived at the embassy to sign six black condolence books. On their way through the embassy, they passed posters showing idyllic scenes of American life: one a view of the New York skyline dominated by the World Trade Centre. The notes attached to the bouquets of red and white carnations carried the same simple messages: "We are with you" and "You'll remain in our hearts forever".

The wave of sympathy – and revulsion at the outrage – extended well beyond Europe. Children knelt in front of the US embassy in Seoul yesterday as Asian nations also came to a standstill. In India an internet website condolence book was opened. At Friday prayers in the biggest mosque in Indonesia, the world's most populous Muslim country, sympathy was expressed for the death of so many civilians. In Australia, trade unionists attending a protest rally in Sydney after the collapse of the country's second biggest airline, paused to observe the silence.

But the closeness of the relationship between the American and British people gave the moments of mourning throughout this country a particularly sombre quality. In London thousands gathered in Trafalgar Square, where the fountains were switched off at the foot of Nelson's Column. All around flags flew at half-mast. Traffic did not just halt but most drivers turned off their engines.

In Oxford Street, an eerie stillness descended one of the busiest roads in Britain as shoppers, tourists and office workers stood to attention.

The bustling heart of Glasgow fell silent as 4,000 people gathered in George Square, which had been covered in gigantic black drapes for a multifaith service which preceded the silence. In Cardiff, workers poured out of local offices to stand respectfully around the war memorial outside the Welsh Assembly's headquarters.

At Edinburgh Castle, workmen dismantling scaffolding built for last month's Military Tattoo raised an American flag; it became the focal point for the silence – which was broken, shortly before its end by a man who began singing the American national anthem. Many of those present wiped tears from their eyes as bright sunlight shone on the castle esplanade.

But it was not just the great cities that were determined to honour the dead. In hundreds of smaller places, tribute was paid. In the village of Dunham Massey, in rural Cheshire, 15 villagers and two passing ramblers stood in a silence broken only by birdsong at the 130-year-old church of St Mark. "God Bless America," said a card pinned to the post office window, accompanied by a small Stars and Stripes flag.

The village is close enough to Manchester to hold its own memories of terror. One of the locals, Hilary Heyworth, 62, recalled how her daughter had been working in the city's centre when the IRA bombed it five years ago. "When she heard about the US she went to pieces," said Mrs Heyworth. The sentiment was shared by the hundreds who gathered, in Albert Square, Manchester. When maroons were launched from the town hall roof, mourners visibly flinched. America's terror has bred that kind of nervousness.

It was not the only place where the explosions in New York and Washington stirred terrible memories. The people of Lockerbie, where 270 people died when Pan Am flight 103 was blown out of the sky in December 1988, stopped to pay their respects; in the High Street people left shops and stood on the pavement, heads bowed, eyes closed.

Tens of thousands of subjects gathered, too, outside Belfast City Hall. And by the buffer line of military vehicles between Protestant and Roman Catholic streets in the Ardoyne district – where loyalist protesters have suspended their two-week campaign to prevent Catholic children going that way to school – a lone Scottish soldier piped a lament on Britain's most disputed patch of ground.

For just three minutes yesterday the world stopped turning. Instead it stood still in a simple but tearful homage.

And yet the result was not depressing. It was a moment of curious enrichment and inspiration.

Millions worldwide mourned yesterday. Among them were the American photographer Koo Stark and her daughter, outside St Paul's Cathedral *Jonathan Evans*

INSIDE

Tariq Ali
Yasmin Alibhai-Brown
Mary Dejevsky
Robert Fisk
Howard Jacobson
Fergal Keane
Donald Macintyre
David Usborne
Natasha Walter

After the mourning, America goes on war footing with troop call-up

George Bush: 'Fight is on'

PRESIDENT BUSH took a step closer to war yesterday by giving the Pentagon authority to mobilise 50,000 reservists after Tuesday's suicide attacks on Washington and New York.

Congress gave him unanimous bipartisan backing to use force to stamp out terrorism, and approved the release of an emergency $40bn (£27bn) fund to help to reconstruct New York and strengthen security.

The Pentagon is activating

BY RUPERT CORNWELL
in Washington

50,000 reservists to help to beef up the protection of airports and other installations around the country, and provide medical and engineering support for the massive rescue and reconstruction effort under way in Manhattan and Washington.

The Senate approved by 96-0 and 98-0 measures to provide the $40bn of federal assistance – double the sum Mr Bush had originally asked for – and authorise force for the war the President has declared on terrorism across the world.

As America geared up for retaliation against the atrocities, the ruling Taliban in Afghanistan vowed to hit back if the country came under attack for harbouring the Saudi dissident Osama bin Laden, who has been identified as a prime suspect in the terror attacks. "We will take revenge if America attacks, through different means," the Taliban's chief spokesman, Abdul Hai Mutamaen, said in Kabul.

Mr Bush later addressed a multidenominational prayer service in Washington's national cathedral, before flying to New York to inspect the damage at first hand and offer his support. "The fight against terrorism is now the focus of my administration," he said.

With America still gripped by fear and anger, life was only slowly regaining a semblance of normality. There was a partial resumption of internal flights, but services into the US by most international airlines were still suspended.

In Britain the Home Secretary, David Blunkett, suggested that a national identity card system might be introduced in response to the attacks on America, while the Foreign Secretary, Jack Straw, confirmed that talks were under way across Europe to tighten extradition laws and combat terrorist groups' activities.

The US Justice Department released the names of the 19 hijackers – not 18 as previously announced – who seized the four aircraft. All are of Middle Eastern origin, some with names native to southern Saudi Arabia and Yemen, where Mr bin Laden originated.

Washington formally requested permission from Pakistan to overfly its territory if necessary to strike at Afghanistan, where Mr bin Laden is thought to be hiding.

9 770951 946962 37

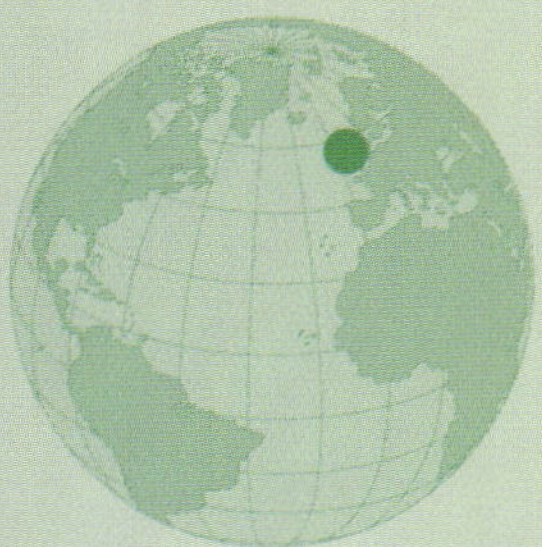

1 **Eine sprachlose Welt, im Schmerz vereint**

2 Die Woche, die die Welt erschütterte

14 Seiten Nachrichten und Analysen – plus 14 Seiten Sonderausgabe des Independent-Magazins

3 Nach der Trauer begibt sich Amerika in den Kriegszustand und beruft Truppen ein

С БЕСПЛАТНЫМ ПРИЛОЖЕНИЕМ ДЛЯ ЧИТАТЕЛЕЙ ГЕРМАНИИ

ШЕМЯКИН
Петербург в руках вандалов с.3

КИДМАН
любовь в клетке с.10

КАФЕЛЬНИКОВ
жена в объятьях сектантов с.12

№ 38 (1091)
Сентябрь 2001 г.
ВАША ГАЗЕТА
Адрес редакции в Интернете: WWW.AIF.RU

Международная телепрограмма плюс кроссворд

АРГУМЕНТЫ И ФАКТЫ

Y 9193
Международное издание

Australia - AUS 2.40; Austria -ÖS 28,00; Belgium - BFR 80,00; Cyprus - CYP 0,85; Czech Republic - CZK 45,0; Denmark - DKR 17,00; France - FF 14,50; Germany - DM 4,00; Greece - DRS 500; Israel - NIS 6,00 (Eilat - 5,00); Italy - ITL 4.800; Luxemburg - LFR 80,0; Malta - LM 0,90; Netherlands - HFL 5,00; Poland - ZL 6,00; Spain - PTS 450; Sweden - SKR 23; Switzerland - SFR 4,0; Turkey - TL 2.200.000; United Kingdom - £ 1,80; USA: New York - USD 0,5, outside New York - USD 0,75

В НОМЕРЕ:

- В Чечне погибли генералы Генштаба с. 4
- А. Шохин. Наше будущее - членство в НАТО с. 4
- Ночные грабители из валютных киосков с. 6
- Капуста и яйца потянули цены вниз с. 9
- Марк Спитц. 7 олимпийских медалей в мусорном контейнере с. 12

«АиФ»-ОПРОС

Как, по вашему мнению, надо поступать с Чечней?

Террористов уничтожать, переговоры вести 50%

Воевать до победного конца 29%

Вывести войска и дать независимость Чечне 21%

Опрос проводился на сайте издательского дома «АиФ» по адресу www.aif.ru

АФОРИЗМ

Террор, остановленный на полпути, опасен. Выжившие полны жаждой мщения.

Дмитрий Волкогонов, российский историк

Призрак терроризма бродит по планете

WWW.AIFNET.RU УНИКАЛЬНАЯ ПОИСКОВАЯ СИСТЕМА НА ВСЕ СЛУЧАИ ЖИЗНИ

1 Das Gespenst des Terrorismus wandert auf dem Planeten

2 Der halbbekämpfte Terrorismus ist gefährlich. Die Überlebenden sehnen sich nach Rache

Argumenti i fakti
www.aif.ru
Russland, Moskau

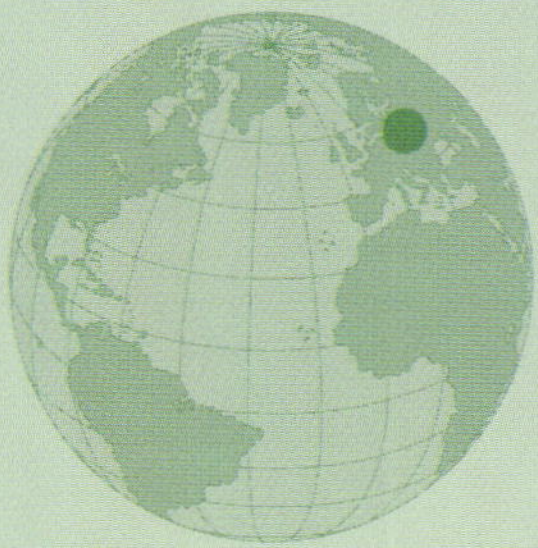

15+

Azeri President Due in Tehran

BAKU (IRNA) – Azeri President Heidar Aliyev is to make a three-day state visit to Tehran as of Monday to hold talks with senior Iranian officials on the disputed legal status of the strategic Caspian Sea, reliable sources said Friday.

During the visit which takes place at the invitation of Iranian President Muhammad Khatami, Tehran and Baku are expected to sign a number of agreements in different fields.

Kayhan International

Burkina Faso for Improved Ties With Iran

OUAGADOUGOU (IRNA) – Burkina Faso's President Blaise Compaor here on Thursday called for expansion of commercial and political relations between Tehran and Ouagadougou.

In a meeting with Hussein Hashemi, heading Iran's parliamentary delegation to the 106th Inter-Parliamentary Union (IPU), Compaore hailed Iranian traders' presence in trade fairs in his country.

VOL. XX. 5936 TEHRAN
Satuday September 15, 2001, Shahrivar 24, 1380, Jamadi-ul-Thani 26, 1422, Price 500 Rials

Kharrazi Says:

Israel Trying to Exploit Terrorist Attacks in U.S.

TEHRAN, Sept. 14 (IRNA) – **Iran's Foreign Minister Kamal Kharrazi said in a telephone conversation with his Austrian counterpart Benita-Maria Ferrero-Waldner on Thursday that Israel is trying to exploit the terrorist attacks in the U.S. for purely provocative purposes.**

He said Israel's behavior in light of the complex regional (Mideast) situation will have negative consequences in the minds of world Muslims and Muslim nations.

He reminded that all Muslim nations had condemned the terrorists attacks in New York and Washington.

The Iranian foreign minister said the international community should prevent Israel from post-facto exploitations that might only serve to further complicate the (Mideast) situation.

He added that the current situation in the Middle East is quite different from what it was in the past which, he observed, warranted "a new approach (to the issue) in the agenda of the world community."

The Austrian minister intimated to the Iranian foreign minister that her government was willing to main continual consultations with Iran on the regional situation.

Iran has vehemently condemned the Kamikaze terrorist attacks in the United States and expressed its deep sorrow and sympathy with the American nation. It has also called for an end to terrorism.

Kamal Kharrazi

Thousands were still missing as rescue crews swarmed over the wreckage of the collapsed World Trade Center's two 110-story towers, where 40,000 people once worked.

In the worst attack on American soil since Pearl Harbor, three hijacked planes slammed into the Pentagon and New York's landmark World Trade Center on Tuesday, demolishing the two 110-story towers that symbolize U.S. financial might.

Terrorist Attacks Condemned ...

Kashani Urges U.S. To Adopt New Approach

TEHRAN, Sept. 14 (IRNA) – **Senior Iranian cleric Ayatollah Muhammad Emami Kashani on Friday condemned what he called "terrorist" attacks in the United States and called for an international move against terrorism.**

Addressing the worshipers attending the weekly Friday congregational prayers, Kashani singled out the Kamikaze attacks on US. landmarks as "tragic" and said: "How can one remain indifferent towards such an incident which has set aflame a large number of innocent men, women and children."

Ayat. Kashani

He said that the Islamic Republic condemns such an "astonishing" incident orchestrated by a unknown number of "terrorists."

Thousands are still missing as rescue crews swarmed over the wreckage of the collapsed World Trade Center's two 110-story towers, where 40,000 people once worked. In the worst attack on American soil since Pearl Harbor, three hijacked planes slammed into the Pentagon and New York's landmark World Trade Center on Tuesday, demolishing the two towers that symbolize U.S. financial might.

Kashani inveighed against the racist Israel and branded it as a "blatant manifestation of state terrorism" he said Israel has infiltrated into the American administration to influence its policies.

He gave a downbeat assessment of the atmosphere created against Muslims in the U.S. following the attacks and argued "why they attribute such actions to Muslims?"

"Does Islam allow such actions? Can an Islamic state jeopardize lives of innocent people?"

"The Zionist regime is attempting to fish in troubled waters. Pressuring the Muslims will bear no fruit," Kashani said, adding, "the incident is worrisome and is condemned, but it should serve to be a lesson for all the powers, especially the U.S., to adopt a new approach."

On Thursday, Iran's Foreign Minister Kamal Kharrazi said Israel is trying to exploit the terrorist attacks in the U.S. for purely provocative purposes.

The Jewish state is not recognized by the Islamic Republic which has always called for the destruction of the racist Israeli regime as the only solution to the turbulent Middle East peace process.

Iran has vehemently condemned the Kamikaze terrorist attacks in the United States and expressed its deep sorrow and sympathy with the American nation. It has also called for an end to terrorism.

Bush Calls Cabinet to Review Military Options

WASHINGTON, Sept. 14 (Reuters) – **President George W. Bush called a cabinet meeting on Friday to review the response to terror attacks that devastated the country before he leads a national day of prayer and gets a first-hand look at damage in New York.**

Bush was to hold his first full cabinet meeting since the attacks by hijacked jets that destroyed the World Trade Center in New York and damaged the Pentagon. Thousands of people were believed killed in what the U.S. president has described as an act of war.

White House spokeswoman Claire Buchan said the 9:30 a.m. (1330 GMT) cabinet meeting would be "reviewing the events and responses to them. (It is) an opportunity to bring all of the people together who have been working shoulder-to-shoulder to respond to what's happened."

Officials said it was not clear whether Bush would be discussing a Pentagon request for authorization to call up as many as 1 million military reservists.

Defense officials said they expected Bush to grant the authority, and that defense secretary Donald Rumsfeld planned to activate between 30,000 and 50,000 for increased protection by jet fighters and for other duties at domestic military bases.

Bush, who is reviewing military options for retaliating for the attacks, declared Friday a national day of prayer and remembrance for the victims. He was to participate in noon services at the Washington's national cathedral.

The dean of the cathedral, Rev. Nathan Baxter, said he would encourage the president to consider "the heart of faith... so that our grief in terms of our responding to this does not cause us to become also the evil we deplore."

Finding justice, he said, sometimes involved violence but that always should be measured, reasonably considered and an act for justice and not just for revenge and anger.

"War... always involves not only the target group but innocent people. We want to be sure that what we do enables peace," Baxter told ABC's "Good Morning America" program.

Bush is also expected to speak at the ceremony. In a proclamation marking the day, Bush called on Americans to remember the victims with noon-

(Continued on Page 7)

Remains of the facade of Two World Trade Center is all that stands after Tuesday's terrorist attack Wednesday.

Russian Premier

Retaliation Won't Solve Terror Threat

MOSCOW, Sept. 14 (AFP) – **Russian Foreign Minister Igor Ivanov warned Friday that US retaliatory strikes for the deadly attacks on Washington and New York would not solve the long-term threat of international terrorism.**

"What we need is long-term cooperation and steps aimed at preventing such tragedies," Ivanov said in an interview with CNN, whose transcript was released by the Russian Foreign Ministry.

"From our point of view, we must present a united response," Ivanov said. "Russia not only offers its sympathy, but also – as President Vladimir Putin has said – is ready to offer all the necessary help."

Ivanov said that Western nations "must jointly develop a global system that would stand in the way of new threats."

"It is absolutely clear that no one nation can solve these problems on its own."

The United States has said it is mulling a military response for Tuesday's attacks, with Saudi multi-millionaire Osama bin Laden – thought to be in hiding in Afghanistan – being the main suspect.

Earlier Friday, Russian Defense Minister Sergei Ivanov ruled out Russia's participation in any joint military reprisal operation.

However, Russia is also keen to see bin Laden taken out, accusing him of funding and training Islamic guerrillas waging a brutal two-year resistance against federal forces in rebel Chechnya.

Separately, the Russian foreign minister said Moscow had no plans to use Tuesday's tragedies as a bargaining chip in ongoing consultations over Washington's plans to construct a missile defense shield.

"Consultations are under way and constructive dialogue is continuing," on missile defense, said Ivanov.

Russia opposes the U.S. project, arguing that it could spark a new nuclear arms race and that it would be unable to protect nations from terrorist strikes such as Tuesday's hit on New York and Washington.

Meanwhile Russia's armed forces' chief of staff said on Friday that Moscow was unlikely to join in any U.S. retaliatory strikes following the terror attacks in New York and Washington, interfax news agency reported.

"The United States has armed forces powerful enough to handle the task by themselves," general Anatoly Kvashnin was quoted as

(Continued on Page 7)

18 Militants Among 23 Killed in Kashmir

SRINAGAR, India, Sept. 14 (Reuters) – **The insurgency in India's Jammu and Kashmir state claimed at least 23 lives, including 14 suspected militants shot dead by Indian soldiers while trying to cross from Pakistan, authorities said on Thursday.**

"Security forces foiled three infiltration bids along the line of control overnight and killed 14 terrorists at Congdor, Pharkian Gali and Tangdhar areas," an army spokesman said, referring to Wednesday night.

The 750-km (470-mile) Line of Control, or ceasefire line, divides Kashmir between arch-foes India and Pakistan.

Later on Thursday Indian police shot dead three militants in another gunbattle in south Kashmir, police said.

Five civilians and a militant also were killed in separate shootouts across the state.

India, which controls 45% of the disputed Himalayan region, blames Pakistan for fomenting the revolt against New Delhi's rule in the country's only Muslim-majority state.

Pakistan, which controls just over a third of Kashmir – China holds the rest – denies direct involvement but says it supports self-determination for the Kashmiri people.

Separatist violence has escalated in the region in recent months, particularly since a July summit between India and Pakistan focused on resolving the dispute ended in deadlock.

Nearly a dozen guerrilla groups have been fighting Indian rule in Kashmir since late 1989.

Officials say that more than 30,000 people have been killed in the years of violence. Separatist organizations put the figure closer to 80,000.

Meanwhile a shadowy militant group in Indian-administered Kashmir has upped the ante in its campaign to impose a strict Islamic dress code, saying it will shoot Muslim women from Friday who refuse to wear a veil.

(Continued on Page 7)

Taliban Claims Advancing on Alliance Stronghold

ISLAMABAD, Sept. 14 (AFP) – **Afghanistan's ruling Taliban forces have moved closer to the opposition-held province of Badakhsan after a 30-kilometer (18.5-mile) advance on the northern front of the country's civil war, a report said Friday.**

Taliban forces captured Dashti-Rubat in Takhar Province and were close to Kalafgan district near Badakhshan after heavy fighting with the opposition forces, the Afghan Islamic Press reported.

Fighting between the rival forces left 19 opposition and seven Taliban soldiers dead, it said quoting an unidentified Taliban spokesman.

It said this was the first major territorial gains on the northern fronts by the hardline militia since the disappearance of opposition commander Ahmed Shah Masood.

Masood, 49, was the target of an assassination plot carried out by two Arabs posing as journalists who detonated a bomb during an interview Sunday in opposition-controlled territory in northeastern Afghanistan.

The opposition denied the reported Taliban advance. Spokesman Muhammad Habeel said the Taliban had captured two hilltops

(Continued on Page 7)

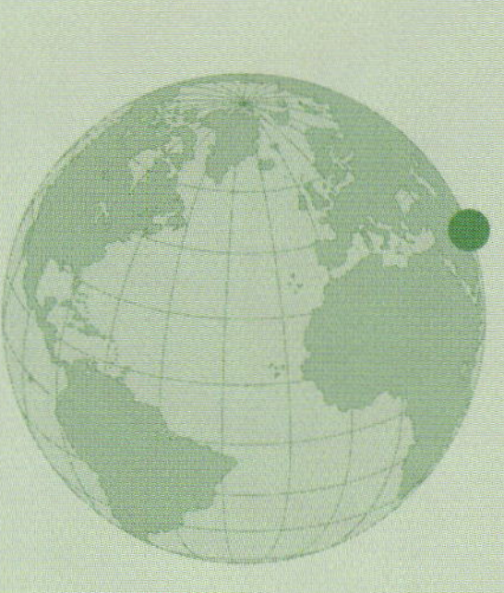

❶ Kharrazi: »Israel versucht die Anschläge in den USA auszunutzen«

❷ Bush ruft das Kabinett zusammen, um militärische Möglichkeiten zu erörtern

❸ Terroristische Attacken verurteilt … Kashani drängt die USA eine neue Vorgehensweise einzuschlagen

❹ Unter den 23 in Kaschmir Getöteten waren 18 Mitglieder militanter Organisationen

❺ Russischer Ministerpräsident: Vergeltung wird keine Lösung der terroristischen Bedrohung sein

Kayhan International
www.kayhannews.com
Iran, Teheran

Impressum

Herausgegeben in Deutschland von
© Verlag Karl Müller GmbH 2002
Venloer Str. 1271
D-50829 Köln
Tel. 0221/13 06 5-0
Fax 0221/13 06 5-210
www.karl-mueller-verlag.de

Gestaltung, Redaktion und Produktion: Büro Norbert Pautner, München

Übersetzungen: Emel Adigüzel (Türkisch), Gabriela Ban (Ungarisch), Heike Barnitzke (Japanisch), Joachim Brauss (Tschechisch), Werner Eder (Indonesisch), Hans Freitag (Schwedisch), Andreas Gruneberg (Chinesisch), Judith Heise (Englisch), Carola Heusinger (Griechisch), Kirsten Hummelmeier (Italienisch), Ele Juhkam (Estnisch), Silja Kaeser (Finnisch), Doreen Krüger (Portugiesisch), Gundula Müller-Wallraf (Englisch), Beate Palubicki (Dänisch), Verena Preßler (Französisch), Onna Riedi (Norwegisch), Anne Schöner (Niederländisch), Sabina Schroeter-Brauss (Tschechisch), Behnaz Hosseini Shokraei (Persisch), Anna Stepien (Polnisch), Johannes Stockinger (Niederländisch), Galo Troya G. (Spanisch), Dick van den Brink (Niederländisch), Hans-Peter Vietze (Mongolisch), Iris Weidlich (Arabisch), Alexander Weingardt (Russisch)

Repro: Fotolitho Varesco, Auer
Druck und Bindung: Mladinska Knjiga Tiskarna, Ljubljana

ISBN 3-89893-052-1

Printed in Slovenia

Bildnachweis

Dank

Die Redaktion bedankt sich ganz herzlich bei den Redakteuren und Mitarbeitern der in diesem Buch veröffentlichten nationalen und internationalen Zeitungen und Magazine für die gute Zusammenarbeit.
Für die außergewöhnlich engagierte Unterstützung bei der Recherche und der Bereitstellung von Abbildungsvorlagen gebührt unser ausdrücklicher Dank der Zeitungsabteilung der Staatsbibliothek zu Berlin, Preußischer Kulturbesitz, dem Archiv des Instituts für Asienkunde (IFA) in Hamburg, der Bibliothek des Osteuropainstituts in München und der Bayerischen Staatsbibliothek in München. Mit Rat und Tat hat uns Jessica Müller-Wallraf bei der Organisation der Übersetzungen zur Seite gestanden.